Politics/America

other *Transaction/Society* readers

Marriages and Families

edited by **Helena Z. Lopata**
Loyola University of Chicago

Social Psychology

edited by **Elliot Aronson** & **Robert Helmreich**
The University of Texas at Austin

a *Transaction/Society* reader

Politics/America

The Cutting Edge of Change

edited by

Walter Dean Burnham
Massachusetts Institute of Technology

D. VAN NOSTRAND COMPANY
New York / Cincinnati / Toronto / London / Melbourne

D. Van Nostrand Company Regional Offices:
New York   Cincinnati   Milbrae

D. Van Nostrand Company International Offices:
London   Toronto   Melbourne

Published by D. Van Nostrand Company
450 West 33rd Street, New York, N.Y. 10001

Published simultaneously in Canada by
Van Nostrand Reinhold Ltd.

10 9 8 7 6 5 4 3 2 1

BIBLIOGRAPHIC NOTE

The year of publication in *trans-Action/Society* for each article in this work is as follows: Abelson, 1968; Bazelon, 1967; Boesel et al., 1969; Burnham (page 118) 1968, (page 125) 1969; Davis, 1968; Dumont, 1970; Eley, 1969; Ennis, 1967; Gamson, 1964; Gehlen, 1969; Greenstein, 1966; Greer, 1971; Hacker, 1964; Hadden et al., 1968; Horowitz (page 17) 1968, (page 27) 1965; Jacob, 1969; Lacy, 1969; Lerman, 1971; Lipset, 1966; Lipset and Raab, 1969; Lipsky, 1969; Lipsky and Olson, 1969; Long, 1968; Lowi, 1970; McMahon, 1971; Marmor, 1968; Maullin, 1971; Melman, 1971; Mondale, 1968; Munger, 1967; Murphy, 1973; Nagel, 1966; Parmenter, 1967; Piven, 1969; Reiss, 1968; Roemer, 1971; Ross et al., 1966; Sigel, 1967; Skedgell, 1966; Skolnick, 1970; Stein, 1969; Steiner, 1971; Sternlieb, 1972; The Walker Commission, 1969; Waskow, 1969; Wildavsky, 1966; Williams, 1967; Wirt, 1970; Wright, 1972.

PICTURE CREDITS

Cover: "Any Thing To Keep Afloat A Little Longer." Woodcut by Joseph Keppler from *Puck*, May 21, 1890.
PART ONE: 9 (detail), Cornell Capa, Magnum. 15, Shelly Rusten. 17, Hugh Rogers. 27, U.S. Army.
PART TWO: 37, © George W. Gardner, 1972. 46, Wayne Miller, Magnum. 55, Inge Morath, Magnum. 65, CBS. 70, 125, United Press International. 82, 105, © George W. Gardner, 1973. 93, Bruce Davidson, Magnum. 118, Bob Dorksen.
PART THREE: 135, 159, 171, United Press International. 140, Charles Harbutt, Magnum. 153, Laurence Fink. 181, Elliott Erwitt, Magnum. 192, Gary Settle, Image.
PART FOUR: 205, 231, Michael Semak. 211, Franklynn Peterson. 220, Paul Sequeira. 226, Bill Owens. 237, Richard Bellak. 246, Mitchell Klein. 253, Helen Nestor. 258, Ed Eckstein. 264, Cornell Capa, Magnum. 272, Enrico Natali.
PART FIVE: 277, Charles Gatewood. 282, 283, 285, 286, 287, 289, 290, John Osborn. 291, John Groth. 299, John Messina. 308, Charles Harbutt, Magnum. 318, Cornell Capa, Magnum. 326, Franklynn Peterson, Sharon Communications. 337, Bill Wingell.
PART SIX: 347, 363, © George W. Gardner, 1973. 352, Michael Alexander. 375, Shelly Rusten. 386, © George W. Gardner, 1972. 393, Anthony Goldschmidt.
PART SEVEN: 395, 406, 422, Paul Sequeira. 399, © George W. Gardner, 1973. 404 (detail), Alan S. Orling. 436, Burt Glinn, Magnum. 440, United Press International.

Foreword

The blunt truth is that there is no such thing as a trade book or a text book—but much more to the point, good books and bad books. It is with that in mind that this collection of articles, based on work previously published in the magazine *trans-Action/Society*, is being made available for the college and university communities.

It is our feeling at Transaction, shared by D. Van Nostrand and hopefully by readers of this book as well, that these analyses of American politics which first appeared in article form in *trans-Action/Society* are of sufficient interest and value to hold up over time and can become both part of the permanent learning experience of the student and, beyond that, part of the permanent corpus of solid materials by which the best of any field is deservedly judged. The text that has resulted from this compilation clearly demonstrates, we believe, the superiority of starting with real world problems, and searching out practical solutions. That the essays fall into generally established patterns of professional disciplines is more an accident than a necessity; it also demonstrates a growing awareness on the part of the basic areas of social science of their larger commitment to the amelioration of the human condition.

The demands upon scholarship and scientific judgment are always stringent—especially so in an era of booming scientific information, to the point of overload. The advantage of these studies is that in every paper there has been an effort to communicate the experience of the crisis of current social and political living. Yet, despite the sense of urgency these contributions exhibit, the editor has chosen them because they have withstood the test of time and match, if not exceed, in durable interest the best of available social science literature. This collection, then, attempts to address fundamental issues and in so doing add to the basic insights derived from a classical literature in the various fields of the social sciences.

Because of the concreteness of these writings, the editor has seen fit to develop at considerable length a theoretical scaffold that links the specific essays themselves. As a result, the text can serve as a valuable series of core readings or as an adjunct anthology. There was nothing slap-dash or random about the selection process, the editing process, or the ideological process that went into this volume. It is our feeling that these essays represent the best in social science thinking and deserve the permanence granted by republication in book form.

The social scientists involved, both as editor and authors of this reader, have gone beyond observation, and have entered into the vital and difficult tasks of explanation and interpretation. The text has defined issues in a way that makes solutions possible. It has provided answers as well as asked the right questions. Thus, this book is dedicated not simply to highlighting political problems for students already inundated with such an awareness but, far more important, establishing guidelines for social solutions based on the social sciences.

Irving Louis Horowitz
Editor-in-Chief
trans-Action/Society

Contents

Preface

Anyone who sets out to edit a collection of articles has to ask himself two questions, both of which are certain to be of importance to the book's audience. First, what special approach to a set of problems do our authors take which is less readily available elsewhere? Second—and intimately related to the first—what, if any, common theme or frame of reference binds together the articles assembled? These questions seem particularly pertinent for a new anthology designed for present-day courses in American government.

The editor's intent in selecting the fifty-one articles that follow was to provide students with a structured sampling of the best that is being written today by practicing political scientists and by others in the social sciences who can shed light on political problems. The articles are supplemented with commentary that attempts to pinpoint the issues they raise and to place those issues in their historico-political context.

As he worked with the materials collected here, the editor became impressed with the sharp difference between any possible combination of them and the "standard" American government reader-texts. There is little discussion here of institutions as such along the old "executive-legislative-judicial" lines. This may surprise some, yet it assuredly reflects the practical concerns of contemporary political scientists. Three major analytical foci emerge in the essays. The first is upon elites who "make things happen," either through outside contributions of expertise or through their carrying out of official roles. The second focus is upon policy issues and agendas in an era of rapid social change, and on the processes and outputs of policy-making. The third emphasis is upon "little people" and their relationship, often adversary, with the structures and outputs of politics and the legal system. These three foci are developed in Parts One through Three, Part Four, and Parts Five through Seven, respectively, in our table of contents.

On the question of a common theme among these articles highlighting a multiplicity of problems, it is the editor's thesis, elaborated in the editorial commentary preceding each section, that the thread of a crisis of political authority runs through these reports.

Justice Holmes commented a century ago that legislation should be seen for what it is: a means by which those having power shift social burdens they find irksome onto the shoulders of those who are unable to resist effectively. Holmes wrote this in criticism of the mythology of social harmony that then, and for a long time afterward, dominated middle-class America, especially the courts. But his point still stands. Society is; there are regularly prescribed patterns of domination on one hand and subordination on the other. And the political system, while it may not be in the crassest sense the "executive committee of the ruling class," is in no way neutral among all groups on the social ladder—not in its structure, its personnel, or its policies.

Of course, no pattern of social stratification or of influence (or lack of influence) on officialdom is wholly static; but in a larger sense this pattern is more or less a constant. Yet if there is anything our political history makes clear, it is that most of the time most people (including most academics) accept things pretty much as they are. To the extent this is so, it follows that people come in large numbers to be sensitive to inequities and injustices only under very special circumstances. Such circumstances are those of a crisis of political authority. In such crises, a great many people come no longer to believe in the moral imperatives which prescribe willing support for existing political structures and willing obedience to the decisions they produce. The essays that follow confirm that it is time to turn to a discussion of forces at work which have precipitated a crisis in contemporary American politics.

The writers represented here are instructive not only for their individual analyses but for their composite voice. Social science has grown enormously in the United States during the past generation. So have the basic problems affecting ordinary people who live in one of the most complex societies ever to emerge in human history. A large pool of well-educated people has come into being since World War II, many of them deeply committed to understanding what is going on in American society and politics. They represent a demand for social-science findings communicated in language which concerned, educated laymen can follow. The authors anthologized here have written out of their need to communicate the data and issues of politics to an audience considerably larger than the usual professional group.

It has been remarked that "Much of sociology is socialism." A throw-away phrase—but like many such it contains an important germ of truth. Criticism from the left has been an integral part of the sociological tradition for more than a century, on both sides of the Atlantic. Intensive professional study of the organizations and myths by which political and social domination-subordination relationships are maintained seems inevitably to produce critical reactions among intellectuals. Modern sociology, from Marx to Durkheim, Weber, and others, was also rooted in Central Europe, among intellectuals who were both cosmopolitan and highly critical of the existing social and political order.

Until recently, however, American political science has had a very different, far more "native-American" tradition. Except for periods of manifest internal crisis such as the 1930s, it has tended to celebrate rather than to criticize the structures and processes of American politics. The writings by political scientists in this book demonstrate, on the whole, how far away from this American celebration the field has recently moved. The political Right virtually does not exist among professional political scientists who publish today. Even Republican Party membership is lightly represented: less than one-fifth of all practising political scientists so identify themselves. But this has been true for a long time. What is new is the extent and depth of critical sensitivity to the existing processes and outputs of "normal politics" which has developed among American political scientists.

In a very real sense, the function of the intellectual approximates that of the canary in a coal mine: by training and temperament hyperalert to pathological developments in society and polity, the intellectual warns of impending crisis before other men sense the danger. Naturally, criticism of existing pieties by intellectuals galvanizes those who are still true believers, and it may have a significant long-term effect in eroding the credibility of those pieties. But such criticism is always more *effect* than *cause* of crisis.

This is a time in our national history when old routines have been undermined and old political formulas lie in ruins, but when the outline of some creative political regeneration is still opaque to our vision. Such a period has its compensations. For a season, we can see further into the heart of things, and further into the distance along some dimensions, than at any other time. As Hegel put it so well, "The Owl of Minerva takes flight at dusk." But it is also true that any transition from one established set of stable social and political routines to another is stressful. Such indeed are "times that try men's souls." It is our lot to live in such times, yet one hopes that the studies in this volume will help readers to understand some of the issues which confront all of us today.

Walter Dean Burnham

Overview

Roots of the Current Crisis in American Politics

The American political system was organized and developed to maturity under social, economic and international conditions which have ceased to exist in our time. It was based upon several primordial elements, the first of which was a belief, revolutionary in its time and for many decades thereafter, in the inherent equality and dignity of the individual. Associated with this was a political machinery which, through federalism and separation of powers, explicitly denied that sovereign power in domestic affairs existed anywhere within it. On the other hand, sovereignty not only existed but was concentrated in the President, so far as the country's relations with foreign powers were concerned. Thirdly, the whole enterprise was based upon the development and maintenance of a very broad consensus within society on fundamentals involving the place of organized religion in the political system, and the dominance of private initiative (and the private sector) generally in the political economy. Without such a consensus the cumbersome machinery would have collapsed; but that is another way of saying that sovereign power in any political State develops historically in response to fundamental conflicts among sharply discrete social groups over control *of society through politics.* It represents the victory of one coalition of such groups over another, and it employs the positive use of state power to consolidate the new group's control—the bourgeoisie over pre-modern feudal and clerical elements, for example—over the social system.

In the American case, we find one spectacular example: the Civil War. Here, for a short season, we find the collapse of the Constitution and the development of sovereign power to an astonishing degree. The episode was temporary, though it left some permanent residues, but it is also exceptionally instructive. Otherwise, however, the social consensus—changing in emphasis and shape as the society was transformed by industrialization—survived. This consensus was, essentially, the ideology of liberal capitalism, coupled after the 1870s with an increasingly explicit racism which justified the restriction of the Southern black to a limbo halfway between the old slavery and genuine citizenship.

When we find ourselves in a political crisis, it is extraordinarily useful to see how often earlier theorists of American politics—particularly those steeped in a juristic-institutional tradition—can illuminate the problem. In 1941 the late E. S. Corwin gave a warning for the future of American politics—and of constitutional liberty in this country, as that term had hitherto been understood. Corwin identified two sea-changes in the context of American politics which had arisen since 1929 and whose implications profoundly disturbed him. The first was the emergence of a permanent federal presence in the private sector, necessitated by the collapse of free-market capitalism in the Great Depression. The second was the permanent mobilization of the United States in world politics, in a context of acute military threat.

Corwin approached these issues from a legalist perspective which many today would describe as old-fashioned. The same is even more true of the warnings which Herbert Hoover continually issued in the 1930s about the dangers of the kind of corporatist syndicalism which the New Deal was bringing into being. Yet in our own day, such warnings may well be taken more and more seriously. We cannot review all of these issues in these few pages; but we can give some indication of their relevance to the current crisis of political authority which we have suggested now grips the United States.

We have argued that the American political system was set up according to a certain conception of liberty which denied the normal existence of sovereign governmental power in domestic affairs. This implied the absence of permanent public regulation of or intervention into the private sector. Yet during industrialization the private sector had created one of the great collectivist organizations of all time, the business corporation. The corporation became, and remains, the dominant form of social organization in the United States. It was not long after the turn of this century that the leaders of corporate capitalism discovered the uses of public authority to achieve some rationalization of their competitive activities and to avoid some of the more ruinous implications of truly free competition. But

the depression which began in 1929 revealed that such marginal public-sector efforts were insufficient to protect even the basic interests of entrepreneurs and management, not to mention those of the rest of society. So permanent public-sector involvement came with the New Deal; but it came without any *basic* change in the political system. That system remained, as before, the essentially non-sovereign collection of middle-class economic and political feudalities which it had been since the end of Reconstruction.

Out of the interaction between this archaic political system and its changed social and economic context came the hybrid phenomenon known as "interest-group liberalism." This in turn promptly received ideological support from political scientists and others who celebrated the virtues of pluralism and veto groups in the political process and of incremental change in policy output. Yet there were two significant problems in this rewriting of Locke, this recasting of atomistic individualism from the level of the individual to the level of the group. The first was that a huge proportion of the American people were not included in the new groupist system. They belonged to no group with political leverage. In fact, even if they were not subject to outright disfranchisement and political persecution—as were Southern blacks—they were excluded from the most elemental mode of participation, voting. Throughout the New Deal and up to the present, these excluded people formed not less than *two-fifths* of the total adult population—concentrated, of course, at the bottom of the socio-economic system. As the late E. E. Schattschneider pithily observed: "The flaw in the pluralist heaven is that the heavenly choir sings with a markedly upper-class accent." It is virtually impossible to overstate the importance of this steep class bias in our politics for the workings of "interest-group liberalism" since the New Deal.

The second major problem of "interest-group liberalism" was accurately pinpointed by Herbert Hoover, when he suggested that it amounts to a kind of unresponsive *syndicalism* which can work oppression on individuals in several ways. Such syndicalism rests upon the creation of large-scale "peak" organizations and ultimately upon power transactions between the top leadership of these organizations and the top leadership of government. Needless to say, the interests of the ordinary individual can, and often do, get lost in this process at all levels—in the "private-sector" organizations themselves, in the interface transactions between peak groups and government, in the shaping of public policy, and in the routine transactions between individual citizens and bureaucracies. When we consider

2

that this applies to individuals who are fortunate enough to be covered by the umbrellas provided by the corporation, the labor union, or other groups active in the pressure system, it is easy to see how much more forcefully it applies to that "other America" which is outside these groups!

"Power speaks to power." If there is one part of the "old politics" which has generated more passionate opposition among Americans than any other, it is this. Such opposition crystallizes, implicitly or explictly, around the belief that there is a common public interest which transcends group negotiations; that this interest is somehow grossly violated by the power game played by peak associations and top-level government people; and that legislation is, or ought to be, the product of more than a temporary balance of power among these organized groups.

The literature of pluralist political science either ignores or categorically denies the existence of such a "public interest" at home, though it finds it easy enough to discover an American "national interest" abroad. But this rejection of the notion of a public interest reveals the extent to which pluralism is bourgeois ideology, simply a logic of justification for an established order of things. The trouble with this line of argument is that it enshrines naked power relationships among group and political elites while arguing that these processes work out for the best because of the operations of a latter-day "invisible hand." It is laissez-faire ideology rewritten for the times. But it is vulnerable when and to the extent that individuals come to disbelieve in this harmony. Further, the long-term workings of this syndicalism themselves destroy public belief in the justness of political solutions and the legitimacy of government itself. At the "end of liberalism," as Theodore Lowi has precisely argued, is a felt lack of justice, of simple human equity in the political system.

Corwin was also apprehensive about the political implications of permanent mobilization of the United States in international politics. President Eisenhower voiced a similar concern in his 1961 farewell address, when he warned against the acquisition of influence, sought or unsought, by the "military-industrial complex." It is a pity that his successors have been so patently insensitive to Eisenhower's warning.

The reason for this concern is inherent in the American constitutional structure. It cannot be said often enough that the American political system is extremely archaic by comparative standards, and that in foreign and military affairs it presupposes that the President will act very much like a seventeenth-century "patriot king." Sweepingly sovereign power is given to the President by the Constitution so far as foreign and military affairs are concerned. Moreover, this power has recently been concentrated in the Executive even beyond the Constitution's very broad grant. Since World War II, a combination of factors—contextual (military threat from the Communist world), ideological (reflexive anti-Communism) and economic (the possibility of large "Keynesian" public-sector expenditures without competition with private enterprise)—have contributed to the development of a colossal military and defense-related organizational structure. This structure ramifies throughout the political system. Four-fifths of all U.S. congressional districts now have defense installations or plants which are of some significance to the local economy. One way to capture graphically the change which has occurred since Corwin wrote is to analyze per capita expenditures on defense, space and military-assistance programs. In current dollars, these amounted to $4.19 per capita in 1935, $89.18 in 1950, $245.97 in 1960 and $387.75 in 1970. Even taking inflation into account, the burden of empire for the average American has grown enormously in the past generation.

The political implications of this immense proliferation in military activity and expenditure are fundamental. Of first importance is the vast new syndicalist "complex" which has come into existence since the New Deal era, based squarely upon the top management of the leading industrial corporations, the political foreign-policy "establishment" around the President and in leading universities, the top Pentagon elite, and the armed-services and appropriations committees of Congress. That group has been actively supported by another major element in the New Deal syndicalist coalition—the top leadership of organized labor, not only on grounds of international anti-Communist ideology but above all because where defense is, there are jobs also. Any effort to organize a domestic political movement calling for reallocation of our scarce resources and budget priorities must recognize the pervasiveness of this "complex" and the multitude of substantial material and ideological interests which are permanently mobilized to support it.

Given the realities of international power politics since World War II, it would be, to say the least, unrealistic to argue that defense and related burdens on American resources can be done away with, or that they are not "needed." But even if we cannot dismantle the "military-industrial-academic" complex, the future of American domestic politics depends in a real sense upon whether this immense set of power concentrations can be tamed and made politically accountable. Perhaps the supreme example of coercions which play upon the little man who is subject to power he cannot control is the drafting of young men to fight a war which was initiated entirely by the President and his narrow elite of military, civilian, and academic advisers.

Although the Vietnam war lends itself to many lines of analysis, the point to be made here is that it has vastly accelerated the domestic political crisis in the United States. The decision to make war in Vietnam reflects the essence of Corwin's warning about the operation of the U.S. political system under conditions of permanent imperial involvement in the outside world. It was an executive decision, made by a President who had campaigned a few months earlier on a pledge not to so decide. The President made war with the advice and consent not of the Senate, as required by the Constitution, but of a rarefied elite of advisers accountable to no one but themselves and the Chief Executive. Yet it was a decision which ordinary people had to pay for: in the case of 50,000 young men, with their lives. And these casualties—no less than the barbarously inhumane methods utilized in the war—contributed immensely to severe alienation among college youth and others in the late 1960s. But these considerations, however important, should not deflect our view from the core of the issue which the war has raised. This issue, baldly put, involves the ascendancy of a narrow executive-military elite in our politics and the absence of any organized institutional means for restraining the exercise of power by that elite.

Lurking just beneath the once-calm surface of American politics, then, is a fundamental constitutional crisis. On the domestic front, the syndicalist politics of groups has produced in dialectical contradiction waves of antagonistic mobilizations and countermobilizations. The final product of the "old politics" of interest-group liberalism is the wavelike spread of acute feelings of relative deprivation among more and more people. This is so not only because such a system "lacks justice" in Lowi's abstract sense, but because concretely it tends to operate only in response to organized pressures and protests. The action and reaction lead to an ever-widening sense of frustration and alienation; power groups proliferate at all levels; and the system "jams" in its practical operation while its very legitimacy suffers cumulative erosion. On the international front, we find ourselves half-republic, half-empire; and one may doubt that this "house divided" can survive indefinitely any

more successfully than did the divided house of which Lincoln spoke a century ago.

Areas of Revitalization and Change

A number of "revolutions" unfolding during the past generation have pushed us toward and beyond the present political crisis. We have already discussed the two most basic—the post-1929 revolution in political economy and the "imperium revolution." But there have been others.

1. The demographic revolution. This revolution is the social and political effect of an enormous exchange of populations since 1945: the urbanization of American blacks (and other groups such as Puerto Ricans and Chicanos) and the massive middle-class flight from central cities to suburbs.

2. The civil-rights revolution and the political mobilization of the black and the poor. This revolution, by "destabilizing" race relations and destroying the repressive compromise of 1877, has also effectively destroyed the old New Deal political coalition.

3. The combined education and media revolutions. Both are products of increased economic affluence in American society. The education revolution has in a sense created the conditions for the emergence of a college-based "class for itself" among young people with common concerns and political values. But the media revolution may prove at least as important. In a curious way, it has permitted people who are physically separated but have common interests and problems to "find" one another. Moreover, it has drastically reduced the costs of political information and—even more subversively, from an official point of view—has permitted ordinary people to judge for themselves the verity of official pronouncements about such events as the Vietnam war. The two revolutions together are producing a large group of Americans who are well-educated, who are politically committed, and who are independent actors in the political arena.

4. Closely associated with the education/media revolution—and the industrial affluence underlying it—is a far-reaching *cultural* revolution. One need not accept all of Charles Reich's pieties or naivetes in *The Greening of America* to realize that, among growing numbers of people—young and not so young—the traditional bonds and moral imperatives of such elemental social groupings as organized religion and the family—not to mention those of the old puritan work ethic—are rapidly dissolving. A worldwide crisis of authority is occuring: as J. H.

Plumb has pointed out, basic social institutions which in one form or another go back to the Neolithic era have suddenly become visibly fragile if not evanescent.

One primary feature of the cultural revolution is that, with all its bizarre and even repellent manifestations, an active search for new meaning is going on in the lives of individuals. When old social myths and paths collapse, when they lose their coercive moral authority, predictably strange things happen to people-in-society. Group struggles and personal anxieties increase drastically. Some people move into politics with the kind of "Puritan saint" commitment of which Michael Walzer has written. Cults flourish, along with chiliastic and millenarian movements. "The end of the world," in one form or another, seems remarkably close at hand to many. Ultimately, the quest is for revitalization: for some new set of social myths and routines which, because people come to believe in them, have the power to reintegrate this social chaos in some new and acceptable order.

Unhappily, such conditions are not the stuff of which political pluralism or incremental bargaining in the policy process are made. They appear, in fact, to be essential ingredients of a truly revolutionary situation. For consciously or not, increasing numbers of people are searching for a reconstruction of themselves through a reconstruction of the social order itself. What they seek they will find, though not necessarily in the form that any individual might either foresee or desire *a priori*. At the same time, what makes revolutions what they are is the fact that this drive for revitalization, for political and social reconstruction, always encounters increasingly desperate resistance not only from established elites but from broad masses of the population. Revolutions are virtually never matters of unanimous consent: the very revitalization which becomes psychically necessary to the person who supports the revolution becomes psychically intolerable to the person who cannot imagine survival without his traditional beliefs.

To the extent that the foregoing has some relationship to today's reality, several propositions can be made about the near future of American politics:

1. The overall thrust of our "revolutions" is to rediscover the worth and dignity of the individual, regardless of his social estate. It is also to attack the fundamental legitimacy of political decisions based upon syndicalist bargains among elites, and of the political processes by which such decisions are made.

2. The political thrust of these revolutions is aimed squarely against the coercive power of Big Organization, whether nominally public or nominally private. One very difficult question is the extent to which such attacks can proceed before they compromise or destroy the capacity of these organizations to perform their functions. In any case, however, the political organization of prisoners in jails, the emergence of "storefront lawyers," and many other signs of the times have come into being to give the little man the elemental leverage on his life that interest group liberalism has denied him.

3. To the extent that the contemporary crisis in American politics is founded in a far-reaching if uneven collapse in traditionally-held values, it can be resolved only through revitalization of some sort. Whatever this revitalization turns out to be, one thing is certain: it will not be "liberal," for Lowi is quite right in claiming that liberalism has really come to an end.

4. It seems increasingly certain, therefore, that American political processes and structures will undergo profound transformation before the end of this century. It is possible that this change, when it occurs, will be revolutionary or counter-revolutionary. In any case, it will be sweeping in practical operation, even though the *forms* of the Constitution may not change very much.

5. There is no reason to suppose, with Charles Reich, that the cultural revolution must succeed, or that revitalization centered around rediscovery of the individual's human, social, and political needs must prevail. Indeed, it is very unlikely to prevail without political organizations which collectively concentrate the power of individuals, and which will therefore articulate new needs in an organizationally familiar way. Every revolution has its counter-revolution, and counter-revolutions sometimes succeed.

The genius of American politics, as history abundantly demonstrates, has resided in the capacity of the system as a whole to undergo renewal and revitalization through critical realignments in the electorate and in the policy structure. Thus far the revolutionary thrust of the present-day changes we have discussed has been contained remarkably well through the existing instrumentalities of politics. But a trade-off is required sooner or later: at some point the old must yield at least partially to the new or it must resort to force, to "breaking the system" in the name of preserving both the system and the ascendancy of the old.

If one thinks as a whole about all of the "revolutions" we have discussed, the most striking thing about them is that they point in increasingly polar-opposite directions. The older revolutions in political economy and world politics, taken together, point to a state with a clearly-defined ruling class based upon an oligarchy of syndicalist elites, a state whose leaders deal with revolutions abroad and with discontent at home in an increasingly militarized, technocratic way. The newer revolutions in media, education, and culture have served to mobilize groups whose former passivity and nonparticipation have been essential preconditions for the smooth operation of the syndicalist welfare-warfare state. The Vietnam war somehow crystallized for the "newer America" what went wrong with our national life under its bipartisan ruling class. It spelled out just how far the syndicalist leadership of the old order was prepared to drift away from the humane premises of the Republic in their pursuit of ideology, interest and, it may be, Empire. It is the dialectical polarization which our revolutions have generated, taken together at the same period in time, which has fueled the present crisis and which has eroded the legitimacy of the existing political order.

Few readers, perhaps, seriously think that all the ills or dysfunctions of a social order undergoing such massive doses of change can be resolved by politics. But few would probably doubt, either, that politics is somehow integrally related to redefining the terms of conflict and compromise among major social forces. It seems to me that we have about reached the point in our national life where a clear breakthrough of the newer forces in American politics can no longer be deferred without catastrophic intermediate-run consequences for the prospects of political freedom in the United States. Political forces such as those which are now on the move represent objective conflicts in society. These conflicts are long-term. Very broadly, they can be settled only by peaceful though rapid change, by violent revolution, or by authoritarian reaction with clearly fascist overtones.

The first alternative presupposes that the rot of syndicalism at home and of imperialism abroad has not gone so far that democratic revitalization must be excluded as a practical option. It presupposes that we have not yet reached the point of no return on our march to construct the *Imperium Americanum*. This may seem to some an heroic assumption, but all the returns are not quite in yet. The second alternative is virtually certain to fail as such: but the danger is very real that parts of the "newer America" may be driven by desperation to violent collisions with the established political order if they cannot gain access to it peacefully. Such collisions would serve, in all probability, to speed up the processes involved in the third "solution,"

one which carries out the implications of syndicalism and militarized foreign policy to their logical extreme. To the extent that "manifest destiny" dominates the political-economy and foreign-policy revolutions of our time—as an orthodox Marxist, for example, might well argue—it must candidly be said that this third option would clearly be the most likely one.

But this is to foreclose a future which has not yet occurred, in the name of a social and political determinism which cannot rest upon an adequate scientific basis. The point is that struggle is going on. It is a struggle over the peaceful penetration of democratic elements into an elite-controlled political system. But in a larger sense, the struggle is for the American soul. On its outcome, in my view, hangs the future of human freedom in the United States. Since these underlying issues are not likely to pass away in our time, it can also be said that the essays in this book—reflecting this struggle in a myriad of often very concrete problem areas—have something to tell us which is not merely transitory. The specific issues may be "period pieces," subject to rapid obsolescence, but the underlying conflict over the political future of this country which they reflect is not.

"Tyranny, like Hell, is not easily conquered." So said Thomas Paine in 1776. The same may be said of any existing power order in society and politics. It is always hard to displace it to any considerable extent—and hardest of all when the displacement is sought by peaceful means within institutional structures. Such structures, after all, exist in large part to protect what is from what might be. The greater and more explicit the gap between the former and the latter, the harder the conflict and the greater the odds which those committed to what might be must face. All of us, I think, will increasingly be called upon to take sides in the period immediately ahead. No one can really dare to say what the outcome of this struggle will be. But it seems virtually certain that the country cannot much longer proceed half-democratic and half-syndicalist, half Republic and half Empire. In the last analysis *it must be governed.* As Hobbes has rightly taught us, people in the mass will prefer anything to anarchy; the erosion of legitimacy which has been shredding this system over the past decade must be halted and reversed one way or another. But how, on what and on whose terms, is America to be governed? That is the central political question of our time.

We have the peculiar fate of living in a time when old routines are undermined and old political formulas collapse in ruins, but when the outline of creative political revitalization is at best shadowy. Such a period has its compensations: for a season, we can see further into the heart of things, and further into the distance along some dimensions, than at any other time. But passing from an old, more or less secure set of social and political routines to another is hard on the nerves, especially when—as at the present—we seem to be almost halfway between the shore we knew and the landfall we are about to make in the fog. In my view, it would be a supreme accomplishment if at the end of this turmoil we had once again managed despite all to regenerate our politics and tame the massive feudal collectivities of "private," military, and bureaucratic-executive power which threaten to overwhelm the rest of our political, social, and human life. Then we might have reconstructed a political and social order which reflected more clearly what America has been all about, an order which realized more perfectly the still unexhausted potential for human liberation promulgated by our Declaration of Independence:

We hold these truths to be self-evident, that all men are created equal, that they are endowed by their Creator with certain unalienable rights, that among these are life, liberty and the pursuit of happiness; that to secure these rights, governments are instituted among men, deriving their just powers from the consent of the governed, that whenever any form of government becomes destructive of these ends, it is the right of the people to alter or abolish it, and to institute new government, laying its foundation on such principles, and organizing its powers in such form, as to them shall seem most likely to effect their safety and happiness.

part one

Social Science and Public Policy

Some readers may think it curious that this book on American politics opens with a selection of essays on the relationship between social scientists and national policy elites. This point of departure is undertaken with certain purposes in mind. To begin with, the student should know that the social and behavioral sciences and their leading practitioners have become significant political forces in their own right. The education revolution has produced far more genuine expertise, far more detailed and accurate knowledge about social and political matters, than laymen realize. It is useful for the student to understand, perhaps for his own career purposes and in any case for the development of his critical intelligence as a citizen, that social science is no longer "purely academic," and that the findings of social and behavioral scientists are becoming of cumulative importance—for good or ill—in the making of public policy.

In addition, the essays that follow provide an excellent introduction to the tremendous complexities and ambiguities of the *contemporary* American political processes of expertise and control. They also permit us to identify some extremely important, difficult problems which expertise and its use raise for our future politics. The ethical problems of sponsored research, for example, which most laymen regard as of interest only to the narrow academic circles involved, have already been apprehended by some undergraduates as raising broad political issues as well.

Our Overview stressed the tremendous durability of the American political system. Yet it is also important to note that our contemporary political hybrid has a very recent birth date, one which falls at some point between March 4, 1933, when Franklin D. Roosevelt was inaugurated, and December 7, 1941, the day on which Pearl Harbor was attacked by the Japanese. Almost nowhere has the essential newness of the political system in its present incarnation been so visible as it was during that brief period. For all practical purposes, there was no educational-governmental complex three decades ago; and, with the partial exception of economics, there was very little of the sometimes rigorous and policy-oriented social science which now exists. Professions such as that of "policy researcher" simply did not exist thirty years ago; and they were still very much in infancy only a decade ago.

The extent to which the picture has changed can best be seen in Senator Mondale's essay which begins this Part. Of course, the Senator is a liberal Democrat, and it is worth noting that the liberal proposals of several years ago have yet to be enacted by Congress. Nevertheless, liberal proposals for funding agencies oriented to the policy sciences and for a social state-of-the-union message reveal something about which there is wide consensus in Washington. There has been an enormous expansion of domestic policy expenditures and programs (and, of course, agencies!) since 1961. The results of these programs have often been different from what their originators expected—and have also quite frequently been disappointing. But if the changed contexts of political economy after 1929 and foreign policy after 1941 produced "revolutions," it is important for us to realize that a third "policy revolution" of huge but as yet undefined scope was launched *at home* during the 1960s. There is food for thought in a Republican President's signing, in 1972, a comprehensive measure to extend aid to higher education. There is more food for thought in the increase in budget expenditures by the Department of Health, Education, and Welfare from $3.4 billion in fiscal 1960 to $61.8 billion in fiscal 1971, (from 4.4% of the 1960 total to 26.4% of the 1971 total). To state the matter in a way that may surprise some readers: while $12.84 was spent in 1960 for direct defense costs to every dollar spent by HEW, by 1971 only $1.24 was spent by the Defense Department for every HEW dollar.

This enormous federal involvement has brought with it a strong urge for rational control, and for the use of technology and science—including social science—to make means-ends relationships more precise and explicit as the stakes involved increase. The same escalating complexity has also produced a strong two-way gravitational undertow. On the one hand, policy-makers gravitate toward expertise wherever they can find it—not merely to permit rational control of costs in the narrow fiscal sense but also to facilitate public policy designs which meet policymakers' definitions of the public or national interest at home and abroad. In short, policymakers are interested (at least ideally) in information and advice which can help close the gap between promise and performance in policy outputs. On the other hand, many social scientists—whether in universities or government or private sector—are drawn into policy research and expert counsel to policymakers. Their motives, of course, are mixed: the call of patriotism, the thrill of being close to power, and the large financial resources which become available are obvious attractions, as, in some cases, are the intellectual challenges involved in designing public policies which attempt to deal with situations of great complexity.

The two-way pull between policymakers and experts yields its own problems and issues. Among them is the skewing of policy advice toward what the decision-maker makes it clear he wants to hear. This skewing, suggested in the first essay here by Horowitz, operates in two ways. First, the policy adviser, wishing to maintain his effectiveness and credibility with his major client, the decision-maker, is under great pressure to accept the basic (often unexamined) value premises on which his client in the policy elite operates. The history of the Vietnam war is replete with this problem. Thus policy alternatives can readily become rapidly narrowed in the name of what may well be "crackpot realism," as C. Wright Mills and Professor Horowitz call it. The dynamics of the decision system itself tend to create self-closure, an increasing isolation of the policy elite and its experts from external public opinion. Again, the history of the Vietnam war is a nearly classic case of what happens to the political system when this self-closure becomes extreme.

But there is a second pattern of skew: government seeks expert advice and can (and often does) pay handsomely for it. Recruitment of policy experts by government necessarily involves a great deal of self-selection which tends to reinforce the political bias of the decision system. Not all social scientists would be willing to accept the practical constraints on their work which come with government—and particularly Defense Department—funding. Horowitz' essay on Project Camelot raises virtually the entire range of these issues, as did the Project itself. Only social scientists who were willing in the name of patriotism or other motives to join in a DOD-sponsored effort to control possible revolution in Chile through behavioral research were part of the project in the first place. Those who objected to this political use of social science—which amounts essentially to an intervention into the internal affairs of other countries—did not participate. But there are always those who will participate. The failure of some social scientists to do so in the Camelot case did nothing more than ensure that criticism of the Project's basic premises would not be likely to achieve an effective voice; so the Project went on until its "cover was blown" and the State Department raised vociferous objections. The other major issue raised by the affair, as Horowitz observes, is that it was essentially "captive" social science from beginning to end; with funding came a very tight control by military and other elites which eventuated in a kind of censorship of the research.

But there is a far more important political effect of all this. In the history of the human race, it has never been so true as at present that knowledge is power. Congress appropriates money, but it is spent overwhelmingly by executive agencies. This has not only contributed to the executive orientation of social scientists, but it has helped to place executive agencies, especially the Defense Department, in a commanding position vis-a-vis Congress. Knowledge thus structured financially and organizationally is a major *political* weapon which has made its own considerable contribution to the contemporary eclipse of congressional in-

fluence over the policymaking process. To a large extent, if "blame" is to be apportioned, it can be said that this has been Congress' fault. It is true in any event that the legislative branch is unlikely again to become truly coordinate in the American institutional scheme unless the majority of its members can define and enforce a *congressional interest as such* and implement it through the development of knowledge resources accountable to it rather than to an executive department. This, of course, would require that Congress not only develop a "collective institutional will" of its own, but create enforceable mechanisms internally by which such a will can be crystallized and made effective. We are unlikely to see a major formal change in the institutional structure of the federal government. And it can be said that any democratic revitalization which stops short of such change will probably require the development of such centralized power and knowledge resources within, or accountable to, the legislature. Whether or not such a major change occurs in the near future, it is useful to view the three essays in this Part as raising issues inherent in this question of expertise and control. These issues are unlikely to go away in the foreseeable future.

America's social goals were well stated by the writers of the Constitution: to "establish justice, insure domestic tranquility, provide for the common defense, promote the general welfare, and secure the blessings of liberty for ourselves and our posterity." But in 1968 we see little domestic tranquility; we see little justice for a substantial number of citizens; and for millions —poorly educated, ill-housed, or otherwise deprived— the blessings of liberty are a cruel jest.

The search for solutions to this modern dilemma leads those of us in government to turn to social research. There is increasing legislative hunger for social-science counsel. Senator Abraham Ribicoff, in major hearings on the urban crisis, called no fewer than 12 social scientists to testify. In order to improve the federal government's social-science research capability, Senator Fred Harris of Oklahoma has reintroduced legislation to establish a national foundation for the social sciences. He seeks to draw the social sciences from the shadow of the National Science Foundation, thus giving them independent status and increased stature.

In government departments, a new kind of administrator is emerging. For example, Daniel P. Moynihan, former Assistant Secretary of Labor, is "one of a new breed of public servants, the social-scientist-politicos, who combine in their backgrounds both social-science training and full-time involvement in political activity." (See "Black Families and the White House," Lee Rainwater and William L. Yancey, *Trans-action* July/August 1966.) Another new political animal in federal departments and agencies is the systems-approach expert, who—by means of cost-effectiveness analysis and other tools—seeks to help decision-makers understand all relevant alternatives and key interactions among them by calculating costs, risks, and potential results associated with each course of action. An example of this new breed is William Gorham, formerly of the Pentagon and the RAND Corporation, and Assistant Secretary for Planning and Evaluation at the Department of Health, Education, and Welfare, who has been appointed head of the Urban Institute, a government-supported independent research center.

The development of these new types of scientist-politicians suggests a governmental institution—an arm of the executive—that can combine a knowledge of sociology, science, history, social psychology, criminology, and social economics. These new specialists can

Reporting on the

place their knowledge in a governmental context, and bring a systems approach to bear on broad social programs.

Early last year I introduced in the Senate the Full Opportunity and Social Accounting Act, which was cosponsored by Senators Clark, Hart, Harris, Inouye, Kennedy of Massachusetts, McCarthy, McGee, Muskie, Nelson, and Proxmire, who is chairman of the Joint Economic Committee. This legislation would draw the social scientists into the inner councils of the Administration; it would foster the use of the systems approach for an overview of the broad range of domestic social programs; and it would establish a system of social accounting to keep a constant check on our domestic social status. Furthermore, it would require a public report of this social audit.

In its statement of policy, the Full Opportunity and Social Accounting Act reaffirms that "it is the continuing policy and responsibility of the federal government, consistent with the primary responsibilities of the state and local government and the private sector, to promote and encourage such conditions as will give every American the opportunity to live in decency and dignity, and to provide a clear and precise picture of whether such conditions are promoted and encouraged in such areas as health, education and training, rehabilitation, housing, vocational opportunities, the arts and humanities, and special assistance for the deprived, the abandoned, and the criminal."

To accomplish this, the legislation would:
—declare social accounting a national goal;
—establish the President's Council of Social Advisers,

Social State of the Union

Walter F. Mondale

comparable in the social sphere to the Council of Economic Advisers in the economic area;

—require the President to submit an annual Social Report to Congress, the social counterpart to his Economic Report; and

—create a joint committee of Congress to examine the substance of the Social Report.

In his Social Report, the President is to detail "the overall progress and effectiveness of federal efforts" toward implementing the policy of the act; review state, local, and private efforts to this end; and present "current and foreseeable needs, programs, and policies and recommendations for legislation."

The three-member Council of Social Advisers, supported by a staff of experts in the social sciences and in those natural sciences concerned with man and his environment, would be empowered to "gather timely and authoritative information and statistical data" and analyze and interpret them. The Council would also appraise the various programs and activities of the federal government and develop priorities for the programs, recommending to the President the most efficient and effective way to allocate federal resources.

The model for this act is the Employment Act of 1946, which has had an indisputably favorable effect on the nation's economy. This economic progress—owing in large part to highly refined economic analysis and indicators—is a powerful argument for using social analysis and measurement.

The Council of Economic Advisers recommends measures to maintain a stable, prosperous, and expanding economy. It operates on four assumptions:

—that welfare (the ultimate objective) is dependent upon the level and health of national economic activity;

—that economic factors can be quantified;

—that action by government can cause specific changes in the national economic condition; and

—that from analysis of economic data it is feasible to recommend specific action to achieve national economic health.

To do its job, the C.E.A. had to develop a system of economic criteria to measure the present and prospective conditions of the economy. It had to increase the expertise and the rigor of the economics discipline in order to reduce the margin of error in economic measurement. It had to develop tools of economic analysis, calling upon the entire community of economists for contributions. It had to proceed with caution so as to command the respect and acceptance of decision-makers. Finally, its recommendations and findings had to be action-oriented.

The same process is now appropriate and necessary in the social endeavors of the federal government. But we should mislead no one: This new job will be far more difficult. There should be no false hopes for instant success. For the most part, economic indicators are hard, cash-register data, and in most indices the dollar is available as a uniform measuring unit. Understandably, it is far easier to count the cash in a workingman's pocket than to measure the quality of his health or education.

A true attempt to apply non-economic measures to the quality of life in America could have a revolutionary impact on government. It might be the first time that government looked at the individual to see what government programs do *to* and *for* him—in other words, to discover the effect, rather than merely to measure the effort, of government programs. For example, we know how many people take advantage of Medicare, but there are no public reports on the quality of this care. The same is true of education, criminal rehabilitation, and much of the poverty effort (although the publication of studies on the effect of Head Start has been a laudable beginning).

At present, our social goals are vague and ill defined. The legislative requirement that the Administration deliver a public social accounting should sharpen the Administration's goals and social planning. This could promote setting long-range goals in, for example, education, health care, and the fight against environmental pollution, and encourage definite periodic progress toward their achievement.

Some argue that this system of progress reports will curb innovation and experimentation. But I think we have little to fear if we use fresh, imaginative ideas. And in fact, the lack of adequate indicators can actually conceal the success of government innovations. Critics of the Job Corps, for example, attack the cost per corpsman, while the Corps' effect on the corpsman's life and potential is ignored.

Some see a danger of the indicators' being manipulated for political ends, or the goals deliberately being set so low that accomplishment will appear spectacular. Of course, our political system is, at every level, vulnerable on this score. But there are checks built into the legislation. It provides for a Joint Congressional Committee empowered to probe deeply into the substance of the Social Report—to examine and criticize the declared goals, to question the philosophy behind the various programs, and to test the adequacy of the indicators. For a demonstration of how effective this legislative tool can be, we need only refer to the transcript of the 1967 hearings of the Joint Committee on the Economic Report chaired by Senator William Proxmire.

There are also other legislative checks on the Administration. The General Accounting Office has won a strong reputation for its auditing of Administration expenditures. Senator Abraham Ribicoff has proposed that this operation be expanded by adding an Office of Legislative Evaluation charged with "evaluating the results of the social and economic programs [Congress] has enacted." The Full Opportunity Act proposes to give the Administration new evaluative and analytical equipment. Certainly Congress should be given comparable legislative tools.

The Administration, with the program-planning-budgeting system directed by the Bureau of the Budget, is already taking limited steps toward improving program evaluation and determining program priorities. And William Gorham, in his work in the Department of Health, Education, and Welfare, has been coordinating a panel working on a "social state of the nation report." No one can guarantee, however, that it will be a permanent institution of government.

Search for a Constituency

As a matter of practical politics, the passage of legislation requires a constituency. Since most laws grow out of a need that has immediacy and relevance for a sizable part of the population, most proposed legislation has a constituency highly motivated to promote its passage. But where is the constituency of legislation that looks to the future—legislation that will have profound impact, yet is currently difficult to understand and in constant danger of being misinterpreted?

To build such a constituency, we must look to the social scientists themselves. And there are other allies as well. At all levels of government, social-welfare organizations and officials are concerned about the effectiveness of programs ranging from welfare to education, from city planning to health care.

The initial job in building a constituency is to bring the legislation to the attention of those for whom it has inherent interest. I have sent letters to 500 social scientists inviting their comment. Furthermore, editorials in media ranging from the *Minneapolis Star* and *Milwaukee Journal* to specialized newsletters have brought encouraging response.

The second step is persuasion, which in this case means education. Few people in policy-making positions are aware of the concept of social accounting—largely because literature on the subject is confined mostly to the academic journals.

The congressional committee is a useful educational device, particularly as an efficient information conduit to the policy-makers. The Full Opportunity and Social Accounting Act has been referred to the Government Operations Committee, which has sent it to Senator Harris's Subcommittee on Governmental Research. In

the summer of 1967 that subcommittee held a unique one-day seminar to explore the ramifications of the proposal. Both that session, and the hearings the subcommittee held later, elicited highly illuminating views from social scientists, present and former government officials, businessmen, and journalists. Above all, the discussions buttressed the need for an institutionalized and on-going review of the state of our nation's social health, at the highest level of government as well as on the community and state levels. In great part the hearings produced more questions than answers, and exposed our ignorance rather than a wealth of information about social processes. But our country is now demanding the answers, and it is essential that we begin asking the right questions.

While the Full Opportunity Act will have a vigorous impact upon government, I believe it will have no less impact on the social sciences. There is every reason to believe that the social sciences—like economics since 1946—will be greatly stimulated by enactment of the legislation. Such legislation may prod many social scientists into devoting increased attention to social problems that have specific relevancy to government. Instead of concentrating solely on research and comment, they will become active participants in policymaking.

Are social scientists up to the task? While most who have written me believe that they are, some are less confident. One social scientist of long experience warned, "The behavioral sciences, in my judgment, are in no real position at this point to give any hard data on social problems or conditions." He added, "There are many promises and pretentions; however, when it comes to delivery, what is usually forthcoming are more requests for further research. . . ."

If social scientists have not developed the necessary sophistication to fully participate in policy determination, then they *must*—and very soon. For government at all levels is going to ask them for advice and value judgments. This responsibility is going to be thrust upon them, and I don't think they are going to refuse it.

I am encouraged by the reports sent to me by social scientists who are involved in both the planning and the evaluation phases of future-looking projects. The work of organizations such as Resources for the Future and the Russell Sage Foundation is well known. And, of course, virtually every major university has a center or institute doing extremely ambitious research on social problems. Others, such as the Center for Research on the Utilization of Scientific Knowledge at the University of Michigan, are devoting their activity to ways of using scientific skills in the social as well as in the natural sciences. The book *Social Indicators* (M.I.T. Press, 1966), edited by Raymond Bauer, shows how researchers can frame the important questions and meet the basic requirements for social accounting.

All this suggests that some social scientists want to become activists—to convert their role from that of observer to that of participant.

The Communication Gap

Today, because much valuable information disappears into the academic journals, many policy-makers remain unaware of its existence. A Council of Social Advisers could probably correct this problem by providing a funnel through which the findings of social-science research would be directed to government.

Of course, government policy-makers shouldn't expect a full range of sophisticated social indicators to be developed overnight, nor should they expect evaluation and analysis that bear the stamp of certainty rather than theory. Scientific progress doesn't work this way. If I read the history of the Council of Economic Advisers correctly, it took that group many years, and experimentation by several Council chairmen, to evolve a satisfactory role in economic analysis and policy recommendation. This will be even more necessary when we are dealing with elusive social values.

Now, a word of warning: There is a history of mistrust on the part of some members of Congress toward the social sciences. This attitude is based partly on unfamiliarity, partly on poor communications between scientists and policy-makers, and partly on the fact that many Congressmen regard themselves as successful practitioners of applied social science—because they have won elections. Institutionalized channels of communication will help break down this mistrust.

Also important is the fact that policy-makers are wary of the political backlash contained in the findings of the social scientists. One dramatic example was the response of policy-makers to the Moynihan Report on the Negro family.

Finally, there are still a substantial number of people who see behavioral-science study as a trend toward the society of Orwell's *1984*. They are wary of invasion of privacy in social research, and fear that data banks will make the individual increasingly vulnerable. These are legitimate concerns, often deeply felt by the social scientists themselves. These concerns demand vigilance. There must be guarantees against misuse of some of the most valuable equipment in social-science research.

But despite these difficulties, it is time to establish an alliance between policy-makers and social scientists. The alliance promises better lives and more individual opportunity through a more orderly approach to the future.

Of this need, former Health, Education, and Welfare Secretary John W. Gardner has said: "We have a great and honored tradition of stumbling into the future. In management of the present, our nation is—as nations go—fairly rational, systematic, and orderly. But when it comes to movement into the future, we are heedless and impulsive. We leap before we look. We act first and think later. We back into next year's problems by studying the solutions to last year's problems."

Bertrand de Jouvenel has written that the 20th century now has the opportunity to devise "a long-term strategy for well-being." As I read the Preamble to the Constitution, it seems to me that this was precisely the goal of the 18th century Constitutional Convention. Today, a vigorous program—backed by the collective political wisdom of the Congress and the technical expertise of the social scientists—finally offers us hope of achieving that goal.

Social Science Yogis and Military Commissars

Irving Louis Horowitz

"The bonds between the government and the universities are . . . an arrangement of convenience, providing the government with politically usable knowledge and the university with badly needed funds." The speaker of these words, Senator J. William Fulbright, went on to warn that such alliances may endanger the universities, may bring about "the surrender of independence, the neglect of teaching, and the distortion of scholarship." Many other distinguished Americans are worried by the growing number of alliances between the military and the university.

The Setting

Instead of the expected disclaimers and denials from university officials, however, in recent months these men—from both the administrative and academic sides—have rushed to take up any slack in doing secret research on campus, asking that the number of projects they are already handling be increased. Arwin A. Dougal, assistant director of the Pentagon's office for research and engineering, has indicated that while some major universities are gravely concerned about academic research for military ends, most universities realize how important "classified research" is to the national security. Indeed, Dougal has said that many professors involved in secret research actually try to retain their security clearances when their projects are completed. Rather than disengaging themselves, they, like many university leaders, are eager to participate to an even greater extent.

Symptomatic of the ever-tightening bond between the military and the social scientist is a "confidential," 53-page document entitled *Report of the Panel on Defense Social and Behavioral Sciences*. It was the offspring of a summer 1967 meeting, in Williamstown, Mass., of members of the Defense Science Board of the National Academy of Sciences. This board is the highest-ranking science advisory group of the Defense Department. The meeting's purpose: to discuss which social-science research could be of most use to the Department of Defense (DoD).

The Report of the Panel on Defense Social and Behavioral Sciences throws a good deal of light on current relations between the national government and the social sciences. Unlike Project Camelot, the abortive academic-military project to investigate counterinsurgency potentials in the Third World, this Report was not inspired by government contractual requests. It is the work of leading social scientists who have been closely connected with federal research. Unlike *Report from Iron Mountain*, this Report can hardly be described as a humanistic hoax. The authors are known, the purpose of the Report explicit, and the consequences clearly appreciated by all concerned. What we have in this Report is a collective statement by eminent social scientists, a statement that can easily be read as the ominous conversion of social science into a service industry of the Pentagon.

Most of the scholars who prepared this Report have one striking similarity—they have powerful and simultaneous academic and government linkages. They move casually and easily from university to federal affiliation —and back again to the university.

The panel's chairman, S. Rains Wallace, the exception, is president of the American Institutes of Research, a nonprofit organization that does research under contract for government agencies, including the DoD.

Gene M. Lyons, who is executive secretary of the Advisory Committee on Government Programs in the Behavioral Sciences of the National Research Council (affiliated with the National Academy of Sciences), is also a professor at Dartmouth College. (He maintains, however, that he attended only one day of the meeting, and as an observer only.)

Peter Dorner, functioning through the Executive Office of the President on the Council of Economic Advisers, is also a professor of economics at the Land Tenure Center of the University of Wisconsin.

Eugene Webb, listed as a professor at Stanford University, is now serving a term as a member of the Institute for Defense Analysis, specifically, its science and technology division.

Other panel members—Harold Guetzkow of Northwestern University; Michael Pearce of the RAND Corporation; anthropologist A. Kimball Romney of Harvard University; and Roger Russell, formerly of Indiana University and now Vice-Chancellor for Academic Affairs at the University of California (Irvine)

—also shift back and forth between the polity and the academy. It is plain, then, that these men have penetrated the political world more deeply than members of past project-dominated research activities.

In addition to this similarity, nearly all of these social scientists have had overseas experience, and are intimately connected with federal use of social science for foreign-area research. Yet, as in the case of Camelot, this common experience does not seem to produce any strong ideological unanimity. The men range from relatively conservative political theorists to avowed pacifists. This underscores the fact that patriotism and professional purpose tend to supersede the political viewpoints or credos these men may adhere to.

The Report

The Report closely follows the memorandum that John S. Foster Jr., director of Defense Research and Engineering of the Department of Defense, issued to the chairman of the panel. Foster's marching orders to the panel members requested that they consider basically four topics: "high-payoff" areas in research and development—"areas of social and behavioral science research in which it would be reasonable to expect great payoffs over the next three to ten years"; research to solve manpower problems; Project THEMIS, a DoD project for upgrading the scientific and engineering capabilities of various academic institutions so they can do better research for the Defense Department; and, finally, broad-ranging government-university relationships.

Before commenting on the Report, let me provide a summary of its findings and recommendations.

To begin with, the Report urges increased effort and funding for research on manpower, in all its aspects; for research on organization studies; for research on decision-making; for increasing the understanding of problems in foreign areas; and for research on man and his physical environment.

■ Under "Manpower," we read, among other things: "In order to make full use of the opportunities provided by Project 100,000 [to make soldiers out of rehabilitated juvenile delinquents] both for the military and for the national economy, we recommend that fully adequate funds be invested to cover all aspects of the military and subsequent civilian experience of the individuals involved."

■ Under "Organization Studies":

"Research on style of leadership and improved methods of training for leadership should be revitalized."

■ Under "Decision-Making":

"Techniques for the improvement of items which might assist in forecasting alliances, neutralities, hostile activities, etc., and for use in tactical decision-making need to be expanded, applied, and tested in the real world."

■ Under "Understanding of Operational Problems in Foreign Areas":

"Despite the difficulties attendant upon research in foreign areas, it must be explicitly recognized that the missions of the DoD cannot be successfully performed in the absence of information on (a) socio-cultural patterns in various areas including beliefs, values, motivations, etc.; (b) the social organization of troops, including political, religious, and economic; (c) the effect of change and innovation upon socio-cultural patterns and socio-cultural organization of groups; (d) study and evaluation of action programs initiated by U.S. or foreign agencies in under-developed countries.

"Solid, precise, comparative, and current empirical data developed in a programmatic rather than diffuse and opportunistic fashion are urgently needed for many areas of the world. This goal should be pursued by: (a) multidisciplinary research teams; (b) series of field studies in relevant countries; (c) strong representation of quantitative and analytic skills; (d) a broad empirical data base."

■ Under "Man and His Physical Environment":

"Continuing and additional research are needed on the effect of special physical and psychological environments upon performance and on possibilities for the enhancement of performance through a better understanding of man's sensory and motor output mechanisms, the development of artificial systems which will aid performance, and the search for drugs or foods which may enhance it."

■ Under "Methodology":

"We recommend increased emphasis upon research in behavioral-science methodology. While this is basic to all of the areas listed above, it needs to be recognized as worthy of investment in its own right. The systematic observation of the many quasi-experimental situations which occur in everyday military activities must be made possible if we are to learn from experience. We recommend that a capability be established in one or more suitable in-house laboratories to address the question of how the logistical problems of such observation can be solved."

■ On government-university relations:

"There is disagreement concerning the involvement of first-rate academic groups in behavioral science research relevant to long-term DoD needs. The task statement implies that DoD has not been successful in enlisting the interest and service of an eminent group of behavioral scientists in most of the areas relevant to it. This panel does not concur. We therefore recommend that the [National Academy of Sciences] Panel on Behavioral and Social Sciences be asked to address this problem and to determine whether, in fact, an acceptable proportion of first-rate academic workers are involved in DoD behavioral-science research."

"More high-quality scientists could probably be interested in DoD problems if DoD would more frequently state its research needs in terms which are meaningful to the investigator rather than to the military. . . . Publicity concerning the distinguished behavioral scientists who have long-term commitments to the DoD should be disseminated as a way of reassuring younger scientists and improving our research image."

The Panelists

Why did these distinguished social scientists accept the assignment from the DoD? Most of them seemed particularly intrigued by the chance to address important issues. They view the work done by the DoD in such areas as racially segregated housing, or the rehabilitation of juvenile delinquents through military participation, as fascinating illustrations of how social science can settle social issues. It is curious how this thirst for the application of social science led the panelists to ignore the *prima facie* fact that the DoD is in the defense business, and that therefore it inevitably tends to assign high priority to military potential and effectiveness. Further, the question of what is important is continually linked to matters of relevance to the DoD. In this way, the question of professional autonomy is transformed into one of patriotic responsibility.

In general, the idealism of social scientists participating in DoD-sponsored research stems from their profound belief in the rectifiability of federal shortcomings, as well as in the perfectibility of society

Why the DoD is No. 1

The Department of Defense (DoD) is the most sought-after and frequently-found sponsor of social-science research. And the DoD is sought and found by the social scientists, not, as is often imagined, the other way around. Customarily, military men provide only grudging acceptance of any need for behavioral research.

There are four distinct reasons why the DoD is sponsoring more and more social-science research.

■ First, money. In fiscal 1968, Congressional appropriations for research and development amount to the monumental sum of $14,971.4 million. Of this, an incredible $13,243.0 million, or about 85 percent, is distributed among three agencies whose primary concern is the military system: the Atomic Energy Commission, the National Aeronautics and Space Administration, and the DoD. The figure for the DoD alone is $6680.0 million. This means that a single federal agency commands nearly two-fifths of the government research dollar. So it is easy to see why so much effort and energy is expended by social scientists trying to capture some of the monies the DoD can experiment with. As bees flock to honey, men flock to money—particularly in an era when costly data-processing and data-gathering strain the conventional sources of financing.

■ Second, the protection that research has when done for the DoD. I am referring to the blanket and indiscriminate way in which Congressional appropriations are made for both basic and applied research. Policy-linked social scientists operate under an umbrella of the secrecy established by the DoD's research agencies. Reasons of security ward off harassment by Congressional committees. Attacks over supposed misallocation of funds and resources—undergone by the National Institutes of Health at the hands of the committee headed by Rep. L.H. Fountain of North Carolina—are spared those academics with Defense Department funding.

This dispensation is strikingly illustrated by the fact that DoD allocations for research and development are not itemized the way allocations are for Health, Education, and Welfare. This auditing cover allows for even more experimenting in DoD spending than its already swollen funds might indicate. Such a *carte blanche* situation probably places far less of a strain on social scientists than would be the case if they worked for other agencies. In the world of research, power provides the illusion of freedom.

■ Third, the relatively blank-check Congressional approach to DoD funds, and the security umbrella of the auditing system, provide social scientists with unlimited resources. DoD allocations are not broken down into sub-agencies, nor are any of their specialized activities or services checked—unlike the usual scrutiny directed at other agencies.

That this fact has not gone entirely unnoticed is shown by the Congressional demand that as of 1968 the DoD be called to account on an appropriation budget.

■ Fourth, the DoD's connection with the "national security" —which protects the DoD and those who work for it— offers great temptations to social researchers interested in the "big news." For it enables the DoD not only to outspend such agencies as the National Science Foundation in university-based activities, but to penetrate areas of non-Defense research that are central only to the social-science researcher. Programs to support juvenile-delinquency research (Project 100,000) and others to upgrade academic institutions (Project THEMIS) are sponsored by the DoD rather than by the Office of Economic Opportunity, and not simply because of their disproportionate fundings. Just as important is the legitimation the DoD can provide for policy-oriented researchers in sensitive areas.

These are the main reasons why many social-science researchers are now enlisting the support of the DoD in their activities—despite the negative publicity surrounding Project Camelot and other such fallen angels.   I.L.H.

---

through the use of social science. Despite the obviousness of the point, what these social scientists forget is that the federal government as well as its agencies is limited by historical and geopolitical circumstances. It is committed to managing cumbersome, overgrown committees and data-gathering agencies. It is committed to a status quo merely for the sake of rational functioning. It can only tinker with innovating ideas. Thus federal agencies will limit investigation simply to what

agent. His designing mentality, his strain toward perfecting, will appear unrealistic in the is immediately useful not out of choice, but from necessity.

The social scientist often imagines he is a policy formulator, an innovating designer. Because of the cumbersome operations of government, he will be frustrated in realizing this self-image and be reduced to one more instrumental light of what he can do. He gets caught up in theoryless applications to immediacy, surrenders the value of confronting men with an image of what *can be,* and simply accepts what others declare *must be.* Thus, what the social scientist knows comes down to what the Defense Department under present circumstances can use.

Although the initiative for this Report came from the social scientists, the DoD provided the structure and direction of its content. To a remarkable degree, the study group accepted DoD premises.

For example, the two major assumptions that influenced its thinking are stated baldly. First, since the DoD's job now embraces new responsibilities, its proper role becomes as much to wage "peacefare" as warfare. Peacefare is spelled out as pacification of total populations, as well as a role in the ideological battle between East and West. Toward such ends, it is maintained, social science can play a vital part.

Nowhere in the document is the possibility considered that the DoD ought not to be in many of these activities—that perhaps the division of labor has placed too great an emphasis upon this one agency of government at the expense of all others. Nor is it anywhere made clear that similar types of educational and antipoverty programs the DoD is engaged in are already under way in other branches of government—that DoD activities might be duplicating and needlessly multiplying the efforts of the Department of Health, Education and Welfare or the National Science Foundation.

The second explicit assumption the group makes is that hardware alone will not win modern wars; Manpower is needed, too. Here the panelists see social science as providing data on the dynamics of cultural change and a framework for the needs and attitudes of other people.

But here, too, there is a remarkable absence of any consideration of the sort of "manpower" deployed in foreign environments; or of the differing responses of overseas peoples to such manpower. The foreign role of the U.S. Defense Department is simply taken as a given, a datum to be exploited for the display of social science information. In this sense, U.S. difficulties with foreign military activities can be interpreted as a mere misunderstanding of the nature of a problem. Expertise and objectivity can then be called upon where a policy design is lacking or failing. Thus even the DoD can mask policy shortcomings behind the fact of a previously inadequate supply of data. In this way, the credibility gap gets converted into a mechanical informational gap. Which is exactly what is done in the Report. All efforts, in other words, are bent to maximizing social science participation rather than to minimizing international conflict.

Still a third assumption of the panel participants—one that is not acknowledged—is that their professional autonomy will not be seriously jeopardized by the very fact of their dependence upon the DoD. Indeed, many scholars seem to have abandoned their primary research interests for the secondary ones that can be funded. And the main responsibility for this shift lies not with the DoD but with the social-science professions and the scholarly community at large.

As one panel member ironically noted, in response to my questionnaire, the position of the DoD is an unhappy reflection of university demands that individual scholars and university presidents pay for expanding university overhead and enlarge graduate programs—rather than any insistence by federal agencies that the nature of social science be transformed. Another panel member indicated that, whatever dishonor may exist in the present relationships between social science and the DoD, the main charge would have to be leveled at the professoriat, rather than at the funding agencies. And while this assignment of priorities in terms of who is responsible for the present era of ill will and mistrust can be easily overdone, and lead to a form of higher apologetics in which there is mutual accusation by the social scientists and government policy-makers, it does seem clear that the simplistic idea that the evil government corrupts the good social scientist is not only an exaggeration but, more often, a deliberate misrepresentation.

The Findings

Reexamining the specific findings of first section of the Report, "High Payoff Research in Development Areas," leaves no doubt that the panelists mean by "high payoff" those potential rewards to be netted by the DoD, rather than advantages to be gained by social scientists. This is made explicit in the section on "Manpower," in which the main issues are contended to concern problems of improving the performance of soldiers equipped with high-level technology. It is in this connection that the panelists heartily approve of Project 100,000. Although (with the exception of two panelists) there is a special cloudiness as to the nature of Project 100,000, the panelists have no doubt that the employment of delinquents in this fashion makes the best use of marginal manpower for a "tremendous payoff" for the future efficiency of the defense establishment.

A number of the Report's recommendations amount to little more than the repetition of basic organizational shibboleths. But even at this level, special problems seem to arise. There is confusion in the minds of the panelists, or at least throughout the Report that they prepared, about what constitutes internal DoD functions as opposed to those belonging to general military functions. The phrase "military establishment" functions as an umbrella disguising this ambiguity. Not only is the relationship between a civilian-led DoD and a "military establishment" unresolved, but beyond that the panelists appear willing to discount the organizational intermingling of the DoD with other governmental agencies—such as the Census Bureau, the Department of Labor, and the Department of Health, Education, and Welfare.

This leads to a tacit acceptance of DoD organizational colonialism. Not only is the DoD urged to be on the lookout for other agencies' collecting similar data and doing similar sorts of analyses, but also an explicit request that the DoD exert a special effort to use the work of outside agencies is included. On behalf of "cooperation," there exists the risk of invasion of privacy, and other dangers encountered when any single department functions as a total system incorporating the findings of other sub-units.

The Report contends that those parts of the armed services responsible for developing basic knowledge about decision-making have done their work well. It is interesting that no examples are given. Moreover, the military and civilian personnel who provide support for decision-making within the military establishment are said to have a rare opportunity to contribute to this steadily-improving use of sound decision-making models for areas like material procurement for frontline battle medical services. Nothing is said about the nature of the conflict to be resolved, or the values employed in such decisions.

While several members of the panel, in response to the questionnaire of mine, indicated that they held this Report to be an indirect resolution of problems raised by Project Camelot, the formulations used in this Report are similar to those used in the Camelot study concerning overseas research.

The Report states: "Comparative organizational work should not be done only within civilian groups such as large-scale building and construction consortia and worldwide airlines systems, but also within foreign military establishments." In Project Camelot, the same desire for military information was paramount. Curiously, no attention is given to whether, in fact, this is a high-payoff research area; or if it is, how this work is to be done without threatening the sovereignty of other nations. In other words, although the Report superficially is dedicated to the principle of maximum use of social science, this principle is not brought into play at the critical point. The ambiguities and doubts raised by previous DoD incursions into the area of foreign social research remain intact and are in no way even partially resolved.

The panelists are dedicated to the principle of high-payoff research, but appear to be disquietingly convinced that this is equivalent to whatever the members of the panel themselves are doing, or whatever their professional specialties are. Thus a high-payoff research area becomes the study of isolation upon individual and group behavior; or the area of simulation of field experiences that the military may encounter; or the study of behavior under conditions of ionizing radiation. It is not incidental that in each instance the panelists themselves have been largely engaged in such kinds of work. One is left with the distinct impression that a larger number of panelists would have yielded only a larger number of "high-payoff" areas, rather than an integrated framework of needs. This leads to a general suspicion that the Report is much more self-serving than a simple review of its propositions indicates.

The references to methodology again raise the specter of Camelot, since it is evident that no general methodology is demonstrated in the Report itself and no genuine innovations are formulated for future methodological directions. There is no discussion of the kind of methodology likely to yield meaningful prediction. Instead, the DoD is simply notified of the correctness of its own biases. We are told that "predictive indicators of a conflict or revolutionary overthrow are examples of the type of data which can gain from control applications." No illustrations of the success of such predictors is given. The purpose turns out to be not so much prediction as control of revolutionary outbreaks. This, then, constitutes the core methodological message of the Report.

Project THEMIS

As for Project THEMIS, designed to upgrade scientific and engineering performances at colleges and universities for the benefit of the Defense Department, the project titles at the institutions already selected do not furnish enough information to assess the actual nature of the research. A proposal of more than $1.1 million for research into "chemical compounds containing highly electro-negative elements" was turned down by the dean of faculties at Portland State College. Said he: "I know what the proposal was talking about. It could very easily be interpreted as a proposal involving biological warfare. The proposal could be construed as committing the university to biological warfare."

Among the universities now contracted for Project THEMIS work is the University of Utah, with the project title "Chemistry of Combustion." Newspaper accounts during the summer of 1967 indicated clearly that this project was aimed at improving missile fuels. Additional illustrations could be given, but the point is clear: Project THEMIS is what it claims to be, a program to involve universities in research useful to the Defense Department.

The panelists assure us that "DoD has been singularly successful at enlisting the interest and services of an eminent group of behavioral scientists in most of the areas relevant to it." They go on to say that, indeed, "the management of behavioral science research in the military department should be complimented for long-term success in building the image of DoD as a good and challenging environment in which to do both basic and applied research." No names are cited to indicate that there are eminent clusters of behavioral scientists working in the DoD. Nor is

there an indication whether "the eminent men" connected with DoD are in fact remotely connected as part-time consultants (like the panelists themselves) or intimately connected with basic work for the government. And even though Foster's letter indicates that there is a problem of recruitment and government-university relations, the panel simply dismisses this as insignificant. Yet members go on to note that the DoD image is perhaps more tarnished than they would like to think; that, for example, the Civil Service Commission discriminates against the behavioral scientist with respect to appointments, and that it is hard to persuade behavioral scientists that the DoD provides a supportive environment for them. Despite the censure of the Civil Service Commission, it is claimed that the DoD has not been as attractive and as successful in social-science recruitment as we were earlier led to believe.

More damaging, perhaps, is the allegation of the panelists that quality control of research at universities is not in any way superior to that exercised within other research sources, such as the DoD. They tend to see "quality control" as something unrelated to university autonomy and its implications for objectivity. Lest there be any ambiguity on this point, they go on to indicate in an extraordinary series of unsupported allegations that the difficulty is not one of social-science autonomy versus the political requirements of any agency of government, but rather one of bad public relations—which is in turn mostly blamed on "Representatives of Civilian Professional Organizations" who lack a clear picture of DoD requirements and yet testify before Congressional committees, which in turn are backed up by social and behavioral scientists who regard such DoD activities as a threat to academic freedom and scientific integrity, and who "are usually ignorant of the work actually being performed under DoD's aegis."

The specific committee hearings referred to are nowhere indicated. Certainly, the various hearings on such proposed measures as a national social science foundation, or on social accounting, do exhibit the highest amount of professional integrity and concern. It might be that DoD intellectuals are concerned precisely over the non-policy research features of such proposed legislation.

Finally, the panelists offer a gentle slap on the wrist to defense research managers who allegedly lack the time to address themselves to these kinds of problems. In short and in sum, the Report ignores questions having to do with social science autonomy as if these were products of misperceptions to be resolved by good will and better public relations between the DoD and the Academy. That such conclusions should be reached by a set of panelists, half of whom are highly placed in academic life, indicates the degree to which closing the gap between the academy and the polity has paradoxically broken down the political capabilities of social science by weakening its autonomous basis.

The panelists have enough firmness of mind to make two unsolicited comments. But the nature of the comments reveals the flabbiness that results from the tendency of social scientists to conceive of their sciences as service activities rather than as scientific activities. They urge, first, that more work be done in the area of potential high-payoff fields of investigation that might have been overlooked in their own Report, given the short time they had available in preparing it. They further urge the establishment of a continuous group with time to examine other areas in greater depth and to discuss them more deliberately, so that high-payoff areas can be teased out and presented for cost considerations. In other words, the unsolicited comments suggest mechanisms for improving these kinds of recommendations and making them permanent. They do not consider whether the nature of social science requirements might be unfit for the bureaucratic specifications of Foster's originating letter.

Advise and Dissent

In some ways, the very tension between social scientists and policy-makers provided each group with a reality test against which basic ideas could be formulated about policy issues. But the very demand for a coalescence of the two, whether in the name of "significant" research or as a straight patriotic obligation, has the effect of corrupting social science and impoverishing policy options.

The question that the Report raises with terrible forcefulness is not so much about the relationship between pure and applied research, but about what the character of application is to be. Applied research is clearly here to stay and is probably the most forceful, singular novel element in American social science in contrast to its European background. What is at stake, however, is a highly refined concept of application that removes theoretical considerations of the character and balance of social forces and private interests from the purview of application. The design of the future replaces the analysis of the present in our "new utopian" world.

The panelists simply do not entertain the possibility that the social world is a behavioral "field" in which decisions have to be made between political goals no less than means. Reports cannot "depoliticalize" social action to such an extent that consequences do not follow and implicit choices are not favored. Innovation without a political goal simply assumes that operations leading to a change from one state to another are a value. The Report does not raise, much less favor, significant political changes in the operations of the DoD; and its innovative efforts are circumscribed to improving rather than to changing. However, efficiency is a limited use of applicability because it assumes rather than tests the adequacy of the social system.

The era of good feelings between the federal government and social science, which characterized the period between the outbreak of World War II and extended through the assassination of President John F. Kennedy, no longer exists. In its place seems to be the era of tight money. The future of "nonprofit" research corporations tied to the DoD is being severely impeded from both sides. Universities such as Pennsylvania, the University of California, and Princeton have taken a hard look at academic involvement in classified research for the Pentagon. Princeton, with its huge stake in international-relations programming, is even considering cancelling its sponsorship of a key research arm, the Institute for Defense Analysis. On the other side, many of the "hard" engineering types have continued to press their doubts as to the usefulness of software research. And this barrage of criticism finds welcome support among high military officers who would just as soon cancel social science projects as carry out their implications.

With respect to the panelists, it must be said that a number of them have indicated their own doubts about the Report. One of the participants has correctly pointed out that the Report has not yet been accepted by the DoD, nor have the findings or the recommendations been endorsed by the National Academy of Sciences. Another member claimed that his main reason for accepting the invitation to serve on the panel was to argue against the Defense Department's involving universities in operations such as Project Camelot. He went on to point out that his mission was unsuccessful, since he obviously did not influence the other panelists.

A third panelist points out that the Camelot type of issue was not, to his recollection at least, a criterion in any discussion of the topics. Yet he strongly disclaims his own participation as well as membership in the National Academy of Science Advisory Committee on Government Programs in the Behavioral Sciences. He also indicates that his panel had nothing but an administrative connection with the National Academy of Sciences, and he, too, seems to indicate that he had an ancillary advisory role rather than an integrated preparatory role.

Trying to gauge the accuracy with which the final Report represented a true consensus of the panelists proved most difficult. While most panelists, with hedging qualifications, agreed that the Report reflected an accurate appraisal of their own views, the question of the actual writeup of the document brought forth a far from consistent response. One panelist claims that "all members contributed to the basic draft of the Report. Each assumed responsibility for composing a section, all of which were then reviewed by the panel as a whole." Another panelist declared his participation only "as an observer," and that he was not involved in any final writeup. Yet a third panelist disclaimed any connection with preparing the Report.

A final, and still different, version was stated as follows: "The report was written by members of the committee and the overall editing and bringing-together responsibility was undertaken by Rains Wallace. One or two members of the committee were assigned to specific topics and drafts were prepared at Williamstown. These went to Wallace, who organized them, did some editing, and sent them back to us. Each person responded and the final version was then prepared by Wallace." In other words, the actual authorship of a document that was released "in confidence" over the names of some of America's most distinguished social scientists is either the work of all and the responsibility of none, or perhaps—as is more likely the case—the work of one or two people and the responsibility of all.

F.A.R. vs DoD

The issuance, even in semi-private form, of this Report reveals the existence of a wide gap between the thinking of the two chief departments involved in sensitive research and in research in foreign areas—namely, the Department of Defense and the Department of State. Indeed, the issuance of this Report is likely to exacerbate the feelings of high officials in the State Department that the Defense Department position represents an encroachment.

The memorandum issued in December 1967 by the Department of State's Foreign Area Research Coordination group (F.A.R.), in which it set forth foreign-area research guidelines, represents a direct rebuke or, at the very least, a serious challenge to the orientation that the Report of the Defense Science Board represents. It is a high point in federal recognition that real problems do exist.

The F.A.R. Report is broken into two different sections with seven propositions in each section. First, under Guidelines for Research Contract Relations Between Government and Universities, are the following:

(1) The government has the responsibility for avoiding actions that would call into question the integrity of American academic institutions as centers of independent teaching and research.

(2) Government research support should always be acknowledged by sponsor, university, and researcher.

(3) Government-supported contract research should, in process and results, ideally be unclassified, but given the practical needs of the nation in the modern world, some portion may be subject to classification. In this case the balance between making work public or classified should lean whenever possible toward making it public.

(4) Agencies should encourage open publication of contract research results.

(5) Government agencies that contract with university researchers should consider designing their projects so as to advance knowledge as well as to meet the immediate policy or action needs.

(6) Government agencies have the obligation of informing the potential researcher of the needs that the research should help meet, and of any special conditions associated with the research contract, and generally of the agency's expectations concerning the research and the researcher.

(7) The government should continue to seek research of the highest possible quality in its contract program.

A second set of seven recommendations is listed under Guidelines for the Conduct of Foreign Area Research Under Government Contract, and these too bear very directly on the panel Report and do so most critically and tellingly.

(1) The government should take special steps to ensure that the parties with which it contracts have the highest qualifications for carrying out research overseas.

(2) The government should work to avert or minimize adverse foreign reactions to its contract research programs conducted overseas.

(3) When a project involves research abroad, it is particularly important that both the supporting agency and the researcher openly acknowledge the auspices and financing of research projects.

(4) The government should under certain circumstances ascertain that the research is acceptable to the host government before proceeding on the research.

(5) The government should encourage cooperation with foreign scholars in its contract research program.

(6) Government agencies should continue to co-ordinate their foreign-area research programs to eliminate duplication and overloading of any one geographical area.

(7) Government agencies should cooperate with academic associations on problems of foreign-area research.

This set of recommendations (with allowances made for the circumstances of their issuance) unquestionably represents the most enlightened position yet taken by a federal agency on the question of the relationship between social science and practical politics. These sets of recommendations not only stand as ethical criteria for the federal government's relationship to social scientists, but—even more decisively—represent a rebuke to precisely the sort of militarization of social science implicit in the panel Report. The reassertion by a major federal policy-making agency of the worth to the government of social science autonomy represented the first significant recognition by a federal agency that Project Camelot was the consequence, not the cause, of the present strains in social science-federal bureaucracy relationships.

The Life and Death of Project Camelot

Irving Louis Horowitz

In June of 1965 — in the midst of the crisis over the Dominican Republic—the United States Ambassador to Chile sent an urgent and angry cable to the State Department. Ambassador Ralph Dungan was confronted with a growing outburst of anti-Americanism from Chilean newspapers and intellectuals. Further, left-wing members of the Chilean Senate had accused the United States of espionage.

The anti-American attacks that agitated Dungan had no direct connection with sending US troops to Santo Domingo. Their target was a mysterious and cloudy American research program called Project Camelot.

Dungan wanted to know from the State Department what Project Camelot was all about. Further, whatever Camelot was, he wanted it stopped because it was fast becoming a *cause célèbre* in Chile (as it soon would throughout capitals of Latin America and in Washington) and Dungan had not been told anything about it—even though it was sponsored by the US Army and involved the tinderbox subjects of counter-revolution and counter-insurgency in Latin America.

Within a few weeks Project Camelot created repercussions from Capitol Hill to the White House. Senator J. William Fulbright, chairman of the Foreign Relations Committee, registered his personal concern about such projects as Camelot because of their "reactionary, backward-looking policy opposed to change. Implicit in Camelot, as in the concept of 'counter-insurgency,' is an assumption that revolutionary movements are dangerous to the interests of the United States and that the United States must be prepared to assist, if not actually to participate in, measures to repress them."

By mid-June the State Department and Defense Department—which had created and funded Camelot—were in open contention over the project and the jurisdiction each department should have over certain foreign policy operations.

On July 8, Project Camelot was killed by Defense Secretary Robert McNamara's office which has a veto power over the military budget. The decision had been made under the President's direction.

On that same day, the director of Camelot's parent body, the Special Operations Research Organization, told a Congressional committee that the research project on revolution and counter-insurgency had taken its name from King Arthur's mythical domain because "It connotes the right sort of things—development of a stable society with peace and justice for all." Whatever Camelot's outcome, there should be no mistaking the deep sincerity behind this appeal for an applied social science pertinent to current policy.

However, Camelot left a horizon of disarray in its wake: an open dispute between State and Defense; fuel for the anti-American fires in Latin America; a cut in US Army research appropriations. In addition, serious and perhaps ominous implications for social science research, bordering on censorship, have been raised by the heated reaction of the executive branch of government.

GLOBAL COUNTER-INSURGENCY

What was Project Camelot? Basically, it was a project for measuring and forecasting the causes of revolutions and insurgency in underdeveloped areas of the world. It also aimed to find ways of eliminating the causes, or coping with the revolutions and insurgencies. Camelot was sponsored by the US Army on a four to six million dollar contract, spaced out over three to four years, with the Special Operations Research Organization (SORO). This agency is nominally under the aegis of American University in Washington, D.C., and does a variety of research for the Army. This includes making analytical surveys of foreign areas; keeping up-to-date information on the military, political, and social complexes of those areas; and maintaining a "rapid response" file for getting immediate information, upon Army request, on any situation deemed militarily important.

Latin America was the first area chosen for concentrated study, but countries on Camelot's four-year list included some in Asia, Africa, and Europe. In a working paper issued on December 5, 1964, at the request of the Office of the Chief of Research and Development, Department of the Army, it was recommended that "comparative historical studies" be made in these countries:

■ (Latin America) Argentina, Bolivia, Brazil, Colombia, Cuba, Dominican Republic, El Salvador, Guatemala, Mexico, Paraguay, Peru, Venezuela.
■ (Middle East) Egypt, Iran, Turkey.
■ (Far East) Korea, Indonesia, Malaysia, Thailand.
■ (Others) France, Greece, Nigeria.

"Survey research and other field studies" were recommended for Bolivia, Colombia, Ecuador, Paraguay, Peru, Venezuela, Iran, Thailand. Preliminary consideration was also being given to a study of the separatist movement in French Canada. It, too, had a code name: Project Revolt.

In a recruiting letter sent to selected scholars all over the world at the end of 1964, Project Camelot's aims were defined as a study to "make it possible to predict and influence politically significant aspects of social change in the developing nations of the world." This would include devising procedures for "assessing the potential for internal war within national societies" and "identify(ing) with increased degrees of confidence, those actions which a government might take to relieve conditions which are assessed as giving rise to a potential for internal war." The letter further stated:

> The US Army has an important mission in the positive and constructive aspects of nation-building in less developed countries as well as a responsibility to assist friendly governments in dealing with active insurgency problems.

Such activities by the US Army were described as "insur-gency prophylaxis" rather than the "sometimes misleading label of counter-insurgency."

Project Camelot was conceived in late 1963 by a group of high-ranking Army officers connected with the Army Research Office of the Department of Defense. They were concerned about new types of warfare springing up around the world. Revolutions in Cuba and Yemen and insurgency movements in Vietnam and the Congo were a far cry from the battles of World War II and also different from the envisioned—and planned for—apocalypse of nuclear war. For the first time in modern warfare, military establishments were not in a position to use the immense arsenals at their disposal—but were, instead, compelled by force of a geopolitical stalemate to increasingly engage in primitive forms of armed combat. The questions of moment for the Army were: Why can't the "hardware" be used? And what alternatives can social science "software" provide?

A well-known Latin American area specialist, Rex Hopper, was chosen as director of Project Camelot. Hopper was a professor of sociology and chairman of the department at Brooklyn College. He had been to Latin America many times over a thirty-year span on research projects and lecture tours, including some under government sponsorship. He was highly recommended for the position by his professional associates in Washington and elsewhere. Hopper had a long-standing interest in problems of revolution and saw in this multi-million dollar contract the possible realization of a life-long scientific ambition.

THE CHILEAN DEBACLE

How did this social science research project create a foreign policy furore? And, at another level, how did such high intentions result in so disastrous an outcome?

The answers involve a network spreading from a professor of anthropology at the University of Pittsburgh, to a professor of sociology at the University of Oslo, and yet a third professor of sociology at the University of Chile in Santiago, Chile. The "showdown" took place in Chile, first within the confines of the university, next on the floor of the Chilean Senate, then in the popular press of Santiago, and finally, behind US embassy walls.

It was ironic that Chile was the scene of wild newspaper tales of spying and academic outrage at scholars being recruited for "spying missions." For the working papers of Project Camelot stipulated as a criterion for study that a country "should show promise of high pay-offs in terms of the kinds of data required." Chile did not meet these requirements—it is not on the preliminary list of nations specified as prospects.

How then did Chile become involved in Project Camelot's affairs? The answer requires consideration of the position of Hugo G. Nutini, assistant professor of anthropology at Pittsburgh, citizen of the United States and former citizen of Chile. His presence in Santiago as a self-identified Camelot representative triggered the climactic chain of events.

Nutini, who inquired about an appointment in Camelot's beginning stages, never was given a regular Camelot appointment. Because he was planning a trip to Chile in April of this year—on other academic business—he was asked to prepare a report concerning possibilities of cooperation from Chilean scholars. In general, it was the kind of survey which has mild results and a modest honorarium attached to it (Nutini was offered $750). But Nutini had an obviously different notion of his role. Despite the limitations and precautions which Rex Hopper placed on his trip, especially Hopper's insistence on its informal nature, Nutini managed to convey the impression of being an official of Project Camelot with the authority to make proposals to prospective Chilean participants. Here was an opportunity to link the country of his birth with the country of his choice.

At about the same time, Johan Galtung, a Norwegian sociologist famous for his research on conflict and conflict resolution in underdeveloped areas, especially in Latin America, entered the picture. Galtung, who was in Chile at the time and associated with the Latin American Faculty of Social Science (FLACSO), received an invitation to participate in a Camelot planning conference scheduled for Washington, D.C., in August 1965. The fee to social scientists attending the conference would be $2,000 for four weeks. Galtung turned down the invitation. He gave several reasons. He could not accept the role of the US Army as a sponsoring agent in a study of counter-insurgency. He could not accept the notion of the Army as an agency of national development; he saw the Army as managing conflict and even promoting conflict. Finally, he could not accept the asymmetry of the project—he found it difficult to understand why there would be studies of counter-insurgency in Latin-America, but no studies of "counter-intervention" (conditions under which Latin American nations might intervene in the affairs of the United States). Galtung was also deeply concerned about the possibility of European scholars being frozen out of Latin American studies by an inundation of sociologists from the United States. Furthermore, he expressed fears that the scale of Camelot honoraria would completely destroy the social science labor market in Latin America.

Galtung had spoken to others in Oslo, Santiago, and throughout Latin America about the project, and he had shown the memorandum of December 1964 to many of his colleagues.

Soon after Nutini arrived in Santiago, he had a conference with Vice-Chancellor Alvaro Bunster of the University of Chile to discuss the character of Project Camelot. Their second meeting, arranged by the vice-chancellor, was also attended by Professor Eduardo Fuenzalida, a sociologist. After a half-hour of exposition by Nutini, Fuenzalida asked him pointblank to specify the ultimate aims of the project, its sponsors, and its military implications. Before Nutini could reply, Professor Fuenzalida, apparently with some drama, pulled a copy of the December 4 circular letter from his briefcase and read a prepared Spanish translation. Simultaneously, the authorities at FLACSO turned over the matter to their associates in the Chilean Senate and in the left-wing Chilean press.

In Washington, under the political pressures of State Department officials and Congressional reaction, Project Camelot was halted in midstream, or more precisely, before it ever really got under way. When the ambassador's communication reached Washington, there was already considerable official ferment about Project Camelot. Senators Fulbright, Morse, and McCarthy soon asked for hearings by the Senate Foreign Relations Committee. Only an agreement between Secretary of Defense McNamara and Secretary of State Rusk to settle their differences on future overseas research projects forestalled Senate action. But in the House of Representatives, a hearing was conducted by the Foreign Affairs Committee on July 8. The SORO director, Theodore Vallance, was questioned by committee members on the worth of Camelot and the matter of military intrusion into foreign policy areas.

That morning, even before Vallance was sworn in as a witness—and without his knowledge—the Defense Department issued a terse announcement terminating Project Camelot. President Johnson had decided the issue in favor of the State Department. In a memo to Secretary Rusk on August 5 the President stipulated that "no government sponsorship of foreign area research should be undertaken which in the judgment of the Secretary of State would adversely affect United States foreign relations."

The State Department has recently established machinery to screen and judge all federally-financed research projects overseas. The policy and research consequences of the Presidential directive will be discussed later.

What effect will the cancellation of Camelot have on the continuing rivalry between Defense and State departments for primacy in foreign policy? How will government sponsorship of future social science research be affected? And was Project Camelot a scholarly protective cover for US Army planning—or a legitimate research operation on a valid research subject independent of sponsorship?

Let us begin with a collective self-portrait of Camelot as the social scientists who directed the project perceived it. There seems to be general consensus on seven points.

■ First, the men who went to work for Camelot felt the need for a large-scale, "big picture" project in social science. They wanted to create a sociology of contemporary relevance which would not suffer from the parochial narrowness of vision to which their own professional backgrounds had generally conditioned them. Most of the men viewed Camelot as a bona fide opportunity to do fundamental research with relatively unlimited funds at their disposal. (No social science project ever before had up to $6,000,000 available.) Under such optimal conditions, these scholars tended not to look a gift horse in the mouth. As one of them put it, there was no desire to inquire too deeply as to the source of the funds or the ultimate purpose of the project.

■ Second, most social scientists affiliated with Camelot felt that there was actually more freedom to do fundamental research under military sponsorship than at a university or college. One man noted that during the 1950's there was far more freedom to do fundamental research in the RAND corporation (an Air Force research organization) than on any campus in America. Indeed, once the protective covering of RAND was adopted, it was almost viewed as a society of Platonist elites or "knowers" permitted to search for truth on behalf of the powerful. In a neoplatonic definition of their situation, the Camelot men hoped that their ideas would be taken seriously by the wielders of power (although, conversely, they were convinced that the armed forces would not accept their preliminary recommendations).

■ Third, many of the Camelot associates felt distinctly uncomfortable with military sponsorship, especially given the present United States military posture. But their reaction to this discomfort was that "the Army has to be educated." This view was sometimes cast in Freudian terms: the Army's bent toward violence ought to be sublimated. Underlying this theme was the notion of the armed forces as an agency for potential social good—the discipline and the order embodied by an army could be channeled into the process of economic and social development in the United States as well as in Latin America.

■ Fourth, there was a profound conviction in the perfectibility of mankind; particularly in the possibility of the military establishment performing a major role in the general process of growth. They sought to correct the intellectual paternalism and parochialism under which Pentagon generals, State Department diplomats, and Defense Department planners seemed to operate.

■ Fifth, a major long-range purpose of Camelot, at least for some of its policy-makers, was to prevent another revolutionary holocaust on a grand scale, such as occurred in Cuba. At the very least, there was a shared belief that *Pax Americana* was severely threatened and its future could be bolstered.

■ Sixth, none of them viewed their role on the project as spying for the United States government, or for anyone else.

■ Seventh, the men on Project Camelot felt that they made heavy sacrifices for social science. Their personal and professional risks were much higher than those taken by university academics. Government work, while well-compensated, remains professionally marginal. It can be terminated abruptly (as indeed was the case) and its project directors are subject to a public scrutiny not customary behind the walls of ivy.

In the main, there was perhaps a keener desire on the part of the directing members of Camelot not to "sell out" than there is among social scientists with regular academic appointments. This concern with the ethics of social science research seemed to be due largely to daily confrontation of the problems of betrayal, treason, secrecy, and abuse of data, in a critical situation. In contrast, even though a university position may be created by federally-sponsored research, the connection with policy matters is often too remote to cause any *crise de conscience*.

THE INSIDERS REPORT

Were the men on Camelot critical of any aspects of the project?

Some had doubts from the outset about the character of the work they would be doing, and about the conditions under which it would be done. It was pointed out, for example, that the US Army tends to exercise a far more stringent intellectual control of research findings than does the US Air Force. As evidence for this, it was stated that SORO generally had fewer "free-wheeling" aspects to its research designs than did RAND (the Air Force-supported research organization). One critic inside SORO went so far as to say that he knew of no SORO research which had a "playful" or unregimented quality, such as one finds at RAND (where for example, computers are used to plan invasions but also to play chess). One staff member said that "the self-conscious seriousness gets to you after a while." "It was all grim stuff," said another.

Another line of criticism was that pressures on the "reformers" (as the men engaged in Camelot research spoke of themselves) to come up with ideas were much stronger than the pressures on the military to actually bring off any policy changes recommended. The social scientists were expected to be social reformers, while the military adjutants were expected to be conservative. It was further felt that the relationship between sponsors and researchers was not one of equals, but rather one of superordinate military needs and subordinate academic roles. On the other hand, some officials were impressed by the disinterestedness of the military, and thought that far from exercising undue influence, the Army personnel were loath to offer opinions.

Another objection was that if one had to work on policy matters—if research is to have international ramifications—it might better be conducted under conventional State Department sponsorship. "After all," one man said, "they are at least nominally committed to civilian political norms." In other words, there was a considerable reluctance to believe that the Defense Department, despite its superior organization, greater financial affluence, and executive influence, would actually improve upon State Department styles of work, or accept recommendations at variance with Pentagon policies.

There seemed to be few, if any, expressions of disrespect for the intrinsic merit of the work contemplated by Camelot, or of disdain for policy-oriented work in general. The scholars engaged in the Camelot effort used two distinct vocabularies. The various Camelot documents reveal a military vocabulary provided with an array of military justifications; often followed (within the same document) by a social science vocabulary offering social science justifications and rationalizations. The dilemma in the Camelot literature from the preliminary report issued in August 1964 until the more advanced document issued in April 1965, is the same: an incomplete amalgamation of the military and sociological vocabularies. (At an early date the project had the code name SPEARPOINT.)

POLICY CONFLICTS OVER CAMELOT

The directors of SORO are concerned that the cancellation of Camelot might mean the end of SORO as well in a wholesale slash of research funds. For while over $1,000,000 was allotted to Camelot each year, the annual budget of SORO, its parent organization, is a good deal less. Although no such action has taken place, SORO's future is being examined. For example, the Senate and House Appropriations Committee blocked a move by the Army to transfer unused Camelot funds to SORO.

However, the end of Project Camelot does not necessarily imply the end of the Special Operations Research Office, nor does it imply an end to research designs which are similar in character to Project Camelot. In fact, the termination of the contract does not even imply an intellectual change of heart on the part of the originating sponsors or key figures of the project.

One of the characteristics of Project Camelot was the number of antagonistic forces it set in motion on grounds of strategy and timing rather than from what may be called considerations of scientific principles.

■ The State Department grounded its opposition to Camelot on the basis of the ultimate authority it has in the area of foreign affairs. There is no published report showing serious criticism of the projected research itself.

■ Congressional opposition seemed to be generated by a concern not to rock any foreign alliances, especially in Latin America. Again, there was no statement about the project's scientific or intellectual grounds.

■ A third group of skeptics, academic social scientists, generally thought that Project Camelot, and studies of the processes of revolution and war in general, were better left in the control of major university centers, and in this way, kept free of direct military supervision.

■ The Army, creator of the project, did nothing to contradict McNamara's order cancelling Project Camelot. Army influentials did not only feel that they had to execute the Defense Department's orders, but they are traditionally dubious of the value of "software" research to support "hardware" systems.

Let us take a closer look at each of these groups which voiced opposition to Project Camelot. A number of issues did not so much hinge upon, as swim about, Project Camelot. In particular, the "jurisdictional" dispute between Defense and State loomed largest.

STATE VS. DEFENSE. In substance, the debate between the Defense Department and the State Department is not unlike that between electricians and bricklayers in the construction of a new apartment house. What "union is responsible for which processes? Less generously, the issue is: who controls what? At the policy level, Camelot was a tool tossed about in a larger power struggle which has been going on in government circles since the end of World War II, when the Defense Department emerged as a competitor for honors as the most powerful bureau of the administrative branch of government.

In some sense, the divisions between Defense and State are outcomes of the rise of ambiguous conflicts such as Korea and Vietnam, in contrast to the more precise and diplomatically controlled "classical" world wars. What are the lines dividing political policy from military posture? Who is the most important representative of the United States abroad: the ambassador or the military attaché in charge of the military mission? When soldiers from foreign lands are sent to the United States for political orientation, should such orientation be within the province of the State Department or of the Defense Department? When under-

cover activities are conducted, should the direction of such activities belong to military or political authorities? Each of these is a strategic question with little pragmatic or historic precedent. Each of these was entwined in the Project Camelot explosion.

It should be plain therefore that the State Department was not simply responding to the recommendations of Chilean left-wingers in urging the cancellation of Camelot. It merely employed the Chilean hostility to "interventionist" projects as an opportunity to redefine the balance of forces and power with the Defense Department. What is clear from this resistance to such projects is not so much a defense of the sovereignty of the nations where ambassadors are stationed, as it is a contention that conventional political channels are sufficient to yield the information desired or deemed necessary.

CONGRESS. In the main, congressional reaction seems to be that Project Camelot was bad because it rocked the diplomatic boat in a sensitive area. Underlying most congressional criticisms is the plain fact that most congressmen are more sympathetic to State Department control of foreign affairs than they are to Defense Department control. In other words, despite military sponsored world junkets, National Guard and State Guard pressures from the home State, and military training in the backgrounds of many

congressmen, the sentiment for political rather than military control is greater. In addition, there is a mounting suspicion in Congress of varying kinds of behavioral science research stemming from hearings into such matters as wiretapping, uses of lie detectors, and truth-in-packaging.

SOCIAL SCIENTISTS. One reason for the violent response to Project Camelot, especially among Latin American scholars, is its sponsorship by the Department of Defense. The fact is that Latin Americans have become quite accustomed to State Department involvements in the internal affairs of various nations. The Defense Department is a newcomer, a dangerous one, inside the Latin American orbit. The train of thought connected to its activities is in terms of international warfare, spying missions, military manipulations, etc. The State Department, for its part, is often a consultative party to shifts in government, and has played an enormous part in either fending off or bringing about *coups d'état*. This State Department role has by now been accepted and even taken for granted. Not so the Defense Department's role. But it is interesting to conjecture on how matter-of-factly Camelot might have been accepted if it had State Department sponsorship.

Social scientists in the United States have, for the most part, been publicly silent on the matter of Camelot. The reasons for this are not hard to find. First, many "giants of the field" are involved in government contract work in one capacity or another. And few souls are in a position to tamper with the gods. Second, most information on Project Camelot has thus far been of a newspaper variety; and professional men are not in a habit of criticizing colleagues on the basis of such information. Third, many social scientists doubtless see nothing wrong or immoral in the Project Camelot designs. And they are therefore more likely to be either confused or angered at the Latin American response than at the directors of Project Camelot. (At the time of the blowup, Camelot people spoke about the "Chilean mess" rather than the "Camelot mess.")

The directors of Project Camelot did not "classify" research materials, so that there would be no stigma of secrecy. And they also tried to hire, and even hired away from academic positions, people well known and respected for their independence of mind. The difficulty is that even though the stigma of secrecy was formally erased, it remained in the attitudes of many of the employees and would-be employees of Project Camelot. They unfortunately thought in terms of secrecy, clearance, missions, and the rest of the professional nonsense that so powerfully afflicts the Washington scientific as well as political ambience.

Further, it is apparent that Project Camelot had much greater difficulty hiring a full-time staff of high professional competence, than in getting part-time, summertime, weekend, and sundry assistance. Few established figures in academic life were willing to surrender the advantages of their positions for the risks of the project.

One of the cloudiest aspects to Project Camelot is the role of American University. Its actual supervision of the contract appears to have begun and ended with the 25 percent overhead on those parts of the contract that a university receives on most federal grants. Thus, while there can be no question as to the "concern and disappointment" of President Hurst R. Anderson of the American University over the demise of Project Camelot, the reasons for this regret do not seem to extend beyond the formal and the financial. No official at American University appears to have been willing to make any statement of responsibility, support, chagrin, opposition, or anything else related to the project. The issues are indeed momentous, and must be faced by all universities at which government sponsored research is conducted: the amount of control a university has over contract work; the role of university officials in the distribution of funds from grants; the relationships that ought to be established once a grant is issued. There is also a major question concerning project directors: are they members of the faculty, and if so, do they have necessary teaching responsibilities and opportunities for tenure as do other faculty members.

The difficulty with American University is that it seems to be remarkably unlike other universities in its permissiveness. The Special Operations Research Office received neither guidance nor support from university officials. From the outset, there seems to have been a "gentleman's agreement" not to inquire or interfere in Project Camelot, but simply to serve as some sort of camouflage. If American University were genuinely autonomous it might have been able to lend highly supportive aid to Project Camelot during the crisis months. As it is, American University maintained an official silence which preserved it from more congressional or executive criticism. This points up some serious flaws in its administrative and financial policies.

The relationship of Camelot to SORO represented a similarly muddled organizational picture. The director of Project Camelot was nominally autonomous and in charge of an organization surpassing in size and importance the overall SORO operation. Yet at the critical point the organizational blueprint served to protect SORO and sacrifice what nominally was its limb. That Camelot happened to be a vital organ may have hurt, especially when Congress blocked the transfer of unused Camelot funds to SORO.

MILITARY. Military reaction to the cancellation of Camelot varied. It should be borne in mind that expenditures on Camelot were minimal in the Army's overall budget and most military leaders are skeptical, to begin with, about the worth of social science research. So there was no open protest about the demise of Camelot. Those officers who have a positive attitude toward social science materials, or are themselves trained in the social sciences, were dismayed. Some had hoped to find "software" alternatives to the "hardware systems" approach applied by the Secretary of Defense to every military-political contingency. These officers saw the attack on Camelot as a double attack—on their role as officers and on their professional standards. But the Army was so clearly treading in new waters that it could scarcely jeopardize the entire structure of military research to preserve one project. This very inability or impotence to preserve Camelot—a situation threatening to other governmental contracts with social scientists—no doubt impressed many armed forces officers.

The claim is made by the Camelot staff (and various military aides) that the critics of the project played into the hands of those sections of the military predisposed to veto any social science recommendations. Then why did the military offer such a huge support to a social science project to begin with? Because $6,000,000 is actually a trifling sum for the Army in an age of multi-billion dollar military establishment. The amount is significantly more important for the social sciences, where such contract awards remain relatively scarce. Thus, there were differing perspectives of the importance of Camelot: an Army view which considered the contract as one of several forms of "software" investment; a social science perception of Project Camelot as the equivalent of the Manhattan Project.

WAS PROJECT CAMELOT WORKABLE?

While most public opposition to Project Camelot focused on its strategy and timing, a considerable amount of private opposition centered on more basic, though theoretical, questions: was Camelot scientifically feasible and ethically correct? No public document or statement contested the possibility that, given the successful completion of the data gathering, Camelot could have, indeed, established basic criteria for measuring the level and potential for internal war in a given nation. Thus, by never challenging the feasibility of the work, the political critics of Project Camelot were providing back-handed compliments to the efficacy of the project.

But much more than political considerations are involved. It is clear that some of the most critical problems presented by Project Camelot are scientific. Although for an extensive analysis of Camelot, the reader would, in fairness, have to be familiar with all of its documents, salient general criticisms can be made without a full reading.

The research design of Camelot was from the outset plagued by ambiguities. It was never quite settled whether the purpose was to study counter-insurgency possibilities, or the revolutionary process. Similarly, it was difficult to determine whether it was to be a study of comparative social structures, a set of case studies of single nations "in depth," or a study of social structure with particular emphasis on the military. In addition, there was a lack of treatment of what indicators were to be used, and whether a given social system in Nation A could be as stable in Nation B.

In one Camelot document there is a general critique of social science for failing to deal with social conflict and social control. While this in itself is admirable, the tenor and context of Camelot's documents make it plain that a "stable society" is considered the norm no less than the desired outcome. The "breakdown of social order" is spoken of accusatively. Stabilizing agencies in developing areas are presumed to be absent. There is no critique of US Army policy in developing areas because the Army is presumed to be a stabilizing agency. The research formulations always assume the legitimacy of Army tasks—"if the US Army is to perform effectively its parts in the US mission of counter-insurgency it must recognize that insurgency represents a breakdown of social order. . . ." But such a proposition has never been doubted—by Army officials or anyone else. The issue is whether such breakdowns are in the nature of the existing system or a product of conspiratorial movements.

The use of hygienic language disguises the anti-revolutionary assumptions under a cloud of powder puff declarations. For example, studies of Paraguay are recommended "because trends in this situation (the Stroessner regime) may also render it 'unique' when analyzed in terms of the transition from 'dictatorship' to political stability." But to speak about changes from dictatorship to stability is an obvious ruse. In this case, it is a tactic to disguise the fact that Paraguay is one of the most vicious, undemocratic (and like most dictatorships, stable) societies in the Western Hemisphere.

These typify the sort of hygienic sociological premises that do not have scientific purposes. They illustrate the confusion of commitments within Project Camelot. Indeed the very absence of emotive words such as revolutionary masses, communism, socialism, and capitalism only serves to intensify the discomfort one must feel on examination of the documents—since the abstract vocabulary disguises, rather than resolves, the problems of international revolution. To have used clearly political rather than military language would not "justify" governmental support. Furthermore, shabby assumptions of academic conventionalism replaced innovative orientations. By adopting a systems approach, the problematic, open-ended aspects of the study of revolutions were largely omitted; and the design of the study became an oppressive curb on the study of the problems inspected.

This points up a critical implication for Camelot (as well as other projects). The importance of the subject being researched does not *per se* determine the importance of the project. A sociology of large-scale relevance and reference is all to the good. It is important that scholars be willing to risk something of their shaky reputations in helping resolve major world social problems. But it is no less urgent that in the process of addressing major problems, the autonomous character of the social science disciplines—their own criteria of worthwhile scholarship—should not be abandoned. Project Camelot lost sight of this "autonomous" social science character.

It never seemed to occur to its personnel to inquire into the desirability for successful revolution. This is just as solid a line of inquiry as the one stressed—the conditions under which revolutionary movements will be able to overthrow a government. Furthermore, they seem not to have thought about inquiring into the role of the United States in these countries. This points up the lack of symmetry. The problem should have been phrased to include the study of "us" as well as "them." It is not possible to make a decent analysis of a situation unless one takes into account the role of all the different people and groups involved in it; and there was no room in the design for such contingency analysis.

In discussing the policy impact on a social science research project, we should not overlook the difference between "contract" work and "grants." Project Camelot commenced with the US Army; that is to say, it was initiated for a practical purpose determined by the client. This differs markedly from the typical academic grant in that its sponsorship had "built-in" ends. The scholar usually *seeks* a grant; in this case the donor, the Army, promoted its own aims. In some measure, the hostility for Project Camelot may be an unconscious reflection of this distinction—a dim feeling that there was something "non-academic," and certainly not disinterested, about Project Camelot, irrespective of the quality of the scholars associated with it.

THE ETHICS OF POLICY RESEARCH

The issue of "scientific rights" versus "social myths" is perennial. Some maintain that the scientist ought not penetrate beyond legally or morally sanctioned limits and others argue that such limits cannot exist for science. In treading on the sensitive issue of national sovereignty, Project Camelot reflects the generalized dilemma. In deference to intelligent researchers, in recognition of them as scholars, they should have been invited by Camelot to air their misgivings and qualms about government (and especially Army sponsored) research—to declare their moral conscience. Instead, they were mistakenly approached as skillful, useful potential employees of a higher body, subject to an authority higher than their scientific calling.

What is central is not the political motives of the sponsor. For social scientists were not being enlisted in an intelligence system for "spying" purposes. But given their professional standing, their great sense of intellectual honor and pride, they could not be "employed" without proper deference for their stature. Professional authority should have prevailed from beginning to end with complete command of the right to thrash out the moral and political dilemmas as researchers saw them. The Army, however respectful and protective of free expression, was "hiring help" and not openly and honestly submitting a problem to the higher professional and scientific authority of social science.

The propriety of the Army to define and delimit all questions, which Camelot should have had a right to examine, was never placed in doubt. This is a tragic precedent; it reflects the arrogance of a consumer of intellectual merchandise. And this relationship of inequality corrupted the lines of authority, and profoundly limited the autonomy of the social scientists involved. It became clear that the social scientist savant was not so much functioning as an applied social scientist as he was supplying information to a powerful client.

The question of who sponsors research is not nearly so decisive as the question of ultimate use of such information. The sponsorship of a project, whether by the United States Army or by the Boy Scouts of America, is by itself neither good nor bad. Sponsorship is good or bad only insofar as the intended outcomes can be pre-determined and the parameters of those intended outcomes tailored to the sponsor's expectations. Those social scientists critical of the project never really denied its freedom and independence, but questioned instead the purpose and character of its intended results.

It would be a gross oversimplification, if not an outright error, to assume that the theoretical problems of Project Camelot derive from any reactionary character of the project designers. The director went far and wide to select a group of men for the advisory board, the core planning group, the summer study group, and the various conference groupings, who in fact were more liberal in their orientations than any random sampling of the sociological profession would likely turn up.

However, in nearly every page of the various working papers, there are assertions which clearly derive from American military policy objectives rather than scientific method. The steady assumption that internal warfare is damaging disregards the possibility that a government may not be in a position to take actions either to relieve or improve mass conditions, or that such actions as are contemplated may be more concerned with reducing conflict than with improving conditions. The added statements above the United States Army and its "important mission in the positive and constructive aspects of nation building . . ." assumes the reality of such a function in an utterly unquestioning and unconvincing form. The first rule of the scientific game is not to make assumptions about friends and enemies in such a way as to promote the use of different criteria for the former and the latter.

The story of Project Camelot was not a confrontation of good versus evil. Obviously, not all men behaved with equal fidelity or with equal civility. Some men were weaker than others, some more callous, and some more stupid. But all of this is extrinsic to the heart of the problem of Camelot: what are and are not the legitimate functions of a scientist?

In conclusion, two important points must be clearly kept in mind and clearly apart. First, Project Camelot was intellectually, and from my own perspective, ideologically unsound. However, and more significantly, Camelot was not cancelled because of its faulty intellectual approaches. Instead, its cancellation came as an act of government censorship, and an expression of the contempt for social science so prevalent among those who need it most. Thus it was political expedience, rather than its lack of scientific merit, that led to the demise of Camelot because it threatened to rock State Department relations with Latin America.

Second, giving the State Department the right to screen and approve government-funded social science research projects on other countries, as the President has ordered, is a supreme act of censorship. Among the agencies that grant funds for such research are the National Institutes of Mental Health, the National Science Foundation, the National Aeronautics and Space Agency, and the Office of Education. Why should the State Department have veto power over the scientific pursuits of men and projects funded by these and other agencies in order to satisfy the policy needs—or policy failures—of the moment? President Johnson's directive is a gross violation of the autonomous nature of science.

We must be careful not to allow social science projects with which we may vociferously disagree on political and ideological grounds to be decimated or dismantled by government fiat. Across the ideological divide is a common social science understanding that the contemporary expression of reason in politics today is applied social science, and that the cancellation of Camelot, however pleasing it may be on political grounds to advocates of a civilian solution to Latin American affairs, represents a decisive setback for social science research.

part two

Public Opinion and the Crisis of Traditional Party Politics

Perhaps the area of American politics that has been most richly illuminated in recent years by the application of empirical research techniques is that of mass inputs into politics: representation schemes, public opinion, and voting behavior. A number of conventional pieties have seen their credibility destroyed or undermined in the process.

One such assumption, which has tended to dominate much of the literature on apportionment, is the notion that if only the stranglehold of the rural parochials could be broken by a one-man-one-vote districting system, all sorts of liberal progress would be made in policy outputs as urban areas received their fair share of representatives. As Hacker points out in his analysis of the probable consequences of congressional reapportionment, however, the Republicans stand to gain more in the long run than the Democrats. If this has not yet materialized to the extent once expected, forces other than those involving redistricting—a secular decline in the proportion of Republican party identifiers in the electorate, for example, and an increasing ascendancy of incumbents in congressional elections—seem largely responsible. In one sense, Hacker pinpoints the actual shift which reapportionment will bring in the 1970s: from country *not to city* but to suburb, from nineteenth-century conservatism *not to liberalism* but to twentieth-century conservatism or middle-of-the-roadism.

It is a striking commentary on the large gaps between opinion, party, and policy in the United States that a major shift in the balance of legislative power should yield so little measurable result. An explanation, it seems to me, lies in the fact that American major parties have been, as we have seen, pragmatic coalitions of regional, economic, and sectoral interests in society. Hitherto in this century they have never been organized in programmatically "liberal-conservative" or "left-right" lines. They have been dominated in their finances, organization, and programs by differing groups in the American upper middle class. Naturally such parties interact with and operate within a public-opinion structure which has now been extremely well documented through the development of scientific survey analysis. Chief among the findings of such analysis—Abelson and Wright present many of them in their essays—is the fact that most Americans do not think about politics in terms of anything like "world views," ideologies, collectively perceived, or sharply held political interests, or even coherent programs.

Thus a second piety which was once held by many political scientists—that of the rational voter who judges programs and candidates and acts independently in terms of his value preferences—is no longer tenable in its old Progressive-Era form. If we find that reapportionment makes so little practical difference in our political life, we are led to examine the behavioral context of party and voter in which representation operates. When we do so, it becomes clear that the electorate is a confused cluster of individuals-in-groups, that it cannot be arrayed intelligibly along any single dimension of left-right, that parties partake of and contribute to this heterogeneity and consequently show little or no differential profile in specific policy areas, especially in the state legislatures. The porosity and protean quality of this system of inputs into the political process would thus extend to supposed conflicts of interest between county, city, and suburbs. There is thus no good reason in such an opinion-electoral system why *any* collective interests of this sort should normally become salient enough among the public to form the base for measurable divisions over public policy.

But empirical social scientists are no more immune to their own versions of "conventional wisdom" than are other mortals. Whenever "public opinion" is discussed without regard to historical time, or to other public opinions in other societies, or as though one were speaking of *the* public opinion structure of Americans, it is always useful to ask three questions. Has it always been so? Must it always be so? Is it so in countries which have very different kinds of party linkages between voters and government? Wright's essay in particular points to the importance of specific issue clusters, and of intensities surrounding them; and clearly, in the case of opinion on Vietnam, a great amount of intensification and polarization is visible across time.

Without wishing to associate Wright with my views, I would argue that the answer to all three questions is no. Such an answer must, of course, be qualified. It seems very probable that the bulk of any population, particularly if it is politically unorganized, has only the most rudimentary idea of what is going on in politics. From their own quite different perspectives, those master political organizers Hitler and Lenin were perfectly clear on this point. But it also seems clear that the extent of politicization, and the breadth and intensity of the public need to consume political information, are dependent variables in the fullest sense of the term. They are heavily dependent upon the specific contexts which the political sociology of a given political system provides at a specific point in historical time. My own research has made it increasingly clear to me that the extent and intensity of politicization among American voters was vastly higher in the period 1854–68 than it is in our own time (so much so as to presuppose a public-opinion structure radically different from that projected by the Survey Research Center or those who worked on the Simulmatics project). While such a view cuts directly athwart that conventional wisdom which assumes some kind of eternal permanence in the public-opinion patterns of 1952–1960, it recognizes that contexts of revolutionary transition in our political life may count for something, after all, in the shaping of public opinion. Certainly the founders of the Republican party—not to mention the founders of modern European mass parties—believed so and acted successfully on that belief.

If American politics is viewed, then, as a dynamic system of action operating through time, the most basic property it has is a long-term cyclical pattern of oscillation between "politics as usual" and a sweeping critical realignment of voters, party coalitions, and policies. This remarkably regular historical oscillation is unique, so far as we can tell, to our political system. It is a characteristic mechanism by which change occurs in this static political world. The analogy to "base and superstructure" seems particularly compelling here. Our socio-economic system is in constant and rapid evolution, largely free from public-sector controls or from feudal or other blockages in the socio-economic system. Our political system has a deeply entrenched tendency toward self-closure and stasis across time. The socio-economic "base" tends to slide out from underneath this relatively inert "superstructure" until a point is reached when the social conflicts generated by change outside the political system conflict with and disrupt the normal political "game." Such political upheavals, which have been spaced about thirty-eight years apart since the beginning of our party system, are "critical realignments"; and these realignments involve nonincremental, very rapid changes in political direction which sometimes approach the stage of revolution.

For reasons which the Overview has attempted to spell out, we now appear to be in the midst of such an upheaval. Realignments are marked by all sorts of "portents and wonders," for example those discussed in this Part for the 1968 election by this writer. Periods of realignment are those in which traditional benchmarks of political analysis and practice appear to fade away. In the contemporary period, much political conflict of a type unprecedented during and after the New Deal has involved the emergence of blacks as a major force in urban politics. Some of the implications are discussed in the essays by Hadden *et al.* and Maullin. Demographic and civil-rights revolutions have not only nationalized Southern politics rapidly, but have also "Southernized" national politics. One result has been the emergence of the Wallace movement among fraternally-deprived lower-status whites which Lipset and Raab discuss. The importance of this white reaction against the Great Society and its civil-rights, welfare, and bussing initiatives is hard to overstate. It is based upon both generalized discontent and a highly specific focus of discontent. The basic question posed by Wallace's supporters is simple, yet thorny: Why should we and our children be expected by well-off liberal bureaucrats, judges, and academics to pay the full cost of the demographics revolution? It becomes even more thorny when one realizes the extent to which the elites and sub-elites have evaded paying any of these costs or "imposing" them on their children: they have the resources to flee, and in the overwhelming majority of cases they have done exactly that.

If the political repercussions are as ugly as a Rizzo victory in the 1971 Philadelphia election, liberal professionals have given little enough evidence that they are willing to entertain the question the Wallace people are asking, much less answer it. They have correspondingly and increasingly forfeited their legitimacy and have left a large part of the political field to George Wallace and Richard Nixon: the Alabama Governor, it is worth noting, won 23.3 percent of all the Democratic primary votes cast in 1972, 51.0 percent in Michigan.

That blacks have been among the chief victims of ghetto-ization and racism should go without saying, just as it should—and must—have positive consequences for the policies we develop. But it is hardly racist to suggest that there have been other victims as well, and that there will continue to be until, for example, public authority is effectively exercised over the decisions made by real estate agencies, banks, and insurance companies. The so-called "race issue" is in fact a cross-cutting farrago of racial, cultural, and class con-flicts. If this were perceived and thought through by liberal academics, professionals and decision-makers, it would require them in the first instance to come to terms with a class prejudice which is the more crippling for being unacknowledged. It is easy to patronize blacks: they have, to the country's lasting shame, been victims of ascriptive oppression throughout our history. It is perhaps harder to accept the human concerns of whites who, after all, have not "made it" in our achieving society. Meritocracy runs deep, the deeper for being unexamined and unacknowledged. Until or unless white liberals work out more satisfactory and comprehensive policies based upon social realities, however displeasing to themselves, they will be in deep trouble with voters who once gave them massive support.

This racial polarization, accompanied by a closely cognate "social-issue" cleavage, has emerged to cross-cut the class stratification of the old New Deal alignment. To these have been added cleavages over Vietnam and the *Imperium*. And there are yet others. The result has been the development of volcanic instability in American voting behavior since the early 1960s. No one issue dominates the entire electorate; many individual issues are capable of producing intense opinions among the electorate. Yet underlying all this has been a steady but by now spectacular decline in the acceptance of many basic social, economic, and political institutions. Accompanying this decline has been a steep growth in anxiety among individuals—to some extent about their economic situation and even their own personal safety, but to a far larger extent about the political stability and political future of this country. It is fair to say that these indicators of disillusion, discontent, and fear have now reached levels unprecedented in modern times. Movements of this kind are precisely what can be expected to occur during an era of critical realignment, especially in its early and intermediate stages. The greater the disruption in the political value system, the more the erosion of legitimacy and the higher these indices should become. The latter are important enough to warrant a short discussion here.

In *Hopes and Fears of the American People*, A. H. Cantril and C. W. Roll present some remarkable findings based upon Gallup polls and a scalar (range: 0–10) "ladder of life" which Mr. Cantril's father devised many years ago. The most impressive of their findings are these. The ladder ratings indicate the respondent's sense of national progress from five years ago to the present and to five years hence. These ratings are particularly valuable because they have a wide comparative dimension (analogous questions have been asked in two dozen countries), and because they have been asked since the 1950s. The overwhelming pattern, as the reader might expect, is one of perceived improvement: things are "better" (the ratings higher) now than five years ago, and are expected to be higher still five years hence. As the authors point out, there have been only two instances in their surveys around the world when this pattern has not obtained: in the Philippines in 1959, and in the United States in 1971. For the first time in these measurements, decline in national prospects from past to present is recorded, along with a projected advance into the future which will do no more than recover the ground lost in the preceding five years. The basic figures are, within this 0–10 range:

	Past	Present	Future
1959	6.5	6.7	7.4
1964	6.1	6.5	7.7
1971	6.2	5.4	6.2

This deterioration of optimism is nearly as striking as the sense of decline in our politics during the recent past. It is obviously and closely related to the political fears of Americans. The strongest 1959–71 increases in things political for which Americans hope are, in order: national unity; solution of environmental problems; law and order; and solution of the drug problem. The greatest increases, in their political fears during this 12-year period have been, in order: political instability at home, up from 3 percent to 26 percent of responses; pollution; lack of law and order; drugs; and racial tensions.

It is also to be expected that major increases across time will have occurred in responses reflecting the individual's sense of political powerlessness, his sense that official elites are dishonest or do not pay attention to his needs, in short, his sense of political alienation. Such evidence is not hard to find. A series of recent polls by Gallup, Harris, and others reveals a dramatic increase in hostile responses toward business corporations, organized religious denominations, and other major social institutions during the past several years. A large increase in responses which involve more specific political alienation is reported by a Harris poll of June 1972. Such feelings are trapped by "projective" questions to which people respond with a yes or no. It is a pity that, as is often the case with commercial polling organizations, there is no agreement-disagreement continuum but rather a simple yes-no dichotomy. But this poll does have a time dimension to it, and its conclusions are clear enough to be reported in part here.

Feelings of Alienation

STATEMENT	Percent Agreeing		Shift
	1966	1972	
The rich get richer, the poor get poorer.	48	68	+20
What you think doesn't count much.	39	53	+14
The people running the country don't really care what happens to people like yourself.	28	50	+22
People who have the power are out to take advantage of you.	X	38	X
You feel left out of things around you.	9	25	+16
Average alienation:	29–31	47	+16 to +18

Average agreement with statements of political alienation has been going up between five and six per cent every two years since this Harris series began in 1966. It is now just under 50 percent. Moreover, alienation is concentrated both socially and politically as one might expect. The 1972 average alienation scores are higher than the national among the following groups, in order: blacks; those with an eighth-grade education or less; big-city residents; union members; people aged 50 or over; and people with less than $5,000 annual income. In short, alienation is growing among those individuals whose position in society is most likely to leave them vulnerable to the exercise of power "from the top" and whose control over their own lives is feeblest. Except for the age-50-and-over group, they are also least likely to vote. Thus the political stratification of alienation is hardly surprising: as of 1972, the average alienation among Nixon supporters was 36, compared with a score of 53 for McGovern supporters and 56 for Wallace supporters.

All this corresponds to the kind of "power deflation" discussed by Chalmers Johnson in his book *Revolutionary Change* as a precondition for such change. It corresponds as well to the kind of "volatilization," intensification of public opinion, and issue cleavages which always characterize realignments. Such trends cannot continue indefinitely: they have already reached levels which bespeak explosive instability at the grass-roots level. Critical realignments are in fact America's equivalent of "revolutionary change," proceeding dialectically from the inertia and self-closure of party and governmental "politics as usual" during stable phases of the electoral cycle. The more intense they are, the clearer the similarity between these events and genuine revolutions.

Essays by Lipset and Raab and by this writer capture some of this process. My essay on "The End of American Party Politics" discusses, speculatively, some alternative scenarios for the immediate future, based upon systematic, largely quantitative analysis of past change in American party politics and voting behavior. In the period since these essays were written, the dialectics of political crisis have continued to work themselves out in ways which are astonishingly similar to earlier periods of crisis in our history. The large outpouring of votes for Wallace and for McGovern in the 1972 Democratic primaries was one result of this deepening crisis. So was the spectacular rejection of established leadership within the Democratic party in 1972.

We have seen that critical realignments occur because of a buildup of new forces in society. To a greater or lesser extent, these forces raise demands which are negations of existing policy and political routines. It is thus very hard for established elites to cope with them affirmatively, since to do so is to repudiate themselves. Moreover, those in power have traditionally had few if any incentives to make such adaptations short of the most extreme crisis. Most of the time, the crisis takes the form of an insurrection within that party which is sociologically most vulnerable to the insurgents. The regulars are not, as a rule, converted but overthrown; and only *after* takeover within a party by a new issue-oriented coalition is the stage set for a sharp polarization in a "critical election" between the two major parties. It was thus in 1856, when the Whig party broke apart and the Republicans emerged on the ruins in the free states; and in 1896, when the victims of colonial economic oppression rose in revolt within the Democratic party and destroyed the Cleveland-Bourbon ascendancy over it; and in 1924–28, when the balance of power within the Democratic party shifted drastically from the old Bryanite-Wilson coalition—nativist, Protestant, and Prohibitionist—to the new urban and ethnic pluralism represented by Al Smith.

So it was also in 1972. The capture of the Democratic party by the McGovern coalition cannot be understood apart from a detailed analysis of the internal contradictions of the New Deal coalition as these developed over time. The catalyst, as we have said, was the Vietnam war, which has been one of the greatest moral issues confronting Americans in modern times. But this war came into being as the result of decisions made by Democratic Presidents, particularly by Lyndon Johnson, not by Republicans. It has been largely supported throughout by groups which remained to the end in adamantine opposition to George McGovern: by the syndicalist leadership of organized labor; by established party regulars whose primary orientation to politics has always—but not completely accurately—been described as pragmatic, non-ideological, and job-oriented; and in largest measure by Southern Democratic politicians. One can hardly understand McGovern's astounding march to the Democratic nomination without keeping at least two points firmly in mind. First, the decisions of the party's established elite were directly responsible for polarizing the party internally, for energizing the influx of newcomers (especially among the young), and ultimately for relinquishing their own control over the party. Lyndon Johnson had achieved the ultimate repudiation: not only did he not attend the 1972 convention, but his name was practically never mentioned by anyone during its operations. Second, the control by the Regulars (and by Johnson's own operatives) of the 1968 convention deferred a repudiation which would have occurred then had the 1972 rules been in effect. But the costs of maintaining this death-grip over the party were catastrophically high, both inside and outside the convention hall. The reform rules of the McGovern commission were one result; the unseating of Mayor Daley and his delegation in 1972 was another; the political destruction of Hubert Humphrey, impaled as he was on the war issue and his support for Johnson's policies, was a third; but far the most important were the overthrow of the structures of power which has dominated the party ever since the New Deal, and the nomination of George McGovern.

It is still too early to undertake any detailed estimate of even the short-term consequences of this transfer of power within America's oldest political party, much less any longer-term consequences. But a few conclusions can already be drawn. The genius of American politics, queer as it may seem to many, has been intimately associated with the phenomenon of critical realignment from the beginning. Realignments have been mechanisms of renewal within the system. Through them parties are substantially remade and renewed. These parties become something quite different from what they were before, yet they retain their traditional identity. It is only through this periodic revival and regeneration of old forms that, so far, the political system has been able to adapt more or less creatively to the demands for change which accumulate at the grass roots over time.

I have frankly doubted in the past, and particularly in the wake of the 1968 and 1972 elections, that enough grassroots political vitality remained in the political system to permit another such revitalization within a major political party. These doubts were candidly expressed in my essay, "The End of American Party Politics." There has been a tremendous and measurable decomposition of party at the grass roots and elsewhere over the past generation, and the observer of 1968 could perhaps be pardoned for thinking that the concentrated power groups which had come to control the Democratic party were too deeply entrenched to be overcome. As it was, the 1972 contest within the Democratic party was a very close and narrowly-decided affair. But the analysis in "The End of American Politics" gave too little emphasis to the possibility that such a renewal as happened at the 1972 Democratic Convention could succeed.

We can now make perhaps four points, even though "conclusions" are not yet possible. First, whatever happens after 1972, it is a fact that the critical-realignment option prevailed at that time over the party-disintegration option. Second, those who felt in 1968 that the defeat of Hubert Humphrey and election of Richard Nixon were necessary to give a chance for renewal to the Democratic party and *hence a new lease of life for the two-party system* seem justified by the long-term result. Third, the Democratic party as it came to be known during and after the New Deal has ceased to exist; another, phoenix-like, must arise from the ashes. Finally, it should be emphasized that, although the new coalition forged at Miami Beach could not defeat the Republicans in 1972, the party's organizational structure will be permanently altered, in ways which are not yet wholly foreseeable. It seems likely too that elections henceforth are likely to be much more explicitly organized around major issues than they have usually been. The battle lines between the "party of order" and the "party of progress" have been drawn on new and sharper issues. Things are not likely ever to be the same again.

Votes Cast and Seats Won

Andrew Hacker

The recent Supreme Court decisions requiring that legislative districts encompass roughly equal populations have roused Congressional ire and promise to play a role in the 1964 Presidential campaign. To be sure, it is not at all clear that all 100 legislative chambers—99 in the states and the House of Representatives in Washington—will have to be so apportioned that the vote cast by any one constituent will be equal in value to that of any other. Judicial delays, legislative moratoriums, and constitutional amendments may emerge to prevent the theory of "one man, one vote" from becoming a practical reality in all parts of the nation. Nevertheless, enough states are in the process of redrawing district lines that there is good reason to believe that lawmaking bodies at both the state and national levels will undergo important changes in character.

The most obvious consequence will be to give a greater voice to suburban voters and to cut down the number of rural representatives. What is less clear is the impact that the equalization of districts will have on the parties. It is therefore of some interest to analyze the results of the last election for the House of Representatives to see what effect, if any, the then-existing inequities had on the results. The outcome in 1962, while not of landslide proportions, was decidedly one-sided; the line-up for the 88th Congress was 258 Democrats to 176 Republicans, with one vacancy to be filled later on. Shortly after the returns were in, the Research Director of the Republican National Committee attempted to explain his party's disappointing showing:

> The fact that Republican candidates got 48 percent of the vote cast nationwide for the House of Representatives but will occupy only 40 percent of the seats in that body is clear evidence that the Republican Party is hurt more than the Democrats by inequities in Congressional districting.

A subsequent letter from the Director of the Arts and Sciences Division of the Republican Party and addressed specifically to political scientists claimed that "had Republican candidates gained as high a percentage of the seats as they did of the vote, there would be 209 Republicans in the House in the 88th Congress—33 more than were elected."

These spokesmen pointed out, correctly, that the Democrats had a disproportionate share of the undersized (and hence overrepresented) districts. From this finding came the Republican charge that their opponents were able to win more seats with an investment of fewer voters-per-seat. The logic behind this theory has undoubted appeal: a party which carries underpopulated districts will obviously be able to pile up victories with minimum expenditure of votes. Yet the key question—one that the Republican researchers failed to ask—is the actual extent to which the final partisan line-up of the House of Representatives resulted from disparities in district size.

In answering this question the basis for analysis will be 430 out of the 435 Congressional districts. The other five — statewide seats in Connecticut, Maryland, Michigan, Ohio, and Texas — can be left out of the study because voters in those states cast ballots for Congressional candidates in their local districts along with the ones they cast for their states' at-large Representatives. When the results of the 430 elections are added together, the following picture emerges:

	Dem.	Rep.
Total votes cast	26,737,000	24,153,000
Total seats won	255	175
Total cast per seat won	105,000	138,000

Thus 33,000 more Republican votes were required to elect a Republican Congressman than a Democrat. This gap is a not unsubstantial one, and it ought to be accounted for.

AT-LARGE ELECTIONS

There were, to begin with, seventeen seats in eight states (Alabama, Alaska, Delaware, Hawaii, New Mexico, Nevada, Vermont, and Wyoming) that elected *all* of their Congressmen at-large in 1962. Democrats won fifteen of these seventeen elections, leaving the Republicans with only two. Yet taken together 822,000 votes were cast for Democratic candidates in these contests and 563,000 for Republicans. Considering that Democrats won all but two of the seats, it emerges that 281,500 Republican votes had to be cast for each seat that party won whereas the Democrats had only to expend 55,000 votes for each seat they captured. This imbalance necessarily contributed to the 33,000 difference in votes per-seat-won between the parties on a national basis. Indeed 5000 of this figure of 33,000 is due to the 17 at-large elections. This leaves a discrepancy of 28,000 to be accounted for.

UNCONTESTED ELECTIONS

More significant is the fact that of the 240 remaining districts won by the Democrats, 53 were uncontested. (The Republicans won only one uncontested election, in Kentucky.) The meaning of this should be obvious. In uncontested Congressional elections, all but a few of them in the South, voting is usually light. These 53 districts, then, provided the Democrats with a large bloc of seats and required only a very low outlay of votes. The 53 uncontested Democrats were elected, on average, by 39,000 votes apiece. (And the one uncontested Republican received 59,000 votes.) The voting figures in these 54 uncontested elections account for most of the votes per-seat-won discrepancy between the two parties. The gap of 28,000 votes per-seat-won is reduced by 20,000 if the 54 uncontested elections are set to one side.

CONTESTED ELECTIONS

Remaining are the 359 contested elections in 41 multi-districted states. In this competitive arena the two parties were quite evenly matched. The Democrats won a total of 187 seats with a total expenditure of 23,864,000 votes and the Republicans secured 172 victories with 23,424,000 votes. For this group of 359 districts, the Democrats had to cast 128,000 votes to win one seat whereas the Republicans had to cast 136,000 votes. *This gap of 8,000 votes per-seat-won is all that remains of the Democratic advantage once the statewide and the uncontested elections are removed from the computations.*

To summarize: For the total group of 430 districts, the Democratic advantage was approximately 33,000 votes per-seat-won. When the 17 statewide contests are eliminated, the advantage falls to 28,000 votes. Take out the uncontested elections, the margin drops to 8,000. It is here that disparities in district-size may be shown to have an effect.

UNEQUAL POPULATIONS

If the Republican concern was primarily over the disparate populations of constituencies, it is easy enough to determine the relative position of each party. Taking the 359 contested districts, the average size of the 187 seats carried by the Democrats was 416,000—smaller than the average Republican district, which was 432,000. It is quite true, then, that Democratic candidates were competing under more favorable circumstances insofar as the majorities they secured were more apt to be in undersized (and there-

fore overrepresented) districts. But how much difference did that advantage—having, on average, 16,000 fewer residents per district—make? Had the 359 contested districts been allocated in relation to each party's share of the total votes cast, the Republican delegation in Congress would have risen to 176 and the Democrats' would have fallen to 183—a transfer of only four Representatives. This is a far cry from the original Republican claim that they had 33 fewer seats than their popular vote entitled them to.

But variations in district-size are not the only means by which a party obtains disproportionate legislative representation. Gerrymandering, which combines cartography, statistical analysis, and political prognostication, also exists. There is prima facie evidence of gerrymandering when a party having the power to draw the election map so deploys district boundaries that its supporters will elect more legislators than their absolute numerical strength would permit were constituencies drawn at random. There is a plentitude of known instances where politicians have, hopefully, gerrymandered. But it is better to measure the results of districting arrangements *after* the voting has taken place. For the best-laid plans of the canniest of gerrymanderers have been known to backfire; and, conversely, partisan advantage can accrue even where there was no manipulative intent behind the districting process.

Votes cast by a party's supporters fall into three categories:

Excess votes are the votes a party's Congressional candidate receives over and above what he needs to win. If he wins by 125,000 to 100,000, then 24,999 of his votes are "excess." Needless to say, no candidate wants to win by only a single vote; some "excess" votes are needed for the sake of comfort and possible recounts. Nevertheless all votes over and above those absolutely needed for victory will be regarded here as "excess," simply to make for ease of computation. A party's "excess" votes, of course, are found only in those districts where that party has won the seat.
"Wasted" votes are all votes received by candidates who ultimately lose. Thus "wasted" Democratic votes are those cast in districts where a Republican wins, and vice-versa.
"Effective" votes are the sum total of a party's votes throughout the country—or within a selected group of districts—after its "excess" and "wasted" votes have been subtracted.

The 1962 Congressional voting, in the 359 contested districts, can be broken down into the three kinds of votes in an effort to determine how effectively each party's support was deployed. The more "excess" votes a party amassed, the greater the indication that it had overlarge majorities in those districts that it carried. Many of these "excess" votes could have been put to good use in districts (sometimes immediately adjoining) where the party's candidate was losing by a narrow margin. The more "wasted" votes contained in a party's total, the greater likelihood that its *defeated* candidates poured a substantial number of votes into their contests but still not enough to win the day for them. Thus a high proportion of "effective" votes means that, on the one hand, a party wins its seats with comfortable but not overlarge majorities; and that, on the other, it expends very few votes in districts that are safely in the hands of the opposition party.

On the basis of this analysis it may be concluded that the Republicans made more effective use of their 23,429,000 votes in the 359 contested districts than the Democrats did with their 23,865,000 votes:

Democrats	Republicans
Excess votes	
5,415,000 (22.6%)	4,975,000 (21.3%)
Wasted votes	
9,842,000 (41.2%)	8,607,000 (36.8%)
Effective votes	
8,607,000 (36.2%)	9,842,000 (41.9%)
23,864,000 (100.0%)	23,424,000 (100.0%)

More Democratic votes were in both the "excess" and the "wasted" categories than was the case with Republicans. This is substantiated by the independent computations that the average winning majority in the 187 districts carried by Democrats was 62.9 percent whereas the average Republican majority in their 172 districts was 60.0 percent. Indeed, 49 of the 187 Democratic victories were with margins of 70 percent or higher whereas only 11 of the Republicans' 172 were. (The Democratic districts with these high majorities were mainly in large Northern cities; only 13 of the 49 were in Southern states.)

DEMOCRATIC EXCESSES

The Democrats had a higher proportion of "excess" votes because overlarge Democratic majorities are naturally clustered in cities, and it is extremely difficult for even a Democratic legislature to find ways and means of transferring segments of these votes to marginal districts elsewhere in the state. By the same token the Republicans have fewer "wasted" votes because they suffer their losses in Democratic strongholds rather than in touch-and-go districts.

The conclusion emerges that had these 359 contested districts been equal in terms of population then the Republicans would actually have won *more* than 176 seats; their "fair" share were seats won proportional to votes cast. In other words, the smaller populations of Democratic districts *not only* gave that party four extra seats in Congress but *also* worked to *offset* the discrimination that party experienced due to ineffective distribution of its voting strength.

In overall terms the Democrats gain more Congressional seats with fewer votes mainly because they reap a harvest of more than 50 uncontested districts. This advantage is further augmented in the statewide elections where the Democrats walked off with most of the prizes. And in the remaining contests Democrats not only have a greater proportion of their votes clustered in undersized districts, but they can use this advantage to more than counterbalance superior Republican "effectiveness" at the polls.

NO NEUTRAL DISTRICT

This analysis also suggests that votes cast for Democratic candidates are more apt to be either "excess" or "wasted" than those going to Republicans. It might be argued that districts where Democratic voters are concentrated should be allowed to be undersized so as to ensure that the electoral scales are balanced even before the ballots are cast. This would be "benign gerrymandering" which—like "reverse discrimination" for Negroes—aims to bring all competitors up to the starting-line on an equal basis. The objection of course is that the principle of equal-sized districts is not intended to equalize the parties but to ensure that all voters have ballots of the same weight when it comes to electing their Congressmen. What does emerge, however, is that there is no such thing as a "neutral" district. *Were equal-sized districts created at random—perhaps with a computer—the result would still be an arrangement under which the Republicans would profit more than the Democrats.*

The Republicans would be well-advised to work for the equalization of districts: they can only profit by such a move. But this will solve only a part—about 25 percent of their problem. They should also try to ensure that statewide elections are held only in those states having a single Congressman. The most important step that must be taken, if seats won are to be in proportion to votes cast, is to bring Republican candidates to the 50-odd districts where the Democrats now walk in without opposition. The advent of two-party competition in what are now one-party areas will, in addition to its other consequences, close the votes-cast-per-seats-won gap that now exists between the parties.

Computers, Polls, and Public Opinion — Some Puzzles and Paradoxes

Robert P. Abelson

Despite a number of unpredictable happenings on the political scene in 1968, public-opinion polls and computers, the twin symbols of voter predictability, seem to be more frequently employed than ever. Indeed, although he had little success with it, Nelson Rockefeller built his whole campaign to impress the Republican delegates on his showing in the polls. In this article I will review several past applications of computers to the study of public opinion, particularly those activities in which I myself have been involved. In the process of this review, a picture of the nature of public political opinion will emerge, a picture that may help resolve the paradox that voter opinion, in response to a political campaign, can be simultaneously predictable and unfathomable.

A couple of years prior to the 1960 Presidential election, the heady notion was in the air of using computers for analysis of voter reactions. Limited funds were available within the Democratic Party to support a foray by Ithiel de Sola Pool, myself, and others into the computerization of public opinion. Our proposal involved two steps: first, we would assemble from archives covering the previous decade a massive public-opinion data bank, tabulating the position of many different types of voters on many different public issues; second, using these data, we would try to predict the consequences of a potential emphasis by the Democratic candidate on any of a number of issues.

Opponents of the project (most of them political experts who felt very uncomfortable at the prospect of computers invading their domain of expertise) freely expressed opinions about the impossibility of doing anything sensible by computer, and the immorality of trying, even if the project were guaranteed not to succeed. Ethics aside, expressions of doubt about the feasibility of our computer project could be summarized by six skeptical questions:

1. *The Validity Question:* Can responses on public-opinion surveys be trusted; that is, do people tell the interviewer what they really think?

2. *The Obsolescence Question:* Don't survey data rapidly become outdated, so that as you accumulate new data in a data bank, the old data grow useless?

3. *The Completeness Question:* How do you know that the surveys are asking the right questions? Or, to put it differently, what happens when a new political issue comes up for which there are no banked data?

4. *The Relative-Importance Question:* How can you tell how important a given issue is for a voter, relative to all the other issues or factors that might be involved in a political campaign?

5. *The Quantitative Prediction Question:* Even if attention is confined to a single issue, how can you predict *how many* voters will be exposed to, and influenced by, an appeal to that issue? Finally,

6. *The Marketing Question:* Even if one knows how many voters might be won over on a given issue, how will that help a candidate to phrase particular appeals on this issue?

It is interesting that these six major questions express no intrinsic doubts about computer technology. To ask whether a computer prognostication of electoral behavior is possible is not to ask whether the *computer* can do it, but rather whether it is possible to solve the technical questions raised in setting up the computations. The role of the computer has been grossly magnified, however, even to the point where *Harper's* Magazine published a mystical account entitled "The People Machine," a sinister title that has since provided gleeful reference material for several anti-Kennedy books including a recent unkind biography of the late Robert F. Kennedy.

But while the answers to the six key questions depend very little upon the nature of computers, they depend a great deal upon the nature of public opinion. Let us take up the thread of the 1960 election project again, to outline our procedures and the results.

From public-opinion survey materials preserved in the Roper Public Opinion Research Center, we accumulated the responses of approximately 100,000 people to an average of about 20 interview items. On the basis of face-sheet information, each respondent was classified as a "voter type," such as, "Eastern, small-town, high-status occupation, white Protestant, male Republican." There were 480 such voter types, the basis upon which, incidentally, Eugene Burdick titled his novel of a computerized candidate *The 480.* We tabulated the percentage of respondents of each voter type favoring, opposing, or having no opinion on each of 50 different issues or candidates. Thus, for any given issue or cluster of issues, for example civil rights, our data bank provided a profile across all 480 voter types of the probable extent of support of the opposing sides on the general issue.

Although we had initially intended to use the data bank for dynamic analyses of many issues in the 1960 campaign, the major task finally commissioned and carried out was the full-scale analysis of the so-called Catholic issue, the effect of John F. Kennedy's Catholicism on the voters.

Obviously, a common-sense analysis of this issue would suggest that a certain number of normally Republican Catholics would vote for Kennedy because of his Catholicism and that a certain number of normally Democratic Protestants would vote against Kennedy because of their anti-Catholicism. These were precisely the two major assumptions incorporated into our computer simulation of the outcome of a hypothetical election based entirely on the Catholic issue.

But note that these assumptions are quantitatively vague, specifying only that "certain numbers" of key voter types should defect to the other side. How did we know *how many* voters would be influenced in the two directions by the Catholic issue? For one direction, defection *away* from the Democrats, we used the part of the data bank containing responses reflecting anti-Catholicism. The usual survey question had been, "If your party nominated an otherwise well-qualified candidate for President who happened to be a Catholic, would you vote for him?" Over 20 percent of Protestant Democrats had said No. Despite some speculation among political analysts about an extra burst of secret anti-Catholicism expressed not to pollsters, but later inside the voting booth, we chose to believe that the percentages expressed in surveys were accurate.

On the other side of the coin, the major survey organizations had neglected to ask the corresponding *pro-*Catholicism question, namely, "If the *other* political party nominated an otherwise well-qualified candidate for President who happened to be a Catholic, would you vote for him?" Since we had no solid information by which to set the rate of defection of Catholic Republicans to the Democrats, we—and here a blush is appropriate—we *guessed.*

Our guess was that one-third of all Republican Catholics would vote for John F. Kennedy. As it turned out, this was not far wrong, being a slight underestimate. In any case, estimates for defection rates on the Catholic issue were available among all voter types. These estimates were aggregated state by state, to generate the predicted effect of the Catholic issue on the entire electorate. Two things were done with these prognostic figures: first, we compared them with Kennedy-Nixon poll standings early in the campaign; second, we compared them with the final vote tallies. Both comparisons led us to the conclusion that the 1960 election could indeed be largely understood as the superposition of the Catholic issue onto traditional party loyalties, since our simple prognoses corresponded well with reality.

On the basis of the comparison with earlier poll results, we had advised Kennedy that by August the Catholic issue had already taken hold with the voters to the full predicted extent, and that therefore (if all our assumptions were correct) he had nothing to lose by calling further attention to his religion with an appeal to fair play. Kennedy followed this kind of advice, which was also available to him from half a dozen other sources, including his own natural inclinations.

The success of our computer simulation suggested

that some of the skeptical questions that had been raised against predictions of this sort could be answered quite satisfactorily.

The Validity Question

The validity question was perhaps the most dramatic. Why wasn't there considerably more anti-Catholic voting than the amount predicted by surveys? Don't social psychologists recognize a clear and large potential discrepancy between public and private attitudes when the private attitude is of low public acceptability, such as religious prejudice? And isn't a public-opinion interview indeed a *public* situation, and voting a private situation?

Admittedly the good fit of our computer prediction to the actual results is not a strong direct test of all the assumptions of the model. Compensating errors are a logical possibility. But in the case of the so-called hidden anti-Catholic vote, there are independent sources of evidence that what anti-Catholic vote there was, was not concealed from pollsters. Why not?

Before attempting a speculative answer, I might note that a comparable conundrum arises in reviewing the 1964 Presidential election. There was supposed to be a secret Goldwater vote unbeknownst to public-opinion interviewers, but that vote did not materialize either.

Let us consider two types of anti-Catholic voters in 1960, the overt and the latent. The overt type had a set of arguments or slogans with which he could convince himself about the danger of a Catholic in the White House. There seems to be no reason why he would have hesitated to express his prejudices, along with supporting argumentation, to an interviewer. Even an attitude that might be unpopular nationally would not seem unpopular to a local enthusiast in contact with many like-minded neighbors. In this connection, it should be noted that public-opinion interviewers run heavily to passive, middle-aged, middle-class local women. These women can readily be perceived by the person with strong opinions as obliging neutral vessels who will carry his messages to City Hall or the state capital or to some vague national consciousness beyond. The interviewers are more likely seen this way than as loyal representatives of an authoritative Establishment that will punish people with unpopular views. Of course, if the interviewee holds strange, idiosyncratic opinions for which he doubts he can count on social support—let us say that he thinks that dolphins should be sent into Haiphong harbor to secretly sabotage Russian ships—then he might hesitate at the prospect of making a fool of himself before the interviewer. But sizable minority opinions are not of this character, since social support is available from friends and neighbors.

These remarks have applied to the case of the confident, overt anti-Catholic. Now imagine another vintage-1960 voter with some suspicion and distrust of Catholics, but also with some uncertainty as to the fairness and propriety of such feelings, some doubt of their relevance to the choice of a President, and no confidence that he could command wholehearted social support for his anti-Catholic feelings. Given the stimulus of a sweet lady interviewer asking whether he, the voter, would be willing to vote for a Catholic nominated by his own party, his response might well be the "fair" answer—that he would of course vote for the good man, Catholic or no. Now picture this voter's twin brother, not exposed to the lady interviewer, but instead to the stimulus of the voting booth presenting his party's Catholic versus the other party's Protestant. Will his suspicion of Catholics now triumph over both fairness and party loyalty because the voting booth is private? To assume that he will is to predict a discrepancy between poll and vote. But since a discrepancy did not appear in our study, this assumption is presumably not correct. Here I submit that the voting booth is not psychologically very private. The voter's family and close friends and perhaps a few acquaintances have probably asked him in advance how he intends to vote and will probably ask afterwards how he *did* vote. A socially undesirable decision in the booth must therefore be cast at the cost of an intent to dissemble when asked about the decision later.

The man who doesn't feel he has a real justification for holding a socially undesirable attitude is therefore in much the same psychological position in the voting booth as he is in the interview situation, albeit one is by appearances more private than the other. In both cases, he must either allow himself to be trapped into making the socially desirable response, or else suffer the social discomfort associated with making an undesirable response.

I do not mean to assert that there are no differences at all between interview and voting-booth situations. There might be a number of people who would vote differently from the way they would poll, but not necessarily all would vote in favor of the less socially desirable response. Some individuals might even use the privacy of the voting booth to guiltily register a conforming response (for example, a pro-minority group vote) that they would be too embarrassed to support in public. This orientation might especially apply to moderate Negro candidates such as Massachusetts Senator Edward Brooke and Cleveland Mayor Carl Stokes. The matter deserves further analysis and study, but I hope I have made one major point successfully, namely that there is no evidence for massive "secret votes" in recent Presidential campaigns. I would further assert that in general the validity of surveys is quite high, although there is a certain kind of exception to which I refer below.

Obsolescence of Data Banks

Returning now to other skeptical questions about computer-aided political prognosis, we come to the possible obsolescence of data banks. Do old surveys really help predict present trends? In our main 1960 simulation, none of the data were gathered later than 1958. Yet the predictions did not substantially suffer on this account, as later replications of the simulation made clear. Of course, the key predictive factors were party loyalty and religion, both highly stable, but still it may be surprising that anti-Catholic sentiments expressed prior to 1958 were germane and predictively valid two years later.

Further surprises were provided by a simulation of the 1964 election results. With data no newer than two years old, we produced a prediction of state-by-state outcomes that was substantially as accurate as the prediction of the 1960 election. More intricate use of the data bank was required, however. For the 1964 election we used data on not one but three political issues: civil rights, nuclear policy, and social-welfare policy.

In brief, we assumed that Republicans who did not support Goldwater on at least two of the three issues would defect to the Democrats, and that Democrats who did not support Johnson on civil rights would defect to the Republicans. The data bank, however, did not contain responses to direct questions such as, "Do you support Goldwater on civil rights?" Instead, the questions on each issue spanned a decade of possibly miscellaneous topical concerns. On civil rights, for example, the questions dealt largely with aspects of the

Supreme Court desegregation ruling of 1954, like "Should the schools in Little Rock, Ark., be integrated now, or should integration be postponed?" Now, one would not *necessarily* expect a high correlation between an anti-integration stand in 1957 and sympathy seven years later with Goldwater's vote against the 1964 Civil Rights Act, to say nothing of the actual behavior of voting for Goldwater. Yet the fairly good predictive accuracy of the 1964 simulation suggests that, at least on the national level, rather old survey items can serve reasonably well as indicators of enduring group dispositions toward stable themes in political life.

With two types of local elections, though, the up-to-dateness of survey data can be a much more serious question. In party primaries, the stabilizing effect of party loyalty is not a factor, and very volatile shifts of candidate strength can appear at the last moment, particularly when discussion of issues is nebulous or absent. In local referenda, likewise, the issues are often unfamiliar and unclear until the 11th-hour introduction of strong arguments. Thus, both primaries and referenda present special difficulties in applied analysis.

Many of the most spectacular apparent failures of polls have been in primaries. "Pollsters Fooled Again," declared the *New York Times* on page 1 of its News of the Week section the Sunday after Eugene McCarthy's stunning showing in the New Hampshire primary, which began the incredible 1968 political season. The idea that pollsters have been tricked by a shrewd electorate makes appealing journalism, but it can tend to perpetuate a serious misrepresentation, as I shall try to show.

In 1964, there were three key Republican primaries, and the polls were wrong in all three cases. In New Hampshire, Rockefeller was supposed to be slightly ahead, but Lodge won easily. In Oregon, Lodge was supposed to be ahead, but Rockefeller won easily. And in crucial California, the final poll had Rockefeller the winner but, of course, Goldwater won.

In 1968, only one primary winner was miscalled by the polls (Robert Kennedy's loss to McCarthy in the close Oregon race), but the percentage predictions were occasionally way off, as in New Hampshire.

The percentage errors in two of the three 1964 cases were much too large to be accounted for by sampling variation, but the clue to what might have gone wrong was that the eventual winner gained five percentage points between the next-to-last poll and the last poll. A late trend was also evident in McCarthy's New Hampshire showing in 1968. This is the basis for what I like to call the First Law of Poll-Watching: *If in a dull primary you see a trend in the polls a week before the election, extrapolate to the result by tripling this trend in the final week.*

The psychological basis for this carefree, slightly tongue-in-cheek rule of thumb is that unless the issues are sharply drawn early, the attributes of the candidates do not usually make a clear impression until the last two weeks before the election. As the day of decision nears, however, any compelling, pithy argument may create a wave of social endorsement for the lucky candidate in whose behalf the argument can be made. With Lodge in the 1964 New Hampshire primary, the pithy argument was that Lodge, unlike the other candidates, was after all a New Englander. With Rockefeller in Oregon, it was that Rockefeller was at least campaigning while Lodge wasn't even clearly interested. In California, the situation was rather more complicated. The campaign commanded sharper interests and loyalties, and no sweeping overall trend was discernible just before the last poll, so the First Law did not apply.

In 1968 in New Hampshire, the simple idea of registering a protest against President Johnson gained rapid currency (though less than half of the voters knew that McCarthy was a "dove"). And in Oregon and elsewhere Robert Kennedy apparently suffered near voting time from the charge that he was ruthless.

Local Referendum Campaigns

With local referendum campaigns, similarly, there is every indication that a strong last-minute amplification of simple, possibly trivial, arguments occurs, carrying the day for one side or the other. Here, too, there are some notable examples of polls seeming to be incorrect. National samples typically show sentiment in favor of water fluoridation at around 60 percent. Yet three out of four local fluoridation referenda lose. The explanation seems to be that before the referendum campaign starts, more positive than negative arguments are known, but during the last two weeks the negative arguments gain wider currency, and a sufficient number of people change from weak pro to weak anti opinions to ensure defeat. I have some very detailed data from a study I did of the water-fluoridation referendum in Berkeley in 1964, which clearly showed this effect.

Two other cases, both notorious, in which polls were accurate in predicting the referendum outcome but were seriously incorrect in calling the percentage margin of victory, were the Proposition 14 vote against fair housing in California in 1964, and the repeal in New York of a civilian police review board in 1966. And lest anyone think from these examples that the illiberal side always wins referenda when the chips are down, I hasten to mention a contrary instance: In California in 1966, a very strict provision (called CLEAN) against obscene literature was leading slightly in the polls yet lost on election day, even while Reagan was romping away with the governorship.

These examples suggest a Second Law of Poll-Watching: *If in a referendum an abstract principle is pitted against a very concrete fear or desire, the concrete side will gain heavily as the campaign nears its conclusion.*

Ordinarily, polls are not taken frequently enough in referendum campaigns to allow extrapolation of last-minute trends. If they were, the experienced poll-watcher could add to this Second Law the triple-trend principle of the First Law—that is, take the percentage gain of the concrete side of the issue in the next-to-last week of the campaign and triple it to predict the final outcome. The reason I suspect that this would work is that the psychological processes involved in last-minute trends are probably similar in referenda and primaries: Just when public attention finally begins to focus lazily on the imminence of voting on a complex matter, a compelling little summarization of what it's all about makes the social rounds.

The feelings involved may range widely in intensity, and the arguments may vary in content from one issue to the next, without disturbing the generalization that in a public confrontation the concrete side of an issue gains voters from the abstract side. The principle of preventive dental hygiene is rather abstract, whereas the various alarms that can be conjured up about fluoride poisoning and impure water are immediate and concrete. In parallel fashion, it is all well and good to declare in principle against pornography, but if it means that someone is going to censor what you read, or worse, take away your copy of *Playboy*, well, then one must stand and be counted.

Now, the discrepancies between abstract and concrete can, to the outside observer, look like sheer hypocrisy, and, on racial issues, conniving bigotry as well.

Yet the voter himself may be blissfully unaware of a discrepancy as he switches from his bland early endorsement of a general principle in an interview to his later concerned support of an application of its contrary, under the stimulus of a pointed campaign exposing him largely to the latter side. Even if he is aware of the discrepancy, it may not disturb him. As political scientist Robert Dahl puts it, "[It is] a common tendency of . . . mankind . . . to qualify universals in application while leaving them intact in rhetoric."

As my preceding remarks have indicated, local campaigns possess a volatility not characteristic of national campaigns. Computerizing local public opinion is therefore more hazardous than computerizing national public opinion. Furthermore, it is an expensive proposition because data-bank information cannot be transferred from one locale to another. Extensive background on the local issues and voters in Berkeley doesn't help you much in predicting the outcome of an election in Indianapolis.

There are quite a number of very interesting psychological questions to be investigated in local referenda or mass public controversies, however, and the construction of computer models whose predictions can be checked against responses from local survey panels is at least one useful way to proceed with such an investigation. To check the predictions of one computer model devised a few years ago by Alex Bernstein and me, I have assembled intensive data from three cities on fluoridation and school-segregation controversies. In this endeavor, we have encountered one peculiar problem that deserves mention, though I will not explore it in detail here. In a local computer model, it is necessary to predict *individual* rather than group opinion changes because there are not enough respondents to construct a large bank of voter types; but when we examine some of these individual changes, however, we find strong evidence of unreliable pseudo-change. Many respondents hop wildly back and forth on the attitude scales from one time to the next, while reporting no exposure to any conversations or persuasive appeals on the issue. It is as if their interview responses are given randomly. This is the phenomenon that sociologists Paul Lazarsfeld and James Coleman refer to as "turnover," and political social psychologists Philip Converse and Milton Rosenberg call "non-attitudes." It is especially prevalent on topics that for uninformed voters

are essentially "nonsense issues," such as water fluoridation, but it occurs to some extent on all issues. And computer simulation models, obviously, will have difficulty in tracing something that isn't there.

Most of what I have said thus far paints a picture of public opinion as disorganized and wishy-washy. But in fact I believe that there are definite simple patterns at work. The forces acting upon public opinion may be viewed as gravitational masses pulling upon a shallow body of water. If more than one force is applied, then the resultant response is often a simple sum of the various appropriate responses. Thus, although the published account of our 1960 and 1964 computer analyses invoke so-called cross-pressure theory, the theory that opposing decisional elements impinging on the voter interact to produce strong motivational effects, I am much more inclined in retrospect to take the view that different issues superpose upon one another *without* mutual interference. Characterizing this view are four simple assumptions:

1. Most issues have so little effect that for practical purposes one may ignore them;

2. One or two issues may have the same effect across all voter types;

3. One or two issues may have different effects across major voter types, effects proportional to measurable susceptibilities to the issue among the various types; and

4. These effects combine additively to determine the final outcome.

What convinces me most strongly of the accuracy of this simple "gravitational" model is the great success of another kind of computer analysis—the election-night computer projections by the television networks of final vote outcomes. (See "How Computers Pick an Election Winner," November, 1966.) In the early projection attempts, a number of pratfalls occurred, but in 1964 and again in 1966 the speed and accuracy of projection were awesome. In the 229 races called in those two election years, each of the two major networks made but two errors. The successful pattern is by now familiar: The bemused announcer, without the slightest understanding of how it's done, and not knowing whether he should believe it himself, reports, "With the polls closed only 20 minutes, and 0 percent of the vote tabulated, the computer already predicts that incumbent Governor Sam Smurch of Idaho will lose to his opponent, Runaway Roberts." And sure enough, when the tabulation is finally in four hours later, Sam Smurch loses.

Observation in a Few Key Districts

On the basis of my experience at NBC in 1964, I can suggest how these minor miracles can be performed. One basic and extremely simple supposition is that a trend observed in a few districts to a large portion of states or even to the whole state. Since the early observation of trends is clearly important to early projection, key districts can be chosen from among those known to have early returns available. But another crucial property of key districts is whether their shifts in voting from election to election have corresponded to the state's shifts over corresponding elections—that is, whether these districts are "swingometric." Suppose that in a state that voted 47 percent Democratic in a previous comparable election, a swingometric precinct that last time went 30 percent Democratic now goes 38 percent Democratic, and one that went 50 percent Democratic now goes 58 percent Democratic. On the basis of only these two pieces of early information, the best guess about the outcome would be a statewide 8 percent swing toward the Democratic side from the previous state results; thus, if in the previous election the Democrats had captured 47 percent of the statewide vote, they would now be predicted to capture 55 percent. Of course, the accuracy depends upon whether these key precincts are in some sense representative of the state, unless *all* precincts have swung the same 8 percent, in which case it doesn't matter which ones you choose for early projection.

If one party's campaign exerts equal attraction on all voter types, it will produce roughly the same amount of swing in all precincts. The projection procedure will then be very "robust," that is, insensitive to the choice of key early precincts. But consider the slightly more subtle situation where the campaign exerts different effects across the state's major population types, say urban versus rural. In that case, the key precincts must be carefully selected to give a balanced picture of swings in both groups. Ideally the selection of key precincts should be deliberately balanced on the basis of the population characteristics known or thought to be important in a swing. Thus, if the state is divided 50-50 between urban and rural population, and key precincts show a 4 percent swing to the Democrats in urban areas and a 6 percent swing to the Republicans

in rural areas, then the projected swing in the state as a whole would be 2 percent in favor of the Republicans.

There are many variations on this basic scheme. Instead of previous voting records, polls throughout the state and in the key precincts can provide the baseline for calculating a probable swing. This polling approach is especially useful in party primaries lacking a historical precedent. The networks have managed to project primary results as well as final election results, although in 1964 and again in 1968 CBS almost goofed in mercurial California with overly quick declarations based too heavily on Southern California key precincts.

That rather simple election-night projection models can work so well is testimony to the simplicity of the major forces operating on the electorate. If a unique constellation of many different forces combined to produce the vote outcome in each separate district, then geographical variation of outcomes would be so high and so apparently unsystematic that any prediction would be hazardous.

Is the view of public opinion I am espousing, with its emphasis on bland simplicity, an unusual view? No, indeed. Professional politicians, and lay and academic analysts of the public mind, have long sounded closely related themes. Herbert McClosky, following an analysis that revealed weak and self-contradictory clusters of public beliefs about democratic norms and practices, put the matter quite sharply. He said, "As intellectuals and students of politics we are disposed both by training and sensibility to take political ideas seriously. . . . We are therefore prone to forget that most people take them less seriously than we do, that they pay little attention to issues, rarely worry about the consistency of their opinions, and spend little or no time thinking about the values, presuppositions and implications which distinguish one political orientation from another."

It seems to me that we can understand and perhaps even sympathize with the general public's failure to organize the political world very well if we realize that there are limits on the typical man's intellectual reach —that his organizing capacities and efforts are usually applied only over a small content area.

Opinion Molecules

To see this pattern, let us postulate the existence of self-contained cognitive units called opinion *molecules*. Each molecule functions for the person holding it by serving most of the purposes an opinion serves. Much has been written about the expressive purposes of opinions and about the psychodynamic functions of more general attitude orientations, but there is a more homey and widespread function that opinions satisfy. Opinions bestow conversational and cognitive security —they give you something to say and think when the topic comes up. To serve this function, as well as some of the deeper psychological functions, the usual minimum-sized, stable opinion molecule seems to require a *fact,* a *feeling,* and a *following*—that is, some item of "information" (which may or may not be objectively correct); some emotional orientation; and some sense that there are others who hold the same opinion.

It is easy to give examples of such molecules: "It's a fact that when my Uncle Charlie had back trouble, he was cured by a chiropractor. You know, I feel that chiropractors have been sneered at too much, and I'm not ashamed to say so, because I know a lot of people who feel the same way." Or again, "Nobody on this block wants to sell to Negroes, and neither do I. The property values would decline." These sorts of opinions are often quite impervious to other levels of argumentation because of their complete, closed, molecular character. It is as if the opinion-holder were saying, "What else could there possibly be to add?"

Certainly the opinion molecule's size will vary, from individual to individual, depending upon habit, education, intelligence, personality, and social context. Sometimes a molecule will have only two components, say just a fact and feeling with no following, as in private little delusions, or a feeling and a following with no essential dependence on variations in fact, as in "Burn, baby, burn." On the other hand, it is quite possible to have larger molecules that include arguments to counter the opposition, qualifications of the opinion, and an organized account of the facts, feelings, and following on the other side.

How elaborate the structure housing an opinion will be depends upon how elaborate the individual requires it to be to serve his purposes. For example, if no counter-arguments are expected, then there is no need to prepare for them. But this is also a matter of cognitive style, varying according to a self-imposed question, "How much do I have to know to be entitled to an opinion?" Presumably, highly educated individuals feel some embarrassment when and if their opinions are revealed as superficial, and therefore are at pains to try to construct them well. But most of the general public feels no such pressure, and there is no realistic reason why they should. Without question, this is a source of great frustration to all those who in some way work to try to increase the public's level of sophistication.

It is possible, as we have seen, to get a lot of mileage out of very simple computer models because the drifts in mass public opinion usually follow simple patterns. In the last analysis, however, despite the fact that any given pattern may be simple, the question of which particular pattern will emerge in a given election campaign is still something of an imponderable. The interpretations placed upon crucial events and personalities —the labels or images, or call them what you will— determine the components available for people's opinion molecules, and these components are never either completely predictable or completely under the control of powerful political figures.

Thus there will always be margin for error in computer prognosis of public opinion, particularly prognoses that try to project too far forward in time. For those still ethically troubled by the political advent of computer analysis, let me add that potential protection against the trivialization of the electoral process is the same as it has always been: an electorate that responds to complex issues in a complex way, a way that defies sterotypes and formulas—and the computers.

Life,Time,and the Fortunes of War
James D.Wright

Unquestionably, the public's attitude toward the Vietnam war has changed greatly in recent years. Commercial polls, media reports and academic studies bear the same message: the war has lost support. But these trend-spotters have left unanswered many questions about the nature of this change. Have the political sentiments articulated at the country club bridge table changed more radically than those voiced at the neighborhood tavern? And if they have, who or what is responsible?—the mass media? Certainly, their editorial viewpoints have undergone concurrent shifts.

But just how powerful are the media? Does a jolting photo-essay of war dead unlock closed minds or lose subscribers? Conversely, could a series of prowar editorials whip up support for a waning cause? Is one medium more effective than another? Is the work-weary lower-income T.V.-watcher any more affected by the evening newscast than the commuting stockbroker is by the news magazine he leafs through enroute to his upper middle-class suburb?

The change in attitudes toward the war coupled with the change in how the war has been reported offers a unique opportunity for social scientists to investigate how mass media and public opinion interact: who influences whom; which is a cause of change and which is a reflection of it.

The period under review here is that from 1964, when President Johnson was swept into office by a huge majority, to 1968 when President Nixon took office, promising to end the war. It was a time when the United States commitment in Vietnam was vastly escalated. The number of troops involved in the war jumped from 40,000 "advisers" to a half-million combat personnel, and in the process, the war was brought home to ever-increasing numbers of people.

Another major phenomenon of the period (no doubt related to the continued escalation) was the rise of large-scale protest against the war. Beginning as a relatively restricted and nonviolent movement in the fall of 1966 with the first big march on Washington, the Movement had taken on a more radical coloration by the summer of 1968. The demands of the protesters changed from the mere end of a senseless war to the end of United States "imperialism" abroad and even the overthrow of "the system" at home. The prominence given to protests in the media cannot but have had an effect on mass sentiment toward the conflict itself.

During the four years from 1964 to 1968, the major media in the country shifted their editorial stance markedly, from a prowar to a fairly obviously antiwar position. This change in the media stance creates an unusual and desirable research situation, because most studies of the influence of the media are forced to deal with them as a constant rather than as a variable.

Fortunately, the University of Michigan's Survey Research Center (SRC) made comprehensive election studies in 1964 and 1968, and the data from them make possible a detailed analysis of the shift in attitudes over the period and of the extent to which the media were responsible.

Before examining these studies, however, it is important to realize the theoretical background against which the analysis must be set, because, in my view, the conclusions to be drawn upset the traditional patterns of speculation about the attitudinal and behavioral impact of the so-called mass media.

There are two characteristic forms of social scientific theory in this area. First, there is the tradition of mass society theorizing. This view links the advance of industrialization and urbanization with breakdowns in the primary social bonds. Upward occupational mobility, a situation presumably endemic to industrial society, is seen as destroying a person's ties with the past—with his parents, his friends and other primary social groups. Meanwhile, increasing urbanization locates individuals in new and unfamiliar milieux in which their old values and attitudes will be inappropriate. These demographic and social psychological processes result in the creation of "mass man," the so-called rootless individual. Lacking strong informal ties to primary social networks, a society of such mass men will be manipulable and public opinion in such a society is believed to be largely "uncrystallized," or, as sociologist William Kornhauser puts it, "available" for manipulation by national political elites. The mass media, then, function mainly as the propaganda arms of these elite groups, with the capability of reaching out and mobilizing mass opinion in support of the elites' goals, whatever these may be.

The second theory contrasts Kornhauser's view. Founded by Paul Lazarsfeld and his associates at Columbia University in the 1940s and early 1950s, it springs from a tradition of political analysis and media research which we may profitably call the "group bases" theory of politics. Lazarsfeld's conception of the relationship between political attitudes and the mass media is summed up in the slogan: reinforcement rather than conversion. In other words, the media are basically successful at reinforcing and articulating already existing opinions or even at creating opinions in areas where none previously existed, but are not so successful at converting individuals from a firmly held opinion to a new one. Lazarsfeld's concept involved a resurrection of the classical sociological image of man as being located amid an array of social and informational networks or primary groups and deriving the major portions of his political ideology and support from those networks. In sharp contrast to the mass-society view, which was then dominant, Lazarsfeld hypothesized that these networks would override the impact of the formal media. Hence, a situation of reinforcement rather than conversion would exist.

Concentric Circles

In 1964, Johan Galtung published an article in *The Journal of Peace Research* which attempted a quasi-synthesis of these two views. In it, Galtung speculates that society, for purposes of political analysis, can best be conceptualized as a series of concentric circles. At the center is a small decision-making nucleus; this is surrounded by a social center, constituted by a core of the well-informed and articulate mass public; these are both finally enclosed by the social periphery, consisting of the majority of the mass public who remain relatively unconcerned with and uninformed about matters of public policy. On its simplest level, Galtung's view is that mass-society theories will tend to describe the state of politics in the periphery and that "social bases" theories will tend to describe politics in the center. Hence, the center (i.e., the middle-aged, males, the well-educated, the high-income, white-collar workers) will consist of a fairly stable and well reinforced body of informed public opinion anchored in ideological communities, which will consequently be immune to overtures made by the media. Those on the periphery (that is the young and the old, females, the poor, the poorly educated, blue-collar workers) will be characteristically amorphous, unconcerned, unreinforced, uncrystallized—in short, more susceptible to media manipulation.

A number of political and social scientists have recently extended the analyses I have outlined above specifically to attitudes toward the war. Seymour Martin Lipset, for example, in an article on Vietnam published in the September-October 1966 issue of *transaction*, asserted that "in the area of foreign policy, most Americans know very little and are only indirectly involved," while Sidney Verba and associates in a 1967 article in *The American Political Science Review*, noted that "most recent academic studies of public attitudes have demonstrated that the public has little information on most issues and that most people do not have thought-out, consistent and firmly held positions on most matters of public policy." Yet in the same article Verba admitted: "We found that the war in Vietnam was a salient problem" and later, "It is our opinion that [these data] represent fairly high levels of information on an issue of foreign policy." Concerning the hypotheses about uncrystallized opinion and manipulability, Lipset asserted that "when it comes to Vietnam basically the opinion data indicate that national policy-makers, particularly the President, have an almost free hand to pursue any policy they think correct and get public support for it." This uncrystallization hypothesis was also elaborated in a 1970 article for *Scientific American* by Philip Converse and Howard Schuman. Finally, Milton Rosenberg joined Verba and Converse in extending these lines of reasoning into specific hypotheses about the role of the media, in their *Vietnam and the Majority: A Dove's Guide*:

In the early years of our Vietnam involvement the news and opinion media fell into voluntary alignment with the government, lending ready support and popularization to the rationale for our overall stance in the international sphere. However, in the last four or five years much media content has been increasingly critical of the Vietnam war. This has probably both reflected and helped to deepen the gradual erosion of the general public's approval (or acceptance) of our involvement in Southeast Asia.

At this point we should take a look at the national print media in the period under review, and clarify exactly how much of a shift occurred in their editorial attitudes. A few illustrations will give an idea of the nature and size of this change. Fortunately, it is readily assessable because approximately 90 percent of the total United States magazine readership (for political information as distinct from entertainment) was concentrated, as of 1968, in seven major magazines: *Life, Look, Time, Newsweek, U.S. News & World Report, Reader's Digest* and the *Saturday Evening Post*.

Until 1966, *Life* magazine was under the editorial direction of that avid Cold Warrior, Henry Luce. Mr. Luce's politics were well reflected in the pages of his magazines: witness the following from a *Life* editorial of early 1963:

We too have some national interests to further. . . and there are lots of places where the average American would like to ease by unilateral action the pains and frustrations of a decade of "alliance diplomacy." In Vietnam, the ghoulish pessimism of the French, plus a deteriorating war, has goaded Washington to reconsider the possibility of stepping up the war. It would also be a pleasure to respond more loftily and unilaterally to the pigmy insults of Castro, of Ghana.

An editorial in the January 8, 1965 issue of *Life* spoke of negotiations as "a euphemism for American withdrawal and a Communist takeover"; in February of 1966, the magazine published an article supporting an escalation, under the title "The War is Worth Winning" (February 25, 1966).

Similar sentiments occurred constantly in Mr. Luce's other major magazine, *Time*, in the same period. From a "non-editorialized" news article of early 1964:

The key to the situation remains the United States struggle to keep South Vietnam from falling to Communism. . . . It has been clear for a long time what would happen if South Vietnam gave way to Communism: the reaction described by the famous "domino theory" would undoubtedly set in (April 3, 1964.).

A mid-1965 *Time* "Essay" clarified the magazine's position still further:

It is sometimes forgotten that Communism still remains an international and aggressive movement, that "infiltration" and "subversion" remain realities. . . . [If the United States were to be pushed out of Vietnam], Americans would only have to make another stand against Asian Communism later, under worse conditions and in less tenable locations (May 14, 1965).

The "Essay" was entitled, "Vietnam: the Right War at the Right Time."

Yet by 1968, both *Time* and *Life* had taken markedly more conciliatory stances. From *Life*:

We urge that this campaign be de-escalated—that the U.S. suspend for the time being the general air attack against the Hanoi-Haiphong industrial and transport system (January 5, 1968).

(Quoting Edwin Reischauer, ambassador to Japan): "We have lost this war in terms of our original objectives. . . ." Is it defeatism to say that? Perhaps: but it is mainly a confession that all the military power in the world can be muscle-bound and useless in some revolutionary situations. Force has its limits and kill ratios are not the measure of its efficiency (February 23, 1968).

By the middle of 1969, *Life* had published the photographs of the previous week's war dead, hardly a clarion call to escalation.

And from *Time*, in August, 1968:

Not all the basic goals of either the U.S. or North Vietnam policy are likely to survive a genuine settlement. . . . Through some combination of a cease-fire, withdrawal and supervision, the guns will eventually fall silent in Vietnam.

The same essay spoke favorably of "integrating the Communists into South Vietnam politics" and described the war as "messy and formless."

Look, too, showed a substantial shift away from support for the war in the four-year period. From an article published early in 1964:

For should South Vietnam be so internally weakened by incessant nightly guerrilla attacks that North Vietnam could absorb it, the bountiful rice harvests of the Mekong delta would well out in life-giving gushers to industrially emerging, but chronically starving, North Vietnam and Red China. Cambodia, Laos, and Thailand would fall like dominoes, and India would be exposed to an Asian Communist bloc for once well-fed and economically viable (January 28, 1964).

Yet by the middle of 1968, *Look* had taken a markedly different stand. In an editorial following seven pages of horrifying war photographs, the editors commented:

Look publishes these photographs to remind you of some things that many Americans seem to have forgotten: that people and nations make mistakes. . . . The Vietnam war has been a mistake, destroying something precious in the word, "America" (May 14, 1968).

The editorial concluded with a call to "wind up our involvement as quickly and as honorably as possible." By late 1969, even the "honorably" qualification was dropped: "We should get out of Vietnam immediately" (J. Robert Moskin, foreign editor, *Look,* November 18, 1969).

Similar shifts are also apparent in *Newsweek* and the *Saturday Evening Post.* (*Newsweek,* for instance, on the occasion of Ho Chi Minh's death in September, 1969, spoke of him as "the George Washington and Abraham Lincoln" of the Vietnamese people.) In the middle of 1964, the *Saturday Evening Post* ran an editorial which included the following:

To pull out of South Vietnam or to accept some glib "solution" as "neutralization" would, as Secretary Rusk has suggested, very likely bring a "major shift in the balance of power." The militant, predatory, and bellicose Communist Chinese regime would be greatly strengthened in power and prestige. . . . The government of the United States in the past has bought untold trouble for future generations of Americans by its failure to appreciate the true dimension of the Communist menace in Asia (June 13, 1964).

Yet by early 1967, the magazine came around to a decidedly different position. Editorializing about President Johnson's professed lack of alternatives in the conduct of the war, the *Post* editors wrote:

The alternative to war is peace; the alternative to bombing civilian villages is to stop bombing civilian villages; the alternative to complaining that one has no choice is to investigate what the choices are (February 11, 1967).

In the same editorial, the *Post* editors endorsed a "permanent and unconditional" bombing halt. In April of 1967 they wrote, "One of the chronic embarrassments of our struggle for Vietnam is that we have been fighting on behalf of a government that doesn't really represent anybody" (April 22, 1967).

Of the Big Seven magazines, only *Reader's Digest* and *U.S. News & World Report* remained relatively hawkish on the war throughout the period. See, for example, the article by Walter Judd in the September 1968 *Reader's Digest,* entitled "No 'Surrender' in the Vietnam Peace Talks," or the *U.S. News* editorial of September 23, 1968. I have not separated the readers of these two magazines—they represent about 15 percent of the total magazine readership—from readers of the more dovish magazines in the analysis that follows.

Obviously, the shifting position of national newspapers is much more difficult to assess. Many of the national circulation newspapers had, however, come out against the war sometime before 1968, among them, the *New York Times,* the *Washington Post,* the *Christian Science Monitor,* the *Atlanta Constitution,* and the *St. Louis Post-Dispatch.* (The *Boston Globe* did an informal study in 1968 of many major American newspapers and found much shifting to more dovish positions. This study is cited in James Aronson's *The Press and the Cold War,* Bobbs-Merrill, 1970.) It is, of course, practically impossible to assess the editorial content of the countless small-town newspapers across the country, but in any case the high-status urban groups are more likely to be attentive to papers such as the *Times,* the *Post,* and so on. And it is, as we shall see, the high-status groups who are our major concern here.

This quite clear and extensive shift on the part of the chief national print media, then, has created a situation highly favorable to the assessment of media impacts on political attitudes. At the most basic level, if the media's editorial opinions do have decisive effects on the public's political attitudes, then we should expect groups with high media attention to be relatively more hawkish in 1964, when the major media were noisily rattling sabres than in 1968, when they had taken a markedly more conciliatory stance. Correlatively, groups with low attention to the media should show considerably less shifting in the four-year period. On the other hand, if the media cannot achieve the easy conversion of that audience, then attention to the media should be basically unrelated to the content and character of a person's opinions about the war in Vietnam.

In November of 1964 (just after the national elections) and in October of 1968 (just prior to the national elections), the Survey Research Center asked the following questions:

Which of the following do you think we should do *now* in Vietnam?

☐ Pull out of Vietnam entirely.

☐ Keep our soldiers in Vietnam but try to end the fighting.

☐ Take a stronger stand, even if it means invading North Vietnam.

The SRC also asked the following questions concerning patterns of media attention in each of the two study years:

We're interested in finding out whether people paid much attention [to the elections] . . . . Take newspapers, for instance—did you read about the campaign in any newspaper? [IF YES] How much did you read articles about the election—regularly, often, from time to time, or once in a great while? . . . How about the radio? . . . How about magazines? . . . How about television?

In 1968 the SRC asked, along with which of the three options the United States should pursue in the conduct of the war, whether the respondent thought our original involvement in Vietnam a mistake. It is interesting to note how markedly dove sentiment varied depending on which question one examines. More than half the sample, for instance, thought the original commitment a mistake, but less than one-fifth chose the pull-out option. Even among the supposedly dovish group who thought we should have stayed out of Vietnam, only one-third favored a pull-out, while about one-fourth chose the stronger stand. An answer that the United States "did the wrong thing" by getting into Vietnam, then, gives the researcher no indication of whether the respondent thinks United States objectives there are worth a further sacrifice of life; the support given the stronger stand is a better indication. Who are the members of the population who would support a further sacrifice of life in the Southeast Asian effort? In order to find out, this report focuses on the third response to the SRC survey question.

The basic distributions for the Vietnam question are presented in Table I.

As the table indicates, the percentage of respondents offering "no opinion" expectedly declined from 41 percent in 1964 to 10 percent in 1968. Part of this decline is because the question was asked in the *post*-election

Sampling Public Opinion on the War

The SRC studies are based upon stratified and clustered probability samples of households of the noninstitutionalized American population of voting age in the contiguous states. The analyses given here are based on the white, non-South responses only. The reason for this is not in any way one of bias. The facts are that both the blacks and the white South are considerably more stable in their support for escalation than is the rest of the population. Among these with an opinion, for instance, escalation received the support of 25 percent (N = 67) of the black respondents in 1964, and 20 percent (N = 153) in 1968. Similarly, among white southerners with an opinion, escalation received the support of 47 percent (N = 202) in 1964, 50 percent (N = 321) in 1968. The reasons for the greater stability of these two groups are interesting but not germane here, and the analysis of trends in support, the inclusion of these groups artificially deflates the actual amount of shifting on the war issue. Consequently, I have omitted them from this analysis with the exception of Table I where the data included represent responses from throughout the nation, and of both races.

Most of the accounts based upon the SRC studies present the second option ("Keep our soldiers in Vietnam but try to end the fighting") as the "status quo" option. There is, however, some question as to whether this is an accurate interpretation. The alternative does rather explicitly specify an attempt to "end the fighting"; insofar as "end the fighting" is taken to mean a cease-fire, then the option is considerably more peace-oriented than the conventional "status quo" label would indicate.

segment of the interview in 1964 and in the *pre*-election interview in 1968; but undoubtedly, another part of the decline reflects a growing public awareness of the war in the four-year period.

One question worth asking is in which camp the "newly awakened" show up; the evidence indicates that they are

Table I — Change in Support for Policy Alternatives in Vietnam from 1964 to 1968

	Pull Out	Stay, End Fighting	Stronger Stand	Don't Know, Other
		Total Sample		
1964	8%	22%	29%	41%
1968	19%	37%	34%	10%
		Of Those With an Opinion		
1964	13%	37%	49%	—
1968	22%	41%	37%	—

likely to be numbered in the anti-war columns. From 1964 to 1968 the stronger stand gained the support of an additional 4.5 percent of the total population compared with a 15-point gain for "end the fighting" and an 11.5-point gain for a pull-out. Although the evidence does not allow a definitive answer, it does suggest that a good portion of the newly awakened reject the stronger stand.

In any case, the substantial differences in the percentage of people responding "don't know—other" makes raw percentage comparisons difficult or misleading. Consequently, the results have been recomputed on the basis of those in the sample who did express an opinion (see the bottom half of Table I), and the remaining tables in this report are based on these recalculations.

One problem with the technique of repercentaging on this basis is that it tends to overestimate the actual hawkish sentiment because, in effect, it assumes that the "don't knows" would be equally distributed across all three response categories, were they to have an opinion. Yet, as I suggested earlier, those without an opinion are in fact more likely to show up in the first and second categories than in the third. Nonetheless, since our concern is with support for the stronger stand, it seems appropriate to overestimate rather than underestimate that support, in keeping with the scientific tradition of erring, if at all, on the conservative side.

Removing those without an opinion leaves us with a reasonably satisfactory portrait of the "more active" public, the group which had at least formulated *some* opinion on a major foreign policy issue, and which comprised 90 percent of the population sampled in 1968. What conclusions can we draw from a comparative analysis of this group in terms of its attention to the national print media?

As indicated in Table I, the overall population shift among those who expressed an opinion on the Vietnam issue was about 12 percentage points over the four-year period. The expectation that the bulk of this shift might be located among the groups with the highest print media attention receives considerable support in Table II. As this clearly indicates,
the 12 percentage-point shift nationwide is caused almost exclusively by major shifts among those segments of the population who pay the greatest attention to the print media. The evidence is particularly persuasive with regard to the magazine readers. As the table suggests, about 25 percent of the population pays more than casual attention to the national newsmagazines. Among that 25 percent, support for escalation declines 20 percentage points. Among the remainder of the population, however, support for escalation declines only marginally (2 percentage points). The indication, then, is that most of the national shifting on the war issue was concentrated in those groups

Table II — Decline in Support for the Stronger Stand by Magazine and Newspaper Readers between 1964 and 1968

	Read Magazines		Read Newspapers	
	Good Many/ Several	Less than Good Many/ Several	Regularly/ Often	Less than Regularly/ Often
1964	54%	41%	56%	43%
1968	34%	39%	39%	36%
Percentage difference	20%	2%	17%	7%

Respondents include white, non-South only, as percentage of those with an opinion.

with the highest print media attention.

Attention to the media, however, is also correlated with a number of other factors, notably social class. A study made by *Newsweek* in 1960, for instance, claimed that almost 90 percent of its male readers were either students or those in white-collar occupations, and reported similar figures for *Time* and *U.S. News & World Report.* My own data indicate that about 34 percent of the total magazine reading is done by college graduates, who represent some 14 percent of the population. Or, to put the argument in another form, about half of the college-educated population in 1968 were accustomed to reading magazines regularly or often for political purposes, as compared to about one-fifth of high-school graduates and about one-tenth of those who had less than a high-school education. And even these figures probably underestimate the gap between the high-status groups and the low-status groups as measured on the media attention variable. For example, "a good many" magazine articles may mean, for the poorly educated, five or six a year, for the better educated, five or six a month, or even a week. There are also probably significant differences in the fashion in which the articles are read and the purposes for which they are used.

But there is little to be gained by belaboring the obvious, that the high-status groups are much more likely to be attentive to the print media than the low-status groups. The possibility that the results displayed in Table II are merely artifacts of an underlying class dimension is addressed in Table III, which deserves detailed inspection.
As an aid to interpretation, I suggest focusing on the "multiple media" variable, listed third. As the table headings indicate, the left-hand side of the table compares those who read both magazines and newspapers regularly or often in 1964 and 1968, while the right-hand side of the table compares those who read neither medium more than occasionally in the two study years. The evidence summarized here clearly indicates an interaction between social class and media attention in their effect on attitudes towards Vietnam.

Table III — Decline in Support for the Stronger Stand by Magazine and Newspaper Readers from the Upper Middle Class (UMC), Lower Middle Class (LMC) and Working Class (WC) from 1964 to 1968

Read Magazines

	Good Many/ Several			Less Than Good Many/Several		
	UMC†	LMC	WC	UMC	LMC	WC
1964	67%	44%	55%	60%	60%	46%
1968	34%	19%	51%	39%	39%	40%
Percentage difference	33%	25%	4%	21%	21%	6%

Read Newspapers

	Regularly/ Often			Less Than Regularly/Often		
	UMC	LMC	WC	UMC	LMC	WC
1964	69%	59%	50%	52%	39%	46%
1968	37%	35%	46%	36%	33%	38%
Percentage difference	32%	24%	4%	16%	6%	8%

Read Multiple Media

	Both Newspapers and Magazines			Neither Newspapers nor Magazines		
	UMC	LMC	WC	UMC	LMC	WC
1964	78%	50%	55%	59%	41%	45%
1968	40%	19%	48%	41%	33%	38%
Percentage difference	38%	31%	7%	18%	8%	7%

Respondents include white, non-South only, as a percentage of those with an opinion.

†Social class as used in the present study involves both an occupational and an income distinction. The working class consists of those in blue-collar occupations; the remaining white-collar workers have been split into upper and lower middle class on the basis of an income distinction with the cutting line at $10,000.

Consider, first, workers who read both media regularly or often. The group indicates a meager 7-percentage-point shift away from support for escalation, which compares to an identical 7-percentage-point shift among the non-reading workers and a 12-percentage-point shift in the population as a whole.

Now, compare the working-class pattern with the pattern shown by the high-status group. Among the reading members of the latter, some 38 percent shifted their position from support for escalation, as contrasted to only an 18-percentage-point shift among the nonreading upper middle class. Clearly, class and media attention interact, or in less technical terms, it can be said that the high-status groups appear to be particularly susceptible to media manipulation. The evidence surely is that the high-status groups "got the message" in both 1964 and in 1968, whereas the low-status groups were barely affected by the changes that had taken place in the media stance.

The introduction of further statistical controls only intensifies the basic finding. For instance, among upper middle-class white Protestant Republicans who read both magazines and newspapers frequently—hardly a peripheral group by any criterion—support for an escalation in Vietnam dropped a full 60 percentage points, from 91 percent support in 1964 to 31 percent support in 1968. Comparable data for the reading section of the working class show that support for escalation ran to 48 percent in 1964 and dropped only 2 percentage points to 46 percent in 1968. This again reaffirms the conclusion that the general drop in support for escalation is mainly caused by the peculiar susceptibility of the upper middle class to media influence.

A possible alternative explanation for these findings might be that the high-status shift occurred independently of the media shift and that the high-status groups simply sougnt out media consonant with their new beliefs. But there is no evidence to indicate any substantial shifting around for a medium consonant with some newfound political attitudes. Twenty-eight percent of the nonmanual workers in both 1964 and 1968 chose the newspaper as their most important source of political information; 11 percent of the group in 1964 and 12 percent in 1968 chose magazines. The magazine readers' attention to particular magazines was not quite so stable: among the nonmanual group, *Life* dropped 9 points (from 20 percent of the total magazine readers who mentioned *Life* as their most important magazine in 1964 to 11 percent who so mentioned it in 1968), *Saturday Evening Post* dropped 7 points, *Reader's Digest* and *Look* stayed the same, *Time* gained 4, *Newsweek* gained 6, and *U.S. News* gained 7. But if the figures do indicate some shifting around among magazines, the shift is by no means decisively in favor of the dovish magazines. Indeed, the hawkish *U.S. News* gained 7 points, while the more dovish *Life* lost 9. If the decline in hawkish sentiment among the high-status groups is the result of some outside factor and those groups have sought out media consonant with this new attitude (a situation which in itself would render the association spurious), there is no sign of such an occurrence in the available data.

At any rate, it is transparently clear that the trend away from a "tougher" stand in the population as a whole is mainly seen in those within the high-status groups who pay close attention to the print media. The argument is highlighted by the virtual absence of any shifting among the working-class population, irrespective of their media attention. This again suggests that the general drop in support for escalation is in fact mainly caused by the special susceptibility of the high-status groups to media influences. To be sure, the high-status groups are more likely to be attentive to print media, but the dramatic shift away from support for escalation is not to be found even among the

61

(admittedly) fewer low-status readers. It is true that the upper middle-class nonreaders also drop considerably in their support for escalation, but the drop is by no means as spectacular as the corresponding one among their more attentive cohorts.

A brief digression is in order here on the question of party identification and city size. Between 1964 and 1968 support for the stronger stand among Republicans fell 29 percentage points, more than twice the 14-point drop for Democrats. The data indicate that this disproportionate Republican shift is chiefly caused by the concentration of white Protestant upper middle-class readers in the GOP ranks. Among working-class Republican newspaper readers, for instance, support for escalation declined only 4 percentage points, by comparison. The examination of support for escalation by party identification, however, uncovers some interesting trends, particularly along the city-size dimension.

As Table IV indicates, urban Democrats show very little shift away from the stronger stand; for every level of media attention, the shift does not substantially differ from the national mean. Rural Democrats who read neither newspapers nor magazines regularly similarly show little shift; 13 points compared to a population mean shift of 12 points. Among Democrats, then, the only disproportionate shift is among rural newspaper readers. The Republican pattern, however, is markedly different. Both urban and rural Republicans with high media attention shift substantially (47 and 38 points respectively); urban nonreaders and rural newspaper readers shift only slightly when compared to the national mean.

This suggests that the Democratic milieu might be called a protective or reinforcing milieu. Urban Democrats appear particularly impervious to media influences, which is to suggest that their environment or the conditions of their existence are likely to be a more important source of political attitudes than, for instance, the media. Or, to put it another way, urban Democrats are likely to exhibit fairly "rational" political attitudes, in that those attitudes appear either to derive from or at least be maintained by their milieu. It is significant that among Democrats, the only group to show any marked shift in the four-year period, is that of rural newspaper readers, who are for all practical purposes without a political milieu which might serve as a source of political attitudes.

Republicans, on the other hand, appear to obtain very little reinforcement from their milieu. Indeed, the only areas of relative stability among the Republican ranks are the urban nonreaders and the rural newspaper readers, and it is a safe bet that the rural Republican newspapers have not "come around" on the war to the extent that the urban newspapers and magazines have. This, then, suggests that Republicans derive less of their attitudes (or reinforcement of their attitudes) from the conditions of their existence, or, again, that Republicans are likely to be relatively less "rational" in their choice of political attitudes. Indeed, the stereotypical Republican monolith appears to be less a function of some special sense of community or class consciousness than a result of their reading more of the same media.

Opinion Conversion

To my mind the relationship between the media and political attitude change needs radical rethinking by social scientists. All the currently held positions are challenged by the evidence I have put forward here. Contrary to the Lazarsfeldian position, the media appear in this instance, at least, to have succeeded in effecting enormous opinion conversions among the high-status groups. In contrast to the claims of the mass-society theory, some segments of the population—notably the supposedly peripheral working class—seem unusually resistant to media manipulation. As for Galtung's theory of a stable center and a volatile periphery, it appears to have things precisely backwards: as

Table IV — Change in Support for the Stronger Stand According to Size of Residential Community, Party Identification and Readership of Magazines and Newspapers from 1964 to 1968

	1964			1968		
	Read Both Magazines & Papers	Read News-papers Only	Read Neither	Read Both Magazines & Papers	Read News-papers Only	Read Neither
Democrats						
Urban	45%	52%	36%	35%	39%	28%
Rural	—	68%	51%	—	43%	38%
Republicans						
Urban	74%	62%	50%	27%	34%	33%
Rural	73%	46%	54%	35%	39%	29%

Urban means a population greater than 10,000.
Respondents include white, non-South only, as a percentage of those with an opinion.

far as the Vietnam issue is concerned, stable opinion lies in the periphery and the manipulable opinion in the center.

One of the first questions to come up is why the high-status groups should be so vulnerable to impressions from the media. Perhaps there may be a greater ability for self-deception among members of the high-status groups, an ability—or perhaps a liability—to pick attitudes and positions out of the media and subsequently convince oneself that they are self-generated. Or it may simply be that the upper middle class attends to the media more seriously than its lower-status cohorts.

Another possibility is that the segment of the national elite which controls the media has very little interest in manipulating the working-class mass and simply concentrates its efforts, apparently most effectively, on the upper middle class. It is, after all, the upper middle class which supports the local and national elites, and whose resources, both financial and technical, are potentially beneficial to the elite group. In the same way that factory foremen are given the "errand boy" tasks of carrying out managerial directives, the upper middle class may be given the task of implementing elite decisions. Even if the metaphor is not apt, it is suggestive.

A third possibility is that, while the media elite may have an *interest* in manipulating the working-class mass, their ability to do so may be severely limited. All of the editorializing in the world, for example, is certain to leave unaffected groups who do not read the editorial page. Even beyond that limitation, the media have to contend with a strongly reinforcing or protective working-class milieu. If, as I have suggested, workers respond mainly to alterations in the basic conditions of community and environment, then it is clear that the media will encounter major difficulties in making inroads among the low-status groups.

A fourth possibility is that the better educated upper middle class is also better trained to be sensitive to predominant elite ideologies. This hypothesis would view the universities more or less as elite-controlled institutions which train an "available" cadre of quasi-political functionaries, the upper middle class, who can be called upon to support the policies of the national elite. This would give the media the mass-society function of serving as the communications and propaganda arm of the elite group, or, to return to the earlier metaphor, simply as foremen who give attitude and policy directives to the upper middle class masses.

There is also the puzzling question of why, given the conventional formulation of working-class attitudes as volatile and unstable, the data presented here indicate precisely the reverse. One possibility, of course, is that the conventional formulation is simply wrong. Another, more conspiratorial in nature, is that the media, seeking to cover their tracks, have hoodwinked their audience—which in-

---

TV—The Common Man's Medium & The Vietnam War

Interestingly enough, attention to television—the poor man's medium—apparently makes very little difference in working-class attitudes toward the war. Like the other media, television leaves the working class largely unaffected. In 1964, for instance, 50 percent of the workers with high television attention (N = 202) supported an escalation, as compared with 48 percent support among those who watched the television infrequently or not at all for political purposes (N = 58). The comparable percentages for 1968 are 41 percent (N = 211) and 40 percent (N = 77) respectively, decreases of 9 and 8 percentage points. Hence, the differences between the working-class watchers and the working-class nonwatchers are minimal for both years. In the middle class, however, the nonwatchers stay about the same for the two study years (46 percent in 1964 [N = 38] and 46 percent in 1968 [N = 65]), while the watchers drop 28 percentage points (from 62 percent support in 1964 [N = 175] to 34 percent in 1968 [N = 217]). Again, this attests to the particular susceptibility of the middle classes to media influences.

---

cludes, obviously, most social scientists—into believing that they are most adept at reaching the low-status groups, all the while secretly manipulating the attitudes of the national upper middle class.

A third possibility, and one I personally think the most likely, is that the data for this report were gathered in times of relatively high political awareness, either just before or just after the national elections. Such a report taps the "mass" when it is, so to speak, at its political best, when attitudes have been most carefully considered, and when information on the major issues is most readily available. It is this more politically aware milieu which exposes the essential stability of mass or working-class opinion on, in this case, the war issue. The suggestion is that, at least among the working-class masses, the widely flaunted "free hand" of the president becomes severely tied down as the election approaches.

A final question remains: Given the degree of acceptance for the "no conversion" hypothesis in the social scientific community, why does the present study find significant media effective—even if localized in high-status groups—when the bulk of the previous evidence has suggested that none are?

First of all, this study considers trends in public opinion and the long-term accumulation of what might otherwise appear to be insignificant opinion changes. Walter Weiss (in a review of media research in the *Handbook of Social Psychology* edited by Gardner Lindzey and Elliot Aronson) has suggested that the "pervasive influence of the media may lead to small, cumulative changes between campaigns. . . the net result may be to affect the dispositions themselves, or to set the perceptual frame in which the campaign is interpreted and responded to." This would suggest that simple cross-sectional surveys may overlook the cumulative influence of the media, i.e., that the media's impact is relatively slight in the short run and hence remains untapped by the standard social science methodology.

But more importantly, examining the issue of the Vietnam War makes it possible to treat the media as a variable rather than as a constant. The major print media have shifted in their position on the war, and it is precisely that shift that makes the conversion hypothesis approachable. But on what other major national issue has such a media shift been apparent? The point, of course, is that in the absence of such a shift, research into the possible conversion effects of the media must leave at the level of speculation the question of what would have happened had the media taken a different position.

To be sure, far too many events occurred in the period from 1964 to 1968 for it to be even remotely a situation where all other things were equal. However, despite the impossibility of a true "ceteris paribus" assumption, the documented media shift still allows us to come much closer to a legitimately controlled research situation than has hitherto been possible with media research.

If the media shift on the war issue is truly indicative of a change in sentiment among one segment of the national elite, then the continuance of the war into the present (and, from all indications, well beyond the present) is indicative of a lack of change in sentiment among another segment of the national elite. This serves to emphasize the existence of significant lines of cleavage, even within the elite group, which is a useful corrective for those accustomed to thinking of the national elite in monolithic terms.

The continuance of the war despite the opposition of the media contains other important lessons, in that it shows the scant power wielded by elites who control mass opinion rather than the major decision-making institutions. Kornhauser, for instance, has stressed the importance of competing elites in maintaining mass access to the elite groups and, although he offers no example, presumably competition between the media elite and the governmental elite would be one such case. Yet, such competition is fairly meaningless when only the one elite controls the decision-making power. The Republican upper middle class, for instance, declined markedly in support for escalation from 1964 to 1968; still, there was virtually no pressure at the Republican convention to nominate a "peace" candidate. The Democrats' attempt to nominate a "peace" candidate needs no further comment here.

How Computers Pick an Election Winner

Robert A. Skedgell

When the American electorate goes to the polls in November many winners of statewide races will be announced on radio and television long before any substantial portion of the tabulated or popular vote is available. Also, many important reasons for their victories will be clear at early stages in the vote counting.

This "clairvoyance" will spring from an extensive use of computerized vote projections, based on quickly reported returns from a small number of selected precincts throughout the country. The radio and television networks will put more trust in, and be more dependent upon, their computers than at any time since they sniffed the first 1960 returns— and proclaimed that the odds were 100 to one that Richard M. Nixon would be the next President of the United States.

One system of computer projections—Vote Profile Analysis used by CBS News—has recorded an average deviation of less than 1 percent in estimating the winners' final percentages in 135 elections. It was developed *after* the 1960 general elections by CBS News, Louis Harris & Associates, and the International Business Machines Corporation. VPA was the first effective and accurate system of drawing scientific samples of the electorate so that a small number of key returns would produce close estimations of election outcomes.

Earlier computer systems were excessively rigid because proper weighting was not given to the individual factors involved. So the first scattered returns from just one or two states tended to unduly influence the vote estimates for the entire nation. The resulting projections for major candidates were inflated—more imputed than computed.

The networks did not suffer great embarrassment over the initial performances of their computerized reporting. They had stashed the machines away practically out of sight of the TV cameras and were prepared to drop them entirely at the first suspicious prognostication; in that event, the computers were to be mere comedy gimmicks, more to be belittled than pitied. If, on the other hand, reasonable fore-

casts seemed to be forthcoming, the broadcasters could claim credit for fathering a rousing advance in the art of election reporting.

Vote Profile Analysis was unveiled in the off-year elections of 1962. The system was applied to 13 key contests in eight states, and it produced accurate results in twelve— up to two hours ahead of the other networks. In the thirteenth race covered that night, the Massachusetts' gubernatorial contest between John Volpe and Endicott Peabody, VPA indicated the outcome as "too close to call." More than a month went by before Volpe was officially designated the winner by a margin of 301 votes out of the total of more than 2,000,000 cast.

VPA Picks Romney

One other VPA projection that same night pointed up the power and value of the new election reporting tool. At 10:05 p.m., Eastern time, CBS News reported—on the basis of VPA—that George Romney was the evident winner over John Swainson. The tabulated vote at that moment read:

SWAINSON 310,000
ROMNEY 236,000

Both Romney and Swainson were as disbelieving as the viewers.

What had happened was that VPA had correctly established that Swainson was running behind his necessary (and expected) strength in Wayne County, and that his showing in the Detroit suburbs was down from two years earlier when he won the governorship. When the computer digested these facts and performed the necessary arithmetic, the projected estimate for Romney came out to 52 percent of the vote. His final, official figure was 51.4 percent.

A modified form of VPA was utilized in the 1964 presidential year in the CBS News coverage of important primary races. From New Hampshire to California, VPA demonstrated its preciseness in pointing to the winners early and accurately. The VPA estimate for Henry Cabot Lodge in the New Hampshire contest was precisely the 35.3 percent of the vote which he officially received; in Oregon, VPA projected that Nelson Rockefeller would win 32.9 percent of the vote, and he won exactly that much.

On November 3, 1964, VPA was put to its first full test—it was applied to a total of 107 contests, including the presidential race in 48 states (excluding Alaska and Hawaii) and the District of Columbia. The average deviation between the final VPA estimates in those 107 races and the final, official returns was less than one percent.

There is no witchcraft about VPA. For all its seeming omniscience, it is simply a formalized effort at systematizing voting data. Its essential function is to measure movement of a particular electorate from their voting history, and to present those findings in an orderly manner. Although it is a sophisticated sampling instrument, it is capable of erring, and proper guidelines must be erected to hold mistakes within acceptable limits.

It is an exercise in simple arithmetic—if there were no rush for the results, it could be done by hand. The computer's contribution to the process—and its only contribution—is to store past voting information for the political units selected; to compare the new results from the special precincts with the old; and to extrapolate an estimate of the final result any time such a projection is requested. Once this point in the process is reached, mortal man takes over to analyze the machine's computations and make judgments based upon political, not arithmetical, knowledge.

Electorate in Miniature

The cornerstone of Vote Profile Analysis is the model of the electorate to be measured in any election. The model is a kind of portrait in miniature of all the voters of a political unit. It has been likened to screening out most of the dots which comprise a newspaper photograph; if a careful selection were made of the dots to remain, the picture would still be recognizable.

As electorates differ from each other, so do models differ. There is no magic formula which will produce a universal model. Each is custom built. For example, the model for the Republican electorate voting in the California primary this year was 90 precincts, selected to represent in their proper proportions the more than 30,000 precincts in the state. In 1964, the model for the Oregon electorate was 42 precincts which served as a microcosm of that state's 3,255 precincts. The number of precincts in a model is set on the basis of having few enough to process quickly on election night, but still enough to represent the state's voters faithfully.

Louis Harris knew from his wide experience in politics and polling that people tend to vote in patterns by groups; the patterns are discernible through the extensive research conducted on voting behavior, and through past polling. The assumption that voters of similar background display similar voting behavior is not to say that all members of a group will vote the same. It simply says that if the rural voters in a state vote 72 percent Democratic, 72 out of every 100 ruralites are performing one way, and 28 out of every 100 are performing another way. Nevertheless, the 72 to 28 ratio is an identifiable pattern which will hold true for all of the rural dwellers in the state.

Every political unit in the nation is made up of groups of voters whose voting patterns can be similarly determined. Harris reasoned that:

—if a small sample could be drawn to represent all of the important groups comprising an electorate by their proportionate voting strengths,

—and if a method could be devised to keep track of their votes on election night,

—and to compare those results with the past voting performance of the same groups,

—then it would be possible to project an accurate result.

To begin with, it would be necessary to determine for each state just what the components of the electorate were, what their history of voting has been, and what proportion of the total vote each group would contribute. In order to accomplish this initial process, teams of researchers pored through Bureau of Census records, demographic reports, and other statistical data. Because there is no central record of precinct results for all states, the researchers had to visit many of the county courthouses around the country and dig out the returns from beneath piles of dust. They studied boundary maps of the precincts to determine if changes had occurred since the last election, for in comparing new returns with the old, it is vital that the perimeters of the current precinct match exactly those of the same precinct as it existed before.

With the initial phase of the research completed, the Louis Harris organization drew up a "recipe" for a model—a specification designed to direct the researchers to the to the kinds of precincts which would ultimately fit the model. If the research indicated that 10 of the model precincts would be metropolitan units, the recipe pointed to the *types* of metropolitan precincts which would qualify as representative of their group.

Each of the precincts in the state models designed for the 1964 elections—nearly 2,000 of them—was classified in four ways:

—by geographic section of the state;

—by the size of community;

—by the ethnic background of a vast majority of the residents;

—and by their religious background.

In Harris' view, each of these four dimensions was a "cutting edge" in the politics of 1964 which would serve to measure political behavior. Economic and social classifications were not used as bases for the VPA controls because of the great difficulty in establishing standards which would apply with equal precision in all sections of the nation. A weekly income of $200 in New York City would produce a standard of living and a political outlook quite different from the same weekly income in a small city elsewhere. The economic status of the model precincts was utilized as an informational guide only and not as a component of the extrapolation formula.

To make certain that the precincts gathered under the terms of the recipe fully qualified for the model, researchers spent many months traveling through and around them. They talked to county and precinct officials and to pastors and rabbis to verify the ethnic and religious background of the residents. They read doorbell names as an additional check.

Blending the Recipe

When the researchers returned from the field, they brought with them data on hundreds of precincts which would meet the technical requirements of the recipe, making them eligible to be among the chosen few to comprise the model. The question then remained: of the hundreds of qualified precincts, which combination of 32 or 40 or 50 would best represent all the voters of the state? For example, of all the precincts classified as predominantly White Anglo-Saxon Protestant, which among them would best portray the political behavior of all of the WASP precincts around the state? Put another way, which combination of precincts meeting all of the weighting criteria of the model would come closest to reproducing or reconstructing the past statewide vote for a particular candidate?

To help find the solution, the computer was put to work running off combination after combination of precincts, averaging their past vote, and comparing them to the statewide average, not for just one past election, but several. The best combinations reproduced past results with only one-tenth or two-tenths of one percent deviation. This process of combining precincts continued section by section until the best grouping for an entire state emerged.

As illustration, VPA for Missouri in the 1964 general elections consisted of 40 precincts assembled to accurately represent more than 4,400 precincts. Missouri was divided into five sections: the St. Louis area and the Kansas City area, the great urban anchor points of the whole state; the rural north, which included St. Joseph; the Ozark country in the southeast; and, the southwest including Springfield. In effect, the geographical map of the state was converted to a political map, with the sectional boundaries marking different kinds of voting behavior.

Since research showed that 33 percent of the electorate resided in the St. Louis area, 33 percent of the model precincts (13 of 40) must be located in that area. Kansas City held 20 percent of the vote (8 of 40 precincts). The remaining three sections of the state produced the other 19 precincts of the model.

This procedure was followed for the other VPA categories: size of place, ethnic composition, and religion. The profile for Missouri showed that 28 percent of the electorate resided in large cities; so 12 of the 40 precincts would come from the large cities. Negro voters would comprise about 8 percent of the vote; so 3 precincts were predominantly Negro.

When the final returns from the Missouri VPA precincts were reported to CBS News election headquarters, and the computer compared those results with the past history of those same precincts, it calculated that Lyndon Johnson would carry the state with a percentage of 63.9. The final, official figure for him was 64.0 percent.

It is seldom necessary to wait for all of the precincts in a particular model to report before the analysts make their decision. More often, those "calls" are made on the basis of partially filled models, when, perhaps, half or fewer of the precincts have reported. It is precisely at this point that the men take over from the machines, bringing their political intelligence to bear on the computer's calculations. In the Missouri election, only 10 of the 40 model precincts had reported at the time that CBS News posted Johnson as the winner.

Because of the four-way classification of Missouri's voters, and because the computer makes a rapid comparison of the new vote with the old, it was easy for the political analysts to determine that the President was running well ahead of Senator Goldwater in each of the five sections of the state, and was getting strong support from all of the major groups of voters. Armed with that kind of detailed information which, of course, the running popular vote total could not provide for hours, the analysts at the CBS News decision desk felt no qualms about picking a winner.

Deceptive Partial Returns

There are times, however, when partial model interpretations can be dangerous, as CBS News, Louis Harris, and IBM discovered last year in the New York City Democratic primary contest. One of the races pitted Oren Lehman against Mario Procaccino for nomination as city controller. When 20 of the 50 VPA precincts had reported their results, there were definite and strong trends for Lehman. Accordingly, the decision was made to post Lehman as the "indicated winner." A little later, as more of the special VPA results came in, the Lehman trend was less strong, and another decision was made to move Lehman from the "indicated" winner's circle to "probable" winner. Still later, when the entire model was complete, the computers calculations suggested to the analysts that the race was, in fact, "too close to call," and Lehman was hence shifted down-

ward another notch. Several hours later, the tabulated vote showed that Procaccino was first catching up, then taking over the lead, and finally was the victor by a slight margin. Procaccino came to the CBS studios to be interviewed in the early morning hours and won the eternal gratitude of all assembled when he refrained from rubbing salt into VPA's wound.

It developed that the city's Jewish Democrats had split their vote sharply in the controller's race, with the Manhattan Jews going strongly for Lehman, and the Bronx and Brooklyn Jews, with a more conservative political tradition, throwing their support to Procaccino, who was running on the so-called "regular party" ticket. When the initial decision was made to name Lehman the "indicated" winner, the special VPA returns from the Manhattan election districts had reported, and they were mistakenly taken as setting the pattern to be expected for all Jewish voters. The subsequent reports from Brooklyn and the Bronx reversed the Lehman trend. Had they been received before or at the same time as the returns from the Manhattan Jewish precincts, the closeness of the race would have been apparent.

Now that computerized vote projections work satisfactorily, the cry is still raised that reporting systems such as VPA take all the fun out of the good old American tradition of waiting for the returns. But it was only a very short time ago that there was considerable, not to say painful, misunderstanding of vote projection. This lack of understanding was fanned inadvertently by the creators of the systems, who found it difficult under the time and competitive pressures of election broadcasting to introduce explanations of the projections with the same impact and prominence as the results. Nowhere was this fact demonstrated more dramatically than in the California Republican primary on June 2, 1964, which squared off Barry Goldwater against Nelson Rockefeller.

At 7:22 p.m., Pacific time, just 22 minutes after some but not all of the polls had closed throughout the state, CBS News reported on the basis of VPA that Goldwater was the winner. What developed through the remainder of that evening, and into the early morning hours of June 3, was enough to try the souls of the CBS News executives who carried the responsibility for the decision.

That decision for Goldwater was based principally on the fact that the first special VPA returns showed him to be making a very strong run in areas where a considerable portion of the Republican electorate resided, especially in Los Angeles County. When the early VPA results were examined by the analysts, it was evident to them that no matter how the vote went in the sections still polling,

Rockefeller just could not catch up.

But almost everyone else, on the basis of early returns, thought Rockefeller would win. The trouble was, the tabulated vote as collected and reported by the Associated Press and United Press International did not reflect Goldwater's strong performance in Los Angeles and in Orange and San Diego counties until many hours after the early evening announcement by CBS that Goldwater had won. In fact, the count by the press services at six o'clock the next morning still did not reflect Goldwater's true strength in the southern counties, and Rockefeller seemed to be holding a slim edge. This incomplete wire service tally gave rise to many confusing reports; one San Francisco paper headlined in its afternoon edition the next day, TV PRATFALL—FAST COUNT. ROCKY SWEEPS INTO LEAD. Appearances notwithstanding, the New York governor had not led at any time.

Ethnics and Ethics

VPA's critics, both professional and lay, have held that it is a divisive force on the body politic; that to report elections in terms of how the various ethnic and religious groups perform is an unhealthy, not to say un-American, approach. Irate viewers called the CBS studios following the New York City elections last year to complain about the undue emphasis they thought had been placed upon what Jewish voters had done, or the Italian-Americans, or the Irish-Americans. It was demonstrable, however, that these groups did behave in voting patterns—they were the "cutting edge" in deciding between two major tickets which were neatly balanced with one Jew each, one Irish-American each, one Italian-American, and one white Anglo-Saxon Protestant.

Another widespread charge leveled at computerized voting projections is that they influence voters in those sections of the country where polls remain open longer; that citizens in the Western states either change their vote to join the so-called bandwagon as reported from the East Coast, or simply decide not to vote at all. Three social scientists, Harold Mendelsohn of the University of Denver and Kurt Lang and Gladys Engel Lang of the State University of New York at Stony Brook, studied a sample of California voters following the 1964 elections to assess the validity of such charges. Their independent investigations could find no basis for the assertions that anyone changed his intention to vote for Johnson because the network broadcasts reported that he was the apparent winner, nor that anyone planning to vote for Goldwater refrained from doing so because it was forecast that he would lose badly.

Mendelsohn had interviewed a voter sample on the night before the election to ascertain their preferences. After the polls closed, he interviewed the same persons to see if anyone had changed his mind. The result was that no matter whether the voters had tuned in election broadcasts, 96 to 97 percent voted as they intended. Not more than 2 percent of those interviewed switched their vote, and those last-minute changes that did occur followed no discernible pattern.

VPA and the other vote projection systems were born of the need to fill the information vacuum existing between the time the polls close and the tabulation of sufficient votes to indicate an election trend. Had VPA been operating in the 1960 presidential race, the public would have known that at the time Kennedy seemed to be piling up a commanding lead, the final result would actually be extremely close.

In many states the vote counting process remains excruciatingly slow. Some precinct officials are content to interrupt the tabulation for dinner, a good night's sleep, and a leisurely completion and reporting of the count on the following morning, just as they have done for years. There have been proposals advanced to bring the states' election laws into some orderly scheme. Some have called for a uniform period of voting across the country; others have asked for a common poll closing time; still others have advocated a much more widespread use of electronic and mechanical ballot counters which have been introduced in places with varying degrees of success.

One day the states' antiquated election machinery will be brought into the twentieth century; but it will not occur this year, nor probably for some time to come. In the meantime, reporters will continue to utilize every means available to them to bring the election stories to the public as quickly and accurately as possible.

Jeffrey K. Hadden, Louis H. Masotti, and Victor Thiessen

The Making of the Negro Mayors

Throughout most of 1967, black power and Vietnam kept this nation in an almost continual state of crisis. The summer months were the longest and hottest in modern U.S. history—many political analysts even felt that the nation was entering its most serious domestic conflict since the Civil War. Over a hundred cities were rocked with violence.

As the summer gave way to autumn, the interest of the nation shifted a little from the summer's riots to the elections on the first Tuesday of November. An unprecedented number of Negroes were running for office, but public attention focused on three elections. In Cleveland, Carl B. Stokes, a lawyer who in 1962 had become the first Democratic Negro legislator in Ohio, was now seeking to become the first Negro mayor of a large American city. In Gary, Ind., another young Negro lawyer, Richard D. Hatcher, was battling the Republican Party's candidate—as well as his own Democratic Party—to become the first Negro mayor of a "medium-sized" city. And in Boston, Louise Day Hicks, a symbol of white backlash, was conducting a "You know where I stand" campaign to capture the mayorality.

Normally, the nation couldn't care less about who would become the next mayors of Cleveland, Gary, and Boston. But the tenseness of the summer months gave these elections enormous significance. If Stokes and Hatcher lost and Hicks won, could Negroes be persuaded to use the power of the ballot box rather than the power of fire bombs?

Fortunately, November 7 proved to be a triumphant day for racial peace. Stokes and Hatcher won squeaker victories, both by margins of only about 1500 votes; in Boston, Kevin H. White defeated Mrs. Hicks by a 12,000 plurality. Labor leader George Meany was exultant—"American voters have rejected racism as a political issue." Negroes in the three cities were also jubilant. In Gary, the most tense of the cities, Richard Hatcher urged the mostly Negro crowd at his headquarters to "cool it." "I urge that the outcome of this election be unmarred by any incident of any kind. . . . If we spoil this victory with any kind of occurrence here tonight, or anywhere in the city, it will be a hollow victory." The evening *was* cool: Joyous Negroes danced and sang in the streets.

But beyond the exultation of victory remain many hard questions. Now that Cleveland and Gary have Negro mayors, just how much difference will it make in solving the many grave problems that these cities face? Will these victories cool militancy in urban ghettos next summer, or will the momentum of frustration prove too great to put on the brakes? A careful analysis of *how* these candidates won office may help provide the answers.

The focus of this report is on Cleveland because:
■ As residents of Cleveland, we are more familiar with the campaign and the election.
■ Cleveland is unique because, in 1965, it had a special census. By matching voting wards with census tracts, we can draw a clearer picture of voting behavior than we could in the other cities, where rapid neighborhood transitions have made 1960 census data quite unreliable in assessing voting patterns. Having examined Cleveland in some detail, we will draw some comparisons with the Gary and Boston elections, then speculate about their significance and implications.

Cleveland—City in Decline

Cleveland has something less than 2,000,000 residents. Among metropolitan areas in America, it ranks eleventh in size. Like many other American cities, the central city of Cleveland is experiencing an absolute decline in population—residents are fleeing from the decaying core to the surrounding suburbs. The city certainly ranks high both in terms of absolute and proportional decline in the central-city population.

Between 1950 and 1960, the population of the central city declined from 914,808 to 876,050, a loss of almost 39,000. By 1965 the population had sunk to 810,858, an additional loss of 65,000. But these figures are only a partial reflection of the changing composition of the population, since new Negro residents coming into the central city helped offset the white exodus. *Between 1950 and 1960, nearly 142,000 white residents left the central city, and an additional 94,000 left between 1960 and 1965—nearly a quarter of a million in just 15 years.*

During the same period the number of Negro residents of Cleveland rose from 147,847 to 279,352— an increase from 16.1 percent to 34.4 percent of the city's population. There is no evidence that this dramatic population redistribution has changed since the special 1965 census. Some suburbanization of Negroes is beginning on the east and southeast side of the city, but the pace is not nearly so dramatic as for whites. In 1960, approximately 97 percent of the Negroes in the metropolitan area lived in the central city. This percentage has probably declined somewhat since then —16,000 Negro residents have moved to East Cleveland. But the basic pattern of segregation in the metropolitan area remains. The development in East Cleveland is little more than an eastward extension of the ghetto, and the older, decaying residential units the Negroes have moved to are hardly "suburban" in character.

While the population composition of Cleveland is changing rapidly, whites are still a significant majority —about 62 percent. Again like many other central cities, a significant percentage of the white population comprises nationality groups that live in segregated sections, with a strong sense of ethnic identity and a deep fear of Negro encroachment. (In 1964, the bussing of Negro students into Murray Hill, an Italian neighborhood, resulted in rioting.)

In 1960, the census classified 43 percent of the central city's white residents as "foreign stock." In that year, five groups—Germans, Poles, Czechs, Hungarians, and Italians—had populations of 25,000 or greater; at least 20 other nationality groups were large enough to have to be contended with in the political arena. But today these ethnic groups—although unwilling to admit it—have become less than the controlling majority they constituted before 1960.

The Cuyahoga River divides Cleveland, physically as well as socially. When Negroes first began to move into the city, during World War I, they occupied the decaying section to the south and east of the central business district. As their numbers grew, they continued pushing in this direction and now occupy the larger part of the eastside (except for some ethnic strongholds). There are no stable, integrated neighborhoods in the central city—only areas in transition from white to black. To the west, the Cuyahoga River constitutes a barrier to Negro penetration.

Ever since 1941, when Frank Lausche was elected, Cleveland has had a succession of basically honest but unimaginative Democratic mayors. These mayors have kept their hold on City Hall by means of a relatively weak coalition of nationality groups. At no point in this 26-year Lausche dynasty did a mayor gather enough power to seriously confront the long-range needs and problems of the city.

By early 1967, the city had seemingly hit rock bottom. A long procession of reporters began arriving to write about its many problems. The racial unrest of the past several years had, during the summer of 1966, culminated in the worst rioting in Cleveland's history. This unrest was continuing to grow as several militant groups were organizing. Urban renewal was a dismal failure; in January, the Department of Housing and Urban Development even cut off the city's urban-renewal funds, the first such action by the Federal Government. The exodus of whites, along with business, shoved the city to the brink of financial disaster. In February, the Moody Bond Survey reduced the city's credit rating. In May, the Federal Government cut off several million dollars of construction funds—because the construction industry had failed to assure equal job opportunities for minority groups. In short, the city was, and remains, in deep trouble. And while most ethnic groups probably continued to believe that Cleveland was the "Best Location in the Nation," the Negro community—and a growing number of whites—were beginning to feel that Cleveland was the "Mistake on the Lake," and that it was time for a change.

Carl Stokes's campaign for mayor was his second try. In 1965, while serving in the state House of Representatives, he came within 2100 votes of defeating Mayor Ralph S. Locher. Stokes had taken advantage of a city-charter provision that lets a candidate file as an independent, and bypass the partisan primaries. Ralph McAllister, then president of the Cleveland School Board, did the same. For his hard line on *de facto* school segregation, however, McAllister had earned the enmity of the Negro community. The Republican candidate was Ralph Perk, the first Republican elected to a county-wide position (auditor) in many years. A second generation Czech-Bohemian, Perk hoped to win by combining his ethnic appeal with his program for the city (Perk's Plan). He had no opposition for his party's nomination. The fourth candidate was Mayor Locher, who had defeated Mark McElroy, county recorder and perennial candidate for something, in the Democratic primary.

It was in the 1965 Democratic primary that the first signs of a "black bloc" vote emerged. The Negroes, who had previously supported incumbent Democratic mayoral candidates, if not enthusiastically at least consistently, made a concerted effort to dump Locher in favor of McElroy. There were two reasons.

■ Locher had supported his police chief after the latter had made some tactless remarks about Negroes. Incensed Negro leaders demanded an audience with the mayor, and when he refused, his office was the scene of demonstrations, sit-ins, and arrests. At that point, as one of the local reporters put it, "Ralph Locher became a dirty name in the ghetto."

■ Stokes, as an independent, and his supporters hoped that the Democratic primary would eliminate the *stronger* candidate, Locher. For then a black bloc would have a good chance of deciding the general election because of an even split in the white vote.

Despite the Negro community's efforts, Locher won the primary and went on to narrowly defeat Stokes. Locher received 37 percent of the vote, Stokes 36 percent, Perk 17 percent, and McAllister 9 percent. Some observers reported that a last-minute whispering campaign in Republican precincts—to the effect that "A vote for Perk is a vote for Stokes"—may have given Locher enough Republican votes to win. The evidence: The popular Perk received only a 17 percent vote in a city where a Republican could be expected something closer to 25 percent. Had Perk gotten anything close to 25 percent, Stokes would have probably been elected two years earlier.

Although he made a strong showing in defeat, Carl Stokes's political future looked bleak. No one expected the Democratic leaders to give Stokes another opportunity to win by means of a split vote. Nor were there other desirable elected offices Stokes could seek. Cleveland has no Negro Congressman—largely because the heavy Negro concentration in the city has been "conveniently" gerrymandered. The only district where Stokes might have had a chance has been represented by Charles Vanik, a popular and liberal white, and as long as Vanik remained in Congress Stokes was locked out. Stokes's state Senate district was predominantly white; and a county or state office seemed politically unrealistic because of his race. So, in 1966, Stokes sought re-election to the state House unopposed.

Between 1965 and 1967, Cleveland went from bad to worse, physically, socially, and financially. With no other immediate possibilities, Stokes began to think about running for mayor again. The big question was whether to risk taking on Locher in the primary—or to file as an independent again.

The Primary Race

In effect, Stokes's decision was made for him. Seth

Taft, slated to be the Republican candidate, told Stokes he would withdraw from the election entirely if Stokes filed as an independent in order to gain the advantage of a three-man general election. Taft had concluded that his best strategy was to face a Negro, *alone,* or a faltering incumbent, *alone,* in the general election. But not both. In a three-man race with Locher and Stokes, Taft correctly assumed that he would be the man in the middle with no chance for victory. (Taft would have preferred to run as an independent—to gain Democratic votes—but the county Republican leader threatened to file *another* Republican candidate unless Taft ran as a Republican.)

Meanwhile, Locher committed blunder after blunder—and Democratic party leaders began to question whether he could actually win another election. In the weeks before filing for the primary, Democratic leaders even pressured Locher to accept a Federal judgeship and clear the way for the president of the city council to run. But the Democratic leaders in Cleveland are not noted for their strength or effectiveness, as is evidenced by the fact that none of the Democratic mayors since 1941 were endorsed by the party when they were first elected. When Locher refused to withdraw, the party reluctantly rallied behind him.

Another Democratic candidate was Frank P. Celeste, former mayor of the Republican westside suburb of Lakewood. Celeste established residency in the city, announced his candidacy early, and—despite pressure from the Democratic Party—remained in the primary race.

There was always the possibility that Celeste would withdraw from the primary, which would leave Stokes facing Locher alone. But the threat of Taft's withdrawal from the general election left Stokes with little choice but to face Locher head-on in the primary. A primary race against Locher and a strong Democrat was more appealing than a general election against Locher and a weak Republican.

Now, in 1965 Stokes had received only about 6000 white votes in the city in a 239,000 voter turnout. To win in the primary, he had to enlarge and consolidate the Negro vote—and increase his white support on the westside and in the eastside ethnic wards.

The first part of his strategy was a massive voter-registration drive in the Negro wards—to reinstate the potential Stokes voters dropped from the rolls for failing to vote since the 1964 Presidential election.

TABLE I

	City Totals			Negro Wards			White Wards			Mixed Wards		
	1965 General	1967 Primary	1967 General	1965 General	1967 Primary	1967 General	1965 General	1967 Primary	1967 General	1965 General	1967 Primary	1967 General
Registered Voters	337,803	326,003	326,003	103,123	99,885	99,885	159,419	152,737	152,737	75,261	73,421	73,421
Turnout	239,479	210,926	257,157	74,396	73,360	79,591	111,129	88,525	119,883	53,962	49,105	57,113
% Turnout	70.9	64.7	78.9	72.1	73.4	79.7	69.7	58.0	78.5	71.7	66.9	77.8
Stokes Votes	85,716	110,769	129,829	63,550	70,575	75,586	3,300	13,495	23,158	18,866	26,699	30,872
% Stokes Votes	35.8	52.5	50.5	85.4	96.2	95.0	3.0	15.2	19.3	35.0	54.4	54.1

The Stokes organization—aided by Martin Luther King Jr. and the Southern Christian Leadership Conference, as well as by a grant (in part earmarked for voter registration) from the Ford Foundation to the Cleveland chapter of CORE—did succeed in registering many Negroes. But there was a similar drive mounted by the Democratic Party on behalf of Locher. (Registration figures are not available by race.)

The second part of the Stokes strategy took him across the polluted Cuyahoga River into the white wards that had given him a mere 3 percent of the vote in 1965. He spoke wherever he would be received —to small groups in private homes, in churches, and in public and private halls. While he was not always received enthusiastically, he did not confront many hostile crowds. He faced the race issue squarely and encouraged his audience to judge him on his ability.

Stokes's campaign received a big boost when the *Plain Dealer,* the largest daily in Ohio, endorsed him. Next, the *Cleveland Press* called for a change in City Hall, but declined to endorse either Stokes or Celeste. But since the polls indicated that Celeste was doing very badly, this amounted to an endorsement of Stokes.

More people voted in this primary than in any other in Cleveland's history. When the ballots were counted, Stokes had 52.5 percent of the votes—he had defeated Locher by a plurality of 18,000 votes. Celeste was the man in the middle, getting only 4 percent of the votes, the lowest of any mayoral candidate in recent Cleveland history.

What produced Stokes's clear victory? Table I (above) reveals the answer. The decisive factor was the size of the Negro turnout. While Negroes constituted only about 40 percent of the voters, 73.4 percent of them turned out, compared with only 58.4 percent of the whites. Predominantly Negro wards cast 96.2 percent of their votes for Stokes. (Actually this figure underrepresents the Negro vote for Stokes, since some of the non-Stokes votes in

these wards were cast by whites. Similarly, the 15.4 percent vote for Stokes in the predominantly white wards slightly overestimates the white vote because of the Negro minority.)

Newspaper and magazine reports of the primary election proclaimed that Stokes could not have won without the white vote. Our own estimate—based on matching wards with census tracts, and allowing for only slight shifts in racial composition in some wards since the 1965 special census—is that Stokes received 16,000 white votes. His margin of victory was 18,000. How would the voting have gone if the third man, Celeste, had not been in the race? Many white voters, feeling that Stokes could not win in a two-man race, might not have bothered to vote at all, so perhaps Stokes would have won by an even larger margin. Thus Stokes's inroad into the white vote was not the decisive factor in his primary victory, although it was important.

Stokes emerged from the primary as the odds-on favorite to win—five weeks later—in the general election. And in the first few days of the campaign, it seemed that Stokes had everything going for him.

■ Stokes was bright, handsome, and articulate. His opponent, Seth Taft, while bright, had never won an election, and his family name, associated with the Taft-Hartley Act, could hardly be an advantage among union members. In addition, he was shy and seemingly uncomfortable in a crowd.

■ Both the *Plain Dealer* and the *Cleveland Press* endorsed Stokes in the general election.

■ The wounds of the primary were quickly (if perhaps superficially) healed, and the Democratic candidates was endorsed by both the Democratic Party and Mayor Locher.

■ Labor—both the A.F.L.-C.I.O. and the Teamsters— also endorsed Stokes.

■ He had a partisan advantage. Of the 326,003 registered voters, only 34,000 (10 percent) were Republican. The closest any Republican mayoral candidate had come to winning was in 1951, when—in a small turnout—William J. McDermott received 45 percent of the vote.

■ Stokes had 90,000 or more Negro votes virtually assured, with little possibility that Taft would make more than slight inroads.

■ Perhaps most important, voting-behavior studies over the years have demonstrated that voters who are confronted by a dilemma react by staying home from the polls. Large numbers of life-long Democrats, faced with voting for a Negro or a Republican by the name of Taft, were likely to stay home.

Had this been a normal election, Democrat Carl Stokes would have won handily. But this was not destined to be a normal election. During the final days of the campaign, Stokes knew he was in a fight for his political life. Those who predicted that the cross-pressures would keep many voters away from the polls forgot that the variable "Negro" had never been involved in an election of this importance.

On Election Day, an estimated 90 percent of those who voted for Locher or Celeste in the Democratic primary shifted to Taft—many pulling a Republican lever for the first time in their life. Was this clearly and unequivocally bigoted backlash? To be sure, bigotry *did* play a major role in the election. But to dismiss the campaign and the election as pure overt bigotry is to miss the significance of what happened in Cleveland and the emerging subtle nature of prejudice in American society.

The Non-Issue of Race

A closer look at the personal characteristics and campaign strategy of Seth Taft, the Republican candidate, reveals the complexity and subtlety of the race issue.

In the final days of the Democratic primary campaign, Taft repeatedly told reporters that he would rather run against Locher and his record than against Carl Stokes. On the evening of the primary, Taft appeared at Stokes's headquarters to congratulate him. As far as he was concerned, Taft said, the campaign issue was, Who could present the most constructive program for change in Cleveland? Further, he said he didn't want people voting for him simply because he was white. A few days later, Taft even presented a strongly-worded statement to his campaign workers:

"The Cuyahoga Democratic party has issued a number of vicious statements concerning the candidacy of Carl Stokes, and others have conducted whisper campaigns. We cannot tolerate injection of race into this campaign. . . . Many people will vote for Carl Stokes because he is a Negro. Many people will vote for me because I am white. I regret this fact. I will work hard to convince people they should not vote on a racial basis."

Seth Taft's programs to solve racial tensions may have been paternalistic, not really perceptive of emerging moods of the ghetto. But one thing is clear—he was not a bigot. Every indication is that he remained uncomfortable about being in a race in which his chances to win depended, in large part, upon a backlash vote.

Whether Taft's attempt to silence the race issue was a deliberate strategy or a reflection of deep personal feelings, it probably enhanced his chances of winning. He knew that he had the hard-core bigot vote. His task was to convince those in the middle that they could vote for him and *not* be bigots.

Stokes, on the other hand, had another kind of problem. While he had to draw more white votes, he also had to retain and, if possible, increase the 73 percent Negro turnout that had delivered him 96 percent of the Negro votes in the primary. Stokes's campaign leaders feared a fall-off in the voter turnout from Negro wards—with good reason. The entire primary campaign had pushed the October 3 date so hard that some Negroes could not understand why Carl Stokes was not mayor on October 4. Full-page newspaper ads paid for by CORE had stated, *"If you don't vote Oct. 3rd, forget it. The man who wins will be the next mayor of Cleveland!"* So Stokes felt he had to remobilize the Negro vote.

The moment came during the question-and-answer period of the second of four debates with Taft in the all-white westside. Stokes said:

"The personal analysis of Seth Taft—and the analysis of many competent political analysts—is that Seth Taft may win the November 7 election, but for only one reason. That reason is that his skin happens to be white."

The predominantly white crowd booed loudly and angrily for several minutes, and throughout the rest of the evening repeatedly interrupted him. Later, Stokes's campaign manager revealed that his candidate's remark was a calculated risk to arouse Negro interest. Stokes probably succeeded, but he also gave Taft supporters an excuse to bring the race issue into the open. And they could claim that it was *Stokes*, not Taft, who was trying to exploit the race issue.

To be sure, *both* candidates exploited the race issue. But, for the most part, it was done rather subtly. Stokes's campaign posters stated, "Let's do Cleveland Proud"—another way of saying, "Let's show the world that Cleveland is capable of rising above racial bigotry." A full-page ad for Stokes stated in bold print, "Vote for Seth Taft. It Would Be Easy, Wouldn't It?" After the debate, Taft was free to accuse Stokes of using the race issue—itself a subtle way of exploiting the issue. Then there was the letter, signed by the leaders of 22 nationality clubs, that was mailed to 40,000 members in the city. It didn't mention race, but comments such as "protecting our way of life," "safeguard our liberty," and "false charges of police brutality" were blatant in their implications. Taft sidestepped comment on the letter.

No matter how much the candidates may have wanted to keep race out of the picture, race turned out to be the most important issue. Both Taft and Stokes could benefit from the issue if they played it right, and both did use it. And although the Stokes's remark at the second debate gave white voters an excuse to vote for Taft without feeling that they were bigots, many whites probably would have found another excuse.

Taft as a Strategist

The fact is that Taft, for all his lackluster qualities, emerged as a strong candidate. He was able to turn many of his liabilities into assets.

■ Taft was able to insulate himself against his Republican identity. He successfully dissociated himself from his uncle's position on labor by pointing to his own active role, as a student, against "right to work" laws. At the same time, he hit hard at Stokes's record as an off again-on again Democrat. This strategy neutralized, at least in part, Taft's first political disadvantage—running as a Republican in a Democratic city.

■ A second liability was that he came from a wealthy family. Taft was an Ivy League intellectual, cast in the role of a "do-gooder." He lived in an exclusive suburb, Pepper Pike, and had bought a modest home in Cleveland only a few weeks before declaring his

candidacy. How, it was frequently asked, could such a man understand the problems of the inner-city and of the poor? Almost invariably the answer was: "Did John F. Kennedy, Franklin D. Roosevelt, and Nelson Rockefeller have to be poor in order to understand and respond to the problems of the poor?" Taft's campaign posters were a side profile that bore a striking resemblance to President Kennedy. Whether he was consciously exploiting the Kennedy image is an open question. But there can be little doubt that when Taft mentioned his Republican heritage, he tried to project an image of the new breed of Republican—John Lindsay and Charles Percy. This image

TABLE II—Percent Stokes Vote by Ward

WHITE WARDS	% Negro	1965 General	1967 Primary	1967 General
1	.6	3.2	17.2	20.5
2	.3	1.9	12.8	17.4
3	.9	2.5	13.6	22.1
4	.3	3.0	18.2	20.9
5	.6	1.7	11.8	17.8
6	.8	2.3	15.1	16.7
7	.6	3.4	16.5	23.7
8	3.0	6.1	24.7	29.3
9	.2	1.9	12.4	16.4
14	1.4	1.1	12.7	13.0
15	1.4	1.2	9.2	14.1
22	5.7	8.1	22.5	26.3
26	1.1	2.8	16.3	19.9
32	2.4	2.9	10.0	15.3
33	.3	2.5	17.7	21.4
Average		3.0	15.2	19.3
NEGRO WARDS				
10	91.3	88.7	97.3	96.7
11	91.8	86.3	95.9	96.0
12	82.7	76.9	90.4	90.5
13	75.2	75.8	90.7	88.4
17	99.0	86.6	98.1	97.9
18	89.3	84.0	96.0	95.7
20	91.0	83.0	95.0	92.8
24	92.6	90.6	98.1	98.1
25	90.9	91.3	98.4	98.2
27	85.7	85.2	95.6	94.0
Average		85.4	96.2	95.0
MIXED WARDS				
16	56.6	50.7	69.9	70.1
19	25.3	29.2	48.0	39.9
21	61.1	55.2	66.3	68.9
23	20.3	9.8	18.2	23.2
28	28.5	26.5	54.8	57.3
29	24.4	26.8	43.2	42.3
30	51.7	51.5	75.3	71.4
31	21.8	16.9	31.8	39.0
Average		35.0	54.4	54.1

didn't come across very well at first, but as he became a seasoned campaigner it became clearer.

■ Another liability was that Taft had never held an elected office. His opponent tried to exploit this—unsuccessfully. Taft could point to 20 years of active civic service, including the fact that he was one of the authors of the Ohio fair-housing law. Then too, the charge gave Taft an opportunity to point out that Stokes had the worst absentee record of anyone in the state legislature. Stokes never successfully answered this charge until the last of their four debates, when he produced a pre-campaign letter from Taft commending him on his legislative service. But this came moments *after* the TV cameras had gone off the air.

■ Still another liability emerged during the campaign. Taft's strategy of discussing programs, not personalities, was seemingly getting him nowhere. He presented specific proposals; Stokes, a skilled debater, succeeded in picking them apart. Stokes himself discussed programs only at a general level and contended that he was best-qualified to "cut the red tape" in Washington. His frequent trips to Washington to confer with top Government officials, before and during the campaign, indicated that he had the inside track.

Taft, realizing at this point that his campaign was not gaining much momentum, suddenly switched gears and began attacking Stokes's record (not Stokes personally). Stokes had claimed he would crack-down on slumlords. Taft discovered that Stokes owned a piece of rental property with several code violations—and that it had not been repaired despite an order from the city. He hit hard at Stokes's absenteeism and his record as a "good" Democrat. He put a "bird-dog" on Stokes and, if Stokes told one group one thing and another group something else, the public heard about it.

The upshot was that in the final days of the campaign Taft captured the momentum. Stokes was easily the more flashy debater and projected a superior image; but Taft emerged as the better strategist.

Should Taft Have Withdrawn?

One may ask whether all of this discussion is really relevant, since the final vote was sharply divided along racial lines. In one sense it *is* irrelevant, since it is possible that a weaker candidate than Taft might have run just as well. It is also possible that a white racist might actually have won. Still, this discussion has buttressed two important points.

■ Taft was not all black, and Stokes was not all white. Taft proved a strong candidate, and—had he been running against Locher instead of Stokes—he might have amassed strong support from Negroes and defeated Locher.

■ By being a strong candidate, Taft made it much easier for many white Democrats, who might otherwise have been cross-pressured into staying home, to come out and vote for him.

Some people felt that Taft should have withdrawn and let Stokes run uncontested. But many of the same people also decried white liberals who, at recent conferences to form coalitions between black-power advocates and the New Left, let black militants castrate them. It is not traditional in American politics that candidates enter a race to lose. Taft was in to win, and he fought a hard and relatively clean campaign—as high a compliment as can be paid to any candidate.

Yet all of this doesn't change the basic nature of the voting. This is clear from the evidence in Table II. Stokes won by holding his black bloc, and increasing his white vote from 15 percent in the primary to almost 20 percent in the general. An enormous amount of the white vote was, whether covert or overt, anti-Negro. It is hard to believe that Catholics, ethnic groups, and laborers who never voted for anyone but a Democrat should suddenly decide to evaluate candidates on their qualifications and programs, and—in overwhelming numbers—decide that the Republican candidate was better qualified. The implication is that they were prejudiced. But to assume that such people perceive themselves as bigots is to oversimplify the nature of prejudice. And to call such people bigots is to make their responses even more rigid—as Carl Stokes discovered after his remark in the second debate with Taft.

This, then, is perhaps an important lesson of the Cleveland election: Bigotry cannot be defeated directly, by telling bigots that they are bigoted. For the most part Stokes learned this lesson well, accumulating as many as 30,000 white votes, nearly five times the number he received in 1965. But another slip like the one in the second debate might have cost him the election.

A few words on the voting for Stokes ward by ward, as shown in the table. Wards 9, 14, and 15—which gave Stokes a comparatively low vote—have the highest concentration of ethnic groups in the city. Not only is there the historical element of prejudice in these areas, but there is the ever-present fear among the residents that Negroes will invade their neighborhoods. (This fear is less a factor in ward 9, which is across the river.)

Wards 26 and 32 also gave Stokes a low percentage of votes, and these wards are also the ones most likely to have Negro migration. They are just to the north of East Cleveland, which is currently undergoing heavy transition, and to the east of ward 27, which in the past few years has changed from white to black. In these two wards, then, high ethnic composition and a fear of Negro migration would seem to account for Stokes's 19.9 and 15.3 percentages.

The highest percentage *for* Stokes in predominantly white areas was in wards 8 and 22. Ward 8 has a growing concentration of Puerto Ricans, and—according to newspaper polls—they voted heavily for Stokes. Ward 22 has a very large automobile-assembly plant that employs many Negroes. Now, in 1965 the ward was 5.7 percent Negro—a large increase from 1960. Since 1965, this percentage has probably grown another 2 or 3 percent. Therefore, if one subtracts the Negro vote that Stokes received in this ward, the size of the white vote is about the same as in other wards.

'Imminent Danger' in Gary

The race for mayor in Gary, Ind., was not overtly racist. Still, the racial issue was much less subtle than it was in Cleveland. When Democratic chairman John G. Krupa refused to support Richard D. Hatcher, the Democratic candidate, it was clear that the reason was race. When the Gary newspaper failed to give similar coverage to both candidates and sometimes failed to print news releases from Hatcher headquarters (ostensibly because press deadlines had not been met), it was clear that race was a factor.

Even though race was rarely mentioned openly, the city polarized. While Stokes had the support of the white-owned newspapers and many white campaign workers, many of Hatcher's white supporters preferred to remain in the background—in part, at least, because they feared reprisals from white racists. Hatcher didn't use the black-power slogan, but to the community the election was a contest between black and white. And when the Justice Department supported Hatcher's claim that the election board had illegally removed some 5000 Negro voters from the registration lists and

added nonexistent whites, the tension in the city became so great that the Governor, feeling that there was "imminent danger" of violence on election night, called up 4000 National Guardsmen.

Negroes constitute an estimated 55 percent of Gary's 180,000 residents, but white voter registration outnumbers Negroes by 2000 or 3000. Like Stokes, Hatcher—in order to win—had to pull some white votes, or have a significantly higher Negro turnout.

The voter turnout and voting patterns in Cleveland and Gary were very similar. In both cities, almost 80 percent of the registered voters turned out at the polls. In the Glen Park and Miller areas, predominantly white neighborhoods, Joseph B. Radigan—Hatcher's opponent—received more than 90 percent of the votes. In the predominantly Negro areas, Hatcher received an estimated 93 percent of the votes. In all, Hatcher received about 4000 white votes, while losing probably 1000 Negro votes, at most, to Radigan. This relatively small white vote was enough to give him victory. If Stokes's miscalculation in bringing race into the Cleveland campaign gave prejudiced whites an excuse to vote for Taft, the glaring way the Democratic Party in Gary tried to defeat Hatcher probably tipped the scales and gave Hatcher some white votes he wouldn't have received otherwise.

The School Issue in Boston

The Boston election, unlike the Cleveland and Gary elections, didn't pose a Negro against a white, but a lackluster candidate—Kevin White—against a 48-year-old grandmother who had gained national attention over the past several years for her stand against school integration. On the surface, Mrs. Hicks seems to be an obvious racial bigot. But she herself has repeatedly denied charges that she is a racist, and many who have followed her closely claim that this description is too simple.

Mrs. Hicks, perhaps more than any other public figure to emerge in recent years, reflects the complex and subtle nature of prejudice in America. Her public denial of bigotry is, in all probability, an honest expression of her self-image. But she is basically unaware of, and unwilling to become informed about, the way her views maintain the barriers of segregation and discrimination in American society. In 1963, when the N.A.A.C.P. asked the Boston School Committee to acknowledge the *de facto* segregation in the schools, she refused to review the evidence. Meeting with the N.A.A.C.P., she abruptly ended the discussion by proclaiming: "There is no *de facto* segregation in Boston's schools. Kindly proceed to educational matters." Later, when the State Board of Education presented a 132-page report on racial imbalance in Massachusetts schools, she lashed out at the report's recommendations without bothering to read it.

Mrs. Hicks, like millions of Americans, holds views on race that are born out of and perpetuated by ignorance. John Spiegel, director of Brandeis University's Lemberg Center for the Study of Violence, has summed up the preliminary report of its study of six cities:

> . . . the attitude of whites seems to be based on ignorance of or indifference to the factual basis of Negro resentment and bitterness. . . . If white populations generally had a fuller appreciation of the just grievances and overwhelming problems of Negroes in the ghetto, they would give stronger support to their city governments to promote change and to correct the circumstances which give rise to strong feelings of resentment now characteristic of ghetto populations.

Prejudice is born not only out of ignorance, but also out of fear. There is much about the Negro ghettos of poverty that causes whites, lacking objective knowledge, to be afraid, and their fear in turn reinforces their prejudice and their inability to hear out and understand the plight of the Negro in America.

In Boston, the voter turnout was heavy (71 percent) but below the turnouts in Cleveland and Gary. White accumulated 53 percent of the vote and a 12,000 plurality. Compared with Stokes and Hatcher, he had an easy victory. But considering Mrs. Hicks's lack of qualifications and the racial overtones of her campaign, Boston also experienced a massive backlash vote. Had it not been for the final days of the campaign—when she pledged, unrealistically, to raise police and firemen's salaries to $10,000 without raising taxes, and came back from Washington with "positive assurance" that nonexistent Federal monies would cover the raises —she might even have won. But throughout the campaign Mrs. Hicks repeatedly revealed her ignorance of fiscal and political matters. Mrs. Hicks had another handicap: She is a woman. The incredible fact that she ran a close race demonstrated again the hard core of prejudice and ignorance in American society.

Now let us consider the broader implications these elections will have on the racial crisis in America. To be sure, the immediate implications are quite different from what they would have been if Stokes and Hatcher had lost and Mrs. Hicks had won. If the elections had gone the other way, Summer '68 might well have begun November 8. As Thomas Pettigrew of Harvard put it a few days before the election, "If Stokes and Hatcher lose and Mrs. Hicks wins, then I just wonder how a white man in this country could ever look a Negro in the eye and say, 'Why don't you make it the way we did, through the political system, rather than burning us down?' "

The Meaning of the Elections

But do these victories really alter the basic nature of the racial crisis? There is, true, some reason for hope. But to assume that anything has been fundamentally altered would be disastrous. First of all, it is by no means clear that these elections will pacify militant Negroes—including those in Cleveland, Gary, and Boston. In Boston, some militants were even encouraging people to vote for Mrs. Hicks— because they felt that her victory would help unify the Negro community against a well-defined foe. In Cleveland, most militants remained less than enthusiastic about the possibility of a Stokes victory. Of the militant groups, only CORE worked hard for him. In Gary alone did the candidate have the solid support of militants—probably because Hatcher refused to explicitly rebuke Stokely Carmichael and H. Rap Brown, and because his opponents repeatedly claimed that Hatcher was a black-power advocate.

If the Stokes and Hatcher victories are to represent a turning point in the racial crisis, they must deliver results. Unfortunately, Hatcher faces an unsympathetic Democratic Party and city council. Stokes has gone a long way toward healing the wounds of the bitter primary, but it remains to be seen whether he will receive eager support for his programs. Some councilmen from ethnic wards will almost certainly buck his programs for fear of alienating their constituencies.

Stokes and Hatcher themselves face a difficult and delicate situation.

■ Their margins of victory were so narrow that they, like Kennedy in 1960, must proceed with great caution.

■ Enthusiasm and promises of change are not the same as the power to implement change. And the two mayors must share power with whites.

■ They must demonstrate to Negroes that their presence in City Hall has made a difference. But if their programs seem too preferential toward Negroes, they run the risk of massive white resistance.

This delicate situation was clearly seen in the early days of the Stokes administration. Of his first ten appointments, only two were Negroes. Although relations with the police have been one of the most sensitive issues in the Negro ghetto, Stokes's choice for a new police chief was Michael Blackwell, a 67-year-old "hardliner." This appointment was intended to ease anxieties in the ethnic neighborhoods, but it was not popular in the Negro ghetto. Blackwell, in his first public address after being sworn in, lashed out at the Supreme Court, state laws, and "publicity-seeking clergy and beatniks" for "crippling law enforcement." Cleveland's Negroes are already beginning to wonder whether a Negro in City Hall is going to make any difference.

Some observers believe that Stokes is basically quite conservative, and point to his sponsorship of anti-riot legislation. To be sure, Stokes's position on many issues remains uncertain, but what does seem fairly clear from his early days in office is that his efforts to gain support in white communities is going to lead to disaffection among Negroes. How much and how quickly is a difficult question.

Race relations is only one of many problems that these two new mayors must face. Stokes has inherited all of the problems that brought national attention to Cleveland last spring—poverty, urban renewal, finance, transportation, air and water pollution, and so on. Hatcher faces similar problems in Gary, and must also cope with one of the nation's worst strongholds of organized crime. If they fail, the responsibility will fall heavier on them than had a white man failed. Some whites will generalize the failures to all Negro politicians, and some Negroes will generalize the failures to the "bankruptcy" of the American political system.

Almost certainly, Washington will be a key factor in determining if these two men succeed. The national Democratic Party has a strong interest in making Stokes and Hatcher look good, for it desperately needs to recapture the disaffected Negro voters before the 1968 national election. But how much can the party deliver? The war in Vietnam is draining enormous national resources and Congress is threatening to slash poverty programs. Even if Federal monies were no problem, there is the question whether *any* of Washington's existing programs are directed at the roots of ghetto unrest. Many informed administrators, scientists, and political analysts feel they are not. And the chances for creative Federal programs seem, at this moment, fairly dim.

Another clear implication of these elections is that white resistance to change remains large and widespread. More than 90 percent of the Democrats in Cleveland who voted for a Democrat in the primary switched, in the general election, to the Republican candidate. Now, not many American cities are currently composed of as many as 35 percent Negroes; the possibility of coalitions to elect other Negro candidates appears, except in a handful of cities, remote. Additional Negro mayoral candidates are almost certain to arise, and many will go down to bitter defeat.

Stokes and Hatcher won because black-voter power coalesced with a relatively small minority of liberal whites. It was not a victory of acceptance or even tolerance of Negroes, but a numerical failure of the powers of discrimination, a failure that resulted in large part because of the massive exodus of whites from the central city. The election of Stokes and Hatcher may break down white resistance to voting for a Negro, but this is, at best, problematical. Also problematical is how bigoted whites will react to the election of a Negro mayor. Their organized efforts to resist change may intensify. As we have already indicated, the pace of white exodus from the central city of Cleveland is already alarming. And an acceleration of this pace could push the city into financial bankruptcy.

America Has Bought a Little Time

In short, while the implications of the November 7 elections are ambiguous, it does seem that the victories of Stokes and Hatcher, and the defeat of Mrs. Hicks, have kept the door open on the growing racial crisis. America has, at best, bought a little time.

On the other hand, we do not find much cause for optimism in those elections—unlike George Meany, and unlike the *New York Times,* which, five days after the election, published a glowing editorial about "the willingness of most voters today to choose men solely on personal quality and impersonal issues." To us, it would seem that the elections have only accelerated the pace of ever-rising expectations among Negroes. And if results don't follow, and rather rapidly, then we believe that the Negro community's frustration with the American political system will almost certainly heighten.

The hard task of demonstrating that Negroes can actually achieve justice and equality in America still lies ahead.

The "Liberation" of Gary, Indiana
Edward Greer

In silhouette, the skyline of Gary, Indiana, could serve as the perfect emblem of America's industrial might—or its industrial pollution. In the half-century since they were built, the great mills of the United States Steel Corporation —once the largest steel complex on earth—have produced more than a quarter-trillion tons of steel. They have also produced one of the highest air pollution rates on earth. Day and night the tall stacks belch out a ruddy smoke that newcomers to the city find almost intolerable.

Apart from its appalling physical presence, the most striking thing about Gary is the very narrow compass in which the people of the city lead their lives. Three-quarters of the total work force is directly employed by the United States Steel Corporation. About 75 percent of all male employment is in durable goods manufacture and in the wholesale-retail trades, and a majority of this labor force is blue-colla.. This means that the cultural tone of the city is solidly working-class.

But not poor. Most Gary workers own their own homes, and the city's median income is 10 percent above the national average. The lives of these people, however, are parochial, circumscribed, on a tight focus. With the exception of the ethnic clubs, the union and the Catholic church, the outstanding social edifices in Gary are its bars, gambling joints and whorehouses.

Company Town

The city of Gary was the largest of all company towns in America. The United States Steel Corporation began construction in 1905, after assembling the necessary parcel of land on the Lake Michigan shore front. Within two years, over $40 million had been invested in the project; by now the figure must be well into the billions.

Gary was built practically from scratch. Swamps had to be dredged and dunes leveled; a belt-line railroad to Chicago had to be constructed, as well as a port for ore ships and of course a vast complex of manufacturing facilities including coke ovens, blast furnaces and an independent electrical power plant. The city was laid out by corporation architects and engineers and largely developed by the corporation-owned Gary Land Company, which did not sell off most of its holdings until the thirties. Even though the original city plan included locations for a variety of civic, cultural and commercial uses (though woefully little for park land), an eminent critic, John W. Reps, points out that it "failed sadly in its attempt to produce a community pattern noticeably different or better than elsewhere."

The corporation planned more than the physical nature of the city. It also had agents advertise in Europe and the South to bring in workers from as many different backgrounds as possible to build the mills and work in them. Today over 50 ethnic groups are represented in the population.

This imported labor was cheap, and it was hoped that cultural differences and language barriers would curtail the growth of a socialist labor movement. The tough, pioneer character of the city and the fact that many of the immigrant workers' families had not yet joined them in this country combined to create a lawless and vice-ridden atmosphere which the corporation did little to curtail. In much more than its genesis and name, then, Gary is indelibly stamped in the mold of its corporate creators.

Labor and the Left

During the course of the First World War, government and vigilante repression broke the back of the Socialist party in small-town America, though it was not very strong to begin with. Simultaneously, however, the Left grew rapidly as a political force among the foreign-born in large urban centers. As the war continued, labor peace was kept by a combination of prosperity (full employment and overtime), pressures for production in the "national interest," and Wilsonian and corporate promises of an extension of democracy in the workplace after the war was over. The promises of a change in priorities proved empty, and in 1919 the long-suppressed grievances of the steelworkers broke forth. Especially among the unskilled immigrant workers, demands for an industrial union, a reduction of the workday from 12 to eight hours and better pay and working conditions sparked a spontaneous movement for an industry-wide strike.

For a time it appeared that the workers would win the Great Steel Strike of 1919, but despite the capable leadership of William Z. Foster the strike was broken. The native white skilled labor aristocracy refused to support it, and the corporation imported blacks from the South to scab in the mills. This defeat helped set back the prospect of militant industrial trade unionism for almost a generation. And meanwhile, racism, a consumer-oriented culture (especially the automobile and relaxed sexual mores) and reforms from above (by the mid-twenties the eight-hour day had been voluntarily granted in the mills) combined to prevent the Left from recovering as a significant social force.

It was in this period between World War I and the depression that a substantial black population came to Gary. Before the war only a handful of black families lived there, and few of them worked in the mills. During World War I, when immigration from abroad was choked off, blacks were encouraged to move to Gary to make up for the labor shortage caused by expanding production. After the war this policy was continued, most spectacularly during the strike, but rather consistently throughout the twenties. In 1920 blacks made up 9.6 percent of the population; in 1930 they were 17.8 percent—and they were proportionately represented in the steel industry work force.

When the CIO was organized during the depression, an interracial alliance was absolutely essential to the task. In Gary a disproportionate number of the union organizers were black; the Communist party's slogan of "black and white unite and fight" proved useful as an organizing tactic. Nevertheless, it was only during World War II (and not as the result of the radicals' efforts) that black workers made a substantial structural advance in the economy. Demography, wartime full employment and labor shortages proved more important to the lot of black workers than their own efforts and those of their allies.

As after the First World War, so after the second, there came a repression to counter the growth of the Left. The Communist component of the trade union movement was wiped out, and in the general atmosphere of the early cold war black people, too, found themselves on the defensive. At the local level in Gary, the remaining trade union leaders made their peace with the corporation (as well as the local racketeers and Democratic party politicians), while various campaigns in the forties to racially integrate the schools and parks failed utterly.

Finally, in the early fifties, the inherently limited nature of the trade union when organized as a purely defensive institution of the working class—and one moreover that fully accepts capitalist property and legal norms—stood fully revealed. The Steelworkers Union gave up its right to strike over local grievances, which the Left had made a key part of its organizing policy, in return for binding arbitration, which better suited the needs and tempers of the emerging labor bureaucrats.

Corporate Racism

The corporation thus regained effective full control over the work process. As a result, the corporation could increase the amount of profit realized per worker. It could also intensify the special oppression of the black workers; foremen could now assign them discriminatorily to the worst tasks without real union opposition. This corporate racism had the additional benefit of weakening the workers' solidarity. For its part, the union abolished shop stewards, replacing them with one full-time elected "griever." This of course further attenuated rank-and-file control over the union bureaucracy, aided in depoliticizing the workers and gave further rein to the union's inclination to mediate worker/employer differences at the point of production, rather than sharpen the lines of struggle in the political economy as a whole.

The corporate and union elites justified this process by substantial wage increases, together with other benefits such as improved pension and welfare plans. For these gains a price was paid. Higher product prices, inflation and a rising tax burden on the workers all ensued from the union's passive acceptance of corporate priorities.

There were extremely important racial consequences as well. For as the union leadership was drawn further and further into complicity with corporate goals, a large segment of the industrial working class found itself in the apparently contradictory position of opposing the needs of the poorest workers for increased social welfare services. A large part of the material basis for white working-class racism originates here. Gary steelworkers, struggling to meet their home mortgage payments, are loath to permit increased assessments for additional municipal services which they view as mostly benefitting black people.

United States Steel

Needless to say, the corporation helped to develop, promote and protect the Gary working class's new ways of viewing itself and its world.

In the mill, the corporation systematically gave the black workers the dirtiest jobs (in the coke plants, for example) and bypassed them for promotion—especially for the key skilled jobs and as foremen. Nor has that policy changed. Although about a third of the employees in the Gary Works are black, and many of them have high seniority, and although virtually all the foremen are promoted directly from the ranks without needing any special qualifications, there are almost no black (or Spanish-speaking) foremen. According to figures submitted by the United States Steel Corporation to the Gary Human Relations Commission, as of 31 March 1968, out of a total of 1,011 first-line supervisors (foremen) only 22 were black.

The corporation not only practices racism directly, it also encourages it indirectly by supporting other discriminatory institutions in Gary. Except for some free professionals and small business, the entire business community is a de facto fief of the corporation. The Gary Chamber of Commerce has never to my knowledge differed from the corporation on any matter of substance, though it was often in its economic self-interest to do so. This has been true even with regard to raising the corporation's property assessment, which would directly benefit local business financially. And in its hiring and sales practices, as well as in its social roles, this group is a leading force for both institutional racism and racist attitudes in the community. For instance, it is well known that the local banks are very reluctant to advance mortgage money in black areas of town, thus assuring their physical decline. White workers then draw the reasonable conclusion that the movement of blacks into their neighborhoods will be at the expense of the value of their homes and react accordingly. The local media, completely dependent financially on the local business community, can fairly be described as overtly racist. The story of the voting fraud conspiracy to prevent the election of the present mayor, Richard Hatcher, a black man, didn't get into the local paper until days after it made the front page of the *New York Times*.

The newspaper publisher is very close to the national Catholic hierarchy and the local bishop, who in turn is closely linked to the local banks. The church is rhetorically moderately liberal at the diocesan level, but among the ethnic parishes the clergy are often overtly racist.

Political Considerations

While the United States Steel Corporation has an annual budget of $5 billion, the city of Gary operates on some $10 million annually. (This figure applies only to municipal government functions; it excludes expenditures by the schools, welfare authorities, the Sanitary Board and the Redevelopment Commission.)

And the power of the city government, as is usually the case in this country, is highly fragmented. Its legal and financial authority is inadequate to carry out the public functions for which it bears responsibility. The power of the mayor is particularly limited. State civil service laws insulate school, welfare, fire and police personnel from the control of City Hall. Administrative agencies control key functions such as urban renewal, the low income housing authority, sanitation, the park system and the board of health. Appointive boards, with long and staggered terms of tenure, hire the administrators of these agencies; and although in the long run a skillful mayor can obtain substantial control over their operations, in the short run (especially if there are sharp policy differences) his power may well be marginal.

Two other structural factors set the context in which local government in Gary—and in America generally—is forced to operate. First, key municipal functions increasingly depend upon federal aid; such is the case with the poverty program, urban renewal, low income housing and, to a substantial degree, welfare, education and even police and sanitation. Thus, the priorities of the federal government increasingly shape the alternatives and options open to local officials, and their real independence is attenuated.

Second, the tax resources of local governments—resting for the most part on comparatively static real estate levies—are less and less able to meet the sharply rising costs of municipal services and operations. These costs reflect the increased social costs of production and welfare, costs that corporations are able to pass on to the general public.

This problem is particularly acute in Gary because of the ability of the corporation to remain grossly underassessed. As a result, there are implacable pressures to resist expansion of municipal services, even if the need for them is critical. In particular, since funds go to maintain existing services, it is virtually impossible for a local government to initiate any substantive innovations unless prior funding is assured. In this context, a sustained response to the urban crisis is prevented not only by a fragmentation of power but also by a lack of economic resources on a scale necessary to obtain significant results.

For the city of Gary, until the election of Mayor Hatcher, it was academic to talk about such considerations as the limits of local government as an instrument of social change and improvement of the general welfare. Before him, municipal government had been more or less content simply to mediate between the rackets on the one hand and the ethnic groups and business community on the other.

The Democratic party, structured through the Lake County machine, was the mechanism for accomplishing a division of spoils and for maintaining at least a formal legitimacy for a government that provided a minimum return to its citizenry. Left alone by the corporation, which subscribed to an inspired policy of live and let live where municipal politics were concerned, this political coalition governed Gary as it saw fit.

In return for the benevolent neutrality of the corporation toward its junior partner, the governing coalition refrained from attempting to raise the corporation's tax assessments or to otherwise insinuate itself into the absolute sovereignty of the corporation over the Gary Works. Air pollution activities were subjected only to token inspection and control, and in the entire history of the city the Building Department never sent an inspector into the mill. (These and other assertions about illegal or shady activities are based on reports from reliable informants and were usually verified by a second source. I served under Mayor Hatcher as director of the Office of Program Coordination until February 1969.)

In this setting—particularly in the absence of a large middle class interested in "good government" reform—politics was little more than a racket, with the city government as the chief spoils. An informal custom grew up that representatives of different ethnic minorities would each hold the mayor's office for one term. The mayor then, in association with the county officials, would supervise the organized crime (mostly gambling, liquor and prostitution) within the community. In effect, the police force and the prosecutor's office were used to erect and centralize a protection racket with the mayor as its director and organized crime as its client. Very large sums of money were involved, as indicated by the fact that one recent mayor was described by Internal Revenue officials as having an estimated annual income while in office of $1.5 million.

Besides the racket of protecting ciminal activity, other sources of funds contributed to the large illicit incomes of city officials. There were almost 1,000 patronage jobs to distribute to supporters or sell to friends. There were proceeds from a myriad of business transactions and contracts carried out under municipal authority. Every aspect of municipal activity was drawn into the cash nexus.

For instance, by local ordinance one had to pass an examination and pay a $150 fee for a contractor's license to do repair or construction work within city limits. The licensing statute was enacted to maintain reasonable standards of performance and thus protect the public. In reality, as late as 1967, passing the exam required few skills, except the ability to come up with $1,200 for the relevant officials, or $1,500 if the applicant was unfortunate enough to have black skin.

Gary municipal affairs also had a racist quality. The black population continued to rise until in the early sixties it composed an absolute majority. Yet the benefits of the system just outlined were restricted to the less scrupulous of the leaders of other ethnic groups, which constituted altogether only 40 percent of the population. The spoils came from all; they were distributed only among whites.

And this was true not only for illegal spoils and patronage but also for legitimate municipal services. As one example, after Hatcher became mayor, one of the major complaints of the white citizenry concerned the sharp decline in the frequency of garbage collection. This resulted, not from a drop in efficiency of the General Services division, as was often charged, but from the fact that the garbage routes were finally equalized between white and black areas.

In short, the city government was itself just another aspect of the institutionalized structure of racism in Gary. To assure the acquiescence of Gary's blacks to the system, traditional mechanisms of repression were used: bought black politicians and ward leaders, token jobs, the threat of violence against rebels and the spreading of a sense of impotence and despair. For instance, it was a Gary tradition for the Democratic machine to contribute $1,500 each week to a black ministers' alliance for them to distribute to needy parishioners—with the tacit understanding that when elections came around they would help deliver the vote.

Hatcher's Campaign

The successful insurgency of Richard Gordon Hatcher destroyed the core of this entire relationship.

Hatcher developed what can best be described as a black united front, inasmuch as it embraced all sectors of the black community by social class, occupation, ideology and temperament. The basis of this united front was a commonly held view that black people as a racial group were discriminated against by the politically dominant forces. Creating it required that Hatcher bridge existing divisions in the black community, which he did by refusing to be drawn into a disavowal of any sector of the black movement either to his left or right—except for those local black politicians who were lackeys of the Democratic machine. Despite immense public pressure, for example, Hatcher refused to condemn Stokley Carmichael, even though scurrilous right-wing literature was widely circulated calling him a tool of Carmichael and Fidel Castro. Actually, the rumor that hurt Hatcher the most was the false assertion that he was secretly engaged to a white campaign worker—and it was so damaging in the black community that special pains had to be taken to overcome it.

Muhammad Ali was brought to the city to campaign for Hatcher, but Hubert Humphrey was not invited because of the bitter opposition of white antiwar elements within his campaign committee. It is worth noting that a substantial portion of Hatcher's financial and technical assistance came from a very small group of white liberals and radicals, who, while they played a role disproportionate to their numbers, suffered significant hostility from their white neighbors for involving themselves openly with Hatcher. Their support, however, made it possible for the campaign to appeal, at least rhetorically, to all the citizens on an interracial basis.

Of course, this support in the white community did not translate into votes. When the count was complete in the general election, only 13 percent of Gary's overwhelmingly Democratic white voters failed to bolt to the Republicans; and if one omits the Jewish professional and business section of town, that percentage falls to 6 percent (in blue-collar Glen Park)—a figure more explicable by polling booth error than goodwill.

Even in the Democratic primary against the incumbent mayor, Hatcher barely won, although he had the support of a large majority of the Spanish-speaking vote and overwhelming support (over 90 percent) of the black vote. His victory was possible, moreover, only because the white vote was split almost down the middle due to the entry of an insurgent and popular "backlash" candidate.

Hatcher's primary victory was particularly impressive given the obstacles he had to face. First, his entire primary campaign was run on less than $50,000, while the machine spent an estimated $500,000 in cash on buying black votes alone. Second, the media was openly hostile to Hatcher. And third, efforts were made to physically intimidate the candidate and his supporters. Death threats were common, and many beatings occurred. Without a doubt, the unprecedented action of the Hatcher organization in forming its own self-defense squads was essential in preventing mass intimidation. It was even necessary on primary day for armed groups to force open polls in black areas that would otherwise have remained inoperative.

These extraordinary methods demonstrated both how tenuous are the democratic rights of black people and what amazing organization and determination are necessary to enforce them when real shifts of power appear to be at stake. When the primary results came in, thousands of black citizens in Gary literally danced in the streets with joy; and everyone believed that the old Gary was gone forever.

Hatcher's Temptations

Immediately after the primary victory, the local alignment of forces was to some degree overshadowed by the rapid interposition of national ones. Until Hatcher won the primary, he was left to sink or swim by himself; after he established his own independent base of power, a new and more complex political process began: his reintegration into the national political system.

The county Democratic machine offered Hatcher a bargain: its support and $100,000 for the general election campaign in return for naming the chief of police, corporation counsel and controller. Naturally, Hatcher refused to accept a deal that would have made him a puppet of the corrupt elements he was determined to oust from power. Thereupon the county machine (and the subdistrict director of the Steelworkers Union) declared itself for, and campaigned for, the Republican.

But the question was not left there. To allow the Democratic party to desert a candidate solely because he was black would make a shambles of its appeal to black America. And dominant liberal forces within the Democratic party clearly had other positive interests in seeing Hatcher elected. Most dramatically, the Kennedy wing of the Democratic party moved rapidly to adopt Hatcher, offering him sorely needed political support, financial backing and technical assistance, without any strings attached. By doing this, it both solidified its already strong support from the black community and made it more reasonable for blacks to continue to place their faith in the Democratic party and in the political system as a whole.

As a necessary response to this development (although it might have happened anyway), the Johnson-Humphrey wing of the Democratic party also offered support. And this meant that the governor of Indiana and the Indiana State Democratic party endorsed Hatcher as well—despite the opposition of the powerful Lake County machine. Thus Hatcher achieved legitimacy within the political system—a legitimacy that he would need when it came to blocking a serious voting fraud plot to prevent his winning the election.

Despite clear evidence of what was happening, the Justice Department nevertheless refused to intervene against this plot until Hatcher's campaign committee sent telegrams to key federal officials warning them that failure to do so would result in a massive race riot for which the federal officials would be held publicly responsible. Only by this unorthodox maneuver, whose credibility rested on Hatcher's known independent appeal and constituency, was the federal executive branch persuaded to enforce the law. Its intervention, striking 5,000 phony names from the voters rolls, guaranteed a Hatcher victory instead of a Hatcher defeat.

The refusal of the Justice Department to move except under what amounted to blackmail indicated that the Johnson-Humphrey wing of the party was not enthusiastic about Hatcher, whose iconoclastic and often radical behavior did not assure that he would behave appropriately after he was in power. But its decision finally to act, together with the readiness of the Kennedy forces to fully back Hatcher, suggests that there was a national strategy into which the Hatcher insurgency could perhaps be fitted.

My own view of that national strategy is that the federal government and the Democratic party were attempting to accommodate themselves to rising black insurgency, and especially electoral insurgency, so as to contain it within the two-party system. This strategy necessitated sacrificing, at least to a degree, vested parochial interests such as entrenched and corrupt machines.

Furthermore, black insurgency from below is potentially a force to rationalize obsolete local governments. The long-term crisis of the cities, itself reflecting a contradiction between public gain and private interest, has called forth the best reform efforts of the corporate liberal elite. Centered in the federal government, with its penumbra of foundations, law firms and universities, the political forces associated with this rationalizing process were most clearly predominant in the Kennedy wing of the Democratic party.

The economic forces whose interests are served by this process are first the banks, insurance companies and other sections of large capital heavily invested in urban property and, more generally, the interests of corporate capital as a whole—whose continued long-range profit and security rest on a stable, integrated and loyal population.

Thus the support given to Hatcher was rational to the system as a whole and not at all peculiar, even though it potentially implied economic and political loss for the corporation, United States Steel, whose operations on the spot might become more difficult. The interests of the governing class as a whole and of particular parts of it often diverge; this gap made it possible for Hatcher to achieve some power within the system. How these national factors would shape the amount and forms of power Hatcher actually obtained became quite evident within his first year of office.

Mosaic of Black Power

When I arrived in the city five months after the inauguration, my first task was to aid in the process of bringing a semblance of order out of what can fairly be described as administrative chaos.

When the new administration took over City Hall in January 1968 it found itself without the keys to offices, with many vital records missing (for example, the file on the United States Steel Corporation in the controller's office) and with a large part of the city government's movable equipment stolen. The police force, for example, had so scavenged the patrol cars for tires and batteries that about 90 percent of them were inoperable. This sort of thing is hardly what one thinks of as a normal process of American government. It seems more appropriate to a bitter ex-colonial power. It is, in fact, exactly what happened as the French left Sekou Toure's Guinea.

There were no funds available. This was because the city council had sharply cut the municipal budget the previous summer in anticipation of a Hatcher victory. It intended, if he lost, to legislate a supplemental appropriation. But when he won without bringing in a council majority with him, its action assured that he would be especially badly crippled in his efforts to run the city government with a modicum of efficiency. Moreover, whenever something went wrong, the media could and did blame the mayor for his lack of concern or ability.

Not only did Richard Hatcher find his position sabotaged by the previous administration even before he arrived, but holdovers, until they were removed from their positions, continued to circumvent his authority by design or accident. And this comparatively unfavorable situation extended to every possible sphere of municipal activities.

Another problem was that the new administrators had to take over the management of a large, unwieldly and obsolete municipal system without the slightest prior executive experience. That there were no black people in Gary with such experience in spite of the high degree of education and intelligence in the black community is explicable only in terms of institutionalized racism—blacks in Gary were never permitted such experiences and occupational roles. Hatcher staffed his key positions with black men who had been schoolteachers, the professional role most closely analogous to running a government bureaucracy. Although several of these men were, in my view, of outstanding ability, they still had to learn everything by trial and error, an arduous and painful way to maintain a complex institution.

Furthermore, this learning process was not made any easier by the unusually heavy demands placed on the time of the mayor and his top aides by the national news media, maneuvering factions of the Democratic party, a multiplicity of civil rights organizations, universities and voluntary associations and others who viewed the mayor as a celebrity to be importuned, exploited or displayed. This outpouring of national interest in a small, parochial city came on top of and was almost equal to, the already heavy work load of the mayor.

Nor were there even clerical personnel to answer the mail and phone calls, let alone rationally respond to the deluge. The municipal budget provided the mayor with a single secretary; it took most of the first summer to make the necessary arrangements to pay for another two secretaries for the mayor's own needs. One result was that as late as June 1968 there was still a two-month backlog of personal mail, which was finally answered by much overtime work.

In addition to these problems there were others, not as common to American politics, such as the threat of violence, which had to be faced as an aspect of daily life. The problem of security was debilitating, especially after the King and Kennedy assassinations. In view of the mayor's aggressive drive against local organized crime, the race hatred whipped up during and after the campaign by the right wing and the history of violence in the steel town, this concern with security was not excessive, and maintaining it was a problem. Since the police were closely linked with the local Right, it was necessary to provide the mayor with private bodyguards. The presence of this armed and foreboding staff impaired efficiency without improving safety, especially since the mayor shrugged off the danger and refused to cooperate with these security efforts.

In addition, the tremendous amounts of aid we were offered by foundations, universities and federal officials proved to be a mixed blessing. The time needed to oversee existing processes was preempted by the complex negotiations surrounding the development and implementation of a panoply of new federal programs. There had never been a Concentrated Employment Program in Gary, nor a Model Cities Program, nor had the poverty program been locally controlled. Some of these programs weren't only new to Gary, they hadn't been implemented anywhere else either. The municipal bureaucracy, which under previous administrations had deliberately spared itself the embarrassment of federal audits, didn't have the slightest idea as to how to utilize or run these complex federal programs. Moreover, none of the experts who brought this largesse to Gary had a clear understanding of how it was to be integrated into the existing municipal system and social structure. These new federal programs sprang up overnight—new bureaucracies, ossified at birth—and their actual purposes and effects bore little relation to the legislative purposes of the congressional statutes that authorized them.

Needless to say, ordinary municipal employees experienced this outside assistance as a source of confusion and additional demoralization, and their efficiency declined further. Even the new leadership was often overwhelmed by, and defensive before, the sophisticated eastern federal bureaucrats and private consultants who clearly wanted only to help out America's first black mayor. The gifts, in other words, carried a fearful price.

Bureaucratic Enemies

Except for the uniformed officials and the schools, which were largely outside the mayor's control, the standing city bureaucracy was a key dilemma for Mayor Hatcher.

The mayor had run on a reform program. His official campaign platform placed "good government" first, ahead of even tax reform and civil rights. Hatcher was deeply committed to eliminating graft and corruption, improving the efficiency of municipal government—especially the delivery of services to those sectors of the citizenry that had been most deprived—and he did not view his regime as merely the substitution of black faces for white ones in positions of power.

But he also had a particular historic injustice to rectify: the gross underrepresentation of blacks in the city government, and their complete exclusion from policy-making positions. Moreover, implicit in his campaign was a promise to reward his followers, who were mostly black. (At least most participants in the campaign assumed such a promise; Hatcher himself never spoke about the matter.)

Consequently, there was tremendous pressure from below to kick out everyone not covered by civil service protection and substitute all black personnel in their places. But to do so would have deepened the hostility of the white population and probably weakened Hatcher's potential leverage in the national Democratic party. He resisted this pressure, asserting that he believed in an interracial administration. However, in addition to this belief (which, as far as I could determine, was genuine), there were other circumstances that dictated his course of action in this matter.

To begin with, it was always a premise of the administration that vital municipal services (police and fire protection, garbage collection, education, public health measures) had to be continued—both because the people of Gary absolutely needed them and because the failure to maintain them would represent a setback for black struggles throughout the country.

It also appeared that with a wholesale and abrupt transition to a totally new work force it would be impossible to continue these services, particularly because of a lack of the necessary skills and experiences among the black population—especially at the level of administration and skilled technical personnel. In this respect Hatcher faced the classic problem faced by all social revolutions and nationalist movements of recent times: after the seizure of power, how is it possible to run a complex society when those who traditionally ran it are now enemies?

The strategy Hatcher employed to meet this problem was the following. The bulk of the old personnel was retained. At the top level of the administration (personal staff, corporation counsel, chief of police, controller) new, trustworthy individuals were brought in. Then, gradually, new department heads were chosen, and new rank-and-file people included. If they had the skill already, they came at the beginning; if they didn't, they were brought in at a rate slow enough to provide for on-the-job training from the holdovers, without disrupting the ongoing functions of the particular department.

The main weakness of this gradualist strategy was that it permitted the old bureaucracy to survive—its institutional base was not destroyed.

The result was that the new political priorities of the administration could not be implemented with any degree of effectiveness in a new municipal political practice. City government remained remarkably like what it had been in the past, at least from the perspective of the average citizen in the community. While the political leadership was tied up with the kinds of problems I noted earlier, the bureaucracy proceeded on its own course, which was basically one of passive resistance. There were two aspects to this: bureaucratic inertia, a sullen rejection of any changes in established routine that might cause conflicts and difficulties for the employees; and active opposition based on politics and racism, to new methods and goals advocated by the mayor.

To cite just one example, the mayor decided to give a very high priority to enforcement of the housing codes, which had never been seriously implemented by preceding administrations. After much hard work, the Building Department was revamped to engage in aggressive inspection work. Cases stopped being "lost," and the number of inspections was increased by 4,000 percent while their quality was improved and standardized. Then it was discovered that cases prepared for legal enforcement were being tabled by the Legal Department on grounds of technical defects.

I personally ascertained that the alleged legal defects were simply untrue. I then assumed that the reason for the legal staff's behavior was that they were overburdened with work. Conferences were held to explain to them the mayor's priorities so they could rearrange their work schedule. Instead, a series of bitter personal fights resulted, culminating in my removal from that area of work since the staff attorneys threatened to resign if there were continued interference with their professional responsibility. In the course of these disputes, both black and white attorneys expressed the opinion that they did not consider themselves a legal aid bureau for Gary's poor, and furthermore the root of the city's housing problem was the indolent and malicious behavior of the tenants. In their view, it was therefore unjust to vigorously enforce the existing statutes against the landlords. Thus, despite the administration's pledge, black ghetto residents did not find their lives ameliorated in this respect.

Gradually, then, the promise of vast change after the new mayor took office came to be seen as illusory. Indeed, what actually occured was much like an African neocolonial entity: new faces, new rhetoric and people whose lives were scarcely affected except in their feelings towards their government.

This outcome was not due to a failure of good faith on the part of the Hatcher administration. Nor does it prove the fallacious maximalist proposition that no amelioration of the people's conditions of life is possible prior to a revolution. Instead, it was due to the decline of the local mass base of the Hatcher administration and the array of national political forces confronting it.

Most black people in Gary were neither prepared nor able to take upon themselves the functions performed for them by specialized bureaucracies. They relied upon the government for education, welfare, public health, police and fire protection, enforcement of the building codes and other standards, maintenance of the public roads and the like. Unable to develop alternative popularly based community institutions to carry on these functions by democratic self-government, the new administration was forced to rely upon the city bureaucracy—forced to pursue the option that could only result in minor changes.

Aborted Liberation

The most significant consequence of the Hatcher administration's failure to transcend the structural terrain on which it functioned was political, the erosion of popular support after the successful mobilization of energies involved in the campaign. The decline of mass participation in the political process contributed in turn to the tendency of the new regime to solve its dilemmas by bureaucratic means or by relying on outside support from the federal government.

The decline in mass support ought not to be confused with a loss of votes in an election. Indeed, Hatcher is now probably as secure politically as the average big city mayor. The point is that the mass of the black population is not actively involved in helping to run the city. Thus, their political experiences are not enlarged, their understanding of the larger society and how it functions has not improved, and they are not being trained to better organize for their own interests. In short, the liberating process of the struggle for office was aborted after the initial goal was achieved— and before it could even begin to confront the profound problems faced by the mass of urban black Americans.

For example, after the inauguration, old supporters found themselves on the outside looking in. For the most part, since there was no organized effort to continue to involve them (and indeed to do so could not but conflict with the dominant strategy of the administration), they had to be content to remain passive onlookers. Moreover, the average citizen put a lot of faith in the mayor and wanted to give him an opportunity to do his job without intruding on the process.

Even among the most politicized rank-and-file elements there was a fear of interfering. Painfully conscious of their lack of training and experience, they were afraid of "blowing it." Instead they maintained a benevolent watchfulness, an attitude reinforced by the sense that Hatcher was unique, that his performance was some kind of test of black people as a race. (Whites were not the only people encouraged by the media to think in these terms.) There were of course some old supporters who were frankly disillusioned: they did not receive the patronage or other assistance they had expected: they were treated rudely by a bureaucratic holdover or were merely unable to reach the ear of a leader who was once accessible as a friend.

The ebbing away of popular participation could be seen most markedly in the Spanish-speaking community, which could not reassure itself with the symbolic satisfaction of having a member of its group in the national spotlight. With even less education and prior opportunity than the blacks, they found that the qualifications barrier to municipal government left them with even less patronage than they felt to be their due reward. This feeling of betrayal was actively supported by the former machine politicians and criminal elements, who consciously evoked ethnic prejudices to isolate the mayor and weaken his popular support.

What happened in the first year of the new administration, then, was a contradiction between efficiency and ethnic solidarity. At each point the mayor felt he had to rely upon the expert bureaucracy, even at the cost of increasing his distance from his mass base. And this conflict manifested itself in a series of inexorable political events (the appointment of outside advisors, for example), each of which further contributed to eroding the popular base of the still new leadership.

As Antonio Gramsci pointed out, beneath this contradiction lies a deeper one: a historic class deprivation—inflicted on the oppressed by the very structure of the existing society—which barred the underclass from access to the skills necessary for it to run the society directly in its own interests and according to its own standard of civilization. Unless an oppressed social group is able to constitute itself as what Gramsci characterizes as a counterhegemonic social bloc, its conquest of state power cannot be much more than a change in leaders. Given the overall relation of forces in the country at large, such an undertaking was beyond the power of the black community in Gary in 1968. Therefore, dominant national political forces were able quickly to reconstitute their overall control.

National Power

What happened to Richard Hatcher in Gary in his first year as mayor raises important questions—questions that might be of only theoretical interest if he were indeed in a unique position. He is not. Carl Stokes, a black, is mayor of Cleveland. Charles Evers, a black, is mayor of Fayette,

Mississippi. Thomas Bradley, a black, very nearly became mayor of Los Angeles. Kenneth Gibson, a black, is now mayor of Newark. The list will grow, and with it the question of how we are to understand the mass participation of blacks in electoral politics in this country and the future of their movement.

I believe that until new concepts are worked out, the best way of understanding this process is by analogy with certain national liberation movements in colonial or neo-colonial countries. Of course, the participants—in Gary as in Newark—are Americans, and they aren't calling for a UN plebiscite. But they were clearly conscious of themselves as using elections as a tool, as a step toward a much larger (though admittedly ill-defined) ultimate goal—a goal whose key elements of economic change, political power, dignity, defense of a "new" culture and so forth are very close to those of colonial peoples. It is because Hatcher embraced these larger objectives (without, of course, using precisely the rhetoric) that his campaign can be thought of as part of a nationalist process that has a trajectory quite similar to that of anticolonial liberation movements.

In its weakened local posture, the Hatcher administration was unable to resist successfully a large degree of cooptation by the national political authorities. Despite a brave vote at the Democratic National Convention for Reverend Channing Philips, Hatcher was essentially forced to cooperate with the national government and Democratic party—even to the extent of calling on the sheriff of Cook County to send deputies to reinforce the local police when a "mini-riot" occurred in the black ghetto.

Without either a nationally coordinated movement or an autonomous base of local insurgency—one capable of carrying out on a mass scale government functions outside the official structure—Hatcher's insurgency was contained within the existing national political system. Or, to express it somewhat differently, the attempt by black forces to use the electoral process to further their national liberation was aborted by a countervailing process of neocolonialism carried out by the federal government. Bluntly speaking, the piecemeal achievement of power through parliamentary means is a fraud—at least as far as black Americans are concerned.

The process by which the national power maintained itself, and even forced the new administration to aid it in doing so, was relatively simple. As the gap between the popular constituency and the new government widened, like many another administration, Hatcher's found itself increasingly forced to rely upon its "accomplishments" to maintain its popularity and to fulfill its deeply held obligation to aid the community.

Lacking adequate autonomous financial resources—the mill remained in private hands, and it still proved impossible to assess it for tax purposes at its true value—accomplishments were necessarily dependent upon obtaining outside funds. In this case, the funds had to come from the federal government, preferably in the form of quick performance projects to maintain popular support and to enable everyone to appear to be doing something to improve matters.

These new programs injected a flow of cash into the community, and they created many new jobs. In his first year in office, the mayor obtained in cash or pledges more federal funds than his entire local budget. Hopes began to be engendered that these programs were the key to solving local problems, while the time spent on preparing them completed the isolation of the leadership from the people.

Then, too, the stress of this forced and artificial growth created endless opportunities for nepotism and even thievery. Men who had never earned a decent living before found themselves as high-paid executives under no requirement to produce any tangible results. Indeed, federal authorities seemed glad to dispense the funds without exercising adequate controls over their expenditures. A situation arose in which those who boasted of how they were hustling the system became prisoners of its largesse.

Even the most honest and courageous leader, such as Mayor Hatcher, could not help but be trapped by the aid offered him by the federal authorities. After all, how can any elected local executive turn down millions of dollars to dispense with as he sees fit to help precisely those people he was elected to aid: The acceptance of the help guaranteed the continuation of bonds of dependence. For without any real autonomous power base, and with new vested interests and expectations created by the flow of funds into the community, and with no available alternate path of development, the relation of power between the local leader and the national state was necessarily and decisively weighted toward the latter.

In Gary, Indiana, within one year after the most prodigious feat in the history of its black population—the conquest of local political power—their insurgency has been almost totally contained. It is indeed difficult to see how the existing administration can extricate itself from its comparative impasse in the absence of fresh national developments, or of a new, more politically coherent popular upsurge from below.

There is, however, no doubt that the struggle waged by the black people of Gary, Indiana, is a landmark on their road to freedom; for the experiences of life and struggle have become another part of their heritage—and thus a promise for us all.

Los Angeles Liberalism
Richard L. Maullin

In November 1970, California voters elected Wilson Riles, a black man, superintendent of public instruction, ousting one of California's leading arch-conservatives, Max Rafferty. Riles' election came as a great surprise because it followed by 17 months the defeat of another black political figure, Los Angeles City Councilman Thomas Bradley, whose inability to turn a primary election lead into a final victory for mayor of Los Angeles, has been attributed to the rejection by white voters of even moderate black candidates. Riles won slightly more than half the votes in suburban white neighborhoods of the city of Los Angeles

where Bradley gained barely 30 percent.

In many respects, the Los Angeles mayoral election that Bradley lost was a primer for the 1970 electoral campaigns. Bradley's opponent, two-term Mayor Samuel W. Yorty, seized upon the "radical liberals" long before the vice-president succeeded in making them his principal bogeymen this past year. And for black candidate Wilson Riles, Tom Bradley's campaign provided many precedents to follow and some important ones to avoid in his attempt to become the first black man elected to a major constitutional or executive office in California history. Greatest of the lessons provided by the Bradley campaign of 1969 was the need "to finesse" the "social issue," which is to say tensions created by changing racial and moral values. The Bradley election showed that the electorate could be frightened by a conscious attempt to conjure up a radical threat with racial undertones. That possibility existed in 1970 as in 1969—as a strategy, as the vice-president's and Max Rafferty's campaigns showed, fear was again to be animated against liberals and blacks. Survey research conducted privately in the California gubernatorial contest indicates that the "social issue," while important as a background factor, may have lost some of the saliency it had in 1969. Yet for Riles, running against an incumbent known for vicious attack precisely on the social issue, the precedents and problems of the Tom Bradley-Sam Yorty election were highly meaningful. The story of Riles' campaign and other seeming reversals of social conservatism in 1970 is in itself fascinating. As a prelude, however, the story of Los Angeles' 1969 mayoral election needs to be examined to highlight the relationships between social attitudes, social science research and the conduct of political campaigns.

The two candidates for mayor of Los Angeles in the spring of 1969 epitomized in their persons and campaign followings important conflicting forces in American society. The incumbent mayor, Samuel William Yorty, a white man with a flamboyant style and a conservative political stance, was strongly challenged by Councilman Thomas Bradley, a black man with liberal support and a cool and dignified manner who had amassed 42 percent of the vote to Yorty's 26 in the primary election earlier.

Yet certain similarities between the two adversaries are also important. Unlike the contrasts, which seemed to mirror national tensions, the similarities between the two candidates derived from the peculiar political world spawned by the ethnic and social character of Los Angeles. Both Yorty, age 60, and Bradley, age 51, were born in the American midlands, Yorty in Nebraska and Bradley in Texas, and both migrated to Los Angeles in the 1920s. Both men came from broken-home, lower-middle-class families; and both men relied on local public education to become men of the law, Yorty as a lawyer and Bradley first as a policeman and later as a lawyer. Both men started their careers as public servants at an early age.

Even their positions on major issues bear some resemblance to each other when viewed in historical perspective. Sam Yorty in the 1930s spoke for Los Angeles' social underdogs, the rural-to-urban migrant, the unionizing worker, the low-paid consumer. His electorates were composed of the little men disdained by the big forces controlling national wealth and claiming social deference. Today, however, as his supporters have become political and social advocates of a status quo in which they are relatively well off, Yorty has moved away from fighting to get things for his clientele to fighting to keep things for it.

By the same token, today Tom Bradley has emerged as an advocate of social justice and equality for those who only marginally benefited from Sam Yorty's earlier political struggles. Bradley's principal following, the black migrants and sons of migrants to Los Angeles, are just beginning to make it. But instead of pushing against a thin line of early pioneers not so unlike the newcomers themselves, they are challenging the white new middle class, a bulky mass of people spread over large homogeneous tracts of single family residences many freeways away, while disputing the nearly white Mexican-Americans of neighboring ghettos for jobs and higher social status. But in a historical and comparative sense, Bradley's and Yorty's public goals have been similar: social and economic opportunity for those who are denied it on the basis of family background and economic status, and an America made strong because of liberty and justice for all.

The special social characteristics of Los Angeles are important as factors in the political conflict of forces represented by Mayor Yorty and Councilman Bradley. The ethnic heterogeneity of the Los Angeles electorate is not by itself especially great. The ethnic breakdown in the city is approximately as follows: Mexican-Americans, 8 percent; Negroes, 18 percent; Jews, 10 percent; Orientals, 3 percent; white Anglo-Saxon gentiles (of predominantly midwestern and border state origin, but with enclaves of Italians, Latin Americans, Slavs and Central Europeans), 61 percent. As a result, the dominant ethnic tone of Los Angeles is that of the Anglo-Saxon small-town midwestern and border states.

More important in designing the peculiar social configuration of Los Angeles have been the high rates of migration —the metropolitan area population increased 54 percent between 1950 and 1960—and the continuing creation of new wealth in different social strata of the population.

Continuous migration has also prevented uniformly strong ties from developing in Los Angeles. Many people, it seems, continue to move about the area, especially if they are not constrained by racial barriers, in a continuous search for the economic and social goals that prompted them to move there in the first place. For many, Los Angeles is where they live, but it is not "home." Even for the more stable, loyalty to place is focused on the homogeneous neighborhood, many of which, in a city of

451 square miles, are five to 25 miles distant from the civic center or other neighborhoods peopled by different ethnic and social types.

American Success Stories

Los Angeles also lacks a commonly acknowledged structure of social deference. Because the city's economy and land resources have absorbed so many migrants successfully, Los Angeles has a large middle-income, high school educated sector living comfortably within the city limits. These tens of thousands of American success stories feel that they owe their well-being to their own efforts. Therefore, they appear less willing to be led in political and social matters by "civic leaders" and "high society" to whom (even if they could identify them) they owe nothing and who are certainly irrelevant to their general life style.

The growth of southern California's population in the early part of the twentieth century led the state's then rather clubby sociopolitical elite to guard the electoral process against ethnic and populist politics thought to be conducive to corruption and mob influence. Partisan political machines in older eastern cities were judged to be a contributing evil, so partisan elections were replaced by nonpartisan contests in many California cities, including Los Angeles.

The nonpartisan nature of Los Angeles elections now seems to encourage local candidacies reflecting the complexity of the city's 1.1 million-person electorate. These elections deny political parties their important function of coalescing the city's diverse social, ethnic and ideological currents behind a limited number of candidate choices. With lessened constraints from organized partisan politics, many groups venture their champion into the mayoral arena. Yet the possibility of victory is held out only to those adept at massaging the moods and opinions of the social majority, a combination of groups likely to change by the issue and over time.

The structure of government also inhibits the formation of a potential power elite of political figures. Legal authority over the social and economic issues affecting Los Angeles is widely dispersed among a welter of jurisdictions. The city and county of Los Angeles have separate police and fire services. Welfare is a state-county concern, and education is controlled by an independent school district whose boundaries are not coterminous with the city's. Smog, largely generated on the freeways and streets of the city, is the problem of state and county agencies. For the vast majority of the Los Angeles electorate, therefore, local political figures, aside from the mayor, have low visibility. They have no publicly displayed partisan labels, and they are not grouped in a coherent body to deal with the multifaceted situations affecting life in Los Angeles.

In short, no effective local power structure of political, business or social elites exists in Los Angeles with sufficient self-assurance, public acknowledgement and legitimacy to operate effectively as a mobilizer of votes in a mass electoral situation. As a result, candidates for major office must face the voter without strong middlemen and mediating institutions that identify the candidate or confer a meaningful endorsement. In this context, the media of mass communication, which deliver the image of the candidates directly to the people, assume great importance. Candidates must rely primarily on skill in the use of mass media, especially television and radio, and on a capacity to sense both what issues are important to the public mood and what is the position of the popular majority on those issues.

Phase and Tactics

To understand the Los Angeles election fully, the campaign must be viewed as a public event of six months' duration. There were three distinct phases of the campaign: the period prior to filing for candidacy when initial financial support was sought and long-range planning begun, then the primary campaign in which four serious contenders prevented any one person from winning with an early majority and finally the Yorty-Bradley runoff two months later. Each phase required a somewhat different strategy and set of tactics by the candidates. In the entire period, however, to quote the California state legislature's annual *Report to the People,* "No single public issue . . . so alarmed and perplexed the people of California as the disorder and lawlessness on [the state's] public campuses."

No matter what other issues were raised about Los Angeles, its leadership and its problems, they inevitably had to compete with student militancy and other law and order issues for the attention of the public. By mid-April, six weeks before the election, in response to the open-ended question, "What is the major problem facing the city of Los Angeles?" carried in a private poll commissioned by the Bradley forces, 39 percent of the replies, the largest grouping of responses in the survey, named an issue related to the campus militancy problem.

Mayor Yorty did not stage an aggressive primary campaign, expecting the opposition candidates to destroy each other. In comparison to Bradley and another contendent, moderate Republican Congressman Alphonzo Bell, who spent $408,000 and $522,000 respectively, Yorty spent relatively little—$285,000. Through February and March, billboards proclaimed him to be "America's Best Mayor," and in his speeches and half-hour TV specials, the mayor concentrated on his "support for the police" and on answering the attacks on his administration by the *Los Angeles Times* and Bradley. For these efforts, Yorty won 26 percent of the vote, about equal to what opinion polls taken by potential opposition from mid-1968 indicated to be his minimum popular following.

Bradley and his managers began the campaign in January with a strategy based on justifiable expectations of a massive black support, as well as several ideological assumptions about the fittingness of a coalition incorporating blacks and Jews, liberal gentiles and Mexican-Americans. Bradley's speeches, charged with reformist rhetoric, accused Yorty of a "total lack of leadership" and referred in vague terms to reforms, which would include the police department. The black-brown aspect of a reformist coalition assumed particular importance for Bradley. But ideological assumptions about the common cause of oppressed minorities could not forever screen out evidence of growing group animosity between Mexican-Americans and blacks as well as abrasive competition for jobs and scarce fruits of social reform. Later, the imperfect fit between the rhetoric of coalition and fact of conflict was to torment Bradley in his relations with the important Mexican-American voting bloc, and Bradley's campaign managers spent countless hours attempting to heal fights among Bradley's squabbling coalition supporters.

Nevertheless, the flaws in Bradley's strategy were slow to appear, and approximately three weeks before the 1 April primary, his campaign seemed to jell. Borrowing a tactic and a line from a primary opponent who had dropped out, Bradley advertised himself as *the* Democratic candidate in an attempt to coalesce Democrats and to overcome the frustrating obstacle of nonpartisanship in the election. (Democratic registration in Los Angeles was roughly 651,000 out of 1.1 million voters.) Fund raising began to pick up as many Democratic party, union and civic leaders began to view Bradley as having some chance for success. Two preprimary polls showing Bradley gaining and taking the lead aided this process.

Bradley at the Peak

Bradley, in fact, was probably at his apogee on 1 April. Solidly backed by white Democratic liberals, as well as by the black voters, the primary that day gave Bradley 294,000 votes (42 percent), Yorty 183,000 (26 percent) and the remainder to the others. Voter turnout was equal to the turnout in the 1965 final mayoral election, approximately 65 percent.

To Bradley's benefit the campaign had been fairly free of open racial inuendos. (Some observers felt, in fact, that only half the voters on 1 April knew Bradley was black, but this was never substantiated through public opinion polling.) The press had taken Bradley's rather detached and cool manner as a virtue, and they played it up in contrast to Yorty's perpetual accusatory brashness. Just enough of the total electorate disliked Yorty and were convinced by Bradley to give him a real chance.

Nevertheless, as the Table (see page 101) shows, the distribution of Bradley's vote according to social and ethnic group provided a bad augury for the runoff, if anyone in his camp had been inclined to read it that way. Bradley emerged from the 1 April primary a national (liberal) hero, apparently riding the crest of a powerful wave of voter support. But the makeup of the support reflected only partial success for his basic strategy of coalition. He successfully monopolized the black vote and raised their turnout. But expectations had been much higher for the Jewish and Mexican-American votes, and a strong black and Mexican-American voters' coalition failed to materialize. Mayor Yorty commented in an interview that if Bradley had done a little better with the brown component of the hoped-for black-brown coalition, Bradley would have been elected in the primary. This might have suggested to Bradley's people that if Mexican-Americans were to support him in the final election it would have to be for reasons other than a desire for a common front with blacks.

As if these signs weren't ominous enough, the last weeks of the primary campaign coincided with a decided worsening of the campus militancy situation, and for the first time during the election campaign, campus incidents with racial content occurred in Los Angeles.

Disturbances by students and black militant organizations continued nationally and locally for the remainder of the campaign, and they succeeded admirably in unsettling the Los Angeles electorate. As mentioned before, private polls taken by Bradley and Yorty indicated that the most important issues for voters in Los Angeles were school disturbances and "law and order." In addition, they showed almost overwhelming support for the Los Angeles police.

Mayor Yorty's counterattack for the third and final stage of the campaign began even as the adverse primary returns were still being counted. Obviously infuriated by his poor showing, Yorty stormed into the city council chamber, where the returns were being reported for the public media, and immediately accused Bradley of being antipolice and of waging a racist campaign to capitalize on the black bloc vote.

Yorty's tone against Bradley was direct and quite

virulent, and it was quickly echoed by some of his supporters who distributed leaflets purporting to show synagogues being bombed by black militants and suggesting that a Bradley victory would bring the same to Los Angeles. Bumper stickers bloomed with the words "Bradley power" and a picture of a black fist raised in the black power gesture. There were newspaper ads that showed Bradley, obviously very black, with the copy asking, "Will your city be safe with this man?" The basic objective, of course, was to discredit the image of Councilman Thomas Bradley by a racist frontal assault.

Nevertheless, as Bradley's private mid-April opinion polling indicated, these tactics had no immediate effect. Some of Yorty's backers, shocked by his poor showing and continuing defensiveness, began to have second thoughts about letting their man shoot from the hip quite as much as his nature prompted him to.

A complete reorganization of the Yorty campaign took place in mid-April. Yorty's campaign committee, co-chaired by conservative Republican party financial leaders Henry Salvatori and Preston Hotchkiss, hired the political management firm of Haig and Associates. Fresh from managing Barry Goldwater, Jr.'s election to Congress, Haig and Associates, led by conservative Republican lawyer Haig Kehaiyan, argued that a more affirmative message from the mayor and tighter control on the various advertising and public relations activities of his campaign were essential. Instead of answering Bradley's charges of incompetence in city government, Kehaiyan's group insisted that the mayor emphasize his commitment to law and order and support for the police and attack Bradley as a tool of radical forces.

To control the public face and voice of the mayor's campaign, Haig and Associates attempted to coordinate the presentation of a "positive" image. As a result, Yorty's theatrics took on a new cast. His speeches satisfied those seeking to hear his view of things in more reasoned tones, while he continued to titillate audiences during question periods with his flamboyant off-the-cuff remarks. In Yorty's words, all this was necessary to keep the press from distorting his position by reporting only his more colorful remarks.

Yorty's campaign managers formed a law enforcement officers' committee, headed by a regular police officer on leave of absence. The committee charged that 90 percent of the police force would resign if Bradley were elected, and to skeptics Yorty urged that they just go up to any policeman and ask if it wasn't true. This group also ran ads in the metropolitan press linking Bradley with several liberal political organizations and these in turn to various militant and Communist groups. Revelations about alleged militants on Bradley's staff were first handled by others, with Yorty echoing the charges like a Greek chorus.

In addition, Kehaiyan, a strong believer in the utility of door-to-door precinct canvassing in areas of potential strength, analyzed the past voting behavior of Los Angeles neighborhoods and then organized numerous Republican volunteers and other conservative groups into a field force to carry personally the new "positive" message. In contrast to Bradley's volunteers, who were more at home with highly verbal "do your thing" politics, Kehaiyan's volunteers seemed like Christian soldiers grimly marching as to war.

Yorty's campaign objective remained the same—to discredit Bradley—but the means were now quite different from the earlier frontal assault. One was to link Bradley to extremist and militant forces so prominent in the news and to cast doubt on Bradley's record as a policeman. The second was to tone down Sam Yorty to make him acceptable to those who had voted against him, *but not for Bradley,* in the primary, or those who did not vote at all.

To some Yorty watchers, his toning down probably seemed the more difficult task. A master of innuendo and the political ad-lib, the mayor has also more than a usual share of irrepressible gall. Yet Yorty has a fantastic survival instinct as well. When pressed, as he was after the primary, he has the capacity to organize all ideas and information in close relation to their possible effect on his basic political goals: survival and new upward chances. Moreover, the message Haig and Associates developed really implied no radical change from what Yorty himself was inclined to say; it just organized it better. Yorty is, after all, a hawk on Vietnam, a propolice hardliner on student militants and a believer in an internal threat posed by American communists. Haig and Associates' concept was as ideological (to the Right) as it was instrumental. Yorty's critics say that his use of Kehaiyan strategy demonstrated a cynical willingness to exploit popular fears and prejudices. His supporters claim Yorty believes what he said. But whatever the truth, the important fact is that he became credible to a majority of the voters.

Bradley's campaign managers, exhilarated by the primary election results, decided to follow a safe and orthodox strategy of not changing what appeared to be a winning campaign unless a serious crisis developed. However, when indications of trouble did show themselves in late April and early May, the Bradley campaign organization proved too inflexible in concept and too amorphous in organization to make needed adjustments in the themes of the campaign or the image of the candidate. Bradley, therefore, continued to emphasize vague liberal reformist slogans while promising to provide Los Angeles with "leadership and integrity." He also hammered away at the corruption for which certain Yorty-appointed city commissioners, but not Yorty, had been indicted. Yet, listening to some of Bradley's followers talk of the mayor, it often seemed that it was Mayor Sam's crass style rather than his supposed misdeeds that really bothered these nouveau cosmopolites who wanted a clean, sophisticated mayor to preside over urbane Los Angeles.

Perceiving Bradley to be in the lead, his campaign managers—with some exceptions—rejected the idea that the two candidates should debate. When local TV offered to carry a Bradley-Yorty encounter, Bradley appointed a committee of six lawyers to negotiate (and evade) the conditions under which the two might meet. Yorty, immediately assuming the pose of the brave sheriff standing nearly alone at the far end of the bar, responded that he would debate anywhere, any time. Later, toward the middle of May, Bradley's managers aborted a chance meeting with Yorty on the rostrum of a local chamber of commerce, even though two previous chance encounters had been judged in Bradley's favor by professional newsmen.

The decision not to debate Sam Yorty was more than a simple tactical one. The arguments over the debate illustrated important differences within Bradley's camp. One position was simply that the front runner never debates a challenger, and since Bradley had done so well in the primary and in published public opinion polls, his views were well supported and there was no need to run the risks of a bad performance. Another participant argued that Bradley would be no match for Yorty's ability to put out faster and better abuse. A third view, argued by a black member of the candidate's inner sanctum, asserted that Bradley would lose even if he won because the public would not tolerate a black man showing up a white man in a face-to-face encounter. Finally, some former Kennedyites, remembering Bob Kennedy's confrontation with Eugene McCarthy more than the 1960 debates, argued that debates are essentially opportunities to project an image directly to the voters and not a contest of wit and intelligence. These people also argued that no matter what the polls or the primary showed, Bradley, a nonincumbent and a black, should always act the hungry challenger eager for opportunities to prove himself.

These arguments carried over into other aspects of the campaign. So long as the campaign tasks were the articulation of liberal social ideas and the projection of Bradley as a man of quiet reason, the previous political experiences and collective liberal assumptions of Bradley's campaign advisers were sufficient to provide direction. But as Yorty's counterattack began to build steam, *using Bradley's liberal supporters and preference for "rational discussion" as arguments against Bradley,* precedents from other liberal campaigns often failed to indicate what to do next. Bradley's campaign had underlying moral assumptions. It argued that Yorty was an opportunistic and corrupt boor and promised to install a regime of personal integrity. These themes, so much a part of a liberal reformer's perspective, actually contributed to the worsening of a key incident signaling Bradley's decline.

The Rothenberg Affair

On 23 April, a Yorty "truth squad" composed of three Los Angeles city councilmen revealed that Don Rothenberg, a campaign coordinator for Tom Bradley, was an ex-Communist who had been a party member as recently as 1956. Bradley strategists, including Maury Weiner, his campaign manager, and Steven Reinhardt, national Democratic committeeman, knew the Rothenberg story would be released, yet they waited for the attack before making any statement or taking any action; they dealt with the problem only after it became a major news story. Then, when first questioned about Don Rothenberg, Tom Bradley did not have a convincing reply. Eventually, a rather weak statement was issued in which Bradley disclaimed knowledge of Rothenberg's past when he was hired but added that he would not fire him. He said, "A man must not be cast aside. He has paid for his mistake . . . he plays no role in deciding issues."

Seizing an opportunity, Yorty began to hammer on the theme that while Tom Bradley might not be a bad guy he was naive and could be manipulated by radical forces. Reporters, even those friendly to Tom Bradley, continued to question him about Rothenberg because, as they indicated later, the question was never really resolved.

The Rothenberg explosion in a national and local environment rife with fear and concern over student disturbances and militant demands marked the point when the Bradley campaign began to sour. Bradley himself agrees that the Rothenberg affair hurt him badly, and he implied that were he to face that issue again he would probably handle it differently. But, Bradley added, if it hadn't been the Rothenberg case, then some other means would have been found to link him maliciously and unjustifiably to extremism. Other key Bradley supporters, while admitting to the harm the incident caused, still maintain that Bradley did the right thing in keeping Rothenberg in spite of Yorty's exploitation of the issue.

Yorty, in a private interview, argued that Rothenberg's presence was just one manifestation of radical and Communist support for Bradley, Yorty was quick to point out that in addition to Rothenberg, whose renunciation of communism Yorty implied was not credible, Gus Hall, leader of the American Communist party, also endorsed Bradley and "even held a meeting of the Western region to instruct the Communists to work for Bradley." For the mayor, nevertheless, Rothenberg was the key to making his point about radical influences over Bradley. It is hard to escape the conclusion of one political reporter that Bradley's handling of the Rothenberg affair was "humanitarian, but politically stupid."

As the contest neared the final four weeks and the pace became exhausting for the candidates, Yorty's campaign seemed to take on the character of Bradley's primary campaign. Fence sitters and their money fell into line, and a winning theme was hit upon.

Some of Bradley's supporters, including staff people lent by other local political figures and leaders of the United Auto Workers, became increasingly uneasy about Bradley's ability to hold his lead after the Rothenberg story broke and Yorty began to exploit it. In their view Bradley needed more stimulating material for his public appearances to make his assertions of energetic leadership more credible. Accordingly, the United Auto Workers brought in both Robert Kennedy's and Eugene McCarthy's principal speech writers to generate a key set of speeches that projected a Kennedy-like forcefulness in the place of Bradley's heretofore unimpassioned, if dedicated tone. Their presence, while ostensibly welcomed by older Bradley hands, in the end added yet more voices to the constant tug and pull between the more optimistic believers in continuity and the more aggressive among Bradley's advisers who wished to change the tone of the campaign.

By deciding to hold the line after the development of the Rothenberg affair, Bradley's campaign managers also seemed to be overlooking many of the implications of the public opinion survey they commissioned for their private use from Opinion Research of California. This survey was conducted one day prior to the breaking of the Rothenberg affair. Even so, the study indicated that a more direct and assertive position by Bradley was needed to answer Yorty's already heavy attacks on the issue of radicalism.

More importantly, the detailed, 66-page Opinion Research study gave Bradley a set of conclusions with potentially broad-reaching and disturbing conclusions:

☐ Bradley's lead was based primarily upon his ability to attract virtually all Negro votes.

☐ Mayor Yorty held a substantial lead among Republican voters and Councilman Bradley held a very strong lead among Democratic voters, but that lead was slight if Negro voters were excluded.

☐ Mayor Yorty would benefit by a high voter turnout.

☐ Although widespread concern existed over the activities of Yorty appointees, most voters did not think that Yorty himself was dishonest or corrupt.

☐ Opinions about Yorty centered on his personality rather than his actions or stands on issues.

☐ Bradley had a favorable image, although most voters did not know much about him or his record and philosophy. At the time of the study, not many voters had formed *strong* opinions about Bradley, pro or con.

☐ Not many voters were inclined to believe Bradley was antipolice, indicating an opportunity to counteract Yorty's charges.

☐ Most voters were satisfied with the level of services in the city of Los Angeles. No single service was universally condemned.

☐ The public image of the Los Angeles Police Department was good, with unfavorable opinions restricted to a small portion of the Negro community.

Moreover, well over a third of the responses to this opinion study cited school problems and law and order as the major local concerns. Only 3.6 percent of the responses of those who said they would vote pointed to corruption and lack of leadership in government—Bradley's theme about Yorty—as an important issue.

Most of these conclusions conflicted with what Bradley thought were the real issues in the campaign so far and with where Bradley thought his support lay. Corruption, concern about police misbehavior, dissatisfaction about the uglification of *arriviste* Los Angeles were notably absent as major public concerns; yet this is what Bradley talked about most. As soon as the opinion survey was received, Bradley's advisers began grappling with its implications. Although an effort was made to beef up Bradley's image as a leader and to reach out to groups in the white majority, the study's implications for a strategy change towards emphasizing Tom Bradley of the Los Angeles Police Department, a hardnose on militant demonstrators, were overwhelmed by the argument that the liberal reformist campaign waged so far was a winner and, the study notwithstanding, no major changes or new efforts were necessary.

In the final analysis, the results of the Opinion Research survey and their interpretation and use by the Bradley campaign underscored the tension that seems to exist between ideological preference and the application of social science techniques and their results. Bradley's people, like other political liberals and like Yorty's men, were not innocent or simple-minded when it came to testing the public's mood. Bradley's staff used all the devices of modern opinion polling, played games of strategy and looked at their candidate in terms of the image he would project over the mass media. Yet when the result of this social science research began to materialize, some of the information was highly disturbing.

One approach to the electorate implied by the Opinion Research survey was to be better than Yorty at his own game. Bradley's team looked at these results, were shocked by this implication and looked away. Their eyes shifted to the page of the report that told them who was ahead on the day of the survey: Bradley, 44 to 37 percent, the rest refusing to answer.

Bradley's men, like most men, did not go into politics simply to merchandise a product; they are political. That is, they are concerned with the use of power to affect values—public and private, material and spiritual. They did not support Bradley only to have his campaigning sanction a rigid, authoritarian approach to police-community problems or student activism. Bradley, undoubtedly, would have rejected such an approach anyway.

Thus, faced with a scientific revelation of public indifference to what they thought were the real issues at stake, they turned back with even greater fervor to the crusade for reform. New position papers, press releases and speeches came out in an unfocused mass telling of corruption, bad police-community relations, pollution and the other standards of a reform campaign today.

But was there only a single implication of the Opinion Research poll's results? The same survey implied other things about potential directions for the remaining weeks of the Bradley campaign, and perhaps about future campaign styles for liberals in the difficult final Vietnam years ahead as well. If Bradley was not a radical, he could take them on strongly, this pool seemed to say, perhaps neutralize Yorty's biggest issue. If Bradley was a policeman and supported true law and order, which he did and which most political liberals do, then he could emphasize that fact clearly, as this poll seemed to invite him to do, without providing distractions about a hard-to-believe corruption he was going to eliminate anyway, once he got in.

In short, this poll told Bradley, as it tells liberals elsewhere, that there are only a few areas where the beliefs, anxieties and concerns of the white middle-class electorate are open for manipulation by liberal candidates. But there are these few. The question might have been asked, "If a fair number of people do not share our view, are there things we can share with them? If there are, will it alienate the *voters* who have so far given us their support?" In Bradley's case, since so much of his strength rested on a unanimous bloc of black votes, it was logical to ask if they had any alternative.

As the final weeks wore on, Yorty found the correct optical language for the nightly television news coverage. At the same time, Bradley became increasingly tired, and his rather stiff television manner turned wooden.

A review of the candidates' public activities and the news for the day for 20 and 21 May highlight the differences in the two candidates' tactical style and basic strategy.

On a day one week before the election, University of California students and demonstrators were dispersed by the National Guard and police using tear gas and shotguns. News stories and film clips showed an American city turned into a battleground under siege; buildings were barricaded by students at the University of California at Santa Cruz, and 250 youths were dispersed near Stanford.

And in the campaign? Yorty reiterated forcefully that Governor Ronald Reagan was right in calling the National Guard to Berkeley. Tom Bradley released his income tax returns for the last five years.

News for the following day, 21 May: draft records were set afire in Los Angeles; Oregon saboteurs dynamited a church, a bank and other buildings; mobs were teargassed at Berkeley; hundreds of students battled police at San Fernando High School in a Los Angeles neighborhood.

And in the campaign? Bradley said that city government corruption was still the main issue while Yorty for the first time in his campaign read a prepared speech in its entirety. In it Yorty said that he could deal with militants better than Bradley and linked the Students for a Democratic Society (SDS) threat with "forces" on Bradley's campaign staff. Whether Yorty and his backers were conscious of this or not, most serious studies of public attitudes towards riot, protest demonstrations and other types of physically assertive political behavior by minorities with grievances (reported best in *Public Opinion Quarterly*) have indicated that roughly between 45 and 60 percent of American whites believe that there is some sort of conspiracy coordinating as well as stimulating protest behavior.

Linking Bradley Up

On the crucial issues of militancy and race, Yorty constantly attempted to link Bradley to the troubles prominent in the news. For example, at a Rotary Club meeting in a predominantly Mexican-American business district, shortly after black militants invaded a Gary, Indiana city council meeting, Yorty said that if Tom Bradley became mayor "the militants could come down and intimidate the City Council . . . I don't want to see that happen in the City of Los Angeles . . . And this could happen, couldn't it? If Bradley got elected, we could have that . . . So I hope that our people will wake up. I'm doing my best to tell them and I need your help in doing it because it's not just my city, it's our city and I think we want to . . . keep the kind of investment climate we've got here now, where people are encouraged to come and where they feel the government is stable and the Police Department will operate and protect them in their rights."

Bradley never ducked the issue of campus unrest and militancy, but his quiet tone and preference for a "reasonable" answer were pale next to Yorty's demagoguery. Bradley would say, "The first step to be taken to solve this problem [campus disorders] is to begin an examination of the fundamental lack of communication and dialogue. Once we do this, we can resolve our difficulties in a proper atmosphere." Yorty's message was simpler: smash them if they show up, and in any case keep their spokesman out of City Hall.

In the end Yorty received 447,000 votes (53.25 percent, and Bradley 392,000 votes (46.74 percent).

There can be little doubt that a backlash factor was at play in public opinion during Los Angeles' election. This attitude, a focused public reaction to a political or social object, was ultimately the most crucial one for determining the vote. It would be a mistake, however, to conclude that backlash was simply and solely rejection of Tom Bradley because of his race. Certainly the national implications of Bradley's defeat and Yorty's victory go beyond simple rejection or vindictiveness on the grounds of race. The election presaged much of 1970's bitterness about "radical liberals" and vice-presidential rhetoric.

Many of Bradley's campaign staff and personal supporters, as well as Bradley himself, explain the defeat by reference to Yorty's successful appeal to racial prejudice and to fear of the unknown consequences that could flow from being governed by a black man. Still Bradley would not have made his bid if he had believed race would be an a priori factor against him. After the campaign Bradley said, "We should have taken on the racial issue frontally, as John Kennedy faced the Catholic issue in 1960, rather than insisting that race was irrelevant, as it most likely is, to being a good mayor." Yet some Bradley supporters, even those who are now quite critical of certain tactical moves in the campaign, feel that even a better-run campaign would have failed in the end.

Yorty's more moderate backers argue that Bradley's blunders, such as the Rothenberg affair, and his poor TV manner allowed Yorty to take the initiative. Race alone, they say, would not have defeated Tom Bradley.

The truth of the matter probably lies somewhere between. Undoubtedly, being black was a drawback for Bradley in dealing with some of the white population. A trade-off could, it is true, exist between the number of real bigots among the whites and the ethnic bloc loyalty of the blacks. Nevertheless, Bradley's race put him at a distinct disadvantage among the white population, which was becoming greatly disturbed by increased social protest in the United

TABLE 1: Percentage of Voters by Social Groups in the Primary and Final Election

Group	% Bradley		% Yorty		% Gain-Loss From Primary To Final Election		% Turnout	
	Primary	Final	Primary	Final	Bradley	Yorty	Primary	Final
Middle- to Upper-Middle-Class Whites	27	32	32	68	+5	+36	63	77
Middle-Class Blacks	85	89	7	10	+4	+3	77	85
Laboring and Lower-Middle-Class Blacks	94	99	4	1	+5	-1	70	79
Laboring and Lower-Middle-Class Mexican-Americans	34	33	30	67	-1	+37	56	70
Lower-Middle to Upper-Middle Class Jews	52	52	18	48	0	+30	62	78

States. Even so, it is important that one remember that Bradley was not overwhelmed in the election even though Sam Yorty mounted what has to have been one of the mos effective exploitations of daily events, underlying suspi cions of minorities and beliefs in conspiracies against the well-being of the American people. In many respects, the Los Angeles election resembled the Carl Stokes election in Cleveland in 1967. The blacks gave their candidate a solid vote, while roughly a third of the whites joined in. The difference, of course—apart from the nature of the campaigns—was that Cleveland is over 40 percent black, while Los Angeles' black community is less than 20 percent of the total population. One national implication raised by Cleveland and Los Angeles is that black candidates in big cities don't lose all white support simply by race alone. Other factors, not always present even in racially troubled United States cities, must be at hand.

Three factors combined to produce the backlash sentiment in Los Angeles, and each of these factors depended in some crucial way on mass media to shape the public expression of backlash.

First, the challenge to established values manifest in the often violent confrontations between students (mostly) and public authorities sensitized a large part of the public, not so much to the points the protesters were raising but to the behavior of the protesters. This is a national phenomenon just as television itself is nationwide. The mass media, by routinely and daily showing protest events, succeeded in proving with visual evidence that the students were running amok instead of studying and that someone—the person the news would fall upon to interview—was "leading" the protest. The fact that local news brought incidents from all over the United States into Los Angeles homes in a regular fashion probably served to intensify concern over the militancy issue. No one in Los Angeles, or Seattle or Mineola for that matter, missed the photograph of black student militants seizing a Cornell University building with rifles and crossed bandoliers. As regards the Los Angeles election, it is important to remember that mass media exposure of these militant student protests began long before the campaign occupied time on television and radio and space in the press. Thus, when candidates came into public focus, really not until shortly before the primary and final elections, the issue most preoccupying the public's mind was the perplexing character of student protest. Students and mass media, in effect, prepared the principal issue for the public and the candidates.

Bradley's argument that other things besides student militancy were important for Los Angeles was evidently unheeded by the voters. The people apparently wanted answers from public officials, regardless of what the city charter or state constitution said about their actual responsibilities. This is probably true nationwide. Paradoxically, being sophisticated enough to distinguish local from national issues may hurt you with the "folks at home" who are wired into a national circuit several hours each night. Yorty, however, was quick to seize upon the public's questioning mood and produced a set of answers to the student protest issue, thus providing the second factor contributing to the backlash sentiment. Ignoring completely the substantive issues raised by the protesters, Yorty assured the public that they were "radicals," "SDS," "anarchists" and "communists" and that the purpose of the protests was to destroy "America," a concept often used by Yorty in its most mythic nationalist connotation.

To convey these "answers" to the greater public—essentially telling the noninvolved "silent majority" who the protesters were and what they were up to—Yorty and his campaign staff relied on the mass media's desire to report his election campaign, a public service paid for by their business, the sale of advertising space and time. Carefully coordinating the free and paid media, Yorty organized public opinion around the problem that local and national opinion polls showed to be a crucial public issue. Once organized, public perplexity and malaise over student military protest were more readily available for conscious expression by the electorate. What the public needed was some object on which they could focus their hostility and fear. That object was Tom Bradley and his followers, the third factor in the creation of a backlash in Los Angeles.

But Bradley alone, or the simple fact of his race, is not a sufficient explanation of why he could become the object of that focus. Bradley and his campaigning had to contribute certain acts and statements in order to link himself negatively to the turbulent public mood. Yorty's role, while catalyzing, was, by itself, insufficient to produce the backlash.

Bradley gave a lot of ground to Yorty. He allowed him to work the issue of militancy—student and racial—at will. It was Yorty who captured the initiative on the police issue in spite of Bradley's 21-year record of service in the Los Angeles Police Department. When Yorty formed an aggressive policeman's committee, only then, and in haste, did Bradley form one. Even then, it lacked strong representation from rank and file policemen. Bradley's campaign spent tens of thousands of dollars on computerized mailing, yet one of its simplest and most effective pieces of literature, a brochure with a picture of Bradley in his police lieutenant's uniform, was developed and mailed only in the twilight of the six-month campaign effort.

Bradley allowed many accusations to go ineffectively answered, though of course he always tried to respond. The Yorty charge of militants in Bradley's campaign is a case in point. There were no white radical New Leftists in the Bradley camp nor any black militants, because both of these groups considered Bradley an Uncle Tom. Indeed, Bradley is a personally conservative person, the antithesis of the radical stereotype. Perhaps the old-time liberals (ironically champions of a new Democratic coalition of Kennedy and McCarthy activists) who were running Bradley's campaign could not bring themselves for ideological-moral reasons to generate the words and the campaign activities necessary to distinguish Bradley *in the public's mind* from forces much further to his left.

Liberal ideological beliefs were, in fact, an important factor in the development of Bradley's candidacy and subsequent campaign. For example, among Bradley's strongest supporters, white and black, a firm belief in rational co-operation for the common good, in which all of America's social groups share on a basis of justice and equality, was the basis for a rejection of the revolutionary rhetoric and occasional violence of the New Left. A deep commitment to individual dignity and to the intrinsic cultural worth of all groups in plural America lay behind the acceptance of Bradley on his merits and the selection of the black-brown-liberal (Jewish) strategy as a key component of the campaign.

Two themes particular in the liberal American credo widely held by Bradley's campaigners seem to have contributed significantly to Bradley's demise. First, the belief in justice and equality led to a reformist view of the police as the front line of justice in America. Los Angeles police had had their brutal and brutalizing moments, apart from the 1965 Watts riot. On 23 June 1967, when President Lyndon B. Johnson visited Los Angeles for a political dinner, the Los Angeles Police Department restrained a large crowd of middle-class war protesters. Excesses occurred, and in hearings before the city council, former policeman Bradley took the police chief and his force to task.

Later, in the Chicago Democratic convention of 1968, other police participated in a many-sided riot as rioters and many of the people who directed Bradley's effort had seen it happen as McCarthy-Kennedy delegates. As a result, reforming the police—not destroying them—became a driving purpose for Bradley's supporters and, one may assume, for Bradley himself. That the police were seemingly expressive of a majority's mood, and had therefore become a

politically sensitive subject indicative of dominant social trends, was lost in the impulse to reform them to a more liberal image of public service. The liberal impulse, in other words, contributed purely and simply to the Bradley's camp missing the political point raised by all sides in the disturbances: more fundamental issues were felt to be at stake than forms and reforms.

Second, the growing assertion of intrinsic worth in the peculiarities and differences among the immigrant, religious and racial groups in America overtly determined Bradley's strategy toward two pivotal social groups in the Los Angeles electorate: the approximately 110,000 Mexican-American voters and the slightly larger number of Jews.

Bradley and his white and black supporters tended to view the Mexican-Americans as a natural ally in the struggle for equality and justice. And to be sure, among the group as a whole, political advocates can be found who champion a sort of romantic cultural nationalism with solidarity toward other colored peoples, but there is also in this group a variety of assimilationist positions as well as a conservative cultural nationalism that rejects contact with outsiders.

Bradley's campaign, however, tended to impose the perspective of the solidarity-oriented cultural nationalists among the Mexican-American population. The black-brown coalition in effect was telling Mexican-American voters that their social and economic goals would only really be achieved when the blacks also received justice. This message negated much of the experience of thousands of Mexican-Americans, who, by virtue of not being black, had greater access to nonghetto housing, higher income and less social hostility from whites than blacks experienced. It is true that Mexican-Americans as a whole have a lower level of educational attainment than blacks, and no one in the Mexican-American community is oblivious to the difficulties of getting a good education in insensitive English-speaking schools. But Bradley's approach to the Mexican-Americans went beyond recognizing the problems. It suggested a means of solution—a black-brown coalition and an emphasis on *chicanismo* (the ambivalent status of being Mexican in an Anglo-American world). To a majority of Mexican-Americans, such a separatist solution was less acceptable than the assimilation implicitly offered by the Yorty forces.

Where Bradley said wait until we are all free, Yorty said, you Mexicans are fine people, "got all the street names in Los Angeles" and I am offering you a chance to get a little closer to good things—jobs, suburbia, a preferred station in the local caste system without having to deal with those aggressive *mayatas* (blacks).

Bradley, in effect, tried to gain Mexican-American support by playing to the brown, poor, equality-demanding—Mexican—side of the Mexican-American group personality. Yorty won his support by appealing to the lower-middle-class, upward-focused, status-oriented and assimilative—American—trend in Mexican-American group behavior. Yorty said in an interview that he treated Mexican-Americans like anyone else. "I gave them jobs, go to their fiestas and try to provide what they are looking for in Los Angeles. Mexicans don't like to be called Brown." Tom Bradley offered the distant prospect of expanding the Los Angeles City Council so that a Mexican-American would have an easier time in getting elected. Bradley said, "I tried to work with Mexican-American leadership, but their conflicts over who was going to get what finally were more than we could handle."

Bradley had more success in his approach to the Jewish population. The liberal creed is widely held among Jews who in Los Angeles, like other major American cities, tend to fall into middle-income professional life or commerce and live in homogeneous clusters. Newspapers, high culture, the manipulation of life by intelligence rather than by force—these are Jewish-liberal things, especially for the highly educated professionals. For these Jewish voters, this is what Tom Bradley tried to identify himself with, and many listened.

But fear of being squeezed between the black and the white *goyim,* while not so liberal an attitude, exists in varying degrees among Jews of all economic brackets. Sam Yorty, for all his demogoguery, is no George Wallace. He said repeatedly that he couldn't understand why everyone was against him in the black community; after all, he integrated city government in 1961. For half the Jews, this was liberal enough. Bradley was all right, it might be said, but recalling the New York school mess and all the charges of black anti-Semitism, these were not normal times. Small groups who have made it in some ways can't afford to take chances in others.

In essence, Tom Bradley contributed to the backlash sentiment by being black in a de facto segregated society, by espousing liberal political views easily interpreted as being soft on militant protesters and in any case less relevant to the immediate interests of potential allies and by employing a person whose previous Communist party connection seemed to back up Yorty's claim that Bradley was in league with campus and racial militants.

No doubt it was easier to convince the white electorate that Bradley was a threat simply because he was black. By and large white people have very little contact with blacks, and too often those they do see are either cleaning the floor or raising a black gloved fist on television. Consequently, as a black candidate, Bradley automatically faced a lower threshold of public suspicion than his white opponent. But Bradley's outspoken liberalism helped push the white electorate over that threshold. Espousing the liberal slant on justice, championing as it does minority causes, Bradley lent himself to the accusation that he would be "their" mayor. Undoubtedly for liberals it is a vile business to be constantly on guard against speaking out on dearly held principles, for fear of adverse voter reaction. But under the reign of one man-one vote, the nonliberals have a majority nationally and in the national microcosm, Los Angeles.

Apocrypha

Every campaign generates apocryphal stories: One of Bradley's white field deputies has a six-year-old daughter who marched up and down her block handing out literature and pitching hard for Tom Bradley. Stopped on the street by a middle-aged woman of Italian descent, the little girl handed her a piece of literature. The woman said, "I hear if Bradley wins all the blacks will take over Los Angeles." Thinking about it for a moment, the little girl replied, "If it's all right with Mr. Bradley, it's all right with me."

The Wallace Whitelash

Seymour Martin Lipset and Earl Raab

The American Independent Party of George C. Wallace brought together in 1968 almost every right-wing extremist group in the country, and undoubtedly recruited many new activists for the rightist cause. Today many of the state parties organized under his aegis have formal legal status and have announced that they intend to nominate candidates for state and local office during the next few years in an effort to build the party. George Wallace himself has sent out a clear signal that he has plans for the future. He has begun to mail the *George Wallace Newsletter* monthly to a mailing list of over one million names which had been assembled during the election. The old address for Wallace activities was Box 1968, Montgomery, Alabama. It is now Box 1972.

The effort to maintain and build the party, however, faces the perennial problem of ideological extremist movements—splits among its supporters. Even during the 1968 campaign, sharp public divisions over local vs. national control occurred in a number of states, usually because complete control over the finances and conduct of the party's work was kept in the hands of coordinators directly appointed by Wallace and responsible to the national headquarters in Montgomery. In some states, two separate organizations existed, both of which endorsed the Wallace candidacy but attacked each other as too radical. Since the 1968 election, two competing national organizations have been created, and again each is attacking the other as extremist.

The group directly linked to Wallace has had two national conventions. The first, held in Dallas in early February, attracted 250 delegates from 44 states and set up a group known as The Association of George C. Wallace Voters. The Dallas meeting was attended by a number of top Wallace aides, including Robert Walter, who represents Wallace in California; Tom Turnipseed, a major figure in the Wallace presidential effort since it started; Dan Smoot, the right-wing radio commentator; and Kent Courtney, the editor of the *Conservative Journal*. The same group met again on May 3 and 4 in Cincinnati, and formally established a new national party to be called The American Party. A Virginian, T. Coleman Andrews, long active on the ultraconservative front, was chosen as chairman. Wallace gave his personal blessing to the new party and its officers. One of his Montgomery aides, Taylor Hardin, who maintains a national office with 20 employees in Montgomery, indicated that the party would have a considerable degree of "central control."

The competing national group met in Louisville on February 22, 1969, and established a new national conservative party to be composed largely of autonomous state parties. As if to emphasize the extent to which it fostered local control, this organization called itself "The National Committee of the Autonomous State Parties, known as the American Independent Party, American Party, Independent Party, Conservative Party, Constitutional Party." This group, or constellation of groups, was united in its opposition to domination by Wallace and his Montgomery aides. Although the former candidate received compliments at the convention, the delegates were much more concerned with building a movement that was not limited to his supporters in 1968. The national chairman of the new group, William K. Shearer of California, editor of the *California Statesman*, had already broken with Wallace during the campaign on the issue of local autonomy. At the Louisville convention, Shearer said:

Governor Wallace has not shown any interest in a national party apart from a personal party. A candidate properly springs from the party and not the party from the candidate. The party should not be candidate-directed. While we have great respect for Mr. Wallace, we do not think there should be a candidate-directed situation. We want our party to survive regardless of what Mr. Wallace does.

The Shearer group also appears to be more conservative on economic issues than the Wallace-dominated one. During the convention, Wallace was criticized for being "too liberal" for his advocacy during the campaign of extended social security and farm parity prices.

The leaders of each faction claim that the other includes extremists. Robert Walters attacked Shearer's group as composed of "radicals and opportunists" and as having "a pretty high nut content." Shearer, on the other hand, has said that he finds many in the Wallace-dominated party "not too savory."

The publications of the competing groups indicate that each is supported by viable segments of the 1968 party. The Shearer National Committee, however, is clearly much weaker financially, since the Wallace national group retained a considerable sum from the 1968 campaign for future activities. It is also unlikely that they can attract many Wallace voters against the opposition of the candidate. The competition for support, however, does give each group an immediate function; and both national organizations appear to be busy holding state and local conventions designed to win over those who were involved in the presidential campaign.

It is difficult to tell how much support the American Party retains. Early in 1969 the party ran a candidate in a special election for Congress in Tennessee's Eighth District. Wallace ran first in this district in the presidential race, but the A.I.P. congressional candidate, William Davis, ran a bad second to the Democrat. The A.I.P. secured 16,319 votes (25 percent) in the congressional race, compared to 32,666 for the Democrat and 15,604 for the Republican. Wallace himself took an active part in the campaign, making speeches for Davis, but he was clearly unable to transfer his presidential support to his follower.

While Davis's showing in Tennessee was fairly respectable, another A.I.P. by-election candidate, Victor Cherven, who ran for the state senate in Contra Costa County in California in late March, secured only 329 out of the 146,409 votes cast. Cherven even ran behind two other minor party nominees. In mid-June, in a by-election for a seat in the California assembly from Monterey, an A.I.P. candidate, Alton F. Osborn, also secured an insignificant vote, 188 out of 46,602. The first effort to contest a congressional seat outside the South failed abysmally, when an American Party candidate in a Montana by-election received half of 1 percent of the vote, 509 out of 88,867 ballots on June 25. Election day, November 4, 1969, produced the best evidence of the inability of the Wallace followers to develop viable local parties. In Virginia, a state in which Wallace had secured 322,203 votes or 23.6 percent in 1968, both rightist parties ran candidates for governor. Dr. William Pennington, the gubernatorial nominee of the Andrews-Wallace American Independent Party obtained 7,059 votes, or .8 percent of the total; and Beverly McDowell, who ran on the Conservative Party ticket of the Shearer segment of the movement, did slightly better, with 9,821 votes, or 1.1 percent of the electorate. Pennington's and McDowell's combined total in 1969 only equalled 5 percent of Wallace's vote in Virginia.

But if Wallace's strength cannot be transferred to local and state candidates, most of it still remains with him on the level of national politics. The Gallup Poll, which chronicled George Wallace's rise in popularity through 1967 and 1968, has continued to examine his possible strength in a future presidential contest. In three national surveys in April, July and September, samples of the electorate were asked how they would now vote in a contest between Nixon, Edward Kennedy and Wallace. Nixon appeared to have gained from both parties, as compared with the 43 percent he received in the 1968 election. His support remained consistently high, 52 percent in April, 52 in July, and 53 in September. Kennedy's backing fluctuated more, 33, 36, 31, as contrasted with the 43 percent that Humphrey had secured. Wallace also dropped, securing 10, 9, and 10 percent in the same three polls. Thus, he lost about a quarter of his support during 1969, but still retains a respectable following for a new campaign. Wallace's social base remains comparable to that which backed him in the election, and he remains a major force in the South, where he pulls 25 percent of the choices as compared with 5 percent in the rest of the country.

Who *did* support George Wallace in 1968? A detailed answer to that question will perhaps tell us more than anything else about his chances for the future, as well as about the potentiality of right-wing extremism in America.

Election Results

Election Day results confirmed the basic predictions of the preelection opinion polls. George Wallace secured almost ten million votes, or about 13.5 percent of the total voting electorate. He captured five states with 45 electoral votes, all of them in the Deep South: Mississippi, Georgia, Alabama, Louisiana and Arkansas. With the exception of Arkansas, which had gone to Johnson in 1964, these were the same states Barry Goldwater won in that year. But Wallace lost two states carried by Goldwater—South Carolina, the home state of Nixon's southern leader, the 1948 Dixiecrat candidate Strom Thurmond, and Arizona, Goldwater's home state.

Since the support for Wallace seemingly declined considerably between early October and Election Day, falling from about 21 percent to 13 percent, an analysis of his actual polling strength is obviously important. Fortunately, the Gallup Poll conducted a national survey immediately after the election in which it inquired both how respondents voted, and whether they had supported another candidate earlier in the campaign. The data of this survey were made available by the Gallup Poll for our analysis. They are particularly useful since it would appear that most voters who had supported Wallace, but shifted to another candidate, did report this fact to Gallup interviewers. Thirteen percent indicated they had voted for Wallace, while another 9 percent stated that they had been for him at an earlier stage in the campaign.

From the national results among whites, it is clear that the data are heavily influenced by the pattern of support in the South. Wallace's voters were most likely to be persons who did not vote in 1964, or who backed Goldwater rather than Johnson. The pattern of an extremist party recruiting heavily from the ranks of nonvoters coincides with the evidence from previous extremist movements both in this country and abroad. Wallace also clearly appealed to those in smaller communities, and his strength was greatest among those with the least education. With respect to income, his backers were more likely to come from the poorer strata than the more well-to-do, although he was slightly weaker among the lowest income class—under $3,000—than among the next highest. He was strongest among those in "service" jobs, a conglomerate which includes police, domestic servants and the military. Of the regular urban occupational classes, his support was highest among the unskilled, followed by the skilled, white collar workers, those in business and managerial pursuits, and professionals, in that order. The number of farmers voting for Wallace was relatively low, a phenomenon stemming from differences between farmers in the South and in the rest of the country. Among manual workers, Wallace was much weaker with union members than nonunionists.

Voting Patterns

The vote behavior with respect to other factors also corresponds in general to preelection predictions. Wallace was backed more heavily by men than by women, a pattern characteristically associated with radical movements, whether of the left or right. Surprisingly, young voters were more likely to prefer him than middle-aged and older ones, with the partial exception that voters in the 25- to 29-year-old

The 1968 Presidential Vote: The Non-South

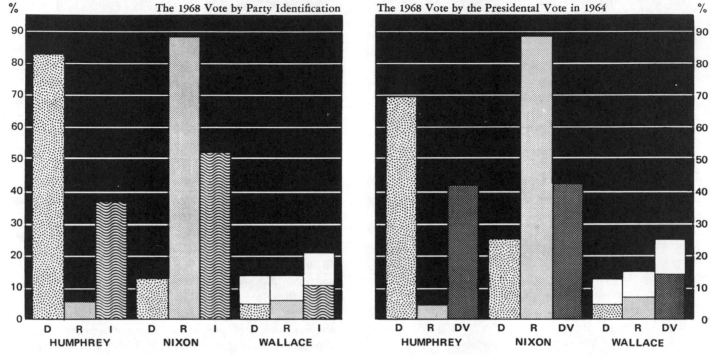

The 1968 Vote by Party Identification

The 1968 Vote by the Presidental Vote in 1964

HUMPHREY   NIXON   WALLACE

The 1968 Presidential Vote: The South

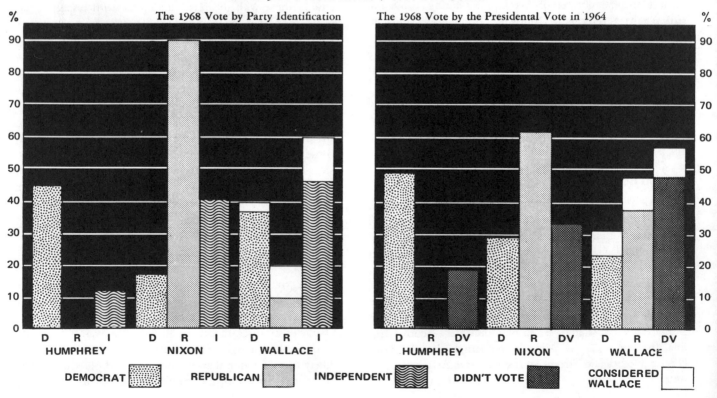

The 1968 Vote by Party Identification

The 1968 Vote by the Presidental Vote in 1964

HUMPHREY   NIXON   WALLACE

DEMOCRAT   REPUBLICAN   INDEPENDENT   DIDN'T VOTE   CONSIDERED WALLACE

category were a bit more likely to prefer Wallace than the 21- to 24-year-old age group. Religion also served to differentiate: Wallace received a higher proportion of the votes of Protestants than Catholics, a product of his strength in the predominantly Protestant South.

Viewed nationally, however, the pattern of support for Wallace is a bit deceiving since so much of his support was in the South. He carried five southern states and received a substantial vote in all the others, plus the border states. To a considerable extent, his movement in the South took on the character of a "preservatist" defense of southern institutions against the threat from the federal government. In most southern states, it was a major party candidacy. In the rest of the country, however, the Wallace movement was a small radical third party, organized around various extreme right-wing groups. While it obviously gave expression to racial concerns, it also included a number of other varieties of the disaffected. One would expect, therefore, differences in the types of voters to whom he appealed in the different sections. The variation in his support in the two sections is presented in graphs 1-4 and Tables 1 and 2.

The variations between the sections are apparent along a number of dimensions. Northern Wallace voters were more likely to come from the ranks of identified and committed Republicans than were those from the South. Thus in the South, a much larger proportion of people who were identified as Democrats (37 percent) than as Republicans (10 percent) voted for him. Conversely in the North, a slightly larger segment of the Republicans voted for him than did Democrats. This emphasis is reversed, however, with respect to the 1964 vote. In both sections, larger proportions of Goldwater voters opted for Wallace than did Johnson supporters. Relatively, however, he did better among the southern Goldwater voters. The seeming contradiction may be explained by the fact that Wallace did best among "independents," and that there were proportionately many more independents in the South than in the North. Southern independents presumably are people who have opted out of the Democratic party toward the right, many of whom voted for Goldwater in 1964 and Wallace in 1968. His greatest support, both North and South, of course, came from the ranks of those who did not vote in 1964. Almost half of the southern nonvoters in the 1964 election who voted in 1968 chose Wallace.

The effect of the social stratification variables were relatively similar in both parts of the country. In general, the better educated, the more well-to-do, and those in middle-

class occupations were less likely to vote for Wallace than voters in the lower echelons.

As far as religion is concerned, nationally Wallace appeared to secure more support among Protestants than Catholics, but a sectional breakdown points up the fact that this was an artifact of the relatively small Catholic population in the South. Outside of the South, Wallace secured more support from Catholics than from Protestants. The pattern appears to be reversed in the South, but the number of Catholics in the sample is too small to sustain a reliable estimate. What is perhaps more significant than the Catholic-Protestant variation is the difference among the Protestant denominations. Wallace's greatest backing, North and South, came from Baptists, followed by "other," presumably mainly fundamentalist sects which have a history of disproportionately backing right-wing groups. Wallace, after all, became the protector of the "southern way of life" and the status of those who bear it, not only for southerners, but for southern migrants to the North. This, apart from education, is one significance of the disproportionate support of Wallace by northern Baptists.

As noted earlier, perhaps the most surprising finding of the polls was the consistent report by Gallup, Harris and the Michigan Survey Research Center that youth, whether defined as 21 to 24 or 21 to 29 years old, were more favorable to the third-party candidate than those in older age groups. Two special surveys of youth opinion also pointed in this direction. One was commissioned by *Fortune* and carried out by the Daniel Yankelovich organization among 718 young people aged 18 to 24 in October 1968. It revealed that among employed youth 25 percent were for Wallace, as compared to 23 for Humphrey, 31 for Nixon and 15 without a choice. Among college students, Wallace received 7 percent of the vote. A secondary analysis of this survey indicated that class and educational level differentiated this youth group as well. Thus 31 percent of young manual workers who were the sons of manual workers were for Wallace, as contrasted with but 6 percent among nonmanuals whose fathers were on the same side of the dividing line. A preelection survey by the Purdue Opinion Poll among a national sample of high school students, reported that Wallace had considerable strength among them as well: 22 percent, backing which came heavily from members of southern, and economically less affluent families.

This "shift to the right" among youth had first been detected among young southerners. Although various surveys had found a pattern of greater youth support for integra-

	Voted for			Consid-ered Wallace	Total Wallace Symp.
	Humphrey	Nixon	Wallace		
OCCUPATION					
Non-manual	42	53	5	5	10
Manual	49	42	9	13	22
Union family	57	34	9	16	25
Nonunion	39	52	9	8	17
EDUCATION					
Grade school or less	53	40	7	10	17
High school or less	43	49	7	9	17
Some college	43	52	5	4	9
INCOME					
less than $3,000	41	53	5	5	11
$3,000-$6,999	46	44	10	9	19
$7,000-$9,999	42	52	6	11	17
$10,000-$14,999	46	47	6	8	14
$15,000 plus	39	58	3	7	10
RELIGION					
Roman Catholic	53	39	8	9	17
Jewish	87	13	—	3	3
Protestant	34	53	6	10	15
Baptist	33	51	16	10	25
Methodist	32	65	3	10	13
Presbyterian	28	68	5	11	15
Lutheran	43	54	3	6	9
Episcopal	40	61	—	5	5
Others	31	59	9	13	22
SIZE OF PLACE					
Rural	37	56	7	11	20
2,500-49,999	43	52	5	6	11
50,000-499,999	44	51	6	5	10
500,000-999,999	46	45	9	6	16
1,000,000 plus	50	44	7	8	15
AGE					
21-25	54	34	13	7	20
26-29	35	54	11	6	17
30-49	43	49	8	14	22
50 plus	43	53	3	5	8
SEX					
Men	43	48	9	11	20
Women	45	51	5	6	11

	Voted for			Consid-ered Wallace	Total Wallace Symp.
	Humphrey	Nixon	Wallace		
OCCUPATION					
Non-manual	22	57	22	14	36
Manual	14	33	53	6	59
Union family	30	30	40	5	45
Nonunion	8	34	58	6	64
EDUCATION					
Grade school or less	23	28	49	8	57
High school or less	21	42	36	11	48
Some college	19	60	21	10	31
INCOME					
less than $3,000	27	30	43	8	51
$3,000-$6,999	18	39	44	5	48
$7,000-$9,999	17	42	42	12	54
$10,000-$14,999	23	63	15	13	28
$15,000 plus	24	62	15	15	29
RELIGION					
Roman Catholic	47	29	24	6	29
Jewish	—	—	—	—	—
Protestant	18	46	36	10	46
Baptist	13	43	45	11	56
Methodist	22	43	35	5	40
Presbyterian	10	76	14	14	29
Lutheran	—	—	—	—	—
Episcopal	—	—	—	—	—
Others	21	25	45	7	52
SIZE OF PLACE					
Rural	17	38	45	4	49
2,500-49,999	21	43	36	8	44
50,000-499,999	23	52	25	9	33
500,000-999,999	31	58	12	3	15
1,000,000 plus	—	—	—	—	—
AGE					
21-25	—	—	—	—	—
26-29	26	37	37	5	42
30-49	14	52	34	8	41
50 plus	26	41	33	10	43
SEX					
Men	24	39	37	11	48
Women	18	51	31	8	39

tion in the South during the forties and fifties, by the 1960's this finding had been inverted, according to two NORC polls reported by Paul Sheatsley and Herbert Hyman. They suggested that southern youth who grew up amid the tensions produced by the school integration battles reacted more negatively than the preceding generations who had not been exposed to such conflicts during their formative political years. And as the issue of government-enforced integration in the schools and neighborhoods spread to the North, white opinion in central city areas, which are usually inhabited by workers, also took on an increased racist character.

What has happened is that increasing numbers of white young people in the South and in many working-class districts of the North have been exposed in recent years to repeated discussions of the supposed threats to their schools and communities posed by integration. They have been reared in homes and neighborhoods where anti-Negro sentiments became increasingly common. Hence, while the upper-middle-class scions of liberal parents were being radicalized to the left by civil rights and Vietnam war issues, a sizeable segment of southern and northern working-class youth were being radicalized to the right. The consequence of such polarization can be seen in the very different behavior of the two groups in the 1968 election campaign.

The indications that the Wallace movement drew heavily among youth are congruent with the evidence from various studies of youth and student politics that suggests young people are disposed to support the more extreme or idealistic version of the politics dominant within their social strata. In Europe, extremist movements both of the right and left have been more likely to secure the support of the young than the democratic parties of the center. Being less committed to existing institutions and parties than older people, and being less inured to the need to compromise in order to attain political objectives, youth are disproportionately attracted to leaders and movements which promise to resolve basic problems quickly and in an absolute fashion.

So much for those who actually voted for Wallace. Equally significant are those who supported Wallace in the campaign but didn't vote for him. Presumably many who shifted from Wallace did so because they thought he could not win, not because they would not have liked to see him as president. This is the uneasiness of the "lost vote." There is also the "expressive" factor, the votes in polls which do not count. Casting a straw vote for Wallace was clearly one method of striking a generalized note of dissatisfaction in certain directions. But since total considerations take over in the voting booth, the nature of the defections becomes one way to measure these dissatisfactions in various quarters. On another level, there is the factor of the social reinforcements that may or may not exist in the voter's milieu and are important for the ability of a third-party candidate to hold his base of support under attack.

The Defectors

In general, Wallace lost most heavily among groups and in areas where he was weak to begin with. Individuals in these groups would find less support for their opinions among their acquaintances, and also would be more likely to feel that a Wallace vote was wasted. In the South, however, almost four-fifths of all those who ever considered voting for Wallace did in fact vote for him. In the North, he lost over half of his initial support: only 43 percent of his original supporters cast a ballot for him. Similarly, Baptists and the small "other" Protestant sects were more likely to remain in the Wallace camp than less pro-Wallace religious groups.

There were certain significant differences in the pattern of defections with respect to social stratification. In the South, middle-class supporters of Wallace were much more likely to move away from him as the campaign progressed. He wound up with 90 percent of his preelection support among southern manual workers, and 61 percent among those in nonmanual occupations. In the North, however, Wallace retained a larger proportion of his middle-class backers (52 percent) than of his working-class followers (42 percent).

The data from the Gallup survey suggest, then, that the very extensive campaign of trade union leaders to reduce Wallace support among their membership actually had an effect in the North. Almost two-thirds (64 percent) of northern trade union members who had backed Wallace initially *did not* vote for him, while over half of those southern unionist workers (52 percent) who had been for him earlier voted for him on Election Day. A similar pattern occurred with respect to the two other measures of stratification, education and income. Wallace retained more backing among the better educated and more affluent of his northern supporters, while in the South these groups were much more likely to have defected by Election Day than the less educated and less privileged.

The variations in the class background of the defectors in the different sections of the country may be a function of varying exposures to reinforcing and cross-pressure stimuli in their respective environments. On the whole we would guess that middle-class Wallace supporters in the North came disproportionately from persons previously committed to extreme rightist ideology and affiliations. Wallace's support among the northern middle-class corresponds in size to that given to the John Birch Society in opinion polls. If we assume that most people who were pro-Birch were pro-Wallace, then presumably Wallace did not break out of this relatively small group. And this group, which was heavily involved in a reinforcing environment, could have been expected to stick with him. In the South, on the other hand, he began with considerable middle-class support gained from people who had been behind the effort to create a conservative Republican party in that section. The majority of them had backed Barry Goldwater in 1964. This large group of affluent southern Wallace-ites encompassed many who had not been involved in extremist activities. And it would seem that the efforts of the southern conservative Republicans (headed by Strom Thurmond) to convince them that a vote for Wallace would help Humphrey were effective. Conversely, among northern manual workers, an inclination to vote for Wallace placed men outside the dominant pattern within their class.

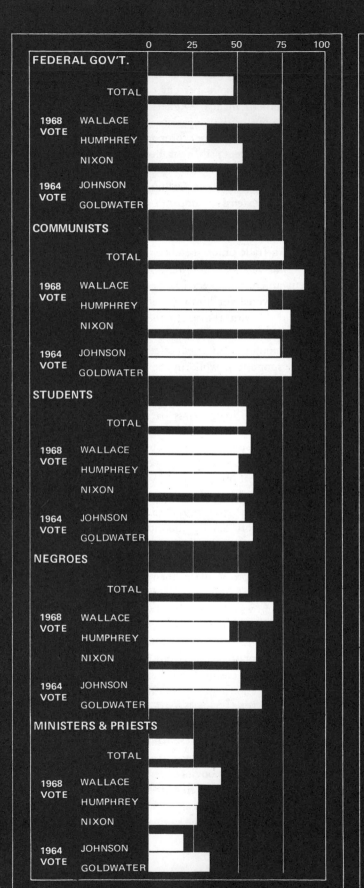

FEDERAL GOV'T.

TOTAL

1968 VOTE
WALLACE
HUMPHREY
NIXON

1964 VOTE
JOHNSON
GOLDWATER

COMMUNISTS

TOTAL

1968 VOTE
WALLACE
HUMPHREY
NIXON

1964 VOTE
JOHNSON
GOLDWATER

STUDENTS

TOTAL

1968 VOTE
WALLACE
HUMPHREY
NIXON

1964 VOTE
JOHNSON
GOLDWATER

NEGROES

TOTAL

1968 VOTE
WALLACE
HUMPHREY
NIXON

1964 VOTE
JOHNSON
GOLDWATER

MINISTERS & PRIESTS

TOTAL

1968 VOTE
WALLACE
HUMPHREY
NIXON

1964 VOTE
JOHNSON
GOLDWATER

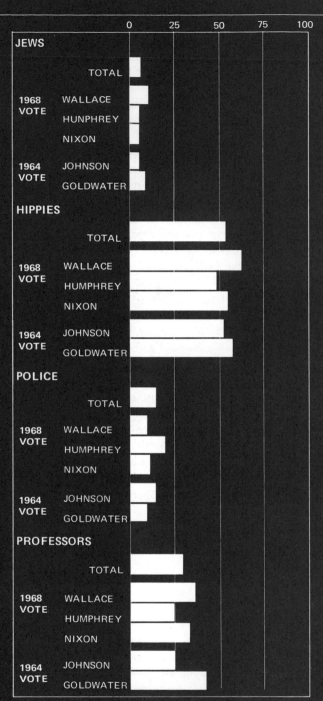

JEWS

TOTAL

1968 VOTE
WALLACE
HUNPHREY
NIXON

1964 VOTE
JOHNSON
GOLDWATER

HIPPIES

TOTAL

1968 VOTE
WALLACE
HUMPHREY
NIXON

1964 VOTE
JOHNSON
GOLDWATER

POLICE

TOTAL

1968 VOTE
WALLACE
HUMPHREY
NIXON

1964 VOTE
JOHNSON
GOLDWATER

PROFESSORS

TOTAL

1968 VOTE
WALLACE
HUMPHREY
NIXON

1964 VOTE
JOHNSON
GOLDWATER

"Which Groups are Responsible for Trouble in the Country?"

1968 and 1964 voters single out "Enemies of the American Way" (by percentage).

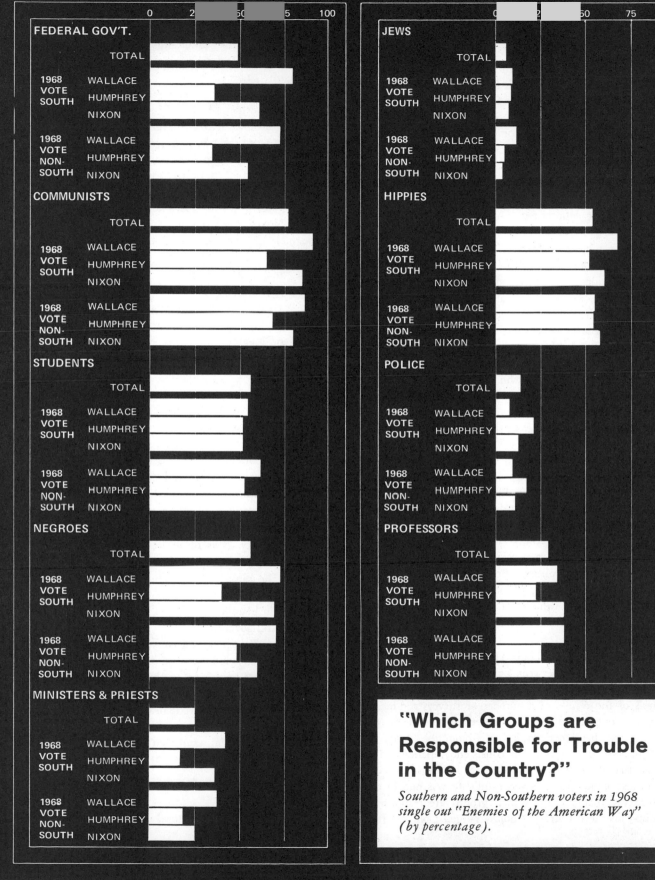

"Which Groups are Responsible for Trouble in the Country?"

Southern and Non-Southern voters in 1968 single out "Enemies of the American Way" (by percentage).

Back to the Home Party

Which of the other two candidates the Wallace defectors voted for clearly depended on background. Three-fifths of those who shifted away from Wallace during the campaign ended up voting for Nixon. But those Wallace backers who decided to vote for one of the major party candidates almost invariably reverted to their traditional party affiliation. The pattern is even clearer when southern Democrats are eliminated. Among the 29 northern Democrats in our sample who defected from Wallace, 90 percent voted for Hubert Humphrey. Humphrey recruited from among the less educated and poorer Wallace voters, Nixon from the more affluent and better educated.

The pattern of shifting among the Wallace voters points up our assumption that Wallace appealed to two very different groups: economic conservatives concerned with repudiating the welfare state, and less affluent supporters of the welfare state who were affected by issues of racial integration and "law and order." As some individuals in each of these groups felt motivated to change their vote, they opted for the candidate who presumably stood closer to their basic economic concerns. The data also point up the difficulty of building a new movement encompassing people with highly disparate sentiments and interests.

After specifying what kinds of groups voted for whom, the most interesting question still remains, especially with respect to deviant and extremist political movements such as Wallace's: What creates the differentials within each of these groups? Why, in other words, do some members of a group vote for a particular candidate, but not others? Quite clearly, members of the same heuristic group or class may vary greatly in their perception of the world, and will therefore differ as to political choice. Since candidates do differ in their ideology and position on particular issues, we should expect that the values of the electorate should help determine which segments of a particular strata end up voting one way or another.

Data collected by the Louis Harris Poll permit us to analyze the connection between political attitudes and voter choice in 1968. The Harris data are derived from a special reanalysis of the results of a number of surveys conducted during the campaign that were prepared by the Harris organization for the American Jewish Committee. Based on 16,915 interviews, it points up consistent variations. The question that best indicated differing political attitudes among those voting for a given candidate was one in the Harris survey that asked, "Which groups are responsible for trouble in the country?" Choices ranged from the federal government to Communists, students, professors, Jews and others. The relevant responses are presented on the preceding pages.

The findings of the Harris organization clearly differentiate the supporters of the different candidates in 1968 and 1964. On most items, the rank order of opinions goes consistently from right to left, from Wallace to Goldwater to Nixon to Johnson to Humphrey. That is, the Wallace supporters show the most right-wing opinions, while the Humphrey ones are most left. As a group those who voted for Goldwater in 1964 are somewhat more "preservatist" than the Nixon supporters in 1968. There is, of course, a considerable overlap. Since none of these items bear on attitudes toward the welfare state, what they attest to is the disdain which rightists feel towards groups identified with social changes they dislike.

The Wallace supporters differ most from the population as a whole with respect to their feelings toward the federal government, Negroes, the Ku Klux Klan, and most surprisingly, "ministers and priests." Although Wallace himself did not devote much attention to attacking the liberal clergy, his followers were seemingly more bothered by their activities than by those of professors. Although the electorate as a whole was inclined to see "students" as a major source of trouble, Wallace backers hardly differed from the supporters of the two other candidates in their feelings. As far as we can judge from these results, they confirm the impression that Wallace appealed strongly to people who identified their distress with changes in race relations, with federal interference, and with changes in religious morality. It is of interest that the Wallace supporters in the South and those in the non-South project essentially the same pattern. The southern differential is very slight with respect to blaming Negroes, still slight but higher in blaming clergymen, and higher yet in blaming the federal government.

Fears that Wallace would convert his following into an extraparliamentary influence on the government and terrorize opponents by taking to the streets—fears based on statements that Wallace himself made during the campaign—have thus far proved unwarranted. Wallace seems largely concerned with maintaining his electoral base for a possible presidential campaign in 1972. The effort to continue control of the party from Montgomery seems to be dedicated to this end.

The Movement in '72

The existence of local electoral parties, even those willing to follow Wallace's lead completely, clearly poses a great problem for him. Wallace's electoral following is evidently much greater than can be mobilized behind the local unknown candidates of the American Party. To maintain the party organizations, they must nominate men for various offices. Yet should such people continue to secure tiny votes, as is likely in most parts of the country, Wallace may find his image as a mass leader severely injured. He seems to recognize this, and though concerned with keeping control over the party organization, he has also stressed the difference between the "movement" and the "party," describing the two as "separate entities" which agree on "purposes and aims." Wallace is emphatic about this: "The *movement* will be here in 1972. The *movement* is solvent and it will be active." Speaking at the Virginia convention of the American Party in mid-July of 1969, he said, "A new party ought to go very slow. It ought to crawl before it walks. It ought to nominate a candidate only if he has a chance to be elected." In Tulsa he again warned his followers to move slowly, if at all, in nominating congressional and local candidates. He argued that if he were elected president in the future he "wouldn't have any trouble getting support from Congress, because most of its [major party] members were for the things he's for."

One aspect of the nonparty "movement" may be the reported expansion of the Citizens Councils of America, whose national headquarters is in Jackson, Mississippi. Its administrator, William J. Simmons, helped direct Wallace's presidential campaign in Mississippi, where he received 65 percent of the vote. In June, 1969, Simmons said:

There has been no erosion in Wallace strength. Wallace articulates the hopes and views of over 99 percent of our members. This state is not enchanted with Nixon, and Wallace sentiment is very strong indeed.

He also reported that the Council, mainly concerned with the maintenance of segregation in the schools had expanded "as a result of backlash generated by campus riots and better grassroots organizational work." The impetus of the Wallace campaign also had obviously helped. The Citizens Councils remain one reservoir of future organizational strength for Wallace.

Moreover, Wallace has attempted to maintain his ties to other groups whose members had backed him in 1968. The Birch Society's principal campaign during 1969 has been against sex education and pornography; Wallace has devoted a considerable part of his talks during the year to the subject. In addition he publicly embraced for the first time the ultraconservative "Christian Crusade" of Billy James Hargis by attending its annual convention.

In his speeches and *Newsletter* Wallace has retained the same combination of "preservatist" moralism and populist economic issues that characterized his presidential campaign. On the one hand, he continues to emphasize the issues of "law and order," "campus radicalism," "military failures in Vietnam," and "the need for local control of schools." On the other hand, speaking in Tulsa, one of the principal centers of the oil industry, he called for tax reform that would benefit the little man, adding that "the $27\frac{1}{2}$ percent oil depletion allowance ought to be looked into." He argued that we must "shift the [tax] burden to the upper-class millionaires, billionaires and tax-exempt foundations." Since this kind of rhetoric flies in the face of the deep-dyed economic conservatives among his supporters, such as the Birchers, it is clear that Wallace's cafeteria of appeals still suffers from the same sort of contradictions that characterized it in 1968, contradictions, it might be added, which have characterized most other right-wing extremist movements in American history.

Righteous Rightists

Another problem that Wallace faces comes from supporters who want to build an extremist movement, rather than an electoral organization for one man's candidacy. This can be seen in the activities of an autonomous youth organization, the National Youth Alliance, formed by those active in Youth for Wallace. As of September, 1969, the NYA claimed 3,000 dues-paying members recruited from the 15,000-person mailing list of the Youth for Wallace student organizations. The group has a more absolutist and militant character than either adult party, and it is much more unashamedly racist. Members wear an "inequality button" emblazoned with the mathematical symbol of inequality. Among other things, the Alliance advocates "white studies" curricula in colleges and universities. According to its national organizer, Louis T. Byers, "The purpose of these will be to demonstrate the nature of mankind. The equality myth will be exploded forever." In an article describing its objectives the then-national vice-president, Dennis C. McMahon, stated that NYA "is an organization with the determination to liquidate the enemies of the American people on the campus and in the community." The tone of this pro-Wallace youth group sounds closer to that of classic fascism than any statements previously made by Wallace's associates. As McMahon wrote,

The National Youth Alliance is an organization that intends to bury the red front once and for all. . . . The NYA is made up of dedicated self-sacrificing young people who are ready to fight, and die if necessary, for the sacred cause.

. . . Now is the time for the Right Front terror to descend on the wretched liberals. In short, the terror of the Left will be met with the greater terror of the Right. . . .

Tar and feathers will be our answer to the pot pusher and these animals will no longer be allowed to prowl and hunt for the minds of American students.

. . . A bright future full of conquest lies ahead of us . . . Soon the NYA will become a household word and the Left will be forced to cower in the sewers underground as they hear the marching steps of the NYA above them.

The racism of NYA leaders includes approval, if not advocacy, of virulent anti-Semitism. Its national headquarters in Washington distributes literature by Francis Parker Yockey, including his book *Imperium,* which defines Jews, Negroes, Indians and other minorities as "parasites" on the Western world. The five members of its adult advisory board have all been involved in anti-Semitic activities. Two of them, Revilo P. Oliver and Richard B. Cotten, were forced out of the Birch Society because of their overt racist and anti-Semitic views. A third, retired Rear Admiral John Crommelein, ran for president on the anti-Semitic National States Rights Party ticket in 1960; while a fourth, retired Marine Lieutenant General Pedro A. Del Valle, is an officer of the Christian Educational Association, which publishes the overtly anti-Semitic paper *Common Sense.* The fifth member of the board, Austin J. App, former English professor at LaSalle College, is a contributing editor to the anti-Semitic magazine *American Mercury.*

Perhaps most interesting of all the problems that Wallace will have to deal with is the fact that the national chairman of his American Party, T. Coleman Andrews, has publicly advocated the Birch Society's version of that hoary international conspiracy, the historic plot of the Illuminati. The Illuminati, which was an organization of Enlightenment intellectuals formed in Bavaria in 1776, and dissolved according to historical record in 1785, has figured in the conspiratorial theories of assorted American right-wing movements as the insiders behind every effort for religious liberalism, economic and social reform since the 1790s. In recent times, both Father Coughlin, the foremost right-wing extremist of the 1930s, and Robert Welch, the head of the Birch Society, have explained various threats to "the American way" from the French Revolution to the Communist movement, as well as the behavior of most key officials of the government, as reflecting the power of this secret cabal of satanically clever plotters. In a newspaper interview following the establishment of the American party in May, Andrews bluntly announced:

I believe in the conspiratorial theory of History. . . . [The Birch Society has been] responsible, respectable. . . . [R]ecently, the Birch Society has begun to prosper. People are beginning to see that its original theories were right. . . . There is an international conspiracy.

Though George Wallace himself has never publicly stated a belief in the conspiracy of the Illuminati (he prefers to talk about the role of Communists, pseudo-intellectuals and the Council on Foreign Relations) the formal organization of his personally controlled national party is headed by a man who has no such hesitation. On May 26, 1969, Wallace formally sanctioned the American Party as the political arm of the movement and said that if he ran for president again it would be under the American Party's banners.

However, while the pulls towards conspiracy theory and towards ideological racism are evident in the background, the logic of the Wallace-ite movement and its future as a mass movement obviously rest on other foundations. S. M. Miller points out that many had been shocked by "the attraction of George Wallace as a presidential candidate to a large number of union members . . . racism appeared to be rampant in the working class." When the vote came, however, racism seemed to have receded before economic concerns. Their disaffection remains nevertheless. As Miller writes, "About half of American families are above the poverty line but below the adequacy level. This group, neither poor nor affluent, composed not only of blue-collar workers but also of many white-collar workers, is hurting and neglected." It is the members of this group that the Wallace-ite movement must grow on if it is to grow, not out of their ideological racism as much as out of their general sense of neglected decline.

Tempered Extremism

Whether the Wallace movement itself will have returned to full or fuller electoral vigor by 1972 depends on a number of factors which emerge from an examination of America's right-wing extremist past. Determinative—not just for the Wallace movement but for any extremist movement—will be the larger historical circumstances. The disaffection of the white working-class and lower middle-class has been noted; if that disaffection grows, and *at the same time* the pressures of an increasingly disaffected black population increase, the soil will of course be fertile for a George Wallace kind of movement. It is the pressure of the emergent black population that provides an essentially preservatist thrust to the social and economic strains of the vulnerable whites. Whether the major political parties can absorb these concomitant pressures in some pragmatic fashion as they have in the past is another conditional factor, which is also partly dependent on historical development.

Wallace, however, is clearly preparing to use another issue in 1972, the responsibility for American defeat in Vietnam. Like others on the right, he has repeatedly argued that if the U.S. government really wanted to win the war, it could do so easily, given America's enormous superiority in resources and weapons technology. Consequently, the only reason we have not won is political: those who have controlled our strategy consciously do not want to win. But, he argued recently, if it "should be that Washington has committed itself to a policy of American withdrawal, irrespective of reciprocal action on the part of the enemy, in effect acknowledging defeat for our forces, which is inconceivable, we feel that such withdrawal should be swiftly accomplished so that casualty losses may be held to a minimum." And he left on October 30 for a three-week tour of Vietnam and Southeast Asia, announcing that he would run in 1972 if Vietnam were turned over to the Communists "in effect or in substance." Clearly Wallace hopes to run in 1972 on the issue that American boys have died needlessly, that they were stabbed in the back by Lyndon Johnson and Richard Nixon.

In order to do so, however, Wallace must keep his movement alive. As he well recognizes, it is subject to the traditional organizational hazards of such a movement, notably fragmentation, and the ascendancy of overt extremist tendencies that will alienate the more respectable leadership and support. During the year following the election, Wallace has performed as though he understood these hazards well. He has avoided expressions of overt extremism. He has attempted to keep his organization formally separated from the fringe groups and more rabid extremists, even those who were in open support of him. In a letter sent to key Wallace lieutenants around the country, asking about the local leadership that might be involved in the next Wallace campaign, James T. Hardin, administrative assistant to Wallace, carefully emphasized that "perhaps of greatest importance, we would like your opinion as to those who demonstrated neither ability nor capability to work with others and who were, in fact, a detriment to the campaign. . . ."

Whether Wallace can succeed in avoiding the organizational hazards of which he seems aware, and whether historical circumstances will be favorable, is of course problematical. But whether his particular movement survives or not, George Wallace has put together and further revealed the nature of those basic elements which must comprise an effective right-wing extremist movement in America.

Election 1968—The Abortive Landslide

Walter Dean Burnham

The 1968 election marks a turning point in American political history. Richard Nixon won the presidency but the ambiguity of the vote reached proportions unusual even for American electoral politics.

By following a rigid periphery vs. center campaign strategy, Nixon lost what was probably a golden opportunity to win the commanding victory the polls had once forecast. The Republicans won the presidency and a dominant majority of state governorships yet they failed to significantly improve their congressional position. The Democratic labor-urban coalition in the industrial states worked surprisingly well but in the end not quite well enough. Humphrey fought a superb campaign in the last six weeks and gained prestige but still he could not overcome the long anti-Administration electoral build-up. And while those supporters of Senator McCarthy who believed Humphrey's defeat essential to their purposes got their wish, their enemies from the Chicago convention remain firmly astride the party saddle. George Wallace, in the end, was quietly dispatched to Alabama but even in defeat he led one of the most impressive third-party showings in the history of the two party system.

These ambiguities faithfully reflect the totality of missed chances, major policy disasters, dissipated majorities, abortive candidacies and exceptionally narrow political choices which have dominated American politics for the last several years. Although deadlock politics has been the norm since 1938, the muffled results of the 1968 election seem even more paradoxical. In the past, *immobilisme* has been a heavy contributor to the survival of American political structures. Whether it will have the same positive effect this time is one of the most significant questions this election has left unanswered.

Even though analysis at this stage is necessarily fragmentary, the cloud of ambiguity can be penetrated and some of the dynamics beneath it perceived. It is worth recalling that just four years ago the Republican party had come dangerously close to losing its position as a usable opposition to which swing voters could feel free to move if they grew disenchanted with the incumbents. President Johnson's 61.3 percent of the vote was a landslide that seemed to foreshadow a long Democratic ascendancy, as did the 1964 party identification in the electorate—53 percent Democratic, 25 percent Republican, 22 percent Independent. Usually such landslides presage victory for the winning party for at

least the next two presidential elections. In 1964, Democratic auguries looked even more favorable since the Goldwater candidacy seriously damaged traditional Republican party loyalties in the Northeast. It seemed clear that a solidly partisan-identified Republican could never win the presidency in any foreseeable future.

Viewed over a time span extending back to 1964, the most dramatic aspect of 1968 was the magnitude and speed of voter defection from the Democratic coalition. Between 1964 and 1968, the net swing to the Republican party was exceptionally high, outranked in a list of 18 election pairs only by the shift from Hoover to Roosevelt and Wilson to Harding (see Table I).

Clearly, the 1964-1968 swing falls into a special category of election type: the landslide which is a vote of no confidence in the incumbent party. Such landslides are rare, and historically have been associated with traumatic experiences felt with abnormal intensity by large numbers of voters.

At first blush it seems anomalous to classify 1968 as a "landslide" since it obviously was not in terms of a two-party division. But examination of the gross shifts in each party's share of the total vote, as well as other factors, suggests that it was in fact a landslide —albeit a negative one.

This is the important reality of the 1968 election. While the magnitude of the gross *Democratic decline* can only be compared with the Republican collapse of 1932, the *Republican gain* over 1964 was so small that Nixon was barely able to win.

This result reflects not only the massive impact of the Wallace vote, but also the decline over the past generation in the Republican party-identified electorate,

Table I

1968 WAS A YEAR OF MASSIVE DEMOCRATIC DEFECTION
Net Partisan Swing in American Presidental Elections, 1892-1968 (Ranked by Magnitude)

Election Pair	Swing	Election Pair	Swing
1928-1932	17.1 D	1924-1928	3.9 D
1916-1920	14.6 R	1892-1896	3.7 R
1964-1968	11.5 R	1932-1936	3.3 D
1960-1964	11.2 D	1952-1956	2.3 R
1956-1960	7.8 D	1944-1948	2.1 R
1936-1940	7.2 R	1940-1944	1.2 R
1948-1952	7.1 R	1896-1900	0.9 R
1900-1904	6.3 R	1920-1924	0.5 D
1912-1916*	5.9 D	1908-1912*	0.1 R

* For analytical purposes the Republican and Progressive percentages of the total vote are combined in Tables I and II.

Table II

A NEGATIVE LANDSLIDE—1968 GOP GAINS WERE
SMALL COMPARED TO LARGE DEMOCRATIC LOSSES
Shifts of 4.9% or More in Winning and Losing Party's
Percentage of the Total Vote, 1892-1968

Losing Party		Gaining Party	
Election Pair	Shift	Election Pair	Shift
1928-1932	–18.6 (R)	1928-1932	+16.6 (D)
1964-1968	–18.2 (D)	1916-1920	+14.2 (R)
1916-1920	–15.1 (D)	1924-1928	+12.0 (D)
1960-1964	–11.1 (R)	1960-1964	+11.3 (D)
1900-1904	– 7.9 (D)	1948-1952	+10.0 (R)
1956-1960	– 7.8 (R)	1936-1940	+ 8.3 (R)
1920-1924	– 6.3 (D)	1892-1896	+ 8.0 (R)
1936-1940	– 6.1 (D)	1956-1960	+ 7.7 (D)
1948-1952	– 5.1 (D)	1904-1908	+ 5.5 (R)
		1964-1968	+ 4.9 (R)

the dislocation of 1964, and Nixon's failure to capitalize on Democratic and Independent disaffection. Granted all these factors, it seems evident that only a political upheaval of near-cataclysmic proportions could have created the conditions in which his election was possible at all.

That this election shares something in common with earlier no-confidence landslides is also suggested by the uniformity of the anti-Democratic shift outside the South, whether measured on a two-party or a three-party basis. The combined effect of the Wallace candidacy and the uniformity of the anti-Democratic swing elsewhere produced three regional bulwarks of support: the Deep South for Wallace, the plains and mountain states for Nixon and New England for Humphrey. These regional polarizations appeared in the 1964 election.

Barry Goldwater's campaign quite clearly polarized the country, not only ideologically but sectionally. In a real sense the Goldwater campaign was an insurrection of local or parochial elements in the American electorate against the cosmopolitans who since the 1930s had controlled the presidential politics of both parties. While the polarization which Goldwater forced upon the American electorate was not widely perceived at the mass base in ideological terms, it was clearly responded to through the social values associated with regional political subcultures. The result was the production of a massive regional tilt from West to East and from South to North. Goldwater's Southern-Western strategy had the expected results, with one important exception: most of "Goldwater country" remained below the 50 percent level of electoral support.

This strategy also had massive and perhaps permanent adverse effects on the Republican party particularly among traditional Republican supporters in the more cosmopolitan regions and sectors of American society.

The results of the 1968 election clearly indicate that this regional tilt has persisted. In an obviously volatile election year, the campaign strategy which Nixon adopted had, it seems, a lot to do with regional persistence. His strategy was, in fact, surprisingly close to Goldwater's, with two major exceptions. First, the extreme racist element associated with the Goldwater effort in the South was, for the most part, cut off from the 1968 Nixon coalition by the Wallace candidacy. And while the Nixon periphery vs. center coalition strategy was still based on the West and South, it was structured by the pragmatic calculations of political technicians rather than by ideological fervor. The fact remains that Nixon, given a once-in-a-generation opportunity to win over large numbers of disaffected cosmopolitans from the Democrats, instead chose a remarkably consistent coalition strategy based upon the more remote areas of American society. With the addition of just enough traditional Republican metropolitan support, he won narrow victories in some industrial states. Although Democrats have occasionally won presidential elections on a similar regional base—Wilson in 1916 and Truman in 1948—1968 marks the second time that Republicans have tried such a coalition, and the first in history in which it produced a Republican victory. The 1964 election may have had more significant long-term consequences for the political system than is often supposed.

One of the elements which made the 1968 election unexpectedly close was Nixon's refusal to make a serious bid for the cosmopolitans who had defected so massively from Goldwater, and the resultant refusal of many of them to give Nixon their support. One indicator of this is Nixon's relatively poor showing in the suburban reaches of the northeastern megalopolis. Lower Merion Township, a bedroom suburb of Philadelphia which is still very "Main Line" in its socio-economic characteristics is probably typical.

As Table III implies, the Republicans are emerging as a party of defense of peripheral social strata and regions against the threat of change. The Democrats, on the other hand, are progressively broadening their base in these social strata and areas which have a vital interest in political modernization and structural transformation. Despite its ambiguous result, the election of 1968 may speed up this process of differentiation.

GOP STRENGTH IN A BEDROOM SUBURB Table III
Political Patterns in Lower Merion Township, 1948-1968:
Transfer of Cosmopolitan Loyalties?

| | Percentage of Vote | | | | Difference From National Percentage | | | |
Year	D	R	Oth.	% D, 2-party	D	R	Oth.	% D, 2-party
1948	22.2	76.4	1.4	22.5	−27.4	+31.3	− 3.9	−29.9
1952	22.9	77.1		22.9	−21.7	+21.7		−21.7
1956	24.2	75.8		24.2	−18.0	+18.0		−18.0
1960	35.6	64.4		35.6	−14.5	+14.5		−14.5
1964	52.7	47.3		52.7	− 8.6	+ 8.6		− 8.6
1968	42.0	55.7	2.3	43.0	− 0.9	+12.3	−11.4	− 7.1

The emergent Democratic coalition is increasingly based on the deprived and nonwhite at the bottom, the younger and better-educated—along with academics and other intellectuals—in the middle, and corporate and financial interests who have accepted the "new economics" and are major partners in the welfare-warfare state at the top. Yet such a coalition of the top and the bottom against the middle still heavily depends on the support of the middle stratum that is growing technologically obsolescent and is also directly on the front lines of our contemporary social wars. Even though George Wallace's penetration of these white-collar and blue-collar workers was substantially checked at the end, they clearly remain among the most potentially volatile elements in the American electorate. Their future partisan allegiance is by no means certain, for as the election returns show, the Republican party has a fundamental problem with its present "image": When the unionized working class becomes disaffiliated from the Democratic party, it does not see Republicanism as a viable option, and hence turns to a third party candidate or to abstention.

The Republican coalition is increasingly becoming composed of the "middle" and technologically-obsolescent peripheries of American society allied against the top and bottom. For many of these voters, significant change in any direction is threatening, and with good reason. But periphery-centered coalitions based on declining social strata have rarely been successful. When they have been, their winning candidates have invariably won less than half of the total vote. Such victories, moreover, have not paved the way for coalitions with great staying power.

Richard Nixon thus faces some extremely tricky political problems, even apart from the overhanging social tensions which alone made his accession to power possible. Governing, which involves both the need to acquire highly skilled personnel to fill key positions and the need to make side-payments to coalitional allies is his first and foremost problem. Skilled personnel are found more and more in the higher reaches of the technical-academic complex. Out of all proportion to their numbers, this complex has in the main contributed to Democratic programs and policies. Whether enough of these people will be available to a Nixon administration will depend, to a large degree, upon the coalitional and policy strategies the new President chooses to adopt. Perhaps the President may govern with some effectiveness without the substantial positive support of opinion-leaders, academics and the technologically sophisticated. But the collapse of the Johnson administration is a warning to any incumbent of the real dangers he may bring upon himself if he follows policies that evoke passionate hostility in most of them. If the periphery-centered strategy of the Nixon campaign is continued and converted into policy, such hostility is very likely to mushroom. If it is abandoned in favor of policy choices which such groups would be likely to at least tacitly support, the periphery-centered elements in his coalition will be tempted to defect.

Nixon's Options Severely Limited

Policy choices and coalitional strategies are intimately related to each other. The need to expand his base of coalitional support, and expand it broadly, is the second of Richard Nixon's problems of choice. Yet his range of options appears to be remarkably limited. A move toward the middle-class political modernizers in both parties is conceivable, but would be a calculated risk carrying very uncertain payoffs with the strong possibility of mass defections within the coalition which elected him. A Whiggish Eisenhower strategy of administrative laissez-faire would probably be ideal from many points of view; however, Nixon is not Eisenhower and the year is not 1955. Any overt movement toward the Wallace following would increase internal tension to the bursting point and destroy any possibility of a positive relationship between the President and the key cosmopolitan influentials whose acquiescence he must have to govern. A policy strategy of calculated ambiguity is probably the most likely way out of these coalitional dilemmas. It remains to be seen whether the press of events will permit the Nixon administration that luxury.

From start to finish, the 1968 election exhibited exceptionally high-levels of public alienation from the old political routines and structures of American electoral politics. Two of the obvious centers of alienation this year were the college-educated young in revolt over Vietnam and a good deal else, and those Southern and blue-collar white elements caught up in the emotions of Negrophobia. There is much evidence, however, that the mood of disenchantment is pervasive.

In the past four years the proportion of Independent identifiers in the electorate have risen rapidly to an all-time high: Independents are to be found among the young, the better-educated and the more affluent. That 43% of the American electorate according to the CBS pre-election poll, would have preferred a choice among candidates different from the one given it is another indicator of alienation. So is the decline in turnout which occurred in many parts of the country. In Massachusetts, for example, turnout declined from 77 percent in 1960 to 72.5 percent in 1964 to 68.5 percent in 1968. Interestingly enough, the decline which appears to have occurred in much of the country this year conforms to a long-standing historical uniformity in American politics. With the exception of the 1856-1860 period, every election in which major third-party candidacies have occurred has been associated with declines in voter participation. The two are probably interrelated: the same widespread public dissatisfaction with the alternatives presented by the two major parties might be expected to manifest itself in abstentions as well as third-party voting.

When all is said and done, the size of the Wallace *ressentiment* movement remains as the most impressive feature of this election; it dramatically shows the disruption of electoral politics through which the country is now passing. While Wallace was not able to win the 20 percent of the vote projected by the surveys, his total of ten million votes—13.7 percent of the total cast—was more than enough to mark his American Independent Party as one of the most significant third-party insurrections in American political history.

Even though its popular support was concentrated in the thirteen states of the greater South, where it won about 57 percent of its nationwide total, the Wal-

IN THIS CENTURY ONLY LAFOLLETTE'S AND ROOSEVELT'S PROGRESSIVES FARED BETTER THAN WALLACE'S AIP	Table IV

American Third Parties, 1832-1968*

Year	Party	Percent of Total Vote
1832	Anti-Masonic	8.0
1848	Free Soil	10.1
1856	American (Know-Nothing)	21.1
1860	Southern Democrat	18.2
1860	Constitutional Union	12.6
1892	Populist	8.5
1912	Progressive	27.4
1912	Socialist	6.0
1924	Progressive	16.6
1968	American Independent	13.7

* Parties winning less than 5% of the total national vote are omitted.

lace movement received about 7.5 percent of the vote outside of this region—a not insignificant share of the whole vote. The AIP is also the first American third party—with the possible exception of the Breckinridge Democrats in 1860—to constitute a major movement on the right rather than on the left.

Definitive academic study of the 1968 election will center most probably on the Wallace movement's impact on American electoral politics. At this time we can only surmise that Wallace's overall effect was to deny Nixon and the Republicans a real rather than an abortive landslide by "spoiling" the major domestic issues (law and order, Negro-white tensions) that were the focal points of greatest discontent with the incumbent Democrats. Such an interpretation tends to support the view that the 1968 election was a partly aborted no-confidence landslide, with the added proviso that both the gross profile of the returns and the limited survey information available suggest a vote of no confidence on the part of many Americans in electoral politics as a whole. The view that the Wallace candidacy further frightened an already unsettled electorate, and frightened a good many voters away from the hard line on law and order, also goes far in explaining Humphrey's near-success in patching the old northern Democratic coalition back together. It is quite understandable that in an abnormally unstructured context, where no candidate is able to develop a differentially positive and reassuring electoral appeal, the voters move back to the safety of established reference groups and traditional routines of electoral behavior.

Large third-party uprisings against the established two-party system have been closely and typically associated with critical political realignments. Realignment comes about in the American context because political party structures and behavioral routines associated with them tend to be static and repetitive over long periods of time. But while politics in America is inherently non-developmental—parties in this country adapt but they do not evolve—the economy and the society evolve rapidly and unevenly. In the process, the disadvantaged and disaffected become more and more numerous, and their demands for political action become more insistent. Eventually the gap between the "old politics" and political demand arising from the consequences of unplanned social change produces a rupture in traditional voting alignments. More often than not, such disruption takes the form, in its earlier stages, of a massive protest movement against established policies, parties and leaders. Third parties reflect politically organizable maladjustments in society which the established order has been unwilling or unable to cope with. In the past they have tended to be way-stations for millions of voters who are *en route* from one major-party coalition to the other.

Wallace and the Republicans

The Wallace movement was centered upon the most explosive and indigestible set of social dislocations the country has had since the Civil War. These dislocations, with racial antagonisms at their core, have raised the few issues in American history which resist incremental or disaggregated solutions. In this respect Wallace's strength in the South, while much more massive than in other parts of the country, is less significant than his penetration of the North—now the vortex of the racial cold war. For it seems clear that the issues involved are going to be fought out at the center of modern American society, in the metropolitan complex rather than at its periphery. With each passing year it seems less likely that the explosive tensions of racial polarization can be settled in the classical American incremental pattern. The New York school strike, after all, may be part of the wave of the future. But to say that these tensions cannot be resolved incrementally is also to say that they will not be resolved at all within the traditional American institutional structure, in which case they will continue to increase. Of course, it is possible to resolve them by fiat. This, however, requires that Americans face up to certain hard questions of sovereign power whose avoidance is the very heart of the American political tradition. It is also possible to resolve these issues through decentralization linked to participatory democracy at the local level. This too would be, in effect, a quasi-revolutionary change in American ways of transacting political business.

Thus the mixture of issues that come from disruptive and unplanned social change, the fruit of millions of private decisions, confronts American politics with very basic challenges. The American political system is Whiggish to its core. It is predicated upon the assumption that fundamental polarizations among antagonistic groups will not often become a cluster of political demands, and that if they do, they can be successfully individualized, fragmented and processed into incremental policy outputs. The political system as a whole can work with minimal success only when this conversion process functions and produces results accepted by the combatants. It seems to be structurally incompatible with any use of political power for authoritative planning and control over the socio-economic system. If problems involving social collectivities cannot be evaded and cannot be adequately resolved in terms of incremental policy outputs resting on individualist social assumptions, the system as a whole will undergo the most profound crisis. So it was in the Civil War era; so it seems to be now.

The Wallace movement or one like it will continue to exist indefinitely as long as the cold war between black and lower-middle-class white communities continues to generate social strains on the current order of magnitude. Only if the Republican party moves toward a semi-Wallaceite position would its political entrepreneurs be absorbed into the existing two-party system. But this kind of movement would not only produce a huge political realignment, it would also augment the potential for civil-war that already exists in this country. If neither party makes a serious effort to win over Wallace's ten million, a racist-populist third party will most probably survive for the indefinite future. From what we know about the political behavior of threatened lower middle-classes, further escalation of our domestic social wars may well ensure a surprisingly bright future for such a third party—that is if the appropriate leadership skills become available.

Nixon has emphasized his commitment to solving metropolitan problems through the medium of private enterprise. But if the domestic policies of 1938 seem to be irrelevant to this problem, it is unlikely that those of 1928 will be any more relevant or productive of viable policy results. Nixon's commitment is, of course, an act of faith in disaggregated individualism as a substitute for social policy; it is a belief that fundamental social problems involving intractable groups can be resolved within the established individualist framework. As such he is touchingly, almost embarrassingly, in the mainstream of the American political tradition. It serves as a convenient reminder that you probably can't get there from here without making a clear break from that tradition.

And so the first clearly partisan Republican president has been elected in this country since 1928 at a time when the disenchantment with traditional American political structures and leadership is pervasive and seems to be growing. If the incoming administration permits its ideology to get the better part of its discretion in foreign policy, and if its private-enterprise policies toward the metropolitan centers provide only palliatives or worse, it will prove not to have been a usable opposition after all. Indeed, it will not have been an opposition at all. The consequences that would follow from this admission, following hard on the heels of the collapse of the Johnson consensus, are not pretty to contemplate. We might then be faced with a really massive popular repudiation of electoral politics as such, and the rise of a popular-totalitarian movement which would seek to destroy the barriers to central political control of society while professing to uphold or restore them. Confronted by accumulated social dislocations so deep and so intractable that no resolution of them is in sight, we have approached the verge of the deepest and most comprehensive crisis in our national history. The way out or through this crisis remains as murky and ambiguous as the results of the aborted landslide of 1968.

The End of American Party Politics

Walter Dean Burnham

American politics has clearly been falling apart in the past decade. We don't have to look hard for the evidence. Mr. Nixon is having as much difficulty controlling his fellow party members in Congress as any of his Democratic predecessors had in controlling theirs. John V. Lindsay, a year after he helped make Spiro Agnew a household word, had to run for mayor as a Liberal and an Independent with the aid of nationally prominent Democrats. Chicago in July of 1968 showed that for large numbers of its activists a major political party can become not just a disappointment, but positively repellant. Ticket-splitting has become widespread as never before, especially among the young; and George C. Wallace, whose third-party movement is the largest in recent American history, continues to demonstrate an unusually stable measure of support.

Vietnam and racial polarization have played large roles in this breakdown, to be sure; but the ultimate causes are rooted much deeper in our history. For some time we have been saying that we live in a "pluralist democracy." And no text on American politics would be complete without a few key code words such as "consensus," "incremental-ism," "bargaining" and "process." Behind it all is a rather benign view of our politics, one that assumes that the complex diversity of the American social structure is fil-tered through the two major parties and buttressed by a con-sensus of middle-class values which produces an electoral politics of low intensity and gradual change. The interplay of interest groups and public officials determines policy in detail. The voter has some leverage on policy, but only in a most diffuse way; and, anyway, he tends to be a pretty apo-litical animal, dominated either by familial or local tradi-tion, on one hand, or by the charisma of attractive candi-dates on the other. All of this is a good thing, of course,

125

since in an affluent time the politics of consensus rules out violence and polarization. It pulls together and supports the existing order of things.

There is no doubt that this description fits "politics as usual," in the United States, but to assume that it fits the whole of American electoral politics is a radical oversimplification. Yet even after these past years of turmoil, few efforts have been made to appraise the peculiar rhythms of American politics in a more realistic way. This article is an attempt to do so by focusing upon two very important and little celebrated aspects of the dynamics of our politics: the phenomena of critical realignments of the electorate and of decomposition of the party in our electoral politics.

As a whole and across time, the reality of American politics appears quite different from a simple vision of pluralist democracy. It is shot through with escalating tensions, periodic electoral convulsions and repeated redefinitions of the rules and general outcomes of the political game. It has also been marked repeatedly by redefinitions—by no means always broadening ones—of those who are permitted to play. And one other very basic characteristic of American party politics that emerges from an historical overview is the profound incapacity of established political leadership to adapt itself to the political demands produced by the losers in America's stormy socioeconomic life. As is well known, American political parties are not instruments of collective purpose, but of electoral success. One major implication of this is that, as organizations, parties are interested in control of offices but not of government in any larger sense. It follows that once successful routines are established or reestablished for office-winning, very little motivation exists among party leaders to disturb the routines of the game. These routines are periodically upset, to be sure, but not by adaptive change within the party system. They are upset by overwhelming external force.

It has been recognized, at least since the publication of V. O. Key's "A Theory of Critical Elections" in 1955, that some elections in our history have been far more important than most in their long-range consequences for the political system. Such elections seem to "decide" clusters of substantive issues in a more clear-cut way than do most of the ordinary varieties. There is even a consensus among historians as to when these turning points in electoral politics took place. The first came in 1800 when Thomas Jefferson overthrew the Federalist hegemony established by Washington, Adams and Hamilton. The second came in 1828 and in the

years afterward, with the election of Andrew Jackson and the democratization of the presidency. The third, of course, was the election of Abraham Lincoln in 1860, an election that culminated a catastrophic polarization of the society as a whole and resulted in civil war. The fourth critical election was that of William McKinley in 1896; this brought to a close the "Civil War" party system and inaugurated a political alignment congenial to the dominance of industrial capitalism over the American political economy. Created in the crucible of one massive depression, this "System of 1896" endured until the collapse of the economy in a second. The election of Franklin D. Roosevelt in 1932 came last in this series, and brought a major realignment of electoral politics and policy-making structures into the now familiar "welfare-pluralist" mode.

Now that the country appears to have entered another period of political upheaval, it seems particularly important not only to identify the phenomena of periodic critical realignments in our electoral politics, but to integrate them into a larger—if still very modest—theory of stasis and movement in American politics. For the realignments focus attention on the dark side of our politics, those moments of tremendous stress and abrupt transformation that remind us that "politics as usual" in the United States is not politics as always, and that American political institutions and leadership, once defined or redefined in a "normal phase" seem *themselves* to contribute to the building of conditions that threaten their overthrow.

To underscore the relevance of critical elections to our own day, one has only to recall that in the past, fundamental realignments in voting behavior have always been signalled by the rise of significant third parties: the Anti-Masons in the 1820s, the Free Soilers in the 1840s and 1850s, the Populists in the 1890s and the LaFollette Progressives in the 1920s. We cannot know whether George Wallace's American Independent Party of 1968 fits into this series, but it is certain—as we shall see below—that the very foundations of American electoral politics have become quite suddenly fluid in the past few years, and that the mass base of our politics has become volatile to a degree unknown in the experience of all but the very oldest living Americans. The Wallace uprising is a major sign of this recent fluidity; but it hardly stands alone.

Third-party protests, perhaps by contrast with major-party bolts, point up the interplay in American politics between the inertia of "normal" established political routines and the pressures arising from the rapidity, unevenness and uncontrolled character of change in the country's dynamic socioeconomic system. All of the third parties prior to and including the 1968 Wallace movement constituted attacks by outsiders, who felt they were outsiders, against an elite frequently viewed in conspiratorial terms. The attacks were made under the banner of high moralistic universals against an established political structure seen as corrupt, undemocratic and manipulated by insiders for their own benefit and that of their supporters. All these parties were perceived by their activists as "movements" that would not only purify the corruption of the current political regime, but replace some of its most important parts. Moreover, they all telegraphed the basic clusters of issues that would dominate politics in the next electoral era: the completion of political democratization in the 1830s, slavery and sectionalism in the late 1840s and 1850s, the struggle between the industrialized and the colonial regions in the 1890s, and welfare liberalism vs. laissez-faire in the 1920s and 1930s. One may well view the American Independent Party in such a context.

The periodic recurrence of third-party forerunners of realignment—and realignments themselves, for that matter—are significantly related to dominant peculiarities of polity and society in the United States. They point to an electorate especially vulnerable to breaking apart, and to a political system in which the sense of common nationhood may be much more nearly skin-deep than is usually appreciated. If there is any evolutionary scale of political modernization at all, the persistence of deep fault lines in our electoral politics suggests pretty strongly that the United States remains a "new nation" to this day in some important political respects. The periodic recurrence of these tensions may also imply that—as dynamically developed as our economic system is—no convincing evidence of *political* development in the United States can be found after the 1860s.

Nationwide critical realignments can only take place around clusters of issues of the most fundamental importance. The most profound of these issues have been cast up in the course of the transition of our Lockeian-liberal commonwealth from an agrarian to an industrial state. The last two major realignments—those of 1893-96 and 1928-36—involved the two great transitional crises of American industrial capitalism, the economic collapses of 1893 and 1929. The second of these modern realignments produced, of course, the broad coalition on which the New Deal's welfarist-pluralist policy was ultimately based. But the first is of immediate concern to us here. For the 1896 adaptation of electoral politics to the im-

peratives of industrial-capitalism involved a set of developments that stand in the sharpest possible contrast to those occurring elsewhere in the Western world at about the same time. Moreover, they set in motion new patterns of behavior in electoral politics that were never entirely overcome even during the New Deal period, and which, as we shall see, have resumed their forward march during the past decade.

As a case in point, let me briefly sketch the political evolution of Pennsylvania—one of the most industrially developed areas on earth—during the 1890-1932 period. There was in this state a preexisting, indeed, preindustrial, pattern of two-party competition, one that had been forged in the Jacksonian era and decisively amended, though not abolished, during the Civil War. Then came the realignment of the 1890s, which, like those of earlier times, was an abrupt process. In the five annual elections from 1888 through November 1892, the Democrats' mean percentage of the total two-party vote was 46.7 percent, while for the five elections beginning in February 1894 it dropped to a mean of 37.8 percent. Moreover, the greatest and most permanent Republican gains during this depression decade occurred where they counted most, numerically: in the metropolitan areas of Philadelphia and Pittsburgh.

The cumulative effect of this realignment and its aftermath was to convert Pennsylvania into a thoroughly one-party state, in which conflict over the basic political issues were duly transferred to the Republican primary after it was established in 1908. By the 1920s this peculiar process had been completed and the Democratic party had become so weakened that, as often as not, the party's nominees for major office were selected by the Republican leadership. But whether so selected or not, their general-election prospects were dismal: of the 80 statewide contests held from 1894 through 1931, a candidate running with Democratic party endorsement won just one. Moreover, with the highly ephemeral exception of Theodore Roosevelt's bolt from the Republican party in 1912, no third parties emerged as general-election substitutes for the ruined Democrats.

The political simplicity which had thus emerged in this industrial heartland of the Northeast by the 1920s was the more extraordinary in that it occurred in an area whose socioeconomic division of labor was as complex and its level of development as high as any in the world. In most other regions of advanced industrialization the emergence of corporate capitalism was associated with the development of mass political parties with high structural cohesion and explicit collective purposes with respect to the control of policy and government. These parties expressed deep conflicts over the direction of public policy, but they also brought about the democratic revolution of Europe, for electoral participation tended to rise along with them. Precisely the opposite occurred in Pennsylvania and, with marginal and short-lived exceptions, the nation. It is no exaggeration to say that the political response to the collectivizing thrust of industrialism in this American state was the elimination of organized partisan combat, an extremely severe decline in electoral participation, the emergence of a Republican "coalition of the whole" and—by no means coincidentally—a highly efficient insulation of the controlling industrial-financial elite from effective or sustained countervailing pressures.

Irrelevant Radicalism

The reasons for the increasing solidity of this "system of 1896" in Pennsylvania are no doubt complex. Clearly, for example, the introduction of the direct primary as an alternative to the general election, which was thereby emptied of any but ritualistic significance, helped to undermine the minority Democrats more and more decisively by destroying their monopoly of opposition. But nationally as well the Democratic party in and after the 1890s was virtually invisible to Pennsylvania voters as a usable opposition. For with the ascendency of the agrarian Populist William Jennings Bryan, the Democratic party was transformed into a vehicle for colonial, periphery-oriented dissent against the industrial-metropolitan center, leaving the Republicans as sole spokesmen for the latter.

This is a paradox that pervades American political history, but it was sharpest in the years around the turn of this century. The United States was so vast that it had little need of economic colonies abroad; in fact it had two major colonial regions within its own borders, the postbellum South and the West. The only kinds of attacks that could be made effective on a *nationwide* basis against the emergent industrialist hegemony—the only attacks that, given the ethnic heterogeneity and extremely rudimentary political socialization of much of the country's industrial working class, could come within striking distance of achieving a popular majority—came out of these colonial areas. Thus "radical" protest in major-party terms came to be associated with the neo-Jacksonian demands of agrarian smallholders and small-town society already confronted by obsolescence. The Democratic party from 1896 to 1932, and in many respects much later, was the national vehicle for these struggles.

The net effect of this was to produce a condition in which—especially, but not entirely on the presidential level—the more economically advanced a state was, the more heavy were its normal Republican majorities likely to be. The nostalgic agrarian-individualist appeals of the national Democratic leadership tended to present the voters of this industrial state with a choice that was not a choice: between an essentially backward-looking provincial party articulating interests in opposition to those of the industrial North and East as a whole, and a "modernizing" party whose doctrines included enthusiastic acceptance of and cooperation with the dominant economic interests of region and nation. Not only did this partitioning of the political universe entail normal and often huge Republican majorities in an economically advanced state like Pennsylvania; the survival of national two-party competition on such a basis helped to ensure that no local reorganization of electoral politics along class lines could effectively occur even within such a state. Such a voting universe had a tendency toward both enormous inbuilt stability and increasing entrenchment in the decades after its creation. Probably no force less overwhelming than the post-1929 collapse of the national economic system would have sufficed to dislodge it. Without such a shock, who can say how, or indeed whether, the "System of 1896" would have come to an end in Pennsylvania and the nation? To ask such a question is to raise yet another. For there is no doubt that in Pennsylvania, as elsewhere, the combination of trauma in 1929-33 and Roosevelt's creative leadership provided the means for overthrowing the old order and for reversing dramatically the depoliticization of electoral politics which had come close to perfection under it. Yet might it not be the case that the dominant pattern of political adaptation to industrialism in the United States has worked to eliminate, by one means or another, the links provided by political parties between voters and rulers? In other words, was the post-1929 reversal permanent or only a transitory phase in our political evolution? And if transitory, what bearing would this fact have on the possible recurrence of critical realignments in the future?

Withering Away of the Parties

The question requires us to turn our attention to the second major dynamic of American electoral politics during this century: the phenomenon of electoral disaggregation, of the breakdown of party loyalty, which in many respects must be seen as the permanent legacy of the fourth party system of 1896-1932. One of the most conspicuous developments of this era, most notably during the 1900-1920 period, was a whole network of changes in the rules of the political game. This is not the place for a thorough treatment and documentation of these peculiarities. One can only mention here some major changes in the rules of the game, and note that one would have no difficulty in arguing that their primary latent function was to ease the transition from a preindustrial universe of competitive, highly organized mass politics to a depoliticized world marked by drastic shrinkage in participation or political leverage by the lower orders of the population. The major changes surely include the following:

■ The introduction of the Australian ballot, which was designed to purify elections but also eliminated a significant function of the older political machines, the printing and distribution of ballots, and eased a transition from party voting to candidate voting.

■ The introduction of the direct primary, which at once stripped the minority party of its monopoly of opposition and weakened the control of party leaders over nominating processes, and again hastened preoccupation of the electorate with candidates rather than parties.

■ The movement toward nonpartisan local elections, often accompanied by a drive to eliminate local bases of representation such as wards in favor of at-large elections, which produced—as Samuel Hays points out—a shift of political power from the grass roots to citywide cosmopolitan elites.

■ The expulsion of almost all blacks, and a very large part of the poor-white population as well, from the southern electorate by a series of legal and extralegal measures such as the poll tax.

■ The introduction of personal registration requirements the burden of which, in faithful compliance with dominant middle-class values, was placed on the individual rather than on public authority, but which effectively disenfranchised large numbers of the poor.

Breakdown of Party Loyalty

Associated with these and other changes in the rules of the game was a profound transformation in voting behavior. There was an impressive growth in the numbers of political independents and ticket-splitters, a growth accompanied by a sea-change among party elites from what Richard Jensen has termed the "militarist" (or ward boss) campaign style to the "mercantilist" (or advertising-packaging) style. Aside from noting that the transition was largely completed as early as 1916, and hence that the practice of "the selling of the president" goes back far earlier than we usually think, these changes too must be left for fuller exposition elsewhere.

Critical realignments, as we have argued, are an indispensable part of a stability-disruption dialectic which has the deepest roots in American political history. Realigning sequences are associated with all sorts of aberrations from the normal workings of American party politics, both in the events leading up to nominations, the nature and style of election campaigning and the final outcome at the polls. This is not surprising, since they arise out of the collision of profound transitional crisis in the socioeconomic system with the immobility of a nondeveloped political system.

At the same time, it seems clear that for realignment to fulfill some of its most essential tension-management functions, for it to be a forum by which the electorate can participate in durable "constitution making," it is essential that political parties not fall below a certain level of coherence and appeal in the electorate. It is obvious that the greater the electoral disaggregation the less effective will be "normal" party politics as an instrument of countervailing influence in an industrial order. Thus, a number of indices of disaggregation significantly declined during the 1930s as the Democratic Party remobilized parts of American society under the stimulus of the New Deal. In view of the fact that political parties during the 1930s and 1940s were once again called upon to assist in a redrawing of the map of American politics and policy-making, this regeneration of partisan voting in the 1932-52 era is hardly surprising. More than that, regeneration was necessary if even the limited collective purposes of the new majority coalition were to be realized.

Even so, the New Deal realignment was far more diffuse, protracted and incomplete than any of its predecessors, a fact of which the more advanced New Dealers were only too keenly aware. It is hard to avoid the impression that one contributing element in this peculiarity of our last realignment was the much higher level of electoral disaggregation in the 1930s and 1940s than had existed at any time prior to the realignment of the 1890s. If one assumes that the end result of a long-term trend toward electoral disaggregation is the complete elimination of political parties as foci that shape voting behavior, then the possibility of critical realignment would, by definition, be eliminated as well. Every election would be dominated by TV packaging, candidate charisma, real or manufactured,

The Emergent Independent Majority 1900-1968

Third party candidates often inspire voters to split their tickets, but the overall trend has been for voters to ignore party labels.

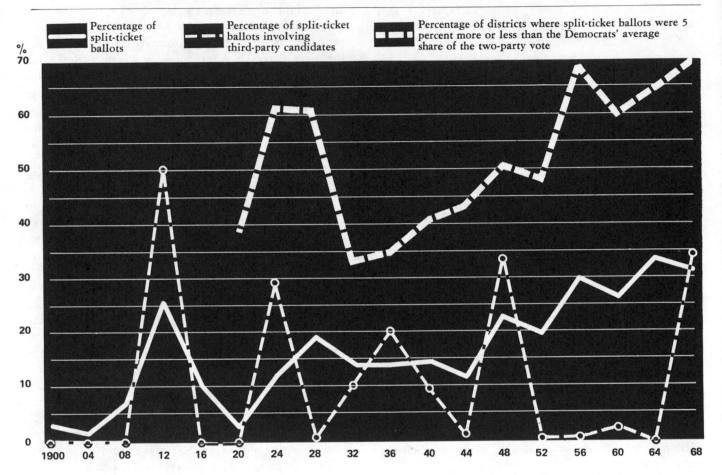

Legend:
- Percentage of split-ticket ballots
- Percentage of split-ticket ballots involving third-party candidates
- Percentage of districts where split-ticket ballots were 5 percent more or less than the Democrats' average share of the two-party vote

and short-term, ad hoc influences. Every election, therefore, would have become deviating or realigning by definition, and American national politics would come to resemble the formless gubernatorial primaries that V. O. Key described in his classic *Southern Politics.*

The New Deal clearly arrested and reversed, to a degree, the march toward electoral disaggregation. But it did so only for the period in which the issues generated by economic scarcity remained central, and the generation traumatized by the collapse of 1929 remained numerically preponderant in the electorate. Since 1952, electoral disaggregation has resumed, in many measurable dimensions, and with redoubled force. The data on this point are overwhelming. Let us examine a few of them.

A primary aspect of electoral disaggregation, of course, is the "pulling apart" over time of the percentages for the

same party but at different levels of election: this is the phenomenon of split-ticket voting. Recombining and reorganizing the data found in two tables of Milton Cummings' excellent study *Congressmen and the Electorate,* and extending the series back and forward in time, we may examine the relationship between presidential and congressional elections during this century.

Such an array captures both the initial upward thrust of disaggregation in the second decade of this century, the peaking in the middle to late 1920s, the recession beginning in 1932, and especially the post-1952 resumption of the upward trend.

Other evidence points precisely in the same direction. It has generally been accepted in survey-research work that generalized partisan identification shows far more stability over time than does actual voting behavior, since the latter is subject to short-term factors associated with each election. What is not so widely understood is that this glacial measure of party identification has suddenly become quite volatile during the 1960s, and particularly during the last half of the decade. In the first place, as both Gallup and Survey Research Center data confirm, the proportion of independents underwent a sudden shift upwards around 1966: while from 1940 to 1965 independents constituted about 20 percent to 22 percent of the electorate, they increased to 29 percent in 1966. At the present time, they outnumber Republicans by 30 percent to 28 percent.

Second, there is a clear unbroken progression in the share that independents have of the total vote along age lines. The younger the age group, the larger the number of independents in it, so that among the 21-29 year olds, according to the most recent Gallup findings this year, 42 percent are independents—an increase of about 10 percent over the first half of the decade, and representing greater numbers of people than identify with either major party. When one reviews the June 1969 Gallup survey of college students, the share is larger still—44 percent. Associated with this quantitative increase in independents seems to be a major qualitative change as well. Examining the data for the 1950s, the authors of *The American Voter* could well argue that independents tended to have lower political awareness and political involvement in general than did identifiers (particularly strong identifiers) of either major party. But the current concentration of independents in the population suggests that this may no longer be the case. They are clearly and disproportionately found not only among the young, and especially among the college young, but also among men, those adults with a college background, people in the professional-managerial strata and, of course, among those with higher incomes. Such groups tend to include those people whose sense of political involvement and efficacy is far higher than that of the population as a whole. Even in the case of the two most conspicuous exceptions to this—the pile-up of independent identifiers in the youngest age group and in the South—it can be persuasively argued that this distribution does not reflect low political awareness and involvement but the reverse: a sudden, in some instances almost violent, increase in both awareness and involvement among southerners and young adults, with the former being associated both with the heavy increase in southern turnout in 1968 and the large Wallace vote polled there.

Third, one can turn to two sets of evidence found in the Survey Research Center's election studies. If the proportion of *strong* party identifiers over time is examined, the same pattern of long-term inertial stability and recent abrupt change can be seen. From 1952 through 1964, the proportion of strong Democratic and Republican party identifiers fluctuated in a narrow range between 36 percent and 40 percent, with a steep downward trend in strong Republican identifiers between 1960 and 1964 being matched by a moderate increase in strong Democratic identifiers. Then in 1966 the proportion of strong identifiers abruptly declines to 28 percent, with the defectors overwhelmingly concentrated among former Democrats. This is almost certainly connected, as is the increase of independent identifiers, with the Vietnam fiasco. While we do not as yet have the 1968 SRC data, the distribution of identifications reported by Gallup suggests the strong probability that this abrupt decline in party loyalty has not been reversed very much since. It is enough here to observe that while the ratio between strong identifiers and independents prior to 1966 was pretty stably fixed at between 1.6 to 1 and 2 to 1 in favor of the former, it is now evidently less than 1 to 1. Both Chicago and Wallace last year were the acting out of these changes in the arena of "popular theater."

Finally, both survey and election data reveal a decline in two other major indices of the relevance of party to voting behavior: split-ticket voting and the choice of the same party's candidates for President across time.

It is evident that the 1960s have been an era of increasingly rapid liquidation of pre-existing party commitments by

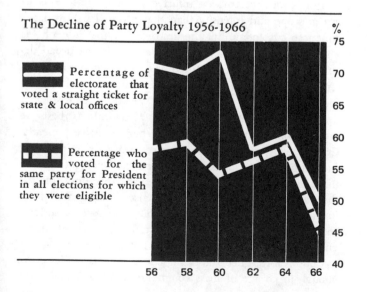

The Decline of Party Loyalty 1956-1966

%

Percentage of electorate that voted a straight ticket for state & local offices

Percentage who voted for the same party for President in all elections for which they were eligible

75
70
65
60
55
50
45
40

56   58   60   62   64   66

individual voters. There is no evidence anywhere to support Kevin Phillips' hypothesis regarding an emergent Republican majority—assuming that such a majority would involve increases in voter identification with the party. More than that, one might well ask whether, if this process of liquidation is indeed a preliminary to realignment, the latter may not take the form of a third-party movement of truly massive and durable proportions.

The evidence lends some credence to the view that American electoral politics is undergoing a long-term transition into routines designed only to fill offices and symbolically affirm "the American way." There also seem to be tendencies for our political parties gradually to evaporate as broad and active intermediaries between the people and their rulers, even as they may well continue to maintain enough organizational strength to screen out the unacceptable or the radical at the nominating stage. It is certain that the significance of party as link between government and the governed has now come once again into serious question. Bathed in the warm glow of diffused affluence, vexed in spirit but enriched economically by our imperial military and space commitments, confronted by the gradually unfolding consequences of social change as vast as it is unplanned, what need have Americans of political parties? More precisely, why do they need parties whose structures, processes and leadership cadres seem to grow more remote and irrelevant to each new crisis?

Future Politics

It seems evident enough that if this long-term trend toward a politics without parties continues, the policy consequences must be profound. One can put the matter with the utmost simplicity: political parties, with all their well-known human and structural shortcomings, are the only devices thus far invented by the wit of Western man that can, with some effectiveness, generate countervailing collective power on behalf of the many individually powerless against the relatively few who are individually or organizationally powerful. Their disappearance as active intermediaries, if not as preliminary screening devices, would only entail the unchallenged ascendancy of the already powerful, unless new structures of collective power were somehow developed to replace them, and unless conditions in America's social structure and political culture came to be such that they could be effectively used. Yet *neither* of these contingencies, despite recent publicity for the term "participatory democracy," is likely to occur under immediately conceivable circumstances in the United States.

It is much more probable that the next chapter of our political history will resemble the metapolitical world of the 1920s.

But, it may be asked, may not a future realignment serve to recrystallize and revitalize political parties in the American system?

The present condition of America contains a number of what Marxists call "internal contradictions," some of which might provide the leverage for a future critical realignment if sufficiently sharp dislocations in everyday life should occur. One of the most important of these, surely, is the conversion—largely through technological change—of the American social stratification system from the older capitalist mixture of upper or "owning" classes, dependent white-collar middle classes and proletarians into a mixture described recently by David Apter: the technologically competent, the technologically obsolescent and the technologically superfluous. It is arguable, in fact, that the history of the Kennedy-Johnson Administrations on the domestic front could be written in terms of a coalition of the top and bottom of this Apter-ite mix against the middle, and the 1968 election as the first stage of a "counter-revolution" of these middle strata against the pressures from both of the other two. Yet the inchoate results of 1968 raise some doubts, to say the least, that it can yet be described as part of a realigning sequence: there was great volatility in this election, but also a remarkable and unexpectedly large element of continuity and voter stability.

It is not hard to find evidence of cumulative social disaster in our metropolitan areas. We went to war with Japan in 1941 over a destruction inflicted on us far less devastating in scope and intensity than that endured by any large American city today. But the destruction came suddenly, as a sharp blow, from a foreign power; while the urban destruction of today has matured as a result of our own internal social and political processes, and it has been unfolding gradually for decades. We have consequently learned somehow to adapt to it piecemeal, as best we can, without changing our lives or our values very greatly. Critical realignments, however, also seem to require sharp, sudden blows as a precondition for their emergence. If we think of realignment as arising from the spreading internal disarray in this country, we should also probably attempt to imagine what kinds of events could produce a sudden, sharp and general escalation in social tensions and threatened deprivations of property, status or values.

Conceivably, ghetto and student upheavals could prove enough in an age of mass communications to create a true critical realignment, but one may doubt it. Student and ghetto rebellions appear to be too narrowly defined socially to have a *direct* impact on the daily lives of the "vast middle," and thus produce transformations in voting behavior that would be both sweeping and permanent. For what happens in times of critical realignment is nothing less than an intense, if temporary, quasi revolutionizing of the vast middle class, a class normally content to be traditionalists or passive-participants in electoral politics.

Yet, even if students and ghetto blacks could do the trick, if they could even begin, with the aid of elements of the technological elite, a process of electoral realignment leftward, what would be the likely consequences? What would the quasi revolutionizing of an insecure, largely urban middle class caught in a brutal squeeze from the top and the bottom of the social system look like? There are already premonitory evidences: the Wallace vote in both southern and nonsouthern areas, as well as an unexpected durability in his *postelection* appeal; the mayoral elections in Los Angeles and Minneapolis this year, and not least, Lindsay's narrow squeak into a second term as mayor of New York City. To the extent that the "great middle" becomes politically mobilized and self-conscious, it moves toward what has been called "urban populism," a stance of organized hostility to blacks, student radicals and cosmopolitan liberal elites. The "great middle" remains, after all, the chief defender of the old-time Lockeian faith; both its material and cultural interests are bound up in this defense. If it should become at all mobilized as a major and cohesive political force in today's conditions, it would do so in the name of a restoration of the ancient truths by force if necessary. A realignment that directly involved this kind of mobilization —as it surely would, should it occur—would very likely have sinister overtones unprecedented in our political history.

Are we left, then, with a choice between the stagnation implicit in the disaggregative trends we have outlined here and convulsive disruption? Is there something basic to the American political system, and extending to its electoral politics, which rules out a middle ground between drift and mastery?

The fact that these questions were raised by Walter Lippmann more than half a century ago—and have indeed been raised in one form or other in every era of major transitional crisis over the past century—is alone enough to suggest an affirmative answer. The phenomena we have described here provide evidence of a partly quantitative sort which seems to point in the same direction. For elec-

toral disaggregation is the negation of party. Further, it is —or rather, reflects—the negation of structural and behavioral conditions in politics under which linkages between the bottom, the middle and the top can exist and produce the effective carrying out of collective power. Critical realignments are evidence not of the presence of such linkages or conditions in the normal state of American electoral politics, but precisely of their absence. Correspondingly, they are not manifestations of democratic accountability, but infrequent and hazardous substitutes for it.

Taken together, both of these phenomena generate support for the inference that American politics in its normal state is the negation of the public order itself, as that term is understood in politically developed nations. We do not have government in our domestic affairs so much as "nonrule." We do not have political parties in the contemporary sense of that term as understood elsewhere in the Western world; we have antiparties instead. Power centrifuges rather than power concentrators, they have been immensely important not as vehicles of social transformation but for its prevention through political means.

The entire setting of the critical realignment phenomenon bears witness to a deep-seated dialectic within the American political system. From the beginning, the American socioeconomic system has developed and transformed itself with an energy and thrust that has no parallel in modern history. The political system, from parties to policy structures, has seen no such development. Indeed, it has shown astonishingly little substantive transformation over time in its methods of operation. In essence, the political system of this "fragment society" remains based today on the same Lockeian formulation that, as Louis Hartz points out, has dominated its entire history. It is predicated upon the maintenance of a high wall of separation between politics and government on one side and the socioeconomic system on the other. It depends for its effective working on the failure of anything approximating internal sovereignty in the European sense to emerge here.

The Lockeian cultural monolith, however, is based upon a social assumption that has come repeatedly into collision with reality. The assumption, of course, is not only that the autonomy of socioeconomic life from political direction is the prescribed fundamental law for the United States, but that this autonomous development will proceed with enough smoothness, uniformity and generally distributed benefits that it will be entirely compatible with the usual functioning of our antique political structures. Yet the high (though far from impermeable) wall of separation between politics and society is periodically threatened with inundations. As the socioeconomic system develops in the context of unchanging institutions of electoral politics and policy formation, dysfunctions become more and more visible. Whole classes, regions or other major sectors of the population are injured or faced with an imminent threat of injury. Finally the triggering event occurs, critical realignments follow, the universe of policy and of electoral coalitions is broadly redefined, and the tensions generated by the crisis receive some resolution. Thus it can be argued that critical realignment as a periodically recurring phenomenon is as centrally related to the workings of such a system as is the archaic and increasingly rudimentary structure of the major parties themselves.

Party vs. Survival

One is finally left with the sense that the twentieth-century decomposition of partisan links in our electoral system also corresponds closely with the contemporary survival needs of what Samuel P. Huntington has called the American "Tudor polity." Electoral disaggregation and the concentration of certain forms of power in the hands of economic, technological and administrative elites are functional for the short-term survival of nonrule in the United States. They may even somehow be related to the gradual emergence of internal sovereignty in this country—though to be sure under not very promising auspices for participatory democracy of any kind. Were such a development to occur, it would not necessarily entail the disappearance or complete suppression of subgroup tensions or violence in American social life, or of group bargaining and pluralism in the policy process. It might even be associated with increases in both. But it would, after all, reflect the ultimate sociopolitical consequences of the persistence of Lockeian individualism into an era of Big Organization: oligarchy at the top, inertia and spasms of self-defense in the middle, and fragmentation at the base. One may well doubt whether political parties or critical realignments need have much place in such a political universe.

part three

National Policy Elites and Their Politics

Essays in this Part deal with significant elements in the shaping of national public policy. As do studies throughout the book, they often cross-cut traditional lines and "loop backward"—and forward—into discussions in other Parts of this work. If most of the essays here probe into the processes by which things get done (or do not get done) in our federal policy-making establishment, they also suggest the importance of behavioral norms and constraints which shape decisions. Taken as a whole, such norms and constraints are of incalculable importance in sustaining the "normal politics" of the post-1941 American hybrid, and in insulating this politics from major change. The interplay between behavioral norms on the one hand and formal institutions and official roles on the other is a matter of perennial fascination and more than occasional discouragement to students of the political process. But beyond that: a systematic study of these realities of human interaction is essential for anyone who wishes to move from the rhetoric of substantial change in our politics toward its reality. This point is especially well made in Dumont's discussion of the governmental bureaucracy.

Turning first to the presidential ascendancy in our political system, we can see some of the materials of which it is constructed. To begin with, there is much of the "divinity that doth hedge a king" in the public response to the office and the men who hold it. Greenstein's essay makes this point forcefully, and it is also implicit in Lipset's discussion of the enormous latitude and initiative which the President has had in molding public opinion on foreign policy. A focus of attention on the President—indeed, a clustering of mythic and symbolic attitudes around him—runs deep in the American value system. There is little enough of the businesslike attitude which people in Great Britain have toward their Prime Minister; but then, the United States does not have a monarch—at least in the formal sense. In this country the symbols of the Head of State are inextricably merged with the politics of presidential government. Presidential ascendancy in the American political system is partly a matter of superior power resources—especially in the foreign and military area, as Wildavsky correctly points out—and partly a matter of knowledge and expertise; at base, it has become a *moral* ascendancy in the public at large. It is this moral element which has permitted charismatic, "heroic" leadership in such executives as Lincoln and the two Roosevelts; such historical episodes have also deeply enriched and entrenched the public mystique of the Presidency.

This mystique creates its own political problems. It is, of course, essential to the health of any political system that it have mythic and symbolic elements which promote solidarity and legitimacy among the masses of the population. But when so much of this mythos centers around a living man who is not a figurehead but rather the most powerful element in government, it can contribute to keeping the public in political tutelage. This has been the case in foreign policy until very recently. As survey after survey has shown, the American public has been conditioned—particularly during the Cold War and the era of bipartisan foreign policy—to accept whatever the President does because as head of government he has secret information which is widely thought (usually wrongly) to be crucial to his decisions. Lipset's discussion captures this conventional wisdom very neatly, and it corresponded closely enough to reality at the time he wrote. The widespread popular and professional opposition to the Vietnam war which subsequently developed had to overcome this mystique first, and only the egregious nature of the President's decisions made it possible at all for this to occur. One small result was to invalidate Lipset's conclusions more and more fully for every year that has passed; this only reinforces the view that all public-opinion structures are more or less artifacts of the historical and political contexts of any given era, however "eternal" they may appear to the analyst at the time.

The mystique has also interacted directly with the institutional-behavioral realities which Wildavsky stresses. The blunt fact is that presidential policy initiatives are vastly more subject to deflection or watering down by veto-group action in the domestic arena than in foreign or military policy. This is in line with the argument in the Overview that the American political system is structured around the denial of *internal* (or domestic) sovereignty while maintaining a full plentitude of *national* sovereignty in the world at large, much of which sovereignty is con-

tained in the Presidency itself. (The reader interested in a judicial exposition of this difference which is still in many ways definitive should consult Justice Sutherland's opinion for the Supreme Court in U.S. v. Curtiss-Wright Export Corp., 299 U.S. 304, 1936). This arrangement corresponds well with the basic functional requisites of a political system which is dominated by a bourgeoisie but where no effectively organized points of resistance to that domination exist. It is not surprising that recent Presidents have turned almost with relief from the turmoils of domestic problems to the apparent certainty—the "unit, secrecy, and dispatch," in Alexander Hamilton's pithy phrase—which the President enjoys in his role as definer and enforcer of the national interest.

The reader can no doubt see obvious long-term potential in all this for converting the President into a functional equivalent of an old-style Emperor, court and all. This is objectively a serious and real enough danger; and it is implicit in the intersection of the new *Imperium* with a very old constitutional scheme. But these issues cut two ways, especially in a crisis situation of the sort we are now living through. For to a unique extent not only policy outputs but the very health of the political system in the United States—and above all its legitimacy—depend upon the acceptance of presidential leadership by the public. An enormous burden is thus placed upon one individual. Not only his policies, but his personality and the extent to which he can project the "moral leadership" of which FDR spoke, contribute to both his personal success and to the vitality and responsiveness of the national policy system in coping with divisive issues.

To a large extent the malaise which now grips American public opinion results from the recent shattering of the presidential idol. This, in turn, can be traced directly to both the decisions and the images of the Presidents who have been in office since November 22, 1963, and especially to Lyndon Johnson's disastrous presidency. The display of self-closure, of righteous disregard for public opinion, and of outright lying which have come from the White House during the past decade explain much of the present crisis of legitimacy. They also explain why in 1972 such large parts of the electorate have persistently been looking, like Diogenes, for an honest man wherever he might be found. But this, in turn, simply reinforces two points we have already established. First, like every major political crisis, the present one is at base a *moral* crisis, one in which the presidency is deeply implicated. Second, it is not revolutionaries who make revolutionary situations: rather, it is established leaders whose decisions push to explicit extremes those elements of normal American politics against which there is growing opposition. By doing this—and established leaderships have had an uncanny way of so acting just before and during realignments throughout our history—the leadership accomplishes two things: it escalates the crisis to the breaking point, and it contributes to its own repudiation. For every charismatic, "revitalizing" president, one can find a repudiated president whose administration became an agony to the whole country. Usually, and by no means accidentally, repudiated presidents have been near predecessors of charismatic presidents.

The problem of remoteness from the public is by no means confined to the White House office and its denizens. It is likewise endemic in the bureaucracy, as Dumont brilliantly traces. Remoteness, of course, is made up of many facets. The bureaucracy's deeply entrenched survival rules are to some extent properties of bureaucratic organizational structures everywhere. But they work with particular force in American political conditions, as anyone who is able to compare, say, Swedish and American responses to "little-man" consumer demand for their services, can tell us. The issue is not only complexity and intricacy of organization and of rule-making; it is also, and more importantly, the tendency of organizations which have no definable sovereign to carve out feudal baronies of their own within the institutional structure, plus a parallel tendency to resist stoutly any outside encroachments. American bureaucratic practice, to the extent that it differs from the activities and responses of public-sector bureaucracies in other Western political systems, is to a large extent a function of what David Bazelon has called "non-rule in America." It is characteristic that Congress felt impelled not long ago to pass a Freedom of Information Act, in an effort to open non-classified bureaucratic files to the interested public; and it is also characteristic that the Act's effectiveness has thus far been at best mixed.

Not surprisingly, suggestions for reform in a "non-rule" climate have been many, among them Dumont's advocacy of "guerrilla administration" staffed by people whose roles are structured around a negation of the bureaucracy's survival rules. Interestingly, such a proposal necessarily implies the creation of instrumentalities of *dual power*—the old regime structure paralleled in one or more of its vital points by another which presumably taps a different and much broader clientele in the mass public. While Dumont could not be classified as revolutionary, the creation of effective structures of dual power has been recognized by analysts everywhere as at least a potentially revolutionary act. It hardly needs saying that the established political leaderships of the cities and states share a decided aversion to a dual power structure. But for our purposes, it cannot be stated forcefully enough that the preconditions for dual power come into being only when the legitimacy of the existing political structure has already undergone severe erosion. And one of the major causes of this erosion, in Chalmers Johnson's phrase this "power deflation," is a growing sense among little people that the existing structure has turned a deaf ear to their vital needs.

Non-rule in the American—or any other—political system has major implications for the core of the political struggle: "who gets what, when, and how." Under conditions of non-rule, it can be presupposed that the basic outcomes of policy will be determined by a balance of forces among organized groups, with the large majority of these organized groups, as the late E. E. Schattschneider insisted, articulating the financial and power interests of the owners of the American economy. For nearly a century, analysts have turned to Congress and the legislative process to study these processes in their purest form, with perspectives ranging from a nearly uncritical acceptance of "pluralism" to sweeping critiques of the process itself and its results. In truth, Congress behaves as one would expect it to behave, granting the primordial importance of "non-rule" and its consequence, the control of public policy domestically by ever-shifting coalitions of upper-middle-class interests. Indeed, since the destruction of the Speaker's centralizing and highly partisan powers in the 1910–11 House and the full incorporation of the seniority rule which paralleled it in time, Congress has pushed non-rule within its own halls to extremes going far beyond what even separation of powers requires. One result of this is the kind of policy controversy—and process, complete with outcome—which Gehlen discusses in her essay on women in Congress. It can be said first that there are very few of them; second, that the seniority rule, being automatic, elevates them to chairmanships if their tenure is long enough; and third, that many of the most important informal processes by which the pies are cut up—the Speaker's "Board of Education," for instance—virtually exclude women.

Any discussion of national policy elites and politics must take notice of the chief characteristics of Congress. Briefly, they are these:

1. Effective decisional power is dispersed centrifugally into committees and subcommittees, with senior members and especially chairman being particularly influential.
2. Party discipline does not exist except on questions

such as the organization of the House at each new Congress; and this is the "reciprocal," indeed the major precondition, of committee ascendancy in legislative policy making, and of the seniority system for recruitment of members and chairmen of committees.

3. There are proportionately far fewer working-class and white-collar people, and women, among members of both houses than in any Western European parliament. The modal profession of national legislators is the law: in recent years, lawyers have comprised between 55 and 60 percent of the membership of both houses.

4. This fragmented decisional process is interpenetrated at every point with organized group influences such as those the drug industry exercised over amphetamine legislation. Interpenetration is also associated with an atmosphere of laxity about financial transactions between legislators and outside business interests which is notorious, and which in its own way has contributed not a little to public cynicism about Congress and the political process generally.

5. Since demands often arise from that public which is outside (and socially beneath) the producer-interest group structure that interpenetrates Congress, it is often the case that legislation is passed which nominally answers the demand but in fact makes little or no change in concrete policy. Politicians are adept at using the legislative machinery to proclaim symbolic recognition of a non-elite group demand while at the same time ensuring that the actual price tag of the legislation is small or non-existent. This, too, is a fruitful source of the credibility gap: the process is so structured as to reinforce systematically a gap between promise and performance.

In this regard, we may take note of Lipsky and Olson's sensitive discussion of the government's increasing use of the Commission device to deal with demands which—like urban riots—have got out of hand. As these authors point out, the commissions operate in an intensely political context; they operate under severe resource constraints, and they are not authoritative but must compete with other groups in the process. As a result, they cannot and do not get to the bottom of things. What they do do, as a matter of fact if not of conscious intent, is to buy time, permitting decision-makers to act not now but later. There is a kind of sameness, an "eternal recurrence" around this process, which has prompted Kenneth Clark to refer to it as "Alice in Wonderland": the same problems, the same investigations, the same conclusions, the same inaction. And indeed,

if one reads the 1922 Illinois Commission report on the 1919 race riot in Chicago together with the Kerner Commission report forty-five years later, it is difficult not to agree with Clark's estimate. Once again, these efforts—which may be well-meaning but are cosmetic in the context of the political process in which they are made—can only serve to raise credibility issues in the minds of the interested public outside.

There may be a curious lesson in all this. The dynamics of the system are such that top decision-makers who wish to engineer any significant change in policy outputs—whether at home or abroad—are driven into a hyperbolic syndrome. They must, in Theodore Lowi's words, first oversell the threat and then oversell the remedy in order to create the conditions for overriding the fragmenting thrust of group action and congressional structure. This dynamic itself leads to loss of credibility and to a sense of outrage when it is found—as it is nearly always found—that the remedy didn't really remove the threat after all. "The last state of that man is worse than the first," since what one really achieves is alienation of those interests who interpret the oversell as threats to themselves on one hand, and the creation of a large resentful group of people with disappointed expectations on the other. Some conservatives have seen this point clearly, and have drawn the inference: the best thing to do is not to raise any expectations in the first place. The Nixon administration has said as much on more than one occasion; and E. C. Banfield's *The Unheavenly City* is filled with policy discussion and policy advice which proceeds from such premises.

There may be something to this conservative approach. If system stability and public legitimacy are to be preserved, then there may well be policy issues which it must leave alone altogether, since their resolution would be subversive of both. But such a philosophy of "you can't get there from here" has another, and possibly very cutting, edge. If demand arises from objective social and economic dislocations and deprivations which have spilled over into the political arena, refusal to meet it on the ground that the system cannot produce the goods wanted can itself contribute to a collapse of that system's political legitimacy. The ultimate test of this will, of course, be empirical; but it will be going on throughout the rest of this century. And very probably the horns of this dilemma will become more and more visible to policy analysts and laymen alike as the historical process unfolds.

The Best-Known American

Fred I. Greenstein

People in the streets around Times Square could hardly believe the news. A man in evening dress said, "It can't be true." There was a steady stream of telephone calls to newspaper offices by persons seeking to verify the news.

(A congressman of an opposing party said): "Oh what a calamity. This is a tremendous shock. . . . Politics are now forgotten in the love all factions had for him as a man."

(On the official day of mourning) . . . public activity was suspended; banks, stores, theaters, and movie houses were closed. At noon, the entire nation observed two minutes of silence in honor of the dead President.

The President described in this newspaper account was not John F. Kennedy, it was Warren G. Harding. Harding was not considered a romantic figure; he was not young, not dead from other than natural causes. But he was the President.

Very similar shock and disturbance was also recorded when Franklin D. Roosevelt died in office in 1945 and there have been reports of similar public reaction to every Presidential death since Lincoln's. The descriptions of psychological responses to presidential deaths are, in general, so identical as to be interchangeable. In each instance the same sense of shock and loss, the public weeping, people acting dazed and disoriented, and showing the symptoms of anxiety.

The public reaction to Kennedy's death is certainly freshest in memory, and was the most completely recorded. It was extensively documented in a national survey conducted immediately after his assassination, three years ago this month. A large majority of the respondents (79 percent) reported that their immediate and "deeply felt" reaction was to think of the President's death as "the loss of someone very close and dear." Half of the national sample acknowledged having wept, many reported such symptoms as loss of appetite (43 percent), insomnia (48 percent), general feelings of nervousness and tension (68 percent). Throughout the following weekend, people were unable or unwilling to carry on normal activities. The average adult spent eight hours on Friday, ten hours on Saturday, eight hours on Sunday, and another eight hours on Monday tuned in on television and radio reports of the assassination and its aftermath.

Of course, Kennedy's comparative youth, his personality, the times, and the tragic manner of his death had much to do with this strong reaction. But Roosevelt, a much older man, died of natural causes, and the effect on the public was in most respects identical.

It may be pointed out that both Kennedy and Roosevelt were colorful, attractive, and controversial men, Presidents in time of crises, men associated with strong policies who tended to rouse passion in both partisans and critics. But what of Harding?

The deaths of other public figures—political leaders, ex-Presidents, religious leaders, entertainment celebrities—do not produce similar reactions, except in very specialized segments of the population.

These extraordinary outbursts of public emotion toward the President are one side of a striking paradox in American political behavior. The other side is the remarkable indifference of most Americans to the sphere of society in which the President is a key actor. This indifference has been documented in endless ways in public opinion surveys:

—80 percent of the electorate do not usually discuss politics.

—90 percent never write public officials.

—45 percent do not know how many senators there are from each state.

—53 percent do not know how long congressmen are elected for; few voters even know who their state congressman is.

How do we account for the seeming inconsistency between public indifference to politics and the profound emotional outpouring that results when the nation's chief political figure dies in office?

There are a number of information sources which shed some light on the matter. First, we possess a good deal of research on public opinion among adults. Then recently there have been significant investigations into children's attitudes toward political authority. Finally, an interesting, if uneven, collection of psychiatric case histories has accumulated over the years, detailing what psychiatric patients have thought, said, and felt about subjects touching on high ranking authorities. Tied together, these three sources—even

if they do not fully resolve the inconsistency—can lead us to some enlightening, if speculative, conclusions about the psychological meaning of the presidency to Americans.

Adult Views about the President

The polls make clear that the President is the best known political figure in the United States. Indeed, he must be the best known person in the nation. This, as we have seen, is not true of other authorities and politicians. More than half of all voters are typically unable to name—or even to recognize the names of—such leading figures as cabinet secretaries, governors of major states, and Supreme Court Justices. In September 1963, less than a year before he received the Republican presidential nomination, Barry Goldwater was unknown to a full 42 percent of a Gallup Poll national sample.

Public officials are less well known than most mass entertainment figures (motion picture stars, television celebrities, athletes), many of whom are familiar to 90 percent or more of the public. But nearly everyone (95 percent) knows the President's name. For many Americans the President provides virtually the sole cognitive link to the political system, a fact related to the consistent ability of twentieth century Presidents to be reelected. (Only two have been defeated; one, Hoover, during a major depression, and the other, Taft, as a result of a major party split.)

A second poll finding is that high public officials are greatly respected in American society. Americans commonly express dislike and distrust of "politicians." But when they are asked to rank occupations according to "general standing," they regularly place such positions as Supreme Court justice, governor, and senator at the top of their rankings, ahead of even the most prestigious civilian role (which happens to be that of physician). Curiously, the presidency itself has never been included in such studies, but, if it were, everything we know would lead us to expect it to be ranked on top.

A third poll finding is that most incumbent Presidents, on most occasions, receive considerably more approval than disapproval. In the case of Presidents Roosevelt, Eisenhower, Kennedy, and Johnson, the regular Gallup Poll assessments of "how good a job the President is doing" *never* found more people disapproving than approving. The only exception has been President Truman; when he took office after Roosevelt's death he received the highest favorable rating ever recorded by the Gallup Poll (87 percent), but at a later point was rated favorably by only 23 percent of the electorate.

A remarkable range of presidential public decorum has proved to be consistent with public approval of the incumbent President—Roosevelt's aristocratic bearing, Eisenhower's folksiness, Kennedy's detached intellectuality and wit, Johnson's use of the idiom of the American Southwest. Yet there evidently are limits to what is considered consistent with the dignity of the presidential role, limits which very probably were transcended in Truman's scrappy partisanship and his occasional public displays of temper.

Fourth, we may note the consistent readiness of citizens to come to the President's support in times of crisis, particularly international crisis. While assessments of the President's performance are generally more positive than negative, his public esteem does fluctuate. Very often the increases in presidential popularity follow fast upon some major presidential action. When the decision was made to resist the Communist invasion of South Korea, President Truman's popularity rose—within the period of a single month—from 37 percent approval to 46 percent approval. Eisenhower's popularity rose from 67 percent to 75 percent during the month of the Suez crisis, and from 52 percent to 58 percent after sending the marines to Lebanon in 1958. Roosevelt's popularity rose from 72 to 84 percent after Pearl Harbor.

More recently, President Johnson's popularity, after suffering a steady erosion during the intensified Vietnamese fighting in the first half of 1966, rose from 50 to 56 percent following the bombing of oil supply dumps in the area of Hanoi and Haiphong.

Even unsuccessful international actions have led to increased presidential popularity. Eisenhower's popularity went up by 6 percentage points after the U-2 incident and the collapse of the Paris summit meetings; Kennedy's by 10 points after the Bay of Pigs invasion. Typically, a rally-around-the-President effect also takes place just after election or reelection, indicating that there is a substance to the familiar metaphor which sees public office as a "mantle" of majesty and authority that has been placed on his shoulders, changing his image. John F. Kennedy had the support of only a fraction of 1 percent more than half of the electorate in November 1960; but by the time of his inauguration, only two months later, 69 percent approved of him.

Finally, there is evidence that citizens perceive and judge the President largely in personal terms. In early 1948 a three-state sample of voters who had already indicated who they wanted elected were asked: "What are the qualities that you think would make him the best man (for President)?" Personal qualities exceeded ideological references more than fourfold. When people were asked during the 1950's what they liked or disliked about President Eisenhower, they most commonly referred to his personal characteristics, conscientiousness, warmth or coldness, physical vigor, sincerity and integrity, religious background and practice. There also were references to policy positions and leadership or lack of it—but together these were less frequent than statements about personal qualities. Comparable evidence exists about Kennedy and Nixon in the 1960 campaign. For both there were substantially fewer references to policy commitments than to the man.

In summary, the surveys show that the President is almost universally known, standing out with far greater clarity than other actors on the political scene; his role seems to be highly respected; his personal popularity fluctuates, but tends generally to be high; support for him increases when he takes decisive action, particularly actions which commit the nation in the international arena; he is perceived and judged to a considerable extent in personal terms.

Children's Views about the President

The President normally is the first public official of whom children become aware. By the age of nine (and usually earlier) virtually every child knows the name of the incumbent President. Like the least informed adults, however, they know very little else about government and politics. But they already share the adult conception of the importance of high political office. Nine-year-olds, asked to rank occupations in terms of importance, place the President at the top, well above such groups as physicians, school teachers, and clergymen. In addition, young children see the President in overwhelmingly favorable terms, thinking of him as benevolent and helpful. The following statements are typical:
—"The President is doing a very good job of helping people to be safe."
—"The President . . . takes care of the U.S."
—"The President has the right to stop bad things before they start."

These early childhood attitudes provide a fascinating problem for analysis. They evidently develop quite subtly, in ways not easy to untangle or explain. Young children are apparently not *taught* to believe the President important and virtuous. In fact, they ordinarily are not explicitly taught about the presidency at all in the early school years. Rather, the notion that the President is "very important" seems unconsciously to build up in the child's mind from casual exposure to such sources as the mass media and adult conversations. The firmness of a young child's belief in the importance of the President, despite absence of accurate information about what he really does, can be seen in this interview conducted in the 1950's, with a seven-year-old:

INTERVIEWER: Have you heard of the President of the United States?
ROBERT: Yes.
I: What is his name?
R: Eisenhower.
I: What does he do?
R: Well, sometimes he . . . well, you know . . . a lot of times when people go away he'll say good-bye and he's on programs and they do work.
I: What kind of work does he do? Do you know any more about it?
R: (After thought) Studying.
I: What sort of things does he study?
R: Like things they gotta do . . . like important . . . what's happening and the weather and all that.
I: Now tell me this. Who is more important, the President of the United States or a doctor?

R: (Pause) The President.
I: Who do you think is more important, the President of the United States or a school teacher?
R: (Emphatically) President!
I: Why is the President more important?
R: They do much more work and they're much importanter. School teacher isn't.
I: (After being told in response to further questions that the President is also more important than a storekeeper and than a general in the army): Who do you think is more important than the President?
R: (Long pause) Lemme see . . . I don't know.

What "information" Robert does have about the Presidency is largely imaginative. It is assembled from the important activities of Robert's older brother, who studies his homework, and from a hazy recollection of the television news broadcasts that transmit somewhat mysterious communications to the adults of the family in the intervals between the children's shows. Yet Robert's basic disposition toward the presidency (which only later will be filled in with specific information) is already well formed.

A rather similar course can be found in the development of political party loyalties. Here also the basic emotional stance—the underlying attitude that "I am a Democrat" or "I am a Republican"—comes first and then gradually the information upon which we might expect such attitudes to be based develops and falls into line.

It has been argued that children's early conceptions of the presidential role provide them with "perceptual filters," which shape their later learning about politics; and that the positive nature of these early conceptions should contribute to a generally favorable orientation toward the political system.

Deeper Feelings About the President

Another source of insight into the psychological meaning of the President to citizens comes from psychiatric literature. Although not very well documented, the suggestions from this source are intriguing and merit further study.

As Freud saw it, the mind tends to thrust out of consciousness distasteful thoughts—such as emotionally painful memories of childhood experiences and unacceptable impulses, many of which are sexual or aggressive. But what is repressed often reappears in other guises—in dreams and neurotic symptoms, and as latent meaning underlying and coloring much of everyday life.

Early conflicts with parents, who are the ultimate authorities in a young child's life, produce much of this repression. Typically there are two inconsistent (in psychiatric jargon "ambivalent") impulses toward family authority that the child forces out of consciousness—the need to be excessively submissive and the need to express hostility, to rebel. In later life, according to this line of psychiatric reasoning, these repressed feelings toward the private authorities of childhood are expressed in citizens' reactions to public authorities such as the President.

There are two reasons why this still imperfectly documented psychiatric reasoning is of interest.

First, psychiatric explanations are especially geared to deal with the seeming paradox of emotional reactions that are out of proportion to the individual's prior attitudes and behavior—for example, intense mourning at the death of an individual one had expressed little feeling toward. In such a case the psychiatrist expects to find that unconscious feelings had been present all along.

Second, even if one does not accept the underlying theory, psychiatric case histories of patients in treatment give unusual insight into feelings and responses that cannot readily be observed in more formal interviews. For example, when President Roosevelt died a number of psychoanalysts reported that their patients reacted in ways that clearly indicated they identified him with one or both of their parents. One analyst found similar associations among his patients even during the less extreme circumstances of the election campaigns of 1948, 1952, and 1956. President Kennedy—in spite of his youth—affected some patients in the same manner, both before and after his death.

What Does the Presidency Mean?

Drawing on the three kinds of research findings, we can suggest several ways in which the President seems to have psychological meaning for citizens:

■ By virtue of being a single highly publicized figure who combines the roles of political leader and head of state the President *simplifies perception* of government and politics. Just as the modern American President has come to be the main source of energy and initiative in the actual workings of the government, he also serves as the main "handle" for providing busy citizens with a sense of what their government is doing. For some citizens the President is virtually the only vehicle for following government and politics, and for children he serves as an instrument of civic learning.

■ The President provides citizens with an *outlet for emotional expression*. In addition to his obvious uses in partisan politics, there are his ceremonial duties and the publicized aspects of his (and his family's) private life. Here again

we have an equivalent to the more dignified displays of symbolic activity associated elsewhere in the world with monarchs. In these aspects of his role the President competes for attention very favorably with such professional celebrities as film stars.

■ The President serves as a *symbol of unity*. The public reaction to a presidential death is a grim instance of the unifying power of the presidency. Despite strong political partisanship, the overwhelming impression that comes through is of the homogeneity of public support. Regret at President Kennedy's death was shared by pro-Kennedy Northern Negroes and anti-Kennedy Southern whites. Another instance, already noted, is the rally-round spirit—the tendency of citizens to come to the support of their President in time of international crisis, regardless of the merits of the dispute.

■ It may well be that in times of crisis, the President serves still another function, providing citizens with a *vicarious means of taking political action*. It seems quite likely that at such times numerous people find themselves "identifying" with the President, at least in the superficial fashion in which we find ourselves taking the part of the hero of a motion picture or novel. To the degree that the President's actions are effective, citizens who identify themselves with him may experience heightened feelings of strength—of being in a world which is not completely dependent upon external circumstances and events.

■ Finally, whether or not one psychically takes the part of the President, it is clear that he serves as a reassuring *symbol of social stability*. For many people, one of the most disturbing aspects of President Kennedy's assassination was the implication that went with it of lack of control—of possible national and international disaster. (As a college student put it, "We're always pushing how civilized we are . . . then here in the United States a President gets assassinated.") This, in effect, is the direct opposite of the crisis situation in which a calm and decisive President by seeming to be in firm command, enhances the citizens' feelings of confidence and security.

It is a caricature of the complex, sprawling, uncoordinated nature of the American political system to see it as a great ship of state, sailing on with the President firmly at the helm. But a great many people find comfort in this oversimplified image.

The Two Presidencies

Aaron Wildavsky

The United States has one President, but it has two presidencies; one presidency is for domestic affairs, and the other is concerned with defense and foreign policy. Since World War II, Presidents have had much greater success in controlling the nation's defense and foreign policies than in dominating its domestic policies. Even Lyndon Johnson has seen his early record of victories in domestic legislation diminish as his concern with foreign affairs grows.

What powers does the President have to control defense and foreign policies and so completely overwhelm those who might wish to thwart him?

The President's normal problem with domestic policy is to get congressional support for the programs he prefers. In foreign affairs, in contrast, he can almost always get support for policies that he believes will protect the nation —but his problem is to find a viable policy.

Whoever they are, whether they begin by caring about foreign policy like Eisenhower and Kennedy or about domestic policies like Truman and Johnson, Presidents soon discover they have more policy preferences in domestic matters than in foreign policy. The Republican and Democratic parties possess a traditional roster of policies, which can easily be adopted by a new President—for example, he can be either for or against Medicare and aid to education. Since existing domestic policy usually changes in only small steps, Presidents find it relatively simple to make minor adjustments. However, although any President knows he supports foreign aid and NATO, the world outside changes much more rapidly than the nation inside—Presidents and their parties have no prior policies on Argentina and the Congo. The world has become a highly intractable place with a whirl of forces we cannot or do not know how to alter.

The Record of Presidential Control

It takes great crises, such as Roosevelt's hundred days in the midst of the depression, or the extraordinary majorities that Barry Goldwater's candidacy willed to Lyndon Johnson, for Presidents to succeed in controlling domestic policy. From the end of the 1930's to the present (what may roughly be called the modern era), Presidents have often been frustrated in their domestic programs. From 1938, when conservatives regrouped their forces, to the time of his death, Franklin Roosevelt did not get a single piece of significant domestic legislation passed. Truman lost out on most of his intense domestic preferences, except perhaps for housing. Since Eisenhower did not ask for much domestic legislation, he did not meet consistent defeat, yet he failed in his general policy of curtailing governmental commitments. Kennedy, of course, faced great difficulties with domestic legislation.

In the realm of foreign policy there has not been a single major issue on which Presidents, when they were serious and determined, have failed. The list of their victories is impressive: entry into the United Nations, the Marshall Plan, NATO, the Truman Doctrine, the decisions to stay out of Indochina in 1954 and to intervene in Vietnam in the 1960's, aid to Poland and Yugoslavia, the test-ban treaty, and many more. Serious setbacks to the President in controlling foreign policy are extraordinary and unusual.

Table I, compiled from the Congressional Quarterly Service tabulation of presidential initiative and congres-

> "In the realm of foreign policy there has not been a single major issue on which Presidents, when they were serious and determined, have failed."

sional response from 1948 through 1964, shows that Presidents have significantly better records in foreign and defense matters than in domestic policies. When refugees and immigration—which Congress considers primarily a domestic concern—are removed from the general foreign policy area, it is clear that Presidents prevail about 70 percent of the time in defense and foreign policy, compared with 40 percent in the domestic sphere.

World Events and Presidential Resources

Power in politics is control over governmental decisions. How does the President manage his control of foreign and defense policy? The answer does not reside in the greater constitutional power in foreign affairs that Presidents have possessed since the founding of the Republic. The answer lies in the changes that have taken place since 1945.

The number of nations with which the United States has diplomatic relations has increased from 53 in 1939 to 113 in 1966. But sheer numbers do not tell enough; the world has also become a much more dangerous place. However remote it may seem at times, our government must always be aware of the possibility of nuclear war.

TABLE I—Congressional Action on Presidential Proposals From 1948-1964.

Policy Area	Congressional Action % Pass	% Fail	Number of Proposals
Domestic policy (natural resources, labor, agriculture, taxes, etc.)	40.2	59.8	2499
Defense policy (defense, disarmament, manpower, misc.)	73.3	26.7	90
Foreign policy	58.5	41.5	655
Immigration, refugees	13.2	86.0	129
Treaties, general foreign relations, State Department, foreign aid	70.8	29.2	445

Source: Congressional Quarterly Service, *Congress and the Nation*, 1945-1964 (Washington, 1965)

Yet the mere existence of great powers with effective thermonuclear weapons would not, in and of itself, vastly increase our rate of interaction with most other nations. We see events in Assam or Burundi as important because they are also part of a larger worldwide contest, called the cold war, in which great powers are rivals for the control or support of other nations. Moreover, the reaction against the blatant isolationism of the 1930's has led to a concern with foreign policy that is worldwide in scope. We are interested in what happens everywhere because we see these events as connected with larger interests involving, at the worst, the possibility of ultimate destruction.

Given the overriding fact that the world is dangerous and that small causes are perceived to have potentially great effects in an unstable world, it follows that Presidents must be interested in relatively "small" matters. So they give Azerbaijan or Lebanon or Vietnam huge amounts of their time. Arthur Schlesinger, Jr., wrote of Kennedy that "in the first two months of his administration he probably spent more time on Laos than on anything else." Few failures in domestic policy, Presidents soon realize, could have as disastrous consequences as any one of dozens of mistakes in the international arena.

The result is that foreign policy concerns tend to drive out domestic policy. Except for occasional questions of domestic prosperity and for civil rights, foreign affairs have consistently higher priority for Presidents. Once, when trying to talk to President Kennedy about natural resources, Secretary of the Interior Stewart Udall remarked, "He's imprisoned by Berlin."

The importance of foreign affairs to Presidents is intensified by the increasing speed of events in the international arena. The event and its consequences follow closely on top of one another. The blunder at the Bay of Pigs is swiftly followed by the near catastrophe of the Cuban missile crisis. Presidents can no longer count on passing along their most difficult problems to their successors. They must expect to face the consequences of their actions—or failure to act—while still in office.

Domestic policy-making is usually based on experimental adjustments to an existing situation. Only a few decisions, such as those involving large dams, irretrievably commit future generations. Decisions in foreign affairs, however, are often perceived to be irreversible. This is expressed, for example, in the fear of escalation or the various "spiral" or "domino" theories of international conflict.

If decisions are perceived to be both important and irreversible, there is every reason for Presidents to devote a great deal of resources to them. Presidents have to be oriented toward the future in the use of their resources. They serve a fixed term in office, and they cannot automatically count on support from the populace, Congress, or the administrative apparatus. They have to be careful, therefore, to husband their resources for pressing future needs. But because the consequences of events in foreign affairs are potentially more grave, faster to manifest themselves, and less easily reversible than in domestic affairs, Presidents are more willing to use up their resources.

The Power to Act

Their formal powers to commit resources in foreign

affairs and defense are vast. Particularly important is their power as Commander-in-Chief to move troops. Faced with situations like the invasion of South Korea or the emplacement of missiles in Cuba, fast action is required. Presidents possess both the formal power to act and the knowledge that elites and the general public expect them to act. Once they have committed American forces, it is difficult for Congress or anyone else to alter the course of events. The Dominican venture is a recent case in point.

Presidential discretion in foreign affairs also makes it difficult (though not impossible) for Congress to restrict their actions. Presidents can use executive agreements instead of treaties, enter into tacit agreements instead of written ones, and otherwise help create *de facto* situations not easily reversed. Presidents also have far greater ability than anyone else to obtain information on developments abroad through the Departments of State and Defense. The need for secrecy in some aspects of foreign and defense policy further restricts the ability of others to compete with Presidents. These things are all well known. What is not so generally appreciated is the growing presidential ability to *use* information to achieve goals.

In the past Presidents were amateurs in military strategy. They could not even get much useful advice outside of the military. As late as the 1930's the number of people outside the military establishment who were professionally engaged in the study of defense policy could be numbered on the fingers. Today there are hundreds of such men. The rise of the defense intellectuals has given the President of the United States enhanced ability to control defense policy. He is no longer dependent on the military for advice. He can choose among defense intellectuals from the research corporations and the academies for alternative sources of advice. He can install these men in his own office. He can play them off against each other or use them to extend spheres of coordination.

Even with these advisers, however, Presidents and Secretaries of Defense might still be too bewildered by the complexity of nuclear situations to take action—unless they had an understanding of the doctrine and concepts of deterrence. But knowledge of doctrine about deterrence has been widely diffused; it can be picked up by any intelligent person who will read books or listen to enough hours of conversation. Whether or not the doctrine is good is a separate question; the point is that civilians can feel they understand what is going on in defense policy. Perhaps the most extraordinary feature of presidential action during the Cuban missile crisis was the degree to which the Commander-in-Chief of the Armed Forces insisted on control-

ling even the smallest moves. From the positioning of ships to the methods of boarding, to the precise words and actions to be taken by individual soldiers and sailors, the President and his civilian advisers were in control.

Although Presidents have rivals for power in foreign affairs, the rivals do not usually succeed. Presidents prevail not only because they may have superior resources but because their potential opponents are weak, divided, or believe that they should not control foreign policy. Let us consider the potential rivals—the general citizenry, special interest groups, the Congress, the military, the so-called military-industrial complex, and the State Department.

Competitors for Control of Policy

■ THE PUBLIC. The general public is much more dependent on Presidents in foreign affairs than in domestic matters. While many people know about the impact of social security and Medicare, few know about politics in Malawi. So it is not surprising that people expect the President to act in foreign affairs and reward him with their confidence. Gallup Polls consistently show that presidential popularity rises after he takes action in a crisis—whether the action is disastrous as in the Bay of Pigs or successful as in the Cuban missile crisis. Decisive action, such as the bombing of oil fields near Haiphong, resulted in a sharp (though temporary) increase in Johnson's popularity.

The Vietnam situation illustrates another problem of public opinion in foreign affairs: it is extremely difficult to get operational policy directions from the general public. It took a long time before any sizable public interest in the subject developed. Nothing short of the large scale involvement of American troops under fire probably could have brought about the current high level of concern. Yet this relatively well developed popular opinion is difficult to interpret. While a majority appear to support President Johnson's policy, it appears that they could easily be persuaded to withdraw from Vietnam if the administration changed its line. Although a sizable majority would support various initiatives to end the war, they would seemingly be appalled if this action led to Communist encroachments elsewhere in Southeast Asia. (See "The President, the Polls, and Vietnam" by Seymour Martin Lipset.)

Although Presidents lead opinion in foreign affairs, they know they will be held accountable for the consequences of their actions. President Johnson has maintained a large commitment in Vietnam. His popularity shoots up now and again in the midst of some imposing action. But the fact that a body of citizens do not like the war comes back to damage his overall popularity. We will support your initiatives, the people seem to say, but we will reserve the right to punish you (or your party) if we do not like the results.

■ SPECIAL INTEREST GROUPS. Opinions are easier to gauge in domestic affairs because, for one thing, there is a stable structure of interest groups that covers virtually all matters of concern. The farm, labor, business, conservation, veteran, civil rights, and other interest groups provide cues when a proposed policy affects them. Thus people who identify with these groups may adopt their views. But in foreign policy matters the interest group structure is weak, unstable, and thin rather than dense. In many matters affecting Africa and Asia, for example, it is hard to think of well-known interest groups. While ephemeral groups arise from time to time to support or protest particular policies, they usually disappear when the immediate problem is resolved. In contrast, longer-lasting elite groups like the Foreign Policy Association and Council on Foreign Relations are composed of people of diverse views; refusal to take strong positions on controversial matters is a condition of their continued viability.

The strongest interest groups are probably the ethnic associations whose members have strong ties with a homeland, as in Poland or Cuba, so they are rarely activated simultaneously on any specific issue. They are most effective when most narrowly and intensely focused—as in the fierce pressure from Jews to recognize the state of Israel. But their relatively small numbers limits their significance to Presidents in the vastly more important general foreign policy picture—as continued aid to the Arab countries shows. Moreover, some ethnic groups may conflict on significant issues such as American acceptance of the Oder-Neisse line separating Poland from what is now East Germany.

■ THE CONGRESS. Congressmen also exercise power in foreign affairs. Yet they are ordinarily not serious competitors with the President because they follow a self-denying ordinance. They do not think it is their job to determine the nation's defense policies. Lewis A. Dexter's extensive interviews with members of the Senate Armed Services Committee, who might be expected to want a voice in defense policy, reveal that they do not desire for men like themselves to run the nation's defense establishment. Aside from a few specific conflicts among the armed services which allow both the possibility and desirablity of direct intervention, the Armed Services Committee constitutes a sort of real estate committee dealing with the regional economic consequences of the location of military facilities.

The congressional appropriations power is potentially a significant resource, but circumstances since the end of World War II have tended to reduce its effectiveness. The appropriations committees and Congress itself might make their will felt by refusing to allot funds unless basic policies were altered. But this has not happened. While Congress makes its traditional small cuts in the military budget, Presidents have mostly found themselves warding off congressional attempts to increase specific items still further.

Most of the time, the administration's refusal to spend has not been seriously challenged. However, there have been occasions when individual legislators or committees have been influential. Senator Henry Jackson in his campaign (with the aid of colleagues on the Joint Committee on Atomic Energy) was able to gain acceptance for the Polaris weapons system and Senator Arthur H. Vandenberg played a part in determining the shape of the Marshall Plan and so on. The few congressmen who are expert in defense policy act, as Samuel P. Huntington says, largely as lobbyists with the executive branch. It is apparently more fruitful for these congressional experts to use their resources in order to get a hearing from the executive than to work on other congressmen.

When an issue involves the actual use or threat of violence, it takes a great deal to convince congressmen not to follow the President's lead. James Robinson's tabulation of foreign and defense policy issues from the late 1930's to 1961 (Table II) shows dominant influence by Congress in only one case out of seven—the 1954 decision not to intervene with armed force in Indochina. In that instance President Eisenhower deliberately sounded out congressional opinion and, finding it negative, decided not to intervene —against the advice of Admiral Radford, chairman of the Joint Chiefs of Staff. This attempt to abandon responsibility did not succeed, as the years of American involvement demonstrate.

■ THE MILITARY. The outstanding feature of the military's participation in making defense policy is their amazing weakness. Whether the policy decisions involve the size of the armed forces, the choice of weapons systems, the total defense budget, or its division into components, the military have not prevailed. Let us take budgetary decisions as representative of the key choices to be made in defense policy. Since the end of World War II the military has not been able to achieve significant (billion dollar) increases in appropriations by their own efforts. Under Truman and Eisenhower defense budgets were determined by what Huntington calls the remainder method: the two Presidents estimated revenues, decided what they could spend on domestic matters, and the remainder was assigned to defense. The usual controversy was between some military and congressional groups supporting much larger expenditures while the President and his executive allies refused. A typical case, involving the desire of the Air Force to increase the number of groups of planes is described by Huntington in *The Common Defense:*

> The FY [fiscal year] 1949 budget provided 48 groups. After the Czech coup, the Administration yielded and backed an Air Force of 55 groups in its spring rearmament program. Congress added additional funds to aid Air Force expansion to 70 groups. The Administration refused to utilize them, however, and in the gathering economy wave of the summer and fall of 1948, the Air Force goal was cut back again to 48 groups. In 1949 the House of Representatives picked up the challenge and appropriated funds for 58 groups. The President impounded the money. In June, 1950, the Air Force had 48 groups.

The great increases in the defense budget were due far more to Stalin and modern technology than to the military. The Korean War resulted in an increase from 12 to 44 billions and much of the rest followed Sputnik and the huge costs of missile programs. Thus modern technology and international conflict put an end to the one major effort to subordinate foreign affairs to domestic policies through the budget.

It could be argued that the President merely ratifies the decisions made by the military and their allies. If the military and/or Congress were united and insistent on defense policy, it would certainly be difficult for Presidents to resist these forces. But it is precisely the disunity of the military that has characterized the entire postwar period. Indeed, the military have not been united on any major matter of defense policy. The apparent unity of the Joint Chiefs of Staff turns out to be illusory. The vast majority of their recommendations appear to be unanimous and are accepted by the Secretary of Defense and the President. But this facade of unity can only be achieved by methods that vitiate the impact of the recommendations. Genuine disagreements are hidden by vague language that commits no one to anything. Mutually contradictory plans are strung together so everyone appears to get something, but nothing is decided. Since it is impossible to agree on really important matters, all sorts of trivia are brought in to make a record of agreement. While it may be true, as Admiral Denfield, a former Chief of Naval Operations, said, that "On nine-tenths of the matters that come before them the Joint Chiefs of Staff

reach agreement themselves," the vastly more important truth is that "normally the *only* disputes are on strategic concepts, the size and composition of forces, and budget matters."

■ MILITARY-INDUSTRIAL. But what about the fabled military-industrial complex? If the military alone is divided and weak, perhaps the giant industrial firms that are so dependent on defense contracts play a large part in making policy.

First, there is an important distinction between the questions "Who will get a given contract?" and "What will our defense policy be?" It is apparent that different answers may be given to these quite different questions. There are literally tens of thousands of defense contractors. They may compete vigorously for business. In the course of this competition, they may wine and dine military officers, use retired generals, seek intervention by their congressmen, place ads in trade journals, and even contribute to political campaigns. The famous TFX controversy—should General Dynamics or Boeing get the expensive contract?—is a larger than life example of the pressures brought to bear in search of lucrative contracts.

But neither the TFX case nor the usual vigorous competition for contracts is involved with the making of substantive defense policy. Vital questions like the size of the defense budget, the choice of strategic programs, massive retaliation vs. a counter-city strategy, and the like were far beyond the policy aims of any company. Industrial firms, then, do not control such decisions, nor is there much evidence that they actually try. No doubt a precipitous and drastic rush to disarmament would meet with opposition from industrial firms among other interests. However, there has never been a time when any significant element in the government considered a disarmament policy to be feasible.

It may appear that industrial firms had no special reason to concern themselves with the government's stance on defense because they agree with the national consensus on resisting communism, maintaining a large defense establishment, and rejecting isolationism. However, this hypothesis about the climate of opinion explains everything and nothing. For every policy that is adopted or rejected can be explained away on the grounds that the cold war climate of opinion dictated what happened. Did the United States fail to intervene with armed force in Vietnam in 1954? That must be because the climate of opinion was against it. Did the United States send troops to Vietnam in the 1960's? That must be because the cold war climate demanded it. If the United States builds more missiles, negotiates a test-ban treaty, intervenes in the Dominican Republic, fails to intervene in a dozen other situations, all these actions fit the hypothesis by definition. The argument is reminiscent of those who defined the Soviet Union as permanently hostile and therefore interpreted increases of Soviet troops as menacing and decreases of troop strength as equally sinister.

If the growth of the military establishment is not directly equated with increasing military control of defense policy, the extraordinary weakness of the professional soldier still requires explanation. Huntington has written about how major military leaders were seduced in the Truman and Eisenhower years into believing that they should bow to the judgment of civilians that the economy could not stand much larger military expenditures. Once the size of the military pie was accepted as a fixed constraint, the military services were compelled to put their major energies into quarreling with one another over who should get the larger share. Given the natural rivalries of the military and their traditional acceptance of civilian rule, the President and his advisers—who could claim responsibility for the broader picture of reconciling defense and domestic policies—had

the upper hand. There are, however, additional explanations to be considered.

The dominant role of the congressional appropriations committee is to be guardian of the treasury. This is manifested in the pride of its members in cutting the President's budget. Thus it was difficult to get this crucial committee to recommend even a few hundred million increase in defense; it was practically impossible to get them to consider the several billion jump that might really have made a difference. A related budgetary matter concerned the planning, programming, and budgeting system introduced by Secretary of Defense McNamara. For if the defense budget contained major categories that crisscrossed the services, only the Secretary of Defense could put it together. Whatever the other debatable consequences of program budgeting, its major consequence was to grant power to the secretary and his civilian advisers.

The subordination of the military through program budgeting is just one symptom of a more general weakness of the military. In the past decade the military has suffered a lack of intellectual skills appropriate to the nuclear age. For no one has (and no one wants) direct experience with

TABLE II—Congressional Involvement in Foreign and Defense Policy Decisions

Issue	Congressional Involvement (High, Low, None)	Initiator (Congress or Executive)	Predominant Influence (Congress or Executive)	Legislation or Resolution (Yes or No)	Violence at Stake (Yes or No)	Decision Time (Long or Short)
Neutrality Legislation, the 1930's	High	Exec	Cong	Yes	No	Long
Lend-Lease, 1941	High	Exec	Exec	Yes	Yes	Long
Aid to Russia, 1941	Low	Exec	Exec	No	No	Long
Repeal of Chinese Exclusion, 1943	High	Cong	Cong	Yes	No	Long
Fulbright Resolution, 1943	High	Cong	Cong	Yes	No	Long
Building the Atomic Bomb, 1944	Low	Exec	Exec	Yes	Yes	Long
Foreign Services Act of 1946	High	Exec	Exec	Yes	No	Long
Truman Doctrine, 1947	High	Exec	Exec	Yes	No	Long
The Marshall Plan, 1947-48	High	Exec	Exec	Yes	No	Long
Berlin Airlift, 1948	None	Exec	Exec	No	Yes	Long
Vandenberg Resolution, 1948	High	Exec	Cong	Yes	No	Long
North Atlantic Treaty, 1947-49	High	Exec	Exec	Yes	No	Long
Korean Decision, 1950	None	Exec	Exec	No	Yes	Short
Japanese Peace Treaty, 1952	High	Exec	Exec	Yes	No	Long
Bohlen Nomination, 1953	High	Exec	Exec	Yes	No	Long
Indo-China, 1954	High	Exec	Cong	No	Yes	Short
Formosan Resolution, 1955	High	Exec	Exec	Yes	Yes	Long
International Finance Corporation, 1956	Low	Exec	Exec	Yes	No	Long
Foreign Aid, 1957	High	Exec	Exec	Yes	No	Long
Reciprocal Trade Agreements, 1958	High	Exec	Exec	Yes	No	Long
Monroney Resolution, 1958	High	Cong	Cong	Yes	No	Long
Cuban Decision, 1961	Low	Exec	Exec	No	Yes	Long

Source: James A. Robinson, *Congress and Foreign Policy-Making* (Homewood, Illinois, 1962)

nuclear war. So the usual military talk about being the only people to have combat experience is not very impressive. Instead, the imaginative creation of possible future wars—in order to avoid them—requires people with a high capacity for abstract thought combined with the ability to manipulate symbols using quantitative methods. West Point has not produced many such men.

■ THE STATE DEPARTMENT. Modern Presidents expect the State Department to carry out their policies. John F. Kennedy felt that State was "in some particular sense 'his' department." If a Secretary of State forgets this, as was apparently the case with James Byrnes under Truman, a President may find another man. But the State Department, especially the Foreign Service, is also a highly professional organization with a life and momentum of its own. If a President does not push hard, he may find his preferences somehow dissipated in time. Arthur Schlesinger fills his book on Kennedy with laments about the bureaucratic inertia and recalcitrance of the State Department.

"The outstanding feature of the military's participation in making defense policy is their amazing weakness. . . . The great increases in the defense budget were due far more to Stalin and modern technology than to the military."

Yet Schlesinger's own account suggests that State could not ordinarily resist the President. At one point, he writes of "the President, himself, increasingly the day-to-day director of American foreign policy." On the next page, we learn that "Kennedy dealt personally with almost every aspect of policy around the globe. He knew more about certain areas than the senior officials at State and probably called as many issues to their attention as they did to his." The President insisted on his way in Laos. He pushed through his policy on the Congo against strong opposition with the State Department. Had Kennedy wanted to get a great deal more initiative out of the State Department, as Schlesinger insists, he could have replaced the Secretary of State, a man who did not command special support in the Democratic party or in Congress. It may be that Kennedy wanted too strongly to run his own foreign policy. Dean Rusk may have known far better than Schlesinger that the one thing Kennedy did not want was a man who might rival him in the field of foreign affairs.

Schlesinger comes closest to the truth when he writes that "the White House could always win any battle it chose over the [Foreign] Service; but the prestige and proficiency of the Service limited the number of battles any White House

would find it profitable to fight." When the President knew what he wanted, he got it. When he was doubtful and perplexed, he sought good advice and frequently did not get that. But there is no evidence that the people on his staff came up with better ideas .The real problem may have been a lack of good ideas anywhere. Kennedy undoubtedly encouraged his staff to prod the State Department. But the President was sufficiently cautious not to push so hard that he got his way when he was not certain what that way should be. In this context Kennedy appears to have played his staff off against elements in the State Department.

The growth of a special White House staff to help Presidents in foreign affairs expresses their need for assistance, their refusal to rely completely on the regular executive agencies, and their ability to find competent men. The deployment of this staff must remain a presidential prerogative, however, if its members are to serve Presidents and not their opponents. Whenever critics do not like existing foreign and defense policies, they are likely to complain that the White House staff is screening out divergent views from the President's attention. Naturally, the critics recommend introducing many more different viewpoints. If the critics could maneuver the President into counting hands all day ("on the one hand and on the other"), they would make it impossible for him to act. Such a viewpoint is also congenial to those who believe that action rather than inaction is the greatest present danger in foreign policy. But Presidents resolutely refuse to become prisoners of their advisers by using them as other people would like. Presidents remain in control of their staff as well as of major foreign policy decisions.

How Complete Is the Control?

Some analysts say that the success of Presidents in controlling foreign policy decisions is largely illusory. It is achieved, they say, by anticipating the reactions of others, and eliminating proposals that would run into severe opposition. There is some truth in this objection. In politics, where transactions are based on a high degree of mutual interdependence, what others may do has to be taken into account. But basing presidential success in foreign and defense policy on anticipated reactions suggests a static situation which does not exist. For if Presidents propose only those policies that would get support in Congress, and Congress opposes them only when it knows that it can muster overwhelming strength, there would never be any conflict. Indeed, there might never be any action.

How can "anticipated reaction" explain the conflict over policies like the Marshall Plan and the test-ban treaty in which severe opposition was overcome only by strenuous efforts? Furthermore, why doesn't "anticipated reaction" work in domestic affairs? One would have to argue that for some reason presidential perception of what would be successful is consistently confused on domestic issues and most always accurate on major foreign policy issues. But the role of "anticipated reactions" should be greater in the more familiar domestic situations, which provide a backlog of experience for forecasting, than in foreign policy with many novel situations such as the Suez crisis or the Rhodesian affair.

Are there significant historical examples which might refute the thesis of presidential control of foreign policy? Foreign aid may be a case in point. For many years, Presidents have struggled to get foreign aid appropriations because of hostility from public and congressional opinion. Yet several billion dollars a year are appropriated regularly despite the evident unpopularity of the program. In the aid programs to Communist countries like Poland and Yugoslavia, the Congress attaches all sorts of restrictions to the aid, but Presidents find ways of getting around them.

What about the example of recognition of Communist China? The sentiment of the country always has been against recognizing Red China or admitting it to the United Nations. But have Presidents wanted to recognize Red China and been hamstrung by opposition? The answer, I suggest, is a qualified "no." By the time recognition of Red China might have become a serious issue for the Truman administration, the war in Korea effectively precluded its consideration. There is no evidence that President Eisenhower or Secretary Dulles ever thought it wise to recognize Red China or help admit her to the United Nations. The Kennedy administration viewed the matter as not of major importance and, considering the opposition, moved cautiously in suggesting change. Then came the war in Vietnam. If the advantages for foreign policy had been perceived to be much higher, then Kennedy or Johnson might have proposed changing American policy toward recognition of Red China.

One possible exception, in the case of Red China, however, does not seem sufficient to invalidate the general thesis that Presidents do considerably better in getting their way in foreign and defense policy than in domestic policies.

The World Influence

The forces impelling Presidents to be concerned with the widest range of foreign and defense policies also affect the ways in which they calculate their power stakes. As Kennedy used to say, "Domestic policy . . . can only defeat us; foreign policy can kill us."

It no longer makes sense for Presidents to "play politics" with foreign and defense policies. In the past, Presidents might have thought that they could gain by prolonged delay or by not acting at all. The problem might disappear or be passed on to their successors. Presidents must now expect to pay the high costs themselves if the world situation deteriorates. The advantages of pursuing a policy that is viable in the world, that will not blow up on Presidents or their fellow citizens, far outweigh any temporary political disadvantages accrued in supporting an initially unpopular policy. Compared with domestic affairs, Presidents engaged in world politics are immensely more concerned with meeting problems on their own terms. Who supports and opposes a policy, though a matter of considerable interest, does not assume the crucial importance that it does in domestic affairs. The best policy Presidents can find is also the best politics.

The fact that there are numerous foreign and defense policy situations competing for a President's attention means that it is worthwhile to organize political activity in order to affect his agenda. For if a President pays more attention to certain problems he may develop different preferences; he may seek and receive different advice; his new calculations may lead him to devote greater resources to seeking a solution. Interested congressmen may exert influence not by directly determining a presidential decision, but indirectly by making it costly for a President to avoid reconsidering the basis for his action. For example, citizen groups, such as those concerned with a change in China policy, may have an impact simply by keeping their proposals on the public agenda. A President may be compelled to reconsider a problem even though he could not overtly be forced to alter the prevailing policy.

In foreign affairs we may be approaching the stage where knowledge is power. There is a tremendous receptivity to good ideas in Washington. Most anyone who can present a convincing rationale for dealing with a hard world finds a ready audience. The best way to convince Presidents to follow a desired policy is to show that it might work. A man like McNamara thrives because he performs; he comes up with answers he can defend. It is, to be sure, extremely difficult to devise good policies or to predict their consequences accurately. Nor is it easy to convince others that a given policy is superior to other alternatives. But it is the way to influence with Presidents. For if they are convinced that the current policy is best, the likelihood of gaining sufficient force to compel a change is quite small. The man who can build better foreign policies will find Presidents beating a path to his door.

Never before in the annals of American political history has a President exhibited such an obvious and intense concern over his public image as indicated by the public opinion polls. President Johnson's well-reported attention to the rise and fall of percentage points raises the question: what are the uses and abuses of polls in affecting the actions of political leaders.

There is a very great difference in the reliability of responses with respect to domestic and foreign affairs. Domestically, the polls indicate that we are dealing with relatively stable attitudes, on issues such as the welfare state, race relations, etc. In addition, when new issues arise such as how to deal with inflation, unemployment, or Medicare, people can react to them in terms of direct personal experience or liberal-conservative predispositions.

Conversely, in the area of foreign policy most Americans know very little, and are only indirectly involved. They have no way of checking on often conflicting reports from countries and regions under contention, nor on public sentiments elsewhere in the world. Consequently, the press and political leaders can have much more influence in determining public opinion on foreign issues than on domestic issues. Whether Tshombe is a villain or a hero, whether the downfall of Nkrumah is good or bad, is defined *for* the average American rather than *by* the average American. If we trace the poll popularity of a single leader, say Tito of Yugoslavia or de Gaulle of France, it becomes clear that the poll variations in the United States follow policy decisions made about him on the basis of whether his actions further or hamper American concerns. In other words, polls do not make policy so much as follow policy in most areas of international affairs.

When it comes to Vietnam, basically the opinion data indicate that national policy-makers, particularly the President, have an almost free hand to pursue any policy they think correct and get public support for it. They can escalate under the justification that this is the only way to prevent a "Communist take-over" in Southeast Asia; they can negotiate with the Viet Cong for a coalition government if this policy is presented as one which will gain peace while avoiding such a presumed take-over. These conclusions do not mean that most people are fickle, but rather that they agree on certain larger objectives, peace without the expansion (or contraction) of communism, and find it necessary to trust the judgment of national leaders as to what is possible given these purposes.

The highly publicized efforts by the President and other foreign policy advocates to interpret the various poll results dealing with the Vietnam conflict—with both hawks and

The President, the Polls, and Vietnam

Seymour Martin Lipset

doves claiming that the American people agree with them —point up the need to clarify the meaning of the polls. Some months ago, a faculty group at various San Francisco Bay Area colleges actually dug down in their own pockets to pay the National Opinion Research Center (NORC) of the University of Chicago to conduct a survey which might clear up some of the confusion. Unfortunately, this survey was no more conclusive than others which have been conducted over the years by other pollsters such as George Gallup, Louis Harris, National Analysts, and the Opinion Research Corporation. The results of most surveys can still be interpreted by both extremes in the foreign policy debate to fit their own preconceptions.

No Pigeonholes for Hawks and Doves

The truth is that the American people as a whole, and many, if not most, individuals cannot be placed in the category of dove or hawk. Two sets of attitudes stand out among the various responses. The great majority of the American people desire peace in Vietnam, do not want war with China, are prepared to accept some sort of compromise truce with the enemy, and, in fact, anticipate a negotiated peace rather than a victory which will see the defeat of the Viet Cong. On the other hand, a substantial majority is strongly hostile to communism and all the Communist countries, including Soviet Russia, Cuba, and China. Almost nobody interviewed by NORC (5 percent or less) believed that our foreign policy toward any one of these countries is "too tough"; a large majority agree with statements that the US is "too soft" in dealing with China and Cuba; almost half think we are "too soft" in our relations with the Russians. Most of those who do not think the policy is "too soft" say it is right.

Most Americans are, in fact, both doves *and* hawks; the more thorough and detailed the querying of opinions, the

more clearly this appears. Early in March of this year, the Gallup Poll asked, "Would you favor or oppose bombing big cities in North Vietnam?" Sixty percent voiced opposition, while only 28 percent favored it. (The NORC study used a similar question and reported 55 percent against bombing cities in North Vietnam and 39 percent in support.) These results would seem to clearly indicate a dove majority against bombing North Vietnam. Yet in the same survey, Gallup also inquired, "Would you favor or oppose *bombing industrial plants and factories* in North Vietnam?" The response distribution was almost precisely opposite to the "bomb North Vietnamese cities" question. Sixty-one percent said they were for the bombing of factories and 26 percent were against. In other words, three-fifths of the American public were for bombing the North Vietnamese factories, but three-fifths (not all the same people) were also against bombing their cities, in March and April. This means that the policy of "strategic" bombing and avoiding

"civilian" targets is generally approved. Thus, when Louis Harris asked about US resumption of bombing in January ("Do you think President Johnson was right or wrong to resume bombing in North Vietnam after the recent pause?") 73 percent said he was right; only 10 percent were opposed. And two months later a National Analysts survey conducted for NBC which inquired, "Should the US continue bombing North Vietnam?" reported almost identical results, 78 percent for continuing; 14 percent for stopping the attacks.

The American public shows a similar general propensity to discriminate among the methods which should be used in fighting the war. Almost the same size majority (68 percent) told National Analysts interviewers that they *opposed* the US using "any nuclear weapons in Vietnam," as *approved* US use of "gas that does not kill people."

Are these illogical or inconsistent responses? No, as in the case of the answers to the bombing questions, they reflect a national mood to do as little as possible to stop communist expansion. The dominant attitude seems to be not to let Vietnam "go Communist" coupled with a desire to end the war as soon as possible, on the most minimal conditions which include a willingness to negotiate directly with the National Liberation Front (NLF).

Peace—yes; Communism—no

The various surveys point up this mixed pattern of responses. Peace sentiments are strong. Almost everyone (88 percent) polled by NORC would favor "American negotiations with the Viet Cong if they were willing to negotiate," and a majority (52 percent for, 36 percent against) would be willing to approve "forming a new government in which the Viet Cong took some part" in order to "end the fighting."

But the *same sample* of respondents who gave these dove answers turned into veritable militant hawks when asked, "If President Johnson were to announce tomorrow that we were going to withdraw from Vietnam and let the Communists take over, would you approve or disapprove?" Four-fifths of the NORC sample, 81 percent, disapproved, as compared with but 15 percent favoring getting out. A goodly majority (56 percent for, 39 percent against) would *not* agree to "gradually withdrawing our troops and letting the South Vietnamese work out their own problems" even though the possibility of a Communist victory was not mentioned in the question.

The willingness of the Americans to fight the war was expressed in the response to a NORC question which first asked respondents to choose among three alternative courses of action: continuing the present situation indefinitely; fighting a major war with hundreds of thousands of casualties; or supporting a withdrawal of American troops which leads to an eventual Communist take-over. Almost half (49 percent) would continue the present situation; 23 percent favored escalation to a major war; and 19 percent would support getting out. However, when the choice was narrowed to either support of escalation to a major war or withdrawal, twice as many (60 percent) chose major war as favored withdrawal. The same aggressive posture is reflected in the answers to an NBC-National Analysts poll, in March, which asked respondents to choose whether we should "pursue a more offensive ground war in Vietnam than we are presently doing, or should we establish defensive positions around the cities we now control?" Over half (55 percent) chose to escalate as compared to 28 percent who favored holding our present lines.

When pollsters' questions remind respondents of the cost of the war in lives and do not mention communism, Americans often support the more pacific alternative; when they are faced with fighting or agreeing to a Communist victory, they opt for continuing the war, and even with escalating if necessary.

Yet, though most Americans ruefully are willing to keep fighting in Vietnam if this is necessary to prevent a complete take-over, or expansion to neighboring countries, they clearly would much prefer not to be there, and are anxious and willing to turn over responsibility to someone else. Back in June 1954, when it first appeared as if the US might send troops to Indo-China, only 20 percent told Gallup interviewers that they would approve sending US soldiers "to help the French fight the Communists in Indo-China." And much more recently, on various occasions, clear majorities have reported to Gallup, Harris, and NORC alike that they would like to see the United Nations take over from the United States, either to fight or settle the war. Thus in the first few months of this year, 70 percent told NORC they would approve the UN or some neutral countries negotiating a peace "with each side holding the territory it now holds"; 74 percent indicated to Gallup interviewers they would approve the UN working out "its own formula for peace in Vietnam"; more people (49 percent) said that the US should submit the Vietnam question to the UN and abide by the UN's decision, *no matter what it is,* than opposed the idea (37 percent); and a UN army for Vietnam and Southeast Asia was approved by a three to one majority (almost identical to the results obtained by Gallup to a similar question a year earlier).

Peace Hopes and the UN

The strength of the sentiment to turn the war over to the United Nations may be seen in the fact that this is the only issue on which poll results indicated that negative judgments of President Johnson far outweighed his support. In September 1965, the Harris Survey reported that 42 percent agreed with the statement, the President was "more wrong than right" in not asking the UN to take over in Vietnam, while only 25 percent thought he was "more right than wrong," and the rest were not sure. A more recent Harris Survey released in early April of this year reports that Americans favor by nearly two to one (50 percent to 27 percent) "turning over the entire Vietnam war to a special three-man United Nations committee for arbitration and a decision binding on all parties."

These attitudes not only reflect ambivalent sentiments about US participation in Vietnam, they also indicate the very strong positive feeling of the overwhelming majority of the American people toward the United Nations. All the surveys have consistently indicated widespread popular support for the UN. (The vociferous rightist critics of American membership in the international body can hardly find more than a small minority to support their views among the general public. Most Americans seem to identify the UN with prospects for world peace, and are willing to do anything to endorse it, including criticizing American foreign policy if a question is worded in such a way as to make the pro-UN response involve such criticism.)

In evaluating the poll responses, it is important to keep in mind that the proportion of Americans who can be considered soft on communism is insignificantly small. Those who approve forming a new government in which the NLF takes part are almost as hard in their attitudes toward Castro, Communist China, and Russia as those who oppose NLF participation. In other words "hard line" anti-Communists are almost as prone to favor dealing with the Viet Cong directly, as those who are generally more favorable to the expansion of relations with Communist countries. For example, 60 percent of those favorable to a coalition with the Viet Cong think our policy toward Castro is "too soft," as compared with 70 percent among those who would not admit the Viet Cong to the government. The response pattern with respect to attitudes toward Communist China and Russia is similar.

What the polls show is that the anti-communism of Americans has little to do with their opinions about how the war in Vietnam should be handled at the tactical level. But, the belief in the need to defeat the Communist enemy, serves to support any actions which the President can argue need to be taken to defeat this enemy. Such attitudes provide a strong reservoir of support for the hawks, and an equally significant impediment for the doves.

These mixed "hawk-dove" sentiments in large measure underlie the general state of opinion concerning President Johnson's handling of the Vietnamese situation. Polls taken before the spring 1966 Buddhist crisis, by Gallup and Harris over the previous year, had indicated approval for the President in the ratio of two to one. The last such pre-crisis survey, Gallup's of late March, indicated that 56 percent approved, while 26 percent disapproved. (The NORC survey taken a little earlier found a comparable division, 61 percent approving and 29 percent disapproving, almost identical to the results reported by the NBC National Analysts poll, also taken in March.)

Who Are the President's Critics?

It is difficult to tell from the available reports of the various surveys whether the critics of President Johnson are disproportionately hawks or doves. It is clear that a large majority both of the extreme hawks, those who favor "carrying the war more into North Vietnam," and of the more pacific doves, those who would "pull our troops out now," tell pollsters they oppose the President's Vietnamese policies. The President, on a number of occasions, has stated that most of those who disapprove of his Vietnamese policies are hawks, rather than doves. And he has interpreted increases in the proportions voicing criticism, such as occurred in May and June of 1966, as reflecting a growth in sentiment to escalate. This may be so, but the President has not presented figures comparing the attitudes of his supporters and opponents on a variety of specific policy issues. This would be the only way to reach a conclusion on this point.

The NORC survey tried to do so but the findings are indecisive and incomplete. Those who "disapprove the way the Johnson administration is handling the situation in Vietnam" are slightly more likely to give dove rather than hawk responses on a few policy questions. However, these data derive from those questions which produced large dove responses among the sample generally, such as negotiate with Viet Cong, form a new government with them.

Most recently, a Gallup survey taken in early June reports that among those who disapprove of Johnson's handling of the situation in Vietnam, 10 percent gave answers which could be categorized under the heading "we should be more aggressive," while 13 percent said that "we should get out." My own interpretation of the data presented by various pollsters is that the proportions of hawks and doves among the President's critics, reported recently by Gallup, has tended to be a relatively stable pattern. That is, the critics have usually contained slightly more doves than

---

"The President makes opinion, he does not follow it. The polls tell him how good a politician he is. They are a weapon against his critics."

---

hawks. It should be stressed, however, that there is always a third group present among the President's critics whose responses cannot be classified in either category.

Clearly, the American people are worried about the Vietnam war. Indeed, they are, according to recent reports, at least twice as concerned over the war as they are over the next leading "issue"—the Negro civil rights issue. When Gallup asked a national sample in December what headline they would most like to see in "tomorrow's paper," almost nine out of ten respondents spontaneously mentioned peace. Almost half (46 percent) specifically said "peace in Vietnam," while another 41 percent stated peace in general. These findings were reiterated in the NORC study which found that more voters (62 percent) said they "worried a great deal" about the war in Vietnam than about any other issue. Only 7 percent said the issue of the war did not worry them at all.

The anxiety and serious thought which Americans devote to the Vietnamese war does not mean that they see any quick or simple way to gain the peace they so ardently desire. They know that we have not been doing well. A CBS-Opinion Research Corporation survey reported in December that when asked which side controlled "most of the land area of South Vietnam," more people said the Viet Cong. *Only 24 percent* thought the US was "making progress toward victory." The bulk of those interviewed also had a reasonably accurate estimate of the numbers of American troops in Vietnam and the casualties suffered by them. Last December, when asked by Gallup, how long they think the war will last, less than 20 percent thought it would end in a year or less; 26 percent guessed at two or three more years; while 36 percent said at least four more years. And when asked by Gallup in January of this year: "Do you think the war will end in a clear-cut victory in Vietnam, or will it end in some sort of compromise settlement?" only 7 percent foresaw a clear-cut victory; 69 percent predicted a compromise ending. This anticipation of a compromise settlement is reflected in the large majorities favoring a negotiated settlement as reported by both Gallup and Harris.

The fact that the government of South Vietnam became involved in serious troubles with its own people in the late spring should not have been too surprising to many Americans. The CBS-National Analysts survey reported in December 1965, that only 22 percent of Americans thought most South Vietnamese are loyal to their present leaders, i.e., the Ky regime. In spite of this lack of belief in popular support for the South Vietnamese government, when this same sample was asked: "Do you think we should have pulled out before American fighting units became involved, or do you think that staying there was the right thing to do?" only 20 percent said we should have pulled out, 65 percent thought staying in Vietnam was right. The ability of people to hold these contradictory beliefs is based on an overriding belief that supporting the war is not specific to Vietnam, but a necessity to stop Communist expansion.

Confusing, but Consistent

The data presented by the various pollsters make it possible for one to argue that the American people are tough, soft, informed, confused, decisive, and indecisive, depending on the case one wants to make. To interpret them in any of these ways, however, would be wrong. These attitudes reflect certain consistent underlying beliefs about peace and Communism which most of the American public, like those who hold office, find difficult to reconcile. Very few are willing to approve actions which they perceive would increase the chances for a larger war, reduce the possibilities for early peace, or encourage Communist expansion into non-Communist areas, inside or outside of Vietnam. And the survey data suggest that most Americans share with their leaders the sense that they are in a morass from which they do not yet see a way out.

The findings of the surveys clearly indicate that the President, while having a relatively free hand in the actual decision-making to escalate or to de-escalate the war, is more restricted when considering the generic issues of action or inaction. He must give the appearance of a man *engagé*, of being certain of what he is doing, i.e., that the anticipated consequences do in fact come about.

The President seems to present his program along two parameters:
■ as part of a plan to secure the peace, particularly if the action involved is actually escalation;
■ pacific actions are presented as ways to contain communism, or even to weaken it.

The President knows that in order to get the support of the American people for a war they wish they never were in, he must continually put his "best peace foot" forward— he continually talks and offers peace, so that he may have public endorsement for war.

And conversely, any effort to make peace, to reach agreement with any Communist state, would best be presented as a way to "contain" Communism, to weaken it by facilitating splits among the various Communist states, or to help change it internally so that it will be less totalitarian, more humane, and less expansionist.

There are, of course, important limits, real limits, on the ability of the President to determine public response. During 1966, his personal popularity and endorsement for the Vietnamese policy dropped sharply—to a point where the percentage indicating support fell to less than 50 percent. A Gallup survey in May indicated only 41 percent of the general public approved "the way Johnson is handling the situation in Vietnam," as against 37 percent who disapproved. This general decline in support was a result of the internal turmoil among the South Vietnamese, and a feeling that the President had become indecisive in his handling of the war. Clearly, there was no way that the President could have prevented the American people from learning of the opposition in the streets to General Ky's government. These events, according to Gallup, led to a sizable increase in the proportion who felt that continued fighting is useless, who viewed the war as lost. Gallup reported as of early June, before the facilities at Haiphong and Hanoi were bombed, that for the first time since the US became heavily engaged in Vietnam, less than half the population, 48 percent supported continuing the war, as compared with 35 percent who were in favor of taking our troops out.

Yet according to the Harris Survey, another effect of the despair over the South Vietnamese turmoil was to increase sharply the numbers of Americans who favored sharp escalation in tactics as a means of ending the war. Thus, *before* the decision was made to bomb installations at Hanoi and Haiphong in June, Harris reported that those in favor of bombing the two cities had increased from 20 percent as of September 1965, to 34 percent in May 1966, while opposition to such bombings had dropped from 47 to 34 percent. Support for blockading North Vietnamese ports, a step not yet taken, jumped from 38 percent in September to 53 percent in May. Those willing to "carry the ground war into North Vietnam at the risk of bringing Red China into the fighting" went up from 28 percent in December 1965 to 38 percent in May.

Once the religious strife was terminated, the President could regain his hold on public opinion by the twin tactics of escalating the bombing raids and emphasizing the military defeats suffered by the Viet Cong, and the presumed demoralization of the Ho government in Hanoi. Gallup reports as of July 1966 show that between early June and mid-July general support for the President jumped from 46 percent to 56 percent and specific endorsement of his role in the Vietnam conflict rose from 41 percent to 49 percent. As of August Harris found that "more than 80 percent favor the bombings of military targets at Hanoi and Haiphong. . . ." Those in favor of intensifying the war effort rose from 47 percent in May to 60 percent in August. These changes underscore the need for Presidential action as a basis of continuing support.

Democratic 'War Losses'

These results do not mean, however, that any course of

decisive action is without great political risks. The deeply felt general anxiety over the continuation and escalation of the war may result in considerable loss of support to the Democrats in the 1966 Congressional elections. A minority, but one large enough to affect the outcome in many districts, is increasingly unhappy. The fact that some of the critics are hawks and others doves, does not change the fact that they may vote for the opposition, or not vote at all as a means of protest. A Harris Survey early in the year reports that "those who disagree with the Administration conduct in Vietnam today say they are likely to vote 52-48 percent Republican next fall."

There are other indications of the diverse ways which the continuation of the war may aid the Republicans and even stimulate right-wing sentiment in the country. On one hand, in July of this year for the first time in many years, a larger group (30 percent) told Gallup interviewers that the Republicans are more likely than the Democrats (22 percent) to keep the US out of World War III. Contrast this result with the finding in October 1964 that 45 percent saw the Democrats as the more pacific party with 22 percent for the Republicans. But the survey data also suggest that the social base for a new wave of McCarthyism may be emerging. In March of this year when asked by national analysts: "Do you agree with the right of an American citizen to demonstrate against the war in Vietnam?" only 34.5 percent agreed, 62 percent opposed. Two earlier surveys, by the Opinion Research Corporation and Gallup in November and December, also yielded results which suggest that the large majority of the public do not view opposition to the war as legitimate, seeing the bulk of the protesters as "communists" or "draft dodgers."

To sum up the implications of the polls, it seems clear that the President holds the trump cards in dealing with the public on foreign policy matters. The public knows they do not know, and feel they must trust the President, for there is no one else on whom they can rely in the international field. There is no equivalent to Dwight Eisenhower around today—an opposition leader with sufficient personal status and international experience to become a counter-center of foreign policy confidence.

If this is so, why does Lyndon Johnson pay so much attention to survey results. Not, I would suspect, to convince himself that he is doing right, or that he is following the wishes of the people. *The President makes opinion, he does not follow it.* His interest in the opinion polls, therefore, reflects his desire to be sure that his approach is reaching the American public in the way he wants them affected.

The polls tell him how good a politician he is. They are also a weapon against his critics. He feels he is under no obligation to make public politically unpalatable information. And, as we have seen, there is enough in the surveys for the President to find justification for whatever policy he wants to pursue in Vietnam, and to tell his political critics that the people are behind him.

The poll data can also enable the President, and other politicians as well, to ignore opposition demonstrations, which are organized by relatively small minorities. Thus, opinion surveys of university student populations, who have provided the main source of organized disagreement, indicate that the overwhelming majority of American students are behind the war. There have been four national surveys of campus opinion, two in 1965 by Louis Harris and *Playboy,* and two in 1966 by Samuel Lubell and Gallup, the latter in June. All of these indicate that a large majority of American students (between two-thirds and three-quarters)

support the war in Vietnam. Faculty opinion, according to a *Playboy* poll, is also behind the war, although by a smaller majority than the students.

As a final point, it may be noted that the opposition to the Vietnamese war is far less than that voiced to the Korean war. As of January 1951, Gallup reported that 66 percent said: "Pull our troops out of Korea as fast as possible" as contrasted with 25 percent who said stay and fight. If the evidence of the polls is to be believed, the American public are far more willing to fight in Asia today than 15 years ago.

The findings presented in this effort to sum up the results of opinion surveys on the Vietnam war may depress many who hope to modify American foreign policy through mobilizing segments of the public in support of various peace movements. It is obvious that such efforts face considerable obstacles, particularly during an on-going war. But ignorance of difficulties is not a virtue, even if knowledge may not suggest a path to influence or victory. ∎

President-elect Nixon has already made two innovations in forming his White House staff. He will not have a press secretary as such; Herb Klein has been appointed director of communications charged with regulating the flow of information from the Departments of State, Defense and other Executive offices. He has also institutionalized the concerns of the city by creating an Office of Urban Affairs, naming Daniel Patrick Moynihan as his special assistant. But what the actual working processes of Nixon's staff will be can be better understood by studying White House staffs of the past.

Early Presidents had to make do with very little professional staff. When Thomas Jefferson entered the White House in 1801, he had one messenger and an occasional secretary—the latter paid out of Jefferson's own pocket, and rarely even in Washington. President Ulysses S. Grant had two professional staffers; and Woodrow Wilson conducted World War I and a major diplomatic effort with seven. When President William McKinley asked a certain J. A. Porter to become his secretary, he was refused— because of "the low recognition value of the job."

Franklin D. Roosevelt, entering the White House in 1933, found that, despite such grave emergencies as the depression and the rise of fascism, things had not changed much. Throughout his first term, he operated with only three professional staff members, three secretaries—(press, appointments, corresponding)—and a small clerical staff. He frequently had to borrow staff members from other departments and agencies, sometimes even moving them to the White House. He also relied on old friends, like Judge Samuel I. Rosenman.

Obviously something had to be done, and in 1936 Roosevelt called upon three political scientists for aid. In 1937, the resulting President's Committee on Administrative Management, under the leadership of Louis Brownlow, submitted a report that led to a major reorganization and expansion of the Presidential staff.

"Where . . ." the committee asked, "can there be found

The White House Staff Bureaucracy
Alex B. Lacy, Jr.

an executive in any way comparable upon whom so much petty work is thrown? Or who is forced to see so many people on related matters and to make so many decisions on . . . incomplete information? How is it humanly possible to know fully the affairs and problems of over 100 separate major agencies . . . ?"

Since the passage of the Reorganization Act of 1939, the total executive office of the President has rapidly grown to match the increased workload. It has now overflowed the old State, War, and Navy building that a few years earlier had housed three major departments. When the Brownlow Committee delivered its report, Roosevelt had 37 White House Office employees, and a budget of about $200,000. By 1967 the budget had increased to nearly $3 million, to support a staff of several hundred.

After 1939, the first big budget jump came in 1947 (from $250,996 in 1946 to $772,122), when President Truman insisted that all White House borrowing of personnel from agencies and departments had to cease. The 1947 budget was therefore the first "honest" White House Office budget. The increase since then has been—with minor exceptions—a steady one. Roosevelt after 1939 operated with an average of eight professional staffers, while Eisenhower and Kennedy both began the Presidency with 21.

Now, nearly three decades after the great change, what, precisely, has been the impact of an expanded staff upon the Presidency? Is the President, as Woodrow Wilson described him in a famous lecture, still free "both in law and conscience to be as big a man as he can"? Or has the Presidential office, as Edward S. Corwin feared, become rigidly bureaucratized and institutionalized?

Since the 1939 reorganization, 169 men have served on the professional White House staff. Typically, they have been (and are) middle-aged; white (only three were Negroes); male (there have been female secretaries, but no female professional staff); from the Eastern half of the United States; with prior experience in federal service; and with at least one Ivy League degree apiece.

Age: The White House staff has tended to be several years younger than other executives in top positions in the federal government, and slightly older than business executives at the time of their first senior appointment in the business world. It is no place for old men—only one (former Senator Walter George) was over 70 at appointment, and he held only a special assignment, and briefly— the White House office is not for young men, either. Only six have been under 30, and the two youngest were 26. Roosevelt had the oldest staff; it averaged five years older than the youngest—its successor, Truman's.

Region: Most White House staffers came from farms and small towns, but followed their careers in the cities, mainly Washington. In their appointments of staff members Presidents, naturally, favor their home regions. Truman relied more than the others on the West North Central States; Kennedy on New England; Johnson on his native Texas. Eisenhower, long removed from his native Midwest, tended to favor businessmen from the Middle Atlantic; and Roosevelt's staff members came from all over, though half had their primary career experience in Washington.

The South and the Mountain and Pacific regions were underrepresented. As an area of career experience, the South Atlantic—almost entirely because it includes Washington—was overrepresented. The Middle Atlantic was overrepresented both as a region of birth and a place of principal experience. Significantly, ten of the staff members were foreign-born—almost 6 percent.

Education: Since 1939, the White House staff has been very well-educated—about the same as other federal executives, and somewhat more advanced than business executives. Under Roosevelt, only a little more than 50 percent had college degrees. Under Truman this rose to 90 percent; it shrank slightly under Eisenhower, to about 84 percent; and under Kennedy and Johnson it has steadied at about 93 percent.

All told, about three out of four had college degrees, and more than half advanced degrees (the majority in law). The Kennedy staff was the best educated: More than 90 percent had bachelor's degrees, two-thirds had advanced degrees, and one of seven was a Ph.D.

The Roosevelt and Truman staffs had fewer Ivy League graduates (21.7 percent Bachelor's degrees, 33 percent advanced) but since Truman about 38 percent of the Bachelor's degrees of staff members, and 62 percent of the advanced degrees have been awarded by Ivy League schools. Harvard leads in all categories; Princeton is second for bachelor's degrees. The Washington area schools, Georgetown and George Washington, are high in the LL.B.'s and M.A.'s.

Experience: The Presidents tended to recruit their staff members from different fields, Ivy League-educated or not. Roosevelt recruited primarily from government and from journalism—getting about a quarter from each. Truman got about half from government. Eisenhower recruited a third from the business world. Kennedy got about two-thirds of his people from government (most with previous staff experience) and the universities. Johnson, too, relied primarily on government service (again, mostly staff men) and the business world.

In each administration many staff members were lawyers, but relatively few depended upon private practice for their incomes before appointment to the White House. None of the Roosevelt and Truman people had been career academics although professors have become quite prominent since then. Eisenhower, naturally, showed preference for military men—several had served under him. Five of his appointees, interestingly, went straight from student status on the college campus to the White House. In all administrations, only one staff member came from organized labor—Roosevelt's Daniel J. Tobin—and he stayed on only a few months.

Politics: Strangely enough, politics has not been an important qualification for staff service. Only 15 of the 169 had been politicians, and most of those 15 were on special assignments. Half served in the administration of

---

AGE DISTRIBUTION & AVERAGE AGE AT APPOINTMENT, WHITE HOUSE OFFICE PROFESSIONAL STAFF, 1939-1967

Age	F.D.R.[1]	H.S.T.[2]	D.D.E.[3]	J.F.K.[4]	L.B.J.[5]
20-29	0	1	4	0	1
30-39	2	6	27	10	4
40-49	4	7	25	12	18
50-59	7	4	22	1	4
60-69	1	1	7	5	2
Over 69	0	0	1	0	0
Average Age	49.6	44.6	45.6	44.9	45.6

[1] Data available for 14 of 16 staff.
[2] Data available for 19 of 22 staff.
[3] Data available for 86 of 86 staff.
[4] Data available for 28 of 28 staff.
[5] Data available for 29 of 33 staff.

---

the only President who had not himself been a professional politician—Eisenhower. As one respondent put it, "There is only room in the White House for one politician."

This does not mean, however, that political know-how has been of little value. Each staff had political-liaison men, and many of those staffers from government service had been involved primarily in politics.

There is no clearcut road to the White House staff. Even friendship does not always help: a majority of staff members had not had a significant working or personal relationship with the President prior to appointment. This was particularly true under Eisenhower.

How were initial contacts made? Most respondents emphasized "chance, circumstance, and a good bit of luck." For example, a Democratic precinct chairman—recently retired—was looking for a research post in Washington, preferably with the CIA, when he happened to bump into an old army buddy then on the Eisenhower staff. He was quickly hired as an assistant, Democratic background and all.

Here are other examples of first contacts:

■ A minor government official gave testimony before a government committee, testimony that impressed Sherman Adams, Eisenhower's chief adviser.

■ One Roosevelt staffer was appointed because Boss Ed Flynn and Henry Wallace felt the President needed someone to stimulate his waning interest in politics.

■ A Truman staffer received appointment because the President remembered a legislative bill the man had written for him when Truman first entered the Senate.

Few have been appointed because of special expertise; few even were the obvious choices—that is, indispensable members of the President's team before the White House (obvious exceptions: Theodore Sorensen, Lawrence O'Brien, Bill Moyers, Walter Jenkins, Sherman Adams). Usually they simply happened to know the right people (generally another staff member) and to be available.

The two Presidents since 1939 who first came to office straight from elections and not because of another President's death—Eisenhower and Kennedy—drew heavily from their original campaign staffs.

Turnover: Roosevelt and Truman, although they had some recruiting and wartime assignment problems, had relatively little turnover. This was generally true of the Eisenhower staff too. The Kennedy staff had the least turnover. The only front-line Kennedy men to leave before the assassination left with the President's blessing to accept other positions in the State Department and the Peace Corps.

If we had comparable statistics, we would probably find that Johnson had the highest turnover rate. Partly of course, this is because he took over the Kennedy staff, and only five Kennedy men stayed until Nixon's election. However, of President Johnson's own 11 early appointees in 1963 and 1964, only three remained to the end. Those who left included key men like Bill Moyers, Walter Jenkins, Jake Jacobsen, Jack Valenti, and Horace Busby.

Salary: After the reorganization of 1939, Roosevelt's staff earned $10,000 a year. With two exceptions, this was still true of the Truman staff in 1948. Salaries crept near $20,000 under Eisenhower, and reached $21,000 under Kennedy. Johnson's top staff aides now receive $30,000, with second-line professional staffers receiving $27,500.

Staffs Vary with the President

The characteristics of the staffs varied, as the Presidents and the times themselves varied. Let us examine them one by one.

Roosevelt dominated every activity of his staff—this is its most impressive characteristic. The staff was an extension of FDR, personally as well as officially. Assignments might seem without reason or purpose, the staff might seem on the brink of chaos—but no one raised a question. Roosevelt initiated the assignments in detail, and personally checked to see that all were carried out (staff members say he never forgot one). All reports were made directly to him. And he was available to all staff members whenever they needed his attention—there was no chain of command.

FDR's relations with his staff were motivated, as Richard Neustadt observed, by "a concern for his position as *the* man in the White House." He believed in action, with "a strong feeling for a cardinal fact in government: that presidents . . . act in the concrete as they meet deadlines set by due dates." His staff members had to be jacks-of-all-trades. None was chosen as a specialist, and none developed pre-emptive influence in any area.

Roosevelt liked to hear differing points of view, and frequently gave two or more staff members the same assignment, and then delighted at their rivalry. Apparently this did not produce permanent hard feelings.

The reorganization plan of 1939 did not radically change the Roosevelt staff. The big change had taken place in 1933-34, because the Presidency and the personality of the President had themselves changed radically. As one staff member said, FDR suddenly needed additional staff in 1933 "because the people began to look to the President as . . . never before—writing to him, calling him."

Even after reorganization, White House Office activity continued to center on the three secretaries. Stephen Early (followed by Jonathan Daniels) was in charge of press relations; Marvin H. McIntyre handled appointments and made arrangements for trips, public appearances, and meetings; Brigadier-General Edwin M. "Pa" Watson was special legman and confidant.

The first three staffmen—James H. Rowe, William H. McReynolds, and Lauchlin Currie—handled whatever tasks were at hand. But the great task of all was to serve as eyes and ears for the President, and be available for anything.

During World War II, the White House Office changed considerably. Judge Samuel I. Rosenman became special counsel to the President. He drafted speeches and messages to Congress, and was responsible for reviewing bills and executive orders. Harry L. Hopkins moved into the White House as special assistant, and was involved in almost every activity during the war years. He actually lived in the President's personal quarters on the second floor. Although his position was a very special one, neither he, nor Judge Rosenman, was ever a chief-of-staff. Hopkins was never a Sherman Adams.

The schedule of FDR's staff was determined by FDR's schedule. The day began with a brief conference with several staff members while he had breakfast. FDR never had regular staff meetings, and the only other time members regularly met wtih him in groups was just before press conferences, when briefings were completed and strategy discussed. After breakfast, the staff was on its own, although called as needed and readily available.

The evenings were for drafting speeches, policy statements, and decision-making, which usually involved Rosenman, playwright Robert E. Sherwood, Hopkins, and borrowed staffers like Benjamin Cohen and Thomas Corcoran. After FDR went to bed, the drafting team frequently worked well into the morning.

Roosevelt was very close to his staffers, and probably socialized with them more than other Presidents did with theirs. Despite its apparent disorder, this may explain why the staff was so effective.

The Roosevelt-Truman transition was traumatic. Truman was unprepared to take over, and unfamiliar with the Roosevelt staff; he had only two of his own men, Matthew Connelly and Harry Vaughan. And the FDR staff was not sure whether he wanted them to stay.

While they hesitated, a number of old Truman friends, mostly from Missouri, turned up and without Truman's authorization tried to take over. One staffer reported, "We wondered if we had a Democratic Harding on our hands." Truman later completely cleared out the newcomers and asked several Roosevelt staff men to stay on.

In a year the staff was decisively reorganized. They continued to be generalists, but fell into fixed areas of assignment from politics to national resources.

Throughout, Truman followed Roosevelt's example by using the three secretaries to handle most recurrent duties. Charles G. Ross was press secretary until his death in December 1950. Matthew Connelly served as appointment's secretary and main political troubleshooter. William D. Hassett continued as corresponding secretary.

Staff work on policy centered on the assistant to the President, and the special counsel to the President. John R. Steelman, persuaded to return to government service by Truman, was the assistant to the President. He served as mediator and coordinator, handling executive family fights and working very closely with the Bureau of the Budget.

Rosenman stayed as special counsel until late 1945. Six months after he left, in June 1946, Clark Clifford took his place—and served four years. He was responsible for writing speeches, and checking bills and executive orders from a legal and policy point of view. Under him and his successor, Charles Murphy, it was the key staff position for policy.

Truman relied on his Cabinet and departments much more than Roosevelt had, keeping his White House staff small. Seldom did more than 11 men report to him directly.

With two exceptions, the administrative assistants were not front-line men in the Truman Administration. In fact, they served primarily as assistants to Murphy, Clifford, and Steelman. In my interviews with Truman men, I soon discovered that most felt that the President should not have more than a dozen reporting to him. Asked "Did you need more men on the staff?" the respondents unanimously replied No.

Like Roosevelt, Truman found that war necessitated special services. In 1950, he appointed W. Averell Harriman as a special assistant to keep the President informed about the Korean conflict. But Harriman never really functioned as a White House Office staff member.

The staff day began with a formal conference—meetings were so regular that everyone sat in the same place. Truman presided, and began by discussing previous reports and handing out new assignments. Then he went around the circle, permitting each member to be heard. The staff was convinced that these meetings were especially important: One said, "Every staff man could hear what his colleagues were doing—be informed, know what was going on."

The President was generally not available to the staff again until 3 P.M.; but 3 to 5 were set aside exclusively for staff and Cabinet, and basic policy matters were discussed.

Truman's staff was made up of very able men, who came to be devoted to him. They were not as intellectual as the Kennedy staff, but Truman probably could not have gotten maximum mileage out of intellectuals; he did get it out of his own group. As one told me, "He had a good concept of staff work. He could delegate. Once he got confidence in a man, he used him to his advantage."

Unlike his immediate predecessors, President Eisenhower had very definite ideas about staff, derived partly from his military experience. He believed in tight organization, efficiency, and keeping as much work as possible off the President. Responding to some critics who felt that the creative chaos of the Roosevelt staff might be better, he noted: "I have been astonished to read some contentions which seem to suggest that smooth organization guarantees that nothing is happening, whereas ferment and disorder indicate progress."

Ike was chief of Staff

Organization was the heart of the Eisenhower White House Office, and Sherman Adams the heart of the organization. He was a real chief of staff. To quote one staffer, "He was the key to the whole thing and he managed everything with a firm hand." In his own book his publisher bills him as "the man who probably exercised more power as a President's confidential adviser and co-ordinator than any other individual in modern times."

The staff was highly structured, with a rigid chain of command and new titles to match. Each man was a specialist.

The basic staff job was to reduce the President's load. Nothing was supposed to go to Ike if it could be handled elsewhere. If it did go to him, it was supposed to be re-

duced to a one-page memo with firm recommendations, and none went without an "O.K., S.A." fixed on it.

Most respondents believed that Adam's reputation as a "hard boss" and "a difficult man to get along with" was well earned. Relations with him were strictly business. Nevertheless, the staff respected him and his ability to make decisions and get work done.

One Eisenhower innovation was a special office to manage the clerical staff, handle correspondence, and—most important—handle national-security and intelligence communications.

Eisenhower formalized the work that had been handled by Clark Clifford for Truman. He had two assistants who were primarily responsible for coordination of national-security policy matters, in addition to the staff secretary who handled communications. They reported directly to Eisenhower and received their assignments directly from him. They worked closely with the staff secretary, and these three usually saw the President daily. As one said: "I seldom saw Adams except in the White House Mess at lunchtime. He may have been 'Assistant President' for domestic affairs, but he had no influence over national-security matters."

Eisenhower made more use of the Cabinet than others had and used the National Security Council "regularly and seriously." It was an important apparatus of coordination for him. He developed and announced all of his national-security and foreign-policy decisions at its meetings so that each department and agency involved knew "how he made the decision, why, and what the rationale was." Working closely with Dulles, for whom he had great respect, Eisenhower exerted his greatest influence as President in the national-security and foreign-policy areas.

Unfortunately, Eisenhower had much less interest in domestic politics, and this made the congressional-liaison unit within the White House Office a very important one. The relatively modest operation of Murphy and his team in the Truman administration gave way to a very elaborate system under General Wilton B. Persons with the able assistance of Bryce Harlow who will undoubtedly be a mainstay of the new Nixon staff. All who worked in legislative liaison for Eisenhower agreed that, especially in the early years, it "was like pulling eye teeth" to get the Republicans in Congress to support the President's program.

The work of the legislative-liaison team was also greatly complicated by Eisenhower's aversion to party politics. One Republican Congressman, asked about patronage under the new Republican administration, complained that not only had he not gotten additional jobs, but that he had lost one that he had under Truman.

The daily schedule of the White House Office under

Adams centered on Adams' schedule, in sharp contrast to the Democratic years when the President's schedule ruled. The typical staff day ran from 7 A.M. to 7 P.M., and the week might include Saturday and Sunday meetings. Adams always wanted the staff there when he came, and he was an "early to bed, early to rise" man—much to their dismay. The staff was grateful that he liked to play golf on Saturdays.

In 1953, Adams held staff meetings every morning; after 1953, usually three a week. Eisenhower rarely attended. In these meetings, Adams gave assignments and outlined the day's work. Those who attended felt that these conferences were very important. General Persons, after he replaced Adams, held very few staff meetings, however. (Adams left in 1958, after he was accused of accepting gifts from industrialist Bernard Goldfine.)

When John F. Kennedy came into office, he had been the recipient of more expert advice about White House organization than any of his predecessors. He immediately decided that he could not operate on the Eisenhower pattern, and his staff organization represented a return to the basic Roosevelt-Truman model. It could not, of course, be a replica of either—because government in the 1960s was very different. And those elements of the Eisenhower experience that proved useful Kennedy did preserve.

From Campaign Staff to White House

Like Nixon in this respect, Kennedy had another advantage over his predecessors: he had already been operating for many months with a very elaborate campaign-staff organization. Most of the appointees to the White House Office staff had already developed work patterns as assistants to Kennedy. He knew what to expect from them, and they knew his expectations, abilities, and needs.

President Kennedy was his own chief of staff. He initiated assignments; received all reports from his top aides; and, as Sorensen has written, "decided what it is he need *not* decide." He much preferred the burdens of close supervision to "being merely a clerk in his own office."

The workload centered on several key offices. The office of special counsel, under Theodore Sorensen, was restored to its former status. Sorensen was primary staff adviser on domestic policy, and speech-writer par excellence.

In foreign policy and national security, Sorensen's counterpart was McGeorge Bundy. Where Eisenhower's national-security advisers had been concerned with organization and coordination of vast and complex activities involving Defense, State, and a dozen other departments and agencies, the Bundy team was primarily concerned with advising Kennedy on policy matters; the President was his own coordinator.

Bundy was assisted by a group of very able men—an average of ten, called by Kennedy his "little State Department." Bundy held the only meetings that even resembled staff conferences in the Kennedy White House— a briefing each morning for key staffers. None of Kennedy's advisers were ever out of touch with foreign policy, and they could shift from domestic assignments to assist in a foreign-policy crisis with relative ease.

Appointments Secretary Kenneth O'Donnell occupied the third office of major importance. He was a political troubleshooter, handled liaison with the Secret Service and F.B.I. and made arrangements for the President's trips. He also kept watch over the White House Office services. Pierre Salinger, in his memoirs, ranks O'Donnell as the most important member of the staff.

Lawrence O'Brien, a first-class political strategist who became Humphrey's campaign manager, was in charge of Kennedy's legislative liaison. Press relations, particularly crucial for Kennedy after his narrow victory of 1960, were handled by another campaign veteran, Pierre Salinger. Arthur Schlesinger Jr.'s position was unique: he was the White House's liaison with intellectuals in general and with Adlai Stevenson in particular. He was not active in the day-to-day work of the White House, he was the idea man, and kept up a steady stream of memoranda.

There was no hierarchy in the Kennedy staff: He reacted against the abundance of titles under Eisenhower. Most staffers were simply "special assistant to the President," and Kennedy remarked that he wished all had that title.

In sharp contrast to most of their predecessors, the Kennedy men were constantly in the news. They made speeches and public appearances; there were detailed and often romantic stories about them in the press; and already three have written memoirs—behavior considered "unheard of" and "not proper" in the Truman and Eisenhower days.

The Johnson staff kept changing all through the time of this study. Until after the 1964 election, President Johnson was not really free to develop his own staff. He kept on as many of the Kennedy people as possible until 1964—and it was this "let us continue" spirit that made the very smooth transition (contrasted to the Roosevelt-Truman trauma) possible. He was also plagued by departures of the key men he did have. Walter Jenkins had been his chief assistant for 20 years; undoubtedly he would have been the key staff member if he had not collapsed after a scandal in 1964. Then, after the election, Jack Valenti and Bill Moyers departed for outside high-pay and high-prestige jobs. During these same three years, most of the Kennedy men were also leaving the staff.

Some preliminary observations can, however, be made about the Johnson style. The President kept firm personal control over the work of the White House Office. More than any President since Roosevelt, he needed a staff that was intensely personal and absolutely attuned to him.

Perhaps because of his difficulties in fitting his staff to his needs, President Johnson has turned to outside advisers more than any other President since Roosevelt. The most important were three Washington lawyers: James Rowe (a Roosevelt administrative assistant), Abe Fortas (now a Supreme Court Justice), and Clark Clifford (who became Secretary of Defense last year).

A Note on the Methodology

The present study is an analysis of the professional staff in the White House. Most of the data were collected through interviews with the men who have served as staffers since 1939. Beginning in early 1966, I interviewed nearly a fifth of them. They included staff members of all five administrations. The interviews lasted an average of about 90 minutes, and the staffers answered questions about staff organizations and work patterns, how they saw their roles in the White House Office, what they had to do with decision-making, how they were recruited, and (in some cases) why they left. The questioning was open-ended; many volunteered information and suggestions.

I sought to determine to what extent the expanding professional staff changed the nature of the presidency—and was changed by it.

What trends and conclusions can we distill from this detailed analysis of the various White House staffs?

Each President since 1939 has had a distinctly different White House operation, and we can expect the same from Richard Nixon. However, each also learned from and built upon his predecessors' work. Thus, Truman rejected the disorder of the Roosevelt staff, but followed its most salient characteristics as he gathered a group of generalists around him and personally supervised them. And although Kennedy rejected the basic tenets of the Eisenhower staff organization, he incorporated the particular aspects that were useful to him.

Despite the differences, there is a strong thread of continuity. Titles and the approaches to work have been different from one administration to the next; but such functions as appointments, press relations, and patronage have steadily formed the spine of the Office.

Each administration has also contributed an increased workload to the next. The Roosevelt staffers worked hard, but between crises had moments to relax; the Kennedy-Johnson staffers have had few such moments, and neither —most likely—will Nixon's. Every assignment is urgent, each mistake costly, every day high-pressure. The workload has increased enormously since 1939; even when measured by such simple criteria as numbers of phone calls and pieces of mail, the present workload is staggering.

The size of the staff—especially in the numbers of assistants backing up the front-line men—has also increased, but not as rapidly as the work. Moreover, to be effective, the President's personal staff must be small. Eisenhower had the largest staff—but even that was only 25; and respondents agree that more would not be useful.

Each choice of a staff member, therefore, has been crucial. In fact, the standards the staffer must meet are often more restrictive than those for cabinet members. The choice often demands subtle and difficult judgments by the President. The 169 staffers studied were an able and well-trained group. There have been very few abject failures among them.

During the past three decades, then, an expanded personal staff in the White House Office has not prevented the President from being, to quote Woodrow Wilson, "both in law and conscience . . . as big a man as he can." In fact, the White House Office staff actually helps him exert his personality as fully as possible, by overcoming the limitations of the office. The staff has helped make the responsibility bearable, the chain of decisions easier, and the consequences a bit more certain. It will be interesting to see if the same holds true for Richard Nixon's staff.

Down the Bureaucracy!

Matthew P. Dumont

There has been a certain tension among the people of our federal city lately. I am not talking about the black population of the district, which becomes visible to the rest of the world only when its rage boils over. I am referring to the public servants who ooze across the Maryland and Virginia lines each day to manipulate the machinery of government.

It has never been a particularly gleeful population, but in the last year or so it has developed a kind of mass involutional melancholia, a peculiar mixture of depression, anxiety and senescence.

As in similarly depressed communities, the young, the healthy and those with good job prospects have tended to migrate. Among those who have departed are a large proportion of that scarce supply of idealistic and pragmatic people who try to work for social change "within the system." They are leaving because they feel unwanted and ineffectual. Let me describe what they are turning their backs on.

Washington is a malaria swamp covered over with buildings of neofascist design and ringed with military bases.

Do you remember Rastignac shaking his fist at Paris from Goriot's grave site? Washington is a city made for fists to be shaken at. Shaken at, not bloodied on. Federal buildings are especially constructed to be impervious to blood. You can rush headlong into a marble balustrade smearing brains and blood and bile three yards wide. But as the lady does on television, with a smile and a few whisks of a damp cloth, the wonderful material will come up as clean and white and sparkling as before.

Some people have tried burning themselves into the concrete. That doesn't work either.

And, as you might have guessed, all that urine on the Pentagon was gone within minutes after the armies of the night retreated.

No, you may, individually or en masse, descend upon the Federal Triangle. You may try to impale and exsanguinate yourselves, flay, crucify and castrate yourselves. You may scream shrill cries or sing "Alice's Restaurant" or chant "Om," but it won't help. The buildings were made to last forever and to forever remain shining and white, the summer sun glaring off their walls, stunning the passersby.

Inside, one might spend eternity hearing the sounds of his own footsteps in the corridors of these buildings and never see his sun-cast shadow. If you took all the corridors in all of the federal buildings in Washington and laid them end to end, and inclined one end slightly and started a billiard ball rolling down, by the time it reached the lower end, the ball would have attained such a velocity that it would hurtle on through space while approaching an infinite mass and thereby destroy the universe. This is not likely to happen because such co-ordination is unheard of among federal agencies. But we will get to that later.

Off the corridors are offices and conference rooms. (There is also a core of mail chutes, telephone lines, elevator shafts, sewer pipes, trash cans and black people, but these are all invisible.) The offices have desks—wooden ones for important people and steel ones for unimportant people. (Otherwise, the distinction is impossible to make unless you could monitor their telephone calls to each other and determine the relative hierarchy depending on whose secretary manages to keep the other party waiting before putting her boss on.)

The offices also contain file cabinets that are filled with paper. The paper is mainly memos—the way people in the federal government communicate to one another. When communication is not necessary, memos "for the record" are written and filed. It has been estimated that the approximate cost in labor and supplies for the typing of a memo is 36¢. The cost in professional time for its preparation is incalculable.

The conference rooms are for conferences. A conference is for the purpose of sharing information among a group of federal officials who have already been apprised of the information to be shared, individually, by memo. Coffee and cigarettes are consumed. By prior arrangement, each participant is, in turn, interrupted by his secretary for an urgent phone call. After the conference additional memos are exchanged.

But let me describe the people who work in the federal government because some mythology must be laid to rest.

They are good people, which is to say that they are no less good than anyone else, which is to say that we are all pretty much cut from the same material and most of it is pretty rotten. I do not wish to be cavalier about the problem of evil, but I will ask you to accept as a premise for this thesis that the differences between the "best of us" and the "worst of us" are no greater than the differences *within* each of us at varying times.

I have been and will be more sober and precise about this issue in other writings, but what I am attempting to convey is a conviction that the great evils of mankind, the genocides and holy wars, the monstrous exploitations and negligences and injustices of societies have less to do with the malice of individuals than with unexamined and unquestioned institutional practices.

I am talking about the Eichmannism —a syndrome wherein individual motives, consciences or goals become irrelevant in the context of organizational behaviors. This can be seen in pure culture in the federal government. There are a host of written rules for behavior for the federal civil servants, but these are rarely salient. It is the unwritten rules, tacit but ever present, subtle but overwhelming, unarticulated but commanding, that determine the behavior of the men and women who buzz out their lives in the spaces defined by the United States government.

These rules are few in number. Rule number one is to *maintain your tenure*. This is at the same time the most significant and the easiest rule to abide by. If you desire to keep a job for several decades and retire from it with an adequate pension, and if you have the capacity to appear at once occupied and inconspicuous, then you can be satisfied as a "fed."

Appearing occupied means walking briskly at all times. It means looking down at your desk rather than up into the distance when thinking. It means always having papers in your hands. Above all, it means, when asked how things are, responding "very hectic" rather than "terrific" or "lousy."

Being inconspicuous means that your competence in appearing occupied should be expressed quietly and without affect. The most intolerable behavior in a civil servant is psychotic behavior. Being psychotic in the federal government is looking people directly in the eye for a moment too long. It is walking around on a weekday without a tie. It is kissing a girl in an elevator. (It doesn't matter whether she is a wife, mistress, secretary or daughter.) It is writing a memo that is excessively detailed, or refusing to write memos. It is laughing too loud or too long at a conference. It is taking a clandestine gulp of wine in a locker room rather than ordering two martinis over lunch. (This explains why there are more suspensions for alcohol-

ism among lower level workers than higher level ones.)

In short, there is no more sensitive indicator of deviant behavior than personnel records of the federal government.

This does not mean that federal officials never vary their behavior. Currently, for example, it is modish to sport the hierarchy (after the protection of your own tenure) is the protection of your superior's tenure rather than the fulfillment of assigned responsibilities. (Obvious exceptions to this rule are J. Edgar Hoover and certain elements in the Department of Defense, who, like physicians and priests, respond to a higher authority.)

The third unwritten rule of federal behavior is to *make sure that all appropriated funds are spent by the end of the fiscal year*. Much of the paper that stuffs the orifices of executive desks has to do with justifications for requests for more money. For money to be returned after such justifications are approved is to imply that the requester, his supervisor and Congress itself were improvident in their demands on the taxpayer's money. It would be like a bum asking for a handout for a cup of coffee. A passerby offers a quarter and the bum returns 15¢ saying, "Coffee is only a dime, schmuck."

Contract hustlers, who abound in Washington, known that their halcyon days are in late spring when agencies are frequently panicked at the realization that they have not exhausted their sideburns and a moustache. The specter of thousands of civil servants looking like Che Guevara may seem exciting, but it has no more significance than cuffless trousers.

You may or may not wish to follow the fashions, but do not initiate them. In general, follow a golden mean of behavior, that is, do what most people seem to be doing. Do it quietly. And if you are not sure how to behave, take annual leave.

The second rule of behavior in the government, and clearly related to the sustenance of your own tenure, is to *keep the boss from getting embarrassed*. That is the single, most important stan-

dard of competence for a federal official. The man who runs interference effectively, who can anticipate and obviate impertinent, urgent or obvious demands from the boss's boss, or from the press, or from the public, or from Congress, will be treasured and rewarded. This is so pervasive a desideratum in a civil servant that the distinction between line and staff activities becomes thin and artificial in the face of it. Your primary function in operating funds and may be in the black by the fiscal year's end. Agencies that administer grant-in-aid programs celebrate end-of-fiscal-year parties with Dionysian abandon when instead of having a surplus of funds they cannot pay all of their obligations.

The only effective way to evaluate a federal program is the rapidity with which money is spent. Federal agencies, no less than purveyors of situation comedies, cigarettes and medical care, are dominated by a marketplace mentality which assumes that you have a good product if the demand exceeds the supply.

The fourth unwritten rule of behavior in government is to *keep the program alive*. It is not appropriate to question the original purposes of the program. Nor is it appropriate to ask if the program has any consonance with its original purposes. It is certainly not appropriate to assume that its purposes have been served. It is only appropriate to assume that once a program has been legislated, funded and staffed it must endure. An unstated and probably unconscious blessing of immortality is bestowed upon the titles that clutter organizational charts in federal agencies.

Congress, with its control of funds, is perceived as a nurturant breast with a supply of vital fluids that may at any time run dry and thus starve the program to death. Such a matter must be looked upon with intense ambivalence, a state of mind associated with schizophrenia in the hostile-dependent offspring. And, indeed, Congress is perceived by federal executives with a mixture of adulation and rage, and, indeed, federal programming is schizophrenic. Like the schizophrenic, federal programs have the capacity to assume pseudomorphic identities, having the outline and form of order and direction and vitality but actually being flat, autistic and encrusted with inorganic matter. Like the schizophrenic, federal programs develop a primitive narcissism that is independent of feedback from the environment other than the provision of life-sustaining funds.

Even programs that are conceived with some imagination as relatively bold and aggressive attempts to institutionalize change, such as Model Cities or Comprehensive Community Mental Health Centers or Community Action Programs, become so preoccupied with survival that compromises in the face of real or imagined criticism from Congress very quickly blunt whatever cutting edges the program may have had.

The fifth and final unwritten rule of federal behavior is to *maintain a stable and well-circumscribed constituency*. With so great a concern for survival in the government, it is necessary to have friends outside of it. One's equity within an agency and a program's equity in Congress are a function of equity with vested interests outside. The most visible and articulate vestedness is best to cultivate. Every agency and every department knows this, as does every successful executive. The constituency not only represents survival credits but has the quality of a significant reference group. The values, purposes and rewards of the federal agent must mesh with those of his program's constituents.

It is easy to see how this works between the Defense Department and the military-industrial complex; between Agriculture and the large, industrialized farming interests; between Labor and the unions; between Commerce and big business. It is obvious that the regulatory commissions of government have a friendly, symbiotic relationship with the organizations they were meant to monitor. It is less clear, however, that the good guys in government, the liberals who run the "social programs," have their exclusive constituents as well. The constituents of welfare programs are not welfare recipients, but social workers. The constituents of education-

al programs are not students, but educators. The constituents of health programs are the providers of health care, not their consumers. The mental health programs of the government are sensitive to the perturbations of mental health professionals and social scientists, not so much to the walking wounded.

In the latter case, for example, to suggest that nonprofessionals should have something to say about the expenditure of millions of research, training and service dollars is to threaten a constituency. And a threatened one is an unfriendly one, which is not good for the program in Congress or for the job possibilities of the executive in the marketplace. As long as the constituency is stable and circumscribed, credits can be counted.

These, then, are the rules of behavior for functionaries in the federal bureaucracy. If they sound familiar, they should. They are not by any means unique to this system. With minor alterations, they serve as the uncodified code of conduct in any organization. They are what sustained every archbureaucrat from Pilate to Eichmann. They explain in large part why the United States government is such a swollen beast, incapable of responding to the unmet needs of so many people.

But only in part. One other feature of the Washington scene must be described before we can say we know enough of it to elaborate a strategy of assault. This has to do with power.

There is a lot of nonsense about power in the government. One sees a black Chrysler with a vinyl top speeding by. A liveried chauffeur, determined and grim, operates the vehicle. In the rear, a gooseneck, high-intensity lamp arched over his shoulder, sits a man studying the *Washington Post*. One is tempted to say, "There goes a man of power."

It is a vain temptation. Power in the government does not reside within gray eminences in black Chryslers. It is a soft, pluralistic business shared by a large number of middle managers. Organizational charts in federal agencies read as if there is a rigid line of authority and control from the top down. It would appear that the secretary of

each department with his designated assistants and deputies would control the behavior of the entire establishment. In fact, there is a huge permanent government that watches with covert bemusement as the political appointees at the top come and go, attempting in their turn to control the behavior of the agencies "responsible to them."

This does not mean that there is not a good deal of respect and deference paid by middle managers to their superiors. But, as in many organizations, this deference can have an empty and superficial quality to it that amounts to mockery. In most hospitals, for example, it is not the doctors who determine what happens to patients, but nurses. Nurses may appear as subordinate to physicians as slaves to their masters, but as soon as the doctor has left the ward the nurse does what she wants to do anyway.

Similarly, in federal agencies, it is the great army of middlemanagers that controls the show. There is not even the built-in accountability of a dead patient for the boss to see.

Power in the government resides less in position and funds than it does in information, which is the medium of exchange. The flow of information is controlled not at the top, but at the middle. There is very little horizontal flow between agencies because of the constant competition for funds, and all vertical flow must be mediated by the bureaucrats who make up the permanent government.

This concentration of power in the middle, controlled by masses of managers who subscribe to the unwritten code of behavior described above, is the reason why the national government is essentially unresponsive. It does not respond to the top or the bottom; it does not respond to ideology. It is a great, indestructible mollusk that absorbs kicks and taunts and seductions and does nothing but grow.

But it's worse than that. The government is righteous. The people who man the bastions of the executive branch (like the rest of us) have the capacity to invest their jobs with their personal identities. Because it is theirs, their function must be defended. Their roles become, in the language of psychiatry, ego-syntonic. Their sense of personal integrity, their consciences, their self-esteem begin to grow into the positions they hold. It is as if their very identities partake of the same definition as their organizationally defined function.

Can you imagine trying to fight a revolution against a huge, righteous marshmallow? Even if you had enough troops not to be suffocated by it, the best you can hope for is to eat it. And, as you all know, you become what you eat. And that is the point. For a revolution to be meaningful it must take into account the nature of organizational life. It must assume that the ideologically pure and the ideologically impure are subject to the same Eichmannesque forces. If a revolution harbors the illusion that a reign of terror will purify a bureaucracy of scoundrels and exploiters, it will fail. It matters little whether bureaucrats are Royalist or Republican, Czarist or Bolshevik, Conservative or Liberal, or what have you. It is the built-in forces of life in a bureaucracy that result in the bureaucracy being so indifferent to suffering and aspiration.

Does this mean that radical change is not possible? No. It means that intelligence and planning must be used, as well as rhetoric, songs, threats, uniforms and all the other trappings of a "movement." The intelligence and planning might orient themselves around a concept of nonalienated revolution that relies on a strategy of guerrilla administration.

This is not meant to be an exclusive strategy. Social change, radical and otherwise, has to be a pluralistic phenomenon. It needs to allow for foxes as well as hedgehogs. This represents one attempt, then, to approach the Great White Marshmallow in such a way that victories are neither impossible nor terrible.

Assuming that power in the federal government is controlled by a vast cadre of middle managers who are essentially homeostatic, and assuming the softness and purposelessness of the system in which they operate, it is conceivable that a critical mass of change agents working within that system may be effective in achieving increasingly significant ad hoc successes.

This requires a group of people who are prepared to work as civil servants but who have little or no concern with the five unwritten rules of behavior of such service. Specifically, their investment in their own jobs carries a very limited liability. The ultimate sanction, being fired, is no sanction at all. Either because they command credentials which will afford them the security they need wherever they work or because they emerge from a generation that has not been tainted by the depression and so have fewer security needs, they are not afraid of being fired.

While they may like the boss, and one may hope they do, they do not see themselves as primarily concerned with saving him from embarrassment.

Spending the program money by the end of the fiscal year and the related rule—keeping the program alive—are significant to them only insofar as the program's purposes mesh with their social consciences, and then only insofar as the program is demonstrating some fealty to those purposes.

Most important, however, is that this critical mass of change agents *not* abide by the rule of maintaining a stable and circumscribed constituency. This is at the same time a liberating principle of behavior and a major strategy of change. It is precisely by broadening the base of the constituencies of federal programs that they will become more responsible to the needs of more people.

This network of communication and collaboration shares as its purpose the frustration of the bureaucracy. But it is the homeostatic, self-serving and elitist aspects of bureaucratic life that are to be frustrated. And this can only be accomplished through the creative tension that emerges from a constant appreciation of unmet needs.

The network of change agents represents a built-in amplifier of those needs either because the agents are, themselves, among the poor, the colored and the young or because they are advocates of them.

It is not critical that the guerrilla administrators who compromise this network be in a position to command funds or program directions. They must simply have access to information, which, you recall, is the medium of exchange in government.

This network, in order to avoid the same traps as the bureaucracy it is meant to frustrate, should never become solidified or rigidified in structure and function. It may have the form of a floating crap game whose location and participation are fluid and changing, but whose purposes and activities are constant. The contacts should remain informal, nonhierarchical and task-oriented. The tasks chosen should be finite, specific, salient and feasible. The makeup of each task force is an ad hoc, self-selected clustering of individuals whose skills or location or access to information suggests their roles. This network of change agents becomes a reference group, but not a brotherhood. There need not be a preoccupation with loyalty, cordiality or steadfastness. They do not even have to be friendly.

This is a rather dry and unromantic strategy of social change. It does not stir one's heart or glands. Where is the image of Parnell pulling his cap low on his forehead as he points his gallant band to the General Post Office? Or Lenin approaching the borders of a trembling Russia in a sealed train? Or Fidel or Che? Or Spartacus, or Mao? Where are the clasped hands and the eyes squinting into a distant line of troops? Where are the songs, the flags, the legends? Where is the courage? Where is the glory?

Such a revolutionary force has nothing of the triumphal arch in it. Nor has it anything of the gallows. It lives without the hope of victory or the fear of defeat. It will yearn for saints and despair of scoundrels, but it will see as its eternal mission the subversion of those systems that force both saints and scoundrels into a common, faceless repression of the human spirit.

Thomas P. Murphy

Executive Branch Lobbying

Lobbying is the process through which representatives of an organization work to change government policies and procedures in ways that will increase the income, power or benefits of that organization. Traditionally, lobbying has been considered the province of industry, labor, farm, medical and veteran interest groups. Now, however, such private organizations have been joined by public interest groups such as Common Cause and Executive Branch lobbyists.

Although not a new governmental phenomenon, federal agency lobbying has now been converted from spasmodic involvement to an institutionalized policy and procedure known as congressional liaison. This activity is classified as "information giving" rather than "lobbying" because Title 18 of the U.S. Code prohibits agencies from lobbying with federal funds. Despite this prohibition, in 1970 the cost of executive branch liaison with Congress exceeded the total *reported* amount of lobbying expenditures by all the industry, union, veteran, medical and public interest groups combined. Industry lobbies the legislative and the executive branches for policy and procedural decisions which will increase profits or provide subsidies; federal agencies attempt in various ways to influence Congress in order to secure appropriations to perform the jobs they believe should be done. Their objective is to establish and maintain a positive relationship with Congress so that the reaction to the agency's legislative and appropriations requests will be favorable. In the stiff competition for scarce resources, federal agencies are as active as universities, cities, counties and states in attempting to influence the legislature to protect their "home" interest. The National Aeronautics and Space Administration (NASA) provides an excellent case study of a congressional liaison office. One of the fastest growing agencies in federal history, NASA attained its highest budgets during the 89th Congress (1965-1966) while the Apollo project was at its peak. This led the agency into extensive contact with Congress.

THE NASA LEGISLATIVE AFFAIRS OFFICE

NASA was created in 1958 and its budget moved from $135 million in fiscal year 1959 to $5.25 billion in fiscal year 1965. From 1961 to 1968 James E. Webb, an experienced government official, served as NASA's administrator. Webb handled the early years of the agency's development very well and his was a complex job; NASA's budget almost doubled annually for several years, and building the agency meant bringing together a number of diverse government organizations into one new research and development organization. In addition, NASA had major involvements with international affairs because of the nature of rockets and satellites; it faced serious public affairs problems and challenges; and it was concerned with many key questions relating to research and development expenditures, patents and contracting problems. Webb's experience in international, budgetary, congressional and managerial affairs made him eminently qualified for the job.

Webb had known most of the key leaders of both parties in the Senate and House for many years. No matter how intensely involved he became with the many missions of NASA, Webb always maintained an alert ear for developments in NASA's external relations and followed closely the performance of his legislative office.

Upon taking office Webb moved Paul Dembling, the long-time general counsel of the National Advisory Committee for Aeronautics, NASA's primary predecessor, into the position of director of congressional affairs. By 1962, the 12 employees of the office were organized into three groups: a correspondence group to answer congressional inquiries; a liaison group to shepherd NASA appropriation and other bills through the two legislative and appropriations committees; and a legislative group to foster NASA relationships with other committees of Congress as well as to explain budgetary reprogrammings to Congress.

in Congress — The NASA Case

Congress gave NASA considerable budgetary freedom because of the unique nature of its mission and the fact that it was hard to predict its costs or timetables. Nevertheless, NASA, like most other major agencies had to undergo annual authorization as well as the appropriation process.

Webb maintained direct personal contact with the chairmen of the NASA committees and with certain other legislators. He carried on a continuous stream of telephone and written communications with key members of the Congress and remained personally available for calls from congressmen.

A fair proportion of the calls from the Hill to the administrator were complaints about requests which had been rejected. This enabled Webb to keep tabs on how effectively his congressional office was operating. Another monitoring device consisted of having his office receive a copy of all written contacts with Congress, regardless of who signed them. His office screened these letters and decided which ones should be brought to his attention.

In 1964 there was a reorganization in NASA which reflected the increasing size and complexity of the program. In order to provide better coordination among some of the externally related key staff offices without further taxing the administrator, Webb named Dr. George L. Simpson, Jr. as assistant deputy administrator. Simpson was to handle the offices of congressional affairs, policy planning, public affairs, international affairs and technology utilization. NASA's Office of Legislative Affairs, which in 1965 and 1966 had 27 employees, developed a system of access to the staff meetings of the three key program offices. Each member of the liaison staff was in a sense an "account executive" for one of these offices and, by keeping up with its problems and developments, was in a better position to represent its interests to the congressional subcommittee which monitored its activities.

One of the most significant problems of a liaison office is to anticipate the problems the agency will face when legislation reaches the Hill each year. For example, in November of 1964, a summary, program area by program area, was made to identify potential trouble spots in the 1965 hearings. The NASA hearing process is extensive because of the large amount of money involved. Yet these hearings involve many witnesses who are primarily technical rather than administratively oriented, while the congressmen and the committee staff members generally do not have technical backgrounds. Administrative policy questions not specifically related to technical subjects, but having implications across the entire agency, are often discussed. One of

the potential weaknesses in the NASA approach to Congress is in briefing these technical people as to the policy implications of a broad spectrum of administrative questions and issues involving NASA. Webb did much to overcome this by his annual congressional briefing to all NASA management officials who were expected to testify at such hearings. This briefing usually was held in early January, just after the President's budget was announced.

Congressional investigations were a special category of activity. For example, in 1965 NASA was involved directly or indirectly in over 15 separate congressional investigations of major scope leading to reports by major committees. Some of these were limited to NASA, whereas others involved broad questions of research and development policy in which NASA was just one of several agencies being investigated.

Many of the investigations were anticipated because they represented unresolved issues from prior years. Another reason for the accuracy of the agency's predictions was that they were based on careful intelligence activity with the staffs of the various House and Senate committees. Since these professional staff personnel are responsible for generating most of the issues for the members of Congress their input was invaluable and helped to preclude too many surprises. In some situations, position papers were prepared and distributed to potential witnesses so they would be informed on agency policy relating to particular questions.

The original organization of NASA's legislative office into three divisions is still in effect. To develop a clearer perspective on the total liaison process, each of these divisions will be reviewed.

CONGRESSIONAL INQUIRIES DIVISION

Written inquiries from Congress were handled in a Congressional Inquiries Division. Most of the requests involved were routine matters facing every congressional affairs office such as referral of resumes on persons seeking employment; general information requests regarding NASA programs; invitations for NASA officials to speak at various programs and functions throughout the nation; complaints, appeals and information requests relating to the award of NASA contracts; and tour, exhibit, and astronaut appearance requests. Requests of the same type came to NASA directly from the public. This meant that the agency had to have a mechanism for responding to general constituent requests for the same services requested by congressmen.

All NASA mail arrived in a central mail room, and all mail bearing a congressional return address was sent automatically to the congressional office regardless of the person to whom it was addressed. The purpose of this procedure was to insure that regardless of the matter involved, someone with a particular concern for how congressional requests were treated was able to oversee the transaction between the agency and Congress.

The same procedure applied to congressional mail addressed to the NASA administrator. All this mail was opened and logged in the congressional office. A control slip was filled out so that there could be close follow-up to insure that timely replies were made. In the case of letters to the administrator, the head of the congressional office would decide whether the administrator's office should become involved immediately or after the data regarding the matter had been gathered and a reply was ready to go back to Congress. In the former case it was processed to the administrator's secretariat where someone close to Mr. Webb would review that decision and either take it to him for policy guidance or provide general guidance to the congressional office. In each case the secretariat had to indicate whether the outgoing letter should be signed by the administrator or by the assistant administrator for legislative affairs. The assistant administrator sometimes overruled the decisions of the secretariat.

One of the devices which the Congressional Inquiries Division had to learn was that even routine requests from the offices of congressmen on NASA's key committees could also be of interest to the Liaison Division which was in regular face-to-face contact with congressmen. After being apprised that a request from a NASA committee member was being considered, the Liaison Division might decide to hand-carry the letter directly to the congressman in order to open up a conversation with him on some other matter of interest to NASA. This was especially true in the case of astronaut appearance requests which were answered in the affirmative. No congressman would refuse to discuss logistics regarding such a visit with the liaison office. In addition, that procedure enabled the liaison office to keep tabs on how the key members were being treated by NASA.

Exhibits

NASA developed and maintained a substantial number of exhibits appropriate for display at such events as high school science fairs, county and state fairs, and teacher conventions. These served to tell NASA's story to the nation. After the initial purchase there was relatively little expenditure other than the cost of shipping and of setting up and dismantling the exhibits. If at all possible, congressional requests for these displays were met. Insufficient time for

making shipping arrangements or unavailability of displays because of other commitments were virtually the only reasons for turning down a request. One firm NASA policy with regard to exhibits was that they could not be used for commercial purposes such as at grand openings of shopping centers.

During 1965, NASA responded positively to 92 of 109 congressional requests for exhibits. Seventy-three requests came from the House and 36 from the Senate. NASA filled 66 (88 percent) of the House requests and 26 (78.8 percent) of those from the Senate, for a combined average of 85 percent. Twenty-one of these requests (20 percent) were from members of the various NASA committees. The agency responded favorably to 18 (86 percent) of these requests, although NASA filled all 11 requests received from the House Committee on Science and Astronautics. The disproportionate number of requests and of approvals for the House Space Committee was directly attributable to the practice of the Congressional Liaison Division staff offering these exhibits to members of the committee during their periodic visits. As a result, committee members were more aware than other congressmen that exhibits existed. When they indicated an interest, the liaison man made sure that their request was met. However, it appears that the agency attempted to fill as many requests as possible without any political consideration.

Speeches

Congressional requests for NASA speakers, other than astronauts, were also responded to affirmatively whenever possible. This was not only a question of being responsive to the congressman, it also increased the general public's knowledge of and interest in the agency and was handled routinely by the Public Affairs Office.

While the agency had a policy of responding favorably to all congressional requests, it appears that requests from the House Committee on Science and Astronautics received higher priority than those from other members of Congress.

However, congressional requests were only one source of requests for speakers. During the six-month period from August 2, 1965, to February 7, 1966, NASA provided personnel for approximately 1,016 speaking engagements; at a rate of 76 per year, congressional requests represented only 3.8 percent of the total. However, only about 50 percent of the general public's requests were honored, as compared with 73.8 percent for Congress. An internal NASA report covering 467 of these meetings in 1965 showed that 188 civic organizations, 115 educational organizations and 164 professional, nontechnical organizations served as sponsors. Attendance ranged from ten to 4,300, and totaled approximately 82,711. Thus, this was a very effective way of reaching a large number of people interested in learning about the NASA program.

Astronaut Appearances

Perhaps the most significant "constituent service" which NASA could provide a congressman was that of arranging for an astronaut to make a public appearance in the congressman's home town or key cities in his district. Such appearances generated a great deal of press, radio and television coverage. Generally the congressman who secured the astronaut introduced him and thereby received a great deal of favorable public exposure. This was a particularly good way to respond to the needs of key congressmen and senators who for one reason or another may have opposed the NASA program or for whom NASA could do little else.

A request from a key senator may even be more significant if that individual serves on more than one committee. Senator Margaret Chase Smith's membership on both the Senate Space Committee and the Senate Appropriations Subcommittee, which handles NASA's appropriations, is a good case in point. She was very sensitive about the fact that Maine, because of its lack of an appropriate industrial base, was not generally able to reap the benefits of NASA procurement contracts. Considering this hard reality and Senator Smith's importance to NASA's programs, it was extremely difficult to deny a request from her for a speaker or an astronaut.

In spite of the potential advantages, for many reasons the number of astronaut appearances arranged for congressmen had to be extremely limited. Congressmen and the general public recognized and generally accepted the fact that the busy training schedule of an astronaut would not allow much time for public relations. NASA had to be mindful of the possible or perceived relationship between some absence from the training program due to a speaking engagement and some later failure in space. Should an astronaut be injured or killed in an accident while en route to such an appearance, many would be quick to point out that it cost four or five hundred thousand dollars to train this individual, only to have his life lost in vain on a public relations mission.

After early enthusiasm, the astronauts did not demonstrate a great deal of interest in this type of assignment. In the first place, most were hesitant to become too closely associated with a particular congressman. Some congressmen attempted to "claim" as their own those astronauts whose home towns were located in their districts. However, they were generally unsuccessful for the reasons already mentioned and the fact that most military men had a number of "home towns" and had been away from most of them for many years.

When a personal appearance by an astronaut is impossible, an attractive alternative is his appearance on a congressmen's taped television program for viewing by the folks back home. This is a relatively simple process after the astronaut is in Washington, and requires only about a half hour of his time. In this way several congressmen could be accommodated in a relatively short time at the House or Senate recording studio. The programs consisted of an introduction, a short briefing by the astronaut, and a question and answer session led by the congressman. The time of the taped interview usually exceeded that of the scheduled program to permit the political leader to edit and select those questions and answers which best served his purpose. The only potential hazard in using the television interview technique is that it may generate requests for personal appearances by the astronauts which the congressman may not be able to arrange.

Congressional requests for astronaut appearances in 1965 were exceeded only by the number of job referrals and publication requests. Twenty-two, or 10 percent, of the 223 congressional requests resulted in an astronaut appearance. Members of committees dealing with NASA were more successful than other members of Congress. Fourteen percent of their requests were filled as opposed to the general congressional acceptance rate of 10 percent. There was, however, some variation in the degree of success experienced by the members of individual committees and subcommittees.

Members of the Senate Appropriations Subcommittee on Independent Offices enjoyed 16.7 percent success, while only 4.3 percent of the requests of members of the Senate Committee on Aeronautical and Space Sciences were filled. The House Committee on Science and Astronautics and the House Appropriations Subcommittee fared much better. The Manned Space Flight Subcommittee members (whose jurisdiction most directly affected the astronauts) had 33.3 percent of their requests filled.

The small total number (22) of astronaut appearances arranged for congressmen by NASA in 1965 does not permit many generalizations. However, NASA was more responsive to requests from members of its own committees than to those who had limited or no contact with the agency.

Personnel Referrals

There are still people who feel that it is necessary, or at least helpful, to be recommended by their congressmen if they are to obtain federal jobs. Both in theory and practice, this has not been a valid assumption. First, contrary to what many people think, the number of positions in any agency that can be filled outside of the civil service selection process is extremely small. At the time of the 1964 presidential election, out of a civilian work force of nearly three million, there were only about 2,200 positions (exclusive of postmaster jobs) which could be filled by means other than the merit selection process. Most of these positions are excluded from the regular selection process because they involve policy determination or a close personal relationship with the agency head or his key officials. Thus, the number of appointments which can be made strictly on political considerations is proportionately quite small.

This is not to suggest, however, that *all* of the other positions in the executive branch are filled without any political consideration. If all other factors are equal and an individual sponsored by a congressman important to the agency is qualified, any agency is more likely to hire the person with a congressional recommendation. However, Civil Service Commission rules and regulations have in many instances prevented the employment of applicants desired by the agency, and these same rules have also provided an available mechanism to refuse to hire a job seeker referred to the agency by Congress.

Another factor which inhibits the employment of persons referred by congressmen is the traditional distrust and distaste career civil servants have for individuals who try to use political connections to get a job. Agency management sees not only the immediate problem of making a position for him, but also the potential problem should it become necessary to take action which would adversely affect such an employee. This hesitance to place the agency in a situation in which a continuing political involvement is possible is extremely strong in an organization such as NASA which is staffed primarily by professional and scientific people.

Most of the placements made by the NASA Office of Legislative Affairs were really repayments by the hiring office for favors done by the congressional office. Weak spots in a presentation may have been strengthened, difficult procurement arrangements may have been resolved, or the Office of Legislative Affairs may have requested that the committee restore funds for purposes they considered important. If a politically-referred applicant was ever hired through the auspices of the personnel office, the congressional liaison office would have wondered what it had done wrong. In a few cases, success was due only to the ability of the assistant administrator for legislative affairs to go directly to program directors and appeal to their organizational conscience to take their "share" of congressional referrals. However, these victories did not come cheaply. Agencies which have a much better record than NASA in these placements have often done so through having a highly placed administrative official establish a series of quotas for its major organizations to take politically referred employees. No such system operated in NASA.

Most congressmen accept the civil service method of filling career-type positions. Often they are somewhat embarrassed by making an employment request and really do not expect a positive response by the agency. Therefore it becomes a matter of the congressmen, and in turn the congressional liaison office and personnel officer, demonstrating to the applicant that a reasonable effort was made to find him a job. This effort usually consists of finding new and sincere sounding verbiage to pass on the same old message, "We just do not have a suitable vacancy for the applicant at this time." This approach usually works quite well in the case of the 62-year-old salesman who wants to "devote the rest of his working career to the public service," but it leaves something to be desired in the case of the 23-year-old law school graduate.

Thus, employment of individuals referred by congressmen has not been used extensively by NASA as a method of developing congressional support. From the congressman's point of view, it appears that in terms of payoff he should spend his efforts in other endeavors. However, he still receives letters requesting employment and must reply to them. He appreciates the help of an agency which can give him a timely reply and evidence of having tried, even if it cannot respond favorably.

Other Constituent Services

The remaining activities labeled "constituent services" consist primarily of providing information. All requests for information are filled. In 1965 there were 1,600 requests for NASA publications; 174 for procurement information; and 96 for statistical information on grants, contracts, flights, astronauts, satellites and other aspects of NASA activity. Members of the NASA committees made 48 (27 percent) of the procurement information requests and 27

(28 percent) of the requests for statistical information, but less than 10 percent of the House members and only 14 percent of the Senate, or a total of less than 11 percent of Congress, is directly assigned to NASA committees.

The Office of Public Affairs usually has developed appropriate information to fill requests for NASA publications, and the liaison office merely selects the material that fits the circumstance and sends it to the congressman for transmittal to his constituent. Requests for procurement information usually come from small businessmen who desire government contracts or who have become entangled with the bureaucracy and need help. Here again, this is common information and can be handled on a routine basis.

There has been, however, more individual and personal involvement in responses by NASA to congressional requests for information concerning the treatment accorded constituents who had contracts. Many times the contractors have not fulfilled the contract and it has been necessary for the agency to withhold the final payment. In this type of situation, there is really nothing the congressman can do, and the agency can only explain the policy to the congressman. These problems are usually handled by junior-level personnel in the liaison office as most of the answers are standardized.

The glamour and interest generated by NASA resulted in an increasing number of congressional requests to arrange tours of Cape Kennedy and Houston for their constituents. Whenever possible, these requests were filled. Requests were denied only if they coincided with certain flight missions which required part or all of the installation to be off-limits. During 1965, the Office of Legislative Affairs arranged for 175 tours of Cape Kennedy and 14 of the Manned Space Center in Houston. Again, both of these centers had well-organized tour offices which merely added these people to their lists. However, some congressionally-referred visitors received extra attention and transportation on their tours.

The services NASA provides for congressmen enable them to satisfy requests from their constituents, so most congressmen appreciate the agency's responsiveness. Since many agencies have not responded effectively to similar requests, this record helps to reenforce the NASA success image developed in the manned lunar flights.

THE CONGRESSIONAL LIAISON DIVISION

The Congressional Liaison Division is responsible specifically for NASA committee relationships, monitoring and analyzing vote records, and maintaining a line of communication to Congress in behalf of the agency. The Congressional Liaison Division involves extensive personal contacts on Capitol Hill. These contacts relate directly to NASA's bills and appropriations and so are more likely to involve the senators and representatives, rather than their staffs. Thus, development of effective techniques for dealing with the committees and individual members of Congress became crucial. However, because of the unique and powerful position occupied by staff personnel, being able to satisfy these key people can on occasion be even more important than contacts with the members of Congress themselves.

Committee Relationships

Different approaches were necessary with regard to the Senate Aeronautical and Space Sciences Committee and the House and Senate Appropriations Subcommittees on Independent Offices. For good reason, neither of these committees could devote the amount of time to NASA that the House Science and Astronautics Committee did. The Appropriations Committees handle appropriations for the entire federal government and even their Independent Offices Subcommittees handle a multiplicity of agencies, including such giants as the Veterans Administration, the Department of Housing and Urban Development, the National Science Foundation and the regulatory agencies, besides NASA. Their role generally does not call for them to go into the agency programs with the depth of understanding that is required by the authorizing committee. Appropriations subcommittees must decide how urgently various agencies need funds, considering the total amount available in a particular year.

Senate legislative committees necessarily spend less time on their function than their House counterparts. There are only 100 senators compared to 435 representatives, yet the Senate must consider all the same problems and legislation considered in the House. This means a senator might be on four committees instead of the one or two on which a representative might serve. Committees therefore tend to meet less often and have fewer members in attendance.

For these reasons the Liaison Division chief tended to handle personally many of the contacts with the two appropriations subcommittees and the Senate Aeronautical and Space Sciences Committee. The assistant administrator or his deputy also worked directly on these contacts. When research or coordination was needed, this was passed on to the man responsible for the operating program area concerned.

The division was concerned that the best available witnesses were present for congressional hearings; that written testimony was prepared in advance according to the rules set down by the committee; that there was a briefing of witnesses on matters of importance to the members of the committee; that witnesses were introduced properly; that the witnesses handled the questions asked at the hearing correctly; that the appropriate persons in the agency were briefed on the outcome of the hearing; and that information requested for the record was provided. They also used their contacts with the committee staff to secure feedback on matters of interest to the committee.

In 1965 alone, 78 NASA witnesses appeared at hearings on 18 separate issues before nine different House and Senate committees. The testimony before the House Committee on Science and Astronautics on the fiscal year 1966 authorization bill, for example, filled 3,233 pages. In addition there was a substantial hearing record in connection with Senate consideration of the authorization bill, of the special inquiry into NASA's post-Apollo plans, and of the appropriation bill.

Congressional Field Trips

During 1965, 32 representatives took a total of 78 field trips, another function for which the Division performed staff and coordination work. Sometimes even official hearings were held in the field at NASA or contractor facilities.

Staff members of the Liaison Division were responsible for arranging these trips and nearly always accompanied the congressmen. They also insured that NASA and contractor employees were appropriately responsive to questions. With regard to contractor employees this was a bit more difficult to accomplish. However, the fact that they too are ultimately affected by congressional decisions usually provided adequate motivation to be responsive.

Field trips reached a zenith with the first Apollo moon flight in July, 1969. NASA invited every member of the House and Senate to Cape Kennedy for that launch. Representative H. R. Gross, Iowa Republican, who serves as Congress's self-appointed economy conscience, prevented the House from adjourning on the day of the launch by objecting to the motion which required unanimous consent. Gross indicated he did not know "a single thing that a member of Congress can contribute . . . by having taken a trip to Florida." Nevertheless, what developed was undoubtedly the largest movement of Congress in history. The Cape Kennedy audience included 230 representatives and 30 senators.

Congressional Notification of Contracts

Very few congressmen turn down the opportunity to issue a press release datelined Washington or to call the contractor to pass on the news of a major contract, implying that they helped to secure it. The ludicrous aspect of this situation is that everyone, except the general public, is aware of the fact that the congressman has not been involved or had any significant impact. The reason for this bit of make-believe is quite simple — publicity and the congressman's need to create the image back home that he is a man who can get things done in Washington. The contract brings additional money and jobs into the district, and he hopes this will be translated into votes for his next election campaign. Thus, it is understandable that congressmen are more than willing to continue this practice and why they are appropriately appreciative of agencies which make it possible for them.

Industry also becomes involved in this political ballet. Many times the firm is advised by the agency three or four weeks in advance of the official announcement. This is especially the case if the agency wants the contractor to start work immediately while contract details are being ironed out. Nevertheless, the contractor acts out his role, displaying surprise and appreciation when the congressman calls to announce the good news. Sometimes the contract is large enough that the White House prefers to make the announcement. Even when the agency is permitted to make the announcement, the White House sometimes dictates *which* senators should be given most of the reflected glory.

There is room for discretion in determining whether the announcement should be made by a particular senator, by both senators, by the congressman from the district affected or some combination of these. These arrangements were worked out on a daily basis by the White House on contracts above a value of over one million dollars. Actually, more than a mere dollar cutoff is involved, since the White House claimed an announcement option on all contracts above the specified level but did not always exercise it. A $500,000 grant in Idaho was often more important politically than a $2,000,000 grant in California.

The foregoing is not meant to suggest that all contracts are awarded without any consideration of or response to political factors. On the contrary, congressmen often have attempted to represent their constituents on contracts, and in some cases political factors may have a bearing upon the final decision. What is suggested, however, is that most contracts are handled routinely between the agency and the contractor, and that the decision is already made by the time the congressman finds out about it.

Preparation of Speeches

Another function of the liaison office which has proven to be quite effective in telling the agency's story is that of preparing speeches for the members of Congress. These speeches are both for presentation to the general public and for introducing and/or supporting NASA's proposals in Congress. Some of these speeches are also used in congressional debates. On occasion the agency will write the speeches for *both* sides of a debate. This is possible because several committee members often ask the committee staff to draft speeches for them. When the annual bill is on the floor, the staff is unable to handle the volume and a helpful liaison man is likely to be asked for assistance. The congressman may or may not know who wrote the speech for him.

Speeches prepared for congressmen to deliver to the public are often based upon input received from the congressmen. For example, one senator might request that the agency emphasize the socioeconomic aspects of the NASA program while another might want to discuss the scientific potential. The most direct and best method of telling the agency's story to Congress is the practice of actually preparing the speech for delivery by the appropriate committee member. This provides the agency the opportunity to identify its needs *to* Congress *through* Congress.

Monitoring Voting Records

To develop positive and friendly relationships with congressmen it is important to "know thy Congressman." One way to develop a feel for a congressmen's political thinking is to analyze his voting record on agency bills. NASA used this tool quite effectively. A rather comprehensive record identified each congressman who voted against NASA, the number of times he voted against the agency and the specific issues which he raised. In cases of doubt, indirect personal approaches were used to determine how the congressman really felt.

All of this information could be used to good advantage. For example, one of the specific problems congressmen faced in the 89th Congress was the charge that the "Great Society" Congress was a rubber-stamp Congress for President Johnson. Opponents in the next election would be sure to charge that the incumbent had never voted against a key Johnson program. This was especially a problem when the freshmen Democrats swept into office in the 1964 Johnson landslide. Many of them won seats in reputedly safe Republican districts. Inquiry showed that congressmen sometimes voted against NASA only to prove they were not rubber-stamp legislators. Since NASA was winning by several hundred votes, it was then possible on *selected* occasions to suggest to members friendly to NASA who needed an anti-administration vote that they could use a particular NASA vote without hurting the agency. This made it easier to solicit a yes vote for NASA during a more closely contested issue. Although this vote record system is not a sophisticated device, it contributes to and is an indication of an effective congressional liaison program.

LEGISLATION DIVISION

The Legislation Division received the NASA authorization and appropriation bills from the General Counsel's office. Then, as required by BOB Circular A-19, it handled clearances from the Bureau of the Budget (BOB) for NASA bills to be presented to Congress. The Division also screened all public bills being considered by Congress for potential impact on NASA and coordinated NASA responses on enrolled enactment reports which on the Bureau of the Budget solicits agency opinions before presidential signature. Consistent with its responsibility to cover general activities of Congress, the Division disseminated an early *NASA Legislative Activities Report* to highlight matters of special NASA interest.

Before NASA could reprogram its funds, it was required to notify its committees. It was almost impossible to know how much certain projects approved by Congress would cost, since they had never been done before, and so a certain amount of financial flexibility was necessary for NASA. NASA's legislation therefore provided that a certain percentage of its research and development appropriation would be transferred to the construction appropriation. Further, money within the appropriation could be redistributed among approved facilities if the NASA committees were advised of the reason why NASA considered this necessary and if the committee did not veto the move during a 30-day waiting period.

As late as 1970 there were still considerable numbers of such transfers of funds in the NASA program. All of these letters were drafted by the Legislation Division in coordination with the operations offices requesting the change, the Budget Office, the Office of the General Counsel and other NASA officials. It might be added that not a single one of these letters was rejected by the committees for lack of detail or specificity. In each case the letter detailed the reason for the requested change, the history of the project, the implications of the inability to make the fund transfer, and the impact on the programs from which the funds would be transferred.

Other congressional committees dealing with general federal administrative practices also took an interest in NASA activities. For example the House and Senate Committees on Government Operations, the Joint Committee on Atomic Energy, the House and Senate Committees on Armed Services, Post Office, and Civil Service, the Small Business Committee, the House and Senate Judiciary Committees were all interested in some aspect of the NASA program ranging from patents and anti-trust questions to legislation relating to federal personnel and pay practices.

The Legislation Division was responsible for monitoring such hearings, providing and briefing witnesses, and insuring that NASA policy positions were expressed and protected. However, it was not possible for the Legislation Division to maintain the intensive relationships with committee staffs that the Liaison Division did with the Space and Appropriations Committees.

HOW NASA FARED IN CONGRESS

Since 90 percent of NASA's budget was distributed to industry and universities on contract, the agency soon became of great interest to Congress for reasons in addition to the size of its budget. The geographic distribution of government contracts, and especially research and development funds, was a major concern in the 1960s because of the assumption by most communities that research and development installations would have a favorable effect upon their area.

In discussing the efforts of the Midwestern Universities Research Association (MURA) to have an AEC accelerator built in Madison, Wisconsin, D. S. Greenberg of *Science* wrote:

When a $150-million research facility is planted on the countryside, all sorts of usually desirable things start to happen to the surrounding area. New industry rushes to the area — as it is now doing, for example, at the previously barren site surrounding NASA's Manned Spacecraft Center in Houston, and other federal agencies take to placing facilities and funds in the region, which is part of the story of the Cambridge and California phenomenon.

Most of the opposition to NASA has been from the economy-minded group in Congress. Not only was NASA

spending giant sums, but it also had an especially serious problem in the geographic distribution of contracts because it dealt mostly with the aerospace industry which has tended to be quite concentrated. For example, in fiscal years 1961 through 1966, NASA contracts awarded to contractors in California totaled just over seven billion dollars — $447 per capita. This must be considered significant for the state as well as for the individual communities involved. A study of the 70 competitive contract awards over $5 million made by NASA from May of 1961 to June 30, 1966, reflected that seven states won 50 of the 70 contracts, including fourteen for California, seven for Florida and Alabama, six for New Jersey and Texas, and five each for New York and Pennsylvania. In self defense, NASA conducted a survey which demonstrated that other states which had the appropriate industrial capacity participated fairly heavily when the subcontracts were awarded. Nevertheless, this is a complex question. Some states with capacity to perform never had a bidding contractor.

NASA was continually compared with the DOD, which has a major impact on each state because of the diversity of its needs. In an article entitled "Military-Industrial Complex," *Newsweek* (June 9, 1969) noted that:

Even more important . . . is the makeup of the armed services and appropriations committees themselves. With few exceptions, the committees are composed of men who either had large defense establishments in their districts when they were appointed or acquired such establishments after they took their seats. The four chairmen are all superpatriotic Southerners whose district or states, as a Washington adage puts it, 'would sink if they got another defense installation.'

The article cited the district of House Armed Services Committee chairman, L. Mendel Rivers, as a dramatic example of this phenomenon. Representative Rivers' district has

an Air Force base, an Army depot, a Naval shipyard, a Marine Air Station, the Paris Island boot camp, two Naval hospitals, a Naval station, a Naval supply center, a Naval weapons station, a fleet ballistic-missile submarine training center, a Polaris missile facility, an Avco Corporation plant, a Lockheed plant, a General Electric plant under construction and an 800 acre plot of ground that has just been purchased by the Sikorsky Aircraft Division of United Aircraft.

Some of these facilities of course predated Rivers. Military payroll in the Rivers' district totaled $2 billion in 1969.

Such efforts on the part of the congressman, who runs on a perennial campaign platform of "Rivers delivers," have not gone unnoticed or unrewarded.

In all fairness to Congress, however, it should be noted this may happen even though no specific pressure is applied. One Pentagon civilian has noted in the same article that the key congressmen do not have to ask. "The military is too smart for them. Do you think Richard Russell [former chairman of the Senate Armed Services Committee] ever asked to have an installation put into Georgia? All he had to do was get appointed chairman and the installations came in." Regardless of who set the process in motion, the congressman or the agency, this type of situation provides ample support for the belief that in some cases factors other than merit are considered in the awarding of government contracts.

Despite these considerations, it is interesting that there is not as much correlation as might be expected between the dollar value of contracts awarded to particular districts and the voting record of their representatives. A review of roll-call voting reveals that seven representatives from the top twenty congressional districts, in terms of NASA contracts, voted against the NASA program 21 times from 1963 through 1965 when almost everyone was for it. Representative Thomas B. Curtis (R-Missouri), whose district ranked sixth in receipt of NASA contracts primarily because the McDonnell Company was located in St. Louis, consistently voted against NASA's authorization and appropriation bills. In fact, representatives of seven of the twenty Congressional districts receiving the greatest volume of NASA dollars voted against NASA with some regularity. All seven of these representatives were conservative Republicans, indicating that ideological considerations were more important to them than federal dollars spent in their districts.

This same phenomenon was even more evident in the Senate. Ten senators from the top ten states in terms of NASA contracts voted against NASA bills or amendments a total of 27 times between 1961 and 1966. The Senate opposition was from both parties, but six Democrats cast 14 of the 27 votes against NASA. Exemplifying the rejection of NASA largesse to their states, senators from New York cast eight votes against NASA, while those from Louisiana, Texas and New Jersey voted against NASA five times each.

Further, of the ten senators who voted against NASA at least nine times on program issues, eight were liberal Democrats. These included Senators Fulbright, Nelson, Neuberger, Clark, McGovern, Proxmire, Douglas and Morse. This could certainly not be considered a regional syndrome, as four are from the Midwest, three from the Far West, one from the East and one from the South.

In summary, the voting evidence leads to four tentative conclusions: first, government contracts do not override strong philosophic positions; second, as long as the voters can be led to believe that the congressman has a significant role in winning contracts, advance notification to congressmen will remain an effective agency tool to build rapport between NASA and Congress; third, where contract decisions are made with an eye to politics, they are as likely to result from executive branch initiative as from specific congressional request; fourth, effective use of public information and congressional liaison offices can enable an agency to create public and congressional support for its program so that individual members of Congress are less likely to challenge it.

CONCLUSION

An agency's congressional fortunes will vary in the long run. NASA rode the crest of the national shock created by Sputnik I. Further, NASA was able to maintain its position only because a successful program was delivered. Eventually it was caught up in the priorities squeeze induced by Vietnam. However, even then the major cuts were made by the executive branch rather than by Congress, where the cuts exceeded 6 percent only once between fiscal years 1959 and 1970 and averaged only slightly over 4 percent.

While the NASA congressional liaison program was effective, its limitations should be made clear. Much of the selling of the program happened at Cape Kennedy, in orbit, and on the way to Venus and the moon. The greatest spokesmen were Mr. Webb, the astronauts, and other top NASA administrators such as Deputy Administrator Hugh L. Dryden and Dr. Robert Seamans, the Associate Administrator who succeeded Dr. Dryden upon his death. Nevertheless, effective handling of the agency's relationship with Congress contributed to the favorable NASA image. No congressional liaison office can sell a program which does not function, and in a sense the function of the office is to help the agency keep from losing on Capitol Hill what it has won from the BOB and the President. The NASA liaison office helped to accomplish that objective.

Women
in
Congress

Frieda L. Gehlen

The United States Senate, someone is always pointing out, is the world's most exclusive club. But no one, as far as I know, has ever coined a cliché in which the House of Representatives figures as "the world's second most exclusive club." Doubtless, there is little enough glory attached to being second on such a scale, but it is still probably true that so far as qualities of matey solidarity are concerned, the House most resembles a congeries of clubs, something like a national Greek-letter fraternity, rather than a more traditional men's club redolent of expensive cigars and deep leather armchairs.

In such an atmosphere, one would expect female members to be not only few and far between, but distinctly uncomfortable as well. And when one recalls that there are in the House many Southerners whose long tenure has elevated them to positions of considerable power, and that many of these same Southerners share quaintly chivalrous notions about the nature and place of womankind, then one might further expect that lady members of the House would be not only uncomfortable but ineffective, except perhaps in those areas that the masculine majority is gracious enough to define as woman's work.

Nevertheless, we know from other times and other circumstances that women often do succeed in furthering themselves and their causes while working in basically masculine settings. The following article does not attempt to deal with all of the ways this might be done. It is rather a descriptive study of one group of women, all members of the United States House of Representatives during a recent session, and of how they fared at the task of being professional politicians.

Did they in fact (were they obliged to) specialize in legislation traditionally thought of as touching on female concerns: child-care and education, health and hospitals, beautification and "culture," consumers' rights and so forth? Did they enjoy free and easy access to the various loci of power in the House, and did they get a crack at holding positions of real power themselves? How did their being women affect their relations with their constituents, and how did it affect their chances for re-election?

These are interesting questions, though *not,* it must be said, because of the vast number of people involved. There have never been many women in the House of Representatives at any time, and at the moments of their greatest number (during the Eighty-fourth, the Eighty-sixth and Eighty-seventh Congresses) there were only seventeen of them. In the Eighty-eighth Congress, with which I shall be most concerned, their number had dropped to eleven, although a twelfth, who will not figure in this discussion, arrived before the end of the last session to serve out the remainder of her deceased husband's term.

Four of the eleven women were married, four were widows of former Congressmen, two were otherwise widowed, and one was divorced, although she had been married at the time of her first election to the office. Their average age was approximately fifty-eight, which was six years older than the average age of the men. They had, again on the average, two or three years of college education, but three of them had done some graduate work and one held a law degree. Three of the women had at least one child of school age at the time of the Eighty-eighth Congress, and in each of these cases a grandmother was pressed into service to help care for the children.

I mention this background information to emphasize the fact that we are not dealing here with stereotypic feminists such as those who agitated for female suffrage a few genera-tions ago, although they *are* still quite feminist in attitude. But they are not typical housewives either. All of those who were not widows of Congressmen had held active positions in either politics or the professions, or both. They are, on the whole, an attractive—in the way that money and training can make women attractive—but not stunning group of upper-middle-class women. Their names, for the record, are: Frances Bolton, Florence Dwyer, Edith Green, Martha Griffiths, Julia Hansen, Elizabeth Kee, Edna Kelly, Catherine May, Charlotte Reid, Katherin St. George, Leonor Sullivan and, the widow who served only a short time, Irene Baker.

The questions of what legislative areas the women specialized in, and of what committees they were assigned to, are both important for this enquiry. Politically, committee assignments are significant because they determine how much legislalive help it is possible to give one's constituents. Also, some committee seats are much better places to begin a climb to leadership than others. If the men do not want women participating fully in the Congress, or holding positions of authority, one of the best ways would be to refuse them decent committee assignments.

Specialization is interesting for cultural reasons. What little writing there is on the role of women in such political positions indicates that they can be expected to concentrate on the so-called "soft" areas of legislative interest: home, children, morality and so on. This, in a sense, is supposed to legitimate their being in a male position and serves to keep them out of the more controversial and power-related areas of interest.

It is true that, over the years, women have been assigned disproportionately to the lesser-status committees; but it is not clear whether this has been because of their being women and discriminated against or simply because they did not have, until recently, as much average tenure as the men. In the Eighty-eighth Congress, however, the women were fairly represented on the higher-status committees. Each of the three most exclusive committees (Rules, Ways and Means and Appropriations) had a woman member. Seven women held positions on the semiexclusive committees, and only two of the women were given only nonexclusive assignments. Four of the women held dual appointments: an exclusive or semiexclusive assignment plus a nonexclusive assignment. Moreover, the average length of "apprenticeship time" on a lesser-status committee was no longer for the women members than for the men.

Yet, did the committee assignments reflect a "feminine bias"? In looking at the evidence, it is very difficult to detect one if it is there.

The eleven women held a total of seventeen committee assignments among them and twenty-two subcommittee positions. (The total of subcommittee positions would be higher if one included Mrs. Bolton, who as ranking Republican on Foreign Affairs sat as an ex officio member of all subcommittees.) Of these assignments, no whole committee can be said to be especially related to the so-called feminine interests and, at the *very* most, only six of the twenty-two subcommittee assignments might be said to fall in that category: consumer affairs, housing, hospitals, Special Education, Indian Affairs and National Parks. Indian Affairs, especially, is a very questionable "traditional" concern of women.

It is possible, however, that the women, unlike their male colleagues, do not specialize in the area of their committee assignment. Consequently, both the women and the men were asked whether the women represented special interests.

The women, when it was put to them directly whether they felt there were certain areas where they did, or were expected to, specialize, rejected the suggestion out of hand. None of them would admit that there were any areas where a woman would be denied an opportunity to concentrate her energies if she were interested enough to prove herself. Furthermore, they were at least hesitant to state that they gravitated to the social issues any more than the men do. One woman suggested that in her experience women were first attracted to politics by these kinds of issues, but that by the time a woman gets to the Congress she has long since learned that she cannot afford such specialization. Two or three others indicated that they would have liked committee assignments in this area, but that politically it was not expedient and they took other posts.

Nor would the men admit to categorizing the women as specialists in social issues. Eighteen Congressmen were asked this question, and only four would admit that they thought the women as a group either should or did specialize in such a manner, and even these four equivocated.

Another means of noticing variations in interests between men and women would be to check whether the women disproportionately sponsored bills related to the expected cultural bias of women's interests. The test was applied by dividing the subject categories into so-called hard, soft and neutral groups and comparing the men and the women on the number of bills that fell in each of these general groupings. The results lend support to the idea that overall the women do differ from the men in their legislative interests and that this difference does come

because of their increased emphasis on social issues. One should also note, however, that the results still do not particularly show that the women "specialize" in such issues. The social or "soft" issues accounted for less than half of the bills introduced, even though this was a significantly greater number, statistically, than the men introduced. Thus, while the evidence provides some basis for arguing that the women have modified the role of Representative toward including some of the usual cultural concerns of women, one can hardly go so far as to say that this is for them a major means of adapting to the role. For some of them, however, it may be a means of reducing stress in a man's world.

Informal Relationships

Close observers of Congress emphasize that informal relationships are of crucial significance to the person who wishes to have a fruitful and active career. "Informal relationship" includes a variety of associations, but the key one is friendship, a relationship of equals based on mutual interests, activities and respect. Now, the usual middle- and upper-middle-class mores hold that, particularly among married people, such friendships are held between members of the same sex, while informal activities among adults of both sexes are considered somewhat questionable when the spouses are not a part of the group.

My evidence on this question is largely gathered from impressions from interviews. But it indicates that the women do indeed face a problem of generalized resistance in informal relationships, but that it varies: some women face more of it than others.

Some few of the women were named by my informants as being acceptable to the men in almost any situation that would be of political concern. Others, by their own admission, felt uncomfortable even stopping in the cloakrooms. But the general impression left is that no woman is as completely acceptable in all situations as a man might be.

The fairly structured small groups such as the freshman clubs, the state delegations and the prayer breakfast group or the Democratic Study Group seem to provide no problem as far as membership is concerned. The women are automatically members of such groups as the delegations and the freshman clubs or classes, and several have been given the honorary position of secretary. These groups, however, are really closer to being formal.

But there is an unknown, and probably shifting, number of small informal groups made up of friends and acquaintances who meet more or less regularly to discuss current legislation, general politics and whatever else comes to mind. They may meet in one of the offices, at a local establishment or in a home. Though some people questioned seemed to know nothing about any such groups, others reported belonging to them. No indication was given that any of the women belonged on a regular basis.

There is, for example, a traditional gathering known as the Board of Education where the Speaker and some of his chosen associates, frequently including the minority leader, gather after a day's session in a special little room deep in the heart of the Capitol to compare notes, have a drink and perhaps plan some strategy. Its title comes from the Speaker's habit of inviting in new members, once or twice, both to teach them some bit of House lore and to learn from them their reactions and attitudes. The men queried on this all agreed that the Board was a place to which women were not likely to be asked. The one woman questioned about it directly—a Democrat with nearly twenty years of seniority—had not even heard the term before.

None of the women denied that the men do meet together informally and that the women are not particularly welcome—and indeed are not invited. However, they have a very interesting way of responding to this form of blocked participation: they define these informal relationships very narrowly as far as their political value is concerned, and then they indicate the variety of other ways in which one can also influence legislation. One very effective woman Democrat, when asked whether there was any problem because she could not go to the gym or be a part of other such informal activities, replied:

> Oh, they may learn some things of the bill that way, but a lot of that becomes available anyway. They don't really decide that much there. If there is anything essential said, some man comes up and tells you. Most of them would be better off back in their offices reading the bills and studying them.

Another woman, a Republican, said, "I think that their camaraderie can sometimes help them, but there are a great many legitimate ways in which we can keep up with such things. . . ." Included in her list of ways to keep up was the cloakroom, or sitting together on the floor. Sometimes knowing their wives was a possible way of being "in."

In the interviews, the term "informal" seems to be used in two rather distinct ways. One has been the principal focus up to this point: it is that in which all parties are seen basically as colleagues and equals. In this sort of relationship, any woman who might be included would fit into the existing male pattern and the attraction between the sexes, or the appreciation of the difference, would not be a major part of the basis for sociability. On the other hand, some of the men recognized that certain women are sought out or included on occasion because they are attractive women. Clearly, this is something other than an informal, yet working, relationship; it is more strictly social. The question was not pursued, but it would be interesting to know whether and how some women could use this social informality for political advantage. Certainly, many of the men recognized *la différence* in other respects. They insisted that the women probably enjoyed some advantages that offset some of the disadvantages of being excluded by informal men's groups. They thought that the women could form their own group—or that they had done so. (In point of fact, the women seem to deliberately shun the idea of being considered a bloc.) Or they stated that the women are treated more courteously and that chivalry might be as beneficial as friendship. (The idea that chivalry is of great value is probably more rationalization than fact except for one important political act: running for reelection. This will be touched upon later.)

In general, however, my sample of Congressmen varied in the degree to which they assigned importance to the fact that a woman could not be a full-fledged part of an informal political network, but to a man they seemed to make the assumption that she would not be. Eleven of the nineteen men felt that this was definitely a handicap, while eight were inclined to view it as less of a problem than many would suppose.

It was a male administrative aide to one of the women who probably summed up the negative side best when he said:

> No woman can quite make it. The power structure doesn't operate that way. So much of the power structure is built around the golf course, the bar, over cards, in the gym shower room, etc. I doubt that the best or most able of women can ever get to the inner circle where there is complete acceptance. There are always some differences. Particularly is this true among the Southerners; she is not accepted there as an equal. Where the men may banter and tease around about an issue—"Hey, Joe, what do you mean by adding that amendment; trying to break the country?" sort of thing—with her they just say, "Why certainly, Mrs. Blank. I'll think about it." But they don't. They give deference, but they don't give any real attention.

While the consensus of the men who were interviewed appeared to be that the women were not really "in" on the total informal network, they agreed that some were much more so than others. As a general rule, the women who were accepted were noted for being rational rather than emotional, articulate, intelligent and not too prudish; that is, the men did not have to modify their own behavior greatly to accommodate them. Even so, it is dubious that any woman would be accepted by all men in their informal groupings. Some indicated that they would find it uncomfortable to have a woman around who acted like a man! And some of the Southerners might not wish to accept women into the informal network at all. Nevertheless, the interesting thing is that those women who have demonstrated the greatest competence, judging by such matters as committee assignments and other honors, are the women who have moved the most toward changing their ascribed role behavior for women to a pattern much more nearly like that of men.

The fact that so much of the House leadership is carried on by informal means is enough in itself to suggest that the women will find it difficult to gain such positions. However, in many respects power in the House is widely diffused due to the committee system. A committee chairman, and even a subcommittee chairman, can, if he or she wishes, wield a great deal of influence.

In the area of committee chairmanships the women face no real difficulty. The position automatically goes to the highest seniority member of that committee on the majority side. Seniority is enough of a sacred principle so that no one has suggested that it be violated simply to keep a woman from holding a chairmanship. During the Eighty-eighth Congress five of the six Democratic women held subcommittee chairmanships. None was a committee chairman, but none had been around long enough to be a ranking member.

Still, can a woman actually claim the power that goes with the position? Can she take informal leadership as well as holding the formal office? Actual evidence here is meager, but it would seem to be, as one man put it, "a matter of personality." This, however, would also be true for a man. Of the four women holding subcommittee chairmanships, two were very definitely wielding real power at the time: Edith Green of the Special Education subcommittee, and Leonor Sullivan of the Consumer Affairs subcommittee and the Panama Canal subcommittee. In the case of Edna Kelly, no one made any comments one way or the other. Mrs. Kee, it would seem, did not exert much leadership.

Mrs. Green and Mrs. Sullivan assuredly ran their own committees. They had the reputation of doing so and it shows also in the *Congressional Record* for the Eighty-eighth Congress. Mrs. Sullivan used the *Record* primarily as a forum for explaining issues with which her committee was concerned, generally in the form of prepared statements or speeches. Defense and explanation of an issue as controversial as the Panama Canal in early 1964 was entirely in her own hands and was quite thoroughly attended to.

Mrs. Green, on the other hand, preferred floor speeches and debate, though she also inserted a good many formal statements. She was active in controlling debate on three rather controversial bills reported out of the Education and Labor Committee: the bill amending the NDEA, the Higher Education Facilities Act and the so-called Juvenile Delinquency Act. Not only did she speak when her own bills were under discussion, but on other bills that dealt with education; though assigned to another committee, she was often in the middle of the discussions.

It is one thing to be a committee chairman due to seniority; it is another to be elected to the party floor leadership. It is here that the women probably face the greatest obstacle in the House. Of course not many men are ever going to make these positions either, but the women do seem to be categorically eliminated from consideration at this time. The women themselves recognize this, but again, rather than admit complete defeat, all put it in the category of one of those things that would happen "some day," but not in the foreseeable future. The men were even more negative. Of the nineteen cases where the men stated an opinion on the matter, fourteen were very negative, though most did cover themselves by not ruling out the possibility. The most common reason was the problem of informal relationships. One cannot, they said, be a party leader without being a part of the inner circle of informal contacts. Other suggested reasons were the ones usually attributed to the sex: too subjective and emotional, too tenacious or too idealistic.

Perhaps a more honest, if less exact, reason was stated by one of the men who said that, knowing the mood of the House, he did not think any woman was likely to get to the leadership positions except by seniority—"not so much because of the informal situations as because there just still exists the feeling among the men that this is a man's job, and it should be reserved for men." And, as another man added, ". . . besides, in caucus there are more of us."

There are a few objective criteria that can be checked that might have some implications for the movement of women into leadership positions. One is whether any of the women are a part of the regional whip system; another is whether any of those of the majority party are ever asked to sit as chairman of the Committee of the Whole during House debate, whether they serve as conferees, or whether they are in any sense a part of the policy-making groups within their own parties. In general these indicate that indeed the women do not participate equally with the men, but that some are involved to a greater degree than the interviews might indicate, particularly in party leadership.

A brief look at how well the women serve their constituents and their chances for reelection indicates that the cultural norms may serve to the advantage of the women on occasion, though the data are only enough to be suggestive. Interviews give the impression that at least some women are more apt than the men to spend personally a great deal of time on their case work, i.e., the problems of individual constituents relating to the government bureaucracies. Perhaps they find this time because they are less included in the informal and leadership groups. But it is also a culturally legitimate female role to be concerned over individual people and their problems. More than half the women made some reference to the satisfaction they got from their case work as one of the basic rewards for staying in the position. Not one of the twenty men queried about the rewards of the job even hinted that case work would be one of them.

Such an interest may have its political rewards as well. Doing one's case work is a very effective way of campaigning for reelection. People remember the representative who was able to do them a favor, and personal attention by the representative is even more apt to bring positive results.

Whether attention to case work has anything to do with it or not, the women do seem to be reelected by slightly safer margins than do the men.

Pentagon Bourgeoisie

Seymour Melman

Military industry in 1970 employed about 3 million persons on work directly traceable to the Department of Defense. In addition, 3.4 million men and women served in the uniformed armed forces and about one million civilians were employed by the Department of Defense, mostly on military bases engaged in research, development, testing, prototype manufacture and supporting activities, and base maintenance. All told, about 22,000 enterprises have been linked to the Department of Defense as performers of contracted work.

People tend to assume that the firms serving the Department of Defense are like other enterprises. But the 25 years of experience enjoyed by these firms has created a new type of enterprise that is basically different in many operating characteristics from the entrepreneurial firm of industrial capitalism. Moreover, the combined effect of this network of enterprises has modified the economy as a whole because of the character and the size of military expenditures.

The autonomous capitalist firm has operated to extend the decision power

of its management by keeping costs down and profits coming. Success has been characteristically measured in terms of percentage of a market, percent of capital investment, or change in the proportion of employees in a given industry. For this extention of decision power, profitability has been calculated and accumulated as a vital source of fresh capital for investment. Thus, during the last half century, firms have become increasingly self-financed, relying increasingly on themselves for accumulation of capital for further investment.

Managing includes decisions on what products to produce; how to accumulate capital; how to design and organize production; the quantity of the product; the price to be charged; and the mode of distribution of the product. Together, these functions constitute management. The autonomy of the private firm rests on the fact that the final veto power over these decisions is in the hands of its own management. This central characteristic has been altered in the military-industrial firm.

From 1946 on, industrial firms were

increasingly linked with military research institutes and with the Department of Defense in conformity with a policy regulation issued by the then Chief of Staff of the United States Army, General Dwight D. Eisenhower. Following that policy memorandum, the Pentagon arranged durable connections between nominally private firms, nominally private research laboratories (profit, university and other non-profit) and the military establishment. Through this period, the Department of Defense proceeded to act in ways that are characteristic of a large, monopolistic buyer—intervening in the internal affairs of the supplying firms to suit its convenience.

The relationship of the Defense Department to these firms is like that of large automotive firms to parts suppliers, or the relation of department stores or mail-order houses to suppliers of products, very often under brand names selected by the buyer. Eisenhower effectively founded the market network he later named the "military-industrial complex," but within the industrial side of the complex management's decisions were increasingly subject to the official *Armed Services Procurement Regulations.*

In 1961, Robert McNamara established, under the Office of the Secretary of Defense, a central administrative office, functionally similar to the type of unit that has operated in central-office-controlled, multidivision, major manufacturing firms. The key element here was the concentration of control in new institutions, like the Defense Supply Agency also set up by McNamara, the impact of which induced a qualitative change in the character of military-industrial enterprise: Final decision power over the main components of managerial control was vested in the new state management apparatus.

Top management at the DOD formally rendered decisions on products. Only the most minor decisions were left to the individual firm. Moreover, the government-based management provided capital, not only by making available land, buildings or machinery, but also by guaranteeing loans obtained from private sources. The extension of the scope and intensity of the state management's control proceeded in every sort of decision-making: on how to produce, on quantity, price and shipment. The net effect was to establish the state management as the holder of the final decision power and also to limit the scope of decision left to the managements of the defense contractors, the subdivisions of the state management.

Within industrial capitalism, subfirms frequently operate under central office control. In the military-industrial system, however, the central office is located in the executive branch of the federal government. It is unprecedented in size, and so is the number of submanagements. By 1968, the Department of Defense industrial system supplied $44 billions of goods and services. This exceeded the combined net sales (in billions) of General Motors ($22.8), General Electric ($8.4), U.S. Steel ($4.6), and DuPont ($3.4). Altogether, this constitutes a form of state capitalism operating under the Department of Defense—hence, the designation "Pentagon capitalism." Internally, the military-industrial complex differs also from the entrepreneurial business; this is best illustrated by the role of profit and cost minimization.

Profit and loss statements are computed in military industry, and a profit category is shown. However, this profit is not a reward for entrepreneurial risk-taking, which is the conventional justification for the profit taken in industrial capitalism. Under conditions of assured (by contract) price and quantity of goods to be delivered to the Department of Defense, there is no risk of the ordinary sort. There may be residual "risk" of not getting further business, but that is another matter. Moreover, profits for a subunit can be readily regulated by the state management which is inclined to regard "profits" of its subunits as a cost to the top controllers.

Within the new military-industrial enterprise, then, the self-correcting mechanisms that characterize the private firm are altered, if not dissolved. When major managerial functions are poorly performed in the ordinary firm, it is the entrepreneurial obligation to correct the malfunction. In the military-industrial firm, this may not be feasible insofar as final decision-making is in the hands of the state management. Thus unusually high costs, or problems in the design of the product, or problems in acquiring sufficient capital are not, in a military-industrial enterprise, necessarily problems for that management.

In the private firm, high costs become important pressures to modify industrial practice. For unduly high cost, as against the cost of alternative methods, can translate into competitive disadvantage and limited profits which means limited options for further capital investment and hence, limited options for further production decision-making by the management. Therefore, the manager of the classic industrial firm is moved to act to minimize costs. This logic operates except where managements, either singly or in concert with others, restrict market competition and shift cost increases to price, while maintaining an acceptable profit margin for all. However, it is ordinarily understood that the latter practice is an alteration of the more characteristic cost-minimizing calculus of the private firm. In the military-industrial firm, cost increases or unusually high costs are dealt with mainly by raising price. The record shows that, on the average, the final price of major weapons systems has been about 3.2 times the initial estimate.

Finally, the conventional firm can move among markets when it finds that its products are not well accepted. No options of this sort exist for the military-industrial firm. For the Department of Defense is the market and the firm may not sell to anyone else except with permission of the Department of Defense—as, for example, to a politically allied foreign military establishment.

These modifications in the self-correcting mechanisms of the classic business firm substantially alter the characteristics of that model entity, distinguishing the military-industrial firm and its controlling state management from the private and autonomous entrepreneurial enterprise.

So much for the complex itself, but the operation of the military-industrial firms also produces a series of unique effects for the economy as a whole. These include distortions of national growth, as well as missed opportunities in terms of depleted industries, services and occupations. From 1945 to 1970, $1,100 billions were expended by the U.S. government for military purposes. This exceeds the 1967 value of all business and residential structures in place on the surface of the

United States. However, the prime effects of the military-industrial activity stem from its economic functional nature.

Ordinarily, in national income accounting, all money-valued goods and services are included in the category Gross National Product. However, because of the character and size of military economic activity, it is important to make an economic-functional differentiation between economic growth that is productive and economic growth that is parasitic.

Productive growth includes goods and services that make up part of what we mean by the standard of living or can be used for further production of whatever sort. Parasitic economic growth refers to goods and services that are not part of the standard of living or cannot be used for further production. Plainly, military goods and services are overwhelmingly in the latter class.

Each year, from 1960 to 1970, 8 to 10 percent of the U.S. Gross National Product has been used for the military. The men and women who did the work were paid, but their products were, upon completion, withdrawn from market exchange. Whatever worth may be attributed to military products on other than economic-functional grounds, it is apparent that you cannot live in, wear or ride an intercontinental missile or an antipersonnel bomb. Neither can such products be used for further production. What seemed a small portion, 10 percent or less, of each year's GNP accumulated to an immense sum from 1945 to 1970.

The full cost to a society of parasitic economic growth is two-fold: First, there is the value of the man-hours, materials and whatever goes into making nonproductive goods or services; second, there is the economic use-value that is lost for standard of living or for further production (as against possible military use-value). Such economic use-value is ordinarily equivalent to the price paid for making nonproductive (or productive) goods. *Therefore, the social cost of parasitic economic growth is that of the resources used up directly plus the productive use-value foregone, or double the price nominally paid.* Thus, the $1,100 billion military outlay by the United States from 1945 to 1970 actually cost the nation $2,200 billion, or the value of total reproducible wealth of the nation (excluding only the land).

A collateral effect of sustained parasitic economic activity in the United States has been to jeopardize the international and the domestic value of the dollar. For the payments made to people for parasitic economic growth are made for goods and services that are not purchasable thereafter. The payments for such goods and services are not "sterilized" economically and are used as claims on those goods that do reach the marketplace. There is no gainsaying the importance of military economic activity as a cause of price instability in today's American society. The 20 percent drop in the purchasing power of the dollar from 1964 to 1970 places its future value in doubt. This means, of course, that the value of money income, savings, insurance and pension funds was diminished by a similar amount; that is, the drop in the value of the dollar saw a corresponding destruction of capital.

The value of the dollar, relative to other currencies, is critically affected by another mechanism. In 1950, the United States Treasury possessed $24 billions in gold bullion. By August, 1970, this had diminished to $11.8 billions. The reason for the drain, despite a sustained favorable balance of trade, was due primarily to the heavy overseas outlays for military and allied purposes during the period 1950 to 1970. The net result was an accumulation of dollars abroad that was not used for purchases from the American economy. Some of these dollars were presented to the U.S. Treasury for redemption in gold. As against $11.8 billions in gold bullion held by the Treasury in August 1970, there were $42 billions of short-term claims by foreigners against the United States reported by American banks. It is plausible to expect that if foreign claimants on United States gold were to attempt massive cashing in of their short-term claims this country would embargo the shipment of gold abroad. The world monetary system would collapse.

It is significant that the annual portion of GNP used for parasitic economic growth is not an average, homogeneous 8 to 10 percent of U.S. goods and services. For example, the military-related institutions and military industry have been using more than half of the nation's technical research talent. Since a missile designer cannot be designing railroad equipment or civilian electronics at the same time, the country has had more missiles but less railroad equipment, civilian electronics and kindred goods.

Only insofar as we understand the consequence of applying half and more of the country's technical research talent to parasitic economic growth can we explain what is otherwise an anomaly: the appearance of technological and economic depletion in many sectors of American industry and services—together with a growth in GNP. The principal industries that are deteriorating now include steel, house-building, ship-building and machinery production of many classes. Deterioration or grossly unsatisfactory performance in services afflicts the telephone and postal systems, the supply of electricity (notably in the northeastern states during the last period) and the performance of medical services.

In 1967, 40.7 percent of the young men examined by Selective Service for military induction were rejected on grounds of physical or educational incapacity. This means that the American economy, with a GNP of one trillion dollars a year, has been short changing the young men and women of this society in education and health care. That is inexplicable, except as we appreciate that $1,100 billion was expended for military and related parasitic purposes over 25 years, and the quality of the manpower was concentrated in military and allied work.

Opportunity cost, the value of something foregone, is one way of assessing the value of goods or services. In the present case, what has been the opportunity cost to American society of expending $1,100 billion for military purposes? Consider that over a period of 20 years this meant a foregone expenditure of $50 billion a year for alternative purposes.

Perhaps even more important than depletion of industries is the depletion of occupations and regions in the economy. Depleted occupations refer, for example, to an unknown but large number of engineers who functioned for many years on behalf of the military and thereby acquired a trained incapacity for functioning in a civilian industrial environment. Depleted regions refer to states, cities and counties which have had a preponderance of military industry and related activity, especially during the decade 1960—1970. By 1970, a slowdown in the rate of military-industrial expenditures, notably in research and development, created depressed areas in regions like the suburbs of Los Angeles, the San Francisco Bay area, Seattle, eastern Long Island and the area around Route 128 in Boston.

The opportunity cost of the military system includes the inability of the United States to provide economic development at home for the 30 million Americans who need it. They need it because of a high infant mortality rate and limited life span, a high incidence of certain epidemic diseases, and limited education and, hence, limited productivity and income. The process

that alters this condition is called economic development. It requires investment in human capital and in physical productive facilities.

In the United States, a process of economic development would require an outlay of about $50,000 for a family of four. Considering 30 million possible candidates, about 60 percent of them white and 40 percent black, the requirement for 7.5 million "equivalent family units" would entail an expenditure of $375 billions over a period of, say, 10 years, or $37.5 billions per year. That sum, it should be noted, compares with estimates of the full annual cost of the Vietnam war at its peak. Obviously, expenditures of $37.5 billions per year for economic development are not conceivable while military budgets use up $70 to $80 billions per year.

The prime limits on the capability of the United States economy are most critically defined in terms of the availability and the use of skilled manpower. To accomplish economic development we need an investment of skilled manpower in the work of enhancing the human capital and productive skills of persons who are economically underdeveloped. The same consideration constrains American participation in economic development in other areas of the world.

The officially budgeted costs of the war in Vietnam include the incremental costs as distinguished from an estimate of the total costs of that war. Thus for 1967, $20 billions; for 1968, $26 billions; for 1969, $29 billions; and for 1970, it is estimated at $23 billions. In 1962, in my book *The Peace Race* I calculated the total cost of economic development for the populations of Africa, Asia and Latin America. My reckoning indicated that an annual capital investment of $22 billions was the cost world-wide for accelerating an economic development process.

Evidently, the incremental military costs—by themselves—to the United

States for the war in Vietnam, from 1967 to 1970, used up a capital sum approximately equal to what I calculated would be required for accelerating economic development in Asia, Africa and Latin America.

For the United States, the policy issue involved in changing from a military-priority economy is not restricted to having a military security system of the present sort as against no military security at all. In fact, many alternatives are conceivable in place of the military security goal of preparing to fight 2½ wars at once, which is the policy that dominated in the 1960s. For example, the United States could conceivably define its foreign policies so as to require a military security force to operate a plausible nuclear deterrent, to guard the shores of the United States, and to have a capability for participating in international peace-keeping. The total manpower required to operate such a force, including supporting staffs and functions, would comprise about one million men, and the cost of operation would be about one-third of the 1970 military budget of $75 billions. A military security concept of this sort opens up the possibility of alternative uses of about $50 billions a year of money and manpower now employed for military and related purposes.

The state management that controls the military-industrial system has applied its considerable influence to counter legislative and other kinds of preparations for conversion of military-industrial employees and facilities to civilian work. By September 1970, Senator Abraham Ribicoff summarized the results of an inquiry by his Subcommittee on Executive Reorganization into the status of capability for conversion to civilian economy among military-industrial firms:

In general, the responses indicated that private industry is not interested in initiating any major attempts at meeting critical public needs. Most industries have no plans or projects designed to apply their resources to civilian problems. Furthermore, they indicated an unwillingness to initiate such actions without a firm commitment from the government that their efforts will quickly reap the financial rewards to which they are accustomed. Otherwise, they appear eager to pursue greater defense contracts or stick to proven commercial products within the private sector . . . After carefully examining the letters as a whole, we found that the need for serious thought and action on conversion has largely been disregarded by most of the business community . . .

For the business units of industrial capitalism, the development of military industry has meant a transformation from the autonomous entrepreneurial firm to the military-industrial enterprise functioning under a state management. For the economy as a whole, the formalization of Pentagon capitalism and the outlays on its behalf have involved parasitic growth on a large scale and at a large opportunity cost. The economy and society as a whole bear the unknown cost of an array of depleted industries, occupations and industrial areas, and the cost of sustaining an economically underdeveloped population of 30 million among 200 million Americans.

Riot Commission Politics

Michael Lipsky and David J. Olson

Speaking before the National Commission on Civil Disorders, better known as the Kerner Commission, Kenneth Clark wondered aloud about the usefulness of what the commissioners and their staff were doing. There had been previous riot commissions, Clark reminded his audience, and they too had issued reports. But the whole undertaking had, for him, an Alice-in-Wonderland quality about it, "with the same moving picture reshown over and over again, the same analysis, the same recommendations, and the same inaction."

Kenneth Clark's skepticism is widely shared. But should we despair with him that riot commission reports are irrelevant? Or should we agree with public officials that riot commissions provide an invaluable service for helping society understand complex events? Or should we think cynically that riot commissions are no more than the tools by which chief executives placate and arouse people? These questions may only be answered by examining the place and function of riot commissions in the political life of the country. What do they really do? And how do they do it? How does one account for the great differences between expectations and results in the lives of recent riot commissions?

These questions open wide areas of disagreement, of course. But generally speaking, riot commissions are usually described in one or more of the following terms:

1. Government officials, it is sometimes thought, create riot commissions to provide authoritative answers to social and economic questions posed by riots, and to provide authoritative recommendations for preventing them in the future. This is certainly what commissions are *supposed* to do, as can be gleaned from reading the formal "charge" to any recent riot commission.

2. Others feel that riot commissions are simply a convenient way for public officials to buy time in which to formulate public policy. A harsher variant of this viewpoint has public officials creating commissions in a deliberate effort to evade political pressures and avoid coming to grips with the problem. A more sophisticated variant has the officials buying time so as not to have to deal with the passions *of the moment*. In the immediate aftermath of a riot, political executives have to conclude that neither the intense anger of blacks nor the intense fear and anger of whites are appropriate pressures or reliable indicators of what they should do.

3. It is said, also, that riot commissions are simply created to exonerate public officials from responsibility for the situation leading to the riot or for their behavior during it. In the recent past a number of commentators have inferred that riot commissions have "whitewashed" public officials.

4. Independent of the validity of the above three positions, it is said that riot commissions are irrelevant to the political process. Essentially this seems to have been the position of Kenneth Clark in his influential commission testimony.

5. Regardless of the reasons for initiating riot commission activity in the first place, it may be said that riot commissions essentially function as interest groups, competing with other interest groups in attempting to influence the political environment in ways favorable to their general orientations.

In recent research on the National Commission on Civil Disorders (Kerner Commission), the Governor's Select Commission on Civil Disorder of the State of New Jersey (New Jersey Commission), and post-riot politics in Newark, Detroit and Milwaukee, we have tried to develop a framework for analyzing some of the above considerations. We conclude that formation of riot commissions gives rise to public expectations which cannot be fulfilled and that riot commissions are charged with incompatible goals which cannot meaningfully be reconciled.

Insofar as this is the case, riot commissions are most profitably viewed as participants in the ongoing political struggle of American race relations. They may make marginal contributions to that struggle by providing status and support for interpretations of riots which may affect the decisions of other political actors. They may also provide information about riots that will influence others, and may lend legitimacy to information which is already available. Riot commissions further may help structure the terms in which debate over issues relating to riots will be pursued.

They are initiated by public officials as part of the executive function, but they are transformed by their constituents and, by virtue of the involvement of commissioners in commission business, they transform themselves into pressure group competitors in the political process.

But before discussing these points it will be useful to review some critical aspects of the Kerner Commission's operations. We will also mention related developments taking place in the New Jersey Commission where appropriate.

First, like other authoritative commissions appointed in recent times, the Kerner Commission was comprised of essentially conservative men. Of the eleven members named by President Lyndon B. Johnson on July 27, 1967, six were elected public officials, the most liberal of whom was Mayor John Lindsay (Republican) of New York City. Governor Otto Kerner, the chairman, was an Illinois Democrat known for his championing of both civil rights legislation and riot control training. Only two Negroes were named to the Commission, Senator Edward Brooke and Roy Wilkins, the most "respectable" of civil-rights leaders. The other members included Chief Herbert Jenkins of Atlanta, who enjoys a reputation for being a progressive among police chiefs; Katherine Peden, who was at the time Kentucky Commissioner of Commerce; and representatives of labor and business: I. W. Abel, President of the United Steel Workers, and Charles B. Thornton of Litton Industries. All of these people are either public officials or the heads of established American institutions. Indeed, as Tom Wicker wrote in his introduction to the Bantam edition of the Kerner Report, "President Johnson in appointing his Commission on Civil Disorders . . . was severely criticized for its moderate character." The McCone Commission, appointed by Governor Pat Brown of California following the Watts riot, and the New Jersey Commission were also made up of reputedly conservative people.

Second, the Kerner Commission began its work amidst conflicting pressures for action. As *The Washington Post* reported, the establishment of the Kerner Commission "followed several days of congressional demands for an investigatory group either from Congress or the White House. Johnson was under pressure to act before conservative opponents in Congress created their own commission." It was quite clear that the thrust of these investigations would be toward discovery of "conspiracies" and techniques of riot suppression.

Third, the research strategy of the Kerner Commission was highly complex and difficult to implement. The President charged it with a number of independent and delicate tasks. The first was to describe accurately what happened in each riot city, and to do it despite an extraordinary diversity of testimony. Adequate handling of this task alone would have had severe political implications. The finding of a conspiracy, for example, would support those skeptics of recent black political developments who would like to discount reports of widespread discontent among black people in American cities. A finding that no conspiracy existed, on the other hand, would lead analysis into the tangled network of social causation in racial matters about which there is great controversy. The President also asked the commission to explain why riots took place in some cities but not in others, even though previous studies on this question had proved to be singularly unsuccessful. Finally the President requested proposals on how to prevent future riots. This may have been the most politically perilous charge of all. It demanded a review and evaluation of reform planning that would have to be convincing to (first) the commissioners and (then) the public. The peril lies in the fact that such a task raises questions of the capacity of this system to respond to social needs and the adequacy of previous programs. This diffuse research agenda had to be accomplished *in less than a year.*

Riot Commissions As Organizations

1. *The Scarcity of Time and Resources.* Such tight schedules are not peculiar to riot commissions, but the Kerner Commission and other recent riot commissions seem particularly hampered by these constraints. It is uncertain whether any riot commission could adequately fulfill the research goals with which they are charged. Almost as soon as commissions are convened, their directors find themselves confronted by critical deadlines. They must hire staff quickly without the luxury of fully assessing their qualifications and before the research agenda has even been completed. One consequence is that generalists, such as lawyers, may be hired over specialists, since staff directors may not know precisely what they want to do. The Kerner Commission was especially hampered because in late August talented people in the academic world were already committed, and because hiring had to proceed in the face of widespread skepticism such as that expressed by Kenneth Clark.

As soon as staff is hired, the pressure is on to collect the data. Investigation must follow quickly upon the occurrence of riots because of the need to interview witnesses while memories are still fresh and because proposed solutions presumably depend upon a research effort. The Kerner Commission decided to obtain information on riots in 20 cities, including environmental background features and interviews with key people, from city officials to militant civil-rights activists. The data-gathering teams went into the field at a time when December 15 was considered the target date for an "interim" report. This meant they had about two months in which to uncover the facts about the riots, the cities in which they occurred, and possible explanations for their occurrence. Obviously, this was too short a time period to obtain sufficient data to develop well-rounded studies, a fact confirmed by the Kerner Commission's decision not to develop all of these profiles for publication. The New Jersey Commission, given less than three months to hire staff and conduct and assemble research, was similarly constrained by time.

Another consequence of having to produce reports under this kind of pressure is that the staff is almost obliged to develop (or simply accept) a general working theory of riot causation to guide the research. The outlines of the theory are familiar to anyone who has looked into almost any recent commission report. It holds that systematic deprivation and discrimination in the past, when added to reasonable expectations of positive change and when accompanied by continued indignities and community resentments, become focused by a single incident or series of incidents into behavior that takes the form of looting and other hostile activities. As a general theory this is perfectly serviceable, but it hardly accounts for the varieties of civil disorders, which Presidents, governors, and others are concerned about. Social scientists, especially, must find this unsatisfactory, since they are interested in explaining variation, rather than explaining why something does or does not exist. The questions of why riots occurred in some cities and not in others, or why riots varied in form and intensity, can be sensibly addressed only through a more rigorous comparative analysis than there was time to undertake in the work of recent riot commissions. Farming out research to social scientists was one way the Kerner Commission attempted to deal with research difficulties, but this was not entirely satisfactory.

As individuals with public constituencies, commissioners have to be assured that their decisions rest upon irrefutable and unambiguous evidence. The time problem intrudes when commission staffs anticipate these needs and try to "build a case," an effort that detracts in some ways from an open research strategy and diverts staff members from other duties. Staffers on the Kerner Commission, for example, had to return to the field to obtain affidavits from witnesses on whose testimony the narrative summaries of disorders rested. Staff investigators of the New Jersey Commission were required to file individual memoranda on every person with whom they talked on commission business. "Building a case" and good research procedures are not necessarily incompatible. But a strain is placed upon mutual satisfaction of both these goals when time is short. Statistics without relevance are collected; time-consuming procedures are honored to make an impression of thoroughness; theories with potential validity are rejected since they cannot be adequately tested, and so on.

Related to the demands for building a case is what happens when commissions begin to focus attention on the single task of producing the final document. At this point, other talents, perhaps antithetical to those of the researcher, are demanded of the staff. These are the ability to work all day and night, the capacity to absorb endless criticism without taking personal affront, and the ability to synthesize the sentiments of the commissioners, or to anticipate their sentiments regarding various issues. These qualities are those of lawyers, of advocates who work under pressure for clients regardless of personal interests or allegiance to material. In this respect commission staff-domination by lawyers may be a necessary rather than an accidentally perverse quality of commissions. But the point remains that those best able to gather and interpret socially relevant data may not perform well in accommodating to the pressures that are brought to bear in writing the final report.

The pressures of time are also incompatible with a rational search for answers. Under rational procedures, study should be followed by conclusions, followed by program suggestions relating to those conclusions. But lack of time required recent riot commissions to formulate their programs at the same time as they were analyzing causes. This is not to say that their conclusions do not follow from the analysis. But this dynamic helps explain why there need not be a relationship between the factual analysis of events and commissions' proposals for change.

Scarcity of resources also contributes to the typical shakiness of the organization of riot commissions. Commissions enjoy no regular budgetary status, nor do they continue to enjoy top executive priority after their creation has served to reassure the executive's constituency that he has acted on the problem. The Kerner Commission, for example, was originally promised sufficient funds to accomplish their task, but it was later discouraged from seeking more money because in late 1967 it had become presidential policy to seek no supplementary appropriations from Congress, and because federal agencies were reluctant to contribute to the commission from their diminished budgets.

2. *Developing Commission Integration.* It is the peculiar dilemma of riot commissions that commissioners are apparently chosen for the diversity of interests they represent, while at the same time they are expected to agree on, and support, a meaningful report about a complex problem with clear ideological overtones. This circumstance sometimes leads the public to assume, quite understandably, that the final report of any given commission will be little more than a collection of bland generalities, or an out-and-out whitewash. If it is the first, it will be because the commissioners were in fact representative of diverse and conflicting interests and were unable to agree on anything controversial. And if it is the second, it will be because they were really chosen by the political leadership for the basic congruence of their views. Either way, the appointment of riot commissions has led to rather unflattering expectations of their work, and often justifiably so, given the extent to which recent commissions have been made up of incumbent or former public officials and bona fide members of high-status organizations such as trade unions, financial conglomerates, or the press.

Riot commissions are made up of men chosen for diversity of interests, and they are inherently temporary. Thus riot commissions are confronted in extraordinary fashion with the problems inherent in all complex organizations —the development of mechanisms of socialization and the development of group norms and values which may overcome tendencies toward fragmentation and disintegration. In practical terms, tendencies toward fragmentation and disintegration in riot commissions may take the forms of developing minority reports and developing destructive tensions between commissioners and staff.

For some commissioners, a minority report represents a threat with which, within limits, they can manipulate other commissioners to modify their views. The strong language of the summary of the Kerner Commission Report, for example, can be attributed to Mayor Lindsay and his staff, who in the weeks just prior to the final approval of the report had come to feel that the commission's approach was not sufficiently hard-hitting. Lindsay seized on the fact that a draft of the summary had not yet been prepared and had his staff develop one. He presented it to the commission as a statement of his position, indicating (it is not clear how explicitly) that he would issue such a statement anyway, if the commission failed to support him. The other commissioners, recognizing that the "summary" prepared by Lindsay reflected the report's contents, and that Lindsay might well release the summary in some form anyway, adopted it as their own. Mayor Lindsay's outspoken comments on the needs of cities may have had the effect of moving some commissioners toward his views in order to keep him in the fold. In any event, it is safe to conclude that the Kerner Commission summary would not have been so dramatic a document if Lindsay had not forced the issue in this way.

But, in a sense, a minority report is an ultimate weapon. One must still account for how commissioners with diverse interests and viewpoints come to identify themselves with the final product of a commission. Under what circumstances do such men permit themselves the luxury of political compromise in endorsing views to which they may not totally subscribe?

One way to explain the surprisingly provocative quality of both the Kerner Commission and the New Jersey Commission reports, given the essentially conservative cast of their members, is that their staff directors explicitly encouraged and engineered the development of *a sense of urgency* within these commissions. Direct exposure to ghetto conditions was perhaps the most successful technique to this end. Members of the Kerner Commission conducted two-day tours of riot areas, sometimes even without the company of the press corps or the guiding hands of city officials. One of the most successful of these took place in Cincinnati on August 30 when Mayor Lindsay and Senator Fred Harris, two of the most liberal members of the commission, met alone with a group of black nationalists. They were frankly informed of the group's dedication to the destruction of American society as now constituted. The confrontation apparently was particularly meaningful for Lindsay and Harris because the nationalists were highly educated men, and so could not be dismissed as being merely frustrated because of restricted mobility.

By the same token, the New Jersey Commission staff arranged for their commissioners to divide into teams of two and accompany antipoverty workers into Newark ghetto homes, bars, and barber shops. Most participants, including chairman Robert Lilley, credited these tours with creating the sense of awareness and alarm about ghetto conditions that was ultimately reflected in the final report.

This facet of commission procedure in part was born of political necessity. Staff research was not immediately available to the commissioners, yet they had to demonstrate to the public that they were doing *something*. One way to do this was to study conditions firsthand. Happily, this also permitted commissioners to learn about ghetto conditions and agree on the nature of ghetto existence before policy papers were prepared and before it became necessary to "take sides."

Exposure to formal witnesses with dramatic testimony was also useful in creating a sence of urgency. Kenneth Clark's appearance before the Kerner Commission was considered influential in offering perspective to the commissioners on their activity. The same effect was produced when the staffs of both the Kerner Commission and the New Jersey Commission circulated articles by Robert Blauner and by Robert Fogelson that were highly critical of the McCone Commission. These articles alerted everyone to the potential public criticism of "wishy-washy" riot reports. Many New Jersey commissioners reported being heavily influenced by the testimony of black shopkeepers whose stores were shot up by New Jersey policemen; shopkeepers, after all, were not likely to be malcontents.

Problems of potential fragmentation threaten commission unity at all stages. Initially, the problem is one of getting commissioners to think of themselves as *commissioners,* not as individual politicians. This is helped, as we saw, by creating a sense of urgency among commission members. In later stages, the problem becomes one of conflicts arising from the fact that commissioners must begin to take stands on matters of public policy.

Considerable conflict did develop in the work of recent commissions at the writing stages, but these conflicts did not erupt to the extent that minority reports were filed or that serious public displays of conflict emerged in the press. The Kerner Commission did not break up over the appropriateness of criticizing major social institutions or over the ultimate tone and emphasis of the report summary, although these were issues of considerable conflict within the commission. Neither did the New Jersey Commission break up over the issue of recommending governmental consolidation for Essex County, although the commission was significantly divided over this issue. Commissioners clearly preferred to accept compromise rather than diminish the total impact of the report because of open conflict or sniping at the document. Members of both commissions have refrained from dissociating themselves from aspects of the reports, and many have actively defended them, despite the controversies they have set off.

Although there were considerable disagreements on the various commissions, what is significant were the areas of agreement. So far as we can discover there was little dispute over the causes of riots. The commissioners agreed that the riots were not results of conspiracies nor mass behavior dominated by criminal or quasi-criminal elements. Rather, these men (and one woman) chosen for their community standing and their connection with established institutions —people, in other words, who were relatively conservative in the literal sense—attributed the riots to long-standing factors of discrimination, deprivation, and neglect. They condemned violence and criminal behavior, but they recognized that riots could be understood as products of central tendencies in American life.

There was also no question that extraordinary measures would have to be taken if the country wanted to deal seriously with the social bases of urban unrest. What debate there was concerned the kinds of measures that would have to be undertaken, and the kinds of criticism of American institutions appropriate for public discussion. But on the whole, these disagreements over the nature of the recommendations are less significant than the commissioners' agreement on the necessity for radical departures from existing public policy. When viewed in the light of the political and social legitimacy commanded by recent riot commissions, this is the significance of recent commission reports.

Apart from the danger of conflict among the commissioners, there is also the possibility of conflict between them and their staffs. In this regard, an important point of tension is the commissioners' need to feel reassured that staff members are free from bias and are presenting their work free from ideological distortion. Commissioners' suspicions apparently focus upon two possibilities. On the one hand, some staff members are feared to be overzealous for social reform, with a corresponding bias emerging in their work. This possibility is somewhat reinforced by the nature of lower-level staff recruitment, where an interest in social reform may be significant in the type of person willing to work for commissions on short notice. The field staff of the Kerner Commission, for example, was made up to a significant degree of young lawyers and returned Peace Corp volunteers. On the other hand, formally bipartisan commissions encounter suspicion that top staff members are really very partisan and have been selected to whitewash elected officials.

The dangers of failure to allay commission suspicions that the staff is overzealous or partisan are two: The commissioners may reject staff work and in the end develop conclusions independent of staff analysis; or, in anticipation of commission antagonism, staff work may be screened to provide commissioners with only "acceptable" material. In either case, the commission runs the risk of staff revolt, the erosion of organizational loyalty among the staff, and divisive public debate inspired by discontented staff.

The Kerner Commission was confronted with all these difficulties. The issue of staff political partisanship arose because some staff members were considered to have developed significant personal stakes in an "Administration outcome" for the final report, and the selection of David Ginsburg as the commission's Executive Director did little to allay concern that the Executive Director would be fronting for the President. Ginsburg is a partner in one of Washington's biggest law firms, has extensive government connections, and was known to participate in White House social circles.

Openness and responsiveness of staff procedures, and symbolic staff appointments, are two strategies available to commission staffs in allaying commissioner fears of partisanship. The staff directors of the Kerner Commission and the New Jersey Commission spent a great deal of energy consulting with commission members about ways in which they wanted to proceed. David Ginsburg and Victor Palmieri, the Deputy Executive Director of the Kerner Commission, were distinctly aware of the possible dangers of commissioners' suspicions. Sanford Jaffe, Executive Director of the New Jersey Commission, also indicated that gaining the confidence of potentially suspicious commissioners was one of his major concerns. In the Kerner Commission, the deep involvement of John Lindsay's assistant, Jay Kriegel, in commission activities contributed to alleviating Republican concerns over a potential "whitewash." The same could be said of the high-level appointments of Richard Nathan and Stephen Kurzman, both of whom had worked for Republican congressmen. Although staff directors of the Kerner Commission insist that these men were not appointed for partisan reasons, their presence was considered by other staff members to have helped reduce fears of partisanship.

Ideological splits between commissioners and staff are more difficult to control and can be quite damaging to ultimate commission influence. The prestige of the McCone Commission, for example, was severely undermined by critics who argued that the conservative cast of the commission substantially ignored the findings of its social science staff and consultants. The writings of Robert Blauner, Robert Fogelson, Paul Jacobs, and Harry Scoble reflect this. During the life of the Kerner Commission, as well, major difficulties emerged over staff suspicions that their analyses were being rejected on conservative grounds.

The most obvious and best publicized example of this commissioner/staff tension revolved around the rejection of a document entitled, "The Harvest of American Racism" drafted by social scientists employed by the Kerner Commission. From all indications, it appears that this draft was rejected for inclusion in the final report not only because its conclusions were radical, but also because documentation for its underlying theory of riot causation was lacking. There was also a problem of communication within the commission. The social scientists were shocked to find the document that they considered only a draft treated as a final product. This was devastating because the social scientists assumed it was clear that adequate documentation had not yet been appended to the theoretical analysis. On the other hand, the chief staff directors of the commission were no less dismayed to receive what they considered an unsubstantiated theoretical piece. The staff directors argued that for commissioners to accept a provocative analysis required, at the very least, that it be grounded in a solid evidential base.

Very shortly after the "Harvest" draft was rejected, the commission changed its timetable to eliminate the interim report and released most of the staff, about 100 people. For some staff members, these three events confirmed their suspicions that the commission was exploiting them without respect for their skills and was leaning toward development of a conservative report that was at odds with the staff members' analysis. Leaks to the press followed, and at least one commission consultant held a press conference to discuss these matters publicly. Thus, for a period in the latter half of December the Kerner Commission was under considerable pressure in the press to deny charges that it was heading in a conservative direction.

Release of the final report allayed these fears. Previously critical staff members now acknowledge this and, indeed, that much of their analysis was woven into the final document. By taking their fears to the press, these staff members may have contributed to the outcome by putting pressure on the commission at a critical time.

3. *The Development of Political Legitimacy.* Initially, riot commissions are charged with generating objective analysis and impartial recommendations based upon this analysis. Initially, commissioners are recruited because of their status, their imputed objectivity and responsibility, and the extent to which they appear to be representative of a spectrum of diverse interests. We have suggested, however, that if commission efforts are to be successful, commissioners must give up some of their self and occupational role interests and develop orientations toward the commission as an organization with a life of its own. As this happens riot commissions adopt strategies to maximize the impact of the final report. We have already mentioned the example of staff directors formulating procedures to discourage minority reports. They recognize that a commission that appears to be substantially divided merely testifies to the complexity of the issue and is supportive of many viewpoints.

An insight into the efforts of riot commissions to develop legitimacy can be found in the tension between pursuit of a "scientific" research strategy (or "scientific" legitimacy) and the political needs of commission work (or "political" legitimacy). Staffs must conduct inquiries so that the commission appears comprehensive in searching for explanations and program proposals, reliable in presentation of evidence, and cognizant of advanced work in various research and program areas. This image must be secured by the staff for the commission whether or not information so obtained is related to questions or answers of commission interest.

Staff directors must conserve scarce time. Yet the staff directors of the Kerner Commission traveled throughout the country to demonstrate (as well as assure) that they had conferred with the broadest base of social scientists and were searching widely for expertise.

Moreover, mechanisms had to be developed to deal with numerous inquiries from people offering their services (for a fee) and research findings. These inquiries and proposals had to be handled in such a way as to give the impression that offers of help were indeed welcome (when in many cases they were not). In this regard the Kerner Commission confronted a problem endemic to most government agencies. But unlike most government agencies, the commission lacked a routine for dealing with these inquiries, the staff to handle them, or the time to evaluate them.

An illustration of this is the case of a prominent research-oriented psychiatrist who submitted his name through his Senator, Edward Brooke, a Kerner Commission member, for one of the top research positions on the commission. He did not receive a reply until some months after the commission was thoroughly staffed. Then he received a formula response, thanking him for his inquiry concerning a "job" at the commission, but explaining that positions were no longer available. The man was insulted, and was subsequently uncooperative with the commission. The peremptory posture assumed by top staff members of the

Kerner Commission of necessity, given the strain under which they operated, was resented in many quarters—both in academic circles and in staffs of subnational commissions. Especially irksome to the Kerner Commission was the fact that from the outset there was general recognition of the time trial the commission would experience; thus the commission was "marked" for exploitation by individuals convinced they could help, or convinced that the commission could help them.

Besides establishing their "scientific" legitimacy, commissions must give the impression that all political groups are given their day in court. Sometimes the motives for hearing certain witnesses are transparently political rather than educational or evidential. The Kerner Commission, for example, took the testimony of many of the black militants whose names appear on the witness list at a period when many chapters in the report already had been approved in relatively final form.

So far, we have been building an argument that the internal political dynamics of riot commissions can be characterized as the gradual development of *a pressure group*. This is particularly curious because, in the first place, riot commissions are established by public officials as objective instrumentalities to provide authoritative answers to questions of concern (thus, they are *government* organizations); and, in the second place, because riot commissions are specifically designed for the representation of *diverse* interests when originally formed.

Nevertheless, this view of riot commissions as developing into pressure groups may help explain both their strengths and weaknesses. Insofar as a diverse group of implicitly responsible, high status individuals subscribe to one interpretation of civil disorders and subscribe to a single set of recommendations, riot commissions may claim a high degree of political legitimacy. This is their strength. But insofar as a riot commission must compete in the political arena without being able to rely upon the organizational status of individual commission members, riot commissions enter an ideological arena where they must compete with other groups in the political process. In that competition, the impact of commissions is predictably marginal. The executive who creates a riot commission assigns to it the function of authoritatively articulating goals for the alleviation of problems of civil disorders. But the goals become authoritative for the larger political system only insofar as they are accepted by other groups for conversion into public policy. In the absence of such acceptance, the recommendations remain only as political demands. They

are purely recommendatory or advisory unless supportive relations can be established with interest groups and other key actors.

Riot Commission Strategy

In attempting to develop political coalitions and influence the political process, riot commissions adopt a variety of strategies to overcome their relatively powerless status. These strategies include: (1) maximizing the visibility and controlling the exposure of the reports; (2) competing for legitimacy; (3) affecting the political environment; and (4) assisting the implementation process.

1. *Maximizing Visibility.* Riot commissions are concerned with creating favorable images of their activities, and attempt to do so by giving maximum visibility to their reports. The tone adopted in the reports reflects this concern. Both the Kerner Commission and the New Jersey Commission elected to develop what appear to be hard-hitting documents. In the Kerner Commission Report, as everyone recalls, "white racism" was identified as the overriding primal cause of conditions leading to riots. This was sensational, assuring a maximum impact for the commission's labors. At the same time, however, the commission report contained almost no criticism of established institutions or programs. Criticism of national-level programs is largely lacking—despite the fact that the federal government is the only locus for the kind of effort that is called for in the report—and criticism is minimized of trade unions, big-city mayors, and other groups who might be expected to do something about the alleged "racism."

The tone achieved by this report was not arrived at accidentally, according to a number of high-level staff members. The commission explicitly decided to produce a moral statement on the evils of racism and implicitly agreed not to specify the institutions perpetuating the condemned racism. Clearly the day-to-day interpersonal brand of racial hostility was not what the Kerner Commission had most in mind when it condemned white racism. The only way that white racism makes sense as a root cause of civil disorders is in terms of its location in and legacy for major American institutions.

The commission apparently avoided criticizing these institutions partly because to do so might destroy the commission's unity (those very institutions being represented on the Kerner Commission in the persons of business leader Thornton, Police Chief Jenkins, labor leader Abel), partly because to criticize these institutions would have involved the commission in nationwide debates with powerful organizations intent on defending themselves, and partly because the commission was dependent upon these institutions to put into effect their recommendations. Thus, criticism of past performances were apparently avoided in the hope that future positive commitments might be forthcoming.

When it comes to manipulating the terms in which commission reports will be received and evaluated, the powers of commissions are extremely limited. The phrase "white racism," for example, which appears but once in the summary of the report, captured the focus of the press to a greater extent than any other single finding reported by the Kerner Commission. From a rereading of the summary, however, it would appear that the commission had hoped that national attention would center on the conclusion that the country was "moving toward two societies, one black, one white—separate and unequal." Similarly, the New Jersey Commission felt obligated to address the issue of official corruption in Newark because of repeated testimony on that subject by commission witnesses. On release of the report, the press, especially in Newark, gave a great deal of attention to the corruption issue, although it had a relatively minor place in the report itself. New Jersey Commission members indicated in interviews that they regretted including the corruption issue at all, because it tended to draw attention away from more important findings of their report.

2. *Competing for Legitimacy.* In attempting to influence other political actors on behalf of their report, riot commissions, as we have seen, try to establish firmly their claims as the authoritative interpreters of civil disorders and as authoritative planners for preventing future civil disorder. These claims do not go uncontested. Other groups have access to the same symbols and similar grounds of legitimacy.

Simply stated, one riot commission often begets another, or two or three. The competing riot commissions have less claim to objectivity or being "official," but they have greater claims to reliable constituencies and the group status that results. These constituencies are, for one reason or another, determined to undermine the monopoly of legitimacy asserted by the riot commissions and attempt to establish legitimacy of their own. They adopt the commission inquiry form in order to capitalize on the acceptability of this political instrument.

The political logic appears to be as follows: if it can be shown that opposite conclusions can emerge from the same kind of investigation of civil disorders, then it can be argued that the conclusion of the authoritative commission was the product of the biases of commissioners. This is all quite explicit, and antagonistic interest groups don't hesitate to use the tactic even when it is patently clear that the "competing commission" is undertaking a biased investigation. Take, for example, the remarks of John J. Heffernan, President of the New Jersey State Patrolmen's Benevolent Association, when he "predicted" the findings of his association's investigation: "We are appalled at the findings of the [New Jersey] riot commission, especially in the interests of law and order. The PBA riot study and investigation committee is certainly going to come up with different findings."

After President Johnson issued an executive order creating the Kerner Commission, the United States Senate authorized the Permanent Subcommittee on Investigations of the Committee on Government Operations (McClellan Committee) "to make a full and complete study and investigation of riots . . . and measures necessary for their immediate and long-range prevention." The McClellan Committee's investigations have attempted to undermine the findings of the Kerner Commission by centering on Office of Economic Opportunity personnel involved in riots, hearing witnesses who allege that there is a conspiracy behind the riots, and generally giving a hostile reception to other witnesses not sympathetic with the committee's more conservative views. That President Johnson himself tried to undermine his own Kerner Commission is perhaps not surprising. The fact that he included in his charge to the (Milton) Eisenhower Commission on the Causes and Prevention of Violence the duty to investigate civil disorders is consistent with his other acts of unsympathetic reception of the Kerner Report. The New Jersey Commission's "Report For Action," released in February of 1968, shortly thereafter triggered the New Jersey State Patrolmen's Benevolent Association's Riot Study Commission report entitled "A Challenge To Conscience." In Detroit, Jerome P. Cavanagh's Mayor's Development Team represented a public response to local civil disorders with most commission members drawn from city agencies and the Mayor's Office. But the Development Team was soon challenged by the New Detroit Committee, a private counterthrust to the public commission. In California, the conservative McCone Commission was countered, both as to its findings and its recommendations, by the California Advisory Committee to the United States Commission on Civil Rights.

These competing commissions employ many of the same

strategies and tactics as official riot commissions in manipulating the symbols of legitimacy. They follow closely the procedures of the initial commissions, including assembling a staff, holding formal hearings, conducting investigations, hearing witnesses, collecting documents, and offering recommendations. In fact, they are often the same witnesses, the same documents, and similar investigations. But their findings and recommendations vary considerably from the conclusions of initial commissions. Riot commissions, whether initial or competing, thus represent ad hoc devices by which on-going antagonistic interests compete for political legitimacy.

3. *Affecting the Political Environment.* In content, commission reports can be analyzed as attempts to reassure various publics in an otherwise unsettled environment. These reassurances may take the form of dispelling popular rumors and myths, or they may take the form of interpreting disturbing events in ways that can be absorbed within traditional American beliefs.

Efforts to reassure various publics begin as soon as commissions are formed. Early testimony plays an important part in giving the appearance that significant interests are being represented. J. Edgar Hoover's statement that he had no evidence of a conspiracy was the only testimony released officially during the first set of Kerner Commission hearings. Then, as if to counteract the information that the chief criminal investigative official of the United States had no evidence of a riot conspiracy, Governor Kerner informed reporters that Sargent Shriver, Director of the Office of Economic Opportunity, and Robert Weaver, Secretary of Housing and Urban Development, both had evidence of the presence of unidentified strangers in neighborhoods shortly before riots broke out. In those days of crisis, it would appear that members of the Kerner Commission wanted to reassure the public that questions of law and order would receive high priority. But, recognizing that Hoover's testimony appeared to preclude a search for confirmation of a theory widely held by some Americans, Governor Kerner "scrambled" the first message in order to protect the commission from early criticism.

Beyond dispelling myths such as those of conspiracy, riot commissions also reaffirm traditionally accepted views of society. They uniformly condemn violence and reaffirm the principles of law and order. They also commonly invoke that series of beliefs in the American creed pertaining to "equality" and "integration." Note the concluding sentence to the Kerner Commission's chapter on the history of Negro protest: "Negro protest for the most part, has been firmly rooted in the basic values of American society, seeking not their destruction, but their fulfillment." Which values? Which America? The statement may have empirical validity when interpreted, but here it has primarily inspirational value.

Of course riot commissions cannot reassure everyone. Reassuring the black community that commissions are sensitive to their feelings about white racism risks arousing the anger of previously uninvolved white groups who violently object to this explanation of riots. Obviously this was the case with the Kerner Commission's focus on "white racism." The New Jersey Commission tried to reassure Newark blacks that their grievances had been heard and would be articulated in the commission report. But this intention was undermined by the controversial nature of its program recommendations. Half of the New Jersey commissioners argued that political consolidation of Essex County was the only means of establishing a tax base that would give Newark the resources to solve its problems. But other commissioners argued against consolidation on the grounds that this would, in effect, preclude the election of a Negro mayor precisely at the time when black people were becoming a majority of the city electorate. The first position risked disturbing white suburbanites upon whose support implementation of commission recommendations rested. The second argument risked reassuring Negroes of electoral success without providing the resources for basic services.

Riot commissions can attempt to quiet unreasonable fears, and reassure segments of the population that their needs are being addressed. But they cannot escape the difficulties that are incurred when controversial program recommendations are considered necessary. Recent commissions have explicitly chosen controversy at the expense of tranquility, but in doing so they have risked arousing political antagonists in the struggle over program recommendations.

These last remarks have been directed toward the more symbolic content of commission activity. More explicitly, riot commissions also attempt to affect the environment in which reports are received by treating gently the riot-related behavior of the executive, and by anticipating the needs of other political actors. Because of their relative powerlessness, commissions are dependent upon the favorable reception of their reports by the executive and other centers of power for maximum impact on the larger political system. However, these same political executives may have been involved in dealing with the control of the civil disorders and with programs related to the basic causes of the disorders. Thus the possibility is raised of commission's having to deal critically with the behavior of the political executives upon whom they are at least partially dependent for the implementation of their recommendations.

One drawback in exonerating the actions of the executive in civil disorders is that it gives credence to competing riot commissions in challenging the initial commission's claims to legitimacy. The New Jersey Commission strongly criticized the city administration in Newark. It left virtually untouched the matter of the Governor's actions at the time of the disorder, which were widely perceived by the black community in Newark to be inflammatory. During the Newark disturbances, Governor Hughes had told reporters that he would draw the line between the law and the jungle, and that riots were criminal and unrelated to civil-rights protests. Naturally enough, city officials in Newark lost no time in pointing out the discrepancy between the commission's statements about the Mayor of Newark and the Governor of New Jersey.

Riot commissions also attempt to further their recommendations by anticipating the needs of other important political actors. The Kerner Commission at one point adopted an end-of-the-year deadline for its interim report in part to obtain consideration in the formulation of the President's budget messages. Later it adopted the President's "message on the cities" as a framework for some of its programmatic recommendations, on the assumption that this would appear to coincide with his legislative goals and thus receive President Johnson's endorsement. The commission also consulted with cabinet officers before releasing its report. This strategy was based on the erroneous assumption that the President would use the commission's recommendations as a tool for furthering his own domestic program.

4. *Strategies for Implementation.* It is appropriate to conclude by mentioning a number of explicit strategies that riot commissions adopt to affect the reception of their product in the political arena. Riot commissions have recently advocated extending commission life in one form or another. The McCone Commission, for example, chose this means for advancing its recommendations. Near the end of the New Jersey Commission's deliberations, a request was made to Governor Richard Hughes to establish an ongoing review body including some members of the commission. A commissioner on Mayor Cavanagh's Development Team indicated that after the MDT issued its report, it was decided that an executive committee composed of the Mayor and five of the Mayor's top assistants should meet peri-odically to review what was happening to the MDT report.

The major drawback to this approach has been the lack of power of the commissions once reports are issued. If riot commissions themselves have relatively little power, then a few of the commission members meeting periodically have even less power in the implementation process. Paul Jacobs suggests that what the periodic review undertaken by the McCone Commission actually accomplished was "defending itself [the commission] against some of the attacks which have been made upon it," and serving a public-relations function. Governor Hughes never granted the request of the New Jersey Commission to be reconstituted as an ongoing review body. In Detroit, the Mayor's Development Team was able to continue meeting periodically, and since many of the members of the MDT were public officials, it was able to participate in the implementation process. The MDT illustrates another aspect to the commission paradox. Commissions comprised of public officials may indeed have power in the implementation process, but they will lack the reputation for objectivity on which their persuasive powers rest.

Commissioners as individuals have attempted to exert pressure on public officials for implementation. In New Jersey, for example, Governor Hughes was threatened by individual members of the commission with public criticism if he continued his failure to respond. Shortly thereafter, the Governor and his staff received members of the commission and in an all-day session virtually wrote the Governor's special message to the legislature. This message, which called for expenditures of $126.1 million on welfare, housing, education, law enforcement and urban problems, incorporated most of the commission's recommendations pertaining to New Jersey state government.

Functions of Commissions

Let us now try to evaluate the assumptions about riot commissions that were identified at the beginning of this essay.

1. Riot commissions are inherently incapable of providing sophisticated answers to the most important questions relating to riots. As government agencies limited in time, resources, and staff, riot commissions can contract for a limited number of empirical studies, investigate the validity of some rumors and myths surrounding civil disorders, and make relatively intelligent judgments in describing riot occurrences. They can also make sound program proposals, though they must do so before critical research has been completed. Recommendations of riot commissions may be

said to be authoritative in the sense that they are comprised of high-status individuals and are accorded high status by the fact that they were created by the chief executive. But their recommendations are authoritative only insofar as the chief executive moves to implement them.

To the extent that the chief executive fails to move toward implementation—as in the case of President Johnson—or to the extent that recommendations go beyond the scope of executive powers—as in the case of the New Jersey recommendations regarding Newark corruption—riot commissions must be seen not as authoritative but as competitive pressure groups in the political process. As such their influence is restricted to the legitimacy that they can capture and the political skills of individual commissioners who attempt to affect implementation.

2. It is rather fruitless to enter the murky area of the motivation of executives who create riot commissions. But our analysis does permit us to say a few things. Whether or not riot commissions are created in order to buy time, it is unquestionable that they do permit public officials to avoid immediate pressures for action and to postpone decisions for many months. Not only does the creation of a commission deflect pressures from the chief executive, but it also improves his bargaining position in a conservative direction by permitting him to claim that he is constrained by other political pressures over which he has little control. In the intense crisis following the riot, people seem to appeal instinctively to the chief executive for leadership. But the opportunity for decisive leadership, for making qualitatively different decisions about national priorities, based on opportunities available only in crisis situations, may not be what the politician desires. Postponement permits the chief executive to wrap himself in the usual constraints of office where politics as usual will continue to obtain. Riot commissions also contribute to cooling of tensions by reassuring various publics in a symbolic way that their needs are being met. This may take the form of calling witnesses representative of various positions, making hortatorical appeals for justice and nonviolence, and so forth.

3. Is there something inherent in riot commissions that supports allegations that they are established to "whitewash" public officials? We may ask this apart from the question of whether some commissions are made up of members picked primarily for their unquestionable support of a chief executive. We think there is a built-in tendency toward the whitewash, to the extent that riot commissions minimize criticism of the public official to whom they must look for primary implementation of the report. Further, for the sake of commission solidarity and to avoid diminishing the report's impact by the airing of dissension, riot commissions minimize criticisms of institutions with which individual commissioners are intimately associated. To some extent, public officials attempt to influence commissions in favorable ways through appointments of political allies and "reliable" individuals to the commission. As we have suggested, however, this strategy will have limited returns because of the fears of partisan bias and the need to make the commission appear "representative."

4 and 5. Kenneth Clark's skepticism over the relevance of riot commissions is essentially justified. Riot commissions are not the authoritative program planners for a community torn by crisis and harvesting the fruits of past social injustice. Neither are they accorded the status that might accrue to them by virtue of the prestige of individual commissioners or the expertise that they command. Rather, starting from the myth that riot commissions will provide authoritative answers to questions of social concern, and that these answers will be widely accepted by politicians who will move to implement them, riot commissions move through a process in which they become just another pressure group among many in the political process. And in influencing that process, their resources are insufficient to prevail in the competition.

The allegation that commissions have repeatedly come to the same analysis, recommended similar programs, and failed to produce action is true, but as criticism it is misdirected. It is not the commissions themselves to which one must look to understand the "Alice-in-Wonderland" atmosphere that Kenneth Clark perceived. One must look to the political process itself—that greater Wonderland in which riot commissions play only a marginal role.

part four

Innovation, Priorities, and Problems in National Public Policies

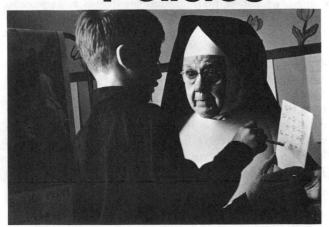

As the reader can see for himself, the line between this and the preceding Part is not very sharp. But we begin to move closer to the arenas of conflict which have been developing in recent years. Perhaps the best point of departure for this discussion is the paradoxical point that sweeping changes have been taking place in public policy over the past decade which, while they have fulfilled the dreams of many liberals in the period extending from the New Deal through the Kennedy years, have also served radically to raise expectations and fears among many groups in the population, and thus have significantly contributed to destabilization of American politics. In retrospect, some liberals might well ponder Goethe's warning: "Let a man take care what he asks for in his youth, for in his age he shall have it." Major changes in domestic policy have, in fact, produced the short-term crisis which Polsby alludes to as the temporary "exhaustion of innovation," seen in the passage by the 89th Congress of bills which had been pending for years or decades.

If there was a New Deal policy revolution in the 1930s and an *Imperium* policy revolution in the 1945–60 period, we have entered a third revolution since 1964. We have no agreed-on name for it yet, but it entails the massive entry of the federal government into the direct provision of goods and services to specific target groups. Perhaps it can be referred to as an "intervention revolution"; in any case, the Great Society programs of the mid-1960s turn out to be more than rhetoric. The basic data are provided by the splendid Brookings Institution study by Charles Schultze et al., *Setting National Priorities: The 1973 Budget.*

It is commonly accepted that a national budget gives an operational definition of the current state of national (public-sector) priorities. Accordingly, trends in the budget should provide clues as to where these priorities are currently heading. The accompanying table

Changing Budgetary Allocations, 1963–1973

CATEGORY OF EXPENDITURE	Billions of $			Percent of Total		
	1963	1970	1973	1963	1970	1973
Defense, space, foreign affairs	58.9	87.7	88.0	52.8	44.2	34.3
Older income-maintenance programs[1]	28.4	49.8	74.9	25.5	25.1	29.2
Major "Great Society" programs[2]	1.7	21.2	35.7	1.5	10.7	13.9
Commerce, transportation, natural resources[3]	7.6	11.6	16.5	6.8	5.8	6.4
President Nixon's new initiatives[4]	. . .	. . .	6.4	. . .	. . .	2.5
Interest (net)	7.7	14.4	15.5	6.9	7.3	6.1
Other programs	7.2	13.6	19.3	6.5	6.5	7.5
Total	111.5	198.3	256.3	100.0	100.0	99.9

EXPENDITURES AS A PERCENT OF FULL EMPLOYMENT GROSS NATIONAL PRODUCT	1963 %	1970 %	1973 %
Defense, space, foreign affairs	9.1	9.0	7.1
All other	8.7	11.3	13.4
Total	18.4	20.3	20.5

[1] Social security and retirement programs, cash public assistance, veterans' benefits, and unemployment benefits.

[2] Such programs as Medicare, Medicaid, loans, and scholarships for higher education, housing subsidies to low- and moderate income families, food stamps, and school lunches.

[3] Excluding programs for environmental protection (ecology) and regional economic development, included under "Great Society" programs.

[4] Revenue sharing, family assistance plan, emergency school assistance.

reveals two elements of "political economy" which are of great importance for such determination of trends. In the first place, the table reveals a stagnation in military-defense-space spending in *absolute* terms between 1970 and 1973, plus a sharp decline in the proportion of such expenditures to the total budget. Corresponding to this is a trend not only toward a rise in older income-maintenance programs (many of New Deal vintage) but a rapid, almost non-incremental increase in expenditures allocated to newer domestic programs. As the Brookings study emphasizes, these programs differ in important ways from earlier ones: for the most part they provide government intermediation in the production of goods and services to targeted groups in the population, rather than cash disbursements. Secondly, President Nixon has made a clean break—one which agitates programmatic conservatives—with earlier Republican public-sector policy as suggested by the special item for his initiatives in the 1973 budget table. But more than that, it is clear that he has accepted the reception of Keynes which

occurred in the Kennedy administration and which is discussed here in Stein's article. Whether one agrees or disagrees with President Nixon's use of these Keynesian economic levers to strike a balance in the eternal tradeoff between inflation and unemployment, there is no doubt that he is using them; and this represents a quite basic change in the Republican approach to managing the economy.

All of this has a profound bearing on the politics of public policy in the 1970s. First, it is important to note that the shift in priorities between defense, space, and foreign affairs on one hand and domestic programs on the other has not only begun but is already well under way. Second, the federal government has undertaken large and growing programmatic responsibilities in the domestic arena which were virtually unknown as late as the beginning of the Kennedy administration. Third, the focus of these new programs has been upon sharply defined sectors of the population—generally, the poor, the aged, and minority groups. Finally, such programs are being undertaken at a time when the economy's growth has markedly slowed down. One of the most important of the Brookings 1973 findings is that already committed program expenditure will significantly outstrip the contributions of currently available generators of revenue (taxes, mostly) throughout most of the 1970s. Professor Schultze and his colleagues conclude from this that (a) tax increases will be needed to pay for increases in costs in the programs which already exist, and (b) there is no room for further program innovation without still further increases in taxation. A necessary corollary of both propositions is that this increased taxation will come because, without it, dangerously high rates of inflation would continue to press on the stability of currency; this would have not only major international ramifications but would injure people on relatively fixed incomes at home. It goes without saying that the 1972 election battles over the size of the defense budget and the issue of tax reform reflected these contextual pressures on policy. It should also be clear that in any case, the pressure of growing domestic demand upon existing public-sector resources will make for sharp conflicts among economic and racial groups in the years ahead; we shall attempt to spell this out later in this volume.

One crucial set of issues deals with the capacity of the system to identify major needs, initiate policy, and produce results which relate in some way to the needs in question. When one thinks of policy formation in these terms, particularly as it concerns "chronic" externally-generated needs rather than "acute" needs which develop within government, several important implications suggest themselves. While the President properly retains much of the ascendancy in policy formation which is conventionally given him, for example, the roles of U.S. Senators and of outside "intellectuals"—professors, intragovernmental experts, and others—become larger. Such actors target emergent needs. In the crucial gestation process, they do the job of thinking out programs which will resolve them.

A good example of this process can be seen in the pages of this Part (particularly when taken in conjunction with Senator Edward Kennedy's book *In Critical Condition*, detailing his efforts in the Senate in the health-care field). It is a notorious fact of life in America that one serious and unexpected illness in a family can wipe it out financially, especially in families whose income lies in that very large range between the poverty line covered by the Great Society health legislation and the well-off who are financially invulnerable. National health insurance proposals, paralleling the British scheme adopted in 1948, have been "around," in and past the gestation stage, for many years. The two essays on the subject in this Part suggest the role of intellectuals in the process.

The first, by Marmor, provides a thoroughgoing critique of the inflationary effects of Medicare and identifies the laissez-faire fee-payment structure of the medical profession as being responsible for this inflation. The implication is clear enough: applying public-good criteria and expenditures to a situation which retains its private-enterprise, commodity-transaction basis will tend to result, among other things, in effectively uncontrollable increases in costs to both the public sector and to private consumers. The second study, by Roemer, carries to their logical conclusion the implications of the contradiction between the realization of public good and the dynamics of private enterprise. If decent health care at socially supportable costs is really to be made available to all, many key elements of private enterprise in the medical profession must be abolished by public authority. Roemer proposes a concrete utopia, an "ideal condition" in which the public good can be realized. He recognizes it as a utopia for the present, but he also emphasizes a major role which such ideal constructs can have in the gestation stage of public policy: they can provide a target, a goal against which intermediate proposals can be judged.

Thus, intellectuals can criticize what is, can reveal why, wherein, and how much existing programs cannot "work," and they can offer blueprints for what might be, blueprints which seem radical at the time, but which provide "targets" or "goals" for a long-range policy effort related to a major need in the larger society. They make decisively important contributions to framing the agenda of concrete policy discussion which may go on for decades. Senators like Kennedy likewise play a major role in such innovations, moved by their own sense of function and, it may well be, by their hopes that presidential lightning will strike them.

In the context of this vision of the policy-initiation process, one additional point about Senators and presidential politics should also be made. Throughout most of the period from the Civil War until the Second World War, the population from which major-party candidates were most frequently recruited was Governor, General, and U.S. Senator in that order, with Vice Presidents *never* chosen unless they had become president first through the death of their predecessor. In our times the political visibility of governors has plummeted (beginning in 1960, none of the major-party candidates nominated for President had had gubernatorial experience). On the other hand, all eight candidates have had senatorial experience; and fully five of these (Nixon three times and Johnson and Humphrey once each) have occupied the vice-presidency. On the other hand, in the years between 1868 through 1944, exactly half of the forty-two major-party candidates were governors at the time of their first presidential nomination, while only three (8%) were Senators. The abrupt, total shift from state-level to national-level political visibility in the nomination process is probably related to, among other things, an emergence of the Senator's role as a national policy spokesman.

Again, one major reason for the sharply increased influence of intellectuals in the gestation stage is the enormously complex, technical framework in which public policy must be articulated these days. A theme of complexity runs throughout our essays on policy advisers, elites, and formulation. While the complexity must be accepted as largely unavoidable—and the role of experts, intellectuals, and others accepted as in some sense permanent—we should be under no illusions about the problems of *political sociology* which these changes have brought in their wake. These are of two major types, which may roughly be classified as functional and class-related.

Big domestic programs are, to a large extent, the consequence of long-term social need; of the gestation process with its corps of executive, senatorial, and intellectual innovators; and of a balance of forces in the political process, both among groups and between the major political parties. Munger's discussion of the changing politics of aid to education captures such movements among political forces particularly well. But in a real sense such programs are cause as well as consequence. Not only do their administrators acquire client groups which help to perpetuate and expand the programs once started; but a very large number of policy professionals are produced by the not-so-simple act of establishing the programs in the first place. These professionals, in turn, have every motivation to sustain and expand the programs germane to their expertise. What occurs, in large part, is a built-in mechanism for developing and exploiting demand among client groups. So far as the Great Society programs are concerned, most of these groups—the poor, the black, the aged—have traditionally been beneath the level of political consciousness or demand, for all intents and purposes. Thomas Jefferson used to comment with some cynicism that it was the office of a good judge to enlarge his jurisdiction; the remark reflects a much broader truth about governmental processes. It can at least

be suspected that the program breakthroughs of the 1960s have tended to generate more and more structured pressure for further policy initiation, and that if one could define an "intensity function" of initiation since 1961, it would describe an upward J-curve across time.

For those who favor further policy innovation and federal involvement, such a functional reality—the reality of how men in politics pull together clienteles or constituents for programs—seems not a problem but rather an opportunity. But life is more complicated than that. Any tendency to create geometrically increasing rates of innovation bears with it considerable potential for generating stress on the political system as a whole. It is precisely this possibility which lies at the heart of recent critiques of liberal policy, for critics like Banfield and Moynihan are concerned that sometimes integuments really *do* burst asunder. In their view, a new kind of "feedback loop" has been constructed during the 1960s which, through interactions between a new policy elite of experts, innovators, and administrators on one hand and their "client groups" or constituencies on the other, threatens to do exactly that to the existing political system. In this collection, Long also strikes a cautionary note which touches on this problem.

For those who believe in radical restructuring of American social, economic, and political structures, such patently bourgeois-conservative views are not likely to be very persuasive. But there is another side to this coin. It is contained in two phrases used by Theodore Lowi in his *The End of Liberalism* and is implicit in his discussion of American apartheid here: "Why Liberal Governments Cannot Plan" and "Why Liberal Governments Cannot Achieve Justice." The latter point will be discussed shortly; the former relates to a very real set of issues involved in the escalation of domestic program innovation *without major restructuring of our political processes.* Conservatives, in order to preserve system stability, may well opt for as little policy innovation as possible. But a non-conservative, too, can recognize that the proliferation of programs and program innovations in recent years has often served not to resolve the problems to which they are supposedly addressed but rather to create more and more unplanned complexity, more and more feudal baronies (complete with Good Lords and villeins) within the existing fragmentation of the American political structure.

In fact conservatives are much more alert to the basic issues here than are "welfare liberals." For they see—correctly, in my opinion—that the rapid expansion of federal responsibilities in domestic policy creates an ever-sharper dialectical contradiction between the existing system's attempt to generate policy in response to demand on one side, and its capacity to survive on the other. Putting the matter in the simplest way: radically expanding federal involvement in domestic resource allocations without correspondingly radical change in structure leads to subinfeudation and a jumble of cross-cutting purposes and effects. Much more is needed in this area than merely adopting the reform—valuable as it is—of a government-wide program budgeting system (PPBS) of the sort Weidenbaum has recommended. Planning of some sort becomes needed in direct positive ratio to the expenditure of money; but planning requires, again, the development of centralized, sovereign power resources which can keep the baronies in line and can integrate them into larger collectives than those of their own intellectuals, bureaucrats, and client groups. To the extent that increases in public-sector activities continue, they will of their own force generate cumulative pressure for a major reorganization of political processes and governmental structures. The expanding functional roles of policy innovators will likewise add their own pressures for new programs with new expenditures. These innovators should, perhaps, develop a more precise sense that their activities—indeed their very existence—point to the establishment of planning and domestic sovereignty out of sheer necessity.

But there is also what I have called a "class-related" factor in policy innovation and policy followthrough. Perhaps this should be rephrased to include not only class but ethnicity and other factors as well, all within the same syndrome. In short, the overwhelming majority of policy innovators, intellectuals, experts, and administrators come from bourgeois social backgrounds—mostly Protestant (WASP) or academic-Jewish—and the bulk of them have been deeply committed to a welfarist-liberal ideology. These characteristics have interacted with the conditions of policy-making and its consequences to produce the "crisis of Justice" which Lowi emphasizes. If there is broad and deep discontent with the fruits of domestic policy among the American public today, a large part of this discontent has so far been tapped more by George Wallace than by George McGovern. It is not difficult to specify the contributions of this "class-ethnic" factor and others in producing domestic discontent, especially among threatened lower-middle-class and blue-collar whites, many of ethnic-Catholic background.

1. Much of the Great Society legislation attempts to deal with the ferocious social pathology which has de-veloped in core cities with black immigration and white flight to the suburbs. This is historically a very recent process in its current form, going back only a few decades.

2. These policies have been fashioned piecemeal in response to especially acute manifestation of social pathology. They have followed closely the basic rubrics of interest-group liberalism: to respond to pressure as it arises.

3. The primary victims of racial discrimination—blacks and other minority groups—have been "colonized," as it were, by white liberals, especially by policy intellectuals. There are excellent cultural reasons for this, especially those having to do with the claims of deprived minorities that they are excluded ascriptively from the human equality which is a central value in the American tradition.

4. On the other hand, the felt needs of lower-middle and working-class whites have been substantially left out of the Great Society programs; such groups are told that their opposition to residential integration and bussing to achieve school integration is immoral and/or unconstitutional.

In a pluralist and fragmented political system, organization begets counterorganization. Programs of the Great-Society variety have been shaped by innovators who have been unable or unwilling to integrate the needs of people who are economically vulnerable but who are also above the poverty line. Quite naturally, the latter have come to see such programs as imposing sacrifices and burdens without adequate justification; and they also see—quite rightly—that the innovators and administrators have used their own superior economic power resources to avoid equal sacrifices by themselves and their families.

These issues involve a very large element of "white racism," to be sure. But they involve other things as well. For a number of reasons it is not so easy to develop client-patron relationships for specific domestic programs affecting the lower-middle and working-class whites as it is for other groups. Partly this is a cultural matter: such whites tend to reject "welfare" on emotional grounds. Partly it is a matter of money: the number of white families with incomes between $6,500 and, say, $11,000 per year is vastly larger than all the "target groups" put together. But partly, it seems to me, very little effort has been made by liberal policy intellectuals and others to come to terms seriously with the whole causal structure which underlies the phenomenon called "white racism." And this is probably due more to the unexamined class, cultural, and ethnic attitudes of policy elites than to any other factor.

Thus, a number of the essays which deal with specific policy areas touch in one way or another on questions which go to the heart of any policy system. Here the studies by Eley, Lowi, and Sternlieb are of particular importance. If one reviews the history of race relations even outside the rural South, the only conclusion which can be drawn is that they have been largely "stable" at the expense of black residential, job, and educational aspirations. The Civil Rights revolution has served to destabilize this situation through a series of piecemeal, incremental adjustments, yet these adjustments have in practical fact left alone the basic *economic* structures which have promoted segregation and black subordination, whatever the rhetoric of legislation or judicial decision has been: this much Eley's article makes particularly clear. Bussing itself is a liberal *pis aller*: it exists only because no will or power resources to cope effectively with residential segregation along economic lines exist. And no wonder: the middle-class drive for economic segregation of residential neighborhoods long preceded the arrival of blacks in metropolitan areas. It is, in fact, one of the strongest and most continuously maintained social processes in American history, emerging as soon as innovations in transportation made it possible a century ago.

The essays in this Part also raise another substantial issue. Is it possible to maintain a line of policy at all in the face of overwhelming majority antagonism? One answer is almost certainly that, in the long run, this cannot be done within the class-implicit rubrics of disaggregated, piecemeal policy innovation, and administration by the middle-class "policy talent pool." This is hardly the place for the editor to spell out the details of a program package in this area. But it is a good place to make the point that only some form of comprehensive, authoritative social planning—involving control by public authority of the economic structures which re-inforce, for example, residential segregation—has any prospect of coping with these immense problems. It should be added that only a policy package which acknowledges the *reality* of "white racism," while attempting to cope with it creatively, has any chance of winning some measure of support among the mass of not-so-well-off white Americans who live in metropolitan areas. Such a package would have to involve equalization of the sacrifices which inevitably follow any transition in the primary modes of social existence; and, so long as the social conditions which lend credence to the prejudices of "white racism" continued to exist, it would probably have to involve enforceable restrictions (insofar as possible, implicit ones of the sort which economic allocations make possible) on populations' movements in metropolitan areas. A tall order indeed! But it is doubtful that the present unstable situation which piecemeal policy-making and unexamined liberal assumptions have interacted to produce will prove *politically* viable, even in the relatively short run. To the extent that government in the United States is ultimately founded on public opinion, then the structure, distribution, and intensity of this opinion must form part of the basic matrix out of which viable policy is made. To structure the situation otherwise is likely—sooner rather than later—to surrender political initiative and control to the Right.

The essays in this Part, then, taken as a whole, shed light upon the contexts, outcomes, and consequences—both intended and unintended—of policy-making in the groupist-liberal state which was built after the Great Depression. They also, it seems to me, prod the reader into thinking out the unexamined assumptions of those concerned, and promote the asking of hard but necessary questions about a possible future for national politics and policy-making in the United States.

Apartheid U.S.A.

Theodore J. Lowi

The United States is over 100 years away from an official apartheid policy. Yet, after more than 20 years of serious involvement by the federal government in the "urban crisis," the social condition of American cities could be little worse if the concerned federal agencies had been staffed all those years by South African agents. A close look at the actual results of federal urban policies gives wonder how there remains any national legitimacy and why the crisis of the 1960s has not been more violent.

The crisis of the 1960s signaled the end of the era that began in the 1930s. Lyndon Johnson was the Herbert Hoover

of this moment of change. As Hoover presided over the wreckage of the depression, Johnson presided over the wreckage of the New Deal. In both crises, the sincere application of established criteria began to yield unexpected, unintended and unacceptable results.

The New Deal was founded on the principle of positive government made possible—that is, acceptable to Americans—by a very special form of decentralization. Ideally, federal funds are to be passed to state and municipal administrators to deal with their problems as they see fit. The legislature is expected to set up a program without giving the administrator any guidance whatsoever for fear of intruding upon state or municipal autonomy. As K.C. Davis puts it, "Congress says, 'Here is a problem. Deal with it.'" The result we generally call enabling legislation.

The New Deal was expected to work effectively and without arbitrariness by putting the new programs in the best of all possible worlds: responsibility will be imposed upon central bureaucrats and decisions will be made miraculously in the public interest merely through the pulling and hauling of organized interests; central government expands; local influence expands as well; everybody gains. It is the providential "hidden hand" of Adam Smith applied to politics.

This neat process has been the prevailing public philosophy for the past generation. Panglossian political scientists describe it with overwhelming approval as pluralism. The Supreme Court has enshrined the essence of the New Deal in American jurisprudence as delegation of power. Most recently, political rhetoricians embrace it as creative federalism, maximum feasible participation, and countervailing power. Thanks to the work of such unlikely comrades as Lyndon Johnson, Arthur Schlesinger, J. K. Galbraith, *Fortune* and the *Wall Street Journal*, the principle of decentralization through delegation became the consensus politics that celebrated the end of the New Deal era in 1968.

What follows is a simple case study of the implementation of the two major federal urban programs in a single city. The case goes far toward explaining why the national regime in the United States is no longer taken to be legitimate by so many black people and why this sense of illegitimacy was so likely to spread eventually to whites. Legitimacy, that elusive but vital underpinning of any stable regime, is that sense of the rightness of the general political order. It is that generalized willingness to view public error or corruption as the result of bad administration. There is probably no way practically to measure legitimacy as such, but one can usually assess roughly the extent to which a regime is less legitimate today then yesterday—just as a doctor may not say precisely what a healthy body is but can know whether it is less healthy now than before.

In this spirit, one can fairly clearly detect a decline in the legitimacy of the regime by noting the rise of instances of repression of Left and Left-sounding activities; one can also detect it by noting the increasing number of political trials and political prisoners, and, more palpably still, the increased infiltration of Left organizations by paid informers. But other indications are not limited to the Left, as for example the increasing numbers of instances of defiance of federal laws—something Southerners have been leading the country in at least since 1954. One can therefore speak of problems of national legitimacy when he begins to sense a general unwillingness to submit political disputes to recognized channels of political settlement, when he sees mediation replaced by direct action.

This case suggests the extent to which the policies of the liberal state are producing its own downfall, and along with that the failure to achieve even a modicum of social justice. Also, in its perverse way, the case also illustrates the effectiveness of planning when governments do define their goals clearly and guide administrators firmly. Tragically the plan was for implementation of an evil policy, apartheid. But through the case perhaps liberals could learn a little something about how to plan for good ends.

Iron City is an urban-industrial area whose corporate boundary surrounds nearly 60,000 residents and whose true metropolitan area includes about 100,000. The history of the development plan of Iron City presents a single, well-documented case of the implementation of explicit racial goals. More than that, the nature of Iron City's official development plans and proposals upon which federal allocations were based serve to document beyond doubt the extraordinary permissiveness of federal urban policy.

Housing Policy in Iron City

The name of the city has been changed to protect the guilty. They are guilty as charged, but no more so than thousands of mayors, councilmen, planners, realtors and builders all over the country. The Iron City situation is extreme and unrepresentative, but it will soon be clear that it provides an ideal laboratory for discovering the nature and limitations of modern federal enabling legislation. Iron City is a southern city, and its development plan fostered racist goals, namely, apartheid, but in doing so its officials only stated the awful truth about the goals of land use development plans in cities all over the country.

In 1950 over 20 percent of Iron City's population was Negro, and they did *not* live in a ghetto. There were neighborhoods of Negroes in virtually every section of town. There was a narrow strip along the river, and there were several strips in the west central and western sections in easy walking distance from the steel and textile mills. There was a largely black neighborhood in the south central section, and there was a larger concentration in the north central section, "across the tracks." (Note the shadings on the map.) There was no Harlem; the implications

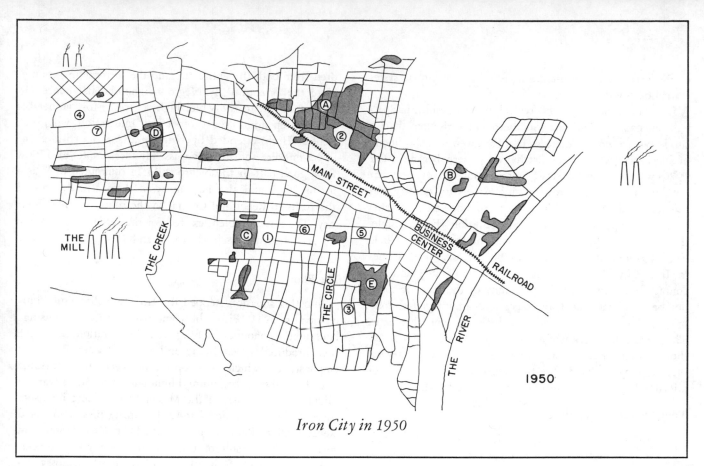

Iron City in 1950

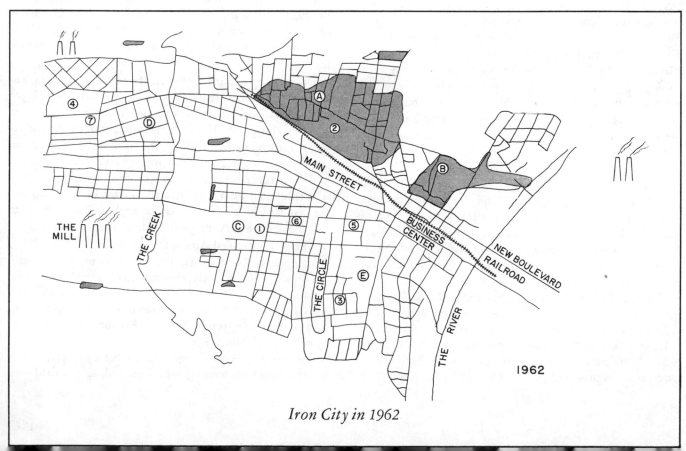

Iron City in 1962

of the very word suggest the nonsouthern origin of systematic housing discrimination.

Iron City's has been the typical Negro residential pattern in stable, middle-size southern cities. Rather than a single Negro section, there were interwoven neighborhoods of black and white. This patchwork pattern began in the 1920s with the slow but steady immigration of Negroes from outlying areas to the growing city. Access to industry and the needs of the wealthier whites for domestic servants made "close quarters" a desired condition. For example, the Negro neighborhoods east and north of The Circle were surrounded on three sides by the wealthiest homes in Iron City. But while the residents tolerated and encouraged in many ways the proximity of the races, it could not be said that Iron City constituted an integrated community. Each neighborhood was distinctly monochromatic. There were no black-white-black-white house patterns, although there were a number of instances when several Negro families lived directly across the street from or alley-to-alley with a larger number of white families.

They "Knew Their Place"

Negroes seemed to accept their back-of-the-bus status and the questionable privileges they had which were unavailable to whites. Crimes committed within the race were not, as a rule, investigated or prosecuted with utmost vigor. Black bootleggers (legal sale of liquor has for years been forbidden in the county) had freer rein to cater to the blacks and the insatiably thirsty white middle class. The raising of a pig or a goat was usually allowed, in violation of public health regulations. The rents tended to run considerably lower. And merchants and newsboys were more permissive in granting or extending petty credit to Negroes. This was the dispersed and highly status-bound social situation as recently as 1950.

Early in that decade, however, most Southerners could see a racial crisis approaching, and for them the problems inherent in the residential pattern were immediately clear. In Iron City each of the major public schools was within walking distance of at least one strip of Negro housing and its complement of school-age children. The map serves to make this graphically clear.

Central High School (1 on the map) offered 9th–12th grade education to the white children who lived east of The Creek. Rebel High (4) served white children living west of The Creek, including some areas not shown on the map. Washington High School (2) taught both junior and senior high school grades (7th–12th) to Negro chil-

dren from both the entire city and the surrounding county. Note the proximity of Negro neighborhoods, hence eligible children, to the white high schools. Most vulnerable to any impending court order for integration would be Central High, attended by virtually all of the children of upper-middle and middle-class families. Note also how far a good half of the Negro children commuted to Washington High and also how many of them actually crossed the paths to Rebel and Central in the course of their journey. The same problem existed for the junior high (3 and 7) and elementary schools (5, 6, and 7).

The Plan

Into this situation stepped the Iron City Planning Commission in 1951. First, the commission analyzed housing, land uses, economic facilities and deterioration. In 1952 they produced a handsome and useful Master Plan, the emphasis of which was upon the need for measures ". . . for arresting beginning blight and correcting advanced blight." On the basis of the Master Plan, a more intensive investigation was ordered toward ultimate production of a Rehabilitation Plan to guide actual implementation and financing. The result of this careful study was a professionally designed, fully illustrated, three-color, glossy paper booklet entitled *Iron City Redevelopment*. The focus of this publication was three areas, designated A, B and E on the map, in which blight had made urban redevelopment necessary.

Upon closer scrutiny, however, the plan reveals itself less a scheme for urban renewal as much as a script for Negro removal. All of the projects proposed in the plan are explicit on this point. The underlying intent to create a ghetto is further highlighted by the inconsistences between the design for Area E, which had relatively few Negroes, and that for Area A, which was predominantly Negro. The latter housing was as blighted as Area E, but, curiously, the standard of blighting was not applied. There the plan called for intensification of use rather than renewal.

The plan identified Area E as:

occupied by Negroes, but the number is too few to justify provisions of proper recreational, school and social facilities. . . . The opportunity to reconstitute the area as a residential district in harmony with its surroundings was the main reason for its selection as the number one redevelopment site.

The second, Area B, was chosen because "a relatively small amount of housing—standard and substandard—exists there"; therefore it would serve as a companion project to . . . [Area E] . . . thus affording home sites for those occupants of [Area E] who are not eligible for relocation in public housing or who, for reasons of their own, prefer single-family or duplex dwellings." Area A, as shown by the intensive survey and the maps published with the plan, contained as much dilapidated and blighted housing as Area E; but Area A was *not* designated an urban redevelopment area in the plan. Although "blighted and depreciating," it was the "center part of the area . . . growing as the focal point of Negro life." Along the main street of this area, extending into Area B, the plan proposed the building of an auditorium, a playfield and other public facilities "to serve [Iron City's] Negro community." Sites were inserted for the three Negro churches which would be removed by the redevelopment of Area E.

Before completion of *Iron City Redevelopment,* implementation projects had begun and were expanding as financing allowed. It was to be a showcase program, and enthusiasm ran high. The first steps, quite rationally, were to acquire housing for those families who were to be displaced. It was perfectly consistent with the city's view of these people that this housing would be public housing. There had been some public housing projects built under depression legislation, but the only meaningful projects were those begun in 1952 under The Housing Act of 1949. On the map the letters A, B, C and D represent the actual locations of these projects. There was never any controversy over the racial distribution of the occupants. Projects A and B were 100 percent Negro; Projects C and D were 100 percent white. By 1955 they were completed and occupied.

Each public housing project was placed carefully. Project A was built in the middle of the largest Negro area.

Public Housing Projects in Iron City

Project	Size (No. of Units)	% Negro in Project	Original Composition of Area	Development Cost
A	160	100	Negro	$1,491,000
B	224	100	Mixed	$2,491,000
C	146	0	Negro	$1,595,000
D	220	0	Negro	$2,300,000

Project B was built in a sparse area, about 50 percent Negro, but marked out in the plan as the area for future expansion of the Negro community. In the area around

Project B, the plan proposed sites for the three new "colored churches" and the "colored auditorium."

Project C, an exclusively white project, was built literally on top of the Negro area around it. While it was relatively inexpensive and contained the fewest number of units, it occupied an eight-square-block area due to its design. According to the executive director of the Greater Iron City Housing Authority, it was "a rather unique design, known in the architectural trade as a crankshaft design, thus providing both front and rear courtyards." This project was cited professionally as an outstanding example of good design. And no wonder! Its maximum utilization of space, although a low-rent project, made it a combination public housing, urban renewal and Negro removal plan par excellence. Project D was also built on top of a blighted Negro neighborhood. While it was a relatively large project, it was not solely responsible for eliminating every Negro from the area, as was Project C.

Meanwhile, renewal of the central city was proceeding at a slower pace; it wasn't until 1956 that implementation projects were fully designed. Two areas, designated by the shaded areas around B and E on the map, were selected for intensive renewal. Most important was Area E, a 56-acre area relatively tightly packed with rickety frame houses, outside toilets, corn or potato plots and Negroes. In the official plan, Area E included the unconnected Negro neighborhood just north of The Circle, as well as the entire shaded area due east of The Circle. Area B was relatively sparsely populated, containing a few shacks which needed removing. In some of these shacks were white unemployables.

Within three years the two urban renewal projects were declared 100 percent accomplished. In the official report to the Urban Renewal Administration, the results were as follows:

Completed Urban Renewal Projects in Iron City

Accomplishment	Activity	For Area E	For Area B
100%	Land Acquisition, No. of Parcels Acquired	168	39
100%	No. of Families Relocated	176	24
100%	No. of Structures Demolished (Site Clearance)	236	33

In Area E every trace of Negro life was removed. As the executive director of the Greater Iron City Housing Authority put it, "In this project, all of the then existing streets were vacated and a new land use map was developed." One entirely new street was put in, several of the narrow lanes (e.g., Saint James' Alley) were covered over, and through connectors were built for a dead-end street or two.

All of Area E has now become prime property. One large supermarket, several neighborhood businesses, and two apartment complexes are operating on renewal land purchased from the authority. To serve the 95 percent white area, an elementary school was constructed, as a consolidation of schools No. 5 and No. 6 which no longer exist. Its large playground and lighted ball field occupy most of the eastern sector of Area E. The renewal effort resulted in an equally impressive campus for the nearby junior high, No. 3. But most of the area was zoned for single family residences, and, as of 1968, the boom in construction of houses in the $25,000–$40,000 range was still in progress.

Area B now enjoys a new elementary school with a field house, lighted ball field, tennis court and playground. The city also built a swimming pool here, but it and the original municipal pool on The River were closed for several years to avoid integration of public facilities. Moreover, though redevelopment sites had been set aside in Area B for the three churches demolished in the redevelopment of Area E, each of the congregations chose locations elsewhere in the Negro community. Similarly, most of the relocating Negroes rejected Area B in favor of Area A, even though it was more densely populated and blighted. Except for the 224 units of new public housing, Area B remains underutilized. Furthermore, the major part of Area B extends north of Project B toward the mountain, where *Iron City Redevelopment* reports that although

> some of the terrain is steep, much of it is gently rolling and well drained. . . . In most southern cities there is a scarcity of vacant land located close to schools and churches and shopping districts and served by city utilities and transportation, land that is suitable and desirable for expansion of Negro neighborhoods or creation of new ones. [Area B] is such an area.

Apparently the Negroes do not agree, and most of the area remains a graded, but raw, expanse of red southern earth on the side of the mountain. This was the one part of the plan that went wrong; this was the voluntary part, not financed by federal agencies.

Yet, as a whole, the plan was an overwhelming success. Well before the 1960 census the large Negro contingent in Area E had been reduced to 5.1 percent of the entire census tract, and this was comprised of a few shanties behind the bottling works and the western edge of the area along The River. In Area C the removal process immediately around Central High was completed with Public Housing Project C. After 1960 some 10 percent of the area was still nonwhite, but this was drying up still further. Removal from Area D was approaching totality. By 1964 removal from all areas west of The Creek was given further assistance by the completion of one federally supported artery running east-west through the city and the inauguration of Iron City's portion of the new north-south Interstate Highway. That brought the nonwhite proportion in the western sectors of the city down to about 3 percent of the total population of those areas.

This is how the situation stood by the end of 1967: west of The Creek and north of Main Street (all around Area D), there remained six Negro families. When a nearby textile mill was closed down some years before, they, as employees, were given the right to buy their houses, and they have chosen to remain. West of The Creek and south of Main Street (the area including The Mill), fewer than 5 percent of the housing units were occupied by Negroes. Virtually every one of these houses is located in isolated and sparse sections along The Creek and behind The Mill, where one can still plant a plot of sorghum, catch a catfish, and, undisturbed, let a 1948 Chevrolet corrode into dust. Closer to the center of things, east of The Creek and south of Main Street, the 1960 distribution of Negroes continues to be reduced. Every last shack is gone from Area E and the entire central section of the white city. Three small pockets remain in the western portion near Area C, and that is all that remains in all of the white city. The last remaining Negro neighborhood of any size, a group of shanties running along The River south of Main Street, was removed by the construction of a City Hall–Police Department–YMCA complex. Area B remains completely nonwhite and underdeveloped. Area A now fills the entire triangle pointing north. It is a ghetto.

The plan enjoyed strong consensus among officials and white citizens. It enjoyed at least the acquiescence and tacit consent of the Negroes whose landlords, in any case, were white. Consensus or not, the plan would have had little chance of success without outside financial assistance. That assistance came, abundantly, from federal programs. And, most importantly, the federal personnel who allocated these funds, and still do, also had access to all the project plans, including the Master Plan and the Renewal Plan. Despite Iron City's open approach to apartheid—nothing was kept secret—federal assistance was never in question.

Relative to the population of Iron City and the size of its annual public sector budget, federal aid was quite substantial—amounting to 20 percent of the municipal budget for a few years. What we have seen here is an honest, straightforward job of federally sponsored physical and social planning. And the results were dramatic. Perhaps only New Haven, Connecticut, a city famous for its redevelopment, has had a higher per capita success ratio.

Direct federal assistance for public housing in Iron City amounted to slightly over $280,000 for the single fiscal year 1966. Each year since the completion of the four projects the city received a similar amount. This varying figure cannot be broken down among the four projects because it is computed on the basis of the "development costs" given above and granted as a lump sum. The Public Housing (recently changed to Housing Assistance) Administration of Housing and Urban Development (HUD) is authorized by law to grant *each year* to any housing authority the difference between expenses (governed by development costs) and income from public housing. Such a subsidy arrangement enabled authorities like Iron City's to borrow from private banks and to refinance through sale of relatively cheap Housing Authority bonds. What is even more significant is that, under the formula, Iron City is authorized to receive a maximum grant of nearly $305,000 per annum. It is a point of pride at the Greater Iron City Housing Authority that the full amount available under the law was never needed or requested. At a minimum estimate of $250,000 per year, federal grants to help carry the public housing have amounted to $3,000,000. And federal public housing grants are never-ending. Each year the total to Iron City goes up another $250,000 or more.

Subsidizing the Rich

Federal assistance for urban renewal, as differentiated from housing assistance, was another indispensable part of the plan. Between 1957 and 1961, by which time virtually everything but land disposition was completed, Iron City received just short of $1,600,000 from the federal government under the urban redevelopment laws. This amounts to an additional subsidy of $400,000 per annum.

The federal housing assistance was at least $300,000 for each year between 1954 or 1955 and 1957. Together with the urban renewal allotments, the total was at least $700,000 during the years of peak planning activity, 1957–1962. This money is the key to the plan's success.

But to this we must also add the resources made available through various other federal agencies. Federal highway assistance added an undetermined amount for new arteries and, incidentally, forced Negroes to move from the western edge of Iron City. The Federal Housing Authority and the Veterans Administration help to finance the lovely homes being built in Area E. It has not been possible to determine whether federal community facilities funds helped remove Negroes from The River where the new City Hall complex now stands. Nor has it been possible to determine if the local banks balked at extending FHA and VA home owner credit to Negroes seeking to build on the mountain side north of Area B. Answers would affect the meaning of the case only marginally.

Tarnished Legitimacy

First, the case bears out what many people have been saying for two decades, that slum removal meant Negro removal. But it goes further. It supports the even more severe contention that the ultimate effects of federal urban policies have been profoundly conservative or separatist, so much so as to vitiate any plans for positive programs of integration through alteration of the physical layout of cities.

Second, it supports the general thesis that a policy of delegation of powers without rule of law will ultimately come to ends profoundly different from those intended by the most libertarian and humanistic of sponsors. Moreover, it supports the unfashionable contention that some of the most cherished instruments of the liberal state may be positively evil—and that a criterion by which this evil can be predicted is the absence of public and explicit legislative standards by which to guide administrative conduct.

Third, the case of Iron City, especially the explicit nature of its racial policy, shows precisely how and why federal policy is ill equipped to govern the cities directly. The permissiveness of federal enabling legislation could do no greater harm to the social future of the cities than if harm were intended. The present disorder in the cities is explained properly by the failure of government and politics, rather than by the inferiority of Negro adjustment. The case demonstrates how national legitimacy can be tarnished to the degree that it is loaned to the cities for discretionary use and how the crisis of public authority is inevitable as long as a political process unguided by law climaxes in abuses such as those catalogued in Iron City. In sum, it helps show why liberal government based on current principles of delegation cannot achieve justice.

217

Every Negro in Iron City knew what was happening. Every Negro in Chicago and New York and Cleveland and Detroit knows the same about his city too. But since northern Negroes are not as docile, does that mean that federal imperium was used completely differently outside the South? True, planning authorities would never so deliberately pursue such obviously racial planning. It is also true that few social plans could be as relatively extensive or as successful as Iron City's. Nonetheless, it is undeniable that misuse of federal programs in ways indistinguishable in principle from the Iron City misuse has been widespread.

Martin Anderson, for example, estimated in 1964 that about two-thirds of all displacements resulting from urban renewal were Negro, Puerto Rican, or some other minority group. In public housing the record is even more somber. First, because the pattern is even clearer, and second, because these projects stand as ever-present symbols of the acts of discrimination by which they were created.

A study by Bernard Weissbrourd for the Center for the Study of Democratic Institutions concluded that ". . . most cities have followed a deliberate program of segregation in public housing. . . ." Until July 1967, many housing administrators followed a rule of "free choice" allowing eligible tenants to wait indefinitely for an apartment, which allowed them also to decline a vacancy on racial grounds. Still more recently it was revealed that the Chicago Housing Authority, with the full knowledge of federal agencies, cleared all proposed public housing sites with that member of the Board of Aldermen whose ward would be affected. Thus, while the whole story cannot be told from official statistics, we may conclude what every urban Negro knows—Iron City is not unique.

Separate but Equal?

According to HUD reports of 1965, only three of New York City's 69 public housing projects were officially listed as all nonwhite or all white in occupancy; but ten of Philadelphia's 40 projects were all nonwhite, and 21 of Chicago's 53, five of Detroit's 12, four of Cleveland's 14, and all of Dallas' ten projects were listed as either all nonwhite or all white. The rest of reality is hidden, because the Public Housing Administration defines an "integrated project" as one in which there are "white and more than one nonwhite, including at least one Negro family." Not only does this system of reporting make it impossible to determine the real number of truly integrated projects, it also serves to maintain local racial policies and prejudices.

The Civil Rights Act of 1965 was supposed to have put an end to such practices, but there is little evidence that it can or will improve the situation in public housing in particular or city housing in general. It was not until July of 1967 that the rule of "free choice" was replaced with a "rule of three," a plan whereby an applicant must take one of the first three available units or be dropped to the bottom of the eligible lists. All of this is undeniable testimony that the practices all along had constituted a "separate but equal" system of federally supported housing.

In June 1967, three years after the 1964 Civil Rights Act and after strenuous efforts by the Johnson Administration, two of Detroit's five segregated projects became "integrated" when one white family moved into each of two totally black projects. At the same time, at least 11 of New York's projects were classified as "integrated" when, in fact, fewer than 15 percent of the units were occupied by families of some race other than the race of the 85 percent majority in that project.

For 33 years the Federal Housing Authority has insured over $110 billion of mortgages to help whites escape, rather than build the city. This confession was made when the FHA instituted a *pilot* program to increase FHA support for housing finance in "economically unsound" areas. And it took the belated 1967 directive on public housing to get them to do that much. These remedial steps came five years after President Kennedy's famous "stroke of the pen" decision aimed at preventing discrimination in publicly supported housing and three years after the first applicable Civil Rights Act. Yet no such legislation or executive decisions can erase the stigma of second-class citizenship placed upon the residents of federal housing programs. Nor can more skillful administration of essentially separatist programs remove the culpability of federal participation in the American local government policy of apartheid. Rather, all of these efforts merely suggest that remedies and correctives are never going to help bad organic laws, because bad organic laws are, quite literally, congenitally defective.

Perhaps it is better to have no new public housing than to have it on the Iron City pattern and at the expense of national legitimacy. With the passing of the Housing Act of 1968 and union agreements to build modular units off-site, some will surely argue that the answers lie in the proper expansion of public housing. But unless steps are taken to prevent the duplication of the patterns reviewed here, more will hardly yield better. Other writers and officials have proposed various solutions. President Johnson suggested creating semipublic corporations to finance public low-cost housing, while Senator Charles Percy would offer incentives to private corporations. These proposals focus on the details of financing and offer further examples of the confusion shared by liberals today concerning forms of law versus essentially technocratic forms of administration for achievement of simple, ordinary justice. Regardless of the means of financing, these programs will produce no lasting social benefit without the rule of law that states unmistakably what administrators can and cannot do, what is to be forbidden, and what is to be achieved. That is the moral of the Iron City story.

Fair Housing Laws—

Unfair Housing Practices

Lynn W. Eley

By the time Congress enacted the Fair Housing Act of 1968, about 62 percent of the nation's population was already covered by some form of local or state fair-housing law. A federal law had been sought mainly because these local and state laws had proved ineffective. The Supreme Court later in 1968 affirmed equal rights for Negroes in renting or buying housing, adding to the scope of fair-housing statutes at all levels. Still, how effective can we expect the new federal legislation to be in opening white neighborhoods to black residents?

Negroes and whites engaged in the fair-housing struggle have been seeking a commitment of public policy as well as changes in private attitudes and behavior. With the attainment of the first goal, the second remains to be seen. It is obvious from a review of the fair-housing struggle at local and state levels that only by changing white attitudes and behavior can we expect Negroes to have the same options as whites in their choice of where and how to live, even given equal *economic* opportunity.

By the 1890's, white America had broken off its flirtation with the concept of racial equality and integration. Patterns of racial segregation in housing were reinforced in the post-Reconstruction era with the tacit consent of government and frequently with its support. As Negroes migrated in growing numbers to the industrial cities of the North and West, they found themselves herded into the slum areas of the central cities, where they replaced Jews, Poles, Italians, and other minority groups who were on the way up in American society. By the end of World War I, patterns of racial segregation were firmly established throughout the country.

Negroes were to be afforded separate but equal schools, public accommodations, and neighborhoods, with the tacit emphasis upon separate. This was a way of minimizing the supposed degrading influence of Negroes on whites. In housing, restrictive covenants forbidding an owner to sell or rent to Negroes were enforceable in courts of law. Home-mortgage and loan policies of the Federal Housing Administration and other government agencies penalized mixed neighborhoods.

The nadir of public policy aimed at securing racial segregation in Northern cities was reached around World War I in the use of local zoning ordinances. In Chicago, for example, the real-estate board's Committee to Study the Invasion of White Residence Districts, in a report issued in April, 1917, asked for "the cooperation of the influential colored citizens" as follows:

Inasmuch as more territory must be provided, it is desired in the interest of all, that each block shall be filled solidly and that further expansion shall be confined to contiguous blocks, and that the present method of obtaining buildings in scattered blocks, be discontinued.

The board did not stop there; the sanction of law was also sought. The board's bulletin of October 1917 reprinted a resolution urging: "the City Council to immediately pass an ordinance under police power whereby further immigration may be stopped until provisions are made and such reasonable restriction of leasing or selling be enforced as to prevent lawlessness, destruction of values and property and loss of life."

The drive for this legislation was suspended when the Supreme Court later that year, in *Buchanan v. Warley,* ruled against a similar ordinance in Louisville, Kentucky. Thereafter, the Chicago real-estate board launched, as its December 1917 bulletin stated, "a propaganda campaign through its individual members to recommend owners' societies in every white block for the purpose of mutual defense." And elsewhere, the authority of government at all levels was generally ranged against Negro Americans.

When the civil-rights movement began to gather momentum in the 1940's and 1950's, Negroes found growing numbers of whites in the North ready to help them gain equal rights. Gradually these forces made headway. In 1948, in *Shelley v. Kraemer,* the Supreme Court held that restrictive covenants could no longer be enforced by the courts. By 1950, in line with that decision, the Federal Housing Administration deleted restrictive covenants from its regulations.

Strategies for Fair Housing

In 1954, with the Supreme Court's decision in the school-desegregation cases, particularly *Brown v. Board of Education,* the civil-rights movement got a tremendous boost. Though the Court's explicit holding was confined to public education, the impact of that decision has been felt in all aspects of Negro-white relations in America—and its course has not yet fully run. It set the stage for the nonviolent demonstrations and the other political and social engagements that have characterized our times ever since.

Open-housing campaigns have drawn much of their inspiration and tactics from the national civil-rights revolution. But until the 1960's virtually all the battles were fought within state and local governments, and most campaigns were waged in core cities of metropolitan areas and in university towns. Public housing projects became the first target of the open-housing forces; they argued that taxes paid by all Americans should not be used for housing closed to some because of race or religion. Builders, realtors and others objected to laws banning discrimination in public housing, but their passage was seldom an occasion for much controversy. By the 1950's, there was a sort of popular moral consensus behind these laws. Rather rapidly, publicly assisted housing was included in those laws and regulations that prohibited discrimination.

It was out of this battle in New York that proponents of open housing began to coordinate their efforts. In 1947, representatives of the New York Society for Ethical Culture, the American Jewish Congress, the NAACP, the American Civil Liberties Union, the Urban League, and several other organizations held a series of meetings to discuss organizational needs. Key leaders realized from earlier experience that combatting discrimination in housing required a high degree of specialized knowledge. Few civil-rights organizations could afford to have a professional staff versed in details of federal and state housing laws or in the complexities of financing in the housing market. In 1948, therefore, 20 organizations agreed to form the New York State Committee on Discrimination in Housing, which from its inception the following January worked toward the passage of local and state legislation banning discrimination in housing.

The Committee soon found that there was a nationwide demand for information and assistance to cope with housing bias. A meeting to plan for a national organization was called by the Committee and the National Association of Intergroup Relations Officials in July, 1950, and it was attended by representatives of 11 national organizations. The title National Committee Against Discrimination in Housing was chosen and the chairmanship was accepted by Dr. Robert C. Weaver, then director of the John Hay Whitney Foundation (and later Secretary of the United States Department of Housing and Urban Development in the Johnson Administration). Since both committees were modestly financed, they used the same staff and office. Eventually the State Committee, its main legislative missions accomplished, went out of existence, while the National Committee developed into an impressive public information and coordinating agency, with over 40 national civil-rights, liberal, and church-related organizations as affiliates.

The idea of extending antidiscrimination statutes to private housing was born in New York City out of the collaborative efforts spearheaded by the State Committee on Discrimination in Housing. Fair-housing laws were urged in the late 1940's and the 1950's as a sequel to fair-employment and fair-education laws, and the terminology was borrowed directly from fair-employment law. The right to shelter of one's own choosing and capacity to pay was in the proponents' view a right of higher priority than the right of government or of other private persons to refuse to sell or rent property to a Negro.

The nation's first fair-housing law was enacted in New York City on December 30, 1957, nearly a decade after the State Committee on Discrimination in Housing had begun its fight. Thereafter, efforts were transferred to the state government and led to the passage of a state law in 1961. Meanwhile fair-housing laws had been adopted in a few other cities and states.

In addition to public and publicly assisted housing these early laws generally covered private "multiple-housing accommodations," variously defined as three, four, five, or more housing units controlled by one person or firm. It proved extremely difficult to win extension of the laws to any part of the private-housing market, which was why the proponents of open housing were willing to settle for regulating the commercial activities of the land developers, builders, realtors, large landlords, lenders, and advertisers. It was also conceded by fair-housing forces that a pattern of discriminatory practices would be much easier to detect and demonstrate in the case of persons and firms associated with housing as a business than in the case of individual homeowners and small landlords.

Broader Coverage Sought by Fair Housing

By the early 1960's, those working for fair-housing laws were emboldened by several legislative victories and heartened because courts were generally upholding the constitutionality of the laws. Even in the two adverse rulings (on laws in the state of Washington and in Toledo, Ohio), the statutes were declared invalid on technical rather than substantive grounds. It was reasonably clear that courts viewed fair-housing laws, if properly drawn, as a legitimate exercise of government power.

On the strength of these successes, fair-housing supporters pushed for coverage of all housing. Prohibition of blockbusting or panic-peddling practices was also sought. In addition to seeking broader coverage, efforts were made to get stronger enforcement powers, particularly as experience under existing laws revealed the serious shortcomings of trying to win compliance by handling violators through administrative investigations, hearings, issuance of cease-and-desist orders, and court imposition of civil and criminal penalties. Following the lead of New York City again, open-housing advocates attempted to obtain legal authority for use of the temporary injunction—a court order which would prevent the sale or rental of housing involved in a discrimination complaint while the complaint was being handled.

Antidiscrimination forces were quite successful, at least until recently, in playing the issue back and forth between the state and local governments—winning a concession in one place, then using it to up the ante in another. In New York, for instance, after passage of the city's law in 1957, efforts were transferred to the state government and led finally to the passage of a state law in 1961. Since then the fair-housing forces have moved back and forth between the city and state political arenas and have secured important strengthening amendments to both laws. Similar patterns may be observed in the activities of fair-housing proponents in Chicago and Illinois; Ann Arbor, Detroit, and Michigan; Berkeley and California; and other cities and states.

The federal government also intervened on the side of integrated housing policy in several states during the Johnson Administration. In 1964, when California voters adopted Proposition 14, which prohibited fair-housing laws, federal officials countered by announcing that federal funds for urban-renewal projects in California would be curtailed, because cities could no longer guarantee that urban-renewal lands would not be used in a discriminatory fashion. In Illinois in 1967, federal officials threatened to withhold funds for the construction of a huge atomic-accelerator plant in a suburb west of Chicago until the state or local governments took legal action to insure equal access to housing for prospective minority employees and their families. Influential politicians opposed the coercion, however, and funds for the plant were finally voted without reference to Illinois' lack of a state fair-housing law. Fair-housing laws have since been passed in several communities in the area of the plant.

Another feature of fair-housing campaigns has been their carefully cultivated bipartisan image. As a rule, fair-housing proposals have had much more support from Democrats than from Republicans, but in most campaigns, at least one Republican officeholder has agreed to have his name listed as a sponsor or co-sponsor. It is doubtful that a federal Fair Housing Act would be on the books now without the support of Senator Everett M. Dirksen and several other Republican Congressmen. Republicans as well as Democrats at all three levels of government may have supported recent proposals by conviction as well as by their realization of the growing political strength of Negroes and allied whites. Other, less honorable considerations may also have been involved.

One of a few instances where a political party played the decisive role in determining what type of legislation would be passed was in Chicago where the Democratic city government tried to persuade the Republican state legislature to take on the onus of passing fair-housing legislation. When it became clear that the state would not do so but that Chicago's problems of race relations demanded dramatic action, Mayor Richard J. Daley jammed an ordinance through the Chicago Council. In most other cities and states, the fair-housing decision has been largely shaped and decided by coalitions of various individuals and community groups, with the political party or parties acting and reacting as part of the total complex of influential forces.

Counteroffensive

Opposition to open-housing laws was generally unorganized until 1963, when voters in Berkeley, California, turned down a fair-housing law. Prior to that time, proponents moved so aggressively and effectively—in New York City and State, Pittsburgh, Colorado, Connecticut, Massachusetts, Oregon, Oberlin, and Ann Arbor—that the opposition did not seem to realize what had happened until a law was on the books. But opposition around the country roused itself after Berkeley, where a council majority in favor of a strong law insisted upon criminal sanctions and as a result galvanized lethargic opponents into equally determined combatants. Perhaps the fair-housing movement at that point would have slowed down anyway for reasons that have produced a deadlock in the larger civil-rights revolution. But it appears that the Berkeley referendum and the subsequent California initiative on Proposition 14 momentarily slowed the movement's momentum.

Real-estate brokers have been the most stubbornly opposed to fair-housing laws. The National Association of Real Estate Boards (NAREB) served as spokesman and strategist for efforts to defeat fair-housing legislation. NAREB labeled the legislation "forced-housing laws," charging that such laws infringe on property rights by forcing people to dispose of their housing to persons they would not ordinarily choose.

By the time of the Proposition 14 drive the following year, the California real-estate group, fresh from its victory in Berkeley, was in high gear. A front organization named the Committee for Home Protection advertised to attract support for its campaign against the recently enacted Rumford Fair Housing Act. One set of ads read in part as follows:

> In September 1963, the Rumford Act became State Law. Heretofore, a man's home was his castle. The Rumford Act makes a man's home subject to the whims of a politically appointed State Board. . . . The politically appointed Commission can FORCE you to sell or rent your home to an individual NOT OF YOUR CHOICE. . . .

The Proposition 14 campaign was successful even beyond the expectations of most realtors, and it sparked a series of referenda against fair housing around the country.

After Berkeley and Proposition 14, opposition tactics were characterized by definite patterns. These usually began with threats to subject a bill to a referendum unless it was killed or watered down. If this failed and a bill was passed to which realtors took substantial exception, they might put the issue to the people; between the Berkeley referendum in April 1963 and early 1968, every popular ballot went against fair-housing legislation—some eight in all.

Another opposition tactic has been to resort to judicial appeal and delay. Opponents have rushed to judges, particularly those known or thought to be sympathetic, to obtain temporary injunctions and agreements to review the legality and validity of fair-housing laws. Opponents have won outright victory in the courts, however, in only one area, and that at the state level. Administrative regulations to forbid discrimination by realtors licensed by the state, have been quashed by the courts as unconstitutional assumptions of legislative authority by the executive. This happened to Rule 9 of the State Corporation and Securities Commission in Michigan and to former Governor Otto Kerner's executive order in Illinois.

Besides these opposition tactics, a whole range of tactics have been adopted to live within the law, but at little outright inconvenience to usual ways of doing business. Some realtors and realtor groups have withdrawn their opposition to fair-housing laws after living under them for a time, and in most of these instances, they have said that the chief reason for their change of heart was the discovery that the laws have not "disrupted" the housing market. In other words, the laws have not yet brought any fundamental change in realtor practices or housing patterns. Realtors have learned to comply with the laws at explicit, formal levels, and yet maintain substantially the same informal practices and patterns.

Realtors' associations in several locations where state or local fair-housing laws have been in operation—among them Chicago, Ann Arbor, Wisconsin, Fort Wayne, and Denver—have officially reversed position and adopted resolutions pledging support and compliance. These conversions are probably in part genuine and in part expedient and tactical. In Ann Arbor, for instance, the conversion statement was accompanied by a plea to fellow realtors to urge local and state government to do the job instead of passing the buck to Washington (this was before the federal law passed).

Present Ambiguities

The ironic political fact of fair-housing legislation at this time seems to be that such laws have won lukewarm public acceptance, but most whites are still unprepared to change their housing practices to permit real integration. At the same time, the decreasing momentum of the civil-rights revolution and the surging Negro drive for independent black power reinforce Negro and white separation, at least in the short run. One may speculate that fair-

housing laws are being passed with greater ease and frequency today mainly because their supporters want them for psychological and symbolic reasons, and opponents and moderates are now persuaded that such laws do not threaten present practice. The function of a fair-housing law is today mainly symbolic and ritualistic. Its existence holds aloft the explicit standard of equal opportunity in housing, confirming the American creed for all of us; but parties on both sides tacitly realize that provisions will not be enforced in a way that basically threatens white neighborhoods. Supporters have the public policy they desire, and opponents have the practice they want to preserve.

This observation applies not only to the enactment and enforcement of a fair-housing law, but to later amendments pressed by fair-housing advocates to extend coverage to additional categories of housing. Whether this situation applies as well to enforcement of the new federal law remains to be seen, but at the moment the popular and political support for energetic and broad-gauged implementation of this legislation appears lacking.

Circumstantial evidence supporting this gloomy verdict is not difficult to find. For one thing, and most important, social scientists and other careful observers have found no direct relationship between the presence or absence of a fair-housing law and the extent of racial integration in a given community or state. Other factors such as the general economic health of the community seem to have greater influence. At the same time, the movement for fair-housing legislation has helped to make integrated housing a subject of attention and concern. The public agitation has apparently improved the general climate in much of the country for acceptance of black families in white neighborhoods. Upper- and middle-class whites seem increasingly disposed to accept black neighbors of similar socioeconomic status. This is still token integration, however, and does not relieve the ghetto conditions in which most Negroes live.

It is also worth comment that fair-housing legislation appears to be less and less an issue of sharp division along partisan political lines. While this has its encouraging aspect, another view is that such legislation has not disrupted much of anything and has therefore lost a good deal of its dangerous political image among whites while retaining symbolic attractiveness for many Negroes; thus politicians are finding it not disadvantageous, and often advantageous, to support new applications of the legislation. In recent instances, such as in Ohio, Michigan, Illinois, and of course on Capitol Hill, fair-housing legislation efforts have picked up important, and in several situations critical, support from Republican officeholders. Ann Arbor's law would not have been passed in 1963, or strengthened in 1965, without Republican support. On the negative side, the bills Republicans are willing to sponsor or vote for are still usually weaker and less comprehensive in coverage than those Democrats are willing to sponsor.

We confront a situation in which a majority of the people of the United States probably oppose integrated housing for any statistically significant numbers of blacks, though on a legal and policy level much of American government has been at least partially converted to the cause of integrated housing. What Daniel P. Moynihan has called "the ethnic disarray" of most of our cities and the hostile attitudes toward Negroes in working class and ethnic neighborhoods severely limit the possibility for open housing. So do the tokenism of the upper-class and middle-class suburbs and the thrust toward black separatism in the Negro ghettos.

It seems fairly clear that we are now witnessing in the area of housing another re-enactment of "An American dilemma"—the painful gap between the professions of the American creed and the reality of racial segregation. Whether the new federal Fair Housing Act, together with the rise of more racially tolerant generations, will lead toward a new day for open housing remains highly questionable.

Death of the American Dream House
George Sternlieb

The private house in America is the focal point of the myth/dream/reality of the good life for its middle classes as well as the aspirants to those anointed ranks. The automobile has lost much of its glamour: the boat, the trailer, the vacation to Europe are separately and together becoming powerful symbols, but their use—and excursions involving their use—begins with the house.

To current blue-collar workers, moreover, the private house is what the old postal savings system or employer-automatic wage deductions for the purchase of Liberty Bonds or Savings Bonds or War Bonds were to previous generations—a form of relatively painless savings. For all but the more affluent in our society, a house is not only a home, it is typically a major repository of capital investment and stored equity. As any imaginative architect will testify, houses are purchased to be sold, not to be lived in. Their ultimate sale represents the edge which makes Social Security and Old Age pensions endurable. Possession of a house makes a man a full citizen of the work group.

In this last generation, workingmen of America have

moved from being renters to owners. The ramifications of this past shift are far from fully explored, but more important to understand now are the present facts and future realities of the housing stock for American workers. Who builds it? For whom? How? Why? And where?

The New Home Business

About 90 percent of all the new private one-family housing under $15,000 built in the United States in 1971, for example, was in the form of mobile home units. This type of configuration will yield approximately 450,000 out of the anticipated 1971 total of two million or so units. Another 400,000 units will be divided nearly evenly between single family homes and multiple family residences supported by government mortgage subsidies under the 235-236 Programs which, depending upon income levels, may bring interest rates down to the 1 percent level. These particular programs are now the primary form of direct federal subsidization of the housing market. (Left out of this discussion are the interminable squabbles on government subsidization of private ownership through preferential tax treatment. Rarely considered are the changes in rents—and possible tax rates—if these nominal windfalls were rectified.)

During the 1930s simple government guarantees of mortgages under the earlier FHA (Federal Housing Administration) programs were sufficient to inspire developers. In more recent years the inflated amounts of government guaranteed indentures, as a function of federal deficits, has increased the interest rate which these bear to the point of making the guarantees in themselves of little use in providing housing. States and municipalities have used the tax-exempt status of their securities with increasing abandon in stepping into the gap. Substantial amounts of housing have been generated under such programs. About a quarter of the states, for example, currently have housing authorities which are financing middle-class housing using tax-exempt securities—and their number is being added to. Again, however, the enormous amount of such tax-exempt securities—windfalls for the rich though they may appear to be—has created a market situation in which the interest rates required to market them is too substantial to permit housing for anything approximating the blue-collar group. In New York City, for example, the Mitchell-Lama Program, which involves tax-exempt 50-year mortgages and local tax exemption up to the 85 percent mark, yields a housing unit renting currently for $90 per month per room. We will come back to why this should be, but for the moment let us accept the case, even though involving perhaps the national high spot in the providing of public housing, as all too characteristic of what has occurred under tax-exempt financing.

In the last decade, the federal government substantially exhausted the potential of even below-market interest rates, which under the 221-d3 Program for example, brought interest rates down to the 3 to 3½ percent level. This too lost its charm and so the 235-236 Programs at the 1 percent level.

Even with these subsidies, however, the absolute costs of amortization involve cash flow requirements of enormous magnitude. Even stretched out over more than lifetime expectancies (50 years with Mitchell-Lama, the 48 years of New Jersey Housing Finance Agency and the like), together with steep rises in local taxation and operating costs, they increasingly leave the working classes out of the spectrum of housing groups that can be accommodated within the present state of the art. In Trenton, New Jersey, for example, 400 units under the 236 Program were just completed at costs of $33,000 per unit. The rents with the full subsidy package approximate $200 a month for two-bedroom units. Since there is an income limit under the 235-236 Program of 135 percent of public-housing admission standards for people who will be subsidized by the program, the answer was to raise the local public-housing limits so that people with incomes of $10,000 and more are presently being housed by a program which was dedicated in its inception to the needs of blue-collar America.

There is a growing body of opinion which holds that the very intervention of governmental subsidy mechanisms into the housing market has served to engender additional increases in the housing costs which they were intended to resolve.

Residential construction costs in America over the last twenty years have never been forced to meet the test of the market. When housing starts to slow down, when land speculators begin to be worried about the inflated values of their holdings, when building-trade workers start shading their prices, the cry comes up that something must be done about housing and a new stimulant is added to the market. This is all in good cause and good conscience. The result, however, is that private conventional housing in much of the Northeast has substantially disappeared at anything under the $25,000 mark; indeed in many of the more affluent suburbs one would have to add another $10,000 to the cost.

In many cases the blue-collar worker finds himself too poor to compete in the unaided market and too rich or sometimes too poor to take advantage of the current forms of government subsidy. There is little in the way of technological innovation which would seem to alter this picture. The answer presently being implemented, in any case, is the lessening of housing quality, size of structure and general lowering of standards; and all of these efforts succeed only at best in momentarily stabilizing prices.

227

The new private house may be the dream of blue-collar America; its reality, however, is drifting away.

The Suburban Squeeze Play

The question of where new housing is to be built is one of the most publicized elements in the current dilemma. It has been highlighted not only in terms of the provision of housing but also for securing a variety of public ends.

There has been a significant upgrading of land use requirements in most suburbs. In the northern half of New Jersey, for example, more than half of all the vacant land zoned for residential purposes requires lots of one or more acres. And this, to any good, concerned citizen is prima facie evidence of the wickedness and sinfulness of the suburbanite. To paraphrase Berthold Brecht: the rich (and the middle-class and the blue-collar worker) may love the poor, but they hate living near them. This is particularly true when their skin color or languages may be different from the mainstream.

Without minimizing the role that prejudice undoubtedly plays in suburban freezeout, one should also not disregard the old-fashioned role of economics. The poor cost more. To use very rough numbers, if one assumes that local realty taxes (which are the main source of revenue for community expenditures) represent at most 25 percent of the rent dollar (and in public housing typically the payments in lieu of local tax are only 10 percent of the gross shelter rent) it becomes very evident that typical local revenues derived from poor families are inadequate to provide the schooling of even one child. This is without attention being paid to any of the other increments in cost generated by the addition of a family. And the same holds true for the blue-collar worker at typical incomes.

In some unique, highly affluent suburbs, liberal forces are at work to crack the suburban barrier. In Princeton, New Jersey, for example, there are presently under consideration more than 500 units of public and low-income housing. The resistance to this addition comes not so much from the affluent of the community as it does from the lingering remnants of blue-collar workers and low-level municipal employees—from the policemen making $10,000 a year and paying 10 percent of it in local taxes, from the maintenance worker working in the local RCA plant and third generation in the community, owning a house and feeling it slipping from his fingers as local taxes increase at a 10 percent-a-year, compounded annually, rate.

The great bulk of government programs which intervene in the municipal sphere at best supply subsidies for capital grants; at worst they tend to involve the community, practically willy-nilly, in greater levels of operating cost. Until, and unless, there is some fiscal packaging of the local costs generated by the additions of moderate and low-income families to the community, the political reality—

"cracking zoning is suicide"—will hold. The recent California court decision, *Serrano et al.* v. *Ivy Baker Priest,* which declared that substantial dependence on local property taxes violated the equal protection clause of the Fourteenth Amendment, may have much more in the way of positive results in opening up the suburbs than all of the efforts at intervention based upon racial equity.

In the meantime, however, the blue-collar workers, particularly those who reside in the older suburbs, guard the walls as best they can from the middle-class aspirants who are fleeing the central city. Certainly this is in substantial part because of prejudice but even more through economic fear.

Racial factors cloak basic economic elements and keep us from coming to political grips with them at great general cost. And for proof that these fears within the parameters of present societal organization are not merely fantasies, the suburban blue collars have only to look at the plight of those of their fellows who remain in the central city.

Trapped in the City

There are many profundities that have been exchanged on the subject of the relatively poor interface between older ethnic minorities, particularly those in the blue-collar occupations/income levels and the black and Puerto Rican populations within central cities. Perhaps so obvious as to be beneath intellectualizing are the impacts of the basic economic elements.

Newark, as in so many other areas, is a clear-cut prototype. The current tax rate is approximately 8 percent of real value. The worker residing in the city—perhaps in one of its white enclaves—or for that matter, since skin color is irrelevant here, the new minority-group home-buyers find that the house, that may have been purchased a dozen years ago and which was looked forward to as the essential cushion for the Florida retirement or as the cash with which to make the down payment on a more desirably sited residence, is instead a dead end. The man that can afford a $1,600 tax bill on a modest $20,000 house doesn't want to live in Newark; the man who can only afford $20,000 for a house can't afford the tax bill. And in neither case is there a bank to grant a mortgage or an insurance company to give essential coverage. The blue-collar worker in Newark is joined by his equivalent on the police department or the fire department in a strong resentment against those who he feels have occasioned this impasse.

There is an interesting variation in owner attitudes towards the central city's problems. In a recent survey of Newark absentee owners, typically of multiple tenancies, viewed their tenants as their prime problem. Resident owners, on the other hand, ranked taxes and tax increases as the premier difficulty and this is a response which is substantially independent of race. Whether in the central city or in some of the older suburbs that are open for mixed occupancy, there are an increasing number of black home-owners typically recruited either from the ranks of the better paid blue-collar workers or equivalent income levels of white-collar and governmental operations. Their attitudes and responses, at least to our surveys, are much more in accord with the economic frame of reference, regardless of their skin color, than they are of any racial element.

The Myth of Home-Ownership

For the first time since the Second World War the level of multiple-tenancy housing starts will exceed that of private one-family houses. In part this is a tribute to the characteristics of our new household formation; the post-war baby boom is rapidly coming to fruition; the children of 1946, 1947, 1948, 1949 are forming the new households of 1971 and must be housed. Typically this takes on the form of the garden apartment house or its equivalent. But these accommodations, in turn, at least according to folklore and for that matter much reality of the recent past, are viewed by consumers as essentially way stations on the life cycle, serving as a temporary abode until (with one-and-a-half children) the migration is made to the one-family tract development. There is increasing evidence that at least for the blue-collar workers in America and for all others of equivalent income this may no longer be a tenable mode.

As pointed out earlier, the well of housing subsidies is beginning to run dry; its effects no longer, at least in the higher-cost areas of the country, adequate in providing modest one-family developments in conventional settings. Again the response in earlier years has been to increase the level of subsidies in one form or another. The question may well be asked, given the political pressures that are so virile in housing, as to whether this process may not be repeated in the future.

World Competition and American Labor

There is a substantial question, however, as to whether Americans still have their old options open to them to choose internal domestic policy on housing as well as other areas. The current economic difficulties of the United States will continue after Vietnam; they will continue regardless of the political complexion of the administration. They might not have occurred quite so quickly with more foresighted economic policies, but it is my thesis that they would have occurred nevertheless.

The gap in wage scales of American production workers as compared with those in hitherto less fortunate parts of the world is not new. In previous years, however, it was buffered by relatively high transportation costs and time lags affecting the foreign competitor. Further, American wage scales for blue-collar employment, particularly, were supported by a level of unparalleled capital intensification and managerial and technological expertise. Now both of these conditions are rapidly dissipating. Japan, Italy and Formosa dominate the Sears Roebuck catalogue.

The development of great supertankers and container ships is being paralleled in terms of dry cargo. The manufacture of labor-intensive products such as brassieres, for example, first shifted to Puerto Rico and now with the minimum wages there moved further afield to Formosa, to Hong Kong, to Singapore. This will be happening to more and more goods.

Other than agricultural products and a few very high cost, high technology items which the United States scale of market and financing have supported (computers and airplanes are cases in point) there are very few things that the United States does so singularly well as to support production workers' wage levels which are at least double those of the competition.

Both American technological innovation and American housing have been supported by the relative cheapness of financing in the United States. In France, for example, housing mortgages of more than 15 years are very rare indeed and conventionally they have been for no more than half the face value of the property. Even our close neighbor Canada until fairly recently has had no financing mechanisms for housing that come even close to matching those available in private United States markets, to say nothing of the government-supported efforts.

But these may be things of the past. We have already seen in the space of not much more than 20 months a very Republican president forced into a series of economic postures earlier antithetical both to his party and to himself. They are probably too little and too late. Over the next five to ten years the basic outer shell of total resources available for domestic programs will be determined much more abroad than they are in Washington. The range of priorities which can be met internally will therefore be shortened.

The sad facts of England indicate that current consumption and large levels of social input supported at the cost of capital investment in crucial industries and economic growth are self-defeating. The Galbraithian thesis, that the pie of American affluence is so very large that the basic requirement is merely a redistribution of the pieces, is an obvious fallacy, if for no other reason than the substantial increase in our labor force resulting from the high birth rate of the post-World War II days.

Where will the jobs come from? Who is going to pay for them? What is going to make their products competitive? The grand cure-all of automation displacement—the growth in service occupations—may run into the same basic problem. Who is going to pay the bill?

Much of the wealth which we have enjoyed has been the product of the exploitation of native raw material and resources, and many of them are exhausted. Their replacements historically, for any of a variety of political reasons, were relatively cheap. But the days of dollar-a-barrel oil, of sheikdoms for a handful of Cadillacs, of bottomless copper mines worked by dollar-a-day labor are over.

In the new operating sheet of the future, the role and the amenities of the blue-collar worker will be subject to very intensive re-evaluation. Home-ownership will be a critical issue, among others, for its day-to-day impact on the working-class family as well as its symbolic meaning. The bitterness between the older blue-collar elements truly sold on affluent America, on the life styles promulgated so victoriously by the mass media, and minority groups striving for economic advance are accentuated by a relatively closed economic universe. It is amazing how much tolerance is generated by a gross national product that increases 5 or 6 percent a year—and how much bigotry is engendered by one that does not.

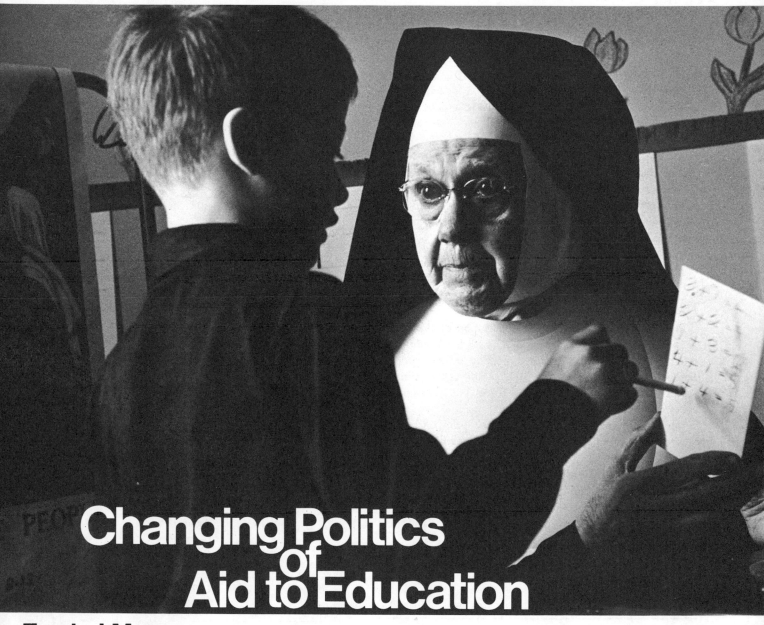

Changing Politics of Aid to Education

Frank J. Munger

This is the story of a major switch in political policy by the Congress of the United States—and an attempt to understand how it came about.

As the 1961 session of Congress neared its end, the then chairman of the House Committee on Education and Labor, Adam Clayton Powell, regretfully asked his colleagues to face "the stark, brutal, and disheartening fact"

that the administration's bill to provide federal aid for school construction was dead. Funds for the restricted purpose of building more classrooms represent about the most restrained form that federal aid to education can take. In 1961 even that modest proposal was more than the nation's legislators were willing to accept.

Four years later in 1965 President Lyndon Johnson

signed a federal aid to education bill with provisions that went far beyond school construction. It was, in the President's words, "an elementary school bill for the children of America," something the federal government had been trying to get, the President noted, "since 1879."

How does Congress make such a major shift in policy? What processes—in the electorate, among groups with a particular stake in the outcome, and in the minds of Congressmen—make the switch possible?

All Americans have an interest in legislation that will change the quality of their children's education. Political scientists have both the citizens' and the specialists' interest in how this particular bill was passed because it gives an opportunity to test a variety of theories about how innovation takes place (or, more often, fails to take place) against the realities of our political system.

The Lineup of Interests

Probably the most prominent explanation of the political process is *interest group theory*. It explains politics as a tugging and hauling among competing interest groups. The policy that exists at any particular time is the point of equilibrium, where the competing forces pull the rope of policy taut.

Interest group theory explains change primarily as the result of shifting alliances among the groups directly concerned. Was this the case with federal aid to education? Would the pattern of groups, for and against federal aid, account for an equilibrium policy of no federal aid in the years before 1965? Did the pattern of alliance shift in that year in ways that could account for the radically new policy?

The history of group alliances on national education policy in the twentieth century goes like this:

MAJOR PROPOSAL	INTEREST GROUPS
1918-1925 Create a cabinet level Department of Education, and grant federal funds to the states for general educational purposes. Defeated.	**For** National Education Association Organized labor Women's groups (including the DAR) Most Protestant denominations **Against** U.S. Chamber of Commerce and other business groups Catholic church Lutheran church National Association for the Advancement of Colored People
1937-1943 Grant federal money for operating expenses, requiring proportionate use of the funds where segregated schools existed. Defeated.	**For** Educators Parent-Teachers Association Organized labor Women's groups (now minus the DAR) Protestants NAACP American Legion Farm groups **Against** Business groups Catholics
1946-1950 Thomas-Hill-Taft bill to authorize federal funds for operating expenses (including teachers' salaries), guarantee proportionate allocations in segregated systems, allow any state that believed the practice constitutional to use the funds for texts and transportation in private schools. Defeated.	**For** Educators PTA Organized labor Women's groups Protestants NAACP American Legion Farm Bureau **Against** Business groups National Catholic Welfare Conference
1954-1957 Grants or loans for school construction only, without reference to segregation and for public schools only. Defeated.	**For** Educators PTA Organized labor Women's groups Protestants Jewish groups **Against** Chamber of Commerce American Legion Farm Bureau NAACP **Officially Neutral** Catholic organizations
1959-61 School construction bills. Defeated.	**For** PTA Women's groups Organized labor Protestants Jews **Against** National Education Association Conservative business groups Catholics NAACP National School Boards Association

1965	For
Concentrated on allocating funds for underprivileged children; provided for benefits to children in parochial schools in the purchase of books and use of supplementary educational centers. Passed.	Education groups Women's groups Organized labor National Council of Churches Catholic Church **Against** Fiscal conservatives Protestants and Other Americans United for Separation of Church and State

For much of the time span presented here there are few changes. Conservatives tended to drift to the *against* side and stay there; the DAR moved there in the 1930's and the American Legion and the Farm Bureau in the 1950's. The NAACP, growing more militantly opposed to any compromise with segregation over the years, moved to the opposition side in 1954. Protestant groups, as long as the "wall of separation" between church and state was not threatened by a proposal to aid Catholic schools, remained steadily in favor. Catholic groups refused to back any bill which did not grant their school systems a share in the funds. The opposing sides were evenly matched, and the result was stalemate.

Three issues served to polarize the lineup:
—segregation;
—fear of federal domination of local school systems;
—aid to parochial schools.
It seemed impossible to design a piece of legislation that could resolve all three.

However, the Supreme Court decisions on segregated schools in the 1950's and the civil rights acts of the early 1960's disposed of the first of the three great dividers; after 1964 civil rights groups were willing to support federal aid, and segregationists were no longer in a position to block it. The question of federal domination was evaded by those bills which provided aid for school construction only, but by 1959 most professional educators were no longer willing to be fobbed off in that way. That year the NEA refused to support a bill which did not provide for teachers' salaries.

The major change in the lineup occurred when the 1965 bill was introduced. The new bill differed in two major ways from its predecessor of 1961:
■ Where the original Kennedy administration bill had specified that only 10 percent of the funds for each state was for instruction of children in low-income families, the 1965 bill made underprivileged children the major focus of its grants.

■ The new bill also included significant benefits for children attending parochial schools—through the emphasis on children of low-income families, through allocations for purchase of library and text books, and through the establishment of supplementary educational centers that parochial school students could also attend.

The focus on underprivileged children allowed for much broader uses of the funds than simply the construction of new classrooms, so the NEA was pacified; and in the climate of the war on poverty the partisans of local school independence were not aroused to their usual strong opposition. The National Council of Churches had also relented somewhat in its stern opposition to any aid for Catholic schools; in 1964 the Council admitted that "Protestants and Orthodox are conscious of the financial difficulties under which their Roman Catholic brethren and others labor in supporting two systems." They were willing to support the compromise that one Protestant spokesman called "a fantastically skillful break in the stalemate" worked out in the 1965 bill.

The 1965 lineup—in which civil rights groups, professional educators, and Catholics moved out of the opposition without provoking a compensatory shift into it by major Protestant organizations—is clearly very different from that of earlier years. It is logical to assume that a shift of this magnitude in the alignment of interest groups is responsible for the change in policy. The case of federal aid to education lends substantial support to the interest group theory of politics.

Party Politics

Interest groups, however they may push and shove, don't actually vote on bills in Congress. They may influence congressmen, but congressmen still do the voting.

There are a great many theories about why congressmen vote the way they do. The interest group theory was one of them, but there are other possibilities. The one we shall examine next is the theory that the strongest single influence on a congressman's vote is his *party affiliation*—that major changes in legislative policy are the result of changes in the party composition of Congress following a decisive election.

The issue of federal aid to education is a strongly partisan one. Broadly speaking, Republicans are against it, and Democrats are for it. One way to measure the partisanship of a particular vote is to see whether much larger percentages of Democratic congressmen vote for a bill than Republican congressmen (or vice versa). In 1948, for example, 86 percent of the Democratic senators and 61.4 percent of the Republican senators voted for federal aid to education; the index of partisanship for the vote is the difference between these two percentages, or 24.6.

If we look at the partisanship index for a number of congressional votes on aid to education, we can demonstrate that it is a partisan issue and has become more so over the years:

Senate Index

1948	1949	1960	1961	1965
24.7	27.6	48.8	50.7	37.0

House Index

1956	1957	1960	1961	1965
14.4	15.5	30.1	63.7	53.3

When an issue is as partisan as this, its fate in Congress should be strongly affected by a decisive election—like the one we had in 1964. When the new Congress convened in 1965, the Democrats had very large majorities in both houses. In the Senate the election did not change the situation; it simply preserved an already existing majority for federal aid. In the House of Representatives, however, the heavy Democratic majorities may have become decisive. The power this majority gave the administration can be shown in one statistic: When the House voted on final passage of the 1965 bill, 190 Northern and Western Democrats divided 187 to 3 for the bill. This wide margin left the bill's managers only 22 votes short of a majority on that specific roll call and only 31 votes short of a majority on any conceivable roll call. The final vote was 263 to 153. In the Senate, the bill passed by 73 to 18.

Public Opinion

Shifting group alignments and changes in party fortune are two plausible ways of explaining the victory for federal aid in 1965. A third possibility is to explain this legislative shift as primarily reflecting a change in *public opinion*. At first sight federal aid to education seems a most unlikely illustration of the power of public opinion. If public opinion compelled Congress to act, we should presumably have had federal aid 30 years ago; public opinion polls have been registering majority support for federal aid all that time. Indeed, political theorist V. O. Key used the case of federal aid as a textbook example of what he called a "permissive consensus" that leaves Congress free to act but does not force it to move.

I believe, however, that the evidence of the opinion polls is misleading, a response to a particular verbal formula rather than an expression of a deeply held opinion. When the wording in the question has been changed, even in quite moderate ways, sharp differences in the responses have occurred. Further, large numbers of people seem to be unaware of or unconcerned by the question; it makes little difference to them whether the state or federal government finances the public schools, so long as adequate funds are found somewhere.

Early in 1965 the American Institute of Public Opinion put the question very sharply to a national sample. AIPO pollsters warned respondents that "during the next few years, taxes to support the public schools will increase sharply, chiefly because there are many more children to educate through high school." Then they asked, "Should the federal government pay more of these costs, or should the state and local communities continue as at present to meet almost all educational expenses for the public schools?" The response to this precisely phrased question was not the usual large majority for federal aid, but an almost even split: 49 percent favored a larger federal contribution, 42 percent urged continued reliance on local and state governments, and 9 percent had no opinion.

People may have been vaguely in favor of federal aid, but not in the deeply convinced way that persuades congressmen. Furthermore, when it came to backing specific pieces of legislation, public support fragmented. The situation facing the administration in 1961 shows the dilemma:

■ Should the bill prohibit aid to segregated schools?
■ Should it provide any benefits for nonpublic schools?
■ Should funds be used for teachers' salaries, for school construction, or for both?

The first issue allows of two alternatives: aid segregated schools or refuse to aid them. Adding the two alternatives to the second issue of nonpublic schools raises the number of options to four. The three positions that are possible for the third dilemma (teachers, buildings, or both) bring the number of options available to bill writers to twelve.

Fortunately for the analyst, an AIPO poll taken in 1961 probed opinion on all twelve of these possibilities:

All public . . only public . . for classrooms	18.3%
All public . . only public . . for salaries	13.9
All public . . only public . . for both	12.5
All public . . also private . . for classrooms	12.6
All public . . also private . . for salaries	8.4
All public . . also private . . for both	8.6
Not segregated . . only public . . for classrooms	7.1
Not segregated . . only public . . for salaries	4.8

Not segregated . . only public . . for both	5.6
Not segregated . . also private . . for classrooms	3.0
Not segregated . . also private . . for salaries	2.5
Not segregated . . also private . . for both	2.7

As we can see, no single alternative had the support of more than 19 percent of the population, and eight different alternatives had the support of at least 5 percent. Under these circumstances it is not surprising that the Kennedy administration found the problem insoluble, and the federal aid bill of 1961 was lost in a House Rules Committee dispute over whether to aid public schools only or to include private schools.

Disputes over aid for construction or aid for salaries—issues of great partisanship in the 1960 presidential election and in the 1961 federal aid fight—seemed to lose their impact later in the decade. Religious and racial controversies have had more enduring significance. Public opinion on these issues, especially religion, remained stable for many years; from 1938 through 1961 generally steady majorities were recorded as opposed to public aid to religious schools. Excluding persons with no opinion and using AIPO data, public attitudes have been:

	Aid to public schools only	Public and parochial
1938	60%	40%
1949	55	45
1961	61	39

But when pollsters asked the same question in 1963, they got some very different answers. In the 1963 survey respondents split 53 percent to 47 percent in *favor* of aiding parochial schools. So we can see quite sharply how four possible versions of the bills would have fared with the public before and after this shift of opinion in regard to parochial schools:

Percentage in favor	1961	1963
All public . . . . only public	44.8%	38.1%
All public . . . . also private	30.1	39.5
Not segregated . . . . only public	17.1	10.1
Not segregated . . . . also private	8.0	12.3

Between 1961 and 1963, there is a small but definite shift from "public only" to "public and parochial" as the solution favored by the largest percentage of people. By 1965 survey results showed a slight additional change: 55 percent now favored aid to parochial schools compared to 45 percent opposed. This shift in long-established opinion opened the door for the federal aid bill of 1965.

Who changed their minds? From 1961 to 1963, the proportion of Protestants favoring aid to private schools increased from 31 percent to 45 percent; of Catholics from 69.5 to 76 percent; of Jews from 2 to 26 percent. The most drastic change in group attitude happened among Jews; the largest number of people who changed their minds were probably Protestants. The remarkable thing is the similarity of the proportions changing: One out of five Protestants, one out of five Catholics, one out of four Jews who had been opposed in the past now favored aid to private schools.

It is not possible, with the data at hand, to do any satisfactory factoring out of the forces involved in this opinion shift. Too many complementary influences are tangled together: the figure of Pope John, the *aggiornamento* within the Catholic church, the Ecumenical Council and the ecumenical movement, the reconsideration of attitudes by Protestant churches, and—not least—the youthful personality of a Catholic President.

By 1963 the preferences of racial and religious groups for the four alternative plans for federal aid stacked up this way:

	All public; only public	All public; also private	Not segregated; only public	Not segregated; also private
White Protestants	50.4%	32.8%	9.7%	7.1%
Negro Protestants	19.8	28.5	14.2	37.5
Catholics	19.5	64.4	4.9	11.2
Jews	43.6	14.3	32.2	11.9

There are sharp contrasts in the way the four groups feel. Separate pluralities appear for three different plans:

■ White Protestants and Jews most favor a plan including all public schools but excluding private schools;

■ Catholics want aid for all public schools, segregated or not, but they also want aid for private schools;

■ Negro Protestants wish to exclude segregated schools, but they are willing to support aid to private schools.

What did this climate of opinion mean to a particular congressman when he came to vote for or against the 1965 bill? If his district was predominantly Protestant, about half his constituents would be disturbed about aid to private schools but a sizable number (33 percent) would go along with an aid bill even with such a provision. A strong-minded congressman could probably back the bill in such a district and survive. If the district included a mixture of Catholics and Protestants, constituency opinion would be evenly divided; this is a situation which leaves a congressman free to act. Congressmen representing predominantly Catholic districts could support the bill with enthusiasm.

Once the passage of the 1964 civil rights bill had effectively removed the dilemma of segregated schools from the education bill, congressmen representing heavily Negro districts could find substantial support for a vote in its favor. The only major group still expressing strong opposition—though not as strong as it once was—was the Jews, but they do not include enough constituents to sway a majority of congressmen. This striking shift of public attitude toward aid to religious schools altered two decades of precedent and prepared the way for the enactment of the 1965 law.

How Policy Changes

This examination of three theories of political change by no means exhausts the range of possible explanations for the passage of the 1965 federal aid to education bill. Policy changes can also be explained in terms of changes in the policy-making institutions: The change in party ratios in the House Committee on Education and Labor in 1959 removed one obstacle to an aid bill, and the enlargement of the House Rules Committee in 1961 was crucial in the committee vote of eight to seven for the bill in 1965.

Explanations of change can also be sought in creative innovation—a new idea cuts through existing obstacles by reshaping perceptions of the problem. The 1965 bill was an ingenious piece of legislative draftsmanship: The idea of shared facilities avoided much of the religious entanglement that had plagued earlier bills; the emphasis on specialized educational programs for children from low-income families avoided the usual partisan controversies over aid to construction only (tolerated by Republicans) or aid to teachers also (favored by Democrats).

This account has not considered the special persuasive skills of a President whom many consider a master of legislative politics. They would undoubtedly interpret the innovation in this and other areas as a result of the leadership of President Johnson.

Clearly, many kinds of influence interact when an innovation of this magnitude occurs. The task remains, however, of trying to sort out which of these factors had the greatest impact on the process. Here the solution is aided by simple chronology. The significant shift in public opinion took place in 1963; it preceded changes in interest group position that did not occur until 1965. In any case, the idea that great numbers of people change their attitudes because of formal statements by the NEA or the National Council of Churches runs counter to everything we know about the way public opinion forms. Nor can the 1963 shift in public opinion be ascribed to presidential leadership; President Kennedy was opposed to public aid to parochial schools. Changing public opinion, then, was a force that preceded, and had an effect on, legislative change.

Shifts in public opinion, even major ones, are not converted into legislation automatically. It is here in the conversion process that all the other components of change come into play. Changes in committee structure, the skill of the legislation's draftsmen, and a persuasive President undoubtedly had much to do with the conversion process. The heavy Democratic victories of 1964 probably served to smooth the passage of the bill, particularly in the House. But the bill didn't pass in 1965 simply because there were more Democrats in the House; in fact, the same percentages of congressmen in each party (98 percent of the Northern Democrats, 43 percent of the Southern Democrats, and 27 percent of the Republicans) could have passed a federal aid to education bill in any Democratic Congress since World War II.

In the final analysis it may well be that federal aid to education is a special case of legislative change: It had been debated longer, been involved in more controversy, and carried a greater potential for basic changes in the federal system than most issues of domestic policy. But with this particular legislation it seems that shifts in public opinion played a major, independent, and unexpected part in helping to secure the enactment of a new law.

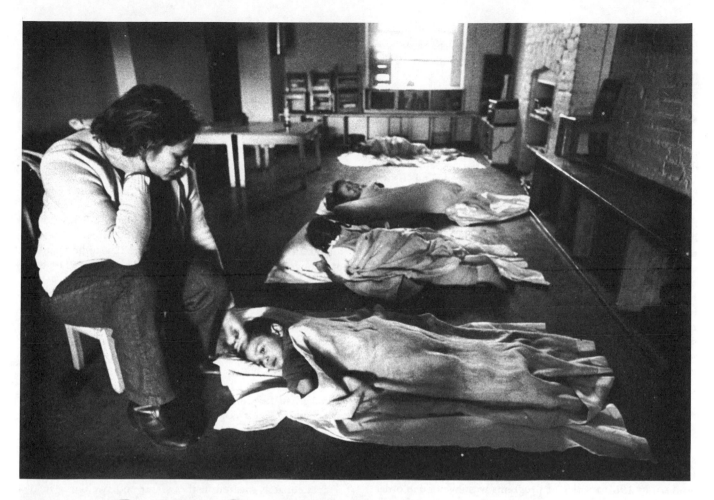

Day Care Centers

Hype or Hope?

Gilbert Y. Steiner

By the end of the 1960s it was evident that under the most prosperous of conditions, public assistance was not about to wither away. A considerable fraction of the population was still outside the sweep of social security's old age pensions, survivors' benefits, or disability insurance, and also outside the sweep of the country's prosperity. "It becomes increasingly clear," the *New York Times* editorialized after the overall level of unemployment in New York City declined to 3.2 percent of the civilian labor force while at the same time the number of welfare clients in the city

climbed to one million, "that the welfare rolls have a life of their own detached from the metropolitan job market."

It is detached from the national job market as well. In 1961, when there were 3.5 million AFDC recipients, unemployment as a percent of the civilian labor force nationally was a high 6.7 percent. By 1968 the national unemployment figure was hovering around a record low 3.4 percent, and there was serious talk among economists about the possible need for a higher rate of unemployment to counteract inflation. But the average monthly number of

AFDC recipients in 1968 was up to 5.7 million, almost 4.4 million of whom were children. In 1969 the monthly recipient total averaged 6.7 million, and for the first six months of 1970 it was 7.9 million.

Public assistance also has a separate life outside the growth of the economy. The gross national product was $520 billion in 1961; in 1969 it was $932 billion. One of the things not expected to rise under those prosperous conditions was payments to relief recipients. Yet total payments in AFDC alone in 1961 were $1,149 million; in 1969 total payments were $3,546 million and rising rapidly.

To put all this another way, it is roughly accurate to say that during the 1960s the unemployment rate was halved, AFDC recipients increased by almost two-thirds, and AFDC money payments doubled. Whatever the relationship between workfare and welfare, it is not the simple one of reduced unemployment making for reduced dependency. How has government responded to this confounding news?

For the most part over the past ten years it has responded by tirelessly tinkering with the old welfare system. Special emphasis has been placed on preparing the welfare population emotionally and vocationally for participation in the labor market, thereby enjoying not only the economic security provided by employment itself, but also the unemployment insurance and survivors' insurance, if needed, which employment gives access to. The first such effort—the professional social service approach characterized by a stated plan emphasizing services over support and rehabilitation over relief—showed no progress after running its full five-year trial period from 1962 to 1967. And so, in 1967 a series of programs was invented in order to push relief clients to work. Work experience, work training, work incentives—whatever the titles and whatever the marginal differences in program content—were all designed, in the catch phrase often used, to move people off the relief rolls and onto the tax rolls. Each program assumed that the gulf between labor force participation with accompanying economic security benefits, on the one side, and relief status, on the other side, was bridgeable.

It was not until 1967, however, that it came to be perfectly acceptable to think of mothers with dependent small children as proper objects of the effort to get the very poor off the relief rolls and onto the tax rolls.

Agreement on this question resulted from the confluence of two separate concerns. One concern was with costs and criticisms. Representative Wilbur Mills, powerful leader of the crucial House Ways and Means Committee, viewed with alarm the costs of an unchecked public assistance program:

I am sure it is not generally known that about 4 or 5 years hence when we get to the fiscal year 1972, the figure will have risen by $2.2 billion to an amount of $6,731,000,000 . . . . If I detect anything in the minds of the American people, it is this. They want us to be certain that when we spend the amounts of money that we do, and of necessity in many cases have to spend, that we spend it in such a way as to promote the public interest, and the public well-being of our people.

Is it . . . in the public interest for welfare to become a way of life?

A different concern motivated an HEW task force, department officials, and some of Mills' legislative colleagues. The task force showed little worry over how many billions of dollars public relief was costing, but did concern itself with the turmoil and deprivation that beset recipients in depressed rural areas and in urban ghettos. Thus, to the Mills conclusion that the costs are prohibitive, there was joined a related HEW conclusion, shared by some members of Congress, that the quality of life on welfare was intolerable.

One congressman with such a view is the only lady member of the Ways and Means Committee, Martha Griffiths. Mrs. Griffiths was especially indignant over the conditions imposed on AFDC mothers.

I find the hypocrisy of those who are now demanding freedom of choice to work or not to work for welfare mothers beyond belief. The truth is these women never have had freedom of choice. They have never been free to work. Their education has been inadequate and the market has been unable to absorb their talents . . . .

Can you imagine any conditions more demoralizing than those welfare mothers live under? Imagine being confined all day every day in a room with falling plaster, inadequately heated in the winter and sweltering in the summer, without enough beds for the family, and with no sheets, the furniture falling apart, a bare bulb in the center of the room as the only light, with no hot water most of the time, plumbing that often does not work, with only the companionship of small children who are often hungry and always inadequately clothed—and, of course, the ever-present rats. To keep one's sanity under such circumstances is a major achievement, and to give children the love and discipline they need for healthy development is superhuman. If one were designing a system to produce alcoholism, crime, and illegitimacy, he could not do better.

Whatever the differing motivation, HEW's task force, Mills and Mrs. Griffiths all pointed in the direction of change from the status quo. And the change agreed upon was abandonment of the heretofore accepted idea that the only employable AFDC recipients were unemployed fathers.

In 1967 the Ways and Means Committee unveiled its social security and welfare bill at about the same time that HEW Secretary John Gardner unveiled his reorganization of the welfare agencies in his department. That reorganization merged the Welfare Administration, the Administration on Aging, and the Vocational Rehabilitation Service into a new agency called the Social and Rehabilitation Service (SRS). To run it, Gardner named Mary Switzer, a veteran commissioner of vocational rehabilitation who was aptly described by a local journalist as "a diligent disciple of work." This bit of tinkering was designed to send the message through the federal welfare bureaucracy that the secretary was receptive to policy change, apparently including a new work emphasis. The great drive to employ dependent mothers and provide day care for their children thus began both in the administration and in Congress two years before President Nixon discovered it anew.

Day Care

Despite an announcement by Miss Switzer in April 1969 that a reduction in the number of people on the welfare rolls is "a top priority of the Social and Rehabilitation Service" which she asked state welfare admistrators "to make yours as well," it was really beyond the power of either Miss Switzer or the state administrators to effect a big breakthrough in the AFDC problem. The key to moving some people off the rolls is employment for the AFDC employable parent. The rub is that even training for employment, a first step, requires an expensive new industry—day care—which now lacks organization, leadership, personnel and money for construction of facilities. Moreover, once the realities of work training and day care programs are examined, it becomes evident that there is not much incentive for a poorly educated AFDC mother to accept training for herself and day care service of uncertain quality for her children.

Training AFDC mothers for employment, actually finding jobs for them, and providing day care facilities for their children present formidable problems. A recent survey of the AFDC population found that 43 percent of the mothers had gone no further than the eighth grade, including 10.6 percent with less than a fifth grade education. Work training that leads to employment at wages adequate to support a family is likely to be prolonged, at best, for this undereducated group.

The realities of the coming crunch in day care are even more troublesome. Day care provisions accompanying the 1967 work incentive (WIN) legislation did not extend to the creation of a federal program authorizing funds for new facilities. There are approximately 46,300 licensed facilities caring for 638,000 children. If every place in every licensed day care facility in the United States were to be reserved for an AFDC child under the age of six, there would be more than one million AFDC children in that age group with no place to go. There would also be consternation among the thousands of non-AFDC mothers with children of that age level who are already in day care centers.

In short, there are not enough facilities—good, bad or indifferent—to accomplish the day care job envisioned by the congressional and administration planners who still talk of moving parents from welfare rolls to payrolls. Representative Fernand St. Germain was undoubtedly right in stating in 1969 that "costs of new facilities are too much for the states to bear alone; centers will only be built in numbers that have any relation to the critical need if federal assistance is forthcoming." No one seems to have foreseen this in 1967, however, and the point never got into the HEW program memorandum that influenced the employable mother discussions and proposals of the House Ways and Means Committee.

But the day care problem goes beyond the matter of adequate space to an important philosophical and political question regarding the appropriate clientele for the service.

There is no political conflict over the proposition that a young mother suddenly widowed and left dependent on social security survivors' benefits should be supported with public funds so that she can stay home and take care of her children. Nor is there congressional discussion or any HEW proposal for day care for those children. If 94.5 percent of AFDC dependency were attributable to death of the father, there would be no congressional interest in day care to speak of.

But, in fact, 94.5 percent of AFDC dependency is not attributable to death of the father; only 5.5 percent is. Most of the political conflict and a good deal of the interest in day care is over whether the public should subsidize those women whom Senator Russell Long once called "brood mares" to stay home, produce more children—some of them born out of wedlock—and raise those children in an atmosphere of dependency.

While medical authorities and professional social workers are still divided philosophically over how accessible day care should be and to whom, Congress in 1967 and President Nixon in 1969 simply embraced the possibility of putting day care to work in the cause of reducing public assistance costs. In other words, political attention has focused less on the practical limits of day care and more on its apparent similarities to baby sitting.

Day care was simply not ready to assume the responsibilities thrust on it by the welfare legislation adopted in 1967, and it was not ready for President Nixon's proposal to expand it in 1969. Whether day care is a socially desirable or even an economical way of freeing low income mothers with limited skills and limited education for work or work training still has not been widely considered. In the few circles where it has been considered, there is no agreement. Both the 1967 legislation and the Nixon proposal for escalation should have been preceded by the development of publicly supported, model day care arrangements that could be copied widely; by attention to questions of recruitment and appropriate educational training for day care personnel; by an inventory of available and needed physical facilities; by the existence of a high-spirited and innovative group of specialists in government or in a private association or both; and by enough experience to expose whatever practical defects may exist in day care as a program to facilitate employment of low income mothers. Instead of meeting these reasonable conditions for escalation, public involvement in day care programs for children, a phenomenon especially of the last ten years, remains unsystematic, haphazard, patchworky.

The Children's Bureau Approach

For many years before 1969, the HEW Children's Bureau ran the bulk of the federal day care program. It did not encourage an approach that would make day care readily available on demand. Stressing that day care can be harmful unless it is part of a broader program overseen by a trained social worker, the bureau defined day care as a child welfare service offering "care and protection." The child in need of day care was identified as one who "has a family problem which makes it impossible for his parents to fulfill their parental responsibilities without supplementary help." The social worker was seen as necessary to help determine whether the family needs day care and if so to develop an appropriate plan for the child, to place the child in a day care program, to determine the fee to be paid by the parents and to provide continuing supervision.

Change comes slowly to child welfare—as to other specialists. Those in the Children's Bureau found it difficult to adjust to the idea of day care available to all comers and especially to low income working mothers. On the one hand, the talk from the top of the bureau has been about the need to face reality in the day care picture—"when," as one bureau chief put it as early as 1967, "thousands of infants and young children are being placed in haphazard situations because their mothers are working." On the other hand, down the line at the bureau the experts continued to emphasize the importance of the intake procedure to insure that children placed in day care "need" the service.

With this approach it might be expected that while the day care expansion movement has ground along slowly, it has ground exceedingly fine. Day care undoubtedly is a risky enterprise. Every center should have a genuinely high-quality, sympathetic environment; no center should be countenanced without clear evidence that such an environment is being created, and all centers that do not give such evidence should be discouraged. The payoff, therefore, for what might seem to be excessive caution by the Children's Bureau could have been a jewel of a limited program and no second or third rate imitations. Then, when money and will were at hand, the jewel could be reproduced.

In fact, no day care activity was discouraged, whether of low quality or not. Caution on the subject of quantity did not work to guarantee quality. Whether or not there would be any day care activity depended on the states, and the federal agency was accommodating, both because it was hard to interest the states in day care at all, and because Congress provided money in fits and starts, rather than in a steady flow. When the money did come, there was an urgent need to spend it.

Funding

Between 1962 and 1965, HEW had only $8.8 million to parcel out to the states for day care. Moreover, it was never able to count on having anything from year to year, so that it is understandable that the federal agency was in no position to threaten the states about the quality of service. The 1962 law required that federal day care money go only to facilities approved or licensed in accordance with state standards. The law said nothing about minimum federal standards. In 1962 a number of states had no day care licensing programs at all; among the states that did, the extent of licensing and the standards used varied considerably. The Children's Bureau's own guidelines were little more than advisory. To raise the quality of day care nationally, the bureau had to fall back on persuasion and consultation, weak tools compared to money.

Licensing

One certain effect of the 1962 requirement that the available federal money go only to licensed facilities was to divert a substantial part of the funds into licensing activity itself and away from actual day care services. For fiscal 1965, for example, 43 percent of the $4 million appropriated for day care was spent on personnel engaged in licensing, while only 36 percent was used to provide day care services in homes or centers. This increased licensing activity has the effect of distorting the picture of growth of day care facilities. In 1960, licensed day care facilities had a reported total capacity of 183,332; in 1965 this had increased to 310,400; in 1967 the figure was up to 473,700; in 1968 to 535,200; and in 1969 to 638,000. There is universal agreement, however, that the growth figure is mostly illusory, a consequence of formerly unlicensed facilities now being licensed.

Moreover, there is more form than substance to licensing decisions. The fact that a day care facility is licensed cannot yet be taken to mean that its physical plant and personnel necessarily satisfy some explicitly defined and universally accepted standards. Like "premium grade" automobile tires, licensed day care facilities can differ sharply in quality—and for the same reason, the absence of industry-wide standards. Licensing studies by public welfare agencies are invariably assigned to new and untrained caseworkers. The results are unpredictable and there is no monitoring body able and authorized to keep a watchful eye on who is being licensed.

Even from those who accept the simplistic assumption that only the absence of child care services and of job or training opportunities preclude AFDC recipients from becoming wage earners, there is no suggestion that just any kind of child care will do. Yet the state of the art in day care is not sufficiently advanced to make it reasonable to expect that states can meet the requirement to provide day care services other than in makeshift, low quality programs. There is clear validity in the complaint of the National Committee for the Day Care of Children that the 1967 legislation was not designed to help children develop mentally and physically, but was "a hastily put together outline for a compulsory, custodial service which is not required to maintain even minimal standards of adequacy."

Challenge from Head Start

Only a month after taking office, President Nixon called for a "national commitment to providing all American children an opportunity for healthful and stimulating development during the first five years of life." A few weeks later secretary of HEW Robert Finch welcomed the delegation of the Head Start program to HEW as the occasion for a new and overdue national commitment to child and parent development. Finch indicated publicly that he was not inclined to put Head Start in the Children's Bureau and instead placed it in a new HEW Office of Child Development (OCD) where the Children's Bureau was also transferred. Social planners in HEW, the Bureau of the Budget and the White House envisioned a new era: day care programs for low income children would be modeled on Head Start; simple custodial arrangements would not be tolerated; parents would be involved. The way for this happy outcome had already been paved by issuance of the Federal Interagency Day Care Requirements, a joint product of HEW and OEO, approved in the summer of 1968.

Things have not worked out. Whatever Finch's initial intention, the day care programs operated by the Children's Bureau never made it to the OCD. In September 1969 a new Community Services Administration was created within the Social and Rehabilitation Service to house all service programs provided public assistance recipients under social security. The Head Start bureau of the OCD, according to the terms of the reorganization, was given some responsibility in Social Security Act day care programs—to participate in policy making and to approve state welfare plans on day care. But effective control of the money and policy in the day care programs remains with the Social and Rehabilitation Service. President Nixon's "commitment to providing all American children an opportunity for health-

ful and stimulating development during the first five years of life" has so far produced more talk than money.

A High Cost Service

There has simply not been enough thinking about the benefits and costs of a good day care program to merit the faith political leaders now express in day care as a dependency-reducing mechanism. Federal day care program requirements are, for the most part, oriented to the idea of day care as a learning experience. They are, therefore, on a collision course with supporters of mass day care as an aspect of the struggle to reduce welfare costs. The high-quality program requirements reject simple warehousing of children, but the prospects for meeting high standards are not good. It seems inevitable that there will be disappointment both for those who think of day care as a welfare economy and for those who think of day care for AFDC children as an important social and educational advance.

Consider the situation in the District of Columbia, which is reasonably typical of the day care problem in large cities. The District Public Welfare Department (DPW) in May 1969 was purchasing child care for 1,056 children, of whom about 400 were children of women in the WIN program. Of the total 1,056 children, 865 were in day care centers, 163—primarily infants too young to be placed in centers—were in family day care homes, and 28 were in in-home care arrangements, a service considered practical only for large families. The total anticipated day care load for the end of fiscal 1969 was 1,262. District day care personnel estimated that 660 AFDC mothers to be referred to WIN during fiscal 1970 (on the basis of 55 per month) would need, on the average, day care for 2 children. These additional 1,320 children would bring the likely number for whom the District would be paying for care to 2,582 by July 1, 1970. Budget requests for day care for fiscal 1970 totaled $3,254,300 in local and federal funds ($1,148,000 of local funds brings $2,106,300 in federal money). Of this amount, about $3 million is for purchase of care, the remainder for administrative expenses. If budget requests were met, the purchase cost of day care in the District would thus be expected to average almost $1,200 per child. Costly as that may seem to be, it represents only a little more than half the actual cost.

It is the beginning of day care wisdom to understand that it is an expensive mechanism and to understand that there are qualitative differences in the care provided. The elegantly stated effort of the DPW is to secure "in addition to good physical care, the kind of exceptionally enriched day care experience that is specifically designed and programmed to stimulate and promote the maximum in emotional, physical, and educational growth and development of the child." Alas, one-third of the centers with which the DPW contracts only "offer primarily custodial and protective care," a code phrase for warehousing. Fees paid day care centers by the District Welfare Department are supposed to be a function of the quality of services offered. Grade A centers are paid $4.00 a day, B centers $3.00 a day, and C centers $2.50 a day. The department's Standards for Day Care Centers say that it uses a fee schedule for two reasons: "to assure that proper value is received for each dollar spent and, secondly, to provide a monetary stimulus to contract day care facilities to up-grade the quality of their services to meet the Department's maximum expectations." Each center's "rating," known only to it and to the Welfare Department, is for "internal use" and is not revealed to the welfare mother because, according to department officials, it would not be fair to the center to do so. A more pertinent question is whether it is fair to the mother, since 25 of the 55 centers from which day care is purchased are graded B or C, and since half of all placements are in B or C centers.

All centers—whether A, B or C—must meet the Health Department's licensing requirements, as well as additional specific standards set down by the Welfare Department in the areas of educational qualifications of personnel, program content, and equipment and furnishings. Yet there are two problems with this seemingly tidy picture. The first is the insistence of close observers that while the Welfare Department's standards for centers look satisfactory on paper, they have not been put into practice very consistently. The second is that even the paper standards will not do when the federal interagency standards become effective July 1, 1971. Spokesmen for the National Capital Area Child Day Care Association (NCACDCA) and District Health Department licensing personnel are critical of the Welfare Department's day care operation. Both suggest there is a lack of awareness in the Welfare Day Care Unit of what constitutes good day care. That high ranking is reserved, in the judgment of these people, for the centers operated by NCACDCA. The critics complain that only the NCACDCA centers can legitimately meet the Welfare Department's own A standards and maintain that the other A centers simply do not meet them. They claim, for example, that one way these latter centers "meet" the educational qualifications for personnel is to list as a director an "absentee"—perhaps a kindergarten teacher in the District of Columbia school system or that of a neighboring county.

No one disputes that most centers in the District cannot meet the Federal Interagency Day Care Requirements—particularly the child-adult ratios and the educational qualifications for staff. Even a good number of the A centers do not meet the child-adult ratio requirements, and the B and C centers meet neither the staff educational qualifications nor the child-adult ratios of the federal

requirements. If the day care centers have not met the federal standards by July 1, 1971, DPW cannot continue making payments on behalf of children for whom it receives federal matching funds. But in the District Welfare Department the view is that the requirements are unrealistic and that widespread complaints from private users who cannot afford the costs involved may result in a lowering of standards.

All the evidence suggests that day care is expensive whether the auspices are public, private or mixed. In a curiously chosen experiment, the Department of Labor decided in 1969 to fund an experimental day care program for its own employees at a time when emphasis was presumably being placed on supporting day care for the welfare poor. Its estimated budget for the first full year of care for 30 children was $100,000, one-third of which was for nonrecurring development costs, including renovation for code compliance, equipment and evaluation. Tuition from the group of working mothers involved amounted to only $7,300, leaving $59,600 of public funds necessary to provide care for 30 children—a subsidy of almost $2,000 per child without considering nonrecurring cost items. Doubling the number of children served the second year would require a budget of $100,000, resulting in an average annual per child cost over the two years of $1,850, or of $2,225, if the renovation and equipment items are not dismissed as readily as the department sought to dismiss them in its official explanation.

The National Capital Area Child Day Care Association estimates costs at almost $2,400 per child per 50-week year. Its standard budget for a 30-child center exceeds $71,000. Tight-fisted budget examiners might effect reductions, but they cannot be consequential unless the pupil teacher ratio is drastically revised. Morever, NCACDCA salary figures are unrealistically low. Head teachers for a 30-child center are hard to come by at $7,300. (See table.)

If these per child costs of desirable day care are projected nationally, the annual bill for all preschool AFDC children must be figured conservatively at $3 billion.

Client Arithmetic

Most women in the District of Columbia WIN program are being trained in clerical skills in anticipation that they will take jobs with the federal government as GS-2s. This is an optimistic view since most trainees have ninth to eleventh grade educations while a GS-2 needs a high school diploma or equivalency or six months' experience and the ability to pass a typing test. That problem aside, the District AFDC mother who completes work incentive training and is placed in a GS-2 job will be better off financially than the mother who stays on welfare. Her gain will be greater the smaller the size of her family. She will have fewer children to support on her fixed earnings, whereas the larger the family on AFDC, the larger the grant.

For many a female head of a family of four in the spring of 1970, however, the work and day care arithmetic was not encouraging as the following illustration shows. If the GS-2 mother has three children and claims four exemptions, about $39 of her monthly salary of $385 is deducted for retirement ($18.50) and for federal ($17) and local ($3.50) taxes, leaving a take home pay of about $346 a month. If two of the three children are in Welfare Department child care arrangements, placed there when the mother entered the WIN program, the mother would pay the department about $6.00 a week toward their care; if the mother had only one child in care, she would pay $5.50. Assuming two children in care, the mother's monthly cost would be about $26, lowering her net earnings to $320.

Suppose, however, that the woman stayed on AFDC. The average benefit for a four-person family on AFDC in the District would bring her $217 monthly. Both the welfare mother and the working mother would be eligible for Medicaid, but only the welfare mother would be eligible for food stamps. For $60 a month she could receive $106 in food stamps, a gain of $46. The welfare mother's child could also receive free lunches at school while the working mother's could not. (The working mother is considerably above the income scale used to determine eligibility for free lunches, although in cases where it is felt children are going hungry, exceptions to the income scale can be made.) A school lunch costs 25 cents in the District's elementary schools. If the welfare child took advantage of the free lunch the mother would save about $5 a month. Thus, the welfare mother would end up with a total of about $268 in welfare, food stamps and school lunches while the working mother would have about $320 a month. In addition, the 1967 welfare amendments allow a welfare mother to earn $30 per month without loss of benefits. The net gain for working full time compared to working only 19 hours a month at the minimum wage is thus reduced to $22. From this, the working mother would have expenses to cover such items as transportation and extra clothes for herself and might have to make some after school care arrangement for her third (school-aged) child.

City Arithmetic

How much work training and day care can save the District of Columbia will depend on how many trainees complete training successfully, get a job and keep it, and on how many children of trainees need child care. The Welfare Department will benefit financially by the AFDC mother's entering a training program and becoming employed as a GS-2 unless the mother has four or more children in day care—which would be most unusual. While it might give the

Standard Day Care Center Budget for Thirty Children for One Year

A. *Personnel*

3 Full-time teachers (head teacher, $7,300; teacher, $7,000; teacher assistant, $4,700)	$19,000
2 Full-time aides ($4,140 each)	8,280
1 Half-time clerk	2,400
Part-time maintenance help (cook, $2,610; janitor, $2,024)	4,634
Substitute (teacher aide, $4,300) and part-time student aide ($1,214)	5,514
Subtotal	$39,828
Fringe benefits (11 percent)	4,381
Total	$44,209

B. *Consultant and Contract Services*

Part-time social worker ($2,500), psychiatric consultant ($5,000), and educational consultant ($1,000)	$8,500
Dietitian	500
Dental and emergency medical service	450
Total	$9,450

C. *Space*

Rent ($1,800); custodial supplies and minor repairs ($1,800)	$3,600

D. *Consumable Supplies*

Office, postage, and miscellaneous (blankets, towels, etc.)	$450
Educational ($400) and health supplies ($30)	430
Food and utensils	4,674
Total	$5,554

E. *Rental, Lease, or Purchase of Equipment*

Children's furniture ($3,000) and office equipment ($200)	$3,200
Equipment: basic (easels, blocks, etc., $1,500); expendable (dolls, puzzles, books, etc., $700); outdoor, with storage ($1,000)	3,200
Total	$6,400

F. *Travel*

Staff ($240) and children's trips ($720)	$960

G. *Other*

Telephone ($36 a month; installation $50)	$482
Insurance (liability, property, and transportation liability)	$700
Total	$1,182
Total project cost	$71,355
Child cost per year	$2,378

Source: Derived from budget of National Capital Area Day Care Association, Inc., Washington, D.C., August 1968.

AFDC mother of three $217 each month, the department would pay only part of her day care cost once she begins working (the department pays all costs for the first three months). With an average cost to the department for day care of $17.50 per child per week, using our hypothetical

GS-2 mother with two children in day care and one in elementary school, the mother would pay $6 a week and the Welfare Department $29 a week for day care. This working mother thus represents a monthly saving to the department of about $56. If, however, the AFDC mother had four children in day care centers and one in elementary school, the mother would pay $6.50 a week toward their care (this figure is the same for three or more children) and the department $63.50. The department would thus spend $273 a month for child care—and save nothing compared to what it would have given her on AFDC to care for her own children at home.

Prospects

What are the prospects for success in turning day care into a program that will reduce the costs of AFDC? They hinge, first, on large numbers of AFDC mothers actually turning out to be trainable and able to be placed in jobs under any conditions and, second, on finding some cheaper substitute for traditional day care centers.

The difficulty in securing the physical facilities and staff needed to develop the traditional centers looked overwhelming to state welfare administrators examining the day care problem in 1967. They did, however, see some hopes for neighborhood day care, a kind of glorified, low income equivalent of the middle class baby-sitting pool. Stimulated by OEO's success in involving poor people in poverty programs, HEW early in 1967 started pushing neighborhood day care demonstration projects using welfare mothers to help care for other welfare mothers' children. This seemingly ideal solution has its own problems. One of them is sanitary and health requirements that, if enforced, disqualify the substandard housing used by many recipients. The unknown emotional condition of the AFDC mother is an equally important problem in this use of the neighborhood care idea. A spokesman for the Welfare Rights Organization warns:

> Do not force mothers to take care of other children. You do not know what kind of problem that parent might have. You do not know whether she gets tired of her own children or not but you are trying to force her to take care of other people's children and forcing the parents to go out in the field and work when you know there is no job.
>
> This is why we have had the disturbance in New York City and across the country. We, the welfare recipients, have tried to keep down that disturbance among our people but the unrest is steadily growing. The welfare recipients are tired. They are tired of people dictating to them telling them how they must live.

Not surprisingly, day care and work training through WIN are lagging as the hoped-for saving graces of public assistance. New York City's experience is instructive. In 1967 the City Council's finance committee concluded that an additional expenditure of $5 million for 50 additional day care centers to accommodate 3,000 additional children was warranted. "The Committee on Finance is informed," said its report, "that many (welfare) mothers would seek employment if they could be assured of proper care of their children while at work. We feel that expansion . . . on a massive scale is called for." The mayor's executive expense budget for day care was thereupon increased by about 60 percent and appropriations in subsequent years have continued at the higher level. But the New York City Department of Social Services—like the U.S. Department of Health, Education, and Welfare—lacks a program for such a rapid expansion of day care. Actual expenditures have lagged. In contrast to the anticipated 50 new centers caring for 3,000 additional children, it was reported in June 1969 that 19 new centers accommodating 790 children had been established.

The national figures resulting from the 1967 amendments are no more encouraging. Like New York City, the federal government has not been able to shovel out the available money. Consider the situation around the time of the Nixon family assistance message. Of a projected June 1969 goal of 102,000 WIN enrollees, only 61,847 were in fact enrolled by the end of that month. Of a projected 100,000 child care arrangements, only about 49,000 children were receiving care at the end of June 1969, and 50 percent of them were receiving care in their own homes. Thus, when President Nixon proposed 150,000 new training slots and 450,000 new day care places in his August 1969 welfare message, the Labor Department and HEW had already found that 18 months after enactment of the 1967 legislation they were unable to meet more than 60 percent of their modest work and training goals or more than 50 percent of their even more modest day care goals.

WIN Loses

The gap between original projections and depressing realities held constant into 1970. The Labor Department first estimated a WIN enrollment level of 150,000 at the close of fiscal 1970, later scaled the figure down to 100,000. And as of February 1970 the cumulative WIN data took the shape of a funnel:

Welfare recipients screened by local agencies for possible referral	1,478,000
Found appropriate for referral to WIN	301,000
Actually referred to WIN	225,000
Enrolled in WIN program	129,000
Employed	22,000

As for day care, 188,000 children were initially expected to be receiving "child care"—which includes care in their own homes by grandmothers or other relatives—on June 30, 1970. The target later was dropped to a more modest

78,000. In May 1970 there were just 61,000 reported in child care, and only about one-fifth of these children were really cared for in a day care facility. Approximately one-half were cared for in their own homes, one-tenth in a relative's home, and the last one-fifth were reported to have "other" arrangements—a category that actually includes "child looks after self."

By July 1970 the House Labor-HEW appropriations subcommittee was discouraged about the progress of work training-day care activity. "It doesn't sound too good," said Chairman Dan Flood (Democrat of Pennsylvania) after hearing the WIN program statistics. The committee proposed a reduction of $50 million from the administration's request for $170 million in 1971 work incentive funds. There was no confusion about either the purpose of the program or its lack of accomplishment:

The objective of the work incentives program is to help people get off the welfare rolls and to place them in productive jobs. While the committee supports the program, it has just not been getting off the ground for several reasons, such as poor day care standards for children.

Unfortunately, the sorry history and the limitations of day care and work training as solutions to the welfare problem could not be faced by the administration's welfare specialists in 1970 because all of their energies were directed toward support for the Nixon family assistance plan. But after a few years it will inevitably be discovered that work training and day care have had little effect on the number of welfare dependents and no depressing effect on public relief costs. Some new solution will then be proposed, but the more realistic approach would be to accept the need for more welfare and to reject continued fantasizing about day care and "workfare" as miracle cures.

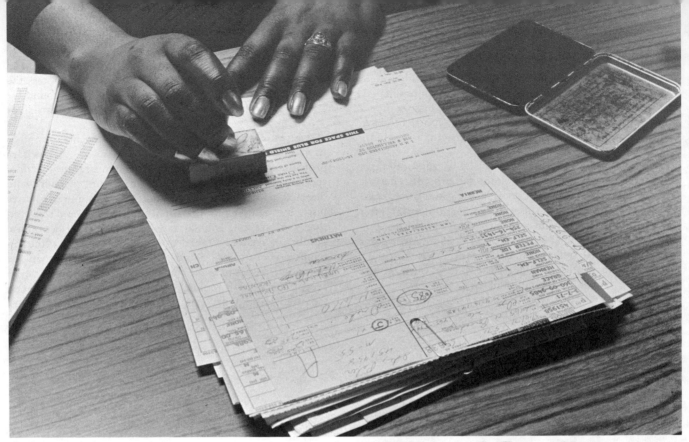

Why Medicare Helped Raise Doctors' Fees

Theodore R. Marmor

After Medicare went into effect on July 1, 1966, the prices of all health services went up. Between December 1965 and December 1966, physicians' fees alone jumped 7.8 percent; from 1959 to 1965, the average yearly increase had been only 2.8 percent. To many people these rising prices seemed more than just a coincidence, and physicians were widely condemned as greedy men soaking the population for each extra dollar. Medicare, the *New Republic* charged, was a "bonanza" for doctors.

Even physicians could not dispute the findings of the Bureau of Labor Statistics that, in 1966, more than a third of American doctors had raised their fees, and that the average increase of this one-third was 25 percent. Whether or not the physicians were also to blame, however, one conclusion was inescapable: Somehow, Medicare itself was partially responsible for the higher medical costs. What was not clear was in what way.

Medicare is a system of health insurance for the

aged. The government helps to pay the hospital charges of people 65 and over (Part A). It also helps to pay the "reasonable" fees of physicians (Part B)—if the elderly sign up for medical insurance and pay a small monthly premium. The Social Security Administration oversees the entire operation; individual insurance companies make and supervise the payments on behalf of the S.S.A.

My own analysis of the government's formula for helping to pay the cost of physicians' services under Part B of Medicare confirms, I believe, that Medicare itself encouraged the increase in physicians' fees. For the formula inadvertently carried with it incentives for physicians to raise their fees. Moreover, this formula was administered with striking laxness.

Originally, supporters of health insurance for the aged envisioned it as helping to pay only hospital bills. Then came the Democratic sweep of 1964, which ensured that some form of Medicare would be approved. Some Republicans, like Congressman John Byrnes of the Ways and Means Committee, thereupon offered programs of health insurance that had two features:
■ they authorized the government to help pay *more* than just hospital bills (many Republicans thought they had been hurt by being identified with the A.M.A.'s stubborn opposition to Medicare); and
■ these bills hadn't a prayer of getting through Congress.
This ploy backfired. Public-opinion polls soon showed that the majority of Americans assumed that the government would pay not just hospital bills for the elderly, but doctors' fees as well.

The upshot was that Medicare was suddenly and surprisingly expanded to include doctors' bills. Over one weekend, with great haste, Congressman Byrnes's staff—with the aid of the Aetna Life Insurance Company—produced a method of paying doctors, which was grafted onto the Medicare program. Unfortunately, President Johnson's administration had little time, in March 1965, to think over the way doctors ought to be paid, and how much.

This payment plan followed Aetna's usual practices and worked as follows:
Medicare would pay 80 percent of the "reasonable" fees that doctors charged. The patient would pay the first $50 (the deductible) and 20 percent of the balance (co-insurance). The rub, of course, was in determining what a reasonable fee was.

Under most current Blue Shield programs, a doctor who repairs (say) a broken leg can be paid a fee up to a specified limit—say, $50. But under Medicare, a doctor sets his own price, within *supposed* limits. He could charge almost anything for repairing a broken leg—$10, $100, $500—and, providing that this fee was deemed "reasonable" by an insurance company, he would be reimbursed.

A "reasonable" charge had to satisfy three criteria:
■ It had to be the "customary" charge for the service, rather than the charge assessed against either very poor patients, or (the greater danger) very wealthy patients.
■ This "customary" charge could not be more than the prevailing rate for the service in the doctor's locality.
■ This "customary" charge could be no higher than what the insurance companies would pay for similar treatment in their own medical plans.

These vague standards gave doctors the best of all possible worlds.

The first thing to make clear is that the Social Security Administration and the private insurance companies had no effective way of determining what a physician's "customary" fee was. For three reasons:
■ Many physicians had not paid as much attention to their sliding fee schedules before. After all, their incomes since World War II had risen not so much because of their increased fees, but because of their working harder, their using new medical procedures, and their use of time-saving devices (like cutting down on house calls). So the sliding-fee schedules of many doctors were not even consistent.
■ In general, doctors do not have one fee for a particular service, like repairing a broken leg. They have a sliding scale of fees—for example, fees for wealthy patients; fees for middle-income patients, or those whose insurance covers the service; and fees for low-income patients, whose Blue Shield coverage is based upon a fixed maximum charge. This fee variation made it extremely difficult for anyone to decide what a physician's "customary" fee was.
■ The insurance companies, despite their early optimism, actually had little useful data on what individual doctors were charging their patients before Medicare.

The result was that many doctors could upgrade their fee schedules before or after Medicare went into effect, without being held to any "customary" fees. And many did.

Why? Simply drawing doctors' attention to their "customary" fees, obviously, could prompt them to raise these fees. Then too, some of their fees may actually have been low compared to those of doctors around them—this was the reason many gave for raising their prices. Furthermore, many doctors were worried that under "government medicine" their "customary" fees would bind them for years to come. If the government would pay "reasonable" fees and no more, to the doctors' way of thinking the government might in the future put a limit on what was reasonable—and hence doctors had to act fast.

In addition, many physicians believed that only with new, higher "customary" fees could they continue to bill wealthy patients for a good deal of money, and still have these fees considered reasonable. And only with these higher fees for the rich, they believed, could they reduce their fees for low-income patients, who even with Medicare might have to pay a stiff amount.

American doctors, in brief, had not been sufficiently informed about how Medicare would work. They had, for instance, no idea of how generously the Social Security Administration and its intermediaries would interpret a "reasonable" fee. And many of them had no idea of how Medicare would work to their benefit.

To begin with, doctors found that they could still charge wealthy patients an "*un*reasonable" fee. The law permitted doctors to bill their patients directly; it then became the patient's responsibility to collect from Medicare. What this meant was that a doctor could charge a rich old man $500 for repairing a broken leg; the man would pay the $500 bill, then send the bill to an insurance company to be reimbursed; the insurance company would pay 80 percent of the "reasonable" charge; and the doctor would have already collected the "unreasonable" difference. The government might not pay "unreasonable" fees, in short, but many patients did.

THE SHARP INCREASE IN PHYSICIANS' FEES

	1964	1965	1966	1967
Physician Fee Index	2.4%	3.8%	7.8%	6.1%
Consumer Price Index	1.3	2.0	3.3	3.1

Nor had very many doctors been informed that, even without raising their fees, their incomes would probably go up under Medicare. For it had been a common practice among physicians to reduce or do away with fees for low-income patients. With Medicare, many poor aged people could now afford to pay, and to pay at a higher level. As one physician in a low-income area wrote in *Medical Economics,* now that he was collecting from the poor, his net yearly income had increased 45 percent. And as one doctor told the *Wall Street Journal,* "Before Medicare I was charging low-income patients only $4 for house calls because I knew they had limited means. But under Medicare I don't dare give them that lower price or the Medicare people will start reimbursing me at $4 for all claims on the grounds that this is my customary fee. So I have to charge them $6 now." Just the fact that low-income patients would pay, and be charged, higher rates meant that the average prices of physicians' services would increase.

There was one last favor that physicians received from Medicare, and that was a partial solution to the problem of patients who don't pay—deadbeats. Confronted with a patient who was a bad credit risk, doctors could bill him directly, and the patient had to pay his bill before he would receive any government benefits. Of course, a patient might decide not to pay anything, even a reduced fee, but he had an impetus—some return on his money, as well as no dunning letters and no visits from a collection agency. (In 1967 this was changed so that patients could send only an itemized bill to an insurance company to be reimbursed.)

In sum, under Medicare doctors got higher average payments—by raising their usual fees, and by charging many low-income patients higher rates than previously; they also retained a way of charging wealthy patients more than the government would reimburse—by having patients suffer the insurance company's decision that a fee was unreasonable; and doctors, for a while, got a higher percentage of paid bills—because some patients could not get reimbursed if they had not already paid their bills.

Thus, despite the doctors' fearful haste to raise their fees, Medicare was really a gift to them. But they didn't get the message in time.

It should not be assumed that American medical organizations cleverly pressured the Johnson Administration for these provisions. The A.M.A. was not fully consulted during the writing of the Medicare law in the Ways and Means Committee. The A.M.A.'s diehard opposition to Medicare led men like committee chairman Wilbur Mills to bar A.M.A. officials from the hearings, where their frantic objections had been of little help in the writing of detailed legislation. And when the Social Security Administration turned to writing up the regulations on the basis of the committee's vague set of guidelines, its intermittent consultations with representatives from the A.M.A. did not produce substantial changes in the payment arrangements. One might more accurately say that Washington's bowing to the presumed preferences of American doctors, coupled with the statutory interpretations of S.S.A. lawyers, produced this payment plan that medical dreams could not have improved on.

Many of the problems with the payment plan were not evident to the S.S.A. even when Medicare began. The assumption that carried the day was that the insurance carriers knew what doctors had been charging, and that profiles of individual doctors' fees were relatively easy to gather.

By March of 1966, though, it finally became evident that a crisis was brewing, so hastily reorganized teams at the S.S.A. got to work. When S.S.A. officials met with the insurance carriers in March, the man from Aetna admitted that he did not have enough bills from any individual doctor to compile data on that doctor's customary fee. "We can get an areawide prevailing fee," he said. "Then, if the charge is above that, we start worrying about its being customary, not before."

Even by July of 1966, not one insurance-company intermediary had the data needed to properly implement the law or the regulations; some of these companies estimate that they will finally have profiles of individual doctors' medical fees only two years after Medicare began.

Although the insurance companies may have misled the committee, in 1965, about their ability to administer the customary-fee standard, the S.S.A. seemed largely unaware of this until nine months after the law had been passed—and three months before it was to begin. A document from the S.S.A. outlining how reasonable charges should be determined was finally sent out to the carriers in July 1966, after the program had begun. By then, the standard for customary fees could not be changed. As the experience of every industrial country shows, the hardest thing in the world is to change a way of paying physicians that they prefer, once it has been conceded.

The price increases that took place in 1966, of course, will raise the fees that Medicare allows American doctors in the future. And these increases, prompted by Medicare, will also increase the prices that insurance companies and private individuals pay for medical services.

The Attempted Exoneration of Medicare

Obviously, the Johnson administration did not want higher medical costs when it passed Medicare. And in its attempt to resolve the controversy about rising costs, a Presidential study exonerated Medicare as the cause. The 1967 *Report to the President on Medical Prices* (the Gorham report), however, rested its findings on two debatable arguments.

■ First, the Johnson administration argued that only a small percentage of the price increases were "unexpected." The administration expected an increase consistent with the past, an increase based upon the 2 to 1 ratio that prevailed between physicians' prices and consumer prices during the postwar period. When the Consumer Price Index rose to 3.3 percent in 1966, doctors' fees were thus expected to rise 6.6 percent.

The administration simplistically assumed that the present and the future would resemble the past. It omitted the crucial consideration peculiar to 1966— that Medicare, by helping low-income, elderly patients pay physicians' fees, assured American doctors substantial increases in income whether they raised their fees or not. Even the A.M.A., in trying to discourage fee increases, estimated that in 1966 doctors' incomes would rise by over $8000 in Florida, $6500 in Michigan, and $3000 in Nevada.

Then too, the fees actually rose 7.8 percent—18 percent more than the expected 6.6 increase.

■ The administration's second argument—that Medicare could not have been responsible for physicians' price increases—rested on premature evidence. The Gorham report pointed out that doctors' fees for five procedures used especially by the aged had increased less than physicians' fees in general, thus apparently showing that Medicare could not have been the crucial cause of these increases. But in July of 1967, the S.S.A. data showed that these gerontological indices were rising in line with other doctors' fees.

Economists might also argue that the laws of supply and demand were responsible for the 1966 price increases. With Medicare paying part of their bills, more elderly people would consult doctors. But here, I think, timing is crucial. Had demand been the key variable, a steeper increase in fees would have occurred *after* the program began. But the rate of fee increases was exactly the same during the first six months of 1966 (pre-Medicare) as they were during the last half of the year (with Medicare): 3.8 percent. Apparently many American doctors raised their fees *not* in response to more crowded offices, but in anticipation of the Medicare program and its formula for paying "reasonable charges."

The lessons we can learn from public medical programs in other countries are not altogether comforting. The experience in Sweden and England shows that governments can seldom change the methods of payment that most doctors in a society prefer. They are unable to innovate in controversial ways (pay by salary, for example), and unable to withstand physicians' demands for change (paying doctors special rates for night calls, as in England in 1965). What's more, these constraints apply to the *unit* of payment (by person, by item of service, by salary units), to the *source* of payment (patient, intermediary, the government), and to the *bases* of differentiating doctors for payment purposes (by type of practice, type of doctor, or type of result). Worldwide, the methods for paying physicians are extraordinarily diverse. What they share is their close resemblance to what the doctors were used to before public programs began, or what doctors were known to prefer.

This strikingly uniform relationship between doctors' preferences and public-payment methods contrasts with the international diversity in physicians' preferences. In Sweden and America, doctors are adamant about being able to charge patients directly, and to charge them on a fee-for-service basis (as opposed to receiving a salary). In England, doctors don't care about the source of payment. A few demand that patients pay some of the medical costs, but not necessarily to the *doctor*.

Further, in paying doctors governments might consider adjusting the amount according to the doctor's specialty (general practitioner versus surgeon, for example), his age, and his type of practice (individual versus group, and so on). But governments can rarely get doctors to accept any differentiation between them that large blocs in the profession don't already accept— like differences in income according to age. Contrari-

wise, in 1966 the British government refused to pay by item-of-service, a demand of the British Medical Association—and could get away with it, because this demand was not fully supported by British doctors.

The Threat of a Doctors' Strike

The state, in short, can seldom make the method of paying physicians conform to its wishes. It has to bargain with men who are suppliers of scarce services, and whose threat of interrupting these services is a powerful political resource.

It is this threat that may basically explain why doctors get their way on payment methods despite the differences in how they press their cases.

Doctors, after all, have nonmonetary reasons for preferring particular methods of payment, and place such considerations above those of total income. And concessions from the government on the method of payment are tangible indications of success for medical organizations to show their members. As for governments, many of them rank expenditure considerations and the avoidance of strikes above considerations about the organization of medical service. So the stage is set for continual concessions to medical preferences. This occurs despite all the lip service that government officials in England, Sweden, and America pay to efficiency. And in all three countries the time that such concessions usually take place is when physicians threaten minimal cooperation with the state. That means at the beginning of public programs (like Medicare) and when medical grievances are expressed in mass protests (such as the general-practitioner strike threat in England during 1965).

Only in countries with much greater supplies of physician services (Israel), or those with revolutionary ideologies (the Soviet Union), or those with populations unused to modern medical practice (the underdeveloped countries), can the threat to the maintenance of public commitments in medicine be called a bluff, the chance be taken that a strike will take place, and emergency substitutes for doctors be offered.

My conclusion is that the *methods* of medical payment will not change in the United States in ways that doctors are known to resent. Retrospectively, this means that the government could not have avoided paying doctors under Medicare on a fee-for-service basis. But the "reasonable" standard for particular services was *not* unavoidable. Nor was the *administration* of "reasonable charges" subject to the same overpowering physician constraints as the choice of the method itself.

What should also be recognized is that changes in the way medical services are organized and financed can be made, however haltingly. When governments pay doctors by a method the doctors prefer, governments should be certain that reforms in medical practice accompany such concessions. One illustration of this is the British government's concession of seniority payments to British general practitioners. No British government had ever wanted such payments; age, clearly, has nothing to do with the quality of medical service. But by making seniority awards contingent upon older physicians' taking refresher courses, the British government saw to it that incentives to improved practice were built into the payment that the British Medical Association demanded and got.

Few concessions of this nature were demanded by the U.S. government in making the Medicare payment policy. The review of fees and the quality of services was left to intermediaries, and there is little reason to believe that the higher prices now paid to doctors by both private citizens and the Medicare program will result in improved medical practices. Doctors' incomes, on the average, are the highest of any medical group in the United States. In 1967, *Medical Economics* estimated that the median physician income, after expenses but before taxes, was $34,000. It would be distressing if government programs further increase physicians' incomes without some assurance that Americans get better value for their money.

Medicare brought doctors increased incomes, an ironic conclusion to a quarter of a century of A.M.A. opposition to any government role in financing personal health services. The fact was that paying doctors at all under Medicare was a surprise to the American government. A good share of the price increases that have taken place since July 1965 can be attributed to that surprise, and the consequent hasty preparation of of the payment method. Surprise will no longer be a problem for the Medicare program. But increasing prices, and the question of medical-care quality, most certainly will.

The strategy of compromise and adjustment to political realities has so long influenced the design of American health legislation that seldom has anyone considered what an ideal helath system might look like. Yet it has become fashionable to recognize that there is a "crisis" in our health services (the White House said so in July 1969) and that the "system" is in need of basic overhauling.

What is it that is basically wrong with the health service system in the United States? What would an ideal but really sound system look like? Aside from high and rising prices, inaccessibility of medical care for the poor and long waits for doctor and dentist appointments for everyone—all of which are symptoms rather than causes—there is little said in answer to the first of these questions. To the second question, one rarely sees any answer at all.

As to the first question, I can be brief. The basic fault in American health service is the descrepancy between our assertion of health care as a basic human right and our practice of treating it as a marketplace commodity. Even when we have taken steps to improve medical care for the poor, as under Medicaid, or for the self-supporting, as under voluntary health insurance plans, we have used a systematized flow of money simply to purchase the services of physicians or hospitals in the open market. We have not organized the provision or "delivery" of health services in the way that other services deemed essential to society have been organized, such as education or protection against fire.

So long as medical care remains a matter of private buying and selling—whether it be from a doctor, a dentist, a pharmacist, a podiatrist, a hospital or a nursing home—it will be subject to all the profit-seeking vicissitudes of the commercial market. This will be true even if the hospital is "nonprofit," because, even without stockholders, it still must make the finanical ends meet. And it will be true in spite of the noblest constraints of medical ethics, which may inhibit open fraud but hardly can influence subconscious monetary incentives.

increase in the demand for medical care in the United States. This has been due not only to the increasing potentialities of medical science but also to the rising knowledge and expectations of people, and the enhanced purchasing power furnished by expanded health insurance. This elevated demand for medical care has been met, of course, by increases in the supply of health care resources—personnel, facilities and equipment—but, as in many commercial markets, at a rate slower than the rate of rising demand. The lag has been caused partly by 30 years of professional obstruction to increasing the output of doctors under the banner of "protecting quality," and partly by the especially high cost of producing medical resources—training doctors, building hospitals and so forth. Because of these educational and capital costs, social funding (mostly

An Ideal Health Care System for America
Milton I. Roemer

state and federal tax revenues) has been called upon, but it has not been forthcoming at a rate commensurate with the needs.

And so we are faced with a mounting shortage of doctors and other health personnel. To cope with it, many ideas formerly rejected are now being implemented. Osteopaths, of decidedly meager educational background, are turned into M.D.'s by law (California), and they are now counted in the national statistics as physicians. Graduates of foreign medical schools—partly foreign nationals and partly Americans denied admission to United States schools—are now welcomed here (about 25 percent of new medical licentiates each year!). Medical care is more and more shifted to the hospital, where large numbers of auxiliary personnel are regularly on hand, conserving the time of the doctor. And diverse new types of health personnel are being trained not merely to help the doctor but to replace him for certain tasks—the physician's assistant, the pediatric associate, the Medex, the nurse practitioner and others.

At the same time, to cope with the medical "crisis," many limited and modest steps are being taken to "change the system." In a variety of forms, these involve the modification of individualistic medical practice toward more organized forms. Group practice of doctors—three or more banding together in a team—is steadily increasing, now engaging the time of about 15 percent of physicians. (While most of this remains private and entrepreneurial, it sets the stage for more socially oriented patterns.) More and more ambulatory care is being sought from hospital outpatient departments or emergency rooms, requiring hospital medical staffs to organize services to meet the demand. In these and other roles, physicians are entering full-time hospital employment in increasing numbers and rates. Neighborhood health centers, offering generalized ambulatory care rather than purely preventive service, are increasing, not only under the auspices of the United States Office of Economic Opportunity (OEO) but under a diversity of local agencies. Medical schools are organizing comprehensive prepaid health care plans based on medical teams, not only for teaching but for demonstration of sound patterns for the future. Even the Nixon administration is calling for the creation of "health maintenance organizations" like the Kaiser Health Plan.

These innovations—and many more (youth clinics, maternity and infant care centers, migrant family clinics and the like)—are all straws in the wind. They depend, however, on private spending, voluntary health insurance or special grants from government and sometimes on philanthropy. Significant as they are, their impact is spotty, and the vast majority of people are not reached. The 63 neighborhood health centers launched by the OEO, for example, alto-

gether reach hardly 1.5 million people in the urban ghettos, while about 30 million Americans are estimated conservatively (15 percent of 200 million) to fall below the poverty line.

The "plight of the patient," as *Time* magazine put it, has many more facets than this. There are the grim and crowded conditions in large urban public hospitals serving the poor—beds in the corridors and packed benches in the clinics. There are the bleak realities in the office of the harassed practitioner in Appalachia. There is the squalor of most state mental hospitals. There is the multibillion dollar wastage each year on worthless (if not harmful) patent medicines, on naturopathic food faddism, or chiropractors and phony curative appliances. But most of all there are the daily inefficiencies of private medical and dental practice, with the design of what *Fortune* magazine calls a "pushcart industry." There are the inducements to unnecessary surgery, made all the more lucrative by much of the undisciplined voluntary health insurance coverage. There are the "shot doctors" who give every indigent patient an

injection, because for this the welfare agency pays an extra fee.

What can be done about all this? At least five major bills have been introduced in the United States Congress to tackle the medical care cost problem, and some of them to go much further. The weakest of them—the "Medicredit" offering of the American Medical Association—would subsidize, from federal monies, voluntary membership of poor people in existing private health insurance plans. Other proposals call for mandatory enrollment in existing plans. The Nixon administration, following the nineteenth century German strategy of requiring employer and worker contributions to these plans, would cover about 90 percent of the population, but substantial deductibles and co-payments by the patient would obviously limit accessibility of low income people to needed care.

The strongest of the proposals—the "Health Security" bill proposed by the late Walter Reuther's Committee of One Hundred and introduced by Senator Edward Kennedy and others—would provide many incentives to modify the system. It would encourage group practice, health maintenance organizations, rural location of doctors, continuing professional education, systematic hospital planning, controls on drug prescribing, increased output of needed health resources and much more. It is clearly the best national health reform legislation ever introduced, using financial support as leverage to modify the health care system. It would certainly move us forward, and it deserves the strongest possible support. Yet, the Kennedy bill would still depend on the effectiveness of various incentives, and we cannot be sure how well they would work. The mainstream of private, entrepreneurial medicine would probably remain predominant for many years. Moreover, much would depend on the ideology and spirit of the government in power, and its delegates at regional, state and local levels.

The Shape of an Ideal System

If an ideal and reasonable system of health care were to be achieved—to answer the second question posed at the outset—what, then, would it look like? Its design need not be so mysterious nor unknowable as some imply.

First of all, in every neighborhood, close to the homes of people, would be a health center staffed by a team of primary health personnel. The doctor would be a generalist—perhaps one of the new "specialists in family practice" or else an internist—working in association with nurses, social workers and clerks. On the team would also be "medical assistants" or "assistant physicians" who would be trained and authorized to handle simple cases on their own—the common cold, the minor injury, the mild gastro-enteritis or the follow-up visit after a previous medical

service. These medical assistants would be supervised by the physician, and, of course, any case not recovering promptly would be referred to the doctor. They would not represent second-class medicine, because they would be properly trained for their duties and would have more time than the doctor to give sympathetic attention to each patient.

At this primary health center all the usual personal preventive services would also be provided. Babies and expectant mothers would get their checkups, immunizations would be given, dietary counseling and health education on various subjects would be offered. Screening tests would also be offered for detection of chronic disease, so that laboratory and X-ray technicians and appropriate equipment would have to be on hand. The basic health and medical record of each patient would be kept here, transferred to another health center if he should move and temporarily lent to a hospital or other facility where he may be referred for care.

Depending on the distribution of the population, each such health center would be intended to serve about 10,000 people. In a sparsely settled rural area, it might be fewer, and in a very densely settled city it might be more. There would be one doctor, in collaboration with the other allied health personnel, for about 2,000 persons; assuming this, a complement of five doctors per 10,000 might be divided between four generalists and a pediatrician. In addition, each health center should have a dental staff—dentists plus dental auxiliaries who, like the New Zealand "dental nurse," would do reparative work as well as prophylaxes on children. An optometrist would also be on the team for visual refractions. Drugs would be dispensed from the pharmacy within the health center.

Each person served by this health center would be attached to a particular doctor and his team of colleagues. Such attachment should ideally be on a geographic district basis, but this should not be rigid. If someone did not like the primary doctor covering his district, he should be free to change to another one in the same health center or, indeed, to a doctor in another center that that was not too far away. Limits would have to be placed on the number of patients a popular doctor could attract, for the protection of quality; up to a certain level, however (perhaps 2,200 persons), the primary doctor should get additional rewards as an inducement to win the confidence of patients. Services of the neighborhood health center should be available 24 hours a day, but no individual doctor should ordinarily have to serve more than an eight-hour day, with the other hours covered on a rotation scheme.

For each four or five such health centers—that is, for population clusters of 40,000 to 50,000—there should be a district hospital. Assuming about three beds per 1,000 for the relatively common conditions handled at this hospital, it would have 120 to 150 beds. This facility would accommodate maternity cases, trauma, abdominal surgery of lesser complexity (appendicitis, hernial repair, gallbladder work), certain psychoneuroses, most cardiovascular cases, severe respiratory infections and the like. It would be staffed by a team of specialists in surgery, internal medicine, orthopedics, obstetrics and gynecology, pediatrics and psychiatry. Normal obstetrical deliveries would be done in the hospital by well-trained midwives—as they are now done in Great Britain with the results better than in America. Anesthesia would also, for the most part, be given by trained nurse-anesthetists working under the supervision of an anesthesiologist. The staff of hospital doctors would be essentially full-time, except for periodic visits they would make as consultants to the affiliated health centers. They would provide ambulatory specialist care through an active outpatient department, to which patients would be referred by doctors at the primary health centers. Except for obvious emergencies, all admissions to the hospital would be made through the outpatient department.

The 120 to 150 beds in the hospital would be organized into "progressively" staged sections for intensive, intermediate and long-term care. The intensive care unit would have all the necessary emergency and monitoring equipment for the severe accident victim, for the postoperative patient, the acute coronary occlusion case and so forth. The highest proportion of beds would be in the intermediate care unit—postoperative surgical patients and most medical patients being diagnosed and treated. The long-term unit would care for patients requiring skilled medical observation and nursing care, but in a chronic or convalescent stage of their illness. In this unit, plenty of provision should be made for diversion and self-help, and an active department of physical and occupational therapy should be attached to it. Patients should not remain here, however, for more than about 30 days, after which they would be transferred to another long-term care institution (extended care facility), if not to their own homes.

In the district hospital, probably near the long-term unit, there should also be provision for some mental patients. If they are not ready for discharge within about 30 days, they would be transferred to a mental hospital. Both the mental hospital and the long-term care institution referred to above would be affiliated with the district hospital administratively and professionally. Thus, the psychiatrist on the district hospital's medical staff would have an appointment on the mental hospital staff, as would the other physicians on the staff of the long-term care institution.

The next echelon of hospital care would be a regional hospital serving populations of about 500,000—in other words, the service areas of about ten district hospitals. Offering about 1.0 bed per 1,000 people, this larger hospital would have about 500 beds and would be devoted to the care of patients with more complex medical or surgical problems. Here is where the chest surgery (heart or lungs) would be done, the more complicated abdominal surgery, the kidney dialyses, the complex diagnostic work-ups. Here also would be an active program of medical research, along with training programs for nurses, technicians and various other types of health personnel. Physicians and others from both the district hospitals and neighborhood health centers would come here also for periodic refresher courses on new developments in medical science.

At the highest echelon, serving the population coming under three to five regional hospitals (that is, from 1½ million to 2½ million people), should be a university medical center. Since this institution would provide the clinical experience for training medical students and certain other health professionals, it must not be limited to acceptance of only the most complex cases, like the regional hospitals. Assuming roughly 0.5 beds per 1,000 (that is, 750 to 1,500 beds), part of these beds would be devoted to simple cases (of the district hospital type), part to complex cases (of the regional hospital type) and part to special diagnostic categories on which the medical school staff was doing research. The latter type of patient might be referred from outside the territory served by each medical center, through intercenter agreements. For certain rare types of cancer, for example, on which critical research might be undertaken, the population required to yield enough patients for good clinical investigation might number ten million to 20 million.

As described above, this "regionalization" network of health centers and hospitals is, of course, oversimplified; a perfectly accurate description would have to be much more elaborate. In the immediate surroundings of each medical center and regional hospital, for example—as well as in the service area of the district hospitals—there would have to be neighborhood health centers, so that each person would have convenient access to a primary doctor. Every hospital, from smallest to largest, would have to provide an outpatient department, not only to furnish specialist consultations but also to cope with emergencies at any hour of the day or night. Moreover, sections for long-term care and psychiatric therapy—as well as the conventional medical, surgical, pediatric and obstetrical departments—would be found in all levels of hospital.

As for care in the patient's home, this would be provided principally by the staff of the local health centers. Physicians would go when necessary—usually for acute emergencies—but most initial or follow-up home visits would be done by broadly trained nurses or medical assistants attached to the health center. If a patient discharged from the hospital must have continuing medically supervised care, this should be provided by the health center staff (aided by any special instructions or advice from the hospital staff) or occasionally by a "home care" staff dispatched directly from the hospital.

This entire network of services, it may be noted, is based on the locations of people's homes in cities, towns or rural areas, but certain health services in an ideal system would have to be provided at places where people are occupied outside their homes. To be convenient for adults and children, therefore, health stations would also be provided at factories or other work places and at schools. These would be for first aid in emergencies, simple follow-up care, health education, immunizations, case-detection screening tests and for other measures that can be more efficiently given where people are congregated. For any significant or continuing medical care, the child or adult would be referred to his local health center.

Economic Support and Administration

How would all this be paid for? Ideally health care should be a public service like schools or roads, paid for from general tax revenues. It is only because of our reluctance to accept this basic concept that we resort to all sorts of other collective devices which still signify individual responsibility, like voluntary health insurance or even social security. These are obviously reasonable methods to collectivize costs, up to a point, but their limitations in achieving comprehensive health care have been all too obvious. Conceivably, because of its political and psychological attractiveness, part of the costs of an ideal health service might be met by a social insurance tax (as is done for about 15 percent of the costs of the British National Health Service), but the great bulk should come from general revenues. These might be divided in some equitable way between federal and state governments. The tax burden should be adjusted according to individual or corporate ability to pay, and the health services offered should bear no relation to the origin of the funds.

For any services rendered within the social program described, there would be no charges made at time of sickness. It is often argued that the patient should bear at least a share of the cost of health services to deter him from unnecessary demands or "abuse." Without going into all the arguments and empirical data about "cost sharing" or "coinsurance" or "deterrent fees" or "deductibles"— whatever term is used—it should simply be realized that the vast majority of medical expenses are determined by the doctor, not the patient, and there is no evidence that cost sharing selectively discourages the unnecessary and not the needed services. This is quite aside from the unequal weight of cost sharing on persons of different wealth, and its administrative awkwardness. Basically, no financial barrier should inhibit the patient from seeking medical care; if he makes demands that are medically and psychosomatically unreasonable, it is up to the doctor to deny the service.

With monies raised from general revenues and no private cost sharing, the fee-for-service method of medical remuneration, with all its incentives to waste, would have no place. Just as nurses, technicians, pathologists or professors are now paid by salaries, so would be all physicians, dentists and everyone else in the health service system. Salaries, of course, should vary, according to qualifications, skills and responsibilities, but each person would be paid for the proper value of his time.

Without the direct financial incentive to hard work of the fee system, how would the quality of medical care be assured, including sympathetic personal concern for the patient? The answer is: the way it is assured in any organization—by a framework of authority and responsibility, backed up by continuous education. Surveillance and reasonable professional controls would also be provided, with rewards and penalties as necessary. It must be realized that in any health care system there can be and should be incentives to excellence in the form of both honor and material rewards.

Another continuous safeguard of medical quality, especially along its personal dimension, should be advisory boards of citizens, made up of both consumers and providers of service, at all echelons of the system. These boards would exercise continuous influence on the appointments of personnel and the operations of the whole health care program. Minority groups should obviously be represented on these boards, but the militant slogan of "consumer control"—generated by today's inequities and professional chauvinism—would be replaced by a reasonable mix of consumer-professional collaboration in policy decisions within an ideal system.

Which brings us to the final topic of this account: the mode of administration of the entire system. Our spectrum of health services in America has conventionally been described as "pluralistic." More accurate would be to describe it as an irrational jungle in which countless vested interests compete for both the private and the public dollar, causing not only distorted allocations of health resources in relation to human needs but all sorts of waste and inefficiency along the way.

To administer the ideal program of health services there would be a single official health agency in each local area. This area is not so easy to define, but it would ideally be synonymous with the catchment area of a regional hospital—about 500,000 population. Subunits within this basic administrative area would operate at the level of a district hospital—that is, for about 50,000 population. Indeed, the health official serving as director for each of these hospitals might properly serve as the overall health director for the corresponding area. Thus, he would not be a "hospital administrator" in the conventional sense, but a "public health director" in the broadest social sense. Under this official would be administrative personnel for managing the hospital, but the functions of the health officer would be much wider. It would be his duty, backed up by the citizen boards mentioned above, to see that the whole health service operates effectively. He would be responsible for quality surveillance and for detection and correction of any deficiencies. He would be constantly alert to the opportunities for health prevention and health promotion, including the whole task of environmental health protection (which this article has not discussed). He would be responsible for coordination of the several parts of the system, through proper use of records, statistics and information exchange. He would observe trends and take steps to plan for the future.

Naturally, the "regional health director" should not be an absolute power but would be responsible to a health official above him. In the American political context, this would be a state health officer, whose responsibilities and duties would be, of course, much broader than they are now. State health officers, aided by a democratically constituted state board of health, would be responsible to a national official. With so large a responsibility, this person should be a member of the president's cabinet—the equivalent to the minister of health found in most countries.

Simplicity from Complexity

All this will strike some people as insufferably bureaucratic or naively utopian, depending on one's ideology. It also might seem hopelessly complicated. In fact, it would be a much simpler health care system than we have now, with its thousands (yes, thousands) of separate agencies for financing or providing different sectors or subsectors of health care. Bureaucratic? Yes. To meet health needs effectively in a complex society of 200 million people demands an organized framework. We take this for granted in much simpler matters, such as operating a post office or a school system. It is all the more necessary if the myriad tasks of assuring good health service are to be carried out. The trend, indeed, over the last 50 or 75 years has been toward increasing health care organization in order to apply the advancing science to increasingly perceived needs. The ideal system described here is essentially only an extension of the direction in which we have been moving.

As for the charge of "utopian," this is a question of timing. The system described could obviously not be achieved in the United States overnight. Even sweeping national legislation could not establish it. Quite aside from the tradition of private entrepreneurial medical practice, with all its inertia and resistance, there is manifestly a nationwide establishment of hospitals and health agencies that would require enormous readjustments to approach the ideal system. This would take great managerial skill and infinitely diplomatic human relationships. It would also require a great deal of money for new construction and new training. And it would take time.

Perhaps the health care system described could not be achieved short of a social revolution? One might be justified in holding this view if it were not for the historical lessons demonstrated in the achievement of a public school system, a sharply graduated income tax and an extensive social security program in all the industrialized capitalistic countries of the world. Each of these vast social developments came in the face of substantial opposition. Each involved invasion of previously sacred rights of private property. Each was part of the program of revolutionary socialist parties before accomplishment.

Regardless of how utopian or unrealistic the ideal health care program may appear, it has importance as a social goal. Only by having a clear goal ahead can one make sound decisions today—decisions along the scores of separate paths on which the health services are becoming organized. By formulating such an ideal system we can recognize that all the legislative measures now being considered in the national Congress—even the most advanced of them—are compromises, middle-of-the-road proposals adjusted to the political realities. The Kennedy "Health Security" bill would undoubtedly be a great step forward, but we need not succumb to the charge that it is a radical proposal. At best, it would provide better economic support and long overdue incentives to move us a little more rapidly toward a reasonable health care system. But we would still have a long way to go to reach an ideal system. The challenge is to see the goal clearly, so that we can decide wisely what specific actions—at local, state and national levels and in all health sectors—would retard and what ones would accelerate our attainment of a really sound health service for America.

257

Cooling Out the Economy

Walter W. McMahon

Unemployment continues to hit hardest those least equipped to bear adversity: unskilled laborers, racial minorities and the poor. At the same time, a slowing but stubborn inflation continues to upset household budgets, especially for those who need medical care and new housing, or who depend on public transportation.

In its efforts to achieve economic stabilization, the administration has devoted more energy to the fight against inflation than to the more recent fight against unemploy-

ment. It has carried on its attack against inflation by curtailing demand, a policy that tends to benefit a different group of people from those who suffer the income loss of unemployment. Yet an attack against unemployment is tantamount to a direct attack against many of our social problems: urban and rural poverty, crime, growing welfare rolls. It is noteworthy that it costs only a little more to employ idle workers than it does to maintain them and their families. Furthermore, unemployment, which these days hovers just below 6 percent, does not hit all groups equally; it is currently about 11 percent for construction workers, about 17 percent for teen-agers, about 9.5 percent for blacks and about 30 percent for black teen-agers. Reducing unemployment would reduce quickly the number of cities designated as "depressed"—currently about 50. It would also contribute to longer-run growth by encouraging investment in new technology. If, instead of relying entirely on curtailing demand, a more comprehensive wage-price or "price-incomes" policy were used to help restrain any continuing inflation, we could reduce both unemployment and the cost of living squeeze. (Such a policy, incidentally, would also help reduce labor unrest, which threatens to result in a steel strike in August.)

The management of the economy is of course fundamental to the public interest. It is also fundamental to President Richard M. Nixon's reelection prospects and to the composition of the next Congress. The Nixon administration attacked inflation with such vigor that it has since found it necessary to counteract the resulting effect by announcing a "full employment budget" designed to stimulate economic activity. Yet tightening of fiscal and monetary policies in 1969 was clearly necessary, for no administration committed to a balanced stabilization policy can allow inflation to run unchecked at rates in excess of 5 to 7 percent. But inflation was curbed at a price, and it is reasonable to ask if the same or better results could not have been achieved at less cost.

In its February *Economic Report* the administration announced that it plans to allow enough slack to remain in the economy throughout 1971 to maintain continuous downward pressure on the rate of inflation. Administration economists, who are aware of the lag between the time a policy is started and the time its effects are felt, plan to have the economy return to full employment "by mid-1972," just in time for elections. Plans for improving conditions in the construction industry were announced, but it is also important to consider other weapons that could be used as part of a price-incomes policy to restrain the more important remaining sources of inflation. The need for a sensible wage-price policy is not a temporary one, for creeping inflation can be expected to remain a problem as long as the economy is kept close to full employment levels. But the social cost of maintaining a pool of 5½ to 6 percent unemployed, as was done throughout the 1958-63 period, is just too high a price to pay for restraining a modest inflation.

The Trade-off Between Unemployment and Inflation

The policy choices open to President Nixon and his key economic advisers are most easily understood by reference to a modified Phillips curve. This curve plots the rate of consumer price increases on one axis and the rate of unemployment on the other, showing that increases in unemployment reflecting slack demand tend to be accompanied by reductions in inflation. A similar trade-off between unemployment and inflation has been found to exist in northern European countries. If refinements are introduced to allow for the effect on wage rates of lagged price increases, labor productivity or profit rate changes, and labor "reserves" (workers who leave the labor force as unemployment increases), it is a permanently useful tool for interpreting economic stabilization policies.

Notice the relatively stable prices throughout 1960-65 appearing low on the curve in Figure 1. This stability was upset by President Lyndon B. Johnson who financed the escalation of the Vietnam War with borrowing rather than with taxes, thereby increasing total demand. Since the economy was already near production capacity and full employment in 1965, excess demand was created, and prices rose throughout 1966-68, as shown to the left along the curve.

Momentum carried the economy upward in the first half of 1969. But President Nixon switched the federal budget to a huge $13.4 billion surplus by midyear and encouraged the most intensive squeeze on credit in the history of the Federal Reserve System. Together these fiscal and monetary policies stopped the upswing, with the upper turning point of industrial production coming early in September 1969.

Then the economy started downward, and unemployment rose. But even though it is well known that the main effect of interest rates in discouraging construction appears only after a lag of six to nine months, monetary policy permitted long-term interest rates to rise on into 1970. As would be expected, the unemployment rate in the construction industry climbed, reaching 12.7 percent by September 1970.

The trough of the recession was reached in November 1970, when real gross national product (GNP) and the industrial production indices were at their low points. Overall unemployment reached its high of 6.2 percent in December. This growing unemployment was stopped by an earlier easing of fiscal policy leading to a $14 billion federal deficit by June 1970. The budget deficit occurred largely because of an increase in unemployment compensation passed by Congress, an automatic increase in unemployment payments as unemployment grew (together a $9 billion increase), expiration of the remaining 5 percent Vietnam War surtax (a $3.5 billion tax decrease) and some automatic reductions in federal income tax receipts as income fell. All of these expenditure increases and tax cuts put purchasing power in the hands of consumers. The increased purchasing power reversed the decline in effective demand within three to six months and contributed heavily to the upturn of the economy in December. Budget deficits are much misunderstood, but they are absolutely vital in filling in the troughs of economic activity, for they leave tax dollars in the hands of consumers and reverse declining demand.

Monetary policy also changed in the summer of 1970, allowing long-term interest rates to decrease a little. This decrease has been reflected in an increase in housing starts, which began in December 1970, consistent with the lag before the first noticeable effects occur that has been estimated to be six to nine months. An increase in other forms of new construction began in January 1971; these are both increases in real investments that can be expected to continue. In fact the enormous pent-up demand for new housing could lead to a significant increase in housing starts in early 1972 because long-term interest rates continue downward right now from 8½ percent toward 6 percent in many cities.

Unfortunately, the steady upward movement of construction costs tends to choke off this demand for new housing. It remains to be seen how effective President Nixon's attempts to do something about the restrictive

practices of some of the American Federation of Labor craft unions and the troublesome markup practices of lumberyards (price increases of 42 percent just since December 1970) will be. But the recovery of the construction industry, not to speak of the welfare of the continuing pool of less skilled and black unemployed construction workers, depends heavily on his success.

In general, then, the administration's effort to prevent first runaway inflation and then massive unemployment has been successful, although we have almost come to take such stabilization for granted. The success of overall stabilization policies, based admittedly on an uneven application of improved economic knowledge, in at least six northern European countries and the United States in the postwar period has been striking. There has in fact been no serious depression or currency breakdown in any of these nations since World War II. President Nixon accepted wholeheartedly the principle of a full employment budget in his January *Budget Message.* Expenditure is to balance with revenue as projected at full employment; this means an actual budget deficit for the new fiscal year following on the $18½ billion for the current fiscal year ending June 30,

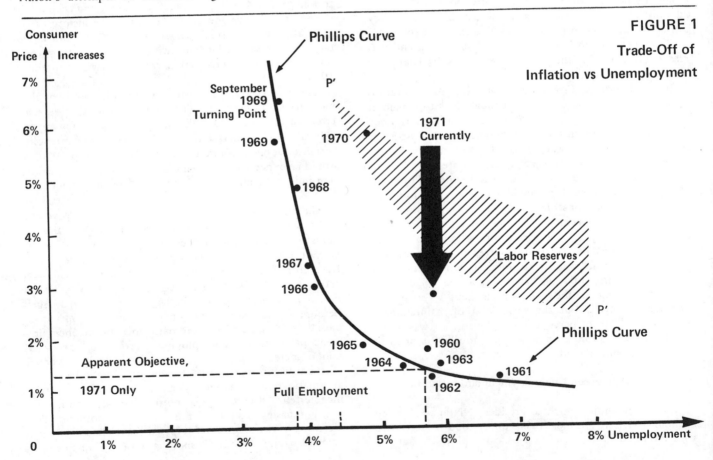

FIGURE 1

Trade-Off of

Inflation vs Unemployment

1971. Therefore, stabilization policy can be expected to take care of the upper and lower ends of the Phillips curve in Figure 1—that is, runaway inflation and massive unemployment—permitting attention to be turned to solving the problems that remain when unemployment is between 3.9 and 4.5 percent.

A Price-Incomes Policy?

Wage-price guideposts were used in the 1962-67 period. After that, apart from some ineffective jawboning and some talk about all-out controls which nobody wants, this approach was dropped. Now, however, the Council of Economic Advisers reports immediately to the Cabinet Committee on Economic Policy any exceptionally inflationary wage and price developments, so that the Cabinet Committee can consider appropriate federal action. The next step should be to articulate a coherent price-incomes policy and subject it to public discussion. Perhaps a few suggestions can be made here about a price-incomes policy that would help improve the trade-off between unemployment and inflation, thereby minimizing unemployment and contributing to the achievement of a sustainable real growth of 4½ percent a year.

From the 1962-67 experience it was learned that wage-price policies work only as a supplement to general fiscal and monetary stabilization policies. When, for example, there is excess demand, as there was in 1967-68, it is unrealistic to expect workers to limit voluntarily their increases in wages to a fixed rate tied to productivity increases (usually about 3.2 percent a year) and firms not to raise their prices unless there is all-out rationing. And at the other extreme when there is considerable unemployment, if it is after a period of rising consumer prices, increases in wages mean that at first workers' real incomes are catching up to the cost of living. But if the slack persists, the guidelines are redundant. A price-incomes policy therefore should probably be used only when the economy is in the middle range of the Phillips curve, as it is now, with unemployment ranging from 3.9 to 6.5 percent.

A price-incomes policy can certainly work to alleviate bottlenecks by increasing supply. One example is medical care. There is an acute need for more doctors, especially general practitioners, pediatricians and internists. Above all, there is an acute need for more doctors in rural areas and urban ghettos. At the same time, medical care prices have risen considerably more rapidly than any other major item in the consumer price index. They stand at 170 on a 1957-59 base of 100, compared to 133 for food and 160 for construction. Part of this may be due to the fact that doctors, rather than the public, control the policies of the Blue Shield plan and of many hospitals, and part may be due to the lower rates of growth of productivity that William J. Baumol and others have suggested may be typical

of many service industries. In any case, from the point of view of the national interest, President Nixon's veto of the doctor training bill is absolutely incomprehensible. For even with government help, it takes a long time to train doctors.

An approach to a price-incomes policy that is appropriate for nonservice industries is to satisfy excess demand by selling government stockpiles and easing import restrictions. In the steel industry, for example, the possibility of easing import quotas was explored by President Nixon. After very large price increases were announced in January 1971, President Nixon, probably as a trial balloon, directed his Cabinet Committee on Economic Policy to reexamine the agreement with Japanese and European Economic Community steel producers that limits their sales of steel in the United States. Since increased steel imports would change the competitive situation, U.S. Steel adopted a somewhat smaller price increase. This is important, because U.S. Steel's prices act as a bench mark for the rest of the industry. Furthermore, the size of the January price increase may influence the policy of the United Steelworkers Union. Had the increases been smaller, the union might have moderated its demands when its contract comes up for negotiation this summer.

Finally, a price-incomes policy is concerned with the economy-wide wage-price escalation, not just with conditions in a few industries. The process goes something like this. Prices depend primarily on total demand, on changes in wages and profit rates and on rates of increase in productivity per man-hour. If high demand should move some prices upward, households will not sit idly by and watch their real incomes deteriorate. There will be pressure for higher wages and salaries, and after a lag these wage rates will be subject to cost of living adjustments. Business firms pass these wage increases along to consumers in the form of a second round of price increases, often with a little additional margin for themselves. This encourages another round of wage increases, which by this time can have become considerably greater than the increase in productivity. Workers see themselves as regaining lost ground, or in Milton Friedman's terms, adjusting to inflationary expectations. If there is unemployment and slack demand, new "safety margins" cannot be built in on each round, and the escalation process must thus slow down.

Some kind of reasonable price and wage criteria that define what is excessive in relation to increases in productivity can help to damp this wage-price escalation. Most research indicates that the guideposts, used during the period 1962-67, did have some effect; Canada is currently having some success with a wage-price policy; and most of the major European countries have used price-incomes policies of different kinds for some time. Of course there is a change in the distribution of real income in favor of entrepreneurs during the period of excess demand, followed by a reduction in profits as labor negotiates cost of living adjustments and catches up, but this is a dynamic effect that any policy must take into account.

The formation of a National Commission on Productivity is certainly a step in the right direction, for increases in productivity will move the modified Phillips curve to the left. Notice the 1970 observation in Figure 1, a year during which productivity grew at only 1 percent and this, combined with 1969's price increases, held the Phillips curve to the right. Then notice the 1971 objective, based on an increase in productivity closer to the more normal rate of 3.2 percent. Increasing productivity means that for any given rate of price increases, there need be less unemployment. The commission should be assigned the task of developing appropriate norms for noninflationary price and wage behavior. But since its responsibility is broader than this, the final responsibility for a price-incomes policy should rest with the Council of Economic Advisers.

New Opportunities for Productivity

Important opportunities for maintaining high rates of growth in productivity lie in the recognition that investment in human capital contributes to productivity and long-run growth. There are other well-known ways of increasing productivity: for example, avoiding recessions, which underutilize plant capacity and white-collar workers, and lead to low investment in new technology; reducing tariffs; reducing by antitrust action barriers to entry into industries; and organizing firms and industries more efficiently. But awareness of the opportunities that exist to increase productivity by investing in human resources is new. Economic research is now flourishing on the connection between investment in education, on-the-job training, health, prisoner rehabilitation, job mobility and productivity in later life. Such investment increases productivity not just in terms of physical output but also in terms of the quality of human life.

Sweden offers an example of a country that through its various social welfare programs has had a very high rate of public investment in human resources accompanied by a vigorous policy of encouraging job mobility. The Swedish economy has been at full employment throughout most of the postwar years, with a pattern of price changes similar to that in the United States, but with a more rapid rate of real economic growth. This faster growth may be partly the result of Sweden's investment in human resources, which allows people to become more productive and encourages more effective utilization of their skills.

Defense Cuts

The cost of the war in Southeast Asia has been estimated at $30 billion a year. There is evidence that expenditures on nondefense public goods are normally curtailed and domestic needs deferred during wars. But it has also been shown that these needs are typically met when the war ends, and many have hoped that the withdrawal from Vietnam would release funds to meet these needs. Yet the budget for fiscal 1972 provides for a remarkably steady outlay compared to fiscal 1971 for military operation and maintenance ($20 billion), military personnel ($20 billion plus $2.4 billion for pay raises), and procurement ($17.9 billion). The defense budget, which reached a peak of $80 billion in fiscal 1970, was cut temporarily by $4 billion in fiscal 1971, and is now budgeted to return to $77.5 billion in the new fiscal year. This cut, together with the dropping of the supersonic transport (SST) led to some temporary unemployment in the West Coast aerospace industry. But the expiration of the surtax on June 30, 1970 left enough purchasing power in consumers' hands to more than compensate for the defense cut. Purchasing power will also be increased by the increase in the standard income tax deduction for 1972 that was part of the tax reform measure passed by Congress in 1969. Thus, the decrease in spending on the war is being offset partly by tax cuts and partly shifted to other defense purposes. And while the decrease in war spending will not lead to unemployment, at the moment it is not directly available to help meet long deferred nondefense needs.

Nor does the administration plan to finance these nondefense needs—domestic education, welfare reform, health care, crime prevention, improvement of environmental quality—by increasing the percentage of GNP spent on social programs. The budget projections through 1975 show public expenditures on nondefense needs remaining at approximately their current 29 percent of GNP, a smaller percentage than occurs in any of the major northern European countries.

Instead, budget increases for public expenditures are to be financed by an $11.6 billion deficit in fiscal 1972 and by the projected growth in the economy. But the budget uses a very optimistic projection for growth, showing the GNP at $1,065 billion in 1972, whereas most economists predict it will be about $1,050 billion. (The first-quarter GNP is $1,020 billion, and about $1,030 billion would have been needed to reach $1,065 billion for the year.) The higher forecast is based on a model constructed by Art Laffer, an economist in the Office of Management and the Budget. His model rests on the debatable assumption that the overall impact of changes in budget policy washes out to zero after the first quarter and that the impact from changes in the quantity of money on consumer and investment spending is instantaneous. Such a model is unlikely to be acceptable to

Arthur Burns, chairman of the Federal Reserve Board, or to many other professional economists. But it does fit in with a certain amount of administration wishful thinking. If the forecast is not attained, the deficits planned for fiscal 1971 and 1972 will be larger than expected.

Further defense cuts, therefore, should not be expected to cause unemployment. Instead they may make it possible to satisfy some of the unmet needs for medical care, education and other social programs.

A Balancing Act

Given the state of economic knowledge, there is no reason the economy cannot be close to full employment and to its potential for real growth without inflation. There is no reason the economic impact of Vietnam cannot be phased out smoothly. The administration has quite properly applied tight monetary and fiscal policies to control inflation. But it has failed to use supplementary programs to ease troublesome bottlenecks, and it lacks a comprehensive price-incomes policy that would include efforts to increase productivity. It also kept long-term interest rates high well past the inflationary peak, maintaining excess slack in the construction industry.

The "mid-course correction" scheduled by the administration in January needs to consider the relation between investment in both new physical equipment and human resources and economic growth. Federal expenditure is not inflationary when the economy is as far away from full employment as it currently is, particularly if further demands are not made on a few bottlenecked sectors. The repeated curtailment of Department of Health, Education, and Welfare expenditure, especially when there are important opportunities to raise productivity through applied research and to develop human resources among the unemployed, appears somewhat shortsighted.

It will take a balancing act to return to full employment and to near potential growth immediately without inflation, but the means are available. It would be unfortunate to have to pay the social cost of maintaining a continuing pool of unemployment together with more inflation than is necessary until mid-1972.

Tax Cut in Camelot

Herbert Stein

Between the time of Herbert Hoover and the time of John F. Kennedy a revolution occurred in American fiscal policy. This revolution was the main ingredient in the transition to the "new economics," the coming of which was widely hailed in the early 1960's as the basis for confidence that full employment and steady growth would be maintained in the future.

The act which more than any other came to symbolize the fiscal revolution was the tax reduction of 1964. On John Kennedy's Inauguration Day in January, 1961, the stage was set for that act. The play had been written, a receptive or at least permissive audience was in its seats, and the actors were in the wings. However, the action was not to begin immediately.

The stage setting was the longest, most serious, period of unemployment since the War. It was almost three-and-a-half years since unemployment had been near the conventional 4 percent measure of high employment. After an abortive recovery from the 1958 recession, unemployment had risen again and was nearing 7 percent on Inauguration Day. Moreover, the recent experience led to the fear that the next recovery, when it came, would also stop short of high employment. Two other items were prominent in the scene. First, tax rates were so high, relative to expenditures, that they would yield a large surplus at high employment. There was room to cut taxes or raise expenditures and still retain the expectation that the budget would be in balance when high employment was regained. Second, the balance-of-payments deficit was believed to require high interest rates in the United States to curb the flow of United States funds to the rest of the world. This meant that the 1960 Democratic campaign formula of easy money with budget surpluses could not be relied upon to achieve high employment because that was a formula for low interest rates. The main, if not exclusive, reliance for economic stimulation would have to be placed on fiscal policy.

There were several possible routes to the conclusion that tax reduction was the appropriate act to be performed on this stage. According to conventional "functional finance" principles, the principles to be found in the textbooks of 1961, when unemployment is high the budget deficit should be increased. With the more cautious principles of the Committee for Economic Development, the 1949 Douglas Committee, and others of the postwar consensus, a large full-employment surplus should be reduced to more moderate size in the absence of strong evidence of inflationary danger. And even if fiscal policy was not to be used to manage the level of economic activity, a balance-of-payments deficit might call for a reduction of taxes, relative to expenditures, in order to raise interest rates and curb the flow of dollars abroad. This idea was commonly advanced in European financial circles. Certainly the combination of excessive unemployment, a large high employment surplus, and a balance-of-payments deficit wrote the script for expansive fiscal policy. And most of the informed audience would have agreed that if the play was to be a success, the main act would have to be tax reduction. Moreover, there were many who wanted taxes reduced.

How the country would receive this act—tax reduction—was more in question but should not have been. That part of the labor movement which expressed opinions on national economic policy, as distinguished from labor policy, had been for fiscal expansion for years. A considerable sector of the business and financial community had come to accept compensatory fiscal policy, if not in totally uninhibited form then in the form of balancing the budget at high employment or in some version of cyclical balancing. Even among those who had not come that far, the desire for tax reduction was so great that they were prepared to swallow its unorthodox fiscal trimmings. Much of the Republican national leadership—outside the Congress—accepted the role of expansionist tax reduction, and although they would not cheer a Democratic Administration for doing it they would not make a great issue of it either. Mr. Nixon's approval of tax reduction as an expansive mea-

sure had been clear in 1958 and 1960.

Of course, there would be opposition, especially in the Congress. Much of the opposition would be partisan and ritualistic, and would require a partisan and ritualistic response. Given their standing in Congress, the opponents could delay the outcome. But they could not prevent it, nor punish those who produced it. In the postwar period, there had been several cases in which Congress had tried, successfully and unsuccessfully, to cut taxes against the opposition of the President. There were no cases of Congressional resistance to tax reduction proposed by the administration.

The players who were to perform the tax reduction were President Kennedy and his advisers. We shall turn to them in a moment. But first it must be made clear that although the setting, the script, and the audience were prepared, the performance was not easy or inevitable. In 1492, it was known that the earth was round. Columbus had neither made it round nor discovered its shape. Others had made long ocean voyages before him, and some, it would appear, had been to America. But it was not inevitable that Columbus should go to America in 1492, and the fact that the times were ripe does not detract from the performance. Decisions still had to be made, and they required courage.

Did the Plot Call for a Tax Cut?

The Kennedy Administration could not be sure that the conditions called for a tax cut according to their own guidebook. By early 1961, the appraisal of the economic situation as one of persistent sluggishness, and not merely transitory recession, was a common one. But this was an economic forecast like many others, and it could be wrong. If it were wrong, a large tax cut might only open the way for the return of inflation. The idea that the balance-of-payments deficit called for reducing taxes rather than balancing the budget was also common. But there was an opposing view that the first essential was to reassure our foreign creditors by pursuing a sound fiscal policy.

Moreover, aside from its appraisal of the economic situation, the administration was not sure that tax-cutting was the role it had been chosen to play. Kennedy, in his inaugural address, had called upon the nation for sacrifice, and this seemed to him inconsistent with tax reduction. In other and perhaps less romantic terms, the administration had promised to improve the nation's educational system, to provide better medical care for the aged, to rebuild the cities, and to do many other things that would cost money. It had promised to accelerate growth, and the prevailing view was that more growth required budget surpluses. There was a long-standing Democratic interest in tax reform to close loopholes. All of these seemed incompatible with tax reduction. To start on the tax-reduction road might keep the administration from reaching more important goals.

Probably most important, the administration could not be sure of the political consequences of cutting taxes when the budget was in deficit. "Fiscal responsibility," symbolized by a balanced budget, had been a commonly used term in the 1960 election campaign, as in previous campaigns for thirty years. The fact that fiscal responsibility was considered to be the property of the Republicans had not prevented the Democrats from winning six of the last eight Presidential elections and thirteen of the last fifteen Congressional elections. Perhaps the public's affection for budget-balancing did not run very deep. But it was something for a President, especially a Democrat, to think about.

By 1961, thirty years of experience, analysis, and discussion had made a tax reduction in the conditions then prevailing not only an available course but a probable one. But the action still had to be taken, and knowing that it could and should be done was different from doing it.

The Pre-Inauguration Kennedy

The most important thing about Kennedy's ideas on fiscal policy before he became President is that they were lightly held. Kennedy has been called the first modern economist in the American Presidency. This may have been true in 1963, but it was not true on Inauguration Day. At that time, Kennedy's fiscal thinking was conventional. He believed in budget-balancing. Although he was aware of circumstances in which the budget could not or should not be balanced, he preferred a balanced budget, being in this respect like most other people but unlike modern economists. But if he brought into the White House no very sophisticated or systematic ideas about compensatory fiscal policy, neither did he bring with him any deep intellectual or emotional commitment to the old ideas. This was partly a matter of his youth. He was not the first Keynesian President on Inauguration Day, but he was the first who was not a pre-Keynesian—the first who had passed the majority of his life in the post-Keynesian world where the old orthodoxy was giving way to the new. This characteristic he shared with his contemporaries. But he had, in addition, special characteristics that helped prepare him to accept the new economics he did not yet know. The son of an extremely wealthy, urban, Catholic family was unlikely to confuse personal budget-balancing with financial acumen or financial acumen with moral virtue. Moreover, there was in his home enough familiarity with the banking and financial community to reveal that its financial precepts were not necessarily Holy Writ. His one course in economics at Harvard had been modern, i.e., post-Keynesian, and although it left no affirmative impression on him, it did nothing to inhibit him from later looking at fiscal policy in a functional way.

Men of an earlier generation of different background, like Eisenhower, could be taught not to make a fetish of balancing the budget, and with strong advice and in clear situations would make fiscal decisions that violated the traditional rules of sound finance. But they could never get over a feeling of discomfort about this, and when there was any reasonable economic case for doing so would lean toward balancing the budget. Moreover, their spontaneous talk, free of speech-writers, would have a much more conventional cast than their actions. Whatever their course, they would prefer to sail under the traditional colors, not simply as a political stratagem but because they found those colors more congenial.

Kennedy Acts Quickly and Surely

Such a person in a position of responsibility would probably have come to tax reduction if confronted with the problems of 1961-1963. But a person like Kennedy, with less firm attachment to the older ideas, would come to the tax cut more surely and quickly.

Kennedy was also free of older ideas of a different kind—in this case traditional, liberal, Democratic ideas. He was not shocked by the fact that some people were very wealthy, or even by the fact that some of them managed, through various tax loopholes, to escape paying very much tax. He was not likely to let a functional fiscal policy for economic expansion get permanently entangled with antirich and anticorporation reformism and thereby alienate the people whose testimony to the soundness of his policy he needed. Unlike Roosevelt, he would not make his program of recovery carry too much burden of reform.

Kennedy's record as a Congressman showed no firm ideas about national fiscal policy and little interest in the subject. When Senator Douglas made his first effort in 1958 to enact an antirecession tax cut, Senator Kennedy voted against it. A few months later, partly on the advice of Professor Seymour Harris of Harvard, he voted for Douglas' second tax-cut proposal—which also failed. Later in his term, Kennedy obtained appointment to the Joint Economic Committee, the Congress' great seminar on fiscal policy, but he did not attend its meetings.

Kennedy campaigned in 1960 as a fiscal conservative. He did not match Roosevelt's 1932 Pittsburgh speech in which the Democratic candidate attempted to take the mantle of sound finance away from Herbert Hoover, but at least he was careful not to arouse conservative sensibilities. In a debate during the West Virginia primary campaign, on May 4, 1960, Senator Humphrey came out for raising income-tax exemptions from $600 to $800 per person. Kennedy replied that he couldn't go around the country urging increased expenditure programs and also say that he was for reducing income taxes that year. "And I don't think, therefore, that at the present time until the economy is moved up, I think it's going to be impossible to reduce income taxes." This exchange prompted Arthur Krock to say, in *The New York Times,* "To those who have carefully noted the public records of the Senators there could have been no surprise in yesterday's evidence that Kennedy is more of a fiscal conservative and is less special-group minded than Humphrey."

The Democratic platform on which Kennedy ran was expansive in monetary policy and restrained in fiscal policy:

> We Democrats believe that our economy can and must grow at an average rate of 5 percent annually, almost twice as fast as our average rate since 1953. We pledge ourselves to policies that will achieve this goal without inflation.
>
> As the first step in speeding economic growth, a Democratic President will put an end to the present high-interest, tight-money policy.

Among the ways to assure that the goal would be achieved without inflation was "budget surpluses in times of high employment."

The campaign discussions on both sides were marked by confusion between the problem of growth, meaning the problem of the rate at which the potential output of the economy rises, and the problem of full employment, meaning the problem of keeping actual output close to its potential. The Democrats seemed to be promising not only to get actual output up to its potential but also to make the potential rise more rapidly than its historical average. That is what the 5 percent goal meant. But the statistics they used to demonstrate the poor performance of the Eisenhower Administration reflected failure to keep output at its potential level, and the remedies they proposed also related mainly to this problem.

In any case, neither the platform nor Kennedy's campaign speeches suggested that Eisenhower's fiscal policy had been too restrictive, in the sense of having too large surpluses, or that the Democrats would behave differently in that respect. Their main fiscal promise was that they were going to spend more. But this spending had its intellectual rationale in Galbraith, rather than in Keynes. That is, it was spending that would divert a larger part of the national output to public purposes from private purposes—not spending that would be undertaken to compensate for a deficiency in private demand and to bring about full employment. Its motivation was not that private spending was inadequate in amount, but that much of it was unworthy in quality.

Both the platform and Kennedy were firm in declaring an intention to finance the enlarged government expenditures within the limits of a balanced budget. After pointing to the needs for larger public programs, the platform said, "We believe, moreover, that except in periods of recession or national emergency, these needs can be met with a balanced budget, with no increase in present tax rates, and with some surplus for the gradual reduction of our national debt. However, the Democrats said that they were prepared to raise taxes if necessary.

Kennedy was even more cautious about the conditions in which a deficit might be justified. They were not merely a "national emergency" but a "grave national emergency" and not merely a "recession" but a "serious recession." However, he held out no promise of debt reduction—at least not in 1961, 1962 or 1963.

The idea of reducing taxes in a recession came up in the October 7, 1960 television debate between the candidates. Mr. Nixon was asked his opinion about what to do in a recession. He mentioned credit expansion as the first move, and then said:

> In addition to that, if we do get into a recessionary period we should move on the part of the economy which is represented by the private sector—and I mean stimulate that part of the economy that can create jobs—the private sector of the economy. This means through tax reform and if necessary tax cuts that will stimulate more jobs.

Asked the same question, Kennedy took the opportunity to give his standard talk against hard money and then turned to fiscal policy:

> If we move into a recession in '61 then I would agree that we have to put more money into the economy, and it can be done by either of the two methods discussed. One is by a program such as aid to education, the other would be to make a judgment of what's the more effective tax program to stimulate our economy.

Kennedy's most developed formulation of a fiscal policy was presented near the end of the campaign, on October 30, in a statement about the international position of the dollar. This statement was intended to assure foreign holders of dollars that the election of Kennedy would not lead to a depreciation of the currency, and also to assure the American business and financial community on the same point. He said:

> First, we are pledged to maintain a balanced budget except in times of national emergency or severe recession. Furthermore, we will seek to maintain a budget surplus in times of prosperity as a brake on inflationary forces. Through the vigorous use of fiscal policies to help con-

trol inflation we will be able to lessen reliance on restrictive monetary policies which hamper growth.

Wherever we are certain that tax revision—including accelerated depreciation—will stimulate investment in new plant and equipment, without damage to our principles of equity, we will proceed with such revision.

We will also carefully examine our entire tax structure in order to close loopholes which are unnecessarily depriving the Government of needed tax revenue, and in order to develop tax policies which will stimulate growth.

In a few words, the Kennedy economics of 1960 was increased expenditures for defense and for public services, financed within a budget that would be balanced in prosperity out of the growing yield of the existing tax system with higher taxes if necessary, and monetary expansion to keep the economy operating close to its rising potential.

Platforms and campaign speeches are notoriously poor indicators of what a candidate thinks or of what he will do if elected. The 1960 program might have been just an election tactic—easy money for the populists, balanced budgets for the conservatives, and more public benefits for everyone. But there is no reason to doubt the sincerity of his belief in the budget-balancing part of the program. And indeed, it would have been most surprising if he had thought anything different in 1960, because the program happened to be not only the old conventional wisdom of Democratic politicians but also the new conventional wisdom of the Democratic intellectuals. For several years, the Joint Economic Committee, on the advice of leading economists, had been promoting the idea of easier money to stimulate the economy, coupled with a budget surplus to prevent inflation and to add to the savings available. This was considered the path to more rapid growth. And the idea that the country badly needed more government spending had been given a new rationale in John Kenneth Galbraith's *The Affluent Society*, one of the most influential economics books of the postwar period.

Some of these ideas were already, during the campaign, in the process of changing. First, it was coming to be realized that the budget already had a very large implicit surplus—would yield a large surplus at high employment—so that there was no need to drive for more fiscal restraint. Second, the persistence of the balance-of-payments problem was suggesting that the easy-money part of the fiscal-monetary program was not timely. Third, the thought was spreading that we were not simply going through another recession but were in a period of persistent stagnation, so that the problem of getting our potential output converted into actual output took precedence over the problem of choosing between public and private use of the output. This appraisal of the situation was to be important when Kennedy took office, but it came too late to influence Kennedy before the election.

Supporting Players—The Kennedy Economists

Kennedy's economists did not dictate either his ideas or his actions in the field of fiscal policy. Nevertheless, he was more influenced by professional economists than his predecessors had been. In part, this was simply the continuation of a rising trend of influence that dated back to Roosevelt and his Brain Trust and ran through the Truman-Keyserling and Eisenhower-Burns relationships. The trend of economists' influence was rising anyway, but it made a leap upward with the Kennedy Administration. Kennedy was especially prepared to accept new ideas. Moreover, he had, for a President, an unusual interest in abstract thinking, read a great deal, enjoyed the company of intellectuals, and was for these reasons open to education by economists.

The economists in turn had exceptional qualities. They were, for one thing, extremely self-confident. Of course, anyone who becomes adviser to a President is likely to be self-confident, but there are degrees of this. The Kennedy economists were, in the main, of that generation which had been most moved intellectually and emotionally by Keynes' *General Theory*. They were neither so old as to have learned it grudgingly and with qualifications nor so young as to have first met it as an already well-established doctrine. They had enlisted as foot soldiers in the Keynesian army at the beginning and risen through the ranks to become marshals. The Keynesian movement had swept economics. Although the meaning of Keynesianism as a doctrine had changed substantially, the esprit de corps of the school remained. Now its leaders were coming to Washington, with this victory behind them, to practice what they had been teaching. They had no reason to doubt that they knew what to do.

This self-confidence helped to make them persuasive with the President. They did not regard their role, however, as merely advising the President. Their role was to bring about the policies they regarded as correct, as long as the issue had not been foreclosed by a decision of the President. They were assiduous in mobilizing support for their views, inside and outside the government, in order to increase the likelihood that the President's decision would be their decision. Once the President's decision was made they were equally vigorous in trying to sell it to the country. In these efforts they were assisted by the presence of like-minded economists in other government agencies, on the staffs of Congressional committees, and to some extent in the press and in organizations of labor and business.

Of course, a President may be influenced by his advisers, but he also chooses his advisers. There is, thus, always some uncertainty about how far the advisers are to be regarded as exerting an independent influence. One of Kennedy's most important advisers, Paul A. Samuelson, put the question this way: "The leaders of this world may seem to be led around through the nose by their economist advisers. But who is pulling and who is pushing? And note this: He who picks his own doctor from an array of competing doctors is in a real sense his own doctor. The Prince often gets to hear what he wants to hear."

The key words here are "array of competing doctors." As far as ideas on fiscal policy were concerned, Kennedy did not choose from an array of competing doctors; he chose from an array of doctors whose ideas were basically the same. If he had chosen six American economists at random, the odds were high that he would have obtained five with the ideas on fiscal policy that his advisers actually had, because those ideas were shared by almost all economists in 1960. As Walter W. Heller later said: "Thus the rationale of the 1964 tax-cut proposal came straight out of the country's postwar economics textbooks." His economic advisers were eminent expositors of the standard economics of their time. They had done much to make it the standard economics. For example, the man who might be regarded as their intellectual leader, Paul A. Samuelson, was also the author of the most popular economics textbook of the postwar period. Kennedy did not choose his advisers to advocate and practice a particular brand of fiscal policy upon which he had already determined. He chose them as representative of the economics of his time, and having done that, he exposed his policy to influence by the economics of that time.

In the fall of 1958, Senator Kennedy began to expand his staff in preparation for the race for the 1960 nomination. Theodore C. Sorensen wrote: "At the same time, with the help of Professor Earl Latham of Amherst College and a graduate student in Cambridge, I initiated at the Senator's request and in his name an informal committee to tap the ideas and information of scholars and thinkers in Massachusetts and elsewhere. Drawn primarily from the Harvard and Massachusetts Institute of Technology faculties, with a smattering of names from other schools and professions, the members of our 'Academic Advisory Committee' held their first organizational meeting with me at the Hotel Commander in Cambridge on December 3, 1958." The economists in this group who later became advisers on fiscal policy to President Kennedy were John Kenneth Galbraith and Seymour Harris, of Harvard, Paul A. Samuelson, of MIT, and James Tobin, of Yale.

Role of the Academic Advisory Committee

What was expected from this committee was more than information and ideas. As Sorensen wrote:

No announcement was made at the time about the committee's formation, but its very existence, when known, helped recruit Kennedy supporters in the liberal intellectual "community" who had leaned to Stevenson or Humphrey. This was in part its purpose, for the liberal intellectuals, with few delegates but many prestigious and articulate voices, could be a formidable foe, as Barkley and Kefauver had learned. Suspicious of Kennedy's father, religion and supposed McCarthy history, they were in these pre-1960 days held in the Stevenson camp by Eleanor Roosevelt and others. Kennedy's "academic advisers" formed an important beachhead on this front.

The Kennedy economists, like most American economists of 1960, believed that the chief economic problem of the country was to achieve and maintain high and rapidly rising total output. That is, the problem was full employment and economic growth. The keys to the management of that problem were fiscal policy and monetary policy, with fiscal policy being the senior partner in the combination. Full employment, or economic stabilization, and economic growth were the main objectives and guides of fiscal policy; budget-balancing was an irrelevancy. The economy was not in need of any basic structural reform, of the character of the National Recovery Act, French planning, or nationalization of industry. In general, the "free market" worked well and was not to be tampered with, but particular issues of government intervention in the market must be considered on their merits and without prejudice. Steps to make the distribution of income more nearly equal were good but they were not the urgent need and not the main road to improving the economic condition of the mass of the population, and they had to be evaluated with due regard for their effects on economic growth.

This set of ideas, which not only justified the big tax cut but also made it the centerpiece of Kennedy's entire economic policy, was the standard economics of 1960. It was Keynesian, but much modified from the American Keynesianism of 1946. What Milton Friedman said in 1966 was already true in 1960: "We are all Keynesians now and nobody is any longer a Keynesian." What had produced this change was the agreement by all parties that both monetary policy and fiscal policy could increasingly affect total spending and the level of total money income. Increasingly after 1951, monetary policy had been reincorporated into Keynesian thinking. Once this happened, the distinction between Keynesians and non-Keynesians ceased to be significant.

Three Ways Kennedy Economic Cast Differed

Within this general consensus of economists there were, of course, differences of emphasis and of degree. Three points distinguished the Kennedy economists from the Eisenhower economists and from a probably small minority of economists in the 1960's.

1. The Kennedy economists were less concerned with the problem of inflation than the Eisenhower economists, to say nothing of Eisenhower himself. Samuelson had foreseen this in 1956 in discussing the economics of Eisenhower:

> I should like to put forward the hypothesis that the relatively minor economic differences between the Republicans and Democrats during 1953-56 has been in the nature of a lucky accident. For reasons that will not necessarily be relevant in the future, *we have been able since 1951 to have a very high degree of prosperity and also to have stable prices*. The drop in farm and other staple prices made this possible.
>
> In the future the dilemma between very high employment and stable prices is likely to reassert itself with increasing force. Then it will be found that the Republicans do differ from the Democrats in the greater weight that they will give to the goal of maintaining an honest dollar in comparison with the clashing goal of keeping unemployment extremely low.
>
> In this clash of ideologies, social welfare functions and not scientific economic principles must play the decisive role.

Samuelson states the choice in a Democratic way. There is also a scientific problem involved in calculating how much additional unemployment, and for how long, would result from "maintaining an honest dollar." Some who would opt for avoiding inflation would say that in the long run such a policy would cost little, if any, additional unemployment. Nevertheless, it was undoubtedly true that the Kennedy economists attached less value to the avoidance of inflation than the Eisenhower economists did.

2. The Kennedy economists were willing to supplement general fiscal-monetary policy with other measures to loosen the constraints under which these general policies operated in achieving high employment. Specifically, they were prepared to "intervene in the market" to a degree that more conservative economists would not have accepted. If confronted with the dilemma that high employment could not be achieved without inflation, they would not be content to choose one horn or the other of the dilemma. They would want to try to remove the dilemma and alter the terms of choice—in this case, by government action to influence the decisions of individuals, businesses, and labor unions in setting wages and prices. If they found that monetary expansion was limited by the need to keep U.S. interest rates high enough so that money would not flow abroad, they would wish to remove that inhibition also, by selective measures to alter the patterns of interest rates, by placing a tax on lending abroad, or by pressure on U.S. lenders.

This willingness to operate directly upon the market should not be exaggerated. In comparison with standard European or Japanese practice, the interventions the Kennedy economists were prepared to recommend were small. But they were prepared to go further than the Eisenhower economists. As Walter Heller later said, "It is hard to study the modern economics of relative prices, resource allocation, and distribution without developing a healthy respect for the market mechanisms. . . . But I do not carry respect to the point of reverence."

3. The Kennedy economists had a high degree of confidence in their ability to forecast economic fluctuations accurately and to adapt fiscal and monetary policy continuously on the basis of these forecasts in order to achieve economic stability within a narrow range. Lack of such confidence was a major element in the preference displayed in the earlier postwar period by the Committee for Economic Development and others to have a largely passive fiscal policy aimed at minimizing the risk of large errors but not at trying to counter forecast fluctuations unless they were large or foreseen with unusual clarity. Walter Heller's main writing on fiscal policy before he became chairman of the Council of Economic Advisers under Kennedy was an argument against this position. His view then, in 1957, was stated mildly:

> No conclusive evidence is available to prove that forecasting techniques are now a thoroughly reliable basis for discretionary stabilization policy. But many new or improved forecasts of important segments of the economy, such as plant and equipment outlays, are now available. The Council of Economic Advisers does not hesitate to invoke "prospective economic conditions" as a basis for discretionary judgments to hold the line on federal taxes. Qualified observers judge our short-term forecasting record as having operated "not too unsuccessfully" in recent years. Guarded optimism as to the future of economic forecasting seems justified.

After his experience on the Council of Economic Advisers, Heller believed that his "guarded optimism" about forecasting had been confirmed:

> In part, this shift from a more passive to a more active policy has been made possible by steady advances in fact-gathering, forecasting techniques, and business practice. Our statistical net is now spread wider and brings in its catch faster. Forecasting has the benefit of not only more refined, computer-assisted methods, but of improved surveys of consumer and investment intentions.

The Kennedy economists did not come to Washington in January, 1961, with a plan for a large permanent tax cut in their briefcases. This became their program only a year-and-a-half later and was their reaction to the developments and the frustrations of the intervening months. But it was the reaction of men who, because of the attitudes described here, were committed to expansionist policies. They were not afraid of overdoing things, because they were not very worried about inflation; they were willing, if necessary, to intervene in the market to control the consequences of inflation if it should come, and they had great confidence in their ability to foresee how much expansionary policy would be enough but not too much.

The effort to stimulate the economy by fiscal policy, culminating in the 1964 tax cut, was smaller and later than the Kennedy economists would have liked. But the fiscal stimulus would almost certainly have been smaller and later without them. Moreover, while the tax cut was being considered, and after it was adopted, they were the chief interpreters of its significance. If the tax cut was a lesson for the future, it was a lesson first seen through their eyes.

Private Initiative in the 'Great Society'

Norton E. Long

America puts a very high value on achievement. It also puts a very high value on equality. The trouble is that, as with rivals in a Western film, there is constant tension between these values—and often open conflict.

How do we solve, or resolve, this tension? In the past, we kept the areas in which equality dominated separate from those in which achievement (or accumulation) dominated. Citizens were given formal equality in law and government, especially in voting privileges, and accepted inequality in the economy. Everyone's vote was supposed to be equal, but the well-to-do could buy more Buicks, or factories, as rewards for more achievement.

This contrast between the formal equality in the political institutions and the actual inequality in the economy led Marxists and many others to call bourgeois democracy a fraud. Focusing on this disparity, Anatole France made the famous comment:

"The law, in its majestic equality, forbids the rich as well as the poor to sleep under bridges, to beg in the streets, and to steal bread."

But today this picture has been radically altered—by the tremendous increase in the availability and importance of public goods and services (such as schools, libraries, police and fire protection, parks, sanitation). Indeed, one of the main problems of our economy may be how to ensure that achievement is encouraged when so many of the things that men value are supposed to be equally available to all. There is a corollary problem: how to keep an unfair share of the public goods, especially good schooling, from going to the wealthy simply because they do have more economic power.

These considerations go to the heart of policy-making, for—from one point of view—all governments, national and local, are really so many devices and institutions for mobilizing and allocating resources, for determining who gives what and gets what and when. So, in its own way, is the market place of private industry. What mix of governmental and private initiatives is most desirable, therefore, depends upon what we want them to accomplish. And how successful our system is depends upon how nearly we achieve our goals of allocation.

Suburbs, the Reward for Achievement

How will achievement be rewarded and encouraged in a society dominated by equality, where public goods are becoming more and more important? So far, the preferred strategy has been suburbanization. In his own suburb the achiever can get a larger return for his money through better schools and services, and more control over his local government, which tends to be composed of people pretty much like himself. He comes into the central city for work, and occasionally for shopping or entertainment, but otherwise lets its stew in its own social problems.

The metropolitan areas, with their many local governments, have become like so many competing residential hotels, with varying qualities of service and different classes of paying guests; and many local politicians have come to act like hotel keepers—competing for the desirable trade, while trying to make sure that undesirables and deadbeats go elsewhere. Even if the politicians rise a notch above this, property-tax considerations will make them act like real-estate men, trying to keep up the value—and raise the income—of the property.

So the metropolitan area has become a patchwork of independent governments offering a wide variety of goods and permissible uses of land. If you pay your money, and are not from an undesirable minority, you can take your choice.

To some people, this state of affairs appears perfectly sensible. It seems to reflect the pluralism of our society; it seems to rescue some measure of quality, variety, and individuality from mass homogenization. But to others it reverberates with the crack of civic doom: It means the fragmentation of the community, political absenteeism, social irresponsibility, tax dodging, and the ghettoization of the poor and colored. Both views have a measure of truth. And they must be reconciled if equality, quality, and achievement are all to remain in our society.

Nationally, it has become possible and even expedient to pass civil-rights legislation, to try to provide equal opportunity, full employment, and open housing, and to make a pass at ending poverty. But many of those who support these national measures also practice local segregation, and therefore unequal rights to public goods. And this segregation obstructs justice. Housing has come to determine education, education to determine jobs, and jobs income. Income, in turn, is the key to housing, and so on around the tightening circle. For Negroes this democracy of the buck—the "free competitive market"—is nullified by that other capitalist ideal, the right to discriminate.

Fragmentation means unrepresentative local governments. Now, the federal government must work through these local governments, and with private enterprise. Consequently, national legislative ideals are easily gutted by the "realism" of local politics and economics. In urban renewal the poor have been *unhoused* by federal subsidies, and the banks *rehoused* with federal subsidies. Since the mayors act as municipal realtors, they try to use federal aid to get more taxes from their real estate (hence, new bank sites) and to get rid of nonpaying tenants (slum dwellers). Why shouldn't they? Federal bureaucrats and congressmen who want to survive in the political game go along. What is often viewed as cynicism is simply the inevitable result of the way the game is structured and played.

Governments can be organized to reflect narrow and selfish interests, but they can also be compelled to aspire to greatness. At present the nation's metropolises, stricken with fiscal anemia, plagued by social absenteeism, and obstructed by the country-club suburb with its toy government, have necessarily become organized on a dog-eat-dog, devil-take-the-hindmost basis. These metropolitan areas contain the overwhelming bulk of the nation's wealth and human talent—but they do not have the structure, the legal power, or even the coordinated theory needed to mobilize this immense strength and wealth behind a meaningful conception of human community. A Great Society will be forever impossible with this metropolitan disorganization, which substitutes the competition of municipal real-estate operators for responsible politics.

As an essential first step, we must create a single political organization for each of our 200-odd metropolitan areas. No smaller divisions have enough means and potential leaders to tackle the full array of local problems facing us. The radical shakeup needed to provide housing, education, and jobs to all requires local leaders who will face these problems. And they must have enough stature, enough of a following, and enough law and money behind them. The federal government cannot achieve major local changes by fiat. The paratroopers at Little Rock and the marshals at Old Miss could coerce, but not persuade. Without the willing cooperation of local leaders, the federal government is almost like an army of occupation. We must have a national system of able local governments to complement a federal government that responds to the national will. The fragmented metropolis we have now is a shattered mirror, utterly incapable of reflecting great or unified national purpose.

It is not enough to put a governmental superstructure, or regional "authority," on top of our divided local governments. Thus Metropolitan Toronto has an overall success in its public-works program that is worthy of Robert Moses—but it has yet to get beyond bricks and mortar to the more important human problems. New York City, big enough for greatness, verges on bankruptcy—until recently, at least, from a lack of purpose and direction. Metropolitan governments *without access to the ample fiscal resources within them* become hardly more than outsized special districts. Great leaders rise where there are great problems, *and* the means and power to solve them. The United States has settlements with untold richness in human talent and material resources. So far they are no more than census statistics with traffic problems, crime, slums, downtown-business districts, and heaps of buildings—without identity, purpose, or direction.

But, again, if fragmentation is a danger, so is homogenization. Metropolitan areas are the only units smaller than states that are nonetheless large enough to have the resources necessary for good government and equal opportunity. But they can also become so many shambling New Yorks, where quality is lost in sodden, equalized mediocrity. Equality of opportunity doesn't have to lead to this—but it can. We can level down as well as up, and wipe out our diversity.

What we must do is look to our principles and priorities. It was inevitable that, when public goods be-

came more and more important in our lives, a powerful drive should develop to maintain the same inequalities in the public sector that there are in the private sector. After all, if parents can buy better food and toys for their children, why should they not also be able to buy safer streets and, especially, better schooling?

But public goods are *not* simply another form of private goods. All children may not be entitled to the best clothes or bicycles, but they *are* entitled to an equal chance at a better life. And this is the nub of the matter: Schools have become gatekeepers to jobs, careers, and opportunities. And when suburbanites demand superior schools for their children, they are demanding superior opportunities and lives for them as well.

Like the English, we have been trying to move from a plutocracy to a meritocracy through education, so that the most able—no matter what their backgrounds—can rise in the social scale. But what this has meant, by and large, is something like scholarships for poor bright boys to go to Oxford and Harvard. The impact of such programs on the opportunities in general is less than spectacular. It does take some of the curse off crass plutocracy, and—despite the anguish of old grads—places some limitation on the ability of the well-heeled to buy success for their children. But it is not enough.

Education in the metropolitan areas is crucial for their future. A Great Society must make full use of its human resources—and it can do this only by improving both education and motivation. It is urgent that we de-ghettoize and improve the metropolitan area's central city. But this, too, cannot be enough—because the central city simply does not have the resources, human and fiscal, to meet its problems. A central city is radically different from a metropolitan area, and the two can never be the same (unless the white middle class should flee the entire metropolitan area—an utterly unlikely possibility). There must be a better, and more democratic, way to achieve quality education than by concentrating it in élite neighborhoods and élite schools A school system based on the resources of an entire metropolitan area might, like a great state university, be able to achieve quality, and diversity as well.

After quality education has been achieved, what then? Education becomes a cruel farce if there are no jobs for the graduates. The mockery and tragedy of much education in arts, music, and other fields comes from the lack of opportunity for adult careers, even when there is no discrimination. Broad avocational interests are fine, but they are not substitutes for jobs.

Now, the number and kinds of jobs are generally limited to what is available within the narrow limits of the private sector. Both the private *and* public sectors must be studied carefully to see whether they can provide jobs and careers for everyone; and, of equal importance, whether this employment makes meaningful use of talent. We need "spiritual" full employment, as well as physical. All of this will require a new system of national, state, and local cooperation and priorities.

The fact is that desirable social goals are often most effectively advanced by both private and public means. Even the Communist countries have begun to recognize the extraordinary advantages of individual and group initiatives, and the deadening routine of hide-bound bureaucracy. Centralized bureaucracies of any kind can become deadly. It is even possible that the state university system of California, one of the outstanding accomplishments of our states, may degenerate into a paper-shuffling civil service as low in morale and originality as the New York City school system. This eventuality is built into the dynamics of centralized administration. The space program and the armed forces have found that they can get much work—and, more important, much-needed new thinking—done for them by the unfettered energies of independent organizations. On the other hand, the Tennessee Valley Authority has provided a public yardstick for private initiative in this country—T.V.A.'s electricity rates can be compared with those of private companies. In this connection, private colleges and universities are providing a yardstick for their state-run counterparts.

The old socialist-capitalist dichotomy of public versus private enterprise is giving way to a realization that we need, and have, a variety of means for achieving desired ends. The profit system is one of the best systems ever evolved for getting unstructured cooperation between people, and it is an essential device for determining costs even in socialist systems. The public responsibility, then, becomes one of creating a general program of goals, and goal supports, that will allow the fullest use of whatever means are best for their attainment. Space is being explored through private, public, and academic cooperation; full employment could be achieved through the same model.

Full employment and the fuller use of talent means not only more jobs for people, but new roles—roles that give people more identity, more meaningful stakes in society. Not least among the needed roles are those of vital neighborhood "actors" and leaders, who can transform neighborhoods into living subcommunities. For instance, the "participant democracy" envisaged by the poverty program would provide such roles, and reduce the pervasive feelings of powerlessness and alienation among slum dwellers. Organized pressure, under competent leaders, has been a historic method for giving people a stake in society and improving their lot.

Under the old Homesteading Act, it was national policy to give farms to those who would make use of the property. This settled the frontier. On the urban frontier we need a similar device—to turn those with no stake in the community into property owners with an equity and interest in their neighborhoods. The Veterans Administration program gave servicemen housing with no down payments and with long-term mortgages. We can do the same in our slums for those who will maintain their own housing and neighborhoods, whether they own homes or cooperative apartments.

For low-income people, ownership is one of the most powerful socializers. The excess costs of maintenance in public housing could be reduced if tenants became owners, and ownership had been earned in a fashion similar to the way the homesteaders earned their farms. Enough new property-owners could transform the gray areas. These men, too, would be the potential neighborhood leaders through whom the "human renewal" that is supposed to accompany urban renewal can become more than an empty phrase.

In the next 20 years, Chicago will add to its population a city the size of Detroit, almost all of it outside the present city limits. From the burgeoning tangle of new and of old jurisdictions, spawned by urban developers, a new urban nation is rising from the old. While most of our attention and funds go into a belated attempt to do something about our central cities, only minor concern and resources are devoted to trying to make sense out of the new America. A few—but only a few—new approaches, like the projected Oakland East and the already building Reston, show how these planned communities could be properly developed.

The poor cannot break the vicious circle of poor housing and poor schools by themselves. New towns, planned communities, are another important way to see that segregation and poverty do not wall them away from the quality public goods.

We are interested in leveling up, and preventing leveling down. We know that segregation promotes the perpetuation of the culture of poverty. This means, at the least, that the poor must have an opportunity to live with the more prosperous in such a way that good neighborhoods will be kept up, that the poor will be enriched, and that nobody will be impoverished.

This leveling up cannot be done piecemeal, with segregated classes, races, or political groups. It cannot be done if every man is left to seek security for himself—this produces only segregation by flight, and racially unbalanced neighborhoods. In our new towns, we need to work out a pattern that will allow the middle class to enjoy good neighborhoods and good schools *without* segregation. If the poor and the black are also to have access to these goods, they must be spread around so as not to seriously jeopardize current standards. For this, we cannot rely either on the real-estate market or the fragmented local political jurisdictions. Only in the well-organized metropolitan areas can a Great Society fully employ the human resources of an urban civilization; only with federal funds and insurance can large-scale new town and tract developments be encouraged and controlled.

And beyond this—and before this—we must have a coherent idea of what the Great Society should be, and do—what our goals are, and how we may best mobilize the means and talents to achieve them.

part five

American Justice as Viewed from the Bottom

Essays in this Part have two common themes. The first is methodological. There has been a very rapidly growing literature on the American legal system which, largely abandoning the old focus on the Supreme Court's interpretations of public law "at the top," approaches its subject in terms of concrete effects on people. To a large extent, this literature is grounded in empirical field work, in which survey analysis plays a very large role. The essays by Jacob, Nagel, Lerman, Ennis, Reiss, and Davis all explicitly rely, to a greater or lesser extent, on survey questionnaires and interviews on the one hand, or quantitative analysis of court inputs and outputs on the other. The second major theme here is that of criticism of American justice on two primary grounds: first, that it is strongly skewed, from police encounters to court decisions, against the poor and the deprived; and second, that it is far behind the times in its failure to incorporate relevant findings of the social sciences in its doctrines and processes.

There is no doubt that much of the criticism is justified. Judge Bazelon's discussion of the courts failure to rethink the ancient M'Naghten rule concerning insanity reveals with particular acuity the extreme slowness of the courts in "receiving" relevant twentieth-century psychiatric findings. Here, as in the case of the Commissions, the observer detects a kind of "Alice in Wonderland" situation. As long ago as 1897, Justice Holmes perceived that the day of narrow legalism unmediated by a sociological sense, was—or should be—drawing to a close. As he observed in his lecture, "The Path of the Law": "For the rational study of the law the black-letter man may be the man of the present, but the man of the future is the man of statistics and the master of economics. It is revolting to have no better reason for a rule of law than that it was laid down in the time of Henry IV. It is still more revolting if the grounds upon which it was laid down have vanished long since, and the rule simply persists from blind imitation of the past." It is precisely this "blind imitation" which Judge Bazelon criticizes in the form of continuing judicial adherence to the M'Naghten rule. So too, Justice Brandeis at length introduced the Supreme Court to a kind of brief which dealt primarily not with doctrinal constructs dear to the heart of "black-letter" lawyers and judges but with social and economic *facts;* in response, the Court at length developed doctrine on the basis of the Brandeis brief in the landmark case, *Muller v. Oregon,* 248 U.S. 412 (1908). Yet the deep reluctance of courts to incorporate social-science findings in their evolution of doctrine persists to this day, despite—or because of?—the Supreme Court's reference to them in the 1954 *Segregation Cases.* Similar factors obtain in the area of child convicts, who are deprived of liberty for behavior which would not be criminally actionable if they were adults. Here we find a judicial unwillingness to accept what must be one of the most basic findings of "forensic sociology": that family units should be kept intact if at all possible, and that breaking them up should be a *last* resort only.

There is likewise no doubt that the administration of justice in the United States tends to be skewed from beginning to end against the poorer people. Such a finding should not occasion surprise, for it is important to understand that in all organized societies the legal system and its administration are essential tools of social and indeed political control. In "class societies" where the ownership of the means of production is mostly in private hands, the same kinds of class biases which exist in political-elite recruitment, political participation, legislative outcomes, and other elements of the political system can be found in the administration of justice as well.

Yet there are at least three rejoinders which can be made to the critical emphasis in this Part. First, judicial decisions over the past forty years have considerably upgraded the lot of the poor and the otherwise disadvantaged in significant ways. The Supreme Court has held over the past decade that all persons charged with a felony are entitled to a formal legal representation by the state if they are too poor to hire their own attorneys; that there are strong procedural hurdles which the prosecution must overcome before confessions can be introduced in court proceedings; and, most recently and spectacularly, that the death penalty as currently operative in state laws is unconstitutional. Nor does this by any means exhaust the list of juridical defenses raised by the Court to protect the rights of arrestees and defendants in criminal proceedings. No one could seriously suppose that such decisions have produced the millennium or that the motto on the Supreme Court building, "Equal Justice Under Law," has been achieved. But anyone who doubts that there has been immense improvement in procedural safeguards for those caught in the toils of the law should read cases such as *Powell v. Alabama* (287 U.S. 45, 1932), involving the notorious trial of the "Scottsboro boys," or *Chambers v. Florida* (309 U.S. 227, 1940), involving third-degree torture to extort a confession from a defendant; he or she can then reflect on what legal practice was like before those cases were handed down, and what it is like now.

The second rejoinder is raised by Judge Bazelon himself. If courts have been slow to adopt relevant social-science findings, a major reason has been what might be called an "interface problem" in which the social scientists are often at fault. Lawyers and judges know what "the law" is; psychiatrists and other social scientists, granted the division of social labor, generally do not. The latter often fail their obligations to the court by attempting on the one hand to be judge, jury, and expert rolled into one, *i.e.*, attempting to go far beyond their own professional competence; on the other, they often give conclusions which are narrowly diagnostic.

As Bazelon points out, one reason why legal rules like M'Naghten survive is that the social sciences are studded with ambiguities. The old question arises: is it a problem of "insufficient knowledge," or is it impossible to adduce knowledge with the precision which has the power to persuade courts and other policy-makers? In any event, the Judge is quite right in pointing out that, at present, social science is sufficiently developed to cast critical—often devastating—light upon the imperfections of present practice, but not sufficiently developed to provide anything approximating "unique solutions" to the concrete problems which those charged with the administration of justice must resolve. The ultimate issue here is exactly what the Judge says it is: society will not divert enough of its resources to mount the kind of massive study effort needed to come closer to the goal of precise expert inputs involving those charged with crime. As matters now stand in the run-of-mine cases involving persons charged with what the law defines as criminal acts, class bias is reinforced both by the usual perfunctory-diagnostic approach of experts to testimony in such matters as those involving insanity, and by the larger-scale judicial reluctance to use social-science findings to modify doctrine.

An additional point concerns the balance between the

rights of the accused and the "rights of society." Every complex, organized society tends to regard certain acts by individuals as criminal: murder, burglary, arson, rape, and so on. In one form or another, it punishes those found guilty accordingly. Social control of antisocial deviant behavior is surely involved as a value here; so is a felt need for revenge against the criminal, as Ennis points out. The latter may strike the well-brought-up liberal as disquietingly primitive, but then crime, particularly violent crime, is pretty primitive too, as Davis' sensational essay on sexual assaults in prisons makes bluntly clear. The ideal, of course, is the elimination of such crime; but alas, not even in the U.S.S.R., in the country of the "new Soviet man," has crime disappeared as its founders prophesied more than fifty years ago.

Still less so in the United States! If we wish to obtain some sense of the power of "law and order" as an issue for Middle Americans—and many others besides—we must begin with two simple but profoundly distressing realities. First, there is much more crime, and more violent crime, in the United States than in any other supposedly advanced industrial society, whatever its social system may be. If we take the homicide rates in 1966 as a case in point, we find that, per 100,000 people, they were 6.0 in the United States, 2.3 in Finland, 1.9 in Hungary, 1.5 in Australia, and 1.3 in neighboring Canada, and 0.7 in England and Wales. Neither density of population nor frontier traditions as such have much to do with such comparisons: it is far safer to walk the streets of Tokyo or London at night than those of New York or Washington; and both Australia and Canada have, with the United States, very recent frontier traditions. The second reality is that, by all measures available to us, all major kinds of crime have increased sharply in this country over the past decade. There is far more of it than there used to be, and the problem of law and order, correspondingly, is by no means simply the artifact of fevered right-wing imaginations. Property "rip-offs" have arisen particularly rapidly, in direct proportion to the epidemic of drug abuse which has swept the United States during the past decade: it costs a lot more to support a "habit" than anyone is likely to make from honest labor.

In *The Unheavenly City,* Banfield makes a great deal of the argument that a substantial part of the poor (especially, one assumes, the black poor) are "lower class" in culture and hence are not likely to be reached effectively by "do-good" government programs to improve their lot. As defined by Banfield, such people bear a close similarity to the class which Marx and Engels described in the *Communist Manifesto* as the *Lumpenproletariat,* "the 'danger-

ous class', the social scum, that passively rotting mass thrown off by the lowest layers of the old society. . . ." But Banfield fails to ask an essential question: why is it that the United States has incomparably the largest such class to be found in any modern industrial society? Why are there—both absolutely and relatively—vastly more "lower class" people in Philadelphia than in Copenhagen, in New York than in London?

Part of the clue to this rests in the fact that violent crime has tended to be concentrated among population strata drawn from the most oppressive feudal-peasant, "underdeveloped" social backgrounds, from Sicilian *mafiosi* to ex-Southern blacks—and ex-Southern whites for that matter. Beyond this, however, it seems clear that there must be some element or elements specific to the American social system itself which explain the existence of what Gunnar Myrdal has called the most disorganized social infrastructure to be found anywhere in the Western world. In my own view, the basic elements involved are several: they include the effects of racial discrimination; the pervasiveness of the American achievement ethic which leaves little ground for the development of disciplined collectivist working-class subcultures and perspectives on society and politics; and the consequent failure of a disciplined, solidaristic working-class political movement to develop in the United States. The failure of political Socialism to emerge as a viable force in this country has always been viewed by consensus theorists as one of the most positive and celebrated features of American politics, but it has worked its dialectically opposite effect: the fragmentation of non-bourgeois elements in the social system has brought with it the largest volume of crimes against persons and property in the Western world. Such crime rates are part—and only part—of the price Americans pay for middle-class liberal ascendancy in this political culture.

Violent crime is everywhere largely a lower-class phenomenon. In most parts of the United States today, it is widely regarded by the middle-class as a black phenomenon as well; as, a century ago, it was associated in the Northeastern cities with Irish immigrants and, half a century ago, with Italians. What permits its widespread identification with race rather than class is the same phenomenon which underlies much of the failure of organization among the lower classes: historically, such classes have been ethnically fragmented to a vastly larger extent than have the middle classes. But however one regards the popular identification of crime with young black males, it is in fact true that they commit a disproportionate share of all violent crimes, and that they constitute a much larger proportion of most prison populations than of the population outside the walls. To an incalculable but significant extent, white middle-class resistance to bussing and to scatter-site low-income housing in middle-class areas is deeply rooted in fear of crime and criminals—not only because of danger to oneself and one's possessions, but because of the physical danger and danger of "social contamination" for one's children. That this is a vicious cycle is obvious. That "black crime" obtains in the United States to a vastly greater extent than in African countries or the West Indies is also obvious—disposing at once of racist explanations for the phenomenon. Yet black crime exists, and its existence is of immense significance as an obstacle to the making of coherent and politically viable social policy in America.

The escalation in U.S. crime rates over the past decade corresponds perfectly with the view that the country is undergoing a major transitional crisis in which traditional "mazeways"—informal patterns of social interaction—are disintegrating. Increases in anomic behavior to "epidemic" proportions are held by Chalmers Johnson to be part of a syndrome leading to "revolutionary change," and by Anthony Wallace to be part of a social-disorganization syndrome which precedes the emergence of large-scale social and political revitalization movements. Since the bulk of the increase (1959-69) has coincided with the eruption of civil disorders, the hypothesis that some sort of general system breakdown is underway receives additional support.

All this will have major importance for the politics of the 1970s. For one thing, increases in perception of crime as a personal threat will very likely produce demands for more and more official force to cope with the problem. As is well known, such Supreme Court decisions as the 1964 *Miranda* case, establishing high barriers to the official use of confessions from detained suspects, have formed a part of President Nixon's campaigns. It was to reverse such decisions— to give law-enforcement officials more leeway in dealing with suspects—that he promised to reconstitute the Court, a promise which has already been very largely carried out. From Hobbes to the present, intelligent students of politics have always understood that widespread anxiety over personal safety breeds repression: men and women fear the "rip-off," and they fear violent, random death even more. If driven to the point, the majority of any population will accept *any* government, *any* repression in preference to what they see as anarchy.

Unfortunately, so long as, and to the extent that, violent crime and anomic, "antisocial" behavior is perceived widely in the white working-class and lower-middle class populations as being a *black* phenomenon, white motivation to keep strangers out of one's own neighborhood, to resist bussing of one's children into black neighborhoods, and in general to keep ghettoization and segregation as they are at present will continue. This may even prove to be irresistible politically. If so, only the political Right can be expected to benefit from the issues which are being raised about crime and drugs. For the Left is in a sense whipsawed by these issues. If it attempts to invoke "law and order" itself as a formula, it compromises itself and thus is likely to forfeit support from blacks and the poor generally. If it attempts to pretend that there is no such problem, or that it is inflated, the daily social experience of white working-class and lower-middle-class people in metropolitan areas will impel them toward conservativism. But if—as is the appropriate course—the left advocates "standby controls" while pushing for a broad program to attack the roots of lower-class disorganization and to reconstruct the domestic social order—well, this requires a great deal of trust and faith on the electorate's part in the short run. The more so since American political culture teaches lower-middle- and working-class people to think in short-run terms. A social system which is "healthy" in its own terms will use the machinery of justice to suppress deviant and anti-social behavior which exceeds socially permissible limits. The more such behavior there is, the more will be the political pressure for suppression, at least up to the point where the system collapses into revolution, civil war, or some other extreme pattern. From the point of view of those who believe constructive change in polity and society to be both possible and necessary, some perverse comfort can perhaps be drawn from the fact that crime has continued to increase during President Nixon's administration, as it did under his predecessors.

Justice Stumbles over Science

David L. Bazelon

Modern criminal law lives almost as much in the shadow of Freud as of Blackstone. For a generation now, law and other social institutions have been receiving revolutionary new information about human beings from the behavioral sciences. This information seldom solves our problems; in fact, it often seems to complicate them.

Some judges and lawyers say that the findings of behavioral science are too revolutionary to be allowed in the courtroom. But I cannot see that we have any choice but to allow them. To quote Havelock Ellis:

. . . However imperfect the microscope may be, would it be better to dispense with the microscope? Much less when we are dealing with criminals, whether in the court of justice or in the prison, or in society generally,

can we afford to dispense with such science of human nature as we may succeed in attaining.

Science does not create complexities for the law—it reveals them.

Are the two systems—law and science—properly informed about and related to each other? We have problems about introducing new knowledge and understanding into the legal system and problems about the differences between the philosophies of science and of law. But as a judge I am primarily troubled by the man in the dock—about how the behavioral sciences are used in our criminal courts.

Over 100 years ago English law produced the M'Naghten rule to be used in deciding whether an accused person should be excused on the ground of insanity. That rule has come to symbolize one of the great debates between

law and the behavioral sciences. M'Naghten provided:

> The party accused must be labouring under such a defect of reason, from disease of the mind, as not to know the nature and quality of the act he was doing, or, if he did know it, that he did not know he was doing what was wrong.

The United States adopted England's M'Naghten rule. In our time it has evoked swelling criticism from psychiatrists who say it places undue emphasis on man's reason and fails to recognize the emotional forces that drive him. A judge on my court put it this way:

> Psychiatry does not conceive that there is a separate little man in the top of one's head called reason whose function it is to guide another unruly little man called instinct, emotion, or impulse in the way he should go. The tendency of psychiatry is to regard what ordinary men call reasoning as a rationalization of behavior rather than the real cause of behavior.

Yet only if a defendant suffers from a defect of reason—of cognition—can he be excused from criminal responsibility under M'Naghten's rule. M'Naghten treats the insanity defense as a hole in the dike of responsibility, to be kept as small as possible lest the dike be weakened.

The Harshness of M'Naghten

A story will illustrate how harshly this rule still operates and how this harshness is rationalized. Seven years ago a young man aged 22, Don White, beat an old woman to death and a few hours later stabbed to death a dockworker whom he had never met before. In neither case did the defendant flee from the scene of the crime. He waited to chat with passers-by and to watch the police come and go.

The court was told about his background. Don White had never lived with his mother. She was only 13 when he was born. When he was four months old, she left him at a railway depot. A porter turned him over to the woman who became his adoptive mother. Despite his superior intelligence—his IQ was about 130—White was expelled from every school he attended. He was in state institutions nine times, with a growing record of violence and delinquency. In 1951 a child psychiatrist said he was suffering from "a very malignant mental illness," that "institutionalization is absolutely necessary," and that "he will almost certainly wind up in prison or in a state mental hospital."

Between his chance meeting in the depot with his adoptive mother and his murderous chance meeting with the dockworker 20 years later, White was the subject of social service and of psychiatric studies time and time again.

What happened when—as we piously say—"he had his day in court?" Despite evidence of serious mental disorder, the defense of insanity was rejected because it was said that he was intelligent—that is, he had a high IQ and knew right from wrong. He was sentenced to die. The appellate court refused to alter the M'Naghten test:

> The question before us is whether we, as the majority of jurisdictions, should refuse to extend absolute immunity from criminal responsibility to persons who, although capable of understanding the nature and quality of their acts (the ability to distinguish between right and wrong), are unable to control their own behavior as a result of mental disease or defect. . . . One argument for such change is that we must take advantage of new developments in psychiatry. [But] there is nothing new about the idea that some people who know what they are doing still cannot control their actions.

"Foundations of justice"

Recognizing that no new knowledge was necessary to see that White was grossly disordered, the court held that the insanity defense "is available only to those persons who have lost contact with reality so completely that they are beyond any of the influences of the criminal law." The court decided to retain the M'Naghten rule since it "better serves the basic purpose of the criminal law—to minimize crime in society. . . . When M'Naghten is used, all who might possibly be deterred from the commission of criminal acts are included within the sanctions of the criminal law."

Another horrible, but not atypical, example of the operation of M'Naghten is the New York case of an 18-year-old college freshman who killed his father. This boy was termed a schizophrenic by the examining psychiatrists. The murder was done several days before the young man was to take his final examinations in college, and apparently one of his psychotic reasons for committing the act was to avoid taking them. His disordered mind had made some connection between escape from taking the examinations, for which he was unprepared, and his hatred of his father and desire to reside again with his mother. On cross-examination, the prosecuting attorney attacked the doctor's diagnosis with a rather traditional line of questioning:

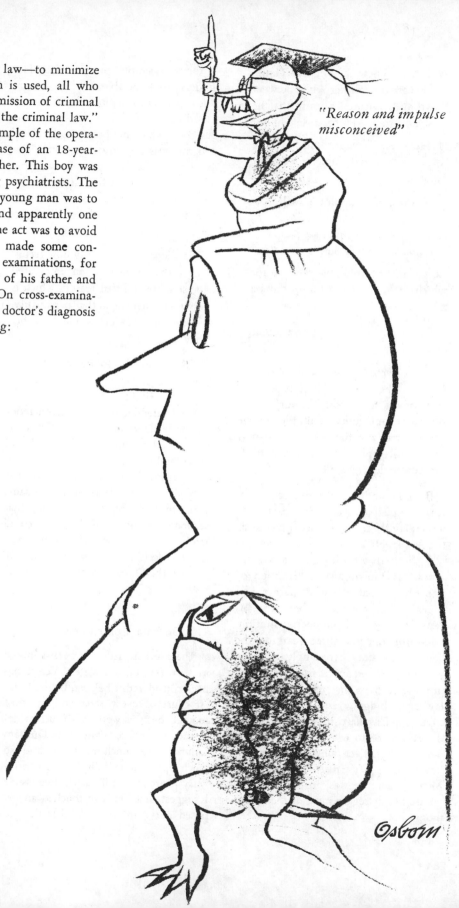

"Reason and impulse misconceived"

Q. . . . First, Doctor, psychiatry is not an exact science, is it?

A. Well, that's a matter of opinion.

Q. Well, let's put it this way, Doctor. Is it generally considered to be an exact science in the same sense that internal medicine or surgery is an exact science?

The prosecutor included an effort to show that the doctor was expressing a mere opinion, that the defendant did not suffer from an "organic" disease, that the doctor's perception of symptoms was "subjective"—and in general that the diagnosis had been made by a psychiatrist rather than an IBM machine.

But most strikingly in this case, the prosecuting attorney pursued a line of questioning based apparently on the assumption that if the boy knew that the knife in his hand when he killed his father was a knife and not a toothbrush, that if when he tried to hitch a ride to his home town on the night of the murder he knew he was headed for Elmira, New York, and not Timbuktu, and so on, *then* he knew what he was doing. Here is an excerpt from the testimony:

Q. . . . He knew then on the Thursday before the murder when he went down and procured a knife that he was procuring a knife, didn't he?

A. He knew he had a knife. But he had a delusional motive when it came to the killing.

Q. Doctor, if you please, will you kindly just answer my question. . . . May I have the last part stricken? *The Court.* Strike it out.

Q. Doctor, he knew the purpose for which he secured the knife, did he not?

A. He had a psychotic motivation at that time.

The Court. Answer the question. More of the same follows, page after page of the transcript. The jury found the defendant guilty of murder in the first degree, and the New York Court of Appeals upheld the ruling and affirmed the death penalty.

I am reminded of the nineteenth century English judge, Lord Bramwell, who quaintly expressed his approval of the M'Naghten rule in these terms:

I think that, although the present law lays down such a definition of madness, that nobody is hardly ever really mad enough to be within it, yet it is a logical and good definition. During my first three years on the bench I became increasingly troubled while passing on and reading cases like the ones I have just recounted. Many lawyers, judges, and jurors were troubled. Psychiatrists were protesting the resistance to use of their new understandings. Even when they were allowed to testify freely in court, the M'Naghten rule was, in effect, an invitation to disregard most of their testimony.

On the simple premise that fact-finders should be able to weigh any and all expert information about the accused's behavior, I wrote an opinion for my court which held that the M'Naghten rule was no longer adequate. That opinion, in the 1954 case of *Durham v. United States,* held that an accused is not criminally responsible "if his act was the product of mental disease or defect." We pointed out that:

The science of psychiatry now recognizes that a man is an integrated personality and that reason, which is only one element in that personality, is not the sole determinant of behavior.

All we sought to do was to give those who are charged with assessing the responsibility of a mentally disordered offender the data which modern understanding requires. Yet Durham raised a controversy in legal and behavioral circles similar to the controversy aroused in wider circles by the Supreme Court's decision of the same year which rejected the old notion that separate treatment of Negroes could really be equal. Opposition to the integration decisions is fast abating. Not so with the Durham decision.

The Durham Controversy

The Durham rule has been adopted in very few of our states. Yet it has been considered, I believe, by the highest court of every state and by most federal courts as well. With such widespread "rejection," why does Durham command so much attention and so much opposition? Why is the controversy it aroused still such a live issue? I suggest that Durham touched an exposed nerve in the administration of criminal justice. We are all troubled by punishing people who suffer from mental and emotional disorders.

There was some amelioration of M'Naghten even before Durham, such as the "irresistible impulse" rule. There has been more since. Nonetheless, there remains a persistent reluctance to include information about sick people. At one level, this could be simple resistance to change. But in all fairness, it seems more complicated. It is a special aspect of the stress which has risen as we have tried to build a better bridge between two systems:

—our legal system, with its reluctance to assimilate knowledge from the behavioral sciences;

—and the behavioral sciences themselves, with their reluctance to clarify the state of the developing body of knowledge about human nature.

Why are professionals on each side failing to adapt? Why does the law find it so difficult to assimilate information which behavioral science has to offer? The principal reason, I believe, is uncertainty about where this information might lead.

We are in that terrible period known as "meanwhile." The behavioral sciences tell us enough to reveal the gross imperfections of present solutions, but not enough to provide perfect alternatives. Furthermore, what we are told is not limited to those recognizably mentally ill. Some light is also shed on those whom the law and society had always thought "bad" rather than "sick." The distinguished British sociologist Barbara Wootton points to the implications:

The creation of the new category of psychopaths is the thin end of what may eventually prove to be an enormously thick wedge: so thick that it threatens to split wide open the fundamental principles upon which our whole penal system is based—undermining the simple propositions . . . as to the responsibility of every sane adult for his own actions, as to his freedom to choose between good and evil and as to his liability to be punished should he prefer evil.

She questions very seriously whether the criminal law, as we know it, can survive the onslaught of new information from psychiatry. My distinguished friend Chief Justice Weintraub of the New Jersey Supreme Court foresees the same problem. He argues that if we allow the psychiatrist to define mental illness for us—and not restrict its legal meaning to knowledge of right and wrong—then he will soon tell us about the factors which affect human behavior. Soon expert witnesses would be testifying about psychological, economic, social, and other matters which cause or contribute to anti-social behavior.

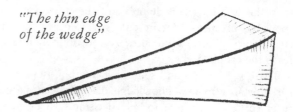

"The thin edge of the wedge"

Information about a defendant's mental disorder may then prove most troubling to the court in seeking a "just" disposition of his case—and may trouble society, too, by revealing that societal disorders contributed to individual disorder. Scientists now generally agree that human behavior is caused rather than willed, that man is most vulnerable in early life, that compared with other species he is capable of learning for an inordinately long period of his life, that he usually responds more readily to reward than to punishment, and that he learns more readily from his peers than from his masters.

Who Is Responsible?

What implications does this information have for our notions of individual responsibility and for our correctional systems? If the information science can give is deeply troubling to our methods of coping with offenders, does this justify us in ignoring it?

Here is a concrete example of the kind of dilemma we face. A few years ago, I served on President Kennedy's Panel on Mental Retardation. I received quite an education since I was the only lawyer in a group that included biologists, geneticists, educators, and psychiatrists. I learned from them for the first time that a disability—retardation, for instance—may arise from wholly unrelated causes, yet produce the same effects. Specifically, my panel colleagues told me, a man may act one way because he has a brain lesion—and we could all understand and forgive the act. But given the same external circumstances, another man may act the same way because of a failure of learning. One who is without identifiable brain damage may become functionally retarded if as an infant or young child he was deprived of a certain minimum of attention, social education, and intellectual stimulation. He will act the same way as the man with the brain lesion.

If this new information is valid, what happens to our notions of morality? Can we call one man responsible be-

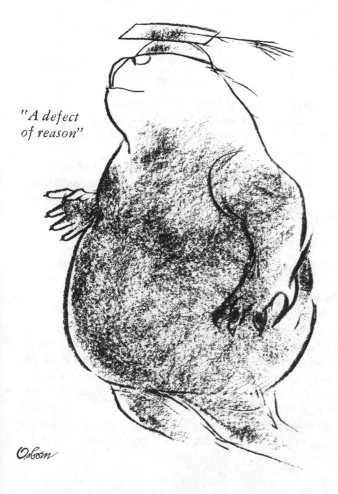

"A defect of reason"

Osborn

cause he is "just plain dumb" and the other man not responsible because of brain damage? Can we continue to condemn people for ignorance? And if not, where does this leave the criminal law?

There is a related and somewhat less philosophical cause for resistance to new knowledge. Each lawyer, judge, and juror conceives his goal to be a decision. All he needs for this is the evidence. The clearer the evidence, the easier the decision. But psychiatry has not yet advanced (perhaps it never will) to the point where it can unequivocally specify what responsibility means. Opinion evidence—especially the opinions of behavioral scientists—is rarely given in black and white. Opinion is, after all, a balance of probabilities. But the psychiatrist sometimes finds this difficult to explain in court. Excerpts from a case transcript will show how a psychiatrist may be berated for inability to give a categorical answer to the prosecutor's questions:

Defense counsel on direct examination: Would you state in your opinion whether there was a causal connection between the mental illness and the crime?

Doctor: In my opinion, there probably was.

Court: No, not probably. I want your expert opinion, not probability. Either you have an expert opinion or you do not.

Doctor: Well, my expert opinion is I do not know for sure.

Court: No, no. That doesn't answer the question.

Counsel: Just give us your opinion—was there a causal connection between the crime and the mental disease?

Doctor: I believe there was.

Court: No. Not what you believe. You must answer the question, Doctor. He is asking for your expert opinion.

Counsel: He said, "I believe there was." I think that is an honest answer.

Court: That is begging the question. I want a direct answer.

Doctor: Does your Honor mean Yes or No?

Court: No, I mean that you must state your opinion. . . . State your expert opinion, not "I believe," or "I guess." . . . Now, I don't want any guessing. If you have an expert opinion, I want it.

Doctor: Yes, my opinion is that the crime is probably the product of illness.

Court: Not probably.

Counsel: We are not concerned with the word "probably." Can you give us your opinion?

Doctor: That is my opinion.

Court: That is not an opinion.

Doctor: I cannot answer Yes or No. I cannot answer it in terms of black and white.

Often the best kind of psychiatric evidence is "merely" opinion. It is an educated, knowledgeable, and often a logical and analytical judgment.

The decision-maker, whether judge or jury, is still left with the ancient and often agonizing tasks of evaluation,

interpretation, and decision. In too many cases, the task of evaluation and interpretation are quickly abandoned, and the decision is reached by a much shorter route.

A short route to decision is to accept whichever expert gives the most clean-cut answers. It is the heart of my thesis that the M'Naghten rule encourages this spurious simplicity, while the facts of the sciences of behavior—at present—often lead toward uncertainty.

The Lonely Half-way Mark

But if the law has not gone half-way to welcome behavioral science into the courtroom, neither have the psychiatrists faced up to their challenge.

What is usually required of the expert is a statement in simple terms of why the accused acted as he did—the psychodynamics of his behavior. In rare instances this is achieved. It occurs most often when the accused or his family has the money to employ a private expert to undertake the comprehensive study required. Then the psychiatrist will learn not only the factors that precipitated the behavior but how the accused became the sort of person he is, and how he must act. This, I repeat, is the exception.

Passing Judgment on Fools

"If a madman or a naturall foole, or a lunatike in the time of his lunacie, or a childe y apparantly hath no knowldge of good nor euil do ki a man, this is no felonious acte . . ."

William Lambarde
Eirenarcha—1581

This rule, in some form, has been in effect in Anglo-Saxon law since the fourteenth century. But the legal definition of insanity—the word itself was coined by a lawyer in 1591 and has no precise medical meaning—has not been settled in 600 years of discussion.

In courts influenced by Anglo-Saxon law, the general test of insanity is the M'Naghten rule: Acquittal on insanity grounds requires that the defendant be so deranged or retarded that he simply not know what he was doing or not know the difference between right and wrong. Most American states use M'Naghten alone, but 17 also allow consideration of the possibility that the criminal act was the result of an "irresistible impulse" to commit an act known to be wrong. New Hampshire and the District of Columbia, however, use respectively, the Pike or Durham rule under which a criminal act is excused if it was the product of a mental disease or defect.

M'Naghten was devised in 1843. Daniel M'Naghten, a Glasgow wood turner with symptoms of elaborate paranoia, set out to kill the Prime Minister, Sir Robert Peel, but in his confusion assassinated instead Edward Drummond, Peel's secretary. The defense called nine medical witnesses who testified to M'Naghten's mental state, and a jury found him "not guilty on the grounds of insanity."

M'Naghten's attack had been the fifth on royalty or its ministers in 40 years, and the decision met bitter resentment in the press and House of Lords. Queen Victoria herself had been attacked in 1840 and 1842. She denounced the decision publicly and privately remarked that she "did not believe that anyone could be insane who wanted to murder a Conservative Prime Minister." The House of Lords called on the 15 judges of the common law courts for an explanation. The result was the statement of the M'Naghten rules.

The crime of Monte W. Durham hardly caused a public furor. Durham, a sometime mental patient, was caught housebreaking in Washington, D.C., in 1951. The resulting opinion of the United States Court of Appeals, written by Judge David Bazelon, attracted a great deal of attention. The judges took the opportunity of Durham's appeal to recast the rules for insanity defense in their jurisdiction to include mental disease or defect. Durham himself was retried under the new rule and again found both sane and guilty. On a second appeal he was freed because the trial judge had told the jury that if they found him insane he would be treated and then would probably be released shortly.

Although Durham has since been considered and rejected in favor of M'Naghten by most of the highest state courts as well as by other federal jurisdictions, it is still strongly debated in medical and legal circles.

Advocates of M'Naghten feel that it provides a clear and convenient standard for jurors. The lack of a standard under Durham, they believe, leaves the jury to rubber-stamp the opinions of the psychiatric witnesses. Nor do they like requiring the state to prove beyond all reasonable doubt that mental illness had nothing to do with the crime in question. They also strongly feel that Durham virtually equates mental abnormality with criminal irresponsibility.

Defenders of Durham conversely argue that M'Naghten senselessly restricts psychiatrists to testimony about cognition, a limited area of human mentality, and also requires them to make a judgment that uncomfortably mixes science and morality. Durham supporters further state that the rule eliminates a legal anomaly created by M'Naghten: under Durham, jurors perform their traditional role as judges of

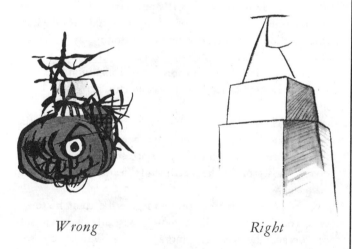

Wrong *Right*

the facts—was the defendant suffering a mental disorder which produced the act?—rather than determining his knowledge of right and wrong, as required by M'Naghten.

The Durham decision cited New Hampshire's Pike rule, which is essentially the same as Durham and has been used there since 1871, but never adopted elsewhere. The basic Durham idea goes back even further—it was first stated in an English case of 1800 in which a man named Hadfield was acquitted of charges of high treason because the jury determined that he was "under the influence of insanity at the time the act was committed." However, the Hadfield decision was not adopted by the courts which until M'Naghten used a 1723 rule under which insanity was defined as the state of mind of an "infant, a brute or a wild beast."

Where it occurs under the Durham rule, the accused may be seen as a sick person and confined to a hospital for treatment, not to a prison for punishment.

Of course it may not be possible for the psychiatrist—or any collection of witnesses—fully to explain *why* the accused acted as he did. The purpose of the Durham rule was to admit a wide range of complexity. But any point in that range, or any uncertainty, may be expressed with clarity.

The task of the expert witness is difficult. He must delve deep into the background of the accused. He must study, analyze, and co-ordinate physical, neurological, and psychological examinations. He must attempt to explain the whole man. He must provide the best explanation of the behavior. He cannot merely attach—or refuse to attach—a few labels or an IQ score. As our court emphasized in 1957:

> Unexplained medical labels—schizophrenia, paranoia, psychosis, neurosis, psychopathy—are not enough. . . . The chief value of an expert's testimony in this field, as in all other fields, rests upon the material from which his opinion is fashioned and the reasoning by which he progresses from his material to his conclusion . . . ; it does not lie in his mere expression of conclusion.

In a more recent case, I had occasion to make the harsh comment that:

> As far as the psychiatric testimony was concerned, [the defendants] might as well have been tried *in absentia*. They were not present in the conclusionary labels of the psychiatrists or in the perfunctory leading questions of counsel.

Why is the psychiatrist prone to give the court his diagnostic conclusion and little more? Basically, I often suspect, because he has little more to give. Our society will not divert enough of its resources to study those charged with crime. This goes to the root of our social system. Our psychiatrists may not be devoted entirely to the rich, but they certainly are seldom familiar with the poor. Most defendants charged with crimes of violence are poor, uneducated, deprived, and segregated. Socially and professionally, most psychiatrists are in the middle class. Psychotherapy has been called the therapy of communication. But many psychiatrists cannot communicate with those accused of crime—and too often they don't try.

Ignorance is compounded by the refusal to admit it. Doctors at one of our federal mental hospitals have often told me in private conversation that they do not have adequate staff and time to make thorough studies of the accused. But once in the courtroom they nevertheless try to live up to our expectations—they will not admit that they do not have all the answers. I sometimes feel that my psychiatrist friends who embrace Durham and then testify beyond their knowledge have done more to warp the Durham concept than the conservative lawyers who oppose it.

Enthusiastic psychiatrists often assume that *they* are being asked to make the moral and legal decision on guilt. They try to become lawyer, judge, jury, and society all rolled into one. They assume they "know" the law and what is good for society and for the accused. They give what we have begun to term "dispositional diagnoses."

Here is an example from a case which came before our court a few years ago. A man was indicted for arson. He gave such a complete written confession that even the police suggested he "was sick and needed psychiatric treatment." The confession revealed the classic symptoms of the sexual pyromaniac. He had been starting fires since he was 12 years old; he had set about 100 of them; the fire at which he had been apprehended was the second he had lit in that house that night.

A psychiatrist submitted the following written report—this and nothing more:

> As a result of this examination and a previous examination . . . it is my opinion that the [accused] is of sound mind. Nothing is elicited which would lead me to the opinion that the act . . . was committed as a result of an irresistible impulse or otherwise as a result of mental illness.

The trial court accepted this report as submitted.

Some time after the appeal to our court was concluded, I met the psychiatrist—whom I knew quite well. I said to him, "John, you examined the pyromaniac—didn't you think he was sick?"

"Sure," he answered, "he was sick as hell."

"And dangerous," I pursued.

"Why, of course."

"Well, why did you tell the court he was of sound mind?"

"Because he was—well, he was not psychotic—he had no delusions or hallucinations—none of the symptomatology of psychosis."

Plainly, this psychiatrist believed that by some absolute legal fiat insanity means psychosis and nothing else. And even after I told him that such was not the law and that his report was therefore terribly misleading, he came forth with this clincher:

I think I would still limit my report to whether or not

Please just answer the question

psychosis was present because it would be too difficult and uncertain to draw the line anywhere else.

Wittingly or not, he was writing the law.

The Science Explosion

I have been concerned principally with the behavioral scientists, the psychiatrists, and the psychologists who are now generally accepted as expert witnesses. But other fields are also contributing new knowledge about human behavior. The biologist, the geneticist, and the biochemist are making fantastic strides in developing information about human personality and the brain.

For a lawyer and a judge, I have had a unique oppor-

tunity to observe and participate in the discussions of some of these scientists. The initial (albeit perhaps misguided) enthusiasm for Durham either pulled or propelled me into their midst. I have not yet extricated myself. So I sit by and hear scientists explain the discovery of the genetic code. I hear them expound on the factors that affect how a human being will develop even before he is born. At the same time I learn that identical cells will act differently depending on the environment in which they are placed. These sciences are now bringing in clues to even more revolutionary findings, as far as ethics and law are concerned. The use of drugs to tranquilize or otherwise influence the mind will have far-reaching implications for our concepts of responsibility and justice.

Full of such facts and speculation, I come back from meetings with scientific groups at the Salk Institute for Biological Studies and various other institutions, and I try to concentrate on the cases which come before me for decision. But I must forget most of what I learned from the sciences of behavior when I judge the behavior of the real human beings who come before our courts.

It seems to me that the criminal law will find it harder and harder not to think about the science explosion. I sometimes wonder how long it will be before our orderly legal processes are shaken by our expanding knowledge of the human being and his behavior. And I wonder whether the biochemist will fare any better in the courtroom than his co-worker, the psychiatrist.

The relations between the individual and society cannot be left to the scientists alone. The criminal law has a role to play. It enforces society's expectations. One might even say that the purpose of the criminal law has been to administer the effects of our disappointed expectations. The law has traditionally sought to reduce the gap between society's expectations and the incapacity of some to fulfill them by minimizing recognition of that incapacity. M'Naghten seems designed to do precisely this. We put our expectations in one compartment and our learned sense of reality in another. There is little communication between the two.

We are fearful that explanation may be taken as tolerance or absolution.

Yet my contention is the opposite. I contend that personal responsibility is linked—indeed locked—to understanding; and that as expectations are altered by growing knowledge, so a utilitarian morality will give way to a humane yet practical morality. A serious inquiry into the defendant's criminal responsibility can provide the catalyst for change.

That inquiry can be compared to a post mortem. The post mortem will not return the dead to life; the trial will not undo a heinous act. But in each case we can learn the causes of failure. And in the trial the entire community can learn—and thereby more clearly understand its responsibility for the act and for the redemption of the actor.

Admittedly the courtroom is not a scientific instrument. But our law libraries are actually man's greatest psychological archive of the natural history of human behavior. Psychological knowledge may reach mankind in many ways. To my mind, the courtroom can become one of the most incisive ways of explaining man and his failings to his fellow men. It can teach us yet again that "no man is an island"; that "though we are not all guilty, we are all responsible."

The Tipped Scales of American Justice

Stuart S. Nagel

The Fourteenth Amendment to the Constitution of the United States asserts that no state or local government shall "deny any person within its jurisdiction the equal protection of the laws." The due process clause of the Fifth Amendment by judicial interpretation provides a similar restraint on the federal government. Other clauses in the Bill of Rights guarantee the right to a lawyer, a grand jury indictment, a speedy trial, and a trial by jury. Do all defendants in American courts get the full benefit of these guarantees?

Many criminologists, lawyers, and other observers say that they do not. The equality before the law guaranteed by the Fourteenth Amendment often turns out in practice to be much like the equality proclaimed on George Orwell's *Animal Farm*—all men are equal, but some groups are more equal than others. Justice, some observers say, may have a blindfold, but it may also have a price, a complexion, a location, and even age and sex; and those with enough money, the right complexion, in the right court, and even sometimes of the right age and the right sex, can often get better treatment. The "least equal" in America are generally those the Fourteenth Amendment was apparently designed specifically to protect—the Negro, the poor, and the ignorant.

The Supreme Court, in an opinion in 1956, stated that "there can be no equal justice where the kind of trial a man gets depends on the amount of money he has." The Attorney General's Committee on Poverty and the Administration of Federal Criminal Justice, headed by Professor Francis A. Allen, then of the University of Michigan Law School, in its 1963 report documented the charge that the poor suffer in the courts because of their poverty. The committee recommended reforms in the bail system, in legal representation, in appeals, and at other steps in the long ladder from arrest to release or conviction.

These propositions would seem to be further supported by common sense. Bail, lawyers, appeals, parole, frequently require money and professional help which are in short supply among the poor. Policemen, prosecutors, judges, and jailors are all human products of our times and nation and, therefore, like the rest of us, are capable of error, prejudice, and "taking the easy way." Our trials are based on the adversary system, in which two more or less evenly matched sides are supposed to meet in the cockpit of a courtroom, under rules designed to insure fair play, and contend until the side with the stronger case wins. How can the indigent, the ignorant, and the victims of discrimination hope to be strong adversaries?

In answer to this question, many prosecutors, law enforcement officers, and editorial writers contend that discrimination in the administration of justice is minor and relatively unimportant. What they believe is much more important—and more damaging—is that safeguards for defendants have already thrown the scales of justice out of balance, and more safeguards could make it almost impossible to get convictions.

Perhaps the picture is muddied partly because not enough broad reliable research has been done on the American system of justice, based on a large, nationwide sample. What has been needed was an analysis of a lot of data taken at all stages of criminal procedure, from all over the country, and including both federal and state cases. This article is based on such an analysis with a concentration on grand larceny and felonious assault cases.

HOW SAFE ARE SAFEGUARDS?

Disparities in justice may appear at any stage of the criminal process—and most groups suffer both apparent advantages and disadvantages from them. For instance, in larceny cases non-indigent defendants are more apt to get probation or suspended sentences than indigent ones, but are also more apt to draw longer sentences if they don't get probation, possibly because of the larger amounts of money which they steal. Also, one defendant's handicap may be another's special privilege. An adult male who does not get a grand jury hearing is possibly being denied a fundamental right; a woman or juvenile who doesn't get one is possibly being given special, informal treatment.

Let us examine these stages briefly, and see what safeguards at each level can mean to an accused.

■ PRELIMINARY HEARING. The preliminary hearing is the first stage on which data are available. The main purpose of a preliminary hearing is to allow the presiding official (police magistrate, justice of the peace, or judge) to decide whether there is enough evidence against the accused to justify further action. If he decides there is not, then an innocent person may be spared considerable humiliation, expense, delay, and inconvenience. The hearing is preliminary to the prosecutor's formal accusation or to a grand jury indictment, which it can prevent. The preliminary hearing also has other advantages for an accused: (1) it deters the use of the third-degree; (2) it allows counsel to appear and plead for the accused, particularly with regard to bail; (3) and it reveals the fact that the accused has been arrested and detained, so that *habeas corpus* (which can bring about immediate release), right to a copy of the complaint, and other guarantees can be secured. In short, the preliminary hearing is a safeguard for the rights of the accused; and its denial is a limitation to those rights.

Of the 1,168 state cases coming from counties that have provisions for preliminary hearings and on which information was available, the accused received no preliminary hearing in 434. In 357 of these he waived his right to a preliminary hearing—possibly without realizing its importance; the rest were recorded as "no preliminary hearing, reason unknown." Information as to the preliminary hearing was not available in the federal data.

■ BAIL. The next important protection for a defendant is the right, or the ability, to be released on bail. Bail reduces his hardship, especially if he is innocent, and gives him a better chance to investigate and prepare his case. Of the 1,552 state cases on which information is available, 44 percent (689) were not released on bail. Of these, 562 were eventually found guilty, 71 found not guilty, and information was not available for 56. Of the 71 not convicted, 20 had stayed in jail for two months or less, 13 for over three months, and we have no information for 38. Five of those not convicted, nor released on bail, in effect served jail terms of six months or more although found guilty of nothing.

■ DEFENSE COUNSEL. Lawyers generally concede that few persons (including lawyers) are capable of properly preparing and arguing their own cases—especially when confined. Having a lawyer, preferably of your own choice, is therefore a fundamental right.

All the state cases were felonies, punishable by more than a year in prison. Yet 183 of the 1,561 cases had no lawyer at all, and only 13 of these were recorded as having waived counsel. (Under the Supreme Court ruling in the famous case of *Gideon versus Wainright*, decided in 1963, all indigent state defendants must hereafter be assigned counsel for any felony. The 1962 data for this study, however, precedes Gideon.) In federal court, all defendants must have counsel of some kind, and the cases were divided according to whether the lawyer was the defendant's own. At least 390 of the 1,151 federal defendants did not have a lawyer of their own choosing.

A lawyer is considered essential for investigation, negotiation with the prosecutor, examination of witnesses, and the presentation of legal and factual arguments to judge and jury. A court-appointed lawyer is better than none, and often better than some, but he can easily suffer from lack of experience, sympathy, enthusiasm, and especially finances and time, since he will probably be appointed late, and may have to take much expense money out of his own pocket.

■ GRAND JURY. What percentage of cases went before a grand jury? Like the preliminary hearing (and the trial) the grand jury process is designed mainly to protect and to minimize the harm done to the innocent. The alternative is to let the prosecutor alone judge whether the accused should be held for trial. The state data did not separate those indicted by a grand jury from those who were not. Of the 915 federal cases involving either grand jury or the prosecutor alone, 344 involved only the prosecutor—although of these only half the defendants formally waived the right to a grand jury hearing.

■ DELAY. The American Law Institute Code of Criminal Procedure provides that if a defendant is held for more than three months without trial due to no fault of his own, then he must be set free without danger of rearrest for the same crime, except for extremely extenuating circumstances. A long delay before trial, especially in jail, can penalize the innocent or over-punish the guilty, as well as make witnesses less available and reliable.

The federal data unfortunately do not distinguish between those who await trial in jail and those who can afford to wait at home. Nevertheless it does reveal that, in-

side or out, there was, for almost half the cases, more than two months delay from arrest until release or trial (whichever came first). In the state cases, of the 405 *not* released on bail, 162 were kept in jail more than two months. (Two months was chosen as the watershed for all cases, half being delayed less, and half more.)

■ TRIAL BY JURY. Generally, there is less chance that twelve jurors will agree unanimously on conviction than one judge (especially a so-called "hanging judge"). Therefore a defendant usually has a greater chance of acquittal before a jury. In addition, if he is a member of a disadvantaged group (uneducated, working-class, or Negro) he stands a much better chance of encountering somebody like himself on a jury than on the bench.

On the other hand, our data show that seeking a jury trial may mean greater delay. It may also mean that if the defendant is found guilty, he is less likely to get probation than if he only had a bench trial. (The stiffer penalties for those convicted by juries may reflect the possibility that the more severe cases come before juries.) But on balance, the chance at a trial by "a jury of his peers" is a strong safeguard of the rights of a defendant.

Nevertheless, in the state data, 63 percent of those cases going to trial did so without a jury; 48 percent of federal trials were held without juries.

■ CONVICTION AND SENTENCING. About four of every five tried defendants, state and local, are found, or plead, guilty. The approximately 20 percent found not guilty, of course, had been put to the expense and anxiety of criminal proceedings. Of those considered guilty, 83 percent pleaded guilty—25 percent to lesser offenses than the original charge, possibly after negotiating with the prosecutor. Almost half the defendants found guilty were given suspended sentences or probation. Slightly more than half of those convicted and sentenced received sentences of more than one year.

THE UNEQUAL DEFENDANTS

These are the major stages in standard criminal procedure. And it is within this framework that disparities because of poverty, race, sex, age, and residence must be understood. The question is not whether the "average" accused person gets complete justice but whether some people and some groups suffer (or benefit) more or less than others—and if so, how and why.

Let us examine some of these disparities.

■ ECONOMIC CLASS. In the state data, "indigent" is defined, generally, to mean not able to afford one's own lawyer—a legalistic rather than a sociological definition. The poor, then, must usually have court-appointed lawyers, or none. In the federal cases, where indigency is not specified, the poor may be defined as those with assigned counsel.

In the pre-sentencing stages, 34 percent of indigents up for felonious assault in state courts did not get preliminary hearings—compared to 21 percent of non-indigents. This was also true, if not as markedly, in state grand larceny cases. Bail, since it requires the ability to raise money, shows the greatest disparity between those who have money and those who do not. About three-quarters of all indigent state cases did not raise bail and stayed locked up, with all this means in unearned punishment and inability to prepare for trial, while 79 percent of non-indigent assault cases, and 69 percent of larceny, did raise bail and got out.

In *having a lawyer,* an interesting reversal occurs; In most states one must be poor to have assigned lawyers, the rich hire their own, and it is the middle group that may be the most apt to be undefended. (Since the *Gideon* decision, as noted, merely having a lawyer is perhaps no longer a major disparity; what *kind* of lawyer, of course, is something else.)

NOTES ON THE STUDY

This article is based on raw data gathered by the American Bar Foundation from state trial court dockets for 1962, in a balanced sample of 194 counties located in all 50 states—a grand total of 11,258 cases of all kinds. The raw data for the federal cases was obtained by the Administrative Office of the United States Courts, and was not a sample, but the complete universe of the 36,265 federal criminal cases decided in 1963. Cases from the District of Columbia and from American territories were excluded, however, in order to confine the data to the 50 states.

The type of crime has a substantial influence on treatment of the criminal, especially at the bail and sentencing stages. So this article concentrates on the two most representative crimes— *larceny,* the most frequently reported crime against property, and *assault,* the most frequently reported against persons. These crimes are also very widespread, being committed by many different kinds of people all over the country. When cases in which the defendant was charged with more than one crime were eliminated, the final sample consisted of 846 assault and 1,103 grand larceny for the states, and for federal offenses, 196 assault and 785 interstate larceny cases. All cases were felonies (except for 51 federal cases of non-aggravated assault).

Felonious assault is generally defined as assault with intent to kill, or to do great bodily harm. Often, studies have shown, the chief difference between it and homicide is that the victim manages to survive.

Grand larceny can be roughly defined as stealing money or property worth more than $50 or $100 (depending on the state) without force or the threat of force.

In the state cases, the indigent were delayed in jail awaiting trial more than the non-indigent. This, obviously, is related to their relative inability to raise bail. In the federal figures delay is measured irrespective of whether or not the defendant is in jail—and here the indigent have *shorter* waits. A court-appointed lawyer would be inclined, apparently, to put in less time and trouble on his case than a private lawyer, and not be as apt to ask for delays; he might also want to get his bail-less client out of jail as soon as possible, and so be less likely to delay the trial.

The federal data show that the indigent are much less likely to have a grand jury indictment than the non-indigent. Perhaps they lack knowledge and are more easily persuaded to waive this right. Perhaps also this ignorance, coupled with appointed attorneys' desires to be rid of their cases, accounts for their relatively high frequency of bench, rather than jury trials. The state indigents also have proportionately fewer jury trials—but here the difference between them and the non-indigent is much less, perhaps because state juries are usually presumed to be of a lower class than federal juries, and middle-class defendants may show less preference for them.

About 90 percent of all indigents studied were found guilty. Though the percentage of non-indigents found guilty was also high, it was consistently lower (averaging about 80 percent). The greatest disparity was in the federal cases, where all indigents had court-appointed lawyers, and this may indicate that poorer representation had something to do with the higher rate of conviction. The poor also tend to feel more helpless, and may be more easily persuaded to plead guilty.

Not only are the indigent found guilty more often, but they are much less likely to be recommended for probation by the probation officer, or be granted probation or suspended sentences by the judge. Of the defendants on whom we had data in this study, a sizeable majority of indigents stayed in jail both before and after trial, unlike non-indigents.

The federal data show that this is true also of those with *no* prior record: 27 percent of the indigent with no prior record were *not* recommended for probation against 16 percent of the non-indigent; 23 percent indigent did *not* receive suspended sentences or probation against 15 percent non-indigent. Among those of both groups with "some" prior record the spread is even greater.

Why these class disparities? They reflect, at least partly, inferior legal help. But even when the lawyer works hard and well, the indigent faces the handicap that he is, and looks, lower class, while those who determine his destiny

—probation officer and judge—are middle-class. Therefore, apart from the other disabilities of the poor, class bias among judicial personnel may work against them.

■ SEX. Are women discriminated against in criminal proceedings as in other walks of life? The findings are much less definite for sex than for poverty, partly because the sample was too small. (Women simply do not commit as many larcenies—and especially assaults—as men.) What differences do emerge seem to be in favor of women, especially in sentencing. It is apparently assumed that women cannot—or, chivalrously, should not—endure as much as men. On the other hand, it is possible that women can be persuaded to give up their rights more easily, and that procedures with them tend to be less formal.

Men are much less likely to be released on bail they can afford than women. In trial, women are more likely to be found innocent, and if guilty more likely to be put on probation or given suspended sentences. Studies in women's prisons have shown that women develop fewer defenses against the pains of incarceration than men and perhaps suffer more, and it is possible that judges and juries know or sense this. Or perhaps they simply find the idea of women in prison, away from their families, offensive.

■ RACE. Most Negroes are poor. A great many poor people are Negroes. So the figures about indigency and race must overlap. But they are not identical, and the differences are important. Generally, the poor suffer even more discrimination than Negroes in criminal justice; and Negroes may suffer more from lack of money than from race.

For instance, a Negro is more likely to get a preliminary hearing than a poor man. He is not as likely as the white defendant to be released on bail, but much more likely to be released than the indigent defendant. Since many Negro defendants are also indigent, the Negro is slightly more likely to have a lawyer than a white defendant, given the indigency prerequisite for receiving a court-appointed lawyer. When the Negro has a lawyer, his lawyer is much more likely to be court-appointed than the lawyers of white defendants. In the federal larceny cases, 52 percent of the Negroes did not have their own lawyers as contrasted to 25 percent of the whites.

Like the indigent, the Negro awaiting trial with his court-appointed lawyer tends to have *less* delay than the white defendant. In fact, being subjected to delay seems to be a sign of high status rather than discrimination. Delay while released on bail may be desired by the defendant because it can benefit the guilty defendant by prolonging his freedom and weakening the memories of witnesses.

The Negro is much less likely than the white to have a grand jury indictment in either federal assault or larceny cases. If he goes to trial he is even more unlikely to have a jury trial. Indeed, 86 percent of the Negroes in federal assault cases failed to receive a jury trial, contrasted to a 26 percent figure for white defendants. It appears that the constitutional rights of a grand jury indictment and of trial by jury are mainly for white men. Perhaps Negroes believe white juries to be more discriminatory than white judges. But it is also possible that Negroes commit the less severe larcenies and assaults, and so do not as often require grand or petit juries.

Negroes, compared to whites, are particularly discriminated against when it comes to probation or suspended sentences. This is evident in the assault convictions, but is more dramatic for larceny; 74 percent of guilty Negroes were imprisoned in state larceny cases, against only 49 percent of guilty whites; in federal larceny cases the score is 54 percent to 40 percent. With prior record held constant, the disparity still holds up.

Why the difference in treatment between Negro assault and Negro larceny? Are not crimes against the person usually considered more reprehensible than those against property? The answer possibly is that larcenies by Negros are more often (than assaults) committed against white men, who are more likely to be worth robbing; but assaults occur most frequently within one's community, in this case against other Negroes. Disparities in sentencing may therefore be double, determined not only by the color of the skin of the criminal, but of his victim too.

It is interesting to note that there is a greater race disparity in federal probation *recommendations* than in probations *granted*. This may be because probation officers deal more subjectively with people, while judges (who are also better educated) tend to put more emphasis on objective factors, like the nature of the crime and the law.

On the other hand, of those actually imprisoned, the Negro defendants (particularly in larceny cases) tended to receive lighter sentences. This may be because, like the indigent defendants, they tend to steal smaller amounts; but it is probably also because the mild white offender is more likely to escape imprisonment altogether.

Generally, and surprisingly, discrimination against the Negro in criminal proceedings was only slightly greater in the South than in the North. It was, however, consistently greater in the South at all stages, pre-trial, trial, and sentencing. Discrimination in the South, predictably, was also greater at the state level than the federal level, possibly because federal judges are more independent of local pressures than state judges.

■ AGE. Younger defendants (below 21 in the state data, 22 in federal) generally are less likely to receive the safeguards the older defendants do, but are more likely to get lighter sentences.

Thus 66 percent of the young did not have their own lawyers in federal assault cases compared to 36 percent of the older defendants. They are less likely to face either grand or trial juries. There is, however, no substantial difference in preliminary hearing or bail. Much of the lack of formal procedure may actually be an advantage, reflecting a protective attitude by the courts toward the young (as toward women), and the belief that informality of procedure diminishes the "criminal" stigma, and leads more easily into rehabilitation. This is, of course, the rationale behind separate juvenile courts. The lack of a personal lawyer probably also reflects some poverty—people 21 and under seldom have much money of their own.

Young defendants are more likely to be recommended for probation, more likely to get it (or suspended sentences), and those few who do go to prison generally receive shorter sentences. (The one exception—longer sentences for youthful federal larcenists who are imprisoned— is probably unrepresentative because of the small sample, or perhaps because only the most hardened cases actually go to federal prison.) Younger people, of course, usually have shorter prior records, and this could count for some of the disparity; but the main reason is probably the belief that the young (again like women) are not as responsible, are more easily rehabilitated, and suffer more hardship in prison.

■ URBAN VS. RURAL, SOUTH VS. NORTH. The sample does not distinguish between *defendants* from the North or the South, the city or the farm—but it does distinguish between *courts* in different locales. Which were the fairest? The answer might sometimes surprise those who automatically accept the stereotype of Northern-urban civil-libertarianism, as opposed to Southern-rural anti-civil-libertarianism.

In the state data, an urban county was defined as one with more than 100,000 population; the federal data used a similar but more sophisticated definition. For both, "South" meant the original eleven states of the Confederacy. The six border states were considered neutral, and the "North" encompassed all the rest. As it developed, most cases (especially the larcenies) were tried in urban courts. Generally, North-South differences in treatment were greater than urban-rural differences.

In preliminary hearing and bail, urban-rural differences were small and inconclusive, but North-South differences were large and consistent—and not to the credit of the North. Thus 38 percent of Northern assaults had no preliminary hearing in spite of laws providing for them, compared to only 10 percent in the South. The South is more traditional toward law and custom, perhaps. The bail difference may also be due to the fact that more Northern defendants were classified as indigents.

Not having any lawyer at all was disproportionately rural and Southern; of the eleven Southern states, eight did not have laws providing for compensated counsel. (*Gideon vs. Wainwright* originated in a Southern state, Florida, and

DISPARITIES IN CRIMINAL PROCEDURE TREATMENT

	DISADVANTAGED GROUPS (Indigents, Negroes, & Less Educated)	PATERNALIZED GROUPS (Juveniles & Females)	INDUSTRIALIZED GROUPS (Northern & Urban Defendants)
SAFEGUARDS FOR THE INNOCENT	Unfavorable, especially as to bail, but favorable as to being provided with a lawyer.	Unfavorable for juveniles especially as to jury trial, but unclear for females.	Unfavorable as to preliminary hearing and delay, but favorable as to providing lawyers. Mixed as to jury trial depending on the crime.
ASSAULT SENTENCING	Unfavorable, especially as to the probation officer decision.	Favorable, especially at the federal level.	Unfavorable as to whether to grant probation, but favorable as to length of imprisonment.
LARCENY SENTENCING	Unfavorable (more so than assault) as to whether to imprison, but favorable as to length of imprisonment.	Favorable, especially at the federal level.	Relatively favorable treatment.

(Based on 1,949 state cases and 981 federal cases from all 50 states for the years 1962-63 in which the defendant was charged with a single charge of assault or of larceny.)

the South will now have to change its ways.) But in the federal cases, where assigned counsel was available, the rural and Southern defendants were *more* apt to have their own hired lawyers than in the cities and the North. That more defendants were labeled indigent in the North, and lawyers cost more there, may be an explanation.

The urban and Northern courts are more congested; defendants wait longer for trial. In the state assault cases, 56 percent of urban defendants sat in jail for more than two months, contrasted to 31 percent of rural defendants, and there is a similar 25 percent spread for federal larceny cases. Much has been written about congestion and delay in urban civil cases, but delay in criminal cases also needs attention, especially in the Northern cities.

In assault cases, jury trials and grand jury indictments are more common in the South than in the North; in larceny cases, however, it is the other way around. (The findings are similar in rural and urban courts, although not as consistent.) Urban and Northern courts are more likely to *imprison* for *assault*; the rural and Southern, for *larceny*. Perhaps these disparities reflect the "frontier" morality still lingering in the open country and the South, in which a man is expected to be prepared to personally defend his honor (and therefore assault is not so terrible) but a crime against property is something else again.

In the congested cities and the North, perhaps, crimes against the person seem more terrible, whereas property tends to be considered corporate and impersonal. Moreover, people in settled areas are more conditioned to rely on professional police, not personal defense and retribution. No great differences exist North and South, urban and rural, in percentages of convictions. But there is a good deal of difference in length of sentences. Rural and Southern courts are harsher, at least at the state level—66 percent of Southern state larceny sentences were for more than a year, contrasted to 35 percent in the North. Assault shows about the same spread. Rural-urban differences are parallel, if less marked. Southern states make the greatest use of capital punishment.

■ FEDERAL VERSUS STATE. Because of different constitutions and judicial interpretations, federal defendants have greater access to the grand jury and to counsel (when the data was collected) than state defendants. Delays are much shorter at the federal level. Shorter delays mean less need for bail, and the grand jury hearing diminishes the importance of the preliminary hearing. A slightly higher percent of federal trials are tried before juries.

Both federal and state trials end in guilty findings (or pleas) about 80 percent of the time; both find assault defendants guilty less often than larceny defendants. Probation and suspended sentences are more common in federal court—but, perhaps because the milder cases are already winnowed out, federal assault sentences are longer.

As detailed earlier, disparities unfavorable to Negroes are slightly greater in the states. Juveniles are more likely to be deprived of safeguards at the federal than the state level—but also given lighter sentences. In the broad outline, however, the same disparity patterns show up in both.

At risk of oversimplification, the major findings of this study are summarized in the accompanying chart.

Significant disparities in the administration of justice do exist. Some groups are more likely than others to receive preliminary hearings, release on bail, better lawyers, grand jury proceedings, jury trials, acquittals, shorter sentences.

Some of these differences are justifiable. The severity of the crime and the prior record, should affect the sentence (though not due process). Women and juveniles should perhaps be given more consideration. Some crimes may have greater importance in one place than another, and minor adjustments made accordingly. Nevertheless, the majority of disparities discussed in this article are probably not socially justifiable and run contrary to our democratic philosophy and to those laws which are supposed to guarantee due process and equal treatment.

CORRECTING THE BALANCE

What can be done about it? Remedies vary with the specific disorder. But these discriminations in the courts partly reflect the same discriminations in our society. The indigent would not get different treatment if there were no indigent; Negroes would not be discriminated against as Negroes if there were no race prejudice. If general American performance matched American oratory and promise, equality in the courts would come quickly enough. Thus the problem of criminal procedure disparities is inherently tied to attempts to remove distinctions that are considered undesirable between the city and the country and the North and the South, and to attempts to further emancipate women, as well as to decrease the numbers of the indigent and the uneducated, and to eliminate general racial discrimination.

Meanwhile, what is being done with regard to a more piecemeal attack on specific disparities?

Partly as the result of the recommendations of such groups as the Attorney General's Committee on Poverty and the Administration of Federal Criminal Justice, the

Vera Foundation in New York City, and the National Bail Conference, the federal courts have been releasing many more people considered trustworthy *without bail,* pending trial. There is some evidence that state courts are starting to follow suit. Illinois now has a law requiring that most defendants waiting trial be released if they can afford a 10 percent down payment on the bail bond—the interest usually charged by commercial bondsmen. Philadelphia, New York, and St. Louis have followed the Vera recommendation to set up bodies that investigate defendants and advise judges whether they are good risks for release without bail. The fact is that judges have almost always had the authority to forego bail for trustworthy defendants—but few have been willing to use it with what little information they could pick up from the bench. In these cities at least they are using it now, and with increasing frequency.

Since *Gideon versus Wainwright,* all felony defendants can probably be assured of *some* kind of representation. In addition, a large scale campaign to provide *competent* counsel has been started by the National Legal Aid and Defender Association, and the American Bar Association. The Administrative Office of the U.S. Courts is currently conducting an educational program to encourage more rational sentencing practices and a statistical program to show more clearly just what those practices are. Though the evidence is very spotty, there does seem to be a general trend, especially in the large cities, toward better trained and better educated policemen, probation officers, and court officials. The civil rights movement, by focusing publicity on disparities, is also bringing change.

Bringing the facts to light can expedite needed change. The disparities exist partly because the facts have been denied, ignored, disbelieved, or simply unknown to a large public. The facts are available, and they keep accumulating. We may reasonably hope that when a similar study is done five or ten years from now it will show less disparity in the administration of criminal justice.

Winners and Losers: Garnishment and Bankruptcy in Wisconsin

Herbert Jacob

The prospect of being dragged into court for not paying one's debts or else pleading bankruptcy in order to evade them looms in the future of thousands of Americans every year. But whether the courts will be the last resort of debt collectors and debt dodgers depends on numerous influences ranging from the attitude of individual communities regarding indebtedness to the life-styles of debtors and creditors.

The courts are the most important contact many citizens have with the government. But whether this political instrument is used to seize wages of those owing money or to help others evade payment by declaring them bankrupt is related to income, the type of debt incurred, job status, to some degree race, and the manner in which the community where the action is taking place views itself.

To find out who uses the courts for garnishment and bankruptcy proceedings, we searched the court records of four Wisconsin cities—Madison, Racine, Kenosha, and Green Bay. In Green Bay, where the number of such proceedings was small, all debtor-creditor cases for a year were recorded. A random sample was taken from the other cities' files.

In all, 454 debtors were interviewed. Another 336 creditors and 401 employers returned completed questionnaires. Interviews with selected attorneys, creditors, collection agencies, and court officials added to the information. From these sources emerged profiles of creditors and debtors and their use of the courts.

Debtor-creditor conflicts usually involve the refusal of the debtor to pay what the creditor feels is due him. The debtor may feel he was cheated or that the creditor didn't live up to the agreement. Unemployment, ill health, a family emergency, or pressure from other creditors to repay them first are other common reasons that people don't pay bills. Sometimes, the debtor simply forgets or no longer wants to pay. In each case, the probability of conflict is high, for most creditors pursue the debtor until he pays. Only when collection costs rise above the amount owed, will most creditors write off the loss.

The typical creditor is a finance company, department store, service station, television repair shop, landlord, hospital, doctor, or even lawyer. A few creditors are personally involved insofar as they themselves extend credit, lend money, or have extensive personal relations with their customers and make a personal effort to collect the loan. Most collectors do not make loans, but are employees of large collection organizations and view collecting as a routine matter.

When most private actions to collect debts fail, the courts stand ready to help creditors: (1) If an article were purchased through a conditional sales contract, the creditor may repossess, sell it, and get a deficiency judgment for the difference between the resale price and the amount still owed on the item from the debtor. (2) The creditor may obtain a judgment so that he can use the sheriff's office in collecting the amount due. The sheriff can seize for sale any articles not exempt under the state law. (3) When, as in many cases, the debtor owns no goods that satisfy the judgment, most states allow the creditor to attach the debtor's wages through wage garnishment. In some states like Wisconsin, creditors may seize the debtor's wages through garnishment even before they obtain a judgment against the debtor.

Under garnishment proceedings, a summons is sent to the debtor's employer, who is then obligated to report whether he owes the debtor any wages. If he does, he must send those wages to court. The debtor may recover some of his wages for living expenses but the bulk of the funds satisfies the debt. A creditor may garnishee his debtor's wages repeatedly until the debt is paid.

Debtors, in turn, have a number of extralegal remedies they can use. In a country where there is free movement and different state laws regarding creditor-debtor relations, the easiest thing for a debtor to do may be to move. Or he may defend his nonpayment in the judgment suit, though this is expensive and rarely successful. But debtors increasingly use a more successful legal measure—promising repayment through a court-approved amortization plan.

Such plans may be available under state law (as in Wisconsin) or through Chapter 13 of the Federal bankruptcy statute. Under the Wisconsin statute, a debtor earning less than $7,500 per year may arrange to repay his debts in full within two years if his creditors consent. During this time, he is protected from wage garnishments and other court actions that seek to collect the debts listed. New debts, however, may be collected as before through judgments or wage garnishments. Under Chapter 13 of the Bankruptcy Act, amortization usually allows the debtor three years to pay. During this time, interest accumulation is stopped and all creditor actions against the debtor are prohibited. New debts as well as old ones may be included in the repayment plan although new debts may be incurred only with the approval of a court-appointed trustee. Chapter 13 also provides for partial payment in satisfaction of the debt.

Bankruptcy provides the final legal escape for the debtor. Bankruptcy is available under Federal law to both the business and nonbusiness debtor. A debtor need not be penniless; he only needs to have debts which he cannot pay as they fall due. Under bankruptcy proceedings, the debtor makes available to the court all nonexempt assets that he possesses for repayment to his creditors.

Nonbusiness bankruptcies usually involve no assets that can be distributed to creditors. After this has been established, the Federal court discharges the debts of the bankrupt and he is no longer legally obligated to repay. (Tax debts, alimony, and child support payments as well as debts incurred through fraud cannot be discharged.) The only limitation to this remedy for debtors is that it may be used only once every six years.

Only a tiny proportion of credit transactions turn into

conflicts between creditor and debtor and only a small proportion of those are eventually brought to court. It is therefore important to identify the conditions under which some people seek to invoke governmental sanctions in their efforts to collect or evade debts. *Four sets of conditions* are readily identifiable and are the subject of analysis here.

■ *Socioeconomic conditions:* A recession (even if slight and local) following a period when credit was freely extended is likely to produce more creditor-debtor conflicts than continued prosperity or a long recession. Likewise, the type of economy in an area is important. Subsistence economies, either in rural or urban slums, do not involve much consumer credit. Factory workers whose employment or earnings are erratic are more likely to be in credit difficulties than white-collar workers whose employment is steadier and whose wages, although lower, are more regular. The availability of credit is also significant. Those living in small towns or cities with few banks and lending institutions may find it more difficult to get credit and also find themselves less tempted to borrow than those living amidst a plethora of lending institutions, constantly inviting them to borrow.

■ *"Civic" or "public" culture of a community:* Some communities have more conservative lending policies than others. Large blocs of citizens may not borrow because they are older and not used to it or because they come from ethnic groups unaccustomed to living on credit. Alternatively, some communities are composed of groups who borrow heavily. In some communities, using the courts comes easily; in others, it involves a morally and culturally difficult decision.

■ *Availability of court action:* In some communities, court action is unlikely because no court sits in the town—all actions must be started in a distant town making litigation inconvenient as well as expensive. Also, some courts are more stringent about requiring representation by lawyers than others. In one town, attorneys may be more available for collection work than in others. Finally, litigation costs vary from town to town, as local judges interpret state laws regarding fees in different ways.

■ *Ability of potential litigants to use remedies:* Different members of a community vary considerably in their ability to use available remedies. They need to know about them. They need the requisite financial resources. They need to be convinced that court action is really appropriate in their situation and to be free of the psychological restraint of shame and the social restraint of retaliation.

Creditor Use of the Courts

In the cities studied, money lenders (principally finance companies), and retailers were the heaviest users of wage garnishments. Hospitals, doctors, and dentists were the third most frequent users in three cities, while in the fourth, landlords were. All other creditors accounted for less than one-third of the wage garnishments docketed in small-claims court.

Creditors, however, do not use wage garnishments in identical ways. Their readiness to use the courts occurs under very different conditions. Finance companies, for example, have the most developed collection system. Ten days after a payment is due, they consider the debtor delinquent and begin efforts to collect. A large repertoire of collection methods are called into play, including overdue notices, telephone calls to the debtor, personal calls to his home, telephone calls to his employer, calls to co-signers of his note (if any), seizure of the collateral for the loan (if any), and wage garnishment. Most of these steps are carried out with minimal assistance by outsiders since their internal organization is structured to accommodate them. Consequently, finance companies almost never use collection agencies. And although they garnishee frequently, they do so only after a long chain of attempts to collect.

Doctors and hospitals are in a different position. Medical ethics downgrade commercial success, and patients reinforce this de-emphasis. Most patients expect a bill; few expect a bill collector to follow. Medical services are something they feel entitled to, regardless of their ability to pay, and therefore even when medical clinics and hospitals have business offices, they do not usually use them for extensive bill-collecting purposes.

Most doctors are not organized for nor do they depend on credit profits. Yet collectively, they probably extend as much credit as finance companies do. As professionals, they dislike spending time collecting delinquent bills. Generally, they wait three months before they consider a bill delinquent. They then send one or two reminders to the patient. They do not call him at home or at work. They have no co-signer through whom to exert pressure; they have no purchases to repossess. They do not even have the time to go to court themselves, so they usually turn delinquent accounts over to a collection agency or attorney. One or two more impersonal attempts are made to collect before the issue goes to court for a judgment and/or wage garnishment. Typically, the doctor and the hospital receive only half the proceeds collected by the agency, the other half being the agency's fee. Most maintain that they pay little attention to what the collection agency does to collect a bill and are unaware that they are garnisheeing their patients' wages. Some say they resort to collection agencies for tax reasons only, since they believe the Internal Revenue Service does not permit them to write off a delinquent account as uncollectable unless court action was attempted.

Retail merchants stand between finance companies and medical men in their use of wage garnishments. Large stores with thousands of accounts have about the same organizational capability of collecting debts as finance companies. Small merchants have to use collection agencies. Like doctors, most retailers do not consider accounts delinquent until 90 days after payment is due and they also have no collateral to repossess since most retail sales are for soft goods. When hard goods such as TVs and refrigerators are sold on credit, the notes are sold by the retailer to a finance company. Retailers, moreover, are sensitive to their customers' opinions of them. Nearly 25 percent of the retailers interviewed were afraid that if they were frequently involved in direct wage garnishments they would lose customers. Almost 50 percent of the doctors expressed similar fears, but no finance company and very few banks and credit unions mentioned this as a reason for not using garnishments more often.

Willingness to use government help in collecting delinquent accounts thus seems to depend, in part, on the organizational resources of creditors, on their dependence on credit for profits, and on restraints produced by customer or patient alienation. Finance companies frequently use the courts because they possess the organizational resources, depend entirely on credit profits, and have little to fear since their customers generally have no other place to borrow. Doctors, hospitals, and retailers differ on all these points from finance companies and, insofar as they differ, are less likely to use the courts. Many, however, are indirectly drawn into court actions by the collection agencies they employ because collection agencies have the same characteristics as finance companies: the organizational resources to sue, their existence depends on collecting, and they have no fear of customer alienation.

The size of the debt is another important variable in the use of the courts. Most bills leading to wage garnishments are relatively large. Only 16 percent involved less than $50. Most were $50-$99, the median was $100-$149. About 20 percent were between $400 and $500, the upper limit of small-claims actions.

Most creditors find that costs are too high for debts of less than $50 to risk wage garnishment proceedings. It costs up to $35 (half in court fees and half in attorney's fees) to collect a bill by garnishment. If the creditor is successful in assessing the garnishment, the debtor pays the court fees. But if the garnishment is unsuccessful—if the creditor puts the wrong employer down on the summons or if he garnishes when the employer does not owe his employee any wages (for example, the day *after* payday rather than the day before)—the creditor must pay the full costs.

Since most debtors earn less than $100 a week, most debts far exceed the amount that can be collected by a single garnishment. Under Wisconsin law, the employer must usually pay the debtor $25 if he is single and $40 if he has dependents before he turns wages over to the court for payment to the creditor. Thus, most garnishments capture $60 or less out of which both the original debt and the court and attorney fees must be paid. In many cases it would take at least three garnishments to satisfy the debt and few debtors are likely to remain on their job beyond two such proceedings. Either they are fired because of the garnishments or quit in order to escape them. Most creditors therefore use wage garnishment to force the debtor to come in and make an arrangement to repay more gradually. As we shall see later, however, these generalizations about the users of garnishment proceedings are not entirely accurate for every city studied, with the locale making a considerable difference.

Debtor Use of the Courts

While creditors are often organizations, the debtors we studied were always individuals. Bankrupts had most often purchased large items such as cars (generally, used cars), appliances, TVs, furniture, and encyclopedias in the three years before going bankrupt. Garnishees, however, reported such purchases far less frequently, mentioning only two luxury items with consistency—home freezers and air conditioners. Medical debts were common to all; 82 percent of the bankrupts and 92 percent of the garnishees reported they were behind in their medical bills. Garnishees were more often protected by medical insurance. While 84 percent said some of their medical bills were paid by insurance, only 66 percent of the Chapter 13's and 57 percent of the bankrupts had similar protection.

Significantly, debtors in our sample who sought court relief were very similar to those who did not. Although garnishees generally had a lower level of indebtedness, and many bankrupts were hopelessly mired in the quicksand of credit, most owed about the same amount of money —between $1,000 and $5,000. (See Table I)

Table I
INDEBTEDNESS OF BANKRUPTS, CHAPTER 13's AND GARNISHEES

Indebtedness	Bankrupts *(N = 196)	Chapter 13's (N = 72)	Garnishees (N = 168)
Up to $999	.5	9.7	25.6
$1000-4999	56.6	73.6	52.4
$5000-9999	20.4	12.4	10.1
Over $10000	22.9	4.2	11.9

* Number of cases

■ Slightly more than half the bankrupts had incomes below $6,000, less than the median family income for the four Wisconsin cities in 1959. Like the garnishees, the vast majority were above the official "poverty" line of $3,000. Most of the Chapter 13's and garnishees reported incomes above $6,000. (See Table II) The most striking difference between the three groups is the frequency of home ownership, with garnishees owning homes more often. This difference may in part be attributed to the loss of homes by bankrupts in the bankruptcy proceedings.

Table II
SELECTED ASSETS OF DEBTORS: TOTAL FAMILY INCOME, HOME OWNERSHIP

Income	Bankrupts	Chapter 13's	Garnishees
Less than $3000	6.2%	6.1%	5.4%
$3000-5999	47.4%	30.7%	33.9%
$6000-9999	40.7%	57.0%	48.2%
Over $10000	5.7%	6.1%	12.5%
Number of cases	209	65	168
Home Ownership			
Own or buying	21.2%	36.4%	42.1%
Number of cases	212	66	171

■ As Table III indicates, garnishees who did not go through bankruptcy court often had larger numbers of wage garnishments levied against them than did bankrupts or Chapter 13's. In fact, many of the bankrupts and Chapter 13's reported neither actual garnishment nor threatened garnishment prior to court relief from their debts.

What then distinguishes those who seek government aid to evade debts from those who don't? Indebtedness and assets do not clearly differentiate the three groups, nor do education and occupation. Most debtors, 84 percent to 87 percent, had at least some high-school education. Most were blue-collar workers—craftsmen, foremen, factory workers, or laborers. A small proportion, ranging from 10 percent of the Chapter 13's to 15 percent of the bankrupts were white-collar workers.

Table III
ACTUAL AND THREATENED GARNISHMENT

Actual Garnishment	Bankrupts	Chapter 13's	Garnishees
None	44.3%	45.3%	—
1-2	28.8%	22.7%	58.1%
3-5	15.6%	17.3%	30.4%
More than 5	11.3%	14.6%	11.5%
Number of cases	214	75	174
Threatened Garnishment			
Yes	55.6%	72.7%	50.3%
Number of cases	214	77	176

Age, however, separates the three groups. Younger debtors go bankrupt more frequently than older ones. Sixty-two percent of the bankrupts were less than 30 years old. Only 43 percent of the Chapter 13's and 37 percent of the garnishees were so young. *A majority of the bankrupts were young men in the early years of their family life who had built up high levels of debt, purchasing most of the items needed to establish a household.* Most did not have more than two children living with them. By contrast, the garnishees were a much older group with well-established homes; often their children had already left home so that they too were usually supporting households with two children or less.

Moreover, a relatively high proportion of the debtors were Negroes. While only 2.5 percent of the total population were black, 16 percent of the garnishees, 12 percent of the Chapter 13's, and 9 percent of the bankrupts were Negroes. This is not surprising given the generally high income of Negroes in the four cities and the likelihood that Negroes are more tempted to overpurchase, because of their previously deprived status and because of the hard-sell techniques. That fewer Negroes take advantage of court relief from their debts results from their being among the least efficacious members of society and that they may know courts only from criminal proceedings.

Neither indebtedness, income, education, nor age distinguish Negroes who seek court relief from debts from those who don't. The difference is principally occupational status, with craftsmen and foremen going to bankruptcy court and mainly factory workers being garnished.

A number of characteristics seemingly related to the occupational status of Negroes are present among the whole sample of debtors. High-job status Negroes are relatively well-integrated at their work place and probably better integrated into the general community than lower-occupation status Negroes. Furthermore, they are probably better linked in communication networks through which they may learn about bankruptcy than are lower-status Negroes. These inferences can't be tested here because the number of Negroes in the sample is too small for more detailed analysis. But these hypotheses should also hold true for the entire group of debtors.

The data indicate that there are significant differences between garnishees and bankrupts in the quantity of information they had and the direction of advice they received about their financial distress. Bankrupts were apparently much better integrated into the legal system than garnishees since twice as many bankrupts as garnishees saw an attorney about a previous garnishment. In addition, those who saw an attorney in the two groups received different advice. Only half the bankrupts were advised to make arrangements to pay their creditors while 75 percent of the garnishees were given that advice. More than 40 percent of the bankrupts were advised by their attorney to go into bankruptcy; less than 20 percent of the garnishees received such advice. Combining the effects of the propensity to see a lawyer and the advice lawyers gave, we find that almost half of the bankrupts were told to take advantage of bankruptcy, while only 5 percent of the garnishees received such advice from a lawyer.

Bankrupts also received different advice from their friends than the garnishees. Far fewer bankrupts reported that their friends advised "doing nothing" or paying their creditors off. Many more reported being advised to see an attorney about their garnishment and a significant proportion (17 percent) were told about bankruptcy, whereas not a single garnishee reported being told about bankruptcy by a friend.

Other data also indicate the importance of integration into a communication network which facilitates the decision to go into bankruptcy. The second most frequent response to "Why did you decide to go into bankruptcy?" was advice from various quarters—most often that advice came from their attorney. In addition, when we asked them where they learned about bankruptcy, lawyers were the most frequently mentioned source of information. Friends, relatives, and people at their place of work followed. The overwhelming proportion of our sample learned about bankruptcy from personal sources rather than from impersonal communications. Indeed, the media were not specifically mentioned by a single one of the almost 200 bankrupt respondents. A final indicator of the importance of personal communications comes from the fact that more than half the bankrupts knew someone else who had gone

through bankruptcy.

These data indicate that bankrupts were integrated into the legal system by a communication network which was conversant with bankruptcy proceedings. Although bankrupts varied greatly in their socioeconomic characteristics, they were linked in a loose communication network. They apparently learned about bankruptcy with relative ease and received support from the various people from whom they heard about bankruptcy. All of this contrasts sharply with the experience of garnishees. Garnishees, although in financial difficulty, were shut out of that network. Thus they did not learn about bankruptcy, were not encouraged to use it, and were not in contact with the professionals who might facilitate their use of it.

Inter-City Variations in Garnishment

Neither creditors nor debtors used the courts to the same extent in the four cities studied. Nor did the variation in garnishment and bankruptcy rates in the four cities conform to social, economic, or partisan factors. (See Table IV) Each of the cities had approximately the same degree of prosperity during the period studied. The proportion of families with incomes in the range where garnishment and bankruptcy most frequently occurs ($3,000-$10,000) was almost identical for Madison, Racine, and Kenosha. Green Bay had slightly more such families but this scarcely explains its *lower* garnishment and bankruptcy rate. All cities had small nonwhite populations. Racine has the largest Negro community consisting of 5.4 percent of its population. Only .9 percent of Green Bay's population was nonwhite, principally Indian. And though there are no available figures on the amount of credit extended in the four cities, the differences in retail sales for the four do not explain the differences in garnishment and bankruptcy rates.

Table IV

GARNISHMENT AND BANKRUPTCY ACTIONS
FOR 12 MONTH PERIOD:

	Madison	Racine	Kenosha	Green Bay
Garnishments	2860	2740	813	130
per 1000 pop.	22.6	30.7	12.0	2.1
Bankruptcies	112	100	63	32
Chapter 13's	37	18	5	7
Total BK-13 per 1000 pop.	1.17	1.32	1.0	.62

The only factor clearly explaining the different rates of garnishment and bankruptcy in the four cities might be called the "public" or "legal" culture. Excluding garnishment and bankruptcy, the frequency with which civil court cases are initiated in the four cities closely follows debtor case rates. (See Table V) The highest rate occurs in Racine, with Madison, Kenosha, and Green Bay following. As expected, the criminal rates differ since they are initiated by public officials. Civil cases, for the most part, are initiated by private citizens. All civil litigation reflects, it then seems, a set of peculiar institutional and cultural patterns that are not evident in the standard socioeconomic indexes ordinarily applied to these cities.

Robert Alford and Harry M. Scoble's study of these four cities and their municipal decision-making processes suggests that they represent distinct political cultures. They label these cultures as (1) *traditional conservatism* (Green Bay), government is essentially passive, a caretaker of law and order, not an active instrument for social or private goals; (2) *traditional liberalism* (Kenosha), "the bargaining process may even extend to traditional services . . .;" (3) *modern conservatism* (Racine), government is legitimately active, but furthering private economic interests that are in the long range public interest, and (4) *modern liberalism* (Madison), "a high level of political involvement · . . . may itself exacerbate conflicts. . . ." Alford and Scoble concentrate on the liberal-conservative dimensions of the four cities, by focusing on the kinds of public decisions made and the range of participation in the decision-making process. When we examine litigation rates, however, the cities cluster on the traditional-modern dimension.

Table V
CIVIL AND CRIMINAL CASES IN FOUR COUNTIES,
JULY 1, 1964-JULY 1, 1965

Civil Cases	Dane (Madison)	Racine	Kenosha	Brown (Green Bay)
County and Circuit Court	1691	817	1203	803
Small Claims Court (minus garnishment)	4203	3024	743	233
Civil Case Rate 1000 pop.	26.5	27.0	19.5	8.2
Criminal Cases (excluding ordinance)	3195	1020	867	722
Rate/1000 pop.	15.8	7.2	8.6	5.8

It appears that Green Bay and Kenosha share low litigation rates because of more traditional public cultures, while Racine and Madison share higher litigation rates because of their more modern public culture. Data from our interviews provide supporting evidence for this conclusion.

Less frequent use of public facilities to settle private conflicts is congruent with the concept of a traditional American public culture. Depending more on personal and less on bureaucratic ways of settling disputes, the traditional culture leads to dependence on personal contact between the principals.

Taking a debtor to court is a highly impersonal proceeding involving the use of public officials as intermediaries and arbiters. Interview data indicate that in Green Bay and Kenosha firms and professionals collecting delinquent accounts depend more on the use of personal contacts, telephone calls to the debtor, or informal arrangements with employers. In Green Bay, where the garnishment rate is lowest, attorneys and creditors often asserted that the city was small enough for everyone to know everyone else, making court action unnecessary. But Green Bay has only 5,000 fewer inhabitants than Kenosha (where no respondents mentioned the intimacy of the town) and is only one-third smaller than Racine which has the highest garnishment rate. Nevertheless, the exaggeration of its small size is significant, since the perception of Green Bay as a small town fits the description of its traditional culture.

The lower garnishment rate also fits Alford's description of these traditional cities as ones in which the business elite does not look upon government as an instrument to obtain private objectives. Passive government and informal bargaining typify many public situations in Green Bay and Kenosha, with the debt-collection process being just one manifestation. In Madison and Racine, creditor-debtor conflicts, like public disputes, more frequently reach official government agencies—in this case, the court—for formal adjudication.

Alford's characterization of these cities leads us to look for differences in the degree to which the people are fiscally traditional.

For the most part, these expectations are confirmed by the debtor interviews. Slightly more debtors in Green Bay than elsewhere thought banks were the best place to borrow money and an overwhelming proportion thought finance companies the worst source of loans.

But Kenosha does not fit the expected pattern, falling instead between Madison and Racine in both ratings. The same is true for actual behavior of the debtors: Fewer Green Bay debtors reported finance companies as their biggest source of loans; the highest proportion using finance companies was in Racine. On another behavioral indicator, more Madison debtors showed an inclination to approve borrowing for a wider range of items than Racine, Kenosha, or Green Bay debtors. The ordering of the cities followed our expectation closely though not exactly: Madison, Racine, Kenosha, Green Bay. Finally, a related indicator showed Green Bay debtors to be more aware of interest rates on their loans than Madison, Kenosha, and Racine debtors—traditional norms of consumer behavior emphasize cost rather than immediacy of purchase. These data support Alford and Scoble's characterization of Green Bay and Kenosha as traditional and Madison and Racine as modern. The patterns distinguishing the public decision-making styles of these cities apparently spill over to private use of judicial agencies by both creditors and debtors.

Traditionalism also affects the legal culture. Only in Green Bay did most of the attorneys handling garnishment cases send out letters to the debtors prior to initiating the court action despite the cases having been extensively worked over by the creditor's collection department or a collection agency. Attorneys in Green Bay were more concerned about avoiding formal court action than attorneys in the other three cities, who reported that they immediately filed for court action unless they knew there had not been an active effort to collect.

Everything cannot be explained by cultural differences between the communities. The higher incidence of Chapter 13 proceedings as compared to bankruptcies in some of the cities is due to different evaluations of Chapter 13 by attorneys and to pressure exerted by the referees in bankruptcy. Where Chapter 13 proceedings are most frequent (in Madison and Racine), debtors report that lawyers often give them a real choice between it and bankruptcy. In Kenosha and Green Bay, lawyers rarely talk about Chapter 13 to bankruptcy clients and since these clients rarely heard of Chapter 13 from other sources, fewer used it.

Differences in attorney behavior are largely accounted for by the pressures they feel from the referee in bankruptcy and their relation to the Chapter 13 trustee, who handles the debtors affairs while he is under the plan. In Madison, the lawyer's preference for Chapter 13 proceedings can be traced to active campaigning in favor of it by the Madison Referee in Bankruptcy. Racine's higher Chapter 13 rate reflects the fact that the trustee was a fellow Racine attorney, readily available on the telephone for consultation. Kenosha attorneys who also had to use the Racine trustee felt that Chapter 13 cases were beyond their

control. They hesitated to incur the slight charge for a call to neighboring Racine. They preferred amortization under state law (although it provided less protection for the debtor) because they could maintain control over the proceedings and keep in close contact with the debtor who might later bring them higher fees in an accident or divorce case. Green Bay and Madison attorneys almost never

---

Is Garnishment Law Constitutional?

The constitutionality of the Wisconsin garnishment statute permitting the seizure of wages without any prior hearing in order to pay a bad debt has been appealed to the United States Supreme Court. The NAACP Defense and Educational Fund, which is the counsel in the case of Sniadash vs. Family Finance Corporation, contends such practice is a violation of due process. The original suit involved the seizure of $32.50 from the $65 weekly pay of Sniadash to pay on a debt of $420.

Under Wisconsin law, the first wage garnishment may be instituted without a hearing, although a hearing must be held before the money is given to the creditor. There must also be a judgment before subsequent garnishments will be ordered by the court. Sixteen other states have laws on the books similar to this.

---

used Wisconsin's amortization proceeding and did not speak of it as a lure to attract clients in better paying cases.

With only four cities, it is statistically impossible to estimate how much of the variation is explained by the political culture, by the legal culture, and by what appear to be accidental variations. Nevertheless, the wide variations discovered among four cities are significant.

This exploration of court usage in wage garnishment and consumer bankruptcy actions shows none of the usual political links between governmental action and private demands. To look for partisan biases of the judges (or referees), for evidence of other attitudinal biases in their decisions, for the linkage between the judicial selection process and court decisions, for the role of other political activities in this process, we would come away convinced that wage garnishment and bankruptcy are totally nonpolitical processes. Only an examination of patronage shows political processes at work, since the referees may appoint at will Chapter 13 trustees and trustees for all bankrupt estates. But Chapter 13 cases don't generate a great deal of revenue for the trustees and most straight bankruptcies by consumers involve either no or very limited assets so that the trustees benefit little from the cases. In the usual *partisan* sense, the processes examined are indeed nonpolitical.

Nevertheless, the courts are very political. Garnishment and bankruptcy cases invoke government power for private ends. Garnishment redistributes millions of dollars each year from the wages of debtors to the accounts of creditors. Bankruptcy results in the cancellation of other millions of dollars of indebtedness. The use of these court procedures also involves frequent harassment and considerable stigmatization. Although garnishment and bankruptcy are considered "private" proceedings, they significantly affect the distribution of material and symbolic values by government in the United States.

Thus it is politically significant that only a few of all eligible creditors and debtors use garnishment and bankruptcy proceedings. It means that government power is used to buoy what many consider to be the socially least desirable form of consumer credit—that extended by finance companies. The experience of wage earners with garnishment is likely to undermine their confidence in the courts as institutions which treat them justly and fairly. On the other hand, the use of bankruptcy by the minority of those eligible for it limits its benefits to the small group which happens to be well integrated into the legal system. Translating these findings to larger cities, it seems likely that in ghetto areas garnishment has even more disadvantageous effects in supporting undesirable credit and bankruptcy is even less used by the masses of alienated consumers who crowd the inner core.

The political process described is quite different from the electoral or legislative political processes political scientists ordinarily study. Instead, it resembles the administrative process which is becoming increasingly significant. The use of agricultural extension services, the use of counseling and educational services by the poor, the use of higher-education facilities by the young raise problems similar to those of court usage. None of these, however, involve, as wage garnishment and bankruptcy do, the dramatic use of the government coercive power for private objectives.

Government power can be invoked through far more routine ways than campaigning in elections. The consumption of government services is based on far different objectives than the ordinary use of government power through partisan means. Court actions, as well as other administrative decisions, frequently affect the core of people's personal behavior, their life-style, or fortune. They can color people's perception of the government and generate support for or alienation from it. We need to know what individuals and groups use such services and how they use them.

Child Convicts

Paul Lerman

About 100 years ago, the state of New Jersey built a special correctional facility to save wayward girls from a life of crime and immorality. Over the years the ethnic and racial backgrounds of the institutionalized girls changed, the educational level of their cottage parent-custodians shifted upward, and the program of correction grew more humane. But the types of offenses that constitute the legal justification for their incarceration in the State Home for Girls have not changed, not appreciably.

The vast majority of the girls in the Home today, as in past years, were accused of misbehavior that would not be considered crimes if committed by adults. They were formally adjudicated and institutionalized as delinquents, but most of them have not committed real criminal acts. Over 80 percent of them in 1969 were institutionalized for the following misdeeds: running away from home, being incorrigible, ungovernable and beyond the control of parents, being truant, engaging in sexual relations, and becoming pregnant. Criminologists classify this mixture of noncriminal acts "juvenile status offenses," since only persons of a juvenile status can be accused, convicted and sentenced as delinquents for committing them. Juvenile status offenses apply to boys as well as girls, and they form the bases for juvenile court proceedings in all 50 states.

Most Americans are probably unaware that juveniles are subject to stricter laws than adults, and to more severe penalties for noncriminal acts than are many adults who commit felonies. This practice, so apparently antithetical to our national conceit of child-centeredness, began well before the Revolution. The Puritans of the Plymouth Bay Colony initiated the practice of defining and treating as criminal children who were "rude, stubborn, and unruly," or who behaved "disobediently and disorderly towards their parents, masters, and governors." In 1824, when the House of Refuge established the first American juvenile correctional institution in New York City, the Board of Managers was granted explicit sanction by the state legislature to hold in custody and correct youths who were leading a "vicious or vagrant life," as well as those convicted of any crime. The first juvenile court statute, passed in Illinois in 1899, continued the tradition of treating juvenile status offenses as criminal by including this class of actions as part of the definition of "delinquency." Other states copied this legislative practice as they boarded the bandwagon of court reform.

My contention that juvenile status offenders are still handled through a *criminal* process will be disputed by many defenders of the current system who argue that the creation of the juvenile court marked a significant break with the past. They contend that juvenile courts were set up to deal with the child and his needs, rather than with his offense. In line with this benign aim, the offense was to be viewed as a symptom of a child's need for special assistance. The juvenile court was designed to save children—not punish them. Only "neglectful" parents were deemed appropriate targets of punishment.

Unfortunately, the laudable intentions of the founders of the court movement have yet to be translated into reality. The United States Supreme Court, in 1967, reached this conclusion; so, too, did the Task Force on Delinquency of the President's Commission on Law Enforcement and the Administration of Justice. Both governmental bodies ruled that juvenile court dispositions were, in effect, sentences that bore a remarkable resemblance to the outcomes of adult criminal proceedings. The Supreme Court was appalled at the idea that 15-year-old Gerald Gault could be deprived of his liberty for up to six years without the benefits of due process of law found in adult courts. The majority was persuaded that the consequences of judicial decisions should be considered, not just the ideals of the founders of the juvenile court.

From an historical perspective, the Supreme Court's ruling appears quite reasonable—although it was 70 years overdue. The juvenile court was grafted onto an existing schema for defining youthful misdeeds as illegal behavior. It was also grafted onto a correctional system that had begun separating youngsters from adults, and boys from girls, for many years before the first juvenile court was established.

Long before there was a juvenile court, the American predilection for utilizing legal coercion to control youthful behavior had been well established. The form of the jurisdictional mandate changed with the emergence of the juvenile court—but the substantive range and scope of youthful liability for noncriminal behavior has not really changed.

Since the Supreme Court ruling in *Gault v. Arizona*, there has been increased concern and debate over the introduction of legal counsel and minimal procedural rights in the operation of the juvenile court. The preoccupation with legal rights in the courtroom has, however, obscured the fact that the sociolegal boundaries of delinquency statutes were unaffected by *Gault*. Nevertheless, some revision of the laws has been undertaken by the states, at least since 1960 when the Second United Nations Congress on the Prevention of Crime and the Treatment of Offenders recommended that juveniles should not be prosecuted as delinquents for behavior which, if exhibited by adults, would not be a matter of legal concern.

One state, New York, even approached a technical compliance with the United Nations standard. In New York, juvenile status offenders are adjudicated with a separate petition alleging a "person in need of supervision" (PINS); traditional criminal offenses use a petition that alleges "delinquency." However, true to American tradition, both types of petitioned young people are locked up in the same detention facilities and reform schools. One of the most "progressive" juvenile court laws in the country was initially enacted with restrictions on mixing, but this was soon amended to permit the change to be merely semantic, not substantive. Besides New York, six other states have amended their juvenile codes to establish a distinctive labeling procedure to distinguish criminal and noncriminal acts. Each of these states (California, Illinois, Kansas, Colorado, Oklahoma and Vermont) has banned *initial* commitment to juvenile reformatories of children within the noncriminal jurisdiction of the court. Whether this ban will be continued in practice (and in the statutes) is uncertain. Meanwhile, young people can still be mixed in detention facilities, transfers to reformatories are technically possible, and subsequent commitments to delinquent institutions are apparently permitted. In addition, it is doubtful whether the public (including teachers and prospective employers) distinguishes between those "in need of supervision" and delinquents.

The Police as Dutch Uncles

If the letter and spirit of American juvenile statutes were rigorously enforced, our delinquency rates and facilities would be in even deeper trouble than they are today. For few American youth would reach adulthood without being liable to its stern proscriptions. However, mitigating devices are used to avoid further overcrowding court dockets and institutions, and to demonstrate that parents and enforcement officials can be humane and child-centered. Adult authorities are permitted to exercise discretionary behavior in processing actions by official petitions. The American system is notorious for its widespread use of unofficial police and judicial recording and supervision of juveniles, whether status offenders or real delinquents. As a matter of historical fact, the hallmark of the American system is the intriguing combination of limitless scope of our delinquency statutes and enormous discretion granted in their enforcement and administration. Our statutes appear to reflect the image of the stern Puritan father, but our officials are permitted to behave like Dutch uncles—if they are so inclined.

Discretionary decision making by law enforcement officials has often been justified on the grounds that it permits an "individualization" of offenders, as well as for reasons of pragmatic efficiency. While this may be true in some cases, it is difficult to read the historical record and not conclude that many juvenile status actions could have been defined as cultural differences and childhood play fads, as well as childhood troubles with home, school and sex. Using the same broad definition of delinquency, reasonable adults have differed—and continue to differ—over the sociolegal meaning of profanity, smoking, drinking, sexual congress, exploring abandoned buildings, playing in forbidden places, idling, hitching rides on buses, trucks and cars, sneaking into shows and subways and so forth. While many judgments about the seriousness of these offenses may appear to be based on the merits of the individual case, delinquency definitions, in practice, employ shifting cultural standards to distinguish between childhood troubles, play fads and neighborhood differences. Today, officials in many communities appear more tolerant of profanity and smoking than those of the 1920s, but there is continuing concern regarding female sexuality, male braggadocio and disrespect of adult authority. In brief, whether or not a youth is defined as delinquent may depend on the era, community and ethnic status of the official—as well as the moral guidelines of individual law enforcers.

National studies of the prevalence of the problem are not readily available. However, we can piece together data that indicate that the problem is not inconsequential. A conservative estimate, based upon analysis of national juvenile court statistics compiled by the United States Children's Bureau, indicates that juvenile status crimes comprise about 25 percent of the children's cases initially appearing before juvenile courts on a formal petition. About one out of every five boys' delinquency petitions and over one-half of all girls' cases are based on charges for which an adult would not be legally liable ever to appear in court.

The formal petitions have an impact on the composition of juvenile facilities, as indicated by the outcomes of legal processing. A review of state and local detention facilities disclosed that 40 to 50 percent of the cases in custody, pending dispositional hearings by judges, consisted of delinquents who had committed no crimes. A study of nearly 20 correctional institutions in various parts of the country revealed that between 25 and 30 percent of their resident delinquent population consisted of young people convicted of a juvenile status offense.

The figures cited do not, however, reveal the number of youths that are treated informally by the police and the courts. Many young people are released with their cases recorded as "station adjustments"; in a similar fashion, thousands of youths are informally dealt with at court intake or at an unofficial court hearing. Even though these cases are not formally adjudicated, unofficial records are maintained and can be used against the children if they have any future run-ins with the police or courts. The number of these official, but nonadjudicated, contacts is difficult to estimate, since our requirements for social bookkeeping are far less stringent than our demands for financial accountability.

One careful study of police contacts in a middle-sized city, cited approvingly by a task force of the President's Commission on Law Enforcement and the Administration of Justice, disclosed that the offense that ranked highest as a delinquent act was "incorrigible, runaway"; "disorderly conduct" was second; "contact suspicion, investigation, and information" ranked third; and "theft" was a poor fourth. In addition to revealing that the police spend a disproportionate amount of their time attending to noncriminal offenses, the study also provides evidence that the problem is most acute in low-income areas of the city. This kind of finding could probably be duplicated in any city—large, small or middle-sized—in the United States.

Legal Treatment of Delinquents without Crimes

A useful way of furthering our understanding of the American approach to dealing with delinquents without crimes is provided by comparing judicial decisions for different types of offenses. This can be done by reanalyzing recent data reported by the Children's Bureau, classifying offenses according to their degree of seriousness. If we use standard FBI terminology, the most serious crimes can be labeled "Part I" and are: homicide, forcible rape, armed robbery, burglary, aggravated assault and theft of more than $50. All other offenses that would be crimes if committed by an adult, but are less serious, can be termed "all other adult types" and labeled "Part II." The third type of offenses, the least serious, are those acts that are "juvenile status offenses." By using these classifications, data reported to the Children's Bureau by the largest cities are reanalyzed to provide the information depicted in the table. Three types of decisions are compared in this analysis: 1) whether or not an official petition is drawn after a complaint has been made; 2) whether or not the juvenile is found guilty, if brought before the court

**Disposition of Juvenile Cases at Three Stages
in the Judicial Process
19 of the 30 Largest Cities, 1965.**

	Part I (Most Serious Adult Offenses)	Part II (All Other Adult Offenses)	Juvenile Status Offenses
% Court Petition after complaint	57% N=(37.420)	33% (52,862)	42% (33,046)
% Convicted — if brought into court	92% N=(21,386)	90% (17,319)	94% (13,857)
% Placed or Committed — if convicted	23% N=(19,667)	18% (15,524)	26% (12,989)

on an official petition; and 3) whether or not the offender is placed or committed to an institution, if convicted. The rates for each decision level are computed for each of the offense classifications.

The table discloses a wide difference between offense classifications at the stage of deciding whether to draw up an official petition (57 percent versus 33 percent and 42 percent). Part I youth are far more likely to be brought into court on a petition, but juvenile status offenders are processed at a higher rate than all other adult types. At the conviction stage the differences are small, but the juvenile status offenders are found guilty more often. At the critical decision point, commitment to an institution, the least serious offenders are more likely to be sent away than are the two other types.

It is apparent that juvenile justice in America's large cities can mete out harsher dispositions for youth who have committed no crimes than for those who violate criminal statutes. Once the petitions are drawn up, juvenile judges appear to function as if degree of seriousness is not an important criterion of judicial decision making. If different types of offenders were sent to different types of institutions, it might be argued that the types of sentences actually varied. In fact, however, all three offender types are generally sent to the same institutions in a particular state—according to their age and sex—for an indeterminate length of time.

Length of Institutionalization

If American juvenile courts do not follow one of the basic components of justice—matching the degree of punishment with the degree of social harm—perhaps the correctional institutions themselves function differently. This outcome is unlikely, however, since the criteria for leaving institutions are not based on the nature of the offense. Length of stay is more likely to be determined by the adjustment to institutional rules and routine, the receptivity of parents or guardians to receiving the children back home, available bed space in cottages and the current treatment ideology. Juvenile status offenders tend to have more family troubles and may actually have greater difficulty in meeting the criteria for release than their delinquent peers. The result is that the delinquents without crimes probably spend more time in institutions designed for delinquent youth than "real" delinquents. Empirical support for this conclusion emerges from a special study of one juvenile jurisdiction, the Manhattan borough of New York City. In a pilot study that focused on a random sample of officially adjudicated male cases appearing in Manhattan Court in 1963, I gathered data on the range, median and average length of stay for boys sent to institutions. In New York, as noted earlier, juvenile status youth are called "PINS" (persons in need of supervision), so I use this classification in comparing this length of institutionalization with that of "delinquents."

The range of institutional stay was two to 28 months for delinquents and four to 48 months for PINS boys; the median was nine months for delinquents and 13 months for PINS; and the average length of stay was 10.7 months for delinquents and 16.3 months for PINS. Regardless of the mode of measurement, it is apparent that institutionalization was proportionately longer for boys convicted and sentenced for juvenile status offenses than for juveniles convicted for criminal-type offenses.

These results on length of stay do not include the detention period, the stage of correctional processing prior to placement in an institution. Analyses of recent detention figures for all five boroughs of New York City revealed the following patterns: 1) PINS boys and girls are more likely to be detained than are delinquents (54 to 31 percent); and 2) once PINS youth are detained they are twice as likely to be detained for more than 30 days than are regular delinquents (50 to 25 percent). It is apparent that juvenile status offenders who receive the special label of "persons in need of supervision" tend to spend more time in custodial facilities at *all* stages of their correctional experience than do delinquents.

Social Characteristics of Offenses and Offenders

The offenses that delinquents without crimes are charged with do not involve a clear victim, as is the case in classical crimes of theft, robbery, burglary and assault. Rather, they involve young people who are themselves liable to be victimized for having childhood troubles or growing up differently. Three major categories appear to be of primary concern: behavior at home, behavior at school and sexual experimentation. "Running away," "incorrigibility," "ungovernability" and "beyond the control of parental supervision" refer to troubles with parents, guardians or relatives. "Growing up in idleness," "truanting" and creating "disturbances" in classrooms refer to troubles with teachers, principals, guidance counselors and school routines. Sexual relations as "minors" and out-of-wedlock pregnancy reflect adult concern with the act and consequences of precocious sexual experimentation. In brief, juvenile status offenses primarily encompass the problems of growing up.

Certain young people in American society are more likely to have these types of troubles with adults: girls, poor youth, rural migrants to the city, underachievers and the less sophisticated. Historically, as well as today, a community's more disadvantaged children are most likely to have their troubles defined as "delinquent." In the 1830s the sons and daughters of Irish immigrants were over-represented in the House of Refuge, the nation's first juvenile correctional institution. In 1971 the sons and daughters of black slum dwellers are disproportionately dealt with as delinquents for experiencing problems in "growing up."

Unlike regular delinquents, juvenile status offenders often find a parent, guardian, relative or teacher as the chief complainant in court. Since juvenile courts have traditionally employed family functioning and stability as primary considerations in rendering dispositions, poor youth with troubles are at a distinct disadvantage compared to their delinquent peers. Mothers and fathers rarely bring their children to courts for robbing or assaulting nonfamily members; however, if their own authority is challenged, many parents are willing to use the power of the state to correct their offspring. In effect, many poor and powerless parents cooperate with the state to stigmatize and punish their children for having problems in growing up.

At least since *Gault*, the system of juvenile justice has been undergoing sharp attacks by legal and social critics. Many of these have pertinence for the processing and handling of juvenile status offenders. The current system has been criticized for the following reasons:

☐ The broad scope of delinquency statutes and juvenile court jurisdictions has permitted the coercive imposition of middle-class standards of child rearing.
☐ A broad definition has enlarged the limits of discretionary authority so that virtually any child can be deemed a delinquent if officials are persuaded that he needs correction.
☐ The presence of juvenile status offenses, as part of the delinquency statutes, provides an easier basis for convicting and incarcerating young people because it is difficult to defend against the vagueness of terms like "incorrigible" and "ungovernable."
☐ The mixing together of delinquents without crimes and real delinquents in detention centers and reform schools helps to provide learning experiences for the non-delinquents on how to become real delinquents.

☐ The public is generally unaware of the differences between "persons in need of supervision" and youths who rob, steal and assault, and thereby is not sensitized to the special needs of status offenders.

☐ Statistics on delinquency are misleading because we are usually unable to differentiate how much of the volume reflects greater public and official concern regarding home, school and sex problems, and how much is actual criminal conduct by juveniles.

☐ Juvenile status offenses do not constitute examples of social harm and, therefore, should not even be the subject of criminal-type sanctions.

☐ Juvenile institutions that house noncriminal offenders constitute the state's human garbage dump for taking care of all kinds of problem children, especially the poor.

☐ Most policemen and judges who make critical decisions about children's troubles are ill equipped to understand their problems or make sound judgments on their behalf.

☐ The current correctional system does not rehabilitate these youths and is therefore a questionable approach.

Two Unintended Consequences

In addition to the reasons cited, there are two unintended consequences that have not been addressed, even by critics. Analysis of the data presented earlier provides evidence that the current system is an unjust one. Youngsters convicted of committing the least serious offenses are dealt with more severely by virtue of their greater length of detention and institutionalization. Any legal system that purports to accord "justice for all" must take into account the degree of punishment that is proportionate to the degree of social harm inflicted. The current system does not meet this minimal standard of justice.

The recent ruling by the U.S. Supreme Court (Gault vs Arizona) found that the juvenile court of Arizona—and by implication the great majority of courts—were procedurally unfair. The court explicity ruled out any consideration of the substantive issues of detention and incarceration. It may have chosen to do so because it sincerely believed that the soundest approach to insuring substantive justice is by making certain that juveniles are granted the constitutional safeguards of due process: the right to confront accusers and cross-examine, the right to counsel, the right to written charges and prior notice, and the right against self-incrimination. While this line of reasoning may turn out to be useful in the long run of history, adherence to this approach would involve acceptance of an undesirable system until the time that substantive justice could catch up with procedural justice. The likelihood that the injustice accorded to youth is not intentional does not change the current or future reality of the court's disposition. Nevertheless, the inclusion of juvenile status offenders as liable to arrest, prosecution, detention and incarceration probably promotes the criminalization of disadvantaged youth. Earlier critics have indicated that incorrigible boys and girls sent to reform schools learn how to behave as homosexuals, thieves, drug users and burglars. But what is the impact at the community level, where young people initially learn the operational meaning of delinquency? From the child's point of view, he learns that occurrences that may be part of his daily life—squabbles at home, truancy and sexual precocity—are just as delinquent as thieving, robbing and assaulting. It must appear that nearly anyone he or she hangs around with is not only a "bad" kid but a delinquent one as well. In fact, there are studies that yield evidence that three-quarters of a generation of slum youth, ages ten to 17, have been officially noted as "delinquent" in a police or court file. It seems reasonable to infer that many of these records contain official legal definitions of essentially noncriminal acts that are done in the family, at school and with peers of the opposite sex.

It would be strange indeed if youth did not define themselves as "bad cats"—just as the officials undoubtedly do. It would be strange, too, if both the officials and the young people (and a segment of their parents) did not build on these invidious definitions by expecting further acts of "delinquency." As children grow older, they engage in a more consistent portrayal of their projected identity—and the officials dutifully record further notations to an expected social history of delinquency. What the officials prophesy is fulfilled in a process that criminalizes the young and justifies the prior actions of the official gatekeepers of the traditional system. Our societal responses unwittingly compound the problem we ostensibly desire to prevent and control—real delinquent behavior.

In the arena of social affairs it appears that negative consequences are more likely to occur when there is a large gap in status, power and resources between the "savers" and those to be "saved." Evidently, colonial-type relationships, cultural misunderstandings and unrestrained coercion can often exacerbate problems, despite the best of intentions. Given this state of affairs, it appears likely that continual coercive intrusion by the state into the lives of youthful ghetto residents can continue to backfire on a large scale.

We have probably been compounding our juvenile problem ever since 1824 when the New York State Legislature granted the Board of Managers of the House of Refuge broad discretionary authority to intervene coercively in the lives of youth until they become 21 years of age—even if they had not committed any criminal acts.

Generations of reformers, professionals and academics have been too eager to praise the philanthropic and rehabilitative intentions of our treatment centers toward poor kids in trouble—and insufficiently sensitive to the actual consequences of an unjust system that aids and abets the criminalization of youth.

Sophisticated defenders of the traditional system are aware of many of these criticisms. They argue that the intent of all efforts in the juvenile field is to help, not to punish, the child. To extend this help they are prepared to use the authority of the state to coerce children who might otherwise be unwilling to make use of existing agencies. Not all acts of juvenile misbehavior that we currently label "status offenses" are attributable to cultural differences. Many youngsters do, in fact, experience troubles in growing up that should be of concern to a humane society. The fundamental issue revolves on how that concern can be expressed so as to yield the maximum social benefits and the minimum social costs. Thus, while the consequences of criminalizing the young and perpetuating an unjust system of juvenile justice should be accorded greater recognition than benign intentions, it would be a serious mistake to propose an alternative policy that did not incorporate a legitimate concern for the welfare of children.

New Policy Perspectives

The issue is worth posing in this fashion because of a recent policy proposal advanced by the President's Commission on Law Enforcement and the Administration of Justice. The commission suggested that "serious consideration should be given complete elimination from the court's jurisdiction of conduct illegal only for a child. Abandoning the possibility of coercive power over a child who is acting in a seriously self-destructive way would mean losing the opportunity of reclamation in a few cases."

Changing delinquency statutes and the jurisdictional scope of the juvenile court to exclude conduct illegal only for a child would certainly be a useful beginning. However, the evidence suggests that the cases of serious self-destructiveness are not "few" in number, and there is reason to believe that many adjudicated and institutionalized young people do require some assistance from a concerned society. By failing to suggest additional policy guidelines for providing the necessary services in a *civil* context, the commission advanced only half a policy and provided only a limited sense of historical perspective.

Traditional American practices towards children in trouble have not been amiss because of our humanitarian concern, but because we coupled this concern with the continuation of prior practices whereby disliked behavior was defined and treated as a criminal offense (that is, delinquent). Unfortunately, our concern has often been linked to the coercive authority of the police powers of the state. The problems of homeless and runaway youths, truants, sex experimenters and others with childhood troubles could have been more consistently defined as *child welfare* problems. Many private agencies did emerge to take care of such children, but they inevitably left the more difficult cases for the state to service as "delinquents." In addition, the private sector never provided the services to match the concern that underlay the excessive demand. The problem of the troublesome juvenile status offender has been inextricably linked to: 1) our failure to broaden governmental responsibility to take care of *all* child welfare problems that were not being cared for by private social agencies; and 2) our failure to hold private agencies accountable for those they did serve with public subsidies. We permitted the police, courts and correctional institutions to function as our residual agency for caring for children in trouble. Many state correctional agencies have become, unwittingly, modern versions of a poorhouse for juveniles. Our *systems* of child welfare and juvenile justice, not just our legal codes, are faulty.

The elimination of juvenile status offenses from the jurisdiction of the juvenile court would probably create an anomalous situation in juvenile jurisprudence if dependency and neglect cases were not also removed. It would be ironic if we left two categories that were clearly noncriminal within a delinquency adjudicatory structure. If they were removed, as they should be, then the juvenile court would be streamlined to deal with a primary function: the just adjudication and disposition of young people alleged to have committed acts that would be criminal if enacted by an adult. Adherence to this limited jurisdiction would aid the court in complying with recent Supreme Court rulings, for adversary proceedings are least suited to problems involving family and childhood troubles.

If these three categories were removed from the traditional system, we would have to evolve a way of thinking about a new public organization that would engage in a variety of functions: fact finding, hearing of complaints, regulatory dispositions and provision of general child care and family services. This new public agency could be empowered to combine many of the existing functions of the court and child welfare departments, with one major prohibition: transfers of temporary custody of children would have to be voluntary on the part of parents, and all contested cases would have to be adjudicated by a civil court. This prohibition would be in harmony with the modern child welfare view of keeping natural families intact, and acting otherwise only when all remedial efforts have clearly failed.

We have regulatory commissions in many areas of social concern in America, thereby sidestepping the usual judicial structure. If there is a legitimate concern in the area of child and family welfare, and society wants to ensure the maintenance of minimum services, then legally we can build on existing systems and traditions to evolve a new kind of regulatory service commission to carry out that end. To ensure that the critical legal rights of parents and children are protected, civil family courts—as in foster and adoption cases—would be available for contest and appeal. However, to ensure that the agencies did not become bureaucratic busybodies, additional thought would have to be given to their policy-making composition, staffing and location.

A major deficiency of many regulatory agencies in this country is that special interests often dominate the administration and proceedings, while affected consumers are only sparsely represented. To ensure that the residents most affected by proposed family and child welfare boards had a major voice in the administration and proceedings, they could be set up with a majority of citizen representatives (including adolescents). In addition, they could be decentralized to function within the geographical boundaries of areas the size of local elementary or junior high school districts. These local boards would be granted the legal rights to hire lay and professional staff, as well as to supervise the administration of hearings and field services.

The setting up of these local boards would require an extensive examination of city, county and state child welfare services to ensure effective cooperation and integration of effort. It is certainly conceivable that many existing family and child welfare services, which are generally administered without citizen advice, could also be incorporated into the activities of the local boards. The problems to be ironed out would of course be substantial, but the effort could force a reconceptualization of local and state responsibilities for providing acceptable, humane and effective family and child welfare services on a broad scale.

Citizen Involvement

The employment of interested local citizens in the daily operation of family and child welfare services is not a totally new idea. Sweden has used local welfare boards to provide a range of services to families and children, including the handling of delinquency cases. While we do not have to copy their broad jurisdictional scope or underrepresentation of blue-collar citizens, a great deal can be learned from this operation. Other Scandinavian countries also use local citizen boards to deal with a range of delinquency offenses. Informed observers indicate that the nonlegal systems in Scandinavia are less primitive and coercive. However, it is difficult to ascertain whether this outcome is due to cultural differences or to the social invention that excludes juvenile courts.

There exist analogues in this country for the use of local citizens in providing services to children in trouble. In recent years there has been an upsurge in the use of citizen-volunteers who function as house parents for home detention facilities, probation officers and intake workers. Besides this use of citizens, New Jersey, for example, has permitted each juvenile court jurisdiction to appoint citizens to Judicial Conference Committees, for the purpose of informally hearing and handling delinquency cases. Some New Jersey counties process up to 50 percent of their court petitions through this alternative to adjudication. All these programs, however, operate under the direct supervision and jurisdiction of the county juvenile court judges, with the cooperation of the chief probation officers. It should be possible to adapt these local innovations to a system that would be independent of the coercive aspects of even the most benign juvenile court operation.

Opposition to Innovation

Quite often it is the powerful opposition of special interest groups, rather than an inability to formulate new and viable proposals for change, that can block beneficial social change. Many judges, probation workers, correction officers, as well as religious and secular child care agencies, would strenuously oppose new social policies and alternatives for handling delinquents without crimes. Their opposition would certainly be understandable, since the proposed changes could have a profound impact on their work. In the process of limiting jurisdiction and altering traditional practices, they could lose status, influence and control over the use of existing resources. Very few interest groups suffer these kinds of losses gladly. Proponents of change should try to understand their problem and act accordingly. However, the differential benefits that might accrue to children and their families should serve as a reminder that the problems of youth and their official and unofficial adult caretakers are not always identical.

Experts' Claims

One proposal in particular can be expected to call forth the ire of these groups, and that is the use of citizens in the administration and provision of services in local boards. Many professional groups—psychiatrists, social workers, psychologists, group therapists and school guidance counselors—have staked out a claim of expertise for the treatment of any "acting out" behavior. The suggestion that citizens should play a significant role in offering assistance undermines that claim. In reply, the professionals might argue that experts—not laymen—should control, administer and staff any programs involving the remediation of childhood troubles. On what grounds might this kind of claim be reasonably questioned?

First, there is nothing about local citizens' control of child and family welfare activities that precludes the hiring of professionals for key tasks, and entrusting them with the operation of the board's program. Many private and public boards in the fields of correction and child welfare have functioned this way in the past.

Second, any claims about an expertise that can be termed a scientific approach to correction are quite premature. There does not now exist a clear-cut body of knowledge that can be ordered in a text or verbally transmitted that will direct any trained practitioner to diagnose and treat effectively such classic problems as truancy, running away and precocious sex experimentation. Unlike the field of medicine, there are no clear-cut prescriptions for professional behavior that can provide an intellectual rationale for expecting a remission of symptoms. There exist bits and pieces of knowledge and practical wisdom, but there is no correctional technology in any acceptable scientific sense.

Third, a reasonable appraisal of evaluations of current approaches to delinquents indicates that there are, in fact, no programs that can claim superiority. The studies do indicate that we can institutionalize far fewer children in treatment centers or reform schools without increasing the risks for individuals or communities; or, if we continue to use institutional programs, young people can be held for shorter periods of time without increasing the risk. The outcome of these appraisals provides a case for an expansion of humane child care activities—not for or against any specific repertoire of intervention techniques.

Fourth, many existing correctional programs are not now controlled by professionals. Untrained juvenile court judges are administratively responsible for detention programs and probation services in more than a majority of the 50 states. Many correctional programs have been headed by political appointees or nonprofessionals. And state legislatures, often dominated by rural legislators, have exercised a very strong influence in the permissible range of program alternatives.

Fifth, the professionalization of officials dealing with delinquent youth does not always lead to happy results. There are studies that indicate that many trained policemen and judges officially process and detain more young people than untrained officials, indicating that their definition of delinquency has been broadened by psychiatric knowledge. At this point in time, there is a distinct danger that excessive professionalization can lead to overintervention in the lives of children and their families.

Sixth, there is no assurance that professionals are any more responsive to the interests and desires of local residents than are untrained judges and probation officers. Citizens, sharing a similar life style and knowledgeable about the problems of growing up in a given community, may be in a better position to enact a *parens patrie* doctrine than are professionals or judges.

Seventh, in ghetto communities, reliance on professional expertise can mean continued dependence on white authority systems. Identification of family and child welfare boards as "our own" may compensate for any lack of expertise by removing the suspicion that any change of behavior by children and parents is for the benefit of the white establishment. The additional community benefits to be gained from caring for "our own" may also outweigh any loss of professional skills. The benefits accruing from indigenous control over local child welfare services would hold for other minority groups living in a discriminatory environment: Indians, Puerto Ricans, Mexicans, hillbillies and French Canadians.

Alternative Policy Proposals

The proposal to create family and child welfare boards to deal with juvenile status offenses may be appealing to many people. However, gaining political acceptance may be quite difficult, since the juvenile justice system would be giving up coercive power in an area that it has controlled for a long period of time. The proposal may appear reasonable, but it may constitute too radical a break with the past for a majority of state legislators. In addition, the interest groups that might push for it are not readily visible. Perhaps participants in the Women's Lib movement, student activists and black power groups might get interested in the issue of injustice against youth, but this is a hope more than a possibility. In the event of overwhelming opposition, there exist two policy proposals that might be more acceptable and could aid in the decriminalization of juvenile status offenses.

The two alternatives function at different ends of the traditional justice system. One proposal, suggested by the President's Task Force on Delinquency, would set up a Youth Service Bureau that would offer local field services and be operated by civil authorities as an alternative to formal adjudication; the second proposal, suggested by William Sheridan of the Department of Health, Education, and Welfare, would prohibit the mixing of juvenile status offenders and classic delinquents in the same institutions. The Youth Service Bureau would function between the police and the court, while the prohibition would function after judicial disposition. Both proposals, separate or in concert, could aid in the decriminalization of our current practices.

However, both proposals would still leave open the possibility of stigmatization of youth who had committed no crimes. The Youth Service Bureau would provide an array of services at the community level, but the court would still have ultimate jurisdiction over its case load, and any competition over jurisdiction would probably be won by the traditional court system. The prohibition of mixing in institutions would, of course, not change the fact that young people were still being adjudicated in the same court as delinquents, even though they had committed no crimes. In addition, the proposal, as currently conceived, does not affect mixing in detention facilities. These limitations are evident in the statutes of states that have recently changed their definitions of "delinquency" (New York, California, Illinois, Colorado, Kansas, Oklahoma and Vermont).

Both proposals deserve support, but they clearly leave the traditional system intact. It is possible that Youth Service Bureaus could be organized with a significant role for citizen participation, thus paving the way for an eventual take-over of legal jurisdiction from the juvenile court for juvenile status offenses (and dependency and neglect cases, too). It is conceivable, too, that any prohibitions of mixing could lead to the increased placement of children in trouble in foster homes and group homes, instead of reform schools, and to the provision of homemaker services and educational programs for harried parents unable to cope with the problems of children. Both short-range proposals could, in practice, evolve a different mode of handling delinquents without crimes.

The adaptation of these two reasonable proposals into an evolutionary strategy is conceivable. But it is also likely they will just be added to the system, without altering its jurisdiction and its stigmatic practices. In the event this occurs, new reformers might entertain the radical strategy that some European countries achieved many years ago—removal of juvenile status offenders from the jurisdiction of the judicial-correctional system and their inclusion into the family and child welfare system.

New Definitions

What is the guarantee that young people will be serviced any more effectively by their removal from the traditional correctional system? The question is valid, but perhaps it underestimates the potency of social definitions. Children, as well as adults, are liable to be treated according to the social category to which they have been assigned. Any shift in the categorization of youth that yields a more positive image can influence such authorities as teachers, employers, military recruiters and housing authority managers. For there is abundant evidence that the stigma of delinquency can have negative consequences for an individual as an adult, as well as during childhood.

It is evident, too, that our old social definitions of what constitutes delinquency have led us to construct a system of juvenile justice that is quite unjust. By failing to make reasonable distinctions and define them precisely, we not only treat juvenile status offenders more harshly but undermine any semblance of ordered justice for *all* illegal behavior committed by juveniles. Maintenance of existing jurisdictional and definitional boundaries helps to perpetuate an unjust system for treating children. That this unjust system may also be a self-defeating one that compounds the original problem should also be taken into account before prematurely concluding that a shift in social labeling procedures is but a minor reform.

We would agree, however, with the conclusion that a mere semantic shift in the social definition of children in trouble is not sufficient. The experience of New York in providing a social label of "person in need of supervision" (PINS)—without providing alternative civil modes for responding to this new distinction—indicates that reform can sometimes take the guise of "word magic." Children are often accused of believing in the intrinsic power of words and oaths; adults can play the game on an even larger scale.

We need alternative social resources for responding to our change in social definitions, if we are at all serious about dealing with the problem. Whether we are willing to pay the financial costs for these alternatives is, of course, problematic. One approach to this issue might be to identify funds currently spent for noncriminal youth in the traditional police, court, and correctional subsystems, and then reallocate the identified dollars into a new child welfare service. This reallocation strategy would not require new funding, but merely a financial shift to follow our new

social definitions and intended responses. The choices would be primarily legal, political, and moral ones and not new economic decisions.

A second strategy for funding a new policy might be based on a more rational approach to the problem. We could attempt to assess the societal "need" for such services and then compute the amount of financial resources required to meet this newly assumed public responsibility. This approach could prove more costly than the reallocation strategy. Conceivably, the strategies of assessed need and reallocation could be combined at the same time or over the years. However, whether we might be willing to tax ourselves to support a more reasonable and moral social policy may turn out to be a critical issue. Perceived in this manner, the problem of defining and responding to children in trouble is as much financial as it is political, legal, and moral. But this, too, is an integral part of the American approach to delinquents without crimes.

Crime, Victims, and the Police

Philip H. Ennis

"A skid row drunk lying in a gutter is crime. So is the killing of an unfaithful wife. A Cosa Nostra conspiracy to bribe public officials is crime. So is a strong-arm robbery...." So states the report of the President's Commission on Law Enforcement and Administration of Justice, commonly known as the Crime Commission report, in pointing out the diversity of crime. Our recent investigation at Chicago's National Opinion Research Center reveals that Americans are also frequent prey to incidents which may not fall firmly within the jurisdiction of criminal law, but which still leave the ordinary citizen with a strong sense of victimization—consumer frauds, landlord-tenant violations, and injury or property damage due to someone else's negligent driving.

With the aid of a new research method for estimating national crime rates (see box, page 321) the Crime Commission study has now confirmed what many have claimed all along—that the rates for a wide range of personal crimes and property offenses are considerably higher than previous figures would indicate. Traditional studies have relied on the police blotter for information. The present research, devised and carried out by the National Opinion Research Center (NORC), tried a survey approach instead. Taking a random sample of 10,000 households during the summer of 1965, we asked people what crimes had been committed against them during the preceding year. The results—roughly 2,100 verified incidents—indicated that as many as half of the people interviewed were victims of offenses which they did not report to the police.

This finding raised several questions. How much did this

very high incidence of unreported offenses alter the picture presented by the standard measures, notably the FBI's Uniform Crime Reports (UCR) index, based only on reported incidents? What was the situation with minor offenses, those not considered in the UCR index? What sorts of crimes tended to go unreported? And why did so many victims fail to contact the authorities? These were some of the issues we attempted to probe.

The Unknown Victims

More than 20 percent of the households surveyed were criminally victimized during the preceding year. This figure includes about *twice as much* major crime as reported by the UCR index. The incidence of minor crimes—simple assaults, petty larcenies, malicious mischiefs, frauds, and so on—is even greater. According to our research, these are at least twice as frequent as major crimes. The UCR index includes seven major crimes, so the proliferation of petty offenses not taken into account by the index makes the discrepancy between that index and the real crime picture even greater than a consideration of major offenses alone would indicate.

Table I compares our figures with the UCR rates for the seven major crimes upon which the index is based—homicide, forcible rape, robbery, aggravated assault, burglary, larceny (over $50), and auto theft. The homicide rate projected by the survey is very close to the UCR rate—not surprising since murder is the crime most likely to be discovered and reported.

The survey estimate of the car theft rate is puzzlingly low. This could be because people report their cars "stolen" to the police and then find that they themselves have "misplaced" the car or that someone else has merely "borrowed" it. They may either forget the incident when interviewed or be too embarrassed to mention it. The relatively high rate of auto thefts reported to the police confirms other studies which show people are more likely to notify the police in this case than they are if they are victims of most other crimes. It may also indicate that people think the police can or will do more about a car theft than about many other offenses.

The startling frequency of reported forcible rape, four times that of the UCR index, underscores the peculiar nature of this crime. It occurs very often among people who know each other—at the extreme, estranged husband and wife—and there appears to be some stigma attached to the victim. Yet among the cases discovered in the survey, too few to be statistically reliable, most were reported to the police. Do the police tend to downgrade the offense

into an assault or a minor sex case or put it into some miscellaneous category? This is a well-known practice for certain other kinds of crime.

TABLE I—ESTIMATED RATES OF MAJOR CRIMES: 1965-1966

Crime	NORC sample: estimated rate per 100,000	Uniform Crime Reports, 1965: individual or residential rates per 100,000
Homicide	3.0	5.1
Forcible rape	42.5	11.6
Robbery	94.0	61.4*
Aggravated assault	218.3	106.6
Burglary	949.1	296.6*
Larceny ($50+)	606.5	267.4*
Car theft	206.2	226.0†
Total	2,119.6	974.7

* The 1965 Uniform Crime Reports show for burglary and larcenies the number of residential and individual crimes. The overall rate per 100,000 population is therefore reduced by the proportion of these crimes that occurred to individuals. Since all robberies to individuals were included in the NORC sample regardless of whether the victim was acting as an individual or as part of an organization, the *total* UCR figure was used for comparison.

† The reduction of the UCR auto theft rate by 10 percent is based on the figures of the Automobile Manufacturers Association, showing that 10 percent of all cars are owned by leasing-rental agencies and private and governmental fleets. The Chicago Police Department's auto theft personnel confirmed that about 7-10 percent of stolen cars recovered were from fleet, rental, and other non-individually owned sources.

To what extent is crime concentrated in the urban environment? To what extent are there regional differences in crime rates? And to what extent are the poor, and especially Negroes, more or less likely to be victims of crime? Behind these questions lie alternative remedial measures, measures which range from city planning and antipoverty programs to the training and organization of police departments and the allocation of their resources throughout the nation.

The Wild, Wild West

The NORC findings presented in the chart above give an overview of the crime rates for central cities in metropolitan areas, for their suburban environs, and for nonmetropolitan areas in the four main regions of the country. The chart shows the crime rate (per 100,000 population) for serious crimes against the person (homicide, rape, robbery, and aggravated assault) and serious crimes against property (burglary, larceny over $50, and vehicle theft).

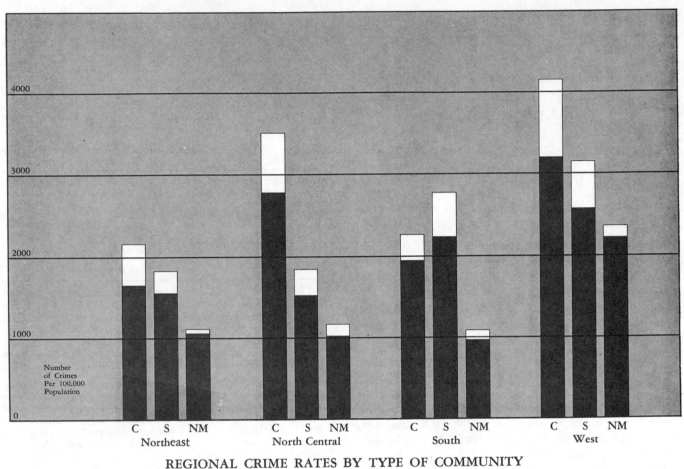

REGIONAL CRIME RATES BY TYPE OF COMMUNITY

☐ Crimes against the person   ■ Crimes against property   C = Central cities   S = Suburban environs   NM = Nonmetropolitan areas

The myth of the wild West is borne out by our figures. Its present crime rate, for both property and personal crimes, is higher than that of any other region of the country. The West has almost twice the rates of the Northeast for all three types of communities. The South, in contrast, does not appear to have the high rate of violent crime that is sometimes alleged.

As one moves from the central city to the suburbs and out into the smaller towns and rural areas, the crime rates decline, but much more drastically for crimes against the person than for property crimes. The metropolitan center has a violent crime rate about *five times* as high as the smaller city and rural areas, but a property crime rate only *twice* as high.

Evidently the city is a more dangerous place than the suburbs or a small town. Yet these figures require some qualification: About 40 percent of the aggravated assaults and rapes (constituting most of the serious crimes against the person) take place *within* the victim's home; and about 45 percent of all the serious crimes against the person are committed by someone familiar to the victim. Random "crime in the streets" by strangers is clearly *not* the main picture that emerges from these figures, even in the urban setting.

Who are the victims? Among lower income groups (under $6,000 per year) Negroes are almost twice as likely as whites to be victims of serious crimes of violence but only very slightly more likely to be victims of property crimes. Our figures show that, per 100,000 population, an estimated 748 low-income Negroes per year will be victims of criminal violence and 1,927 victims of property offenses, whereas the numbers for whites in the same income bracket are 402 and 1,829. The situation is exactly reversed for upper income groups. The wealthier Negro is not much more like-

320

Finding the Victims

The study reported here is one of the major research efforts to have provided hard figures for the President's Crime Commission report. Its survey approach originated from well-known difficulties with police statistics. Those difficulties included the lack of comparability of criminal statistics in different cities; the fact that "crime waves" could be made to appear and disappear with changes in the system of reporting; the failure to include some kinds of criminal activities in statistical reports or to differentially report certain types of crimes; and, perhaps most important, the impossibility of estimating how much crime was not being reported to the police.

The excellent work of the FBI's Uniform Crime Reports, upon which the UCR index of major crime is based, repaired only some of these difficulties because these reports still drew on local police records. Was there another way to measure crime that did not rely on the police? Could a survey method do the job? These were the questions that D. Gale Johnson, dean of the social sciences at The University of Chicago, asked Peter H. Rossi, director of the National Opinion Research Center (NORC), in 1962.

The inquiry was of more than academic interest, for Chicago's crime statistics had just been jogged upward by the new police superintendent, Orlando Wilson, pointing out in dramatic fashion all the difficulties just outlined. In Chicago, as well as nationally, important policy questions—what resources had to be given to the police and how they were to be allocated—depended upon accurate social bookkeeping on the amount and distribution of crime.

After considerable experimentation NORC concluded that a survey of individual *victims* of crime could feasibly supply national estimates. Moreover, such estimates were now imperative. The crime problem was becoming more serious daily, and the President's commission had already begun its investigation.

The study's focus on individual victims meant that some crimes could not be measured. People were simply not going to report their participation in illegal activities such as violation of gambling, game, or liquor laws, abortion, or the use of narcotics. Crimes against corporations or other large institutions were also excluded.

Crimes of violence and property crimes against the individual were the main targets. Defining such crimes turned out to be a problem. For example, many people said they had been "robbed" (personally held up) when in fact they had been "burglarized" (had had property stolen from their homes, cars, etc.). Was a fist fight in the schoolyard really an assault? Was being given a bad check by a friend a fraud, a basis for a civil law suit, or just a private matter? Was the man's coat really taken, or did he leave it in the bar? A "stolen" pocketbook may simply have been lost, and a "consumer fraud" have been no more than sharp dealing.

A variety of tactics were used to identify and reduce these potential errors. First, interviewers were instructed to allow the respondents plenty of time to recollect about each type of crime. Then, when an incident was recalled, the special questionnaire form probed intensively into the matter—what had happened, when and where, whether there were witnesses, whether the police were called, the extent of injuries, loss, and damage, and the direct and indirect costs. Was there an arrest, a trial? If not, what was the outcome?

The 3,400 "crimes" reported in the interviews were then reviewed by two different staff members, evaluating each case independently. To check this evaluation procedure, a team of lawyers from the American Bar Foundation and two detectives from the Chicago police department were asked to make independent evaluations of NORC's interviews. The results were most encouraging, with substantial agreement in between 75 and 80 percent of the cases.

The evaluation outcome reduced the initial 3,400 reported victimizations to about 2,100. These 2,100 offenses—ranging all the way from murder to victimizing incidents typically treated as private matters—were felt to realistically represent the experience of the American people with crime.

---

ly than the white to be a victim of a violent crime, but he is considerably more likely to have property stolen. His chances of losing property are 3,024 in 100,000, whereas the figure is only 1,765 for whites in the same income bracket. Burglary is the most common property crime against more affluent Negroes. The implication is that ghetto neighborhoods in which poor and richer Negroes live side by side make the latter more vulnerable to property losses than are higher income whites, who can live in more economically homogeneous areas.

Despite the fact then that per capita offense rates are generally acknowledged to be higher among Negroes than among whites, the incidence of whites being victimized by Negroes—an image frequently conjured up by the specter of "crime in the streets"—is relatively infrequent. Negroes tend instead to commit offenses against members of their own race. The same is true of whites. Further, to the extent that crime is interracial at all, Negroes are more likely to be victims of white offenders than vice versa. Our figures show that only 12 percent of the offenses against whites in

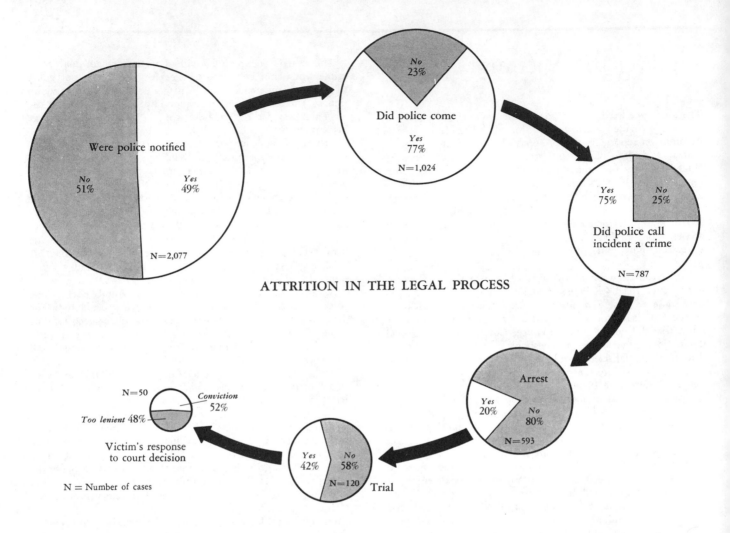

ATTRITION IN THE LEGAL PROCESS

Were police notified
No 51%   Yes 49%
N=2,077

Did police come
No 23%
Yes 77%
N=1,024

Did police call incident a crime
Yes 75%   No 25%
N=787

Arrest
Yes 20%   No 80%
N=593

Trial
Yes 42%   No 58%
N=120

Victim's response to court decision
N=50
Conviction 52%
Too lenient 48%

N = Number of cases

our sample were committed by nonwhites, whereas 19 percent of the nonwhite victims reported that the persons who committed offenses against them were white.

Who Calls the Police?

What happens when a person is victimized? How often are law enforcement and judicial authorities involved? What changes occur in the victim's attitude and behavior as a result of the incident?

If the "right thing" to do is to call the police when you have been a victim of a crime, and there is considerable pressure to do just that, why is it that half the victimizations were not reported to the police?

The more serious the crime, the more likely it is to be reported: 65 percent of the aggravated assaults in our sample were reported to the police, but only 46 percent of the simple assaults; 60 percent of the grand larcenies, but

only 37 percent of the petty larcenies. Insurance recovery also appears to play a role in the very high rate of reported auto thefts (89 percent) and reported victimizations that are the result of automobile negligence (71 percent). Victims of offenses at the border of the criminal law apparently do not think the police should be involved. Only 10 percent of the consumer fraud victims called the police, whereas 26 percent of the ordinary fraud victims (mainly those of bad checks) did so.

Those victims who said they did not notify the police were asked why. Their reasons fell into four fairly distinct categories. The first was the belief that the incident was not a police matter. These victims (34 percent) did not want the offender to be harmed by the police or thought that the incident was a private, not a criminal, affair. Two percent of the nonreporting victims feared reprisal, either physically from the offender's friends or economically from cancellation of or increases in rates of insurance. Nine percent did not want to take the time or trouble to get involved with the police, did not know whether they should call the police, or were too confused to do so. Finally, a substantial 55 percent of the nonreporting victims failed to notify the authorities because of their attitudes toward police effectiveness. These people believed the police could not do anything about the incident, would not catch the offenders, or would not want to be bothered.

The distribution of these four types of reasons for failure to notify police varies by type of crime and by the social characteristics of the victim, but two points are clear. First, there is strong resistance to invoking the law enforcement process even in matters that are clearly criminal. Second, there is considerable skepticism as to the effectiveness of police action.

The Attrition of Justice

A clue to this skepticism lies in the events which follow a call to the police. All the victims who reported an offense were asked how the police reacted and how far the case proceeded up the judicial ladder—arrest, trial, sentencing, and so forth. We have simplified the process into six stages:

■ Given a "real" victimization, the police were or were not notified.

■ Once notified, the police either came to the scene of the victimization (or in some other way acknowledged the event) or failed to do so.

■ Once they arrived, the police did or did not regard the incident as a crime.

■ Regarding the matter as a crime, the police did or did not make an arrest.

■ Once an arrest was made, there was or was not a trial (including plea of guilty).

■ The outcome of the trial was to free the suspect (or punish him "too leniently") or to find him guilty and give him the "proper" punishment.

The figure on page 40 shows the tremendous attrition as the cases proceed from the bottom of the "iceberg," the initial victimization, to the top, the trial and sentencing. Failure of the police to heed a call and their rejection of the incident as a crime account for a large proportion of this attrition. Also noteworthy are the low arrest and trial rates. Once the offender is brought to trial, however, the outcome appears more balanced. About half the offenders were treated too leniently in the victim's view, but the other half were convicted and given "proper" punishment.

Satisfaction and Revenge

How do the victims feel about this truncated legal process? Do they feel that the situation is their own fault and accept it, or are they dissatisfied with the relatively frequent failure of the police to apprehend the offender? When the victims were asked their feelings about the outcome of the incident, only 18 percent said they were very satisfied; another 19 percent were somewhat satisfied; 24 percent were somewhat dissatisfied; and 35 percent were very dissatisfied (4 percent gave no answer).

The level of satisfaction was closely related to how far the case went judicially. (See Table II.) People who did not call the police at all were the most dissatisfied. If they called and the police did not come, about the same percentage were very dissatisfied; but peculiarly, there were more who reported that they were satisfied. An arrest lowered the dissatisfaction level, but the dramatic differences appeared when the offender was brought to trial. If he was acquitted or given too lenient a penalty (in the victim's view), dissatisfaction ran high; if he was con-

TABLE II—DEGREE OF SATISFACTION WITH OUTCOME OF OFFENSE

Disposition of case	Very satisfied	Somewhat satisfied	Somewhat dissatisfied	Very dissatisfied
No notification of police	13%	18%	28%	41%
Police did not respond to notification	22	22	18	38
Police did not consider incident a crime	24	26	24	26
Crime, but no arrest	20	23	27	30
Arrest, but no trial	33	21	22	24
Acquittal or too lenient penalty	17	13	26	44
Conviction and "proper" penalty	60	16	12	12

victed and given the "proper" penalty, the victim was generally quite pleased. This suggests that the ordinary citizen's sense of justice includes a vengeful element—a desire for punishment over and above monetary compensation for loss. Advocates of rehabilitation rather than retribution for criminals might well take such public sentiments into account.

Quite independent of the judicial outcome of the case is its impact on the daily life and feelings of the victim and his family. Slightly more than 40 percent of the victims reported increased suspicion and distrustfulness along with intensified personal and household security measures. It appears that it is the unpredictability of the event and the sense of invasion by strangers rather than the seriousness of the crime that engenders this mistrust. With these strong feelings and the frequent lack of knowledge about the identity of the offender, victimization may well exacerbate existing prejudice against the groups typically blamed for social disorder and crime.

Police Popularity Poll

How does the public feel about the police? The survey asked all the crime victims and a comparably large sample of nonvictims a series of questions probing their attitudes on how well the local police do their job, how respectful they are toward the citizenry, and how honest they are. Items concerning the limits of police authority and exploring the functions of the police were also included.

Several conclusions emerged. Upper income groups are consistently more favorable in their evaluation of the police and are more in favor of augmenting their power than those with lower incomes. Negroes at all income levels show strong negative attitudes toward the police. (See Tables III and IV.)

Table III shows rather clearly that Negroes, regardless of income, estimate police effectiveness lower than whites do, with Negro women being even more critical than Negro men of the job the police are doing. Furthermore, Negroes show a smaller shift in attitude with increasing income than do whites, who are more favorable in their opinion of police effectiveness as their income rises.

Table IV shows that Negroes are also sharply more critical than whites are of police honesty. Here there are no income differences in attitude among white males. Women at higher income levels, both white and Negro, appear to be relatively less suspicious of police honesty. It is difficult to say how much these attitude differences are attributable to actual experience with police corruption and how much

they express degrees of general hostility to the police. In either case the results indicate a more negative attitude toward the police among Negroes than among whites.

TABLE III—POSITIVE OPINIONS ON LOCAL POLICE EFFECTIVENESS
(Percentage who think police do an excellent or good job in enforcing the law)

	White		Nonwhite	
Sex	Less than $6,000	$6,000 or more	Less than $6,000	$6,000 or more
Male	67%	72%	54%	56%
Female	66	74	39	43

TABLE IV—OPINIONS ON THE HONESTY OF NEIGHBORHOOD POLICE

	Males			
	White		Nonwhite	
Police are ...	Less than $6,000	$6,000 or more	Less than $6,000	$6,000 or more
Almost all honest	65%	67%	33%	33%
Most honest, few corrupt	24	26	47	41
Almost all corrupt	3	1	9	19
Don't know	8	6	11	7

	Females			
	White		Nonwhite	
Police are ...	Less than $6,000	$6,000 or more	Less than $6,000	$6,000 or more
Almost all honest	57%	65%	24%	35%
Most honest, few corrupt	27	29	54	49
Almost all corrupt	2	0	10	4
Don't know	14	6	12	12

The next question probed a more personal attitude toward the police—their respectfulness toward "people like yourself." Almost 14 percent of the Negroes answered that it was "not so good." Less than 3 percent of the whites chose this response. This represents a much more critical attitude by Negroes than by whites, with hardly any differences by sex or income. There is some tendency, however, for very low income people of both races and sexes to feel that the police are not sufficiently respectful to them.

One further conclusion is more tentative. It appears that there is no *one* underlying attitude toward the police. The police have many and sometimes only slightly related jobs to do in society. For example, they have a role both in suppressing organized gambling and in maintaining civil order. Most people (73 percent) feel the police should stop gambling even though it brings a good deal of money into the community. A significant minority (21 percent) feel the police should act only on complaints, and only 2 percent said the police should not interfere with gambling at all. With respect to police control of demonstrations for civil and political rights, on the other hand, a slight majority (54 percent) say police should not interfere if the protests are peaceful; 40 percent say police should stop all demonstrations; and 3 percent feel demonstrations should be allowed under any and all circumstances. Negroes are much more permissive about demonstrations than whites, and somewhat more permissive about gambling. Among lower income Negroes there is a significant relation between permissiveness on gambling and a strong prodemonstration attitude. But whites show no such consistent attitudes on the two issues. They tend to favor police intervention in gambling but not in rights demonstrations.

A more dramatic example of discontinuities in attitudes toward police has to do with limitations on their power. A national cross-section of citizens was asked:

■ "Recently some cities have added civilian review boards to their police departments. Some people say such boards offer the public needed protection against the police, and others say these boards are unnecessary and would interfere with good police work and morale. In general, would you be in favor of civilian review boards or opposed to them?"

In favor 45%
Opposed 35
Don't know 20

■ "Do you favor giving the police more power to question people, do you think they have enough power already, or would you like to see some of their power to question people curtailed?"

Police should have more power 52%
Have enough power already 43
Should curtail power 5

■ "The police sometimes have a hard time deciding if there is enough evidence to arrest a suspect. In general, do you think it is better for them to risk arresting an innocent person rather than letting the criminal get away, or is it better for them to be really sure they are getting the right person before they make an arrest?"

Risk arresting innocent 42%
Be really sure 58

■ "The Supreme Court has recently ruled that in criminal cases the police may not question a suspect without his lawyer being present, unless the suspect agrees to be questioned without a lawyer. Are you in favor of this Supreme Court decision or opposed to it?"

In favor 65%
Opposed 35

The significance of these results is their lack of consensus. On none of the questions is there overwhelming agreement or disagreement. Opinions are split almost in half, with the exception that hardly anyone is in favor of curtailing present police powers. The advocates of extending police authority in questioning suspects are almost balanced by those who think the police have enough power to do their job. Further, there is lack of internal agreement on the specific facets of the question. Being in favor of a civilian review board does not necessarily make a person support the Supreme Court decision on interrogation of suspects. Nor does a preference for having the police risk arresting the innocent rather than letting a criminal go free strongly predict being in favor of granting more power to the police in questioning people.

It is not clear why attitudes toward the police are so scattered. Perhaps police power is too new an issue on the national scene to have its components hammered into a clear and cohesive whole. Local variations in police practices may also blur the situation. It appears we are only at the beginning of a long process of relocating the police in the political spectrum.

As the federal presence in local law enforcement enlarges, both the shape of crime and the nature of law enforcement itself will change. Accurate crime statistics will be essential in monitoring these changes and in evaluating the worth of new programs designed to protect the public from the growing threat of invasion and victimization by criminal acts.

Police Brutality—
Answers to Key Questions
Albert J. Reiss, Jr.

"For three years, there has been through the courts and the streets a dreary procession of citizens with broken heads and bruised bodies against few of whom was violence needed to effect an arrest. Many of them had done nothing to deserve an arrest. In a majority of such cases, no complaint was made. If the victim complains, his charge is generally dismissed. The police are practically above the law."

This statement was published in 1903, and its author was the Hon. Frank Moss, a former police commissioner of New York City. Clearly, today's charges of police brutality and mistreatment of citizens have a precedent in American history—but never before has the issue of police brutality assumed the public urgency it has today. In Newark, in Detroit, in Watts, in Harlem, and, in fact, in practically every city that has had a civil disturbance, "deep hostility between police and ghetto" was, reports the Kerner Commission, "a primary cause of the riots."

Whether or not the police accept the words "police brutality," the public now wants some plain answers to some plain questions. How widespread is police mistreatment of citizens? Is it on the increase? Why do policemen mistreat citizens? Do the police mistreat Negroes more than whites?

To find some answers, 36 people working for the Center of Research on Social Organization observed police-citizen encounters in the cities of Boston, Chicago, and Washington, D.C. For seven days a week, for seven weeks during the summer of 1966, these observers, with police permission, sat in patrol cars and monitored booking and lockup procedures in high-crime precincts.

Obtaining information about police mistreatment of citizens is no simple matter. National and state civil-rights commissions receive hundreds of complaints charging mistreatment—but proving these allegations is difficult. The few local civilian-review boards, such as the one in Philadelphia, have not produced any significant volume of complaints leading to the dismissal or disciplining of policemen for alleged brutality. Generally, police chiefs are silent on the matter, or answer charges of brutality with vague statements that they will investigate any complaints brought to their attention. Rank-and-file policemen are usually more outspoken: They often insinuate that charges of brutality are part of a conspiracy against them, and against law and order.

The Meaning of Brutality

What citizens mean by police brutality covers the full range of police practices. These practices, contrary to the impression of many civil-rights activists, are not newly devised to deal with Negroes in our urban ghettos. They are ways in which the police have traditionally behaved in dealing with certain citizens, particularly those in the lower classes. The most common of these practices are:
—the use of profane and abusive language,
—commands to move on or get home,
—stopping and questioning people on the street or searching them and their cars,
—threats to use force if not obeyed,
—prodding with a nightstick or approaching with a pistol, and
—the actual use of physical force or violence itself.

Citizens and the police do not always agree on what constitutes proper police practice. What is "proper," or what is "brutal," it need hardly be pointed out, is more a matter of judgment about what someone did than a description of what police do. What is important is not the practice itself but what it means to the citizen. What citizens object to and call "police brutality" is really the judgment that they have not been treated with the full rights and dignity owing citizens in a democratic society. Any practice that degrades their status, that restricts their freedom, that annoys or harasses them, or that uses physical force is frequently seen as unnecessary and unwarranted. More often than not, they are probably right.

Many police practices serve only to degrade the citizen's sense of himself and his status. This is particularly true with regard to the way the police use language. Most citizens who have contact with the police object less to their use of four-letter words than to *how* the policeman talks to them. Particularly objectionable is the habit policemen have of "talking down" to citizens, of calling them names that deprecate them in their own eyes and those of others. More than one Negro citizen has complained: "They talk down to me as if I had no name—like 'boy' or 'man' or whatever, or they call me 'Jack' or by my first name. They don't show me no respect."

Members of minority groups and those seen as nonconformists, for whatever reason, are the most likely targets of status degradation. Someone who has been drinking may be told he is a "bum" or a "shitty wino." A woman walking alone may be called a "whore." And a man who doesn't happen to meet a policeman's standard of how one should look or dress may be met with the remark, "What's the matter, you a queer?" A white migrant from the South may be called a "hillbilly" or "shitkicker"; a Puerto Rican, a "pork chop"; a young boy, a "punk kid." When the policeman does not use words of status degradation, his manner may be degrading. Citizens want to be treated as people, not as "nonpersons" who are talked about as if they were not present.

That many Negroes believe that the police have degraded their status is clear from surveys in Watts, Newark, and Detroit. One out of every five Negroes in our center's post-riot survey in Detroit reports that the police have "talked down to him." More than one in ten says a policeman has "called me a bad name."

To be treated as "suspicious" is not only degrading, but is also a form of harassment and a restriction on the right to move freely. The harassing tactics of the police—dispersing social street-gatherings, the indiscriminate stopping of Negroes on foot or in cars, and commands to move on or go home—are particularly common in ghetto areas.

Young people are the most likely targets of harassing orders to disperse or move on. Particularly in summer, ghetto youths are likely to spend lots of time in public places. Given the inadequacy of their housing and the absence of community facilities, the street corner is often their social center. As the police cruise the busy streets of the ghetto, they frequently shout at groups of teenagers to "get going" or "get home." Our observations of police practices show that *white as well as Negro youths* are often harassed in this way.

Frequently the policeman may leave the car and threaten or force youths to move on. For example, one summer evening as the scout car cruised a busy street of a white slum, the patrolmen observed three white boys and a girl on a corner. When told to move on, they mumbled and grumbled in undertones, angering the police by their failure to comply. As they slowly moved off, the officers pushed them along the street. Suddenly one of the white patrolmen took a lighted cigarette from a 15-year-old boy and stuck it in his face, pushing him forward as he did so. When the youngsters did move on, one policeman remarked to the observer that the girl was "nothing but a whore." Such tactics can only intensify resentment toward the police.

Police harassment is not confined to youth. One in every four adult Negroes in Detroit claims he has been stopped and questioned by the police without good reason. The same proportion claim they have been stopped in their cars. One in five says he has been searched unnecessarily; and one in six says that his car was searched for no good reason. The members of an interracial couple, particularly a Negro man accompanying a white woman, are perhaps the most vulnerable to harassment.

What citizens regard as police brutality many policemen consider necessary for law enforcement. While degrading epithets and abusive language may no longer be considered proper by either police commanders or citizens, they often disagree about other practices related to law enforcement. For example, although many citizens see "stop and question" or "stop and frisk" procedures as harassment, police commanders usually regard them merely as "aggressive prevention" to curb crime.

Physical Force—or Self-Defense?

The nub of the police-brutality issue seems to lie in police use of physical force. By law, the police have the right to use such force if necessary to make an arrest, to keep the peace, or to maintain public order. But just how much force is necessary or proper?

This was the crucial problem we attempted to answer by placing observers in the patrol cars and in the precincts. Our 36 observers, divided equally between Chicago, Boston, and Washington, were responsible for reporting the details of all situations where police used physical force against a citizen. To ensure the observation of a large number of encounters, two high-crime police precincts were monitored in Boston and Chicago; four in Washington. At least one precinct was composed of primarily Negro residents, another primarily of whites. Where possible, we also tried to select precincts with considerable variation in social-class composition. Given the criterion of a high-crime rate, however, people of low socio-economic status predominated in most of the areas surveyed.

The law fails to provide simple rules about what—and how much—force that policemen can properly use. The American Bar Foundation's study *Arrest,* by Wayne La Fave, put the matter rather well, stating that the courts of all states would undoubtedly agree that in making an arrest a policeman should use only that amount of force he reasonably believes necessary. But La Fave also pointed out that there is no agreement on the question of when it is better to let the suspect escape than to employ "deadly" force.

Even in those states where the use of deadly force is limited by law, the kinds of physical force a policeman may use are not clearly defined. No kind of force is categorically denied a policeman, since he is always permitted to use deadly force in self-defense.

This right to protect himself often leads the policeman to argue self-defense whenever he uses force. We found that many policemen, whether or not the facts justify it, regularly follow their use of force with the charge that the citizen was assaulting a policeman or resisting arrest. Our observers also found that some policemen even carry pistols and knives that they have confiscated while searching citizens; they carry them so they may be placed at a scene should it be necessary to establish a case of self-defense.

Of course, not all cases of force involve the use of *unnecessary* force. Each instance of force reported by our observers was examined and judged to be either necessary or unnecessary. Cases involving simple restraint—holding a man by the arm—were deliberately excluded from consideration, even though a policeman's right to do so can, in many instances, be challenged. In judging when police force is "unwarranted," "unreasonable," or "undue," we rather deliberately selected only those cases in which a policeman struck the citizen with his hands, fist, feet, or body, or where he used a weapon of some kind—such as a nightstick or a pistol. In these cases, had the policeman been found to have used physical force improperly, he could have been arrested on complaint and, like any other citizen, charged with a simple or aggravated assault. A physical assault on a citizen was judged to be "improper" or "unnecessary" only if force was used in one or more of the following ways:

■ If a policeman physically assaulted a citizen and then failed to make an arrest; proper use involves an arrest.

■ If the citizen being arrested did not, by word or deed, resist the policeman; force should be used only if it is necessary to make the arrest.

■ If the policeman, even though there was resistance to the arrest, could easily have restrained the citizen in other ways.

■ If a large number of policemen were present and could have assisted in subduing the citizen in the station, in lockup, and in the interrogation rooms.

■ If an offender was handcuffed and made no attempt to flee or offer violent resistance.

■ If the citizen resisted arrest, but the use of force continued even after the citizen was subdued.

In the seven-week period, we found 37 cases in which force was used improperly. In all, 44 citizens had been assaulted. In 15 of these cases, no one was arrested. Of these, 8 had offered no verbal or physical resistance whatsoever, while 7 had.

An arrest was made in 22 of the cases. In 13, force was exercised in the station house when at least four other policemen were present. In two cases, there was no verbal or physical resistance to the arrest, but force was still applied. In two other cases, the police applied force to a handcuffed offender in a field setting. And in five situations, the offender did resist arrest, but the policeman continued to use force even after he had been subdued.

Just how serious was the improper use of force in these 44 cases? Naturally there were differences in degree of injury. In about one-half of the cases, the citizen appeared little more than physically bruised; in three cases, the amount of force was so great that the citizen had to be hospitalized. Despite the fact that cases can easily be selected for their dramatic rather than their representative quality, I want to present a few to give a sense of what the observers saw and reported as undue use of force.

Observing on Patrol

In the following two cases, the citizens offered no physical or verbal resistance, and the two white policemen made no arrest. It is the only instance in which the observers saw the same two policemen using force improperly more than once.

The police precinct in which these incidents occurred is typical of those found in some of our larger cities, where the patrolmen move routinely from gold coast to slum. There are little islands of the rich and poor, of old Americans and new, of recent migrants and old settlers. One moves from high-rise areas of middle- and upper-income whites through an area of the really old Americans—Indians—to an enclave of the recently arrived. The recently arrived are primarily those the policemen call "hillbillies" (migrants from Kentucky and Tennessee) and "porkchops" (Puerto Ricans). There are ethnic islands of Germans and Swedes. Although there is a small area where Negroes live, it is principally a precinct of whites. The police in the district are, with one exception, white.

On a Friday in the middle of July, the observer arrived for the 4 to 12 midnight watch. The beat car that had been randomly chosen carried two white patrolmen—one with 14 years of experience in the precinct, the other with three.

The watch began rather routinely as the policemen cruised the district. Their first radio dispatch came at about 5:30 P.M. They were told to investigate two drunks in a cemetery. On arriving they found two white men "sleeping one off." Without questioning the men, the older policeman began to search one of them, ripping his shirt and hitting him in the groin with a nightstick. The younger policeman, as he searched the second, ripped away the seat of his trousers, exposing his buttocks. The policemen then prodded the men toward the cemetery fence and forced them to climb it, laughing at the plight of the drunk with the exposed buttocks. As the drunks went over the fence, one policemen shouted, "I ought to run you fuckers in!" The other remarked to the observer, "Those assholes won't be back; a bunch of shitty winos."

Not long after they returned to their car, the policemen stopped a woman who had made a left turn improperly. She was treated very politely, and the younger policeman, who wrote the ticket, later commented to the observer, "Nice lady." At 7:30 they were dispatched to check a suspicious auto. After a quick check, the car was marked abandoned.

Shortly after a 30-minute break for a 7:30 "lunch," the two policemen received a dispatch to take a burglary report. Arriving at a slum walkup, the police entered a room where an obviously drunk white man in his late 40s insisted that someone had entered and stolen his food and liquor. He kept insisting that it had been taken and that he had been forced to borrow money to buy beer. The younger policeman, who took the report, kept harassing the man, alternating between mocking and badgering him rhetorical questions. "You say your name is Half-A-Wit [for Hathaway]? Do you sleep with niggers? How did you vote on the bond issue? Are you sure that's all that's missing? Are you a virgin yet?" The man responded to all of this with the seeming vagueness and joviality of the intoxicated, expressing gratitude for the policemen's help as they left. The older policeman remarked to the observer as they left, "Ain't drunks funny?"

For the next hour little happened, but as the two were moving across the precinct shortly after 10 P.M., a white man and a woman in their 50s flagged them down. Since they were obviously "substantial" middle-class citizens of the district, the policemen listened to their complaints that a Negro man was causing trouble inside the public-transport station from which they had just emerged. The woman said that he had sworn at her. The older policeman remarked, "What's a nigger doing up here? He should be down on Franklin Road!"

With that, they ran into the station and grabbed the Negro man who was inside. Without questioning him, they shoved him into a phone booth and began beating him with their fists and a flashlight. They also hit him in the groin. Then they dragged him out and kept him on his knees. He pleaded that he had just been released from a mental hospital that day and, begging not to be hit again, asked them to let him return to the hospital. One policeman said: "Don't you like us, nigger? I like to beat niggers and rip out their eyes." They took him outside to their patrol car. Then they decided to put him on a bus, telling him that he was returning to the hospital; they deliberately put him on a bus going in the opposite direction. Just before the Negro boarded the bus, he said, "You police just like to shoot and beat people." The first policeman replied, "Get moving, nigger, or I'll shoot you." The man was crying and bleeding as he was put on the bus. Leaving the scene, the younger policeman commented, "He won't be back."

For the rest of the evening, the two policemen kept looking for drunks and harassing any they found. They concluded the evening by being dispatched to an address where, they were told, a man was being held for the police. No one answered their knock. They left.

The station house has long been suspected of harboring questionable police practices. Interrogation-room procedures have been attacked, particularly because of the methods the police have used to get confessions. The drama of the confession in the interrogation room has been complete with bright lights and physical torture. Whether or not such practices have ever existed on the scale suggested by popular accounts, confessions in recent years, even by accounts of offenders, have rarely been accompanied by such high drama. But recently the interrogation room has come under fire again for its failure to protect the constitutional rights of the suspect to remain silent and to have legal counsel.

Backstage at the Station

The police station, however, is more than just a series of cubicles called interrogation rooms. There are other rooms and usually a lockup as well. Many of these are also hidden from public view. It is not surprising, then, that one-third of all the observations of the undue use of force occurred within the station.

In any station there normally are several policemen present who should be able to deal with almost any situation requiring force that arises. In many of the situations that were observed, as many as seven and eight policemen were present, most of whom simply stood by and watched force being used. The custom among policemen, it appeared, is that you intervene only if a fellow policeman needs help, or if you have been personally offended or affronted by those involved.

Force is used unnecessarily at many different points and places in the station. The citizen who is not co-operative during the booking process may be pushed or shoved, have his handcuffs twisted with a night-stick, have his foot stomped, or be pulled by the hair. All of these practices were reported by policemen as ways of obtaining "cooperation." But it was clear that the booking could have been completed without any of this harassment.

The lockup was the scene of some of the most severe applications of force. Two of the three cases requiring hospitalization came about when an offender was "worked over" in the lockup. To be sure, the arrested are not always cooperative when they get in the lockup, and force may be necessary to place them in a cell. But the amount of force observed hardly seemed necessary.

One evening an observer was present in the lockup when two white policemen came in with a white man. The suspect had been handcuffed and brought to the station because he had proved obstreperous after being arrested for a traffic violation. Apparently he had been drinking. While waiting in the lockup, the man began to urinate on the floor. In response, the policemen began to beat the man. They jumped him, knocked him down, and beat his head against the concrete floor. He required emergency treatment at a nearby hospital.

At times a policeman may be involved in a kind of escalation of force. Using force appropriately for an arrest in the field seemingly sets the stage for its later use, improperly, in the station. The following case illustrates how such a situation may develop:

Within a large city's high-crime rate precinct, occupied mostly by Negroes, the police responded to an "officer in trouble" call. It is difficult to imagine a call that brings a more immediate response, so a large number of police cars immediately converged at an intersection of a busy public street where a bus had been stopped. Near the bus, a white policeman was holding two young Negroes at gun point. The police-man reported that he had responded to a summons from the white bus-driver complaining that the boys had refused to pay their fares and had used obscene language. The policeman also reported that the boys swore at him, and one swung at him while the other drew a screwdriver and started toward him. At that point, he said, he drew his pistol.

The policemen placed one of the offenders in hand-cuffs and began to transport both of them to the sta-tion. While driving to the station, the driver of one car noted that the other policeman, transporting the other boy, was struggling with him. The first police-man stopped and entered the other patrol car. The observer reported that he kept hitting the boy who was handcuffed until the boy appeared completely sub-dued. The boy kept saying, "You don't have any right to beat me. I don't care if you kill me."

After the policemen got the offenders to the station, although the boys no longer resisted them, the police began to beat them while they were handcuffed in an interrogation room. One of the boys hollered: "You can't beat me like this! I'm only a kid, and my hands are tied." Later one of the policemen commented to the observer: "On the street you can't beat them. But when you get to the station, you can instill some re-spect in them."

Cases where the offender resists an arrest provide perhaps the most difficulty in judging the legitimacy of the force applied. An encounter that began as a dispatch to a disturbance at a private residence was one case about which there could be honest difference in judgment. On arrival, the policemen—one white, the other Negro—met a white woman who claimed that her husband, who was in the back yard and drunk, had beaten her. She asked the policemen to "take him in." The observer reported that the police found the man in the house. When they attempted to take him, he resisted by placing his hands between the door jamb. Both policemen then grabbed him. The Negro policeman said, "We're going to have trouble, so let's finish it right here." He grabbed the offender and knocked him down. Both policemen then wrestled with the man, handcuffed him, and took him to the station. As they did so, one of the policemen remarked, "These sons of bitches want to fight, so you have to break them quick."

A Minimal Picture?

The reader, as well as most police administrators, may be skeptical about reports that policemen used force in the presence of observers. Indeed, one police administrator, indignant over reports of undue use of force in his department, seemed more concerned that the policemen had permitted themselves to be observed behaving improperly than he was about their improper behavior. When demanding to know the names of the policemen who had used force improperly so he could discharge them—a demand we could not meet, since we were bound to protect our sources of information —he remarked, "Any officer who is stupid enough to behave that way in the presence of outsiders deserves to be fired."

There were and are a number of reasons why our observers were able to see policemen behaving improperly. We entered each department with the full cooperation of the top administrators. So far as the men in the line were concerned, our chief interest was in how citizens behave toward the police, a main object of our study. Many policemen, given their strong feelings against citizens, fail to see that their own behavior is equally open to observation. Furthermore, our observers are trained to fit into a role of trust— one that is genuine, since most observers are actually sympathetic to the plight of the policeman, if not to his behavior.

Finally, and this is a fact all too easily forgotten, people cannot change their behavior in the presence of others as easily as many think. This is particularly true when people become deeply involved in certain situations. The policeman not only comes to "trust" the observer in the law-enforcement situation—regarding him as a source of additional help if necessary— but, when he becomes involved in a dispute with a citizen, he easily forgets that an observer is present. Partly because he does not know what else to do, in such situations the policeman behaves "normally." But should one cling to the notion that most policemen modify their behavior in the presence of outsiders, one is left with the uncomfortable conclusion that our cases represent a minimal picture of actual misbehavior.

Superficially it might seem that the use of an excessive amount of force against citizens is low. In only 37 of 3826 encounters observed did the police use undue force. Of the 4604 white citizens in these encounters, 27 experienced an excessive amount of force —a rate of 5.9 for every 1000 citizens involved. The comparable rate for 5960 Negroes, of whom 17 experienced an excessive amount of force, is 2.8. Thus, whether one considers these rates high or low, the fact is that the *rate of excessive force for all white citizens in encounters with the police is twice that for Negro citizens.*

A rate depends, however, upon selecting a population that is logically the target of force. What we have just given is a rate for *all* citizens involved in encounters with the police. But many of these citizens are not logical targets of force. Many, for example, simply call the police to complain about crimes against themselves or their property. And others are merely witnesses to crimes.

The more logical target population consists of citizens whom the police allege to be offenders—a population of suspects. In our study, there were 643 white suspects, 27 of whom experienced undue use of force. This yields an abuse rate of 41.9 per 1000 white suspects. The comparable rate for 751 Negro suspects, of whom 17 experienced undue use of force, is 22.6 per 1000. If one accepts these rates as reasonably reliable estimates of the undue force against suspects, then there should be little doubt that in major metropolitan areas the sort of behavior commonly called "police brutality" is far from rare.

Popular impression casts police brutality as a racial matter—white police mistreating Negro citizens. The fact is that white suspects are more liable to being treated improperly by the police than Negro suspects are. This, however, should not be confused with the chances a citizen takes of being mistreated. In two of the cities we studied, Negroes are a minority. The chances, then, that any Negro has of being treated improperly are, perhaps, more nearly comparable to that for whites. If the rates are comparable, then one might say that the application of force unnecessarily by the police operates without respect to the race of an offender.

Many people believe that the race of the policeman must affect his use of force, particularly since many white policemen express prejudice against Negroes.

Our own work shows that in the police precincts made up largely of Negro citizens, over three-fourths of the policemen express prejudice against Negroes. Only 1 percent express sympathetic attitudes. But as sociologists and social psychologists have often shown, prejudice and attitudes do not necessarily carry over into discriminatory actions.

Our findings show that there is little difference between the rate of force used by white and by Negro policemen. Of the 54 policemen observed using too much force, 45 were white and 9 were Negro. For every 100 white policemen, 8.7 will use force; for every 100 Negro policemen, 9.8 will. What this really means, though, is that about one in every 10 policemen in high-crime rate areas of cities sometimes uses force unnecessarily.

Yet, one may ask, doesn't prejudice enter into the use of force? Didn't some of the policemen who were observed utter prejudiced statements toward Negroes and other minority-group members? Of course they did. But the question of whether it was their prejudice or some other factor that motivated them to mistreat Negroes is not so easily answered.

Still, even though our figures show that a white suspect is more liable to encounter violence, one may ask whether white policemen victimize Negroes more than whites. We found, for the most part, that they do not. Policemen, both Negro and white, are most likely to exercise force against members of their *own* race:

—67 percent of the citizens victimized by white policemen were white.

—71 percent of the citizens victimized by Negro policemen were Negro.

To interpret these statistics correctly, however, one should take into account the differences in opportunity policemen have to use force against members of their own and other races. Negro policemen, in the three cities we studied, were far *less* likely to police white citizens than white policemen were to police Negroes. Negro policemen usually policed other Negroes, while white policemen policed both whites and Negroes about equally. In total numbers, then, more white policemen than Negro policemen used force against Negroes. But this is explained by the fact that whites make up 85 percent of the police force, and more than 50 percent of all policemen policing Negroes.

Though no precise estimates are possible, the facts just given suggest that white policemen, even though they are prejudiced toward Negroes, do not discriminate against Negroes in the excessive use of force. The use of force by the police is more readily explained by police culture than it is by the policeman's race. Indeed, in the few cases where we observed a Negro policeman using unnecessary force against white citizens, there was no evidence that he did so because of his race.

The disparity between our findings and the public's sense that Negroes are the main victims of police brutality can easily be resolved if one asks how the public becomes aware of the police misusing force.

The Victims and the Turf

Fifty years ago, the immigrants to our cities—Eastern and Southern Europeans such as the Poles and the Italians—complained about police brutality. Today the new immigrants to our cities—mostly Negroes from the rural South—raise their voices through the civil-rights movement, through black-nationalist and other race-conscious organizations. There is no comparable voice for white citizens since, except for the Puerto Ricans, they now lack the nationality organizations that were once formed to promote and protect the interests of their immigrant forbears.

Although policemen do not seem to select their victims according to race, two facts stand out. All victims were offenders, and all were from the lower class. Concentrating as we did on high-crime rate areas of cities, we do not have a representative sample of residents in any city. Nonetheless, we observed a sizable minority of middle- and upper-status citizens, some of whom were offenders. But since no middle- or upper-class offender, white or Negro, was the victim of an excessive amount of force, it appears that the lower class bears the brunt of victimization by the police.

The most likely victim of excessive force is a lower-class man of either race. No white woman and only two Negro women were victimized. The difference between the risk assumed by white and by Negro women can be accounted for by the fact that far more Negro women are processed as suspects or offenders.

Whether or not a policeman uses force unnecessarily depends upon the social setting in which the encounter takes place. Of the 37 instances of excessive force, 37 percent took place in police-controlled settings, such as the patrol car or the precinct station. Public places, usually streets, accounted for 41 percent, and 16 percent took place in a private residence. The remaining 6 percent occurred in commercial settings. This is not, of course, a random sample of settings where the police encounter suspects.

What is most obvious, and most disturbing, is that the police are very likely to use force in settings that they control. Although only 18 percent of all situations involving suspects ever ended up at the station house, 32 percent of all situations where an excessive amount of force was used took place in the police station.

No one who accepts the fact that the police sometimes use an excessive amount of force should be surprised by our finding that they often select their own turf. What should be apparent to the nation's police administrators, however, is that these settings are under their command and control. Controlling the police in the field, where the policeman is away from direct supervision, is understandably difficult. But the station house is the police administrator's domain. The fact that one in three instances of excessive force took place in settings that can be directly controlled should cause concern among police officials.

The presence of citizens who might serve as witnesses against a policeman should deter him from undue use of force. Indeed, procedures for the review of police conduct are based on the presumption that one can get this kind of testimony. Otherwise, one is left simply with a citizen complaint and contrary testimony by the policeman—a situation in which it is very difficult to prove the citizen's allegation.

In most situations involving the use of excessive force, there were witnesses. In our 37 cases, there were bystanders present three-fourths of the time. But in only one situation did the group present sympathize with the citizen and threaten to report the policeman. A complaint was filed on that incident—the only one of the 37 observed instances of undue force in which a formal complaint was filed.

All in all, the situations where excessive force was used were devoid of bystanders who did not have a stake in being "against" the offender. Generally, they were fellow policemen, or fellow offenders whose truthfulness could be easily challenged. When a policeman uses undue force, then, he usually does not risk a complaint against himself or testimony from witnesses who favor the complainant against the policeman. This, as much as anything, probably accounts for the low rate of formal complaints against policemen who use force unnecessarily.

A striking fact is that in more than one-half of all instances of undue coercion, at least one other policeman was present who did not participate in the use of force. This shows that, for the most part, the police do not restrain their fellow policemen. On the contrary, there were times when their very presence encouraged the use of force. One man brought into the lockup for threatening a policeman with a pistol was so severely beaten by this policeman that he required hospitalization. During the beating, some fellow policemen propped the man up, while others shouted encouragement. Though the official police code does not legitimate this practice, police culture does.

Victims—Defiant or Deviant

Now, are there characteristics of the offender or his behavior that precipitate the use of excessive force by the police? Superficially, yes. Almost one-half of the cases involved open defiance of police authority (39 percent) or resisting arrest (9 percent). Open defiance of police authority, however, is what the policeman defines as *his* authority, not necessarily "official" authority. Indeed in 40 percent of the cases that the police considered open defiance, the policeman never executed an arrest—a somewhat surprising fact for those who assume that policemen generally "cover" improper use of force with a "bona-fide" arrest and a charge of resisting arrest.

But it is still of interest to know what a policeman *sees* as defiance. Often he seems threatened by a simple refusal to acquiesce to his own authority. A policeman beat a handcuffed offender because, when told to sit, the offender did not sit down. One Negro woman was soundly slapped for her refusal to approach the police car and identify herself.

Important as a threat to his authority may appear to the policeman, there were many more of these instances in which the policeman did *not* respond with the use of force. The important issue seems to be whether the policeman manages to assert his authority despite the threat to it. I suspect that policemen are more likely to respond with excessive force when they define the situation as one in which there remains a question as to who is "in charge."

Similarly, some evidence indicates that harassment of deviants plays a role in the undue use of force. Incidents involving drunks made up 27 percent of all incidents of improper use of force; an additional 5 percent involved homosexuals or narcotics users. Since deviants generally remain silent victims to avoid public exposure of their deviance, they are particularly susceptible to the use of excessive force.

It is clear, though, that the police encounter many situations involving deviants where no force is used. Generally they respond to them routinely. What is surprising, then, is that the police do not mistreat deviants more than they do. The explanation may lie in the kind of relationships the police have with deviants. Many are valuable to the police because they serve as informers. To mistreat them severely would be to cut off a major source of police intelligence. At the same time, deviants are easily controlled by harassment.

Clearly, we have seen that police mistreatment of citizens exists. It is, however, on the increase?

Citizen complaints against the police are common, and allegations that the police use force improperly are frequent. There is evidence that physical brutality exists today. But there is also evidence, from the history of our cities, that the police have long engaged in the use of unnecessary physical force. No one can say with confidence whether there is more or less of it today than there was at the turn of the century.

What we lack is evidence that would permit us to calculate comparative rates of police misuse of force for different periods of American history. Only recently have we begun to count and report the volume of complaints against the police. And the research reported in this article represents the only attempt to estimate the amount of police mistreatment by actual observation of what the police do to citizens.

Lack of Information

Police chiefs are notoriously reluctant to disclose information that would allow us to assess the nature and volume of complaints against the police. Only a few departments have begun to report something about citizen complaints. And these give us very little information.

Consider, for example, the 1966 Annual Report released by the New Orleans Police Department. It tells us that there were 208 cases of "alleged police misconduct on which action was taken." It fails to tell us whether there were any allegations that are *not* included among these cases. Are these all the allegations that came to the attention of the department? Or are they only those the department chose to review as "police disciplinary matters"? Of the 208 cases the department considered "disciplinary matters," the report tells us that no disciplinary action was taken in 106 cases. There were 11 cases that resulted in 14 dismissals; 56 cases that resulted in 72 suspensions, fines, or loss of days; and 35 cases involving 52 written or verbal "reprimands" or "cautionings."

The failure of the report to tell us the charge against the policeman is a significant omission. We cannot tell how many of these allegations involved improper use of force, how many involved verbal abuse or harassment, how many involved police felonies or misdemeanors, and so on. In such reports, the defensive posture of the nation's police departments is all too apparent. Although the 1966 report of the New Orleans Police Department tells us much about what the police allege were the felonies and misdemeanors by citizens of New Orleans, it tells us nothing about what citizens allege was misconduct by the police!

Many responsible people believe that the use of physical brutality by the police is on the wane. They point to the fact that, at least outside the South, there are more reports of other forms of police mistreatment of citizens than reports of undue physical coercion. They also suggest that third-degree interrogations and curbstone justice with the nightstick are less common. It does not seem unreasonable, then, to assume that police practices that degrade a citizen's status or that harass him and restrict his freedom are more common than police misuse of force. But that may have always been so.

Whether or not the policeman's "sense of justice" and his use of unnecessary force have changed remains an open question. Forms may change while practices go on. To move misuse from the street to the station house, or from the interrogation room to the lockup, changes the place but not the practice itself.

Our ignorance of just what goes on between police and citizens poses one of the central issues in policing today: How can we make the police accountable to the citizenry in a democratic society and yet not hamstring them in their legitimate pursuit of law and order? There are no simple answers.

Police departments are organizations that process people. All people-processing organizations face certain common problems. But the police administrator faces a problem in controlling practice with clients that is not found in most other organizations. The problem is that police contact with citizens occurs in the community, where direct supervision is not possible. Assuming our unwillingness to spend resources for almost one-to-one supervision, the problem for the police commander is to make policemen behave properly when they are not under direct supervision. He also faces the problem of making them behave properly in the station house as well.

Historically, we have found but one way—apart from supervision—that deals with this problem. That solution is professionalization of workers. Perhaps only through the professionalization of the police can we hope to solve the problem of police malpractice.

But lest anyone optimistically assume that professionalization will eliminate police malpractice altogether, we should keep in mind that problems of malpractice also occur regularly in both law and medicine.

Sexual Assaults in the Philadelphia Prison System and Sheriff's Vans

Alan J. Davis

In the summer of 1968, Joseph F. Mitchell, a slightly-built 19-year-old, was brought to trial before Alexander F. Barbieri, judge of the Court of Common Pleas No. 8 in Philadelphia County. Mitchell's lawyer, Joseph E. Alessandroni, told Judge Barbieri that his client, while being transported in a sheriff's van, had been repeatedly raped by a gang of criminals. A few weeks later, Alessandroni informed the judge that George Di-Angelo, a slender 21-year-old whom Barbieri had committed to the Philadelphia Detention Center merely for

pre-sentence evaluation, had been sexually assaulted within minutes of his admission.

Judge Barbieri thereupon appointed me, then Chief Assistant District Attorney of Philadelphia, to investigate these allegations. Police Commissioner Frank L. Rizzo started a parallel investigation; then these two investigations were merged.

In the Philadelphia prison system there are three facilities: the Detention Center, Holmesburg Prison, and the House of Correction. The period we chose to study was from June 1966 to July 31, 1968—a little over two years. Out of the 60,000 inmates who passed through the prison system in those 26 months, we interviewed 3,304—virtually all of them inmates during the period of our investigation. We also interviewed 561 out of the 570 custodial employees. We took 130 written statements from those who had given us important information, and gave polygraph ("lie-detector") examinations to 45 of them. We asked 26 employees to take polygraph tests: 25 refused, and the one employee who took the test "passed." We asked 48 inmates: seven refused, and of the 41 remaining, 10 failed the test and 31 passed. (We ignored the statements of those prisoners and employees who either would not take the test or who failed it.) In addition, we interviewed several people whom we believed had special information, and we reviewed all of the reports dealing with homosexuality issued by the prison system since June 1966. Finally, we made a number of detailed personal inspections of the prison facilities and of the sheriff's vans.

In brief, we found that sexual assaults in the Philadelphia prison system are epidemic. As Superintendent Hendrick and three of the wardens admitted, virtually every slightly-built young man committed by the courts is sexually approached within a day or two after his admission to prison. Many of these young men are repeatedly raped by gangs of inmates. Others, because of the threat of gang rape, seek protection by entering into a homosexual relationship with an individual tormentor. Only the tougher and more hardened young men, and those few so obviously frail that they are immediately locked up for their own protection, escape homosexual rape.

After a young man has been raped, he is marked as a sexual victim for the duration of his confinement. This mark follows him from institution to institution. Many of these young men return to their communities ashamed, and full of hatred.

This, then, is the sexual system that exists in the Philadelphia prisons. It is a system that imposes a punishment that is not, and could not be, included in the sentence of the court. Indeed, it is a system under which the least hardened criminals, and many men later found to be innocent, suffer the most.

A few typical examples of such sexual assaults may convey the enormity of the problem. In an early draft of our report, an attempt was made to couch this illustrative material in sociological, medical, and legal terminology less offensive than the raw, ugly language used by the witness and victims. This approach was abandoned. The incidents are raw and ugly. Any attempt to prettify them would be hypocrisy.

A witness describes the ordeal of *William McNichol*, 24 years old and mentally disturbed:

"That was June 11th, I was assigned to E Dorm. Right after the light went out I saw this colored male, Cheyenne—I think his last name is Boone. He went over and was talking to this kid and slapped him in the face with a belt. He was saying come on back with us and the kid kept saying I don't want to. After being slapped with the belt he walked back with Cheyenne and another colored fellow named Horse. They were walking him back into E Dorm. They were telling him to put his hand down and stop crying so the guard will not know what is going on. I looked up a couple of times. They had the kid on the floor. About 12 fellows took turns with him. This went on for about two hours.

"After this he came back to his bed and he was crying and he stated that 'They all took turns on me.' He laid there for about 20 minutes and Cheyenne came over to the kid's bed and pulled his pants down and

---

A Note on This Report

This article is based on the results of a three-month investigation conducted jointly by the Philadelphia District Attorney's office and the Police Department, under the supervision of the author. It culminated in a 103-page report submitted to Judge Alexander F. Barbieri and the public on Sept. 11, 1968. More than half of the report contains detailed recommendations for controlling sexual assaults and for the general reform of the Philadelphia prison system. Many of these recommendations are now being implemented by the city administration. This article relates only to those portions of the report analyzing sexual assaults and comparing the physical and psychological characteristics of the victims and aggressors.

got on top of him and raped him again. When he got done Horse did it again and then about four or five others got on him. While one of the guys was on him, raping him, Horse came over and said, 'Open your mouth and suck on this and don't bite it.' He then put his penis in his mouth and made him suck on it. The kid was hollering that he was gagging and Horse stated, 'you better not bite it or I will kick your teeth out.'

"While they had this kid they also had a kid named William in another section in E Dorm. He had his pants off and he was bent over and they were taking turns on him. This was Horse, Cheyenne, and about seven other colored fellows. Two of the seven were brothers.

"Horse came back and stated, 'Boy, I got two virgins in one night. Maybe I should make it three.' At this time he was standing over me. I stated, 'What are you looking at?' and he said 'We'll save him for tomorrow night.' "

Julius Brown, 18 years old:
"Brown stated that he has been in Holmesburg since March 29, 1968, and that about a week and a half ago, on Thursday, he was in I block; his cell was number 926. On this date, in the morning after breakfast, James Williams called him into his cell; he went into William's cell. Donald Reese was in there also. Further that he had owed Williams four cartons of cigarettes. Williams said to him that he would have to give the cigarettes back right now or he would have to give them something else. He [Brown] then started to walk out of the cell and Williams pushed him down. Williams picked up the window pole, Reese picked up a bench and stood blocking the door. Reese told him that if he goes to the guard they are going to get him anyway; there were other men outside the cell.

"Further that he walked out of the cell, they were all around him and walked to cell 971, and they pushed him inside. He went over and sat on the toilet seat. Twin [Roger Jones] came into the cell, they made him lay down on the floor, and Twin pulled his [Brown's] pants down and made him lay face down. Twin pushed his [Brown's] legs apart and Twin put his penis into his [Brown's] rectum. He was on him until he discharged. When he got through, Brown saw that he was bleeding from the rectum. Then Twin, Williams, Reese, and McDuffy told him that if he went to the guard their boys would get him to D block, and he was scared then to tell the guard. Further that he did cry out when Twin did this to him, but the guard wouldn't be able to hear him because the block is long.

"Brown went on to say that the next day after chow [breakfast] James Williams, McDuffy, Ike (Isaiah Franklin), and Leftenant got him in cell 972 [Roger Jones's cell]. They told him that everything is cool now as long as he doesn't tell. Further that he had never been in jail before and he was too scared to tell anybody. Then four of them did it to him—they put their penises into his rectum, James first, Ike second, Leftenant third, McDuffy fourth. Twin did not bother him that time. That after they did this he was bleeding and got sick.

"That night, Roach [Thomas Roach] came into his cell and changed with his partner. Roach told him that he would have to do it. When the guard came to check the cells, Roach turned over so he wouldn't be recognized. After the guard counted and left, Roach got on top of him, put his penis into his [Brown's] rectum, and discharged."

Nineteen-Year-Old Is Beaten

Charles Williams, 19 years old:
"On Tuesday morning, the first week of June at about 9:30 A.M., I was in my cell 412 on D block and I had started to clean up. A tall, heavy-set fella came into the cell and asked for a mirror and shaving brush and a comb, and that my cell partner said he could borrow.

"He then said that he heard something about me concerning homosexual acts. I told him what he had heard was not true. He then started to threaten me and if I didn't submit to him. Then I hit him with my fist in his face before he could hit me. Then about three more men came into the cell, and they started to beat me up, too. I fought back the best I could and then I fell on the floor and I got kicked in the ribs. Three guys were holding me while the other one tore my pants off; I continued to fight until one of the guys knocked me out. One of the guys was holding me on the floor and had my arm pinned to the floor. And about seven or eight guys came into the cell and they took turns sticking their penis up my ass. When they finished they left my cell, and I was still laying on the floor."

Clarence Garlick, 26 years old:
"Back in April this year, about 10:30 A.M. I was in my cell 455 on block D when Joe Lovett came into my cell. I was laying on my bed. When he came in I jumped up. He told me to get greased up. I told me I wasn't going to do nothing. He told me, 'You're go-

ing to do something.' He started punching me. I had backed up into a corner of the cell. He seen some mineral-oil grease I had on the table and he reached over and handed it to me saying, 'Put this on.' I put some on and layed down on the bed. He took out his penis and got on top of me. After he did what he wanted to do he got up and got some toilet paper and wiped himself off and went out of the cell.''

"This is the second incident. He came to me on July 18, 1968, in the morning about 10 o'clock. I was standing up in the doorway of my cell, 455. He told me to 'Get it fixed.' I told him I wasn't going to do nothing, that today was my birthday. He walked on away.'

"The next day, on the 19th, he came to me again. I was in my cell, this was about the same time. He stated, 'Today isn't your birthday, you're going to do something.' I told him I wasn't going to do anything. He started punching me again. I told him I was going to call the guard. He stated, 'Go ahead and call, you'll only call him one time and I'll knock you out.' He got the grease from off the table and handed it to me, told me to put some on, which I did. I laid down on the bed, he took out his penis and got on top. A friend he walks with, Kincaid, was standing out by the door, he was laughing. Joe got up after he got through, got toilet paper and wiped himself off. He then walked out of the cell.''

During the 26-month period, we found, there had been 156 sexual assaults that could be documented and substantiated—through institutional records, polygraph examinations, or other corroboration. Seven of the assaults took place in the sheriff's vans, 149 in the prisons. Of the sexual assaults, 82 consisted of buggery; 19 of fellatio; and 55 of attempts and coercive solicitations to commit sexual acts. There were assaults on at least 97 different victims by at least 176 different aggressors. With unidentified victims and aggressors, there were 109 different victims and 276 different aggressors.

For various reasons, these figures represent only the top of the iceberg.

■ Our investigators, as mentioned, interviewed only a twentieth of the inmates who passed through the prison system. We discovered 94 assaults—excluding those reported in institutional records. This suggests that if all 60,000 inmates had been interviewed, 20 times 94—or 1880—additional assaults would have come to light.

■ Almost all of the victims still in prison were so terrified of retaliation by other prisoners that they were very reluctant to cooperate with us.

■ Many guards discouraged complaints by indicating that they did not want to be bothered. One victim screamed for over an hour while he was being gang-raped in his cell; the block guard ignored the screams and laughed at the victim when the rape was over. The inmates who reported this passed a polygraph examination. The guard who had been named refused to take the test.

Then too, some guards put pressure on victims not to complain—such complaints, after all, would indicate that the guards were failing in their duty. We found many cases where victims, after filing complaints, had "voluntarily" refused to prosecute, and a number of them told us that guards urged them to rely on prison discipline rather than to bring the facts out into the open. Very often, these guards asked the victim if he wanted his parents and friends to find out about his humiliation.

■ Without prompting from the prison guards, many victims and their families wanted to avoid the shame and dishonor they believed would follow such a complaint.

■ Inmates have little faith in the ability of a guard to protect them from retaliation should they complain. Their fears are justified by the lack of supervision by guards, and the inadequate facilities to provide security for complainants.

■ Inmates who complain are themselves punished by the prison system. It is usual procedure to place a victim of a sexual assault on "lock-in feed-in," obstensibly for his own protection. This means that after a complaint is made, and especially if it is pressed, the complainant is locked in his cell all day, fed in his cell, and not permitted recreation, television, or exercise until it is determined that he is safe from retaliation. Many victims consider this "solitary confinement" worse than a homosexual relationship with one aggressor.

■ Sometimes very little comes of a complaint. Some compaints are just not acted upon; action, when taken, usually consists of putting the aggressor in the "hole" for 30 days or less. Meanwhile, the victim also is usually locked in, and looks forward—when released—to terror from the aggressor's friends, and from the aggressor himself when he is let out of the "hole." Finally,

■ Many of the victims themselves distrust and are

The Sheriff's Vans

The sheriff of Philadelphia County is responsible for transporting prisoners between the courts and the various county and state prisons. For this purpose, there are five sheriff's vans and seven station wagons. Only five inmates can be carried in each station wagon. Some 35 to 40 inmates are crammed into each van. Since hundreds of prisoners must be transported back and forth each day, the vans do most of the work.

Investigators are in complete accord with the following essay written by one articulate inmate who had traveled on the vans some 50 times:

"Prisoners confined in Philadelphia's three prisons commute from their institutions to the courts by way of a prison van. The van is a truck externally resembling the sort of refrigerated delivery truck that delivers meat to food stores. The body of the truck has no windows. At the very top of the truck there is a tiny row of slots purportedly for ventilating purposes.

"Winter—The van is parked overnight in the House of Correction. At eight o'clock in the morning the van driver picks it up and drives it to the Detention Center. There, some 40 prisoners, who have been waiting since six o'clock (packed like sardines in a steel-barred can), are loaded into the van. It has only seating capacity for 15 people. The rest must make themselves 'comfortable' as best they can. There are no handholds. There is no heat. It is freezing with an intensity so great that some prisoners relinquish their seats: The pain of frozen iron pressed against their backsides is unendurable. Packed into the mass of men they may find a little warmth jammed together. The trip from northeast Philadelphia is an hour of grinding stops and bumping halts. The standing men are tossed about inside the van. There is no light in the vehicle and the darkness is punctured by the grunts and groans.

"Summer—The prison van is a sweltering cauldron of red-hot cast iron. The packed bodies of men stink. Prisoners who were arrested in winter are still in their heavy clothes. The sun winks occasionally through the narrow slits on top, but the outside air remains aloof, not wishing to contaminate itself with this Dante's Inferno on wheels.

"Some Interesting Highlights—Riding in the prison van is virtually the only time in a prisoner's detention that he is completely unsupervised, and some strange things do occur. If anyone is homosexually inclined, and it is summer, a stinking sex orgy may take place in the dim confines of the van. Sometimes this is with mutual consent, sometimes by coercion. All the time it is done with utter disregard for the feelings of the other men in the van, who cannot even avert their faces. Sometimes a prisoner who is going to be a [state] witness is accidentally thrown into the company of the very people he is going to testify against. Threats and even violence

break out. The van drivers roll merrily on their way, blissfully unaware of what is taking place.

"The prisoners are alone in their walled-up cage, alone with their dry bologna sandwiches that must serve as sustenance for the next 24 hours. No cooked meal awaits them at the Detention Center when they return from court at night, only the same bologna sandwich. On the return trip from court, the van drops prisoners off at Holmesburg, the Detention Center, and the House of Correction, in that order. At Holmesburg the van drives into a walled-off enclosure that is barred by two massive solid doors and topped by solid concrete and steel. Believe me, it's a very snug fit. It generally takes between 15 to 20 minutes of paperwork until the van is allowed to proceed, and during this time the already high temperature rises sharply, the atmosphere becomes completely stagnant, and the waiting becomes interminable and finally unbearable. The prisoners scream and bang on the sides of the van but there is no relief. The time never gets any shorter, sometimes it gets longer.

"It is difficult to comprehend how the city justifies the van as treatment for untried, unconvicted, unsentenced men, who are the bulk of its passengers.

"I know, as a matter of fact, that the Interstate Commerce Commission requires that certain minimum space be provided for each individual hog shipped in commerce. Couldn't untried prisoners get the same that a pig gets?

"I have written these few words not out of bitterness, but out of the experience of 50 trips.

"I was there, Charlie."

Dennis Cujdik, a 17-year-old charged only with being a runaway from home, describes his ride on the van:

"I was at 1801 Vine in a cell when four Negro boys started bothering me for not having underwear on. Then when we got on the sheriff's van and started moving they told everyone that I didn't have on underwear. As the van was moving they started getting close to me. One of them touched me and I told them to please stop.

"All of a sudden a coat was thrown over my face and when I tried to pull it off I was viciously punched in the face for around ten minutes. I fell to the floor and they kicked me all over my body, including my head and my privates. They ripped my pants from me and five or six of them held me down and took turns fucking me.

"My insides feel sore and my body hurts, my head hurts, and I feel sick in the stomach. Each time they stopped I tried to call for help, but they put their hands over my mouth so that I couldn't make a sound. While they held me, they burned my leg with a cigarette. When the van stopped at the prison, they wiped the blood from me with my shirt. They threatened my life and said they would get me in D1 if I told anyone what happened. They said that if they didn't get me in D1 they'd get me in the van again. When the door opened they pushed me to the back so they could get out first. At first, I told the guard I tripped and fell, but then I thought I'd better tell the truth. I pointed out those who beat me up. A doctor looked at me and said I'd have to go to the hospital. They took pictures of the bruises on my body, and I could just about breathe because my nose and jaw seemed to be broken in many different places. I was asked by the lieutenant to write down what happened, and this is exactly what happened."

Why has this situation been allowed to continue for so long, despite the fact that it was brought to the attention of public officials at least two years ago? The answer is simple: The responsible city officials have blatantly neglected their duty.

---

hostile to constituted authority, and could not bring themselves to cooperate by filing a complaint.

Taking all of these facts into consideration, we conservatively estimate that the true number of assaults in the 26-month period was about 2000. Indeed, one guard put the number at 250 a year in the Detention Center alone.

Of the estimated 2000 assaults that occurred, 156 of which were documented, the inmates reported only 96 to prison authorities. Of this 96, only 64 were mentioned in the prison records. Of these 64, only 40 resulted in internal discipline against the aggressors; and only 26 incidents were reported to the police for prosecution.

Consensual Homosexuality Excluded

Now, in our study of sexual assaults we excluded any that were cases of truly "consensual" homosexuality. Nonetheless, it was hard to separate consensual homosexuality from rape, since many continuing and isolated homosexual liaisons originated from a gang rape, or from the ever-present threat of gang rape. Similarly, many individual homosexual acts were possible only because of the fear-charged atmosphere. Thus, a threat of rape, expressed or implied, would prompt an already fearful young man to submit. Prison officials are too quick to label such activities "consensual."

At the opposite end of the spectrum from innocent victims of homosexual rape are the male prostitutes. These homosexuals—known as "sissys," "freaks," or "girls"—were supposed to be segregated from the general prison population, yet they were readily available. We learned of repeated instances where homosexual "security" cells were left unguarded by a staff that was too small or too indifferent, or who turned their backs so that certain favored inmates could have sexual relations.

Many of these male prostitutes were created not only by force and the threat of force, but by bribery. The fact is that a person with economic advantage in prison often uses it to gain sexual advantage. Typically, an experienced inmate will give cigarettes, candy, sedatives, stainless-steel blades, or extra food pilfered from the kitchen to an inexperienced inmate, and after a few days the veteran will demand sexual repayment. It is also typical for a veteran to entice a young man into gambling, have him roll up large debts, and then tell the youth to "pay or fuck." An initial sexual act stamps the victim as a "punk boy," and he is pressed into prostitution for the remainder of his imprisonment.

Despite the important role that economic advantage plays in the creation of homosexuality, it is virtually impossible to obliterate economic distinctions between inmates. Even a small accumulation of money or luxuries gives an inmate substantial economic advantage: In the prison economy, a shopworker earns 15 to 25 cents a day; half of the inmates have no prison jobs at all, and most inmates get little or no material help from friends or relatives outside the prison.

It is the duty of prison officials to reduce the economic power that any inmate might exercise over another inmate. Yet we discovered one area in which Philadelphia prison officials, either through neglect or indifference, disregarded this duty. As a result, at least one inmate became so powerful economically that he was able to choose, as cellmates, a series of young men he found attractive, and then use bribery to sexually subvert each one.

The University of Pennsylvania and a private concern operate a large laboratory on H block of Holmesburg Prison, where they test inmates' reactions to new medicines and to experimental commercial products like soaps, shaving creams, suntan lotions, and toilet tissue. The prisoners are excellent "human guinea pigs" (1) because they live under controlled conditions, and (2) because they will submit to tests for a fraction of the fee that a free individual would demand. Prison officials—because there is very little other activity for the prisoners, and because the laboratory pays 20 percent of the inmates' wages to the prison system—have allowed the project to expand to the extent that it constitutes a separate government within the prison system.

All the inmates at Holmesburg wanted to "get on the tests" because, by prison standards, they can earn a fortune. Just by wearing a chemical patch on his back, for example, a prisoner can earn $10 to $15 a week. By participating in some tests that last longer, a prisoner—for doing almost nothing—will receive over $100. Altogether, the Holmesburg inmates earn more than $250,000 a year from the project. A few prisoners end up with bodies crazyquilted with motley scars and skin patches, but to these men, in the context of a prison economy, it seems well worth it.

To save money another way, the operators of the project also use inmates as laboratory assistants. An experienced assistant, working an eight-hour day, will get $100 a month—in the prison economy, the equivalent of a millionaire's income. Even a few prison guards are employed in the project, after their regular hours, and they work side by side with the prisoners.

University of Pennsylvania Project Disastrous

Generally, the "U. of P." project has had a disastrous effect upon the operations of Holmesburg Prison; it is one of the reasons why morale of the employees is at the lowest in that institution. The disproportionate wealth and power in the hands of a few inmates leads to favoritism, bribery and jealousy among the guards, resulting in disrespect for supervisory authority and prison regulations. What is more, the project contributed to homosexuality in the prison.

Stanley Randall, a 38-year-old con man serving a four- to eleven-year sentence, was employed in laboratory cell 806, H block, as an assistant. Although prison and laboratory officials at first denied it, Randall had the power to decide which inmates would serve as subjects on various tests. Since the 806 cell disbursed $10,000 to $20,000 a year, Randall's power was considerable.

Randall's special taste was newly admitted young inmates. Through his influence with the guard staff he had his pick of these young men assigned to him as cellmates—and for as long as he wished. When his victims moved in, Randall solicited them to engage in sexual acts in return for his giving them a steady stream of luxuries and for "getting them on the tests." At least half a dozen of these inmates submitted, and went on to profit handsomely from the University of Pennsylvania project.

Although top prison officials assured us that no inmate was permitted to earn more than $1200 a year, and that $400 was unusually high, in six months Ran-

dall's present cellmate had earned over $800. The record was held by a prior cellmate of Randall's, who had earned $1740 in just 11 months. When we asked university project managers about these high incomes, they told us they had never heard of any $1200-a-year-limit. The prison's accounting office had apparently never heard of this $1200-a-year limit either, because that office had credited these high amounts to the accounts of Randall's cellmates.

How had Randall managed to get his choice of cellmates? One guard told us that H-block guards had been instructed by "higher ups" not to interfere in the affairs of inmates working for the U. of P. Another guard reported he had received such instructions, and said they had come from the guard lieutenant. The lieutenant denied this, and agreed to take a lie-detector test. Later he reversed his position and refused. Randall admitted he had often given cigars to this lieutenant.

Other inmates besides Randall exploited their powerful positions. One inmate worker, for example, forged test results and fee vouchers, and got fees for inmates who had not actually been test subjects. It also seems that at least a few guards were also corrupted.

As a result of our investigation, prison officials have relieved the powerful inmate workers of their positions with the U. of P. project. They are also considering phasing out the project entirely.

How did sexual aggressors in the prisons differ from their victims? On the average, aggressors tended to be older, heavier, taller, and more serious offenders. Data on hundreds of victims and aggressors yielded the following comparisons:

	Victims	Aggressors
Average Age	20.75	23.67
Average Height	5'8¼"	5'9"
Average Weight	140.9	157.2

Both victims and aggressors tended to be younger than the average inmate, as comparison with the following table shows:

Average Age of Prisoners (July 31, 1968)	
Detention Center	27.9
Holmesburg	29.3
House of Correction	28.9
All Prisons	28.8

Yet although aggressors on the average are older and larger than victims, these differences are rather slight. In many cases, there may be no differences, and in others they are reversed. Still, after having observed hundreds of victims and aggressors we believe that there are other, more subjective, physical criteria which can be used to differentiate between aggressors and victims:

- Victims tend to look young for their age.
- Victims tend to look less athletic, and less physically coordinated.
- Victims tend to be better-looking.

A comparison of 164 aggressors and 103 victims showed that 68 percent of the former and only 38 percent of the latter had been charged with serious felonies. Among aggressors, violent assaultive felonies were particularly common. Thus, 14 aggressors had been charged with rape, but only three victims; six aggressors had been charged with weapons offenses, and no victims; 34 aggressors with robbery and aggravated robbery, but only eight victims; and seven aggressors with assault with intent to kill, but only one victim. As many victims as aggressors, however, had been charged with homicide. On the other hand, many more victims than aggressors were charged with relatively less serious offenses, such as the larceny of a car, going AWOL from the armed forces, violating parole, and delinquency.

We also made a study of the 129 documented assaults in which the races of both aggressors and victims had been ascertained, and found that a disproportionate number involved Negro aggressors and white victims:

Type of Incident	Number of Incidents	Percentage
White Aggressors & White Victims	20	15%
Negro Aggressors & Negro Victims	37	29%
White Aggressors & Negro Victims	0	0%
Negro Aggressors & White Victims	72	56%
Total	129	100%

These statistics in part reflect the fact that 80 percent of the inmates are Negro—it is safer for a member of a majority group to single out for attack a member of a minority group. Then too, Negro victims seemed more reluctant than white victims to disclose assaults by Negro aggressors. But it also seems true that current racial tensions and hostilities in the outside community are aggravated in a criminal population.

Now, we are not professionally qualified to offer a scientific theory to explain the sexual aggression in the Philadelphia prison system. We have, however, reached certain conclusions that should be recorded for possible use by psychiatrists, psychologists, and social scientists. The conclusions and the analysis set forth are based upon our observations, upon pertinent literature, and upon discussions with a psychiatrist and a psychologist who are experts in forensic psychology.

- We were struck by the fact that the typical sexual aggressor does not consider himself to be a homosexual, or even to have engaged in homosexual acts. This seems to be based upon his startlingly primitive view of sexual relationships, one that defines as male whichever partner is aggressive and as homosexual whichever partner is passive.
- It appears that need for sexual release is not the primary motive of a sexual aggressor. After all, in a sexually segregated population, autoeroticism would seem a much easier and more "normal" method of release than homosexual rape. As recent studies have shown (Masters and Johnson, *Human Sexual Response*, 1966), autoerotic stimulation yields a measure of physical release and pleasure similar to that yielded by sexual intercourse.
- A primary goal of the sexual aggressor, it is clear, is the conquest and degradation of his victim. We repeatedly found that aggressors used such language as "Fight or fuck," "We're going to take your manhood," "You'll have to give up some face," and "We're gonna make a girl out of you." Some of the assaults were reminiscent of the custom in some ancient societies of castrating or buggering a defeated enemy.
- Another primary goal of many of the aggressors, it appears, is to retain membership in the groups led by militant sexual aggressors. This is particularly true of some of the participants in gang rapes. Lacking identification with such groups, as many of the aggressors know, they themselves would become victims. And finally,
- Most of the aggressors seem to be members of a subculture that has found most nonsexual avenues of asserting their masculinity closed to them. To them, job success, raising a family, and achieving the respect of other men socially have been largely beyond reach. Only sexual and physical prowess stands between them

and a feeling of emasculation. When the fact of imprisonment, and the emptiness of prison life, knock from under them whatever props to their masculinity they may have had, they became almost totally dependent for self-esteem upon an assertion of their sexual and physical potency.

In sum, sexual assaults, as opposed to consensual homosexuality, are not primarily caused by sexual deprivation. They are expressions of anger and aggression prompted by the same basic frustrations that exist in the community, and which very probably were significant factors in producing the rapes, robberies, and other violent offenses for which the bulk of the aggressors were convicted. These frustrations can be summarized as an inability to achieve masculine identification and pride through avenues other than sex. When these frustrations are intensified by imprisonment, and superimposed upon hostility between the races and a simplistic view of all sex as an act of aggression and subjugation, then the result is assaults on members of the same sex.

Assuming that this analysis is valid, then the principal psychological causes of sexual assaults in the Philadelphia prison system are deeply rooted in the community—in that millions of American men, throughout their lives, are deprived of any effective way of achieving masculine self-identification through avenues other than physical aggression and sex. They belong to a class of men who rarely have meaningful work, successful families, or opportunities for constructive emotional expression and individual creativity. Therefore, although sexual assaults within a prison system may be controlled by intensive supervision and effective programing, the pathology at the root of sexual assaults will not be eliminated until fundamental changes are made in the outside community.

part six

Local Government and Community Control

In recent seasons, one often heard ·the phrase —shouted, whispered, sung—"Power to the people!" One rarely heard the logical retort: power to *what* people? The essays in this Part raise a number of very basic questions about power, influence, and participation in local politics. We can begin by acknowledging that city government is huge, bureaucratic, and unresponsive. The conventional liberal solution to this state of affairs is the provision of essential *political* attributes to urban neighborhoods: institutional structure, command over local resources, territoriality and, of course, democratic choice by the neighborhood's people of their local political elites. Some such formulation lies at the base of a large part of the burgeoning professional literature on community control, and something like it pervaded the policy-making response of the Johnson Administration in setting up the OEO in response to the "urban crisis." One may readily agree that—under the right conditions—neighborhood institutionalization can be a useful tool for achieving greater social solidarity and reducing the anomic "you-can't-fight city-hall" syndrome. Still, the prime question remains: How realistic is this drive for "community control" as a political goal in a highly concentrated, vertically stratified class society?

There are some major conflicts, contradictions, and paradoxes in the critical literature on the metropolitan conurbation. Whenever we see a professional literature which is shot through with such contradictions, we are entitled to suspect that crucial underlying problem areas have escaped perception by experts and policy-makers. One such major conflict which is evident from several essays that follow here is that neighborhoods need institutional and resource inputs because city government is "too big," too unresponsive; New York City is the classic, horrible example of the consequences. On the other hand, the literature of the metropolitan crisis is replete with arguments and pleas that the political boundaries *breaking up* the metropolitan area have contributed in key ways to the crisis, and that they must be transcended. In "dividing the indivisible," to use Theodore Lowi's phrase, suburbs are hived off both from each other and from the central city: government is thus not "too big," but "too small," and by a wide margin. Who is right? Pretty clearly, both "blind men" are seeing parts of the same "elephant"; each is right in his own frame of reference. Can you have it both ways? This is a more difficult question. What causes the manifest political pathology which threatens the American metropolitan region? To this question we can provide some tentative, if necessarily very broad answers.

Basic settlement patterns in American metropolitan regions are determined by cultural imperatives whose realization is made possible by radical inequalities in economic resources among population groups. This settlement pattern has been developing for a century or more, as historical studies by Sam B. Warner and others have revealed. A process has been at work during this period in which those who could afford to do so set up neighborhoods which were homogeneous in class terms and, until rather recently, relatively homogeneous in ethnic terms as well. Referred to by some as "the urban frontier," and by others as "the quest for the rural ideal," suburbanization—the drive to create such social homogeneities—has been one of the most powerful, persistent social and demographic determinants of American urban history. One is tempted to say that it has existed and remains potent because of a cultural and economic heterogeneity in American life which verges on anarchy. The homogeneous middle-class white neighborhood informally performs a whole network of social-control functions which are prized by its inhabitants. So, for better or worse, does any homogeneous neighborhood at any class level. This movement began long before there were significant numbers of blacks in American cities; it is, if anything, reinforced in today's context by the association of negritude with lower-class status in the minds of middle-class whites.

If suburbanization as a deterministic historical process has gone on ever since the invention of the streetcar, a politically crucial intervening variable has materialized in the century since. Until about World War I, as Lowi has shown, the extension of suburban domains had not reached the corporate limits of the central city. Thereafter, however, it spilled across these invisible but tremendously potent boundaries; shortly thereafter, operating under the universally-accepted ideology of "local control," and "local self-government," the corporate boundaries of the American big city stopped expanding. The present central city is typically big enough to be "unresponsive" even to lower-middle-class people, not to mention lower-class and poor people, yet it falls short of commanding the natural resource base of the metropolitan area. The middle-class white evacuation from the core city during the past generation—leaving the inner-city to fill up with the poor, segregated racial minorities, and others—has produced our current urban crisis. It is well known that until very recently, federal programs—conspicuously in the housing field, but scarcely less in the "national-defense" road-building programs of the 1950s and 1960s—have themselves contributed massively to the crisis.

We need to address ourselves here to two major questions. First, what produces unresponsiveness and policy drift and stagnation in cities, and hence the drive for "community control"? Second, what can we say about "community control" itself? The first question can be partly, but only partly, answered in terms of a scarcity and a declining volume of financial resources available to big-city government to perform elementary collective services. But Wirt's essay on politics in San Francisco, by taking an extreme case, reflects a much deeper source of political malaise. Briefly stated, this malaise is rooted in "hyperpluralism," that is, in the absence of *any* effective institutional mechanism for centralizing political power even in the limited corporate boundaries of the city. San Francisco is an extreme case of "hyperpluralism" in action, in large part, because Progressive-Era reforms destroyed political parties on the local level. This leads us, in turn, to pause for a moment to examine such reforms and the contexts in which they arose.

The period from 1900 to the end of the First World War was marked by a number of fundamental political changes which, carried out in accordance with democratic political rhetoric, helped in fact to break what little leverage the lower classes had on the political system. It is common textbook knowledge that Progressive-Era reforms in municipal government grew out of protest against the excesses and iniquities of the urban machine. It is perhaps less often realized that the struggle for "purification" and democratization was a combined class and ethnocultural struggle. At its end, in a great many cities, was the replacement of "politics" by "administration"; of parties by nonpartisanship; of ward control over fire, police, and school activities by rationalized bureaucratic, "professional" standards which were city-wide; and of ward representation in the city council by at-large representation. These reforms went beyond undermining and eventually destroying machine politics; more importantly, they were means through which a highly class-conscious upper bourgeoisie could remake city politics in their own cultural image. In California, the Progressive-Era reforming spirit was at its most intense and effective.

"Hyperpluralism" and feudalization or balkanization of the urban political process along sectoral and ethnic lines was the long-term consequence. The liquidation of such centralist controls as Boss Reuff exercised over San Francisco at the turn of the century was precisely comparable to the liquidation in 1910 of Speaker Joseph Cannon's powers, and occurred at about the same time. The latter created a House of Representatives which, in E. E. Schattschneider's words, looked very much like a legislature which had been stripped of its powers of decision. The former created a city government which looked much the same way. Nothing could be more congenial, ultimately, to the short-term purposes of the Big Establishment to which Wirt refers, for the fragmentation which followed made it as a rule quite unnecessary for its members to organize in any coherent political way in order to get what they wanted. "Nondecisions" did their work for them.

What one finds again and again after 1900—in urban politics and elsewhere throughout the political system—is a rapid spread of anti-sovereign government even within the narrow sphere of the city or the somewhat broader sphere of the state. When one destroys centralized political machinery, one does not create an apolitical utopia. Instead, one creates a form of *feudalism,* or, rather, a rich proliferation of feudalisms involving the interests of business, labor, ethnic, and other organized groups with a stake in determining relatively narrow ranges of policy outcomes. One of the attributes of this, or any feudalism is that those who are not under the umbrella of one or another organized group, those who do not have a "good lord" to defend their interests, find themselves without leverage on decisions—and nondecisions—which affect their lives in very direct ways.

And so one has that remarkable *deja vu* sense that, after decades of reform, the urban bureaucracies remain unresponsive; we return once again to concepts of community control—a control which in rudimentary form had existed in the bad old days of the urban machine, a control which

it was the stated purpose of many progressive reforms around 1910 to eradicate. The response is natural enough; it finds expression in Waskow's advocacy of community control of police. It is also more than implicit in Piven's discussion of civil-servant political mobilization in New York, of which the Ocean Hill-Brownsville school controversy of the late 1960s is a prime example. Yet if the core problems in this area directly involve the theory and practice of pluralist non-sovereignty verging on anarchy, why should one expect that feudalized bureaucracies without effective masters should be anything *but* unresponsive?

There are some excruciating dilemmas involved in the concept and practice of "community control," whether of the police or any other official resource. On the one hand, we find the imperatives for centralization, rationalization, and bureaucratic standardization which exist in governmental activity, on the other the imperatives for "maximum feasible participation" by the inarticulate and the poor. But even these patent contradictions are as nothing when weighed against the crucial question, *whose* community control? We have argued here that the American suburb is a preeminently successful example of community control in action. Originally designed to achieve such control informally, it later acquired the corporate independence needed to do a more perfect job of protecting its inhabitants from the social chaos which lurked just over the city line.

But *this* isn't what most advocates of community control have in mind. Mayor John Lindsay and educator Simeon Golar may have favored community control in New York's Ocean Hill-Brownsville school dispute between the local poor (black-Puerto Rican) community and the United Federation of Teachers, but they were strongly opposed to the community control which middle-class Jewish residents of Forest Hills, in New York's borough of Queens, wished to exercise to keep lower-class, high-rise housing out of their neighborhood. Obviously, many people in HEW, OEO, and elsewhere want community control when it favors one group but not when it favors another. A problem of distributive justice is thus presented nakedly. Resolution is possible, but *not* in terms of a disaggregated, operationally feudalized liberalism which ultimately responds only to organization and to pressure. And if the philosophical problem of justice in such cases cannot be resolved within the rubrics of orthodox interest-group liberalism, still less is it amenable to viable *political* solution. Indeed, the two intersect. For what motivates the residents of Forest Hills are the sense that an injustice is being committed against them by government, the belief that their claims for community autonomy are being rejected by "unresponsive bureaucracy" in City Hall and in Washington, and an acute anxiety as to the resulting practical consequences.

The upshot, again, is that organization begets counterorganization. In the process, "cosmopolitans" lose their legitimacy as leaders and cue-givers for "parochials," and the latter react at the polls by electing Right-winger Louise Day Hicks in Boston, as Ross et al., point out, and by rejecting fluoridation referenda, as discussed pointedly by Gamson. Such countermobilization, too, is part of "free democratic politics"; it's playing the game strictly according to the rules. As Ross et al. rightly suggest in the Boston case, an important part of the process by which racial segregation is reinforced lies in "parochial" white desires to keep neighborhoods homogeneous, i.e., to exercise community control!

If organization begets counterorganization, it is also true that this groupist escalation can and often does lead to a deadlock. For pluralism has implicitly presupposed two things about group struggle which are no longer very relevant. It has assumed in the first place that organized groups in the policy arena will compromise or negotiate their differences. Secondly, it has assumed that only some groups will be organized. As critics have frequently pointed out, the universe of organized groups described and celebrated by David B. Truman's The Governmental Process and other such studies is a universe of social and economic elites. To what extent does the survival of American non-sovereign political fragmentation—the "normal" American way of doing political business—depend upon this strong class skew in the pressure system? We don't know for sure as yet, but it is possible to have definite suspicions. So long as "everybody" was not mobilized politically, pluralism could continue to function and a "hidden hand"—very nearly the political equivalent of Adam Smith's capitalist "hidden hand" in economics—could go about its beneficent work.

One of the most remarkable aspects of the contemporary urban political scene is the rapid growth and mobilization of groups which were never heard of in the far-off pluralist Golden Age of the Eisenhower Administration. As we have suggested, a good deal of federal "Great Society" policy is aimed directly at mobilizing the poor and the deprived. But as this has occurred—and as the discussion by Wirt, Waskow, and Piven make clear—the groups thus mobilized and countermobilized do not fit the old incremental-bargaining model of pluralist group theory. Many of

their conflicts are of a "zero-sum" kind, or at least are so perceived by the people concerned. The strains on policy are correspondingly large, and the pressure for an intensely politicized stalemate grows. In the short run, the drift toward feudalized "protective associations"—for example, the police, the sanitation workers, and the teachers in New York City, each dominated by a single lower-middle or working-class ethnic group—is sharply intensified. It is no wonder that there is such a radical difference between Nathan Glazer's and Daniel P. Moynihan's Beyond the Melting Pot in its first (1963) and second (1970) editions. The introduction to the first edition is filled with the optimistic conventional wisdom of the early 1960s concerning ethnic and racial integration in New York City. The second edition opens with gloom, alarm, and pessimism—and no wonder.

But if the drift toward feudalization is intensified by this intensely politicized wave of group mobilizations, it seems reasonable to suppose that there are forces at work which will not allow it to develop indefinitely. Sigel's discussion of the present and possible roles of citizen's advisory councils suggests one way by which the weight of expertise can be shifted from the existing official governmental structure to citizens' groups which need such information to articulate their demands intelligently but cannot provide the information themselves.

Beyond this, as Lipsky observes, is the point which was made for years by the prince of community organizers, the late Saul Alinsky. For effective pressure to be exercised by the disadvantaged, they must find ways of developing their own organizations; these organizations must be durable and must have strategies and personnel (including experts in the art of pressure on officialdoms and establishments) for the long haul. It was my argument earlier that there are dynamics in the policy system itself, as "unleashed" since 1963, which provide important continuing incentives for such group organizations to form and to be effective, at least within limits. But implicit in this argument is the more-than-suspicion that both the problems and the mobilizations point directly toward an assertion of sovereign, accountable, and central control over basic definitions of policy in the years ahead. The feudalization of power resources which the American system of "non-rule" has spawned has been significantly reinforced by the "Great Society's" attempts to cope with social problems within the structural and behavioral limits of fragmented liberalism. But leaving philosophical issues of distributive justice entirely aside, it is difficult to see on purely practical administrative and political grounds that this process can continue much longer. It is not possible to say at the moment how and through what means the process can be arrested and reversed. But it will be—not because some of us wish it to be, but from the sheer necessities of the case. In the immediate future, we can anticipate that antagonistic non-elite mobilizations will continue, that pressures on the policy system will increase, and that our domestic politics will be snarled and loaded with intensity—nowhere more so than in the metropolitan political arena.

Alioto and the Politics of Hyperpluralism

Frederick M. Wirt

Because, as Alexander Hamilton noted, men are not angels, government is needed; but from the beginning the makers of American charters have been almost obsessed by fears of too much government. The Platonic method of controlling arbitrary power—by recruiting only moral men—has found limited use in our history. It is Aristotle who informs the American political tradition: the division of power so that no one gets too much—power is set against power, ambition against ambition and interest against interest. The hope is that in this way, "Nobody gets everything, nobody gets nothing, everybody gets something."

Few American cities have embraced this traditional principle more enthusiastically than San Francisco. Here the politics of public decision-making proceeds in a context of such fragmentation of power that the traditional principle has come to its logical end—powerlessness. In this article, part of a larger work in progress, I treat but one question: How are political decisions made here? The answers tell us much about the adaptability of this political structure to meet emergent community problems and to respond to group demands.

Political decisions are our focus, those having a public impact and those most often in the domain of government. Decisions that arise out of private organizations also have public consequences, of course, and hence they too are a part of the pool of political decisions. When the Transamerica Corporation decides to erect a gigantic skyscraper in downtown San Francisco, it's going to have immense effect on many city dwellers. Although I won't discuss this sort of decision here, one has to keep in mind that this world of private decision-makers exists and that it is made up of both a Big Establishment and a Small Establishment. The distinction is not merely the amounts of money available to each. The Big E is peopled by financial and industrial capitalists and managers whose interests run far beyond the Bay to the nation and the world. The Small E centers on the group whose financial interests extend only to the Bay Area, and particularly the city itself.

The Big E pays little attention to San Francisco politics or its government, while many in the Small E do so with perserverance and fascination. Both have material interests at stake in local government, of course, but the Big E's are long-run, while the Small E's are short-run. Both cooperate on cultural, civic and generally nonpolitical matters. And in the last analysis, one can safely suppose that it is this constellation of private interests that makes many if not most of the decisions that involve the allocation of values in this community and that therefore affect most people most enduringly. Government, however, often has to deal with many of the problems that arise as the result of these private decisions. Local government may have little to do with the origins of such problems; it may not help in the takeoff, but only in the flight—and often only when cries of "Mayday! Mayday!" fill the air.

Barking Party Politics

For anyone accustomed to the frenetic party politics of such big American cities as Chicago, Detroit, New York and Boston, the party politics of California cities must seem mysterious, if only because of their absence. Like the dog in the Sherlock Holmes story, they are important because

they do *not* bark. One finds traces of their presence in party leader titles and in announcements of committee meetings. But such spoor lead to nothing at all.

The evanescent nature of California parties arises from the state's distinctive political culture. Its central feature is a distrust of politics and politicians and a magical belief that if you give something a different name, you can change its essential quality—like the Victorians calling chicken breast "white meat." But the abolition of political parties didn't make politicians and politics vanish. They only shifted their field of operations into what Eugene C. Lee has described in *The Politics of Nonpartisanship* as a "politics of acquaintance" in which one's political loyalties and values are shaped by friends and neighbors, or by specific interests close to one's heart or pocketbook.

Such is the politics of the city of San Francisco today, although it was not always so. During and for a while after the New Deal, the Irish totally dominated Democratic politics; but in the post–World War II period their dominance began to loosen. Both parties now reveal a high degree of factionalism, and it is not uncommon to see interparty coalitions on behalf of specific candidates or issues.

Among the Democrats there had been hopes in the late 1950s that the California Democratic Council (CDC) would permanently consolidate and lead a liberal movement. The CDC now controls the party's Central Committee in the county (identical with the city as the two are consolidated). But the fervor generated by Adlai Stevenson has diffused lately, so much so that in the 1968 presidential primary, Democrats provided Humphrey, Kennedy and McCarthy with slates of delegates.

This fragmentation is well illustrated in the 1967 election of the dominant political figure of San Francisco today, Mayor Joseph Alioto. First of all, the basic rule of the game in such races is that victory is by plurality—highest takes all. This plurality system clearly militates against coalitions, which would be needed if a runoff election were required to achieve a majority winner. Fragmentation is thereby enhanced. Thus in the 1967 contest there were three candidates: Alioto; Jack Morrison, Democratic member of the Board of Supervisors (the legislative body under city-county consolidation); and Harold Dobbs, the Republican. All of this, remember, was formally nonpartisan.

The 1967 Mayorality Race

Alioto's victory that fall was deliberately built on the support of a number of factions. When the rising Democratic leader, State Senator Eugene McAteer, died in the spring of 1967 on the verge of certain election as mayor, portions of his following gravitated to various places. Some of his chief lieutenants are said to have suggested a Small E member as candidate, but he declined and endorsed Alioto, who at that point was little known publicly, despite solid duty on the school board and a legal career in anti-monopoly law that had made him a multimillionaire.

Alioto thereupon inherited much of McAteer's organization, which included both traditional conservative Democrats and some CDC members. But the main CDC support was and still is behind Congressman Phillip Burton who supported Supervisor Jack Morrison against Alioto. Organized labor, in this town where labor is very important politically, swung from the CDC to back Alioto; the resulting tensions between Burton and Alioto have not yet been resolved. Alioto made the usual swing of ethnic areas, but he worked especially hard and successfully to lure black votes away from Morrison, the expected heir. Thus the mayor drew his support from different factions of the Democratic party—the conservative and usually more affluent Irish, the labor unions, the upper-middle-class intellectuals and the ghetto blacks.

In the Republican party, a conservative-liberal factionalism is more evident. In the last decades the party has lost electoral support gradually (registration is now heavily Democratic), but there is little agreement among their leaders why this is so. One answer might be that young moderates and liberals complain they receive insufficient support from the more conservative and well-heeled party members whose tolerance of deviance from old-line Republicans is nil.

For example, take the cases of John Burton, a liberal Democrat like his brother Phillip, and Caspar Weinberger, a liberal Republican—two young men whom the city sent to the state legislature. Weinberger's career was outstanding (he was voted the best freshman legislator), but his law firm is said to have received little support from Republican clients in the city who were unhappy about the young legislator's occasional straying from the party fold on votes. In contrast, Burton is said to have gone to Sacramento on a retainer from a number of unions; his law firm prospered, and there seemed to be more forgiveness from his constituents for his party deviations.

The Republican candidate in the 1967 mayoral race, Harold Dobbs, was a longtime supervisor who had lost once before in this contest. His party was heavily outnumbered, there was little party organization, and his conservative image cost him votes. Indeed, liberal Republican leaders privately reported they backed Alioto, thereby providing him yet another bloc of support. Further, Alioto played the two candidates off against one another, alleging that "a vote for Morrison is a vote for Dobbs," which is to say, Democrats supporting the sure-to-lose Democrat would split the majority, giving it all to Dobbs.

In all this confusion party structure, predictably, has only a paper existence. There is no cadre of precinct or ward workers except that provided by each candidate or, in times past, the CDC. The candidates also do the bulk of their own fund-raising. There is a Central Committee, currently regarded among Democrats as being controlled by Congressman Burton, but no one seems to know why such control is important. In ostensibly nonpartisan elections the committee doesn't endorse candidates; formally this is illegal, but informally there is fear of driving away Republican support. While the committee does take stands on some issues, they are seldom, if ever, publicized. In this world of form without substance—not unlike the smile of Alice's Cheshire cat—the struggles to control the Central Committee seem meaningless, a mark of the politician's propensity to grab any loose marbles lying around.

Urban Political Issues

Quite obviously, however, the lack of meaningful party machinery has done nothing to inhibit the rise of a turbulent local politics. The central issues are not unlike those of any urban area in America. There is a tension between the demands upon government to spend more money and the taxpayers' desire to keep the rates down. Taxes have increased significantly recently; when on the eve of the fall 1969 election citizens were hit by large tax increases, almost every bond issue failed.

Conservation has a special power to arouse San Franciscans because of the city's remarkably beautiful setting. The citizens are peculiarly narcissistic about that beauty, even beyond Oliver Wendell Holmes's observation that "the center of Earth's gravity runs through every small town in America." But then, they have much to be narcissistic about. A poll in late 1969 showed Americans rating San Francisco above all other cities, primarily for its natural beauty.

Local governments' efforts to satisfy different ethnic interests have given a distinctive shape to urban politics all over America, and San Francisco is no exception. With the third highest percentage of foreign-born or foreign-stock population of any city in America (behind New York and Boston), a special part of San Francisco's mystique has been the notion of its tolerance for differing ethnic ways of life. Somehow the flooding into this port from the time of the forty-niners onward has created a tradition of a haven of diversity, an oasis of equal treatment for restless migrants from points as removed as Malta and Samoa.

But that image of equal treatment is not the reality. The reality is certainly less hollow than in the Mississippi Delta or along the Rio Grande—but equality is still far away. And it certainly wasn't there to begin with. The forty-niners were a bloodthirsty, gold-grubbing lot who believed in equality—among Anglo-Americans. If you were Mexican, Indian or Chinese, and had by some miracle staked out a claim, the odds were excellent that one of those forty-niners would either steal it from you or shoot you for it. This city's subsequent history of tolerance is not all that heartwarming either. Before the turn of the century, one successful mayoral candidate ran on a platform openly advocating violence against the Chinese; Mayor Alioto frequently cites this as evidence of the city's great strides in ethnic amity. One bit of ethnic nastiness that San Francisco does seem to have escaped is the anti-Irish prejudice of the East's Yankee Establishment, possibly because there never was much of that Establishment here.

But refraining from killing one another is not the same thing as tolerance or equality. Today there is a high degree of ethnic enmity, or at least rivalry, mainly because of the persistence of ethnic ties that scholars once thought had been assimilated out of existence. The persistence creates friction for Chinese and Negroes. And possibly the most underplayed story of consequence for the political future of California is the political awakening of the Chicano.

Black, yellow and brown demands for power are new elements in the ethnic politics of San Francisco, but here, as elsewhere, they must operate within the restraining context of more favored ethnic groups—the Irish and Italians. For most of this century the Irish have dominated the politics of the city, and their names are legion in the lists of civil service. In days past, the Byzantine intricacies of San Francisco's government and regulations were passed on as daily fare to Irish children, immensely improving their chances of passing the civil service exams and of maintaining themselves thereafter. Politicians who went to Saint Ignatius High School and thence to the University of San Francisco (both Catholic) joined an "old boys" circuit of influence not unlike that of the private school and Ivy League in the East.

Italian names are becoming somewhat more prominent in city politics, partly because of the success of Joseph Alioto,

although he was not the first Italian mayor. A glance at the roster of City Hall clerks and of patrolmen might find the Italian presence looming larger now than it did a quarter century or more ago. But their voice has not become sufficiently dominant to speak of "ethnic succession"—yet.

Special mention should be made in this brief ethnic survey of the position of the Jews of San Francisco, for the city *has* been more open to them than probably any other in America. Their names appear not merely in the sponsorship of cultural, educational and civic groups and causes. They appear also in the politics of both parties, although especially the Democratic, as "fat cat" donors, as behind-the-scene influentials in the Small E and, occasionally, as prominent public officials. None of them when interviewed seems to have a clear reason of why this openness should be so. Most trace it to the haste with which San Francisco developed after the gold rush. Many of the now leading Jewish families came here together at about that time. In any event, they are now very nearly the Brahmins of San Francisco. They are still blackballed at some social clubs, but they also support and sit on the boards of Roman Catholic colleges.

Elections without Parties

In this context of invisible parties and turbulent ethnic politics, the election process is much like the start of those long-distance races; everybody is on his own, eyes straight ahead, and there's a considerable amount of jostling in the pack. Candidates raise their own funds, rarely coalesce with other candidates in a slate, and strive earnestly to reach across party and ethnic lines. With all elections at-large, many candidates for a given office, and no runoff, the impression provided the voter is best characterized by the local practice of slapping one's posters on buildings, fences and poles. On election day the city's walls create a kaleidoscope of jarring, confusing and possibly self-defeating posters.

One consequence of such partyless politics is reminiscent of what V. O. Key found in his study, *Southern Politics*. Because the party does not bind its candidates to a common program, temporary coalitions of voters support a given candidate but fall away by the next election, thereby rendering impossible any accountability for program. What mandate could be perceived, for example, in the at-large 1965 election of Peter Tamaras for supervisor? An incumbent—and until 1967 most of the supervisors elected were incumbents—he was supported by business, Congressman Burton and Cyril Magnin—conservative, very liberal and moderate liberal. He received the largest vote—60 percent—but this represented only 37 percent of the registered voters, 23 percent of those over 21 and 17.2 percent of the total population. With only small minorities contributing to his election and with a contingent of supporters many of whom hardly speak to one another, how does one measure Supervisor Tamaras's responsibility in the use of his office?

The system emphasizes responsiveness, if not responsibility. The major vote-getting device of San Franciscan candidates is to appear before neighborhood groups and ethnic clubs seeking their endorsements. Politicians do this in every city of course, but there are always some groups who are judged not worth battling for. In San Francisco, however, a basic informal rule is that the candidate *must* confront these groups. Night after night he follows an unending sequence of group meetings where he briefly states his qualifications. Sometimes he will have secured the endorsement ahead of time, but even when he has it he must show up anyway. Once there, as often as not, he is jammed into a reception room to wait his turn, along with the other candidates. It's all rather like those freshmen nervously waiting in their rooms on the night when fraternities give out their bids. The number of groups is extraordinary; their diversity is staggering: ethnics, taxpayers, neighborhood home-owners, conservationists, businessmen, unions and even homosexuals (who are interested in the candidate's sensitivity to civil rights).

If this system encourages responsiveness to local interests, it is questionable whether it also furthers responsibility in the use of power. A candidate cannot be certain what combination of interests most clearly supports him. He may know the region of the votes and he may know which groups endorsed him, but he can't be certain which worked for him and which did not. As the parties have no internal discipline, they cannot provide any clear-cut image of responsibility for the voters and cannot impose a sense of purpose upon their members' task of governance. Even if the parties were to attempt it, the structural obstacles embodied in the city charter are immense.

Government by Nondecision

In 1932 the voters approved a charter whose primary purpose was to prevent widespread corruption. It succeeded admirably. Indeed, the charter divided the power and structure of governance into so many pieces that if officials wanted to be corrupted, the game would hardly be worth the candle. But as charter critics now say, the price for achieving this honesty was to make San Francisco's governors impotent, robbing them of co-ordinated instruments for meeting crucial urban problems as they emerged. The cover of the League of Women Voters' excellent 1967 volume wryly caught the essence of the city's government. A Calder-like mobile is shown with figures frozen in mid-air but interconnected in inexplicable ways by lines zooming all over the place. A mobile is a thing of beauty, but, as countless observers of the city have complained, "It's a hell of a way to run a railroad."

The charter combines some features of the strong mayor, weak mayor, chief administrative officer and commission forms of governing. To control corruption, members of the legislative Board of Supervisors are elected in off years and at-large in a part-time office for staggered terms. Innumerable boards and commissions, designed to maximize citizen participation—long before the current interest in "participatory democracy"—exercise powers independent of the mayor, except in that he appoints them; some are very responsive to him, however, as the mayor is said to run the police department through the police commission. (Some see these commissions as a throwback to the old vigilante committees of a century ago.) Further, the chief administrative officer (CAO) has limited administrative power; he has no financial or appointive authority; at the same time, however, because he cannot be removed except for serious cause, the CAO is literally appointed for life.

The comptroller has probably the greatest administrative power—all of which leaves the mayor with little formal power short of appointment and budget-making, and even that is limited under a charter that mandates extensive civil service and merit systems. Supervisors are supposed to function exclusively as legislators; indeed, under penalty of law, they cannot advise administrators on the ordinances they originate. Meanwhile, the CAO supervises several city departments, commissions administer yet other functions, and the school board, though appointed by the mayor, is independent of the formal government.

Strangely enough, electoral participation in such a hodgepodge is both expensive and limited. Note that the CAO, comptroller and other administrative officials of considerable power do not stand for election. With long tenure and profound knowledge of the uses of the charter, they may have more real influence than the mayor or supervisors—yet they are virtually untouchable by the electorate. As if in compensation, however, San Francisco's charter offers the citizens 65 elective offices, 18 directly elected at-large and 47 in effect confirmed by the electorate, usually after appointment by the mayor.

But the greatest influence of the electorate lies in the referendum. Every time even the most minor charter change —often only administrative—is required, there must be a referendum. Though only a tiny minority of San Franciscans understand the minutiae of these proposals, at every election they are confronted with 10 to 20 of them. Eugene Lee has concisely indicated the consequences for the political system when

> the charter . . . is full of administrative detail which necessitates bringing to the voters countless matters on which they cannot and should not be expected to be properly informed. The politics of charter amendment are dominated by the fact that city elections involve a relatively light turnout, and of those who turn out thousands do not vote on the ballot propositions. Therefore, small groups in the city are able to influence the character of the charter far out of proportion to their numbers.

The referendum might seem an excellent way to work out democracy's basic premises about popular sovereignty, but it creates serious problems for the total polity. The referendum is essentially a method for resolving a conflict, but another and far more frequently used method lies in the process of political parties. In normal party operations the politician, driven by the necessity to construct majorities, strives to ameliorate the sharp edges of intergroup conflict. Usually this means a search for compromise, some broader ground on which competing groups can live. In this process, a compromise requires groups under that party label to work together in order to protect the party's tenure.

But in the absence of parties and with the substitution of the referendum, something else happens. Recent studies by Gerald M. Pomper and by David W. Abbott (the latter on New York's referendum on the civilian review board) argue that this decision-making device polarizes all segments of the public, particularly the ethnic groups. Without any overriding concern to further the political party's control of government and without the party agents moving among competing groups searching for a viable compromise, each group feels more alone, insecure and hence hostile and suspicious of suggestions that it modify its views. The use of party to ameliorate group conflict has its vices, too, as even the casual student of contemporary urban affairs must know. Yet the reformist urge to democratize public decision-making by decentralizing it should not be accepted without recognition that its price is a heightened polarization and perhaps a deadening immobility.

In a highly pluralistic nation, the accumulated price of such fractionated decision-making is considerable. In a highly pluralistic city such as San Francisco, the price has become *non*decision-making. When successful policy outcome rests necessarily upon the agreement of so many disparate private groups and public authorities, the power of one component to block any action is magnified. Over time, consequently, only minor policy adjustments are possible, and it is highly doubtful whether these add up to an adequate response to deep and widespread community problems. Instead, the bulk of public policy-making is done by civil servants beyond the reach of the electorate. Each of these functionaries can affect only small sections of the government, but cumulatively their little decisions comprise the totality of public policy. Moreover, the central drift of the pattern of these decisions can best be characterized as nondecision. And the decision not to act has as much public consequence as the decision to act.

What San Francisco has, then, is government by clerks. That feature of urban life is not distinctive to "the city," of course, but the clerical power is enhanced by the relative absence of instruments for maintaining clerical responsibility. The political party, not being there, cannot perform that function. Civil service or charter status makes for immunity from election or recall. Indeed, the city workers' union is a sufficient power in itself to affect electoral outcomes for offices and referenda.

The immunity of the clerks seems an invitation to public corruption. Yet in recent decades this has not been the case at all. The one recent instance of corruption, that of the city assessor, involved relatively small amounts of public money for himself, and $9 million has since been recovered from favored taxpayers. Far more characteristic are the CAO and controller. Although removed from the electorate, everyone regards them as possessing a high degree of competence and probity. While this government of clerks may be incapacitated, it is certainly not dishonest.

An experienced bureaucrat once highlighted the problem by an example that would be ridiculous if it weren't true. If a scrap of paper blew in front of the City Hall steps, it could not be swept up until a jurisdictional decision was made as to the appropriate agency. If found on the sidewalk, it would belong to the street-cleaning department; if on the stairs, to the building superintendent; and if on the lawn, to the agency for recreation and parks.

What of the mayor? The position is pretty much what he makes it by the force of his character and personality. He may define his role as that of Chief Greeter for the city, and given the flow of the world's notables through this port (film companies are shooting all over town now), he could well fill his time. If he has higher ambitions, he could play the role of Rising Politico, spending a lot of time in Sacramento or Washington or other watering places of politicians. The two roles are not exclusive, of course, although no San Francisco mayor has gone to higher state or national office since the days of "Sunny Jim" Rolph in the 1920s. Earl Warren, non-Californians should note, came from Alameda County across the Bay.

Joseph Alioto entered office with a splash, clearly trying to rise above these limited roles—without, however, ignoring them. His advisors report him as wearing a multiplicity of hats—ceremonial, public relations officer, carrier of some authority, concerned about crucial urban problems. Keenly aware of the charter and political limitations of his office, Alioto tries to use to the utmost that power which may ultimately be the prime one for all executives, public and private. This is the power to persuade.

"A Man of Energy and Ideas"

People close to the mayor say he approaches his work with several basic notions of the community. He sees it as a matrix of pluralist conflict in which every day a host of issues—usually small—agitates the body politic and in which invisible groups are constantly winning and losing. The manipulation of these issues is necessary to enhance the mayor's power, even when the most he can do is get the contenders to sit down and talk. In this view, the mayor's office requires more legislative than executive work, more bargaining among equals than issuing authoritative demands.

This might seem to make him powerless, because not controlling a hierarchy of powers in the Weberian model, he must haggle and bargain. Instead, the mayor's influence over the outcome of policy conflicts rests on his ability to persuade others to find a satisfactory compromise or set of trade-offs among contending groups. Such is the potential in the mayor's office of this city—and perhaps of most, if not all, cities in America.

But for this model to work effectively, the mayor needs not merely persuasiveness but information. Alioto is said to have developed a personal network of supporters in many commissions and departments who provide information on happenings in their bailiwicks. Other mayors here did not do this. Newsmen form another part of that network of information. The mayor's flamboyant style makes good copy, and the press often returns the favor in its kind. The intelligence network provides him not merely with data on what is or may be happening and on who wants what; it also allows him to communicate to the government and community the image he desires—as one advisor put it, that of "a man of energy and class."

As a part of his concern to use the office's potential more fully, Alioto is said to have wanted to break out of the "City Hall syndrome" of problem-solving, that is, the usual practice of getting the bureaucrats together to discuss a new problem. Although little emerged from this practice, it did provide newspaper copy which gave the impression that something was being done. Instead, Mayor Alioto looks to other experts to contribute to his decisions. He actively seeks out the views of special groups. He has made special efforts to reach out to the black community and to create an image of helpfulness. But as much as he asks for advice, this of course is not the same thing as being able to translate the advice and views into hard policy.

High Ambition Has a Price

Other means have to be found for that. Thus, in the final year of the Johnson administration, as a solid Humphrey supporter, Alioto was poking into every crevice of the federal government for funds for community projects. While successful at times in Washington, he was often stymied by agencies and interests back home. The failure to obtain a Model Cities program occurred primarily because city agencies failed to meet federal deadlines—despite Alioto's urgings. Private business provides only a fraction of the summer or permanent jobs needed to attack hard-core poverty among the young. His supporters claim, however, that he sought help for some city problems from business contacts made during his legal career.

Yet another force of possible use in translating public preferences into public policies lay in his reputation as a rising politico. From the day of his election, Alioto has been surrounded by excited expectations that he would go on to higher things politically. This possibility of increased eminence may have attracted some of the independent power-holders of city government who simply like to be associated with future governors or senators. But this rising politico role exacted a price—the time and energy it took away from the city. Administrators are more likely to move when the mayor leans on them persuasively and continually, a likelihood diminished when part of his time must be spent considering his political future. Whatever this role may do for the mayor in the future, it limits his present power to persuade.

As we have indicated, that power is a fragile thing—in president or mayor—and this has certainly been the case with Alioto. *Look* magazine's allegations of his supposed connections with the Mafia dealt him a serious blow. Following close upon this attack, the Republican attorney general of the state of Washington claimed that Alioto had improperly split fees with a former Democratic attorney general in some utility cases Alioto had handled for that state. The mayor promptly and energetically rebutted both charges, in the first mounting a multimillion dollar damage suit and in the second opening all his books for examination to underline his claim that nothing illegal or unethical was involved. But state polls show that his political future has been hurt. It was tough enough as it was. Seemingly intent upon the governor's chair, he already faced two major obstacles—Jess Unruh's desire for the job and Ronald Reagan's immense popularity. In January 1970 Alioto declined to run.

The role of Rising Politico, then, probably offers little to help a mayor in his efforts to strengthen his persuasiveness and to impose some programmatic unity on the city. The fragmentation of power makes it difficult to construct a convincing record as administrator which could be trumpeted to the state. The resources needed to work hard at future eminence diminish his influence in the city administration. Setbacks in his political aspirations may well diminish it further.

Who Defines the Urban Crisis?

I take time for this consideration of Alioto's administration not because he is one of the more charismatic mayors in the city's history to have adopted the role of Chief Persuader, but because with all his local popularity, energy, publicity and serious effort, the problems of the city remain unsolved. Ethnic conflict is increasing, and the militants in each of these groups become more dominant, more resistant to compromise, more irreconcilable. The housing shortage becomes more severe, the tax load heavier and discontent with the nature of emerging urban life more evident in more segments of the public.

The point is not, however, that all this is the mayor's fault but that these problems are increasing in spite of, not because of, the mayor's effort and that this condition afflicts every mayor in America today. Most American mayors find it difficult to provide the leadership and the resources to cure an appalling list of urban ills. Urban reformists, in their drive for administrative unification and centralization, pay little attention to the need for strengthening the mayor's power to form coalitions of interests to meet major urban problems. That function is rather left to

the vagaries of mayoral character and temperament.

Where then does one find such an integrative force? San Francisco's mayor, whoever holds the office, may only be the least equipped of the lot to provide political unification. And yet leadership for these tasks emerges from no other single group or combination of groups in the community. The business influence of "the Downtowners" and the Chamber of Commerce has waned recently as other groups' voices are being heard. Unions, particularly the powerful city workers, consider proposals for the mobilization of power to meet current problems as a threat to the interests currently vested in the charter. Ethnic groups have eyes only for their own kind. The major corporations, whose gleaming—and often ugly—buildings increasingly fill the downtown, are more interested in defending their interests at the state, national and international levels. Meanwhile, the local government with its multiple points of seeming access to the city's pluralist society does not provide access to those claiming new needs and new problems. Against these the government is insulated, droning on, with little effective leadership.

In November 1969 almost every major element of the city publicly attested to the validity of the preceding analysis by swamping an effort to reform the city charter. Sixty-three percent opposed reform, and probably only the League of Women Voters supported it. Each of the other major groups in the community found some portion of the revision so seriously threatening that they advised their members to vote "No." The reforms sought to strengthen the mayor's office, unify the commissions' powers and in other ways combine the resources of local government to meet the issues of 1970 and not those of 1932. It failed, reform leaders resigned, and the event explains much of the failure of contemporary reform proposals for urban government.

These proposals have traditionally emphasized upper-middle-class values of efficiency and rationality. These values are to be maximized by structures designed to centralize power in visible positions filled by professionally trained personnel. The ideal is reflected in the city manager government concept, where a professional isolated from ostensibly grubby political influences is set free to administer efficiently the corporation of government, much in the way the business corporation's managing director operates. But such a proposal is seldom accepted in America's largest cities; none over 800,000 uses it, and the bigger ones adopted it three or more decades ago. The reason lies in another set of values embedded in prevailing institutions which reflect the very pluralistic and ethnic composition of these big cities.

The city workers of San Francisco furnish a prime example. Their interest lies not merely in a job but in the identity, success and hopes of an ethnic group. When persons of other ethnic identities talk reform, any appeal to general values of rationality and responsibility seems merely a camouflage to those threatened. Conversely, when the attacks on special interest come from emergent ethnic groups levying new claims for a shred of the resources from the body politic, ethnic prejudices and political principles merge in an indistinguishable fashion.

Those protected are not merely ethnic groups, of course. Taxpayers fear changes, although as one looks at the taxpayers' plight around the country it's hard to see how reform could squeeze them any harder than they already are. Business groups, used to a special and favorable connection with the licensing and taxing power of cities, find some administrative reform proposals equally threatening. Protectors of a particular cultural institution, such as the museums, warily eye reformist notions about unification of the control of all cultural programs. City workers, used to having their way on wages and pensions in an electorate where their own vote bulks large, see nothing but loss if such decisions are to be made legislatively.

If reformists in San Francisco still have hope, their best strategy may lie in publicizing how unbearable are the costs of maintaining the status quo, how really *unprotected* they are under this system. When citizens defeated completion of the Embarcadero Freeway a few years ago, they demonstrated a widespread refusal to accept the costs of the loss of beauty just to save the time of motorists. Although San Francisco and other American cities have not yet accepted it, there is however another cost—widespread but subtle—arising from the system's inability to respond to critical physical, social and economic needs. All San Franciscans have this in common—they pay for systematic failure to respond by higher taxes, deteriorating environment, rising crime rate, worse living conditions, traffic congestion and the rest.

Comes the Earthquake

All pay for this, but the poor pay more than most, a different kind of regressive "tax" system, when one conceives taxes as something more than what tax assessors levy. Taxed in this fashion but unable to move a system toward some kind of tax equity, the disadvantaged cannot, like their ancestors, withhold taxes and cry, "No taxation without representation!" Smog, congestion, crime and sweatshops cannot be withheld. One can endure them or strike out blindly. In the latter case, the city may yet pay for its failure to recognize a present cost common to all.

Reform may occur in another, more macabre way. Disaster often generates change. The commission form of government was born out of a hurricane in Galveston a half century ago. Reforms at the national level have often if not predominantly proceeded from large-scale disaster, as witness something as major as the New Deal legislation or as minor as the Drug Control Act of 1962. Unfortunately for reformists, one cannot stage a disaster, so for most American cities the strategy is meaningless. However, the city of San Francisco sits on the major earthquake line of the San Andreas fault, and geologists anticipate an earthquake any day or month or year—but soon. When one imagines this city's little mobile of a government trying to cope with the effects of such a cataclysm, he can only shudder, but one result will surely be that dangling figures will fall. In that case, by one of the ironies which delight intellectuals, that Nature which has made the Bay so beautiful in the past may in the future help make local government effective.

Such speculation should not be regarded as a signal to the League of Women Voters and other reformers to set off dynamite blasts underground. It does suggest, however, the extraordinary tenacity of the government which has become so adapted to San Francisco's pluralist community. A less drastic strategy for meeting reformists' definition of crisis may be turning toward the federal government. Federal monies provide at least one kind of resource for building new power bases for groups formerly disadvantaged. This may be in rural Mississippi (as I have found) or in the depths of the Oakland ghettos (as Aaron Wildavsky is finding). Traditional groups have their power bases in the local charter or in traditional ways of operating, but emergent groups may find their power base in yet another source, the federal government. Yet another player will then have been added to the urban team but at the cost of a drastic diminution of the role of city government in policy-making that affects its citizens.

It is partly a question of where pluralists pressures arising out of the city are to have their focus. Reformists call for strengthening local government so that the myriad of needs arising from the community can be met and handled there. Others argue that this strengthening cannot take place because the city's vested power bastions can fight off new demands. They want to bypass the city and go to Washington to focus pressure, for the group denied access to local government can achieve power through some national program. It is, of course, another question, how the "locals" and the "feds" are going to agree what decisions should be made.

Federal intervention to meet the problems of specific groups now disadvantaged seems more likely to work than efforts to rearrange the total structure through charter reform. If it does work, American federalism will once again have demonstrated its extraordinary versatility in adapting to new demands. In such a fashion, too, the contention of political pluralists may find some vindication, even though federal programs to date have been far too limited to do more than begin the process of helping disadvantaged groups. In this context, San Francisco provides a severe test of the adaptability of federalism. Its fragmentation of governmental power and structure, its absence of party organization and processes for the task of welding the seams of a pluralist system, its government by clerks which enfolds in its crevices a variety of special interests—all provide a politics of pluralism with a vengeance.

But, like almost everything else in San Francisco, it is fascinating to gaze at.

Citizens Committees—
Advice vs. Consent
Roberta S. Sigel

Does any citizen have a direct voice in determining the government policies that affect his everyday life? What can he do or say about such matters as air pollution, transportation, the racial composition of the inner city? The fact is that citizens are seldom consulted when government initiates policies which have major impact on their lives.

The war on poverty legislation is an exception—it insisted that no federal money be given to local anti-poverty agencies unless the poor were among those drawing up the programs. This authorization of "maximum feasible participation" has become a hot political issue in Washington and in communities across the country.

But aside from this pioneering effort, it is rare that

citizen opinion is asked for. This state of affairs is disturbing. In practical terms, hired experts cannot do a useful job unless they know what people want and need; in the absence of vital feedback, experts often prescribe what they think people ought to have—and this is often inadequate or unfeasible. Also, what happens to our concept of democracy under such conditions? In what sense is a government elected by only a fragment of the populace and dominated by salaried technicians a "government of the people, by the people, and for the people?"

In the 1840's Alexis de Tocqueville pinned his faith in the survival of democracy on the existence of institutions such as the town meeting where the citizen "learns to know the laws by participating in the act of legislation; and takes a lesson in the forms of government from governing." But the town meeting has almost completely disappeared from the American scene, and people who are concerned about citizen participation in government have tried to find some viable alternative.

One such alternative is the *citizens advisory committee,* which is proliferating at every level of government and is especially evident in the war on poverty.

CAC's come in a variety of forms. One is the advisory committee of all the illustrious names and power figures in the community. It meets only a few times on no regular schedule, and advice is only sought on plans previously drawn up by public officials. It is a ratifying committee, not a study committee or policy initiating committee.

Another type of advisory committee is frequently called into existence by civic officials concerned about such matters as schools, race relations, and neighborhood conservation. It is a real working committee, or at least its subcommittees are. The members try to develop their own plans rather than merely ratifying blueprints issued by a mayor or school superintendent.

For a period of 18 months I watched one such committee—known as Community Planning for Community Schools—go about its job to make recommendations for a community high school in a rundown, quasi-slum neighborhood in one of the major cities of the United States. The group was set up by the superintendent of schools. Its task, formulated by the superintendent, was to help design not only a new high school but a blueprint for uplifting the whole community, adults as well as youth, through the joint resources of the school, community agencies, and the people residing in the area.

The superintendent charged the committee "to dream big" and produce "something that actually materializes within a limited period of time." Freedom to plan, however, did not include drawing up a budget, selecting a site for the new high school, or making its plans mandatory on the school board. The committee was purely advisory; what it possessed in freedom to plan and dream, it lacked in power and responsibility.

This limitation notwithstanding, in the end it produced a comprehensive blueprint for a community high school and for services and facilities (such as a family center) which went beyond the original assignment and made a valuable contribution to educational planning. The new high school is in operation today, and some of the extra services have become operative; but the recommended large family center may never be built, at least not in the format visualized by the committee.

What then can we say about the usefulness of CAC's? To answer that we must distinguish between two factors:
■ The process of decision making—was it the most efficient, speedy, and purposeful way of planning?
■ The quality of the product—did a better community plan evolve because citizens were involved?
Finally, it must also be borne in mind that advisory committees must fulfill another function—to involve the community. So we must ask a third question: Did they really involve the community, and how did they affect it?

Before turning to the last two questions, an analysis of this committee's decision-making processes may help to understand the potential contributions—and limitations—of citizen advisers in other cities and situations.

The Decision-Making Process

In general, the decision-making process of this group was characterized by:
—slowness;
—acceptance of administrative goals;
—great dependence on experts.
There followed:
—a failure to generate new ideas of their own;
—an absence of conflict;
—very little use of negotiating techniques.

To some of the more knowledgeable members, the committee went about its work with excruciating deliberateness. Each subcommittee spent weeks and months gathering facts before it tackled actual recommendations. They called in *outside* experts, listened to them and usually accepted (without further checking) the facts and figures produced by the experts. They also sent delegates out to gather information, then sat through endless recitals of the results at their meetings. They also studied past reports and recommendations of other citizens committees, further slowing down the process. The staff, consisting of two professional educators called "coordinators," had prepared background material which could well have shortened this fact-finding period. But they dared not push them on uninterested members lest they be accused of that gravest of educational sins, "manipulating the group."

This study group approach seems to be characteristic of committees composed of lower echelon personnel. Advisory groups studded with big names often have neither the time nor inclination for dreary leg work. They rely on their own or the administration's staff to prepare the material.

Acceptance of Administrative Goals

It must be remembered that the committee was not formed as a result of any deep-felt citizen urge to organize and do something about the neighborhood. Rather, it was called into action by an administrative agency. The community itself had not voiced any urgency. Some of the people, notably those with children in school, might have been concerned about school overcrowding and neighborhood deterioration, but it is doubtful they had specific plans to solve their problems by building a new high school, let alone a community high school. Here, as with other CAC's, citizens did not initiate, citizens responded. And because it was the professionals, not the citizens, who initiated, they also set the committee's goal: to build a community high school dedicated to community uplifting. Citizens were told to suggest ways to do it, but not asked *whether* it should be done. Not once during the entire 18 months do I recall a single member ever challenging the concept of a community high school—or suggesting that responsibility for community uplift should be elsewhere.

This acquiescence to professionally-determined goals did not come about because the group consisted exclusively of "yes" men but precisely because most were citizens and not professionals. They simply lacked imagination or expertise to redefine the committee's task. The professionals set the goal, and the members accepted it.

When the time came for making concrete proposals, the *inside* experts appeared. Committee members staked out areas of expertise; for example, someone from the city's public library system was full of definite plans for the high school library, and he would lapse into silence while the public health people urged the need for dental clinics. What was involved here was not simply mutual back-scratching, but a willingness to defer to each other's special knowledge. Inside experts like these were enormously influential in shaping the final plans.

These inside experts left their marks on the final recommendations in two ways: They furnished basic ideas, and they determined the emphasis of the report. For example, one subcommittee on auxiliary school services had a public health doctor on its roll. Because of his enthusiasm and the information he had at his command, better health care became one of the major goals of the committee; it overshadowed many other auxiliary services and finally became the aim of one-half of the committee's total package of recommendations.

A committee member from the park department surveyed existing park facilities at the request of his subcommittee.

He then talked so persistently about the need for nature study that the committee recommended a nature study area next to the new high school. Pushing his idea even further, the committee also suggested training students for work as landscape gardeners, tree cutters, and horticulturists. It is unlikely that this recommendation would have occurred to the committee without the information that the city needed such workers—information which had been supplied by the same park department staffer.

The outside experts appeared once more at later sessions; professional educators from Detroit and nearby, professors of social welfare, agency heads, local ministers, came and spoke at length. Rarely did the committee members have the energy—or the expertise—after the lectures to question the speaker. As a result, many of the experts' recommendations also found their way into the final report.

What about the non-expert—the housewife, the shopkeeper, the local politician? Their roles were limited; they did not originate any of the major features of the plan. What they contributed was a specific, human, local perspective on the expert recommendations. Non-experts frequently "humanized" technical plans. For instance, several experts had the idea that with the shortage of personnel in many nursing homes, training nurses aides would be a useful feature of the curriculum. It took the protest of Negro members to show them how Negro parents feel about low status jobs, how very deeply they wanted their children prepared for white collar jobs. Other non-experts contributed specific viewpoints from the Negro, the local politicians, etc. These viewpoints were not unknown to the planners, but their ramifications and intensity were unknown. The contributions of the non-experts led to modification of some ideas, some minor additions, and some different emphasis at points. However, the substance of the recommendations was made by the experts.

This reliance on experts may be one reason why innovation seems to be notoriously absent from most CAC reports. Many recommendations are carbon copies of allegedly successful experiments undertaken elsewhere, others are rehashes of recommendations previously made in the same community. If such repetition seems wasteful and unoriginal, it must be noted that repetition occurred only because of unmet demands.

The Atmosphere of Sweet Reasonableness

All of these decisions were reached in a spirit of quiet, peaceful accommodation. The conflict that is the essence of political decision-making was almost completely absent.

Why? Part of the answer is the subject matter itself—

everyone agrees that education is "a good thing." Few citizens are threatened by a better school as they might be by an urban renewal project. Furthermore, the members of this committee were simply making a plan, not allocating resources from a limited budget. The point where political conflict usually arises—where one project must be chosen at the expense of another—is never reached by a purely advisory committee.

Another factor which contributed to the conflict-free atmosphere was the personnel itself. First, generally, only those friendly to the goal were on the board. Second, working after hours, on their own time, they put a premium on cooperativeness, and combativeness was viewed as obstructionism in their effort to expedite the committee's work. Third, lay members relied heavily on expert advice while the experts deferred to each other's judgments. Fourth, those few lay citizens opposed to professional recommendations lacked the skills and background with which to combat the professionals.

There may be still another reason why committees of this type show so little conflict—the members have only a limited stake in how it all turns out. Their personal goals, their passions, are not engaged. Urban renewal committees, in contrast, experience bitter conflict precisely because members' life styles are at stake.

Traditional decision-making techniques such as bargaining, compromising, and conceding of points were notoriously absent. But why should they have been employed? Where a group has no internal conflict there is no need to compromise or to concede. But—and this point needs to be stressed—the group did not even utilize negotiating techniques where they seemed appropriate. For example, even though they made elaborate provisions for community reorganization, they never sounded out the community on how it would react to being reorganized. In fact, they ignored the outside world altogether.

In part this behavior can be explained on the basis of political naiveté. Reform-minded citizens, often imbued with the righteousness of their cause, assume that whatever is righteous will come to pass, that it will please the powers-that-be as much as it pleases themselves. The naiveté can be clearly seen in the failure to establish liaison with city hall and community agencies in planning for the family center. No wonder city hall vetoed the family center.

The Quality of the Decision

By and large, the report produced by Community Planning for Community Schools was all the superintendent said it was—"comprehensive, extensive, thorough." But not much was original or innovative. For the most part the advisory committee did not initiate, it reiterated. Fortunately, most of the report was solid and meritorious.

The report also exuded an air of community reform. What the committee meant by "uplift" boiled down to helping a lower class Negro community assimilate the customs of the urban middle class. It rarely occurred to this (or any) advisory committee that a neat plot of grass, or a sanitary supermarket may not have been top priorities for the community they wished to serve. What the committee picked out as areas of great discontent—segregated schools, dilapidated housing, lack of city services—did not distress the local residents as deeply as the committee members supposed; poor people sometimes accept the harsh realities of their lives with more equanimity than the committee members would believe possible.

When we surveyed area residents directly, we found that most were much too involved in immediate, personal problems to have much concern left for community needs. This observation does not, I think, invalidate the committee's work. In a very large measure the needs for social reforms are always articulated by community leaders; dissatisfaction with the status quo is perhaps the stuff leaders are made of.

The plan produced by this citizens group, then, was a serious, useful, workmanlike proposal that grappled with real community problems. But what about the larger purpose of citizens advisory groups, their use as a way of drawing citizens into active participation in government?

First, how completely did the committee represent the community for which it planned? The school people made an honest effort to recruit typical area residents to the committee, but they did not succeed. The unemployed, the assembly line worker, the ADC mother were not on the committee. Some lower class housewives were, some people of little education and limited income were, but not many of them. And those few were not average residents; they were people who had actively participated in previous community projects, people who belonged to PTA's and block organizations. The great majority of the members were middle class citizens appointed because they previously had shown an interest in the schools or because they represented major interests in the community or because they were from important racial and religious groups in the area.

Who Serves on Community Action Committees?

Most of the 183 committee members came from three major sources: church and social service agencies like the Lutheran Social Service, the Legal Aid Bureau, the Detroit

Urban League, and the YWCA (42 members); public school teachers and staff (40 members); and local residents, including housewives and local party leaders (47 members). The city sent along two representatives from agencies like the City Plan Commission, the departments of parks, health, and police, and the public library. A sprinkling of members represented local business and the United Auto Workers (eight members); colleges and universities sent six people; and students and unemployed youth contributed 12 more. Neither this nor any other advisory committee is truly representative of the urban poor.

Yet at the risk of appearing to be anti-democratic, I would like to suggest that it is naive and even cruel to expect the inarticulate masses to devise urban renewal schemes, library plans, or what have you. This is not to say that citizens groups should not strive for better balance, but simply to admit that the bulk of the members must continue to be those with skill and experience in dealing with complex community problems.

Saying that most disadvantaged people lack some of the necessary equipment for helping in policy formulation for social change is not to say they should be excluded from such planning. On some levels poor people can be utilized and should be utilized more fully—for the action, for implementation, and even perhaps for goal formulation. The least appropriate level is the one at which general goals have to be translated into technical and detailed blueprints. And that, after all, is the task which confronts large CAC's.

For that reason, among others, officials fail when they systematically hunt for CAC members among "the great inarticulate masses." Nor does it follow that "the great inarticulate masses" really would be heard if they could be enticed to serve on a CAC. Merely adding a dozen disadvantaged people to a board is no guarantee that they will have plans and speak up; nor does it guarantee that other members will really listen with an open mind. This is not to say that future CAC's and other social planning agencies should not strive for better balance, so that even the barely articulate can be heard. It is merely a word of caution not to expect much initiative from those who have been robbed of initiative. Washington is to be commended for stipulating that poor people shall have "the maximum feasible participation" in the war on poverty—the question is merely what is feasible.

What about the committee's influence on government? Citizens' recommendations do not have to be accepted, but it is unlikely that they will be brushed off lightly. The Detroit school board accepted committee recommendations

entirely. The school has been built. Other parts of the report are still in the political arena; they must compete with other projects; the voters must be induced to authorize the necessary funds; officials to coordinate themselves, etc. In this political process, much of the report will undoubtedly be lost. But this is a fate shared with many governmental agencies, and we do not call their recommendations uninfluential simply because they are not all enacted into legislation. A citizens advisory group, then, can provide a channel for making plans at least at effective as those produced by the city's own agencies and experts.

The Ones Who Care

What about the impact on citizens at large? If we are asking whether the committee's work got the man in the street or the average resident of the specific neighborhood directly involved and excited, the answer can only be "no." If we ask a more limited question—were more people feeling involved in their community after the committee's work than before—the answer is probably "yes."

The greatest impact, of course, was on the committee members themselves. Membership was a profound learning experience. Some members had no firsthand knowledge of the old high school, others knew little of the complexities of education, and some were not aware of either. Many knew only too well that the old school was not good enough, but did not realize how housing patterns, homes, and the neighborhood environment contributed to the problem. Some committee members had heard vaguely about slum schools, dropouts, and children who could not attend school for lack of shoes—these were the members who came to meetings from air-conditioned offices and modern houses in the suburbs. As one of them put it:

> To me problems like this high school were someone else's problems. I didn't have the faintest idea of the magnitude of the problem. Nor did I have any idea of the large number of people involved. The problem is no longer academic for me. I am really involved.

One small businessman, who arrived at the first meeting eager to save tax money by chopping away at "frills," learned how quality schools require spending. An executive, whose vision of high school extended only to preparation for college, learned to support a broad curriculum that would meet the needs of *all* the children in the community. It may be that these insights developed because the committee's processes were so slow. The cumbersome, time-consuming fact gathering turned out to be a necessary part of the learning process—it takes time to shed preconceptions and acquire new points of view.

Nor did this learning process stop with the committee membership. Most members that I interviewed believe that ideas filtered down to the rest of the community. One member made a point of mentioning the committee's work at all local block and community council meetings. Another talked about the work with her neighbors and at the PTA.

A businessman-member would discuss the work with several colleagues at lunch; they would discuss it with other people they met during the day. The businessman also joined a discussion group at his church, and helped draw fellow members into an active interest in the committee's work and in other civic problems.

As one member said, "Maybe we only influenced 10 percent of the community, but don't discount the 10 percent. They are the ones who care."

Rent Strikes
Poor Man's Weapon

Michael Lipsky

The poor lack not only money, but power. Low-income political groups may be thought of as politically impoverished. In the bargaining arena of city politics the poor have little to trade.

Protest has come to be an important part of the politics of low-income minorities. By attempting to enlarge the conflict, and bring outside pressures to bear on their concerns, protest has developed as one tactic the poor can use to exert power and gain greater control over their lives. Since the sit-in movement of 1960, Negro civil-rights strategists have used protest to bring about political change, and so have groups associated with the war on poverty. Saul Alinsky's Industrial Areas Foundation continues to receive invitations to help organize low-income communities because it has demonstrated that it can mobilize poor people around the tactics of protest.

The Harlem rent strikes of 1963 and 1964, organized by Jesse Gray, a dynamic black leader who has been agitating about slum housing for more than 15 years, affected some tenants in approximately 150 Harlem tenements. Following the March on Washington in August, 1963, the rent strikes played on the liberal sympathies of New Yorkers who were just beginning to re-examine the conditions of New York City slums. Through a combination of appeal and threat, Jesse Gray mounted a movement that succeeded in changing the orientation of some city services, obtained greater *legal* rights for organized tenants, and resulted in obtaining repairs in a minority of the buildings in which tenants struck. Along with rent strikes conducted by Mobilization for Youth, a pre-war poverty program, the rent strikes managed to project images of thousands of aroused tenants to a concerned public, and to somewhat anxious reform-oriented city officials.

The rent strikes did not succeed in obtaining fundamental goals. Most buildings in which tenants struck remained in disrepair, or deteriorated even further. City housing officials became more responsive to housing problems, but general programs to repair slum housing remained as remote as ever. Perhaps most significant, the rent strike movement, after a hectic initial winter, quickly petered out when cold weather again swept the Harlem streets. Focusing upon the rent strikes may help explain why this protest failed, and why protest in general is not a reliable political weapon.

Protest Has Long-Range Limits

Protest as a political tactic is limited because protest leaders must appeal to four constituencies at the same time. A protest leader must:

(1) nurture and sustain an organization composed of people who may not always agree with his program or style;

(2) adapt to the mass media—choose strategies and voice goals that will give him as much favorable exposure as possible;

(3) try to develop and sustain the protest's impact on third parties—the general public, sympathetic liberals, or anyone who can put pressure on those with power; and

(4) try to influence directly the targets of the protest—those who have the power to give him what he wants.

The tensions that result from the leader's need to manipulate four constituencies at once are the basic reason why protest is an unreliable political tactic, unlikely to prove successful in the long run.

Protest activity may be defined as a political activity designed to dramatize an objection to some policies or conditions, using unconventional showmanship or display and aimed at obtaining rewards from the political system while working within that system. The problem of the powerless is that they have little to bargain with, and must acquire resources. Fifteen people sitting in the Mayor's Office cannot, of themselves, hope to move City Hall. But through the publicity they get, or the reaction they evoke, they may politically activate a wider public to which the city administration is sensitive.

The tactic of activating third parties to enter the political process is most important to relatively powerless groups, although it is available to all. Obviously any organization which can call upon a large membership to engage in political activity—a trade union on strike, for example—has some degree of power. But the poor in individual neighborhoods frequently cannot exert such power. Neighborhood political groups may not have mass followings, or may not be able to rely on membership participation in political struggles. In such cases they may be able to activate other political forces in the city to enter the conflict on their behalf. However, the contradictions of the protest process suggest that even this tactic—now widely employed by various low-income groups—cannot be relied upon.

Take, for example, the problem of protest leaders and their constituents. If poor people are to be organized for protest activities, their involvement must be sustained by the symbolic and intangible rewards of participation in protest action, and by the promises of material rewards that protest leaders extend. Yet a leadership style suited to providing protesters with the intangible rewards of participating in rebellious political movements is sometimes incompatible with a style designed to secure tangible benefits for protest group members.

Furthermore, the need of protest leaders to develop a distinctive style in order to overcome the lack of involvement of potential group members diffuses as well as consolidates support. People who want psychological gratification (such as revenge or public notice and acknowledgment), but have little hope of material rewards, will be attracted to a militant leader. They want angry rhetoric and denunciation. On the other hand, those people who depend on the political system for tangible benefits, and therefore believe in it and cooperate with it to some extent, are likely to want moderate leadership. Groups that materially profit from participation in the system will not accept men who question the whole system. Yet the cohesion of relatively powerless groups may be strengthened by militant, ideological leadership that questions the rules of the game, that challenges their morality and legitimacy.

On the other hand, the fact that the sympathies and support of third parties are essential to the success of protesters may make the protesters' fear of retribution, where justified, an asset. For when people put themselves in danger by complaining, they are more likely to gain widespread sympathy. The cattle-prod and police-dog tactics of Alabama police in breaking up demonstrations a few years ago brought immediate response and support from around the country.

In short, the nature of protesters curtails the flexibility of protest leadership. Leaders must limit their public actions to preserve their basis of support. They must also limit protest in line with what they can reasonably expect of their followers. The poor cannot be expected to engage in activities that require much money. The anxieties developed throughout their lives—such as loss of job, fear of police, or danger of eviction—also limit the scope of protest. Negro protest in the South was limited by such retributions or anxieties about facing reprisals.

Jesse Gray was able to gain sympathy for the rent strikers because he was able to project an image of people willing to risk eviction in order to protest against the (rarely identified) slumlords, who exploited them, or the city, whose iceberg pace aided landlords rather than forced them to make repairs. In fact, Gray used an underutilized provision of the law which protected tenants against eviction if they paid their rent to court. It was one of the great strengths of the rent strikes that the image of danger to tenants was projected, while the tenants remained somewhat secure and within the legal process. This fortunate combination is not readily transferable to other cases in which protest activity is contemplated.

Apart from problems relating to manipulation of protest group members, protest leaders must command at least some resources. For instance, skilled professionals must be made available to protest organizations. Lawyers are needed to help protesters use the judicial process, and to handle court cases. The effectiveness of a protest organization may depend upon a combination of an ability to threaten the political system and an ability to exercise legal rights. The organization may either pay lawyers or depend on volunteers. In the case of the rent strikes, dependence on volunteer lawyers was finally abandoned—there were not enough available, and those who were willing could not survive long without payment.

Other professionals may be needed in other protest circumstances. A group trying to protest against an urban-renewal project, for example, will need architects and city planners to present a viable alternative to the city's plan.

Financial resources not only pay lawyers, but allow a minimum program of political activity. In the Harlem rent strikes, dues assessed against the protesters were low and were not collected systematically. Lawyers often complained that tenants were unwilling to pay incidental and minor fees, such as the $2 charge to subpoena departmental records. Obtaining money for mimeo flyers, supplies, rent, telephones, and a small payroll became major problems. The fact that Jesse Gray spent a great deal of time trying to organize new groups, and speaking all over the city, prevented him from paying attention to organizational details. Furthermore, he did not or could not develop assistants who could assume the organizational burden.

Lack of money can sometimes be made up for by passionate support. Lawyers, office help, and block organizers did come forth to work voluntarily for the rent strike. But such help is unreliable and usually transient. When spring came, volunteers vanished rapidly and did not return the following winter. Volunteer assistance usually comes from the more educated and skilled who can get other jobs, at good salaries. The diehards of *ad hoc* political groups are usually those who have no place else to go, nothing else to do.

Lack of money also can be overcome with skilled nonprofessionals; but usually they are scarce. The college students, Negro and white, who staffed the rent-strike offices, handled paper work and press releases, and served as neighborhood organizers, were vital to the strike's success. Not only could they communicate with tenants, but they were relatively sophisticated about the operations of the city government and the communications media. They could help tenants with city agencies, and tell reporters that they wanted to hear. They also maintained contacts with other civil rights and liberal organizations. Other workers might have eventually acquired these skills and contacts, but these student organizers allowed the movement to go into action quickly, on a city-wide scale, and with a large volume of cases. One of the casualties of "black power" has been the exclusion of skilled white college students from potentially useful roles of this kind.

Like the proverbial tree that falls unheard in the forest, protest, politically speaking, does not exist unless it is projected and perceived. To the extent that a successful protest depends on appealing to, or perhaps also threatening, other groups in the community, publicity through the public media will set the limits of how far that protest activity will go toward success. (A number of writers, in fact, have noticed that the success of a protest seems directly related to publicity outside the immediate protest area.) If the communications media either ignore the protest or play it down, it will not succeed.

When the protest *is* covered, the way it is given publicity will influence all participants including the protesters themselves. Therefore, it is vital that a leader know what the media consider newsworthy, and be familiar with the prejudices and desires of those who determine what is to be covered and how much.

Media's Demands May Be Destructive

But media requirements are often contradictory and hard to meet. TV wants spot news, perhaps 30 seconds' worth; newspapers want somewhat more than that, and long stories may appear only in weekly neighborhood or ethnic papers. Reporters want topical newsworthiness in the short run—the more exciting the better. They will even stretch to get it. But after that they want evidence, accuracy, and reliability. The leader who was too accommodating in the beginning may come to be portrayed as an irresponsible liar.

This conflict was well illustrated in the rent strike. Jesse Gray and the reporters developed an almost symbiotic relationship. They wanted fresh, dramatic news on the growth of the strike—and Gray was happy to give them progress reports he did not, and could not, substantiate.

Actually, just keeping the strikes going in a limited number of buildings would have been a considerable feat. Yet reporters wanted more than that—they wanted growth. Gray, of course, had other reasons for reporting that the strike was spreading—he knew that such reports, if believed, would help pressure city officials. In misrepresenting the facts, Gray was encouraged by sympathetic reporters—in the long run actually undermining his case. As a *New York Times* reporter explained, "We had an interest

in keeping it going."

Having encouraged Gray to go out on a limb and overstate the support he had, the reporters later were just as eager for documentation. It was not forthcoming. Gray consistently failed to produce a reliable list of rent-strike buildings that could withstand independent verification. He took the reporters only to those buildings he considered "safe." And the newspapers that had themselves strongly contributed to the inflation of Gray's claims then helped deflate them and denied him press coverage.

The clash between the needs of these two constituencies —the media and the protesters—often puts great strain on leaders. The old-line leader who appeals to his followers because of his apparent responsibility, integrity, and restraint will not capture the necessary headlines. On the other hand, the leader who finds militant rhetoric a useful weapon for organizing some people will find the media only too eager to carry his more inflammatory statements. But this portrayal of him as an uncompromising firebrand (often meant for a limited audience and as a limited tactic) will alienate him from people he may need for broad support, and may work toward excluding him from bargaining with city officials.

If a leader takes strong or extreme positions, he may win followers and newspaper space, but alienate the protest's target. Exclusion from the councils of bargaining or decision-making can have serious consequences for protest leaders, since the targets can then concentrate on satisfying the aroused public and civic groups, while ignoring the demands of the protesters.

What a protest leader must do to get support from third parties will also often conflict with what he must do to retain the interest and support of his followers. For instance, when Negro leaders actually engage in direct bargaining with politicians, they may find their supporters outraged or discouraged, and slipping away. They need militancy to arouse support; they need support to bargain; but if they bargain, they may seem to betray that militancy, and lose support. Yet bargaining at some point may be necessary to obtain objectives from city politicians. These tensions can be minimized to some extent by a protest organization's having divided leadership. One leader may bargain with city officials, while another continues rhetorical guerilla warfare.

Divided leadership may also prove useful in solving the problem that James Q. Wilson has noted: "The militant displays an unwillingness to perform those administrative tasks which are necessary to operate an organization." The nuts and bolts of administrative detail are vital. If protest depends primarily on a leader's charisma, as the rent strikes did to some extent, allocating responsibility (already difficult because of lack of skilled personnel) can become a

major problem. In the rent strike, somebody had to co-
ordinate court appearances for tenants and lawyers; somebody had to subpoena Building and Health Department
records and collect money to pay for them; and somebody
had to be alert to the fact that, through landlord duplicity
or tenant neglect, tenants might face immediate eviction
and require emergency legal assistance. Jesse Gray was often
unable, or unwilling, to concentrate of these details. In
part failures of these kinds are forced on the protest leader,
who must give higher priority to publicity and arousing
support than to administrative detail. However, divided
leadership can help separate responsibility for administration from responsibility for mobilization.

Strain between militancy to gain and maintain support
and reasonableness to obtain concessions can also be diminished by successful "public relations." Protest groups
may understand the same words differently than city officials. Imperatives to march or burn are usually not the commands frightened whites sometimes think they are.

Bargaining Is for Insiders

Protest success depends partly upon enlarging the number of groups and individuals who are concerned about the
issues. It also depends upon ability to influence the shape
of the decision, not merely whether or not there will be a
decision. This is one reason why protest is more likely to
succeed when groups are trying to veto a decision (say, to
stop construction of an expressway), than when they try to
initiate projects (say, to establish low-cost transportation
systems for a neighborhood).

Protest groups are often excluded from the bargaining
arena because the civic groups and city officials who make
decisions in various policy areas have developed relationships over long periods of time, for mutual benefit. Inter-
lopers are not admitted to these councils easily. Men in
power do not like to sit down with people they consider
rogues. They do not seek the dubious pleasure of being denounced, and are uneasy in the presence of people whose
class, race, or manners are unfamiliar. They may make opportunities available for "consultation," or even "confrontation," but decisions will be made behind closed doors
where the nature of the decision is not open to discussion
by "outsiders."

As noted before, relatively powerless protest groups
seldom have enough people of high status to work for
their proposals. Good causes sometimes attract such people,
but seldom for long. Therefore protest groups hardly ever
have the expertise and experience they need, including
professionals in such fields as law, architecture, accounting,
education, and how to get government money. This is one
area in which the "political impoverishment" of low-in-

come groups is most clearly observed. Protest groups may
learn how to dramatize issues, but they cannot present data
or proposals that public officials consider "objective" or
"reasonable." Few men can be both passionate advocate
and persuasive arbiter at the same time.

Ultimately the success of a protest depends on the targets.

Many of the forces that inhibit protest leaders from influencing target groups have already been mentioned: the
protesters' lack of status, experience, and resources in bargaining; the conflict between the rhetoric that will inspire
and hold supporters, and what will open the door to meaningful bargaining; conflicting press demands, and so on.

But there is an additional factor that constrains protest
organizations that deal with public agencies. As many students of organizations have pointed out, public agencies
and the men who run them are concerned with maintaining and enhancing the agency's position. This means protecting the agency from criticism and budget cuts, and attempting to increase the agency's status and scope. This
piece of conventional wisdom has great importance for a
protest group which can only succeed by getting others to
apply pressure on public policy. Public agencies are most
responsive to their regular critics and immediate organizational allies. Thus if they can deflect pressure from these,
their reference groups, they can ease the pressure brought
by protest *without meeting any of the protest demands.*

At least six tactics are available to targets that are inclined to respond in some way to protests. They may respond with symbolic satisfactions. Typical, in city politics,
is the ribbon-cutting, street-corner ceremony, or the Mayor's
walking press conference. When tension builds up in Harlem, Mayor Lindsay walks the streets and talks to the people. Such occasions are not only used to build support, but
to persuade the residents that attention is being directed to
their problems.

City agencies establish special machinery and procedures
to prepare symbolic means for handling protest crises. For
instance, in those New York departments having to do
with housing, top officials, a press secretary, and one or
two others will devote whatever time is necessary to collecting information and responding quickly to reporters'
inquiries about a developing crisis. This is useful for tenants: It means that if they can create enough concern, they
can cut through red tape. It is also useful for officials who
want to appear ready to take action.

During the New York rent strikes, city officials responded by: initiating an anti-rat campaign; proposing ways to
"legalize" rent strikes (already legal under certain conditions); starting a program to permit the city to make repairs; and contracting for a costly university study to re-

view housing code enforcement procedures. Some of these steps were of distinct advantage to tenants, although none was directed at the overall slum problem. It is important to note, however, that the announcement of these programs served to deflect pressure by reassuring civic groups and a liberal public that something was being done. Regardless of how well-meaning public officials are, real changes in conditions are secondary to the general agency need to develop a response to protest that will "take the heat off."

■ Another tactic available to public officials is to give token satisfactions. When city officials respond, with much publicity, to a few cases brought to them, they can appear to be meeting protest demands, while actually meeting only those few cases. If a child is bitten by a rat, and enough hue and cry is raised, the rats in that apartment or building may be exterminated, with much fanfare. The building next door remains infested.

Such tokenism may give the appearance of great improvement, while actually impeding real overall progress by alleviating public concern. Tokenism is particularly attractive to reporters and television news directors, who are able to dramatize individual cases convincingly. General situations are notoriously hard to dramatize.

■ To blunt protest drives, protest targets may also work to change their internal procedures and organization. This tactic is similar to the preceding one. By developing means to concentrate on those cases that are most dramatic, or seem to pose the greatest threats, city officials can effectively wear down the cutting-edges of protest.

As noted, all New York City agencies have informal arrangements to deal with such crisis cases. During the rent strikes two new programs were developed by the city whereby officials could enter buildings to make repairs and exterminate rats on an emergency basis. Previously, officials had been confined to trying to find the landlords and to taking them to court (a time-consuming, ineffective process that has been almost universally criticized by knowledgeable observers). These new programs were highly significant developments because they expanded the scope of governmental responsibility. They acknowledged, in a sense, that slum conditions are a social disease requiring public intervention.

At the same time, these innovations served the purposes of administrators who needed the power to make repairs in the worst housing cases. If public officials can act quickly in the most desperate situations that come to their attention, pressure for more general attacks on housing problems can be deflected.

The new programs could never significantly affect the 800,000 deteriorating apartments in New York City. The new programs can operate only so long as the number of crises are relatively limited. Crisis treatment for everyone would mean shifting resources from routine services. If all cases receive priority, then none can.

The new programs, however welcomed by some individual tenants, help agencies to "cool off" crises quicker. This also may be the function of police review boards and internal complaint bureaus. Problems can be handled more expeditiously with such mechanisms while agency personnel behavior remains unaffected.

■ Target groups may plead that their hands are tied—because of laws or stubborn superiors, or lack of resources or authority. They may be sympathetic, but what can they do? Besides, "If-I-give-it-to-you-I-have-to-give-it-to-everyone."

Illustratively, at various times during the rent strike, city officials claimed they did not have funds for emergency repairs (although they found funds later), and lacked authority to enter buildings to make emergency repairs (although the city later acted to make emergency repairs under provisions of a law available for over 60 years). This tactic is persuasive; everyone knows that cities are broke, and limited by state law. But if pressure rises, funds for specific, relatively inexpensive programs, or expansion of existing programs, can often be found.

■ Targets may use their extensive resources and contacts to discredit protest leaders and organizations: "They don't really have the people behind them"; they are acting "criminally"; they are "left-wing." These allegations can cool the sympathies of the vital third parties, whether or not there is any truth behind them. City officials, especially, can use this device in their contacts with civic groups and communication media, with which they are mutually dependent for support and assistance. Some city officials can downgrade protesters while others appear sympathetic to the protesters' demands.

■ Finally, target groups may postpone action—time is on their side. Public sympathy cools quickly, and issues are soon forgotten. Moreover, because low-income protest groups have difficulty sustaining organization (for reasons suggested above), they are particularly affected by delays. The threat represented by protest dissipates with time, the difficulty of managing for constituencies increases as more and more information circulates, and the inherent instability of protest groups makes it unlikely that they will be able to take effective action when decisions are finally announced.

Survey Research as Procrastination

The best way to procrastinate is to commit the subject to "study." By the time the study is ready, if ever, the protest group will probably not be around to criticize or press for implementation of proposals. The higher the status of the study group, the less capable low-status protest groups will be able to effectively challenge the final product. Furthermore, officials retain the option of rejecting or failing to accept the reports of study groups, a practice developed to an art by the Johnson administration.

This is not to say that surveys, research and study groups are to be identified solely as delaying tactics. They are often desirable, even necessary, to document need and mobilize public and pressure group support. But postponement, for whatever reason, will always change the pressures on policy-makers, usually in directions unfavorable to protest results.

Groups without power can attempt to gain influence through protest. I have argued that protest will be successful to the extent that the protesters can get third parties to put pressure on the targets. But protest leaders have severe problems in trying to meet the needs and desires of four separate and often conflicting constituencies—their supporters, the mass media, the interested and vital third parties, and the targets of the protest.

By definition, relatively powerless groups have few resources, and therefore little probability of success. But to survive at all and to arouse the third parties, they need at least some resources. Even to get these minimal resources, conflicting demands limit the leader's effectiveness. And when, finally, public officials are forced to recognize protest activity, it is not to meet the demands, but to satisfy other groups that have influence.

Edelman has written that, in practice, regulatory policy consists of reassuring mass publics symbolically while at the same time dispensing tangible concessions only to narrow interest groups. Complementing Edelman, I have suggested that public officials give symbolic reassurances to protest groups, rather than real concessions, because those on whom they most depend will be satisfied with appearances of action. Rent strikers wanted to see repairs in their apartments and dramatic improvements in slum housing; but the wider publics that most influence city officials could be satisfied simply by the appearance of reform. And when city officials had satisfied the publics this way, they could then resist or ignore the protesters' demands for other or more profound changes.

Kenneth Clark, in *Dark Ghetto,* has observed that the illusion of having power, when unaccompanied by material rewards, leads to feelings of helplessness and reinforces political apathy in the ghetto. If the poor and politically weak protest to acquire influence that will help change their lives and conditions, only to find that little comes from all that risk and trouble, then apathy or hostility toward conventional political methods may result.

If the arguments presented in this article are convincing, then those militant civil-rights leaders who insist that protest is a shallow foundation on which to build longterm, concrete gains are essentially correct. But their accompanying arguments—the fickleness of the white liberal, the difficulty of changing discriminatory institutions as opposed to discriminatory laws—are only part of the explanation for the essential failure of protest. An analysis of the politics involved strongly suggests that protest is best understood by concentrating on problems of managing diverse protest constituencies.

It may be, therefore, that Saul Alinsky is on soundest ground when he recommends protest as a tactic to build an organization, which can then command its own power. Protest also may be recommended to increase or change the political consciousness of people, or to gain short run goals in a potentially sympathetic political environment. This may be the most significant contribution of the black power movement—the development of group consciousness which provides a more cohesive political base. But ultimately relatively powerless groups cannot rely on the protest process alone to help them obtain long-run goals, or general improvements in conditions. What they need for long-run success are stable political resources—in a word, power. The American political system is theoretically open; but it is closed, for many reasons suggested here, to politically impoverished groups. While politicians continue to affirm the right to dissent or protest within reason, the political process in which protest takes place remains highly restricted.

Community Control
of the Police

Arthur I. Waskow

In almost every American metropolis, the police no longer are under civilian control—that is to say, democratic public control. Whether it be constant harassment of black youth in Los Angeles and white youth in Washington, brutal repression of white dissidents in Chicago and beating of peaceful Black Panthers in New York, refusal to obey the orders of a black mayor in Cleveland and those of a white president of the Board of Education in Philadelphia, or failure to answer routine calls for assistance from black neighborhoods of

Detroit and white neighborhoods of Baltimore, it is clear that there are many people in the metropolitan areas who do not believe they can make the police respond to their needs. The problem is clearer and more chronic in black neighborhoods—the consciousness of it is clearer there, so that it is seen not as a "failure" but as the successful accomplishment by the police of their mission as an occupation army. But parts of the white community—the young, dissident middle-class liberal peaceniks, even such Establishments as

those that try to set up civilian review boards, even such ethnic working-class communities as those that threw rocks at Martin Luther King's Chicago marches—feel unable to control their police. Increasingly, the police control themselves—almost in the fashion of the Prussian military traditionally so dreaded by democracies. (The fear of police autonomy has probably been because the police were expected to act autonomously in relation to the blacks, the Spanish-speaking and the poor. Only recently have parts of the middle class found themselves powerless vis-à-vis the police.)

There are two ways the police gain their autonomy: First, by constructing a police subculture of lifelong policemen, they insulate themselves against informal social controls—defining their own norms, defending, rewarding and promoting policemen who adhere to these regardless of public pressures or orders from above, insisting that policemen are "professionals" who should be trained by "professionals," so that civilians are increasingly excluded even from police academies. Secondly, they have, on the basis of this subculture, organized quasi unions with considerable political power, which have been able to "negotiate" practical autonomy on most occasions.

"Professionalized" Cops

During the period from the 1940s to about 1965, when liberal criticism of the police focused on "brutality" toward black people, the liberal solutions were: psychological screening to exclude sadists; human relations training to soften racial "prejudice"; professionalization to reduce "lower-class" or "untrained" reliance on naked violence; and civilian review boards to discipline violators of professional norms. All have failed. Among the most "professional" big city forces has been that of Los Angeles; among those most carefully screened to exclude sadists has been that of Chicago; among those with a "strong" civilian review board has been that of Philadelphia.

There are at least three major possible directions in which to go to achieve the kind of change in police forces that seems necessary to restore democratic, civilian control over the police:

1. Formal restructuring of metropolitan police departments into federations of neighborhood police forces, with control of each neighborhood force in the hands of neighborhood people through election of commissions.

2. Creation of countervailing organizations (in effect, "trade unions" of those policed) responsible to a real political base, able to hear grievances and force change.

3. Transformation of the police "profession" and role so as to end the isolation of policemen from the rest of the community, and thus to establish de facto community control by chiefly informal means.

The neighborhood control approach could be institutionalized by election of neighborhood or precinct police commissions which would 1) appoint high precinct officers (perhaps with approval of metropolitan headquarters, the mayor or a civil service commission); 2) approve the assignment in the precinct of new policemen and be able to require transfers out; 3) discipline officers, perhaps with the concurrence of a city-wide appeal board; and 4) set basic policy on law enforcement priorities in the neighborhood.

Neighborhood Control

Such an arrangement would respond first of all to the possibility that no great metropolis can be democratically governed from City Hall; that departments of education, police, zoning and the like may become far too bureaucratic and too insulated from popular pressures and fresh ideas if they try to govern from a single center a public of more than 100,000 people. It would thus accept the traditions of rural counties and suburban towns that find electing the sheriff or closely supervising the town police workable. Secondly, neighborhood control would respond to the concentration of the black populations in particular neighborhoods, and would thus attempt to deal at least with the "occupation army" aspect of a white-governed police force in black areas. It might also make working-class ethnic neighborhoods and middle- or "new-class" neighborhoods more able to shape their own police forces, and might even provide a framework for dealing with the difficulties that the "youth minority" face with policemen.

As far as the black neighborhoods are concerned, elected precinct commissions with the powers described would make possible great changes in the policemen who walk or ride the beat. Policemen might be chosen from the neighborhood and required to live in it. Black recruits are likely to be far more numerous if the police do not in fact bear the stigma of an occupying army, and they are far more likely to feel and act like members of the black community when they are no longer under pressure from a white-bossed headquarters and overwhelmingly white colleagues. Neighborhoods where back yards and recreation cellars are scarce might decide that enforcement of laws against playing ball in an alley or loitering to talk on the street would not be high-priority matters, and that enforcement of laws for decent housing would. Policemen would be much more likely to take seriously and answer promptly calls for their help. Drunks in the inner city might be taken home to their families like drunks in the suburbs, instead of beaten mercilessly and dumped in jail. The cries of "Nigger!" and "Boy!" would be much less frequent. The black community would almost certainly be living much more comfortably with its police.

The idea of neighborhood control of the police has raised objections on two related "territorial" grounds: that major differences in style of law enforcement would plague any one person as he moved around the metropolis, and that "hot pursuit" questions (and other similar negotiation problems of the neighborhood forces) would be much worse. Both these "difficulties" exist now in rural and suburban jurisdictions, and can only be said to be new in the sense that population density might make a difference. It is true that shifts from one neighborhood to another come more quickly than from town to town and that more people do in fact move from one neighborhood to another during their daily lives. But it should be noted that already, in a city like Washington where U.S. park police, capitol police, White House police and metropolitan police have major geographically distinct jurisdictions within the District of Columbia, solutions for "hot pursuit" and similar problems have been worked out. With reference to the problem of different styles in law enforcement, it seems already true that within a single city there are great differences from neighborhood to neighborhood, especially in the regulation of street conduct—but they are defined by policemen, not the public.

It might also be objected that neighborhood control of the police would destroy some city-wide institutions that ought to be protected. Not necessarily: for example, such divisions as fingerprint files and modus-operandi files, homicide squad and arson squad could still function under metropolitan police headquarters.

Finally, would neighborhood control in itself—regardless of the decisions made by the elected commissions—require changes in the role of the policeman? Perhaps the most politically ticklish question would arise around the function of the policeman as protector of property. In neighborhoods filled with property owners, that role would be supported; but in neighborhoods of the poor, would the residents put great store in the protection of property? It is precisely the fear that they would not that has motivated many property holders to insist that the poor should be policed by outside authority rather than police themselves. But first of all, the poor might turn out to want their few miserable possessions protected as desperately as the rich want their great hoards guarded. The poor might even be prepared to say that all property—that of the wealthy as well as their own—should be protected. The present ideological commitment of the middle class to protect giant property that it does not own suggests that for long-range reasons, intelligently or stupidly conceived, people will protect even interests that in some ways may damage them.

Countervailing Power

The possibility of control of the police through countervailing power is based on two recent models: the emergence of the Community Alert Patrols (CAPs) in Watts and elsewhere as checks on the police, and the Community Review Board created by the Mexican-American community in Denver. Both are vastly different from the conventional neutral civilian review boards, in that they are explicitly based not on a quasi-judicial model but on the necessity of having independent political power to confront that of the police forces. Both assume that the police are themselves either an independent political force or an arm of a powerful establishment, not a neutral peacekeeping body.

Thus both approaches seek some external political support for pressing grievances against the police. In the Denver case, *chicano* organizations investigate charges of illegitimate or unjust police behavior and, where they regard the charges as well founded, demand punishment of the officers and back up their demands with political pressure (publicity, threatened loss of votes, threatened disorder and others). As for the CAPs, they used the endemic anger of young black men against the behavior of the police in the black community to energize youth patrols that accompany the police on their rounds to take detailed notes and photographs of their behavior. Where the patrols felt the police acted badly, they filed complaints and sometimes tried to turn on some political heat to achieve redress. The Watts CAP tried, notably, to combine the insurgent political energy of the black community with the outside political (i.e., financial) support of the federal government, and thus to box in the police force. But what the Watts CAP hoped to gain from the federal tie in political ability to resist enormous hostility from the police, was lost in the weakening of ties with the black community itself. The CAP's legitimacy within Watts declined; and then, when the Los Angeles police department brought its political power to bear, the federal government backed off.

Nevertheless, the countervailing-power approach may have some advantages over neighborhood control. Perhaps the major one is that it can be undertaken without agreement of those in power, whereas the neighborhood-control model requires governmental acquiescence. It should also be noted that it does not need to be tied to a neighborhood base. Where a given community that feels itself the powerless object of police power, not the defining subject, is scattered across a city, then a countervailing organization along the lines of the Denver Crusade for Justice could be useful. And finally, some activists have argued that at least in the short run it is wiser to organize the powerless to oppose police power than to grasp it—on the grounds that power over one police precinct, or even many, in the absence of drastic social change in other spheres of life, may simply make fuzzy the face of the enemy, require the poor to police themselves in the patterns demanded by the unchanged spheres of social power, and thus stultify movements for more basic change.

As suggested above, the isolation of the police into an angry and frequently frightened subculture with a tight and effective political "face" is at least as important a factor in preventing democratic control as is the formal command hierarchy and its ties to the metropolitan white power structures. So it may be just as important to work for community control by cracking this informal "blue curtain" as it is to change the formal power relations and command hierarchies.

In examining ways to crack the "career" subculture, an important distinction should be kept in mind: the distinction between on-the-street peacekeeping and the more formal and "organized" policing of systematic off-street crime. These are quite different roles of the people we call "policemen."

In the first case, it seems relatively easy to argue that the police should not be "professionals" or career men. The role of peacekeeper on the beat is not a highly technical or specialized one, but depends rather on a fairly widespread and certainly nonprofessional skill in conciliatory human relations. The "false professionalization" of the role is due in part to an effort by policemen to defend their jobs and careers, and in part to the attempt of middle-class liberals to "upgrade" and "retrain" working-class policemen, on the theory that the "uneducated cop" was typically brutal or racist. This process could be reversed; peacekeepers could be recruited for a term of not more than three years from a broad cross-section of the public—especially and deliberately from among women as well as men, and from a wide age range, so as to emphasize the peacekeeping rather than the force-dispensing function. Such peacekeepers would probably not carry firearms, but would probably be trained in such defensive tactics as judo. They should probably wear uniforms quite unmilitary in style, be required to live in the community and keep up strong social contacts in it, and so on. Thus the community should see them as quite unlike traditional "policemen," and this perception should be accurate. Their command line should be totally divorced from that of the regular "police" department, and ideally would run to a neighborhood commission of the kind described above.

If it is true, as has frequently been claimed, that those who volunteer for police duty are especially self-selected for tendencies to sadism, then even a short-term volunteer process might not change the police enough, and one might have to think about selection of police by lottery from the whole population. But most of the evidence suggests that recruitment for the police proceeds on so many different appeals that if sadism is widespread, or becomes widespread on particular occasions, that is because it is learned on the job from other officers and from the nature of the role. If that is so, reducing the "career" line to three years would greatly weaken the informal social pressures from older policemen, and transforming the role would change the direction of the pressures.

The peacekeepers would deal with such traditional worries of the patrolman as family fights, conflicts between a tavern owner and unruly customers or between sleeping old people and singing youngsters. Indeed, some police authorities say patrolmen spend 80 percent of their time on such matters—and resent it terribly. For they are taught that their function is to Enforce the Law, not calm people down. Thus they tend to be bad at what they feel is a waste of their time and training—and of course even worse at it when they are strangers to or contemptuous of the community they are doing it in. Peacekeepers who are recruited for that precise job would do it better.

"Downtown" Policemen

Along with the transformation of the neighborhood street police, there should be a reexamination of the "downtown" policemen. Here there are two issues: Should these men be under neighborhood control? and does their work require professional expertise and training?

On the issue of where to locate authority, the answer seems clear from the kinds of crimes these men must handle: large-scale, quasi-business, "organized" crime; systematic refusal of large-scale land or factory owners to obey laws concerning adequate housing, adequate pollution control, and so forth; embezzlement, tax evasion and other white-collar crimes. It does not seem possible or appropriate to cope with these on a neighborhood basis. Indeed, many such categories of crime are already dealt with on a federal basis, and certainly metropolitan or even regional policing makes sense in these areas. The policemen involved would rarely if ever need to be "on the street" in any particular neighborhood, and their work would affect much wider areas; therefore wider areas should be governed.

"Professional" Danger

But this issue of size leaves open the issue of professionalization. On one hand, there is evidence in this realm of police work—from the growing use of large-scale private detective agencies, the growing importance of electronic detectors and computer analysis of financial accounts—that public police have not kept pace with the degree of technical expertise now required by much of the public. But on the other hand, there is the necessity of making sure that national, regional or metropolitan police forces, as well as neighborhood peacekeepers, are kept under civilian control—a necessity not easily achieved as the history of the FBI makes clear and one that itself will require considerable social innovation. Whether there is any way to meet the requirement for technical skill while still preventing the emergence of a "professional" career subculture in this kind of police work is not clear, and will require further study. If the ultimate goal is not merely representative but participatory democracy, then deprofessionalization of even the technical police must be sought.

Model-building is not enough; we must also examine the politics of change toward one or another of these models of community control of the police.

The only city in which a sustained demand for neighborhood control along the lines of Model I has turned into a serious political issue seems to be Washington, D.C. There the Black United Front has demanded neighborhood election of precinct police commissions—in the context of a series of homicides of civilians (almost all black) by policemen (all white) and the killing of a white policeman by a black civilian. The BUF demand was picked up by a group of black businessmen, some black clergymen and a number of white and racially mixed groups in the city, including the Democratic Central Committee. In the total absence even of a fiction of city-wide democratic control over the police, the claims of neighborhood democracy have been strengthened. The strongest pressure has come from upsurges of rage from the black community after each homicide of a black civilian has been ruled "justifiable." Opposition to neighborhood control has come from the police, the white business community, the two large newspapers and the southern congressmen who control the city's budget. Washington's city government has tried to appease both "law and order" and "community control" pressures by issuing slightly stronger restrictions on police use of guns, by calling for new advisory precinct boards and so forth. Their efforts have had little effect.

Efforts in the direction of Model II have come almost entirely from black or Spanish-speaking communities (perhaps in a few Appalachian white "ghettos" like uptown Chicago), with only momentary outside support from the federal government or foundations.

The radical deprofessionalizing of some police roles, as in Model III, seems not to have become a political issue anywhere; but the splitting of police functions into several distinct roles and the recruitment of more "community" people (but no effort toward democratization of the command line) has been urged by the president's crime commission. A "community participation" (but not control) project in Washington, developed by outside agencies (the National Institute of Mental Health, especially) to test the crime commission's proposals, has triggered considerable enmity from neighborhood organizers on the ground that it will simply extend and intensify police control over the community (through informers, for example), rather than the reverse.

Obviously, what political strategy is developed in achieving community control over police depends heavily on which model one intends to pursue, and which end result within them one hopes to achieve. Let us assume, however, that a decision is made to pursue a combination of Models I and III—which together seem to offer the fullest control over a police force to those in the neighborhood—by transforming both the formal lines of command and the informal interpersonal processes to converge on the community.

With that goal in view, it would make sense to strive immediately to set up Model II. Such a countervailing "community union to police the police" could then become not simply a grievance-processing organization, but also a continuous pressure group for the adoption of a Model I/III arrangement *in the form of a present version of what the future Model I/III control would look like.* Imagine an open-ended community group that anyone in a given police precinct could join, the directors of which would be periodically elected, and that would be funded by neighborhood "dues" and, perhaps, matching foundation grants. Such a strong community union to police the police could 1) itself put peacekeepers on the street —unarmed, distinctively uniformed, oriented to conflict resolution rather than enforcing the law, including women, young dropouts and clergymen; 2) itself patrol the police, taking evidence of bad behavior and offering to settle problems instead of the police; 3) hear and investigate and judge complaints; 4) mobilize political pressure for the transfer of bad policemen, bad precinct commanders and others; and 5) keep up constant pressure for the transfer of power over the neighborhood police to the neighborhood itself. It must be clear that such a community union to police the police would be a focus of intense political conflict, including great hostility and possibly physical danger from the police. But if the groundwork in organizing community support for a Model I/III arrangement had been well done, the very intensity of political conflict over a strong Model II might persuade the city to allow Model I/III to be established. In any case, it is hard to see how democratic civilian control over a staff of armed men who are widely believed to hold a monopol over legitimate violence and who are well organized in a separate subculture and a strong political force can be reestablished without intense political conflict.

Militant Civil Servants in New York City

Frances Fox Piven

Not long ago, thousands of people massed in front of New York's City Hall and sang "Solidarity Forever." The image was of workers marching against Pinkertons. But the ranks were middle-class civil servants, and their solidarity was directed against the black and Puerto Rican poor. The issue on this occasion was school decentralization, but that is only one of a host of issues currently galvanizing white civil servants and dividing them from the enlarging minorities in the cities.

The rising militancy of public employees needs no documenting here. New York's 60,000 school teachers have been shutting down the school system regularly; this fall it was the Day Care Center workers; slowdowns by police and firemen are becoming commonplace. And if public employees are more militant in New York, where they are the most numerous and best organized, public unions across the country are catching up. Teachers prevented schools from opening this fall in Illinois, Ohio, Indiana, Massachusetts, Pennsylvania, New Hampshire, Michigan, New York, Pennsylvania, Connecticut, Rhode Island, Wisconsin, Minnesota, Utah and Tennessee. Last year Detroit's police were hit by the "blue flu"; while Cleveland's police threatened outright rebellion against Mayor Carl B. Stokes. In Atlanta the firemen went on strike; in Newark the police and firemen simultaneously called in sick.

These events are not, as they are sometimes described, simply contests between unions and the "general public." The keenest struggle is with residents of the central-city ghettos (who in any case now form a substantial segment of the "general public" in most big cities). Police, firemen, teachers and public-welfare workers increasingly complain about "harassment" in the ghettos. For their part, growing numbers of the black poor view police, firemen, teachers, public-welfare workers and other city employees as their oppressors.

The emerging conflict is not difficult to explain. Whites and blacks are pitted against each other in a struggle for the occupational and political benefits attached to public employment. Whites now have the bulk of these benefits, and blacks want a greater share of them. Nor is it only jobs that are at stake. Organized public employees have become a powerful force shaping the policies of municipal agencies, but the policies that suit employees often run counter to ghetto interests. We may be entering another phase in the long and tragic history of antagonism between the black poor and the white working class in America.

The Ethnic Stake-out

Municipal jobs have always been an important resource in the cultivation of political power. As successive waves of immigrants settled in the cities, their votes were exchanged for jobs and other favors, permitting established party leaders to develop and maintain control despite the disruptive potential of new and unaffiliated populations. The exchange also facilitated the integration of immigrant groups into the economic and political structures of the city, yielding them both a measure of influence and some occupational rewards. Public employment was a major channel of mobility for the Italian, the Irish and the Jew, each of whom, by successively taking over whole sectors of the public services, gave various municipal agencies their distinctly ethnic coloration. Now blacks are the newcomers. But they come at a time when public employment has been preempted by older groups and is held fast through civil-service provisions and collective-bargaining contracts. Most public jobs are no longer allocated in exchange for political allegiance, but through a "merit" system based on formal qualifications.

The development of the civil-service merit system in municipalities at the turn of the century (the federal government adopted it in 1883) is usually credited to the efforts of reformers who sought to improve the quality of municipal services, to eliminate graft and to dislodge machine leaders. At least some of the employees in all cities with more than 500,000 inhabitants are now under civil service; in about half of these cities, virtually all employees have such protections.

Although the civil service originated in the struggle between party leaders and reformers for control of public employment, it launched municipal employees as an independent force. As municipal services expanded, the enlarging numbers of public employees began to form associations. Often these originated as benevolent societies, such as New York's Patrolmen's Benevolent Association which formed in the 1890s. Protected by the merit system, these organizations of public employees gradually gained some influence in their own right, and they exerted that influence at both the municipal and the state level to shape legislation and to monitor personnel policies so as to protect and advance their occupational interests.

Shortly after World War I, when the trade union movement was growing rapidly, public employees made their first major thrust toward unionization in the famous Boston police strike. About 1,100 of the 1,400-man force struck, goaded by the refusal of city officials to grant pay raises despite rapid inflation and despite the favorable recommendations of a commission appointed to appraise police demands. The strike precipitated widespread disorder in the streets of Boston. Official reactions were swift and savage. Calvin Coolidge, then governor, became a national hero as he moved to break the strike under the banner, "There is no right to strike against the public safety by anybody, anywhere, anytime." Virtually the entire police force was fired (and the few loyal men were granted pay raises). More important, the numerous police unions that had sprouted up in other cities, many of them affiliated with the American Federation of Labor, were scuttled. Public unionism did not recover its impetus until well after World War II.

In the meantime, civil-service associations relied mainly on lobbying to press their interests and, as their membership grew, they became an effective force in party politics. Although the mode of their involvement in party politics varied from place to place and from time to time, the sheer numbers of organized public employees made political leaders loath to ignore them. One measure of their impact is the number of major party leaders who rose from their ranks. In New York City, for example, Mayor William O'Dwyer was a former policeman; Abe Beame, the Democratic candidate for mayor in 1965, was a former schoolteacher, and Paul Screvane, his competitor for the Democratic mayoralty nomination in that same year, began as a sanitation worker.

Public Unionism

Now unionism is on the rise again, signalling a new phase in the political development of public employee groups. It is even spreading rapidly to the more professional services, such as education and welfare, whose employees have traditionally resisted the working-class connotation of unionism. The American Federation of Teachers has organized so many teachers as to force the National Educational Association, which considers itself a professional association, into a militant stance (including endorsing boycotts and strikes by its members). In New York, firemen last year successfully wrested the right to strike from their parent International Association of Firefighters, and the Patrolmen's Benevolent Association is exploring the possibility of an affiliation with the AFL-CIO. The American Federation of State, County, and Municipal Employees—half of whose members work for municipalities— is one of the fastest-growing affiliates of the AFL-CIO, having increased its membership by 70 percent in the last four years. Overall, unions of public employees are adding 1,000 new members every working day, according to a member of the National Labor Relations Board.

By becoming part of the labor movement, public employees are augmenting their influence in two ways. First, they can call for support from other unions, and that support can be a substantial force. New York's teachers were backed in the struggle against school decentralization by the Central Labor Council, which represents 1.2 million workers. (The Central Labor Council, headed by a top official from the electricians' union, and with an overwhelmingly white membership, also had its own interest in the school issue: the Board of Education disperses over $1 billion annually for maintenance and construction. Under a system of community control, contracts might be awarded to black businesses or to contractors who hire black workers. Some black labor officials, seeing themselves allied against their own communities, broke ranks with the Central Labor Council over the decentralization issue.)

Unionism also means that public employees feel justified in using the disruptive leverage of the strike. Transit workers bring a metropolis to a standstill; teachers close down the schools; sanitation men bury a city under mounds of garbage. With each such crisis, the cry goes up for new legislative controls. But it is hard to see how laws will prevent strikes, unless the political climate becomes much more repressive. So far political leaders have been reluctant to invoke the full penalties permitted by existing law for fear of alienating organized labor. Thus New York State's Condon-Wadlin Law, enacted in 1947, was not used and was finally replaced by the "model" Taylor law which, as the experience of the last three years shows, works no better. Theodore Kheel, one of the nation's most noted labor arbitrators, in pronouncing the failure of the new law, pointed out that the state Public Employment Relations Board, established under the Taylor law to arbitrate disputes, took no action on either of the New York City teacher strikes. The *New York Times* concluded with alarm that "The virus of irresponsibility is racing through New York's unionized civil service," and "There is no end, short of draining the municipal treasury and turning taxpayers into refugees or relief recipients. . . ."

Public unions must be controlled, so the argument goes, because they are uniquely capable of paralyzing the cities and gouging the public as the price of restoring services. In a recent decision, New York's highest court held that a legislative classification differentiating between public and private industry was reasonable and constitutional, thus justifying prohibitions on the right of public employees to strike. The courts unanimously held that public employees could "by the exercise of naked power" obtain gains "wholly disproportionate to the services rendered by them."

As a practical matter, however, these distinctions between public and private employees do not hold up. Strikes in the public and private sectors rely on the same forms of leverage, though in varying degrees. Private-sector strikes result in economic losses, but so do strikes in the municipal services (for example, transit stoppages). Even teachers and welfare workers exert some economic pressure, although they rely more heavily on another form of leverage—the cries of a severely inconvenienced and discomfitted populace—to force government to settle their grievances. But private strikes of milk or fuel deliveries, of steel workers or transportation workers, also discomfit large sectors of the population and generate pressure for government to intervene and force a settlement.

Nor is it true that the coercive power of municipal unions enables them to obtain more favorable settlements than private unions. If, under the pressure of a strike in municipal services, the public is often unmindful of the impact of settlements on taxes, the public is equally unmindful of the eventual costs to consumers of settlements in the private sector. Industrial strikes are by no means necessarily less disruptive than public strikes or less coercive in pressing for a greater share of the public's dollar.

Blanket Security

Despite the continuing controversy over the right to strike, it is not the root of the trouble over municipal employment. Rather it is that the gains won by employees after long years of struggle now seem to be in jeopardy.

In fact, some groups of public employees had managed to secure substantial control over their working conditions long before they began to unionize, and in many cases long before comparable gains had been secured by workers in the private sector. These victories were won by intensive lobbying and by the assiduous cultivation of influence in the political parties at the municipal and state levels.

In the past, except where wages were concerned, other groups in the cities rarely became sufficiently aroused to block efforts by public employees to advance their interests. On issues such as tenure of working conditions or career advancement, and even retirement (which does not involve immediate costs) the civil services associations were able to make substantial strides by using conventional means of political influence.

First, with their jobs secured by the merit system, public workers in many agencies went on to win the principle of "promotion from within." This principle, together with promotion criteria that favored longevity, assured the career advancement of those already employed. But such a system of promotion, because it has the consequence of restricting outsiders to the bottom rank of public employment, is being opposed by new groups. When proponents of school decentralization insist that these requirements be waived to place black people in supervisory or administrative positions, spokesmen for the New York school supervisors' association answer that it will "turn the clock back 100 years and reinstate the spoils system."

In some municipal agencies, moreover, newcomers are even barred from lower-level jobs. Building inspectors in New York City are required to have five years' experience in the building trades, but few black people can get into the building trades. Police associations oppose any "lowering" of hiring standards, proposed as a way of facilitating entrance by minority groups, arguing that the complexity of modern law enforcement calls for even higher educational standards. (Police have even objected to lowering the physical height requirement, which now excludes many Puerto Ricans.) When New York City recently announced that impoverished people would be granted up to 12 extra points on civil-service tests for 50 low-paying jobs in anti-poverty agencies, the very meagerness of the concession cast in relief the system of exclusion it was to modify.

Public employees have also been successful in preempting some of the future resources of the city. Demands for improved retirement and pension plans, for example, are prominent: New York's transit workers recently settled for a contract that awarded pension pay on the basis of a time-and-a-half provision during their last year of employment, and the police are demanding the right to retire after 15 years. Such benefits are often won more easily than wage demands, for it is less onerous for a mayor to make concessions payable under a later administration.

Obviously, elaborate entrance and promotion requirements now limit access by blacks to municipal jobs. Indeed, one can almost measure the strength of public employee associations in different cities by their success in securing such requirements, and in keeping minority members out. In New York, where municipal workers are numerous and well organized, 90 percent of the teachers are white; in Detroit, Philadelphia, and Chicago, where municipal employees are not well organized, 25 to 40 percent of the teachers are black.

Mortgaged Treasuries

The number of jobs at stake is vast, and black demands are mounting. New York City employs 325,000 people, and personnel costs naturally account for the lion's share (about 60 percent) of a municipal budget topping $6 billion. And the share is growing: the number of public employees continues to rise (up 60 percent in New York City since the end of World War II), and wages and benefits are also rising. The question is not whether these costs are legitimate—but who will benefit by them. For as blacks become more numerous in cities, they will come to power only to find the treasuries mortgaged to earlier groups.

Unionization has been important mainly (but not exclusively) in the area of wages, where public employees often lagged behind organized private workers. Relying as they did on political influence, they were blocked by taxpayer groups who usually opposed higher municipal salaries. However, with unionization and strike power, public employees are no longer dependent on the vicissitudes of interest-group politics to get higher wages, and so, as the *New York Times* notes with horror, they have begun to "leap frog" each other in salary demands.

Unionization is also enabling large numbers of municipal workers who hold less coveted jobs to move forward. By and large, hospital workers, clerks and janitors, for example, were left behind in the process of advancement through the civil services and through party politics. In New York City, many of these workers have now been organized by District 37 of the State, County and Mu-

nicipal Employees Union. Furthermore, because these are low-paid, low-prestige jobs, they are often held by blacks who constitute about 25 percent of District 37s membership. (This helps to explain why Victor Gotbaum, the outspoken head of District Council 37, bucked the Central Labor Council in the school decentralization fight.) And following the path of earlier public employee groups, District 37 is beginning to press for a series of civil service reforms to enable its members to move up the muncipal career ladder. The much publicized struggles of the garbage workers in Memphis, and the hospital workers in Charlotte are efforts by low-paid blacks who, by using militant union tactics, are making their first advances.

Competition for jobs and money is by no means the worst of the struggle between the ghetto and public employees. In the course of securing their occupational interests, some groups of public employees have come to exercise substantial control over their agencies, and that control is now being challenged, too. The struggle over school decentralization in a number of cities is a prime example.

Public employees have been able to win considerable influence over the tasks they perform and other conditions of work. Many civil-service positions are now enshrined in codified descriptions which make both the job-holder and the work he performs relatively invulnerable to outside interference, even by political leaders. Furthermore, substantial discretion is inherent in many civil-service tasks, partly because legislative mandates are obscure, and partly because many civil-service positions require the occupants to be "professionals," enabling them to resist interference on the ground that they are "experts."

Public employees often use both the codified protection of their jobs and their powers of discretion to resist policy changes that alter the nature of their work. When former Mayor Robert Wagner asked the police department to patrol housing projects, the police refused and were supported by the police commissioner. School personnel effectively defeated desegregation policies by simply failing to inform ghetto parents of their right to enroll their children in white schools, and by discouraging those parents who tried to do so. The combined effect of procedural safeguards and professional discretion is suggested by the often-noted dilemma of a board of education that is simultaneously too centralized and too decentralized: it is hamstrung by regulations that seem to limit policy options, while its personnel retain the license to undermine central directives.

If some public employees have always had the ability to undermine policies, they now want the right to set policies, usually on the ground that as professionals they know what's best. Thus teachers recently demanded that the New York City Board of Education expand the "More Effective Schools" program, and that they be granted the right to remove "disruptive" children from their classrooms. Threatened by the efforts of ghetto parents to free their children from an unresponsive educational system, the union became the major force opposing school decentralization. Similarly, New York's striking welfare workers bargained for (but have not yet won) the right to join the commissioner in formulating agency policies, arguing that 8,000 case workers ought to have a say in policy decisions. The Patrolmen's Benevolent Association has begun issuing its own instructions to policemen on how the law should be enforced, to countermand Mayor John Lindsay's presumed indulgence of looters and demonstrators. And only through a full-scale public campaign was the mayor able to override the PBA's stubborn resistance to a "fourth platoon" permitting heavier scheduling of policemen during high crime hours. All of these ventures by the unions represent incursions on matters of municipal policy. That they are made under the banner of professional commitment to public service should not obscure the fact that they will entrench and enhance the position of the public employees involved.

In part, demands in the policy area are being provoked by the feeling among public employees that they must defend their agencies against black assailants. The black masses are very dependent on public services, but these services have been conspicuously unresponsive to them, and have even become instruments of white antagonism, as when police services take on the character of an army of occupation in the ghetto. The fierce fight waged by the New York Patrolmen's Benevolent Association against a civilian review board reveals the intensity of the conflict over the control of municipal agencies. In education and public welfare, the effects of cleavage between white staff and black recipients are even more pervasive and tragic, for by blocking and distorting the delivery of these services white staffs virtually fix the life chances of the black poor.

Jobs and services have always been the grist of urban politics. By entrenching and enlarging control over municipal agencies, white-controlled public-employee unions are also blocking a traditional avenue by which newcomers become assimilated into the urban political and economic system. Politicians who depend on the black vote have not been oblivious to this obstruction. One response has been to generate new systems of services to be staffed by blacks. By establishing these services under separate administrative

auspices and by calling them "experimental," political leaders have tried to avoid aggravating white public employees. Thus the national Democratic administration which took office in 1960 created a series of new programs for the inner city in the fields of delinquency, mental health, poverty, education and the like. Federal guidelines required that blacks have a large share of the new jobs and policy positions (e.g., "maximum feasible participation of the poor"). In general, these "demonstration" programs have been more responsive than traditional municipal agencies to black interests. Of course, the white-dominated city bureaucracies fought for control of the new programs and sometimes won: at the least, they obtained a substantial share of the new funds as compensation. But regardless of who has control, the new programs are miniscule compared with existing municipal programs. If anything, the antipoverty program has made more visible just how little blacks do control, thus precipitating some of the current wrangles over control of traditional municipal programs.

Ironies of History

There are ironies in these developments. Reformers struggled to free municipal services from the vicissitudes of party politics; now some politicians are struggling to free municipal services from the vicissitudes of employee control. The advent and (at this writing) likely defeat of the Lindsay administration in New York City is a good illustration, for it exposed and escalated the conflict between blacks and whites. Lindsay campaigned against the old Democratic regime to which the unions were tied. His election was made possible by the defection of almost half of the black voters from Democratic ranks, and by middle- and upper-class support. It was to these groups that he appealed in his campaign and to which he is now trying to respond through his public posture and policies. To the black voter, he has been a politician who walked in the ghetto streets, who allowed the welfare rolls to rise, who attempted to assert control over the police force and to decentralize the school system; to the middle and upper classes, he has been a reformer and innovator who revamped the city's bureaucratic structures and appointed prestigious outsiders to high administrative posts. Appeals to both constituencies led him to do battle with the public unions regularly, for these moves threaten the control exerted by employee groups over municipal services. These battle have activated race and ethnic loyalties so fierce as to seem to rupture the city; and the possibility that Lindsay has even alienated the largely liberal Jewish vote exposes the intensity of the struggles for control of municipal benefits. Similar alliances between the black poor and affluent whites are also appearing in other cities (Cleveland, Detroit, Gary) with similar reactions from public employees, and white ethnic groups generally.

There is still another irony, for the militancy and radical rhetoric of the rapidly growing public unions have led some observers to define them as the vanguard of a re-awakened labor movement. Bayard Rustin and A. Philip Randolph were recently moved to applaud the New York teachers' union for "having clearly demonstrated that trade unionism can play a useful part in obtaining needed facilities for . . . radically improving the quality of education for all children." One could wish the applause were justified; one could wish that white workers were allies of the black masses. But it is turning out that most advances by the public unions are being made at the expense of the black masses. As it now stands, there is only so much in the way of jobs, services and control over policy to be divided up. As one black spokesman said of the struggle between the UFT and the Ocean Hill-Brownsville govern-

ing board, "The name of the game is money and power for blacks!" Or, he might have added, for whites.

But the bitterest irony of all is that the struggle between whites and blacks is being played out within the narrow limits of the resources available in municipalities. There is nothing unreasonable in white employees' pressing to hold and expand the gains they have won, which in any case are not so munificent. What is unreasonable is that their gains are being made at the expense of blacks, not at the expense of affluent and powerful sectors of the society. How to shift the struggle from the arena of municipal jobs and services to the arena in which national and corporate wealth are divvied up is hardly clear. But one thing is clear. The burden of shifting the struggle should not fall on blacks, for they are only now getting their first chance at a share of what the city has to offer. Confined to the municipal sphere, blacks will oppose the advances of the white unions and fight for what others got before them. And they may have cause to worry—not only that the stakes of municipal politics are limited, but that all of the stakes may be claimed before they have joined the game.

Negro Neighbors– Banned in Boston

J. Michael Ross, Thomas Crawford, and Thomas Pettigrew

A big woman, her voice is small, almost piping, and it starts to break when she talks about "civil-rights leaders using our children, using our schools." When she gets to "little children being bussed all across the city," she seems half a syllable from tears. "Why?" she keeps asking, for she sees no reason. "What will Negroes learn by sitting in class with white children?"

"Boston's Louise Day Hicks," Ira Mothner, *Look*, Feb. 22, 1966

For four years now an intense struggle has raged in Boston over the best methods for achieving—or not achieving—school desegregation. Officially, the argument is not about the virtues of desegregation itself, or about any other aspect of discrimination. Most Bostonians agree (at least publicly) to the desirability or at least inevitability of righting old social wrongs. The specific school conflict is focused, as it has been in many American cities, on "bussing"—whether children should be transported out of their own neighborhoods to more distant schools to achieve racial balance.

But the fury with which the contending forces attack and counterattack, and the passions, accusations, and national publicity that have resulted show clearly that far more lies beneath the surface than is obvious, or will be admitted. Much of the controversy has swirled around the program and personality of one person—Mrs. Louise Day Hicks of the Boston School Committee, an implacable foe of bussing and similar methods of effecting school desegregation. She has become a national figure for her stand, a symbol of stand-patism, a "Joan of Arc" to those who resist social change—even though she denies any such intention. Her triumphs at the polls mark her today as the most politically successful opponent of racial change outside the South. (She has been elected three times to the School Committee and the last two times received about two-thirds of the vote.)

Obviously the "Hicks phenomenon" has significance far beyond Massachusetts. The weathervane that swings with the passions aroused by the campaigns, arguments, and elections in Boston may show which way the wind is starting to blow elsewhere in America. Groups of aroused resisters have been formed in other large cities to fight bussing; pro-segregation housing legislation has been approved by large majorities in Akron, Detroit, and California; and many Northern politicians have attempted to engage in Hicks-style campaigns, even while insisting that they are in favor of the *legitimate* interests of Negroes.

The "Neighborhood" Dilemma

But is the Hicks phenomenon really a clear indication of "blatant" bigotry in the Northern cities? Is it symptomatic of a new era of explicit white resistance to civil rights?

A study of the issue that we conducted in Boston indicates that pure racism is far too simple an explanation. It is not open bigotry, nor the never-proven "white backlash," nor even the simple, much proclaimed desire to support neighborhood schools that has won Mrs. Hick's elections for her. It is something much deeper and more meaningful for our times—*the perception of a threat to familiar, secure, and comfortable ways*. The hard resistance to this perceived threat has formed not around *school* segregation, which is an outpost, but around *neighborhood* segregation, which is the inner citadel. In the magic words "neighborhood schools," the emphasis is on the first, not the second, word.

Mrs. Hicks first ran in 1961 as a reform candidate who wanted "to serve the youth of the city" and "to keep politics out of the School Committee." But by 1963 she had discovered the political value of opposing the moderate requests of Boston's relatively small Negro community (about 11 percent of the population). She ran in 1963 as a "neighborhood school" defender and garnered 69 percent of the vote, easily leading the ticket. After two more years of publicized rejection of Negro requests, she got 64 percent of the vote in 1965, and again ran at the head of the ticket.

This last triumph evoked strong reactions. The Roman Catholic Archdiocesan *Pilot* bluntly charged that the Hicks following had voted ". . . against the rightful claims of the Boston Negro for the education of his children." The defeated Negro candidate, Melvin King, remarked, "A little bit of democracy died in Boston yesterday"; the election results were, he maintained, proof ". . . of bigotry and racism in the city." Joseph Alsop, the national columnist, hurled the strongest salvo: "A sinister election . . . overwhelmingly re-elected on a platform of covert yet rather pronounced racial prejudice, . . . she . . . resembles the late Joseph R. McCarthy dressed up as a Pollyanna."

On election night Mrs. Hicks herself said simply: "The people are speaking tonight. . . . I am of the people. I don't need any pipelines to know what they want."

Are They Bigots?

The Hicks supporters deny bigotry—even those officeholders and voters who have consistently opposed racial change say that bigotry is not involved. Typical of supporters is the white man who says, "I've really got my doubts about all this racial balancing of schools. But don't get me wrong—I have nothing against Negroes, and I wouldn't mind having my children go to school with a few Negro children." Mrs. Hicks says she is not even opposed to desegregation—merely wants it to come "naturally," without harming neighborhood schools.

In their broad social characteristics, however, the pro-Hicks white resisters (who would like to see Mrs. Hicks become mayor) resemble their Southern counterparts. Compared to other Bostonians they are as a group less educated, poorer, and older.

But in their other characteristics, even the pro-Hicks group bears little resemblance to conservative Southerners. According to national surveys, our Boston sample as a whole (despite being roughly two-to-one for Mrs. Hicks) showed *less* blatant prejudice against Negroes than white Northerners in general. Only 12 percent thought Negroes not as intelligent as whites; only 16 percent said they "disliked Negroes as a group." And 95 percent believed that "Negroes should have as good a chance as white people to get any kind of job."

This acceptance extended in part to schools. All 317 of our respondents were asked: "Do you think white students and Negro students should go to the same schools or to separate schools?" Only 7 percent of the total preferred separate schools; only 9 percent of even the pro-Hicks group chose separate schools. What about parents? Each of those with children already in (or about to enroll in) Boston's public schools was asked if he had "any objection to sending his children to a school where *a few* of the children are Negro." Only 1 percent objected.

But where we probed beyond abstractions and token integration, a different picture began to emerge. Thus, 22 percent of parents objected to sending their children to a school where *half* of the student body was Negro; 64 percent objected to sending their children to a school where *more than half* was Negro. Differences between pro-Hicks, partial supporters, and anti-Hicks groups became sharper. At each level of education, pro-Hicks parents objected to their children enrolling in a predominantly-Negro school more strongly than anti-Hicks parents.

Many said they were not against desegregation, merely against the way it was coming about. They deplored the methods, they deplored the speed. Sixty-two percent of all 317 thought "civil rights leaders are trying to push too fast"; 52 percent believed that the protest actions had been "generally violent"; and 48 percent asserted that "the actions Negroes have taken, on the whole *hurt* their cause." Even when educational levels were held constant, the pro-Hicks respondents agreed with these statements to a considerably greater extent than the anti-Hicks group, with the partial supporters falling between.

Inconsistencies were rife. Almost two-thirds realized that "racial imbalance does exist in the Boston public schools," and nearly half believed that "racial imbalance in schools hurts the education of children." Yet large majorities still favored "neighborhood schools," opposed bussing, and insisted that "Negro children are getting equal educational opportunities in Boston's public schools."

These inconsistencies suggest that white Northerners are surprisingly misinformed and uninformed about how interracial education might actually be achieved. So much heat and emphasis has been focused on "bussing" (a method, incidentally, not very popular among Negro parents themselves), that alternative, superior methods are not only seldom considered, but most people do not even know that they exist. We asked in our pilot work for opinions about other mixing techniques—re-drawing district lines, strategically locating new schools, pairing white and Negro schools, and building large "campus park" school facilities to serve large areas. Most people had no opinions about them; most had not even heard of them. When told, they failed to see any connection between these alternatives and the problem.

Nationwide polls find much the same situation in other cities. This fact points to the possibility of some reduction in white resistance to desegregation in the North when the public's information level on the issue is raised. It might be well, also, to avoid head-on confrontations over single, emotionally charged issues when alternatives that might accomplish the same ends are available.

The much touted "white backlash," the white counter-attack to Negro civil rights activities, though much prophesied during the George Wallace and Barry Goldwater ascendancies, never materialized for Goldwater, and has never been confirmed by social science research.

Is There a White Backlash?

Actually, an array of surveys during the critical years 1963-65 has shown a *gain* in popular acceptance and favor for Negro rights; apparently Americans will come to condemn injustice if they are continually reminded that it exists.

For instance, the Louis Harris poll showed a steadily mounting majority in favor of the Civil Rights Act. In November 1963, 63 percent favored it; this rose to 68 percent by February 1964, and to 70 percent by May 1964 —a 7 percent rise during six months when the so-called "backlash" was supposedly in full swing. According to a more recent Harris survey, not even the Watts riots brought on a white backlash. Between August of 1963 and August 1965, the national sample of whites who thought that "most Negroes believe in non-violent action" rose by 6 percent (from 53 to 59 percent) in spite of Watts, and other disorders.

Consider, too, the results of surveys by the National Opinion Research Center specifically designed to test for any "backlash." An intensive study of racial attitudes throughout the United States was conducted in December of 1963; it was followed up in the summer of 1964 by re-interviewing those sample members who lived in large Northern, industrial areas where the "backlash" was presumably endemic. Yet these follow-up interviews revealed that basic attitudes toward the *goals* of racial change had not shifted. Those whites who had previously favored the desegregation of schools, public facilities, and neighborhoods still favored it; those who had previously opposed it, still opposed it. As in our Boston data, there were negative sentiments expressed about the *means* of achieving racial change, but this was nothing new; such sentiments are expressed by many white Americans each time a new protest technique—sit-ins, freedom rides, street demonstrations—is introduced.

Our Boston data are consistent with these national findings. We did not conduct interviews in 1963; but our respondents reported marked uniformity in their voting for or against Mrs. Hicks in 1963 and 1965. What was more important was that the feelings we uncovered about Mrs. Hicks and racial balance in schools were related to personality and political attitudes that went far beyond race. The same kind of people who were most strongly for Mrs. Hicks and the status quo were also most strongly in agreement with such statements as:

—If a child is unusual in any way, his parents should get him to be more like other children.

—Things are pretty good nowadays—it is best to keep things the way they are.

—We should be sympathetic with mental patients but we cannot expect to understand their odd behavior.

This is conservatism speaking—not bigotry *per se.* Civil rights become involved only insofar as they represent the threat of unsettling change.

Strong affinities do exist, however, between these basic personality and political orientations of the pro-Hicks people and the general position advanced by the far right in recent years. At the heart is a predisposition to halt and condemn many of the liberal policies of the last 34 years. There is a feeling of discomfort and confusion, and an inability to understand or cope with social change. "There is a stir in the land," noted Senator Goldwater during the 1964 election campaign. "There is a mood of uneasiness. We feel adrift in an uncharted land and stormy sea. We feel we have lost our way."

The Goldwater thesis hammered away at moral deficiencies: "The moral fiber of the American people is beset by rot and decay." Similarly, our pro-Hicks respondents most often agreed that: "The facts on crime and sexual immorality show that we will have to crack down harder on young people if we are going to save our moral standards." The more educated pro-Hicks supporters typically rejected liberal ideology and distrusted the liberal intellectual who "frowns on the policeman and fawns on the social psychologist." (As social psychologists ourselves, we can assure everyone that no one has "fawned on" us lately!) They most frequently believed that the government places "too much" attention upon "problems such as housing, unemployment, and education," and that "a lot of professors and government experts have too much influence on too many things nowadays."

In local issues, these negative attitudes are much more potent than on the national scene, where life, death, and national prosperity are also involved. In local elections, therefore, they can often determine who will win, in spite of what happened to Goldwater. Note, too, that among our Boston respondents less than a third "would like to see" her assume the responsible office of mayor, while over two-thirds registered their discontent by voting for her for the lesser office of school committeewoman.

This feeling of discontent definitely underlies many of the attempts to resist change that we witness in our cities today. And the discontent is strongly felt by many in the white urban electorate. In the Boston School Committee elections the pro-Hicks minority of discontents were joined by a larger and less extreme group, who would not vote for Mrs. Hicks for the higher, if local, office of mayor, but did vote for her on the immediate, tense, issue of bussing—and insured her a large majority.

Love Thy Neighborhood School

A third theory about the pro-Hicks vote holds that bigotry is not at all involved—that parents of school children are merely expressing strong preference for neighborhood schools.

First, as our data has already demonstrated, bigotry, though not as blatant as some expected, though often disguised behind rationalizations, *is* involved—at each educational level the followers of Mrs. Hicks are more anti-Negro than her opponents.

The second contention, however, does contain a kernel of truth. Neighborhood schools are popular, and bussing is unpopular. Further, the pro-Hicks people are slightly more often speaking from personal concern: 25 percent of the pro-Hicks group, compared to 16 percent of partial supporters and only 10 percent of the anti-Hicks group, actually do, or will soon, send their own children to the public schools.

On the other hand even 25 percent is not a large percentage; it still leaves 75 percent animated by something besides direct involvement with public school affairs. Mrs. Hicks herself sent her own children to parochial schools.

What then does animate them? To repeat, our study indicates strongly that behind the resistance to school desegregation lies the greater fear of neighborhood desegregation; and even beyond that, fear that the old, good ways of life will change if Negroes move in. This concern may be especially acute in a city so identified with Catholic immigrants, who have put such great emphasis on neighbor-

389

hood life, church, and ethnic identity. To the extent that she seems to be a champion of the old, tight, "good" neighborhoods, Mrs. Hicks has tapped a responsive nerve. (It should be noted parenthetically that Mrs. Hicks is more than the embattled housewife fighting for the little children as she is often portrayed. Her father was a very influential and popular Irish politician; her background and training were heavily political; she was a lawyer active in public affairs long before nomination for the school committee. She is quite aware of the political and emotional implications of what she is doing.)

The Housing Hurdle

The neighborhood roots of the Hicks supporters are deeper and stronger than those of her partial supporters, and especially of her detractors. Half of the pro-Hicks group owned their own homes, compared to 37 percent of partial supporters, and 29 percent of her critics. Even more striking, 42 percent of her supporters had owned those homes for more than 10 years—while the same percentage of the anti-Hicks group had rented, and lived, at the same address less than four years. In various ways, the anti-Hicks groups showed least attachment to their neighborhoods: they least often had relatives living nearby, or spent time chatting with neighbors; they were most likely to have been born outside Boston.

Once we openly discussed housing integration, much of the fog that habitually surrounds Northern racial prejudice was dissipated—even among the well-educated. Statements were relatively frank and revealing. At each educational level, pro-Hicks supporters agreed more than others that "it is best to keep" Negroes "in their own districts and schools" and that "white people have a right to keep Negroes out of their neighborhoods if they want to." They also volunteered more unfavorable comments about the prospect of "a Negro with the same income and education" moving into their blocks. Indeed, these three housing questions evoked the largest and most consistent differences between our three groups.

Housing segregation is self-perpetuating. Since it inhibits the association of the races as equals, and limits the chances of white residents to really get to know Negroes as neighbors and fellow human beings, it tends to reinforce the stereotypes that support segregation. Much of the fear of neighborhood integration must stem from the lack of simple contacts with Negroes in the past and present. Not illogically, the strongest resisters of change, the pro-Hicks people, when matched with others of equal education, reported far

more often than the others that they lived in all-white neighborhoods. Further, they were far less likely to "know personally a Negro professional." No wonder, as noted, they reacted unfavorably to the prospect that a Negro, even with the same income and education, might move close by; they seldom, if ever, had known such a Negro.

To summarize briefly:

■ Are the Hicks supporters open bigots? Not precisely. Support for Mrs. Hicks *is* strongest among the most anti-Negro respondents, but even here the anti-Negro views are not generally "blatant"—nor do strong anti-Negro feelings characterize all of her supporters.

■ Do their attitudes symptomize a "white backlash?" No —there is no evidence that these anti-desegregation attitudes are new, or newly reinforced—and this supports other studies throughout the nation.

■ Was the pro-Hicks vote purely a desire to maintain "neighborhood schools?" Hardly. Neighborhood schools are popular, but they are by no means at the heart of the controversy.

■ It is not fear of school desegregation but of neighborhood desegregation that drives the people who support Mrs. Hicks.

What can be done? Many northern educators, caught in the cross-fire, argue that they are being punished for a social problem beyond their control or responsibility, and that school desegregation must and should wait on neighborhood desegregation—what Mrs. Hicks calls the "natural" solution. Yet our data suggest that white resistance to interracial neighborhoods is actually far stronger and more entrenched than resistance to school desegregation. To let the weaker bastion wait until the stronger one falls would delay desegregation and could defeat it for a long time.

Intense pressure for desegregation in public schools will undoubtedly build up throughout the nation. Residential desegregation—even with new federal legislation—will move too slowly to help the schools much. Generally, racial change in education in the urban North will precede, not follow, change in housing patterns.

Therefore, the bitter struggles over schools that have raged from Boston to Oakland will continue. How can they be alleviated—and resolved? Data from our survey offers a possible way—one that has already proven effective even in the reluctant South.

To put it bluntly, money is the Achilles heel of bigotry. Negro leaders have known this for some time and have used it effectively in boycotts. Racial conflict can give a city a bad image and hurts its economy, as Little Rock and New

Orleans learned. Racial attitudes and economic interest can come into conflict; and when segregation begins to cost money, even the most committed stand-patter can suddenly come to see things in a new light.

Last year Massachusetts enacted a statute that can deny state funds to any school district that practices racial imbalance. The 1964 Civil Rights Act gives similar, if less explicit, powers to the U.S. Commissioner of Education. Indeed, state officials are currently withholding educational funds from Boston's public schools pending positive action by the School Committee on racial balance. The Massachusetts Department of Education has even supplied the committee with a carefully devised redistricting plan. At this writing, the School Committee continues to resist, but time is running out. Boston taxpayers have recently been warned that if the funds are not soon released their property taxes will rise again.

How deep seated are these racial attitudes then? Are they more than pocketbook deep? If the Boston taxpayer can only have the lady if he also takes the tiger—Mrs. Hicks and greatly increased taxes—will he still choose her?

The Money Question

We asked our 317 sample members if they agreed or disagreed with the following statement: "Although taxes may go up, it is better to lose state aid to Boston public schools than to bring about racial balance in the schools." Only 17 percent of our total sample agreed; for the vast majority, lower taxes easily outranked school segregation in importance. Only a minority of even the pro-Hicks group was willing to pay more taxes for segregated schools. And among the partial supporters of Mrs. Hicks who provide her electoral majority, only one-fifth was willing to pay the price.

However, the withholding of federal and state funds from recalcitrant school districts is difficult, and may, for a number of reasons, prove unpopular, unwieldy, and impractical. The emphasis then should include not only a stick but a carrot as well—such as awarding extra funds only for those endeavors which definitely further school desegregation. For instance, new school construction could be financed only after it was demonstrated that the location of proposed schools contributed significantly to racial balance.

More help must come from the suburbs, the "white nooses around the Negro's neck." Most of the action has taken place in the central cities where the Negroes are concentrated, while the white suburbs, with their separate school systems, have remained aloof, though full of good advice. (In Boston, Mrs. Hicks has been denounced roundly by white liberals—who live in the suburbs and cannot vote against her.) Carrot legislation could be helpful here also: state and federal funds could finance transportation of students from crowded inner schools across district lines to suburban schools, recompensing both; through legislation and subsidies, encouragement could be given for the construction of joint campus parks along borders, sharing facilities. Without such carrot legislation, cooperation between city and suburb will probably not materialize.

The struggle over school desegregation will be with us a long time, and will heat up before it cools down. But the general tactics that might bring victory are:

■ School desegregation should itself be made a primary objective; it should not be required to wait until residential desegregation, change of heart, or the millenium are accomplished first.

■ Money pressure should be applied. Federal and state funds should be withheld from school districts which do not comply with laws against discrimination in schooling.

■ The carrot of public money may be even more effective than the stick. Extra funds for construction, facilities, and faculty which actively promote desegregation should be offered and awarded.

■ Bussing is not the only method to achieve racial balance. All methods which achieve the same result might be tried —careful placement of new schools, changing boundaries, the large area campus park principle, and so on.

■ Cooperation between suburbs and the central city, and across boundaries, should be encouraged, through the use or withholding of public monies. School segregation is a metropolitan, not an inner city, problem.

When questions of public policy are submitted to a community-wide referendum, they face a most uncertain fate. Furious passions can be aroused when the most commonplace proposals are put to a vote. The outcome may, and very often does, contradict the overwhelming recommendation of the experts. One proposal which has been studied systematically is fluoridation. The Harvard School of Public Health has studied eighteen New England communities where fluoridation was put to a vote; it was approved in only four. I am no expert on how to win a fluoridation referendum, but on the basis of this study I am prepared to offer some observations on what not to do.

The opposition to fluoridation is varied. Among the active opponents there are disingenuous professionals, sincere but rather emotional individuals, and calm and rational opponents who object on grounds of individual rights or public policy. Among those who vote against fluoridation are all of the above plus those who are confused and unconvinced by either side.

Those who vote for fluoridation are also varied—many confuse fluoridation with some water purification process such as chlorination. It is difficult to specify that any given strategy will be effective without specifying the audience and the characteristics of the community involved.

Even with these limitations, a common theme runs through many of the unsuccessful attempts to have fluoridation adopted by public vote. A hypothetical community, with a composite of the errors made in many of the communities studied, will serve as an example. While many extraneous complicating factors have been omitted, Fluoradale is not simply a "straw town" set up for easy criticism. The actions described have all taken place in one or more actual communities studied.

Different researchers have reached a considerable amount of agreement on why people vote for or against fluoridation. Substantial difference on the degree to which they feel that they are able to control the important forces in their lives appear between those who vote for and those who vote against. This has been variously characterized as alienation, feelings of deprivation, and a low sense of political efficacy. Essentially, those who vote against fluoridation seem to have greater feelings of helplessness than do those who vote in favor.

One other contrast between those who vote for and those who vote against is worth bringing out. Some proponents have incorrectly argued that opponents are anti-scientific. This assumes that opponents perceive scientific unanimity on this issue and refuse to respect it. In fact,

How to Lose a Referendum

The Case of Fluoridation

William A. Gamson

there is evidence that many of those who vote against fluoridation see the "experts" as divided on the merits of the proposal. How, one might ask, can they continue to do so in spite of endorsement by the United States Public Health Service, the American Medical Association, and the American Dental Association?

To answer this it is necessary to make a distinction between "experts" and "authorities." Many active opponents perceive such organizations as the AMA and the ADA not as technical experts, but as medical "authorities" with the power to punish individual doctors and dentists who do not follow their policies. Furthermore, they frequently do not believe that these organizations use their power in a disinterested fashion. They may easily interpret the self-interested actions of the AMA on such issues as medical care for the aged as evidence for such a belief. On the other hand, when an occasional doctor or dentist opposes fluori-

physicians and dentists in town. One of the dentists points out that fluoridation does poorly on referenda and that it would be wise to try to have fluoridation adopted directly by the town council. Up to this point, no opposition has developed, and everyone is generally optimistic.

The council is sympathetic although one member has some doubts, and they decide to hold a public hearing on the proposal. In response to a notice in the paper, an unexpectedly large number of people attend the hearing, and most of them are hostile to fluoridation. Proponents are heckled and asked hostile questions from the floor. One opponent, a retired chiropractor, asks to be allowed to testify. The health officer argues that he is unqualified. "There is no sense in letting a lot of scientifically untrained people shoot off their mouths about this," he tells the council. Several people in the audience loudly object, and the meeting threatens to get out of hand. One of the councilmen most sympathetic to fluoridation makes a short speech about democracy. "This is a public hearing, and anyone here who wishes to speak may do so," he announces.

The retired chiropractor makes a moderate plea. "There is a lot of controversy about this question of fluoridation, and I think we should study it thoroughly before we adopt it. In a lot of places, they've tried to rush it through and suppress the opposition. I hope the people of Fluoradale will be given a chance to hear both sides and decide for themselves on this question."

The health officer is annoyed at the response of the partisan audience. He reasserts the technical nature of the question and the lack of qualifications of the average citizen to pass judgment on a scientific matter. He is willing to take the word of reputable scientific organizations on faith; why should those so much less qualified than he insist on exercising their own judgment?

After lengthy discussion the council decides to place the question on the ballot at the next town election, and a study committee is formed to publish an impartial report. The health officer, another physician, and a dentist are appointed along with the chiropractor and another opponent, a housewife.

The active proponents begin mobilizing quickly by forming a committee. They contact all the physicians and dentists except for one retired and rather senile physician who has lived in Fluoradale all his life. They also approach various civic organizations. The Chamber of Commerce and one of the service clubs promise support. They begin publishing advertisements over the names of most of the leading business and civic leaders including three council members.

dation, he may be seen as a technically qualified "expert" with the courage to oppose the "authorities." These partisan opponents then will see the authorities as united but the experts as divided. In a less explicit fashion, many ordinary voters may be unconsciously making this kind of distinction.

CRACKPOTS AND CONTROVERSY

The health officer in Fluoradale is a conscientious, intelligent, but somewhat rigid person. He is aware that fluoridation has been a controversial issue in many places, but he sees no reason why it can not be adopted in Fluoradale if it is handled correctly. In his view, opposition in these other communities has come from a handful of "crackpots" who have managed to scare or hoodwink a gullible populace. Fluoradale is a pretty sensible town and while it has its crackpots, no one will take them seriously.

The health officer goes to other health officials and finds that they favor fluoridation as well. He also contacts various

The proponents see their campaign as educational rather than political. They point out that the majority of the study committee (which also published a two-man minority report) recommended fluoridation. They decide to hold a large public meeting to present their side. The active opponents bring in an anti-fluoridation "expert" from outside the community and ask that he be heard. The proponents charge that he is a "quack," and say that this is their meeting—an educational forum, not a debate. Opponents claim that this is a deliberate effort to keep the people from being told both sides. Finally, the proponents consent to questions from the floor; a free-wheeling debate ensues in which both sides grow highly emotional. Anti-fluoridation speakers repeatedly challenge the motives of the proponents.

As the controversy in the community grows more heated, several of the civic leaders among the original endorsers ask that their names be removed from the advertisements. They begin to let it be known that they are neutral on the issue but intend to see that both sides are heard. The health officer, in a letter to the paper, suggests that "neutralism is immoral when an issue of right or wrong is involved."

The opposition campaign begins to gather momentum. They point to the array of community leaders and medical people who endorse the proposal as evidence of the powerful forces involved. The defectors to neutrality are seen as men of conscience who are really opposed but do not have sufficient courage to buck the "powers." The elderly physician, who was not contacted by the pro-fluoridation committee, publishes a letter attacking fluoridation and the endorsing physicians. This is used as evidence of how an "expert" who is beyond the reach of sanctions will act. Any privately expressed doubt by a doctor or dentist on any grounds is viewed as his "honest," unpressured opinion.

The pro-fluoridation partisans follow the policy of not responding to opponents' charges "to avoid dignifying such hogwash." People whose normal skepticism would lead them to dismiss the usual flamboyant stories of pipe corrosion, deaths from cancer, dying goldfish, and stillbirths are left in some doubt under the atmosphere of mistrust generated by the campaign.

On election day fluoridation is beaten decisively. The nature of the campaign leaves most community leaders—even those who were active proponents—feeling that it would be a bad thing for the community to have the issue brought up again.

The unsuccessful campaign in Fluoradale is not intended to illustrate any specific tactical "don'ts" or to comment on the general wisdom of getting endorsements from civic leaders, of avoiding referenda, of answering opponent charges, or of any of the other specific acts that were performed. Such specific tactical considerations largely depend on the conditions existing at a given time.

"Don'ts" should center on certain characteristic ways in which many active proponents view the controversy:

■ Don't assume that all opponents are the same—that they are stupid, emotional crackpots. For every person whom this description fits, you'll convince a dozen more whom it doesn't fit to vote against it.

■ Don't assume that the mere multiplication of medical and political authorities will convince doubters that the experts agree. Attitudes of trust or distrust toward the influence held by such authorities may be decisive. Endorsements of fluoridation by them may be given a different meaning by potential opponents.

■ Don't assume that those who are influential on other issues will necessarily be influential on fluoridation. An individual who wields a great deal of power on a sewage or a school bond proposal may or may not be able to influence the outcome of a fluoridation vote.

■ Don't be annoyed at implicit or explicit challenges to your own role as an expert. By allowing themselves to be baited by hostile questions, some active proponents seem to confirm opposition charges of high-handedness or concealment.

The story of Fluoradale illustrates a more general "don't" growing out of the earlier discussion of sources of opposition. Many people in many communities are likely to have feelings of political helplessness. These are insufficient in themselves to turn someone against fluoridation. The fact that such differences between voting proponents and opponents exist seems to indicate that there is something about the fluoridation issue that makes these feelings noticeable.

This something may be inherent in the nature of the issue—its technical quality or some other feature—and beyond the control of anything proponents do in a campaign. On the other hand, it may be that the posture which partisans take may make these feelings salient in relations to fluoridation and other issues. Well-intended actions in a fluoridation campaign can have unintended consequences.

Most of us are annoyed and righteous when someone who is unqualified challenges our opinion on a subject on which we feel we are to some degree expert. This kind of legitimate "arrogance" is more refreshing than false humility. But legitimate or not, it is a poor posture to take on fluoridation or any other issue which will eventually be decided by public vote.

part seven

The Limits of Usual Politics

We all know that the decade of the 1960s in the United States was marked by a huge outpouring of political unrest and violence. The essays in this Part explore some of the underlying causal factors, as well as certain responses to and consequences of this unrest. The debacle has been massive enough to produce a flood of reports by official commissions, from the Warren Commission report on the assassination of President Kennedy (1964), through the report of the National Advisory Commission on Civil Disorders (1968), to the Walker Commission report, *Rights in Conflict* (1968), the report of the National Commission on the Causes and Prevention of Violence, *To Establish Justice, to Insure Domestic Tranquility* (1969), to the report of the President's Commission on Campus Unrest (1970). Ancillary to these reports have been such remarkable compendia as the Violence Commission's staff reports, *The History of Violence in America* (1969) and *Assassination and Political Violence* (1970), as well as monographs on special subjects such as the staff report to the Violence Commission, *Shoot-Out in Cleveland* (1969). In subject matter, in comprehensiveness, and in volume, these reports have been unprecedented in American history. Surely Skolnick is right in thinking that, even if they produce no short-term effects, they will prove a rich mine of information for years to come. They tell us a great deal about where we have been going; and they have an official *imprimatur* which is by no means without political value, as Marx's utilization of British factory commission reports in the writing of *Capital* should remind us.

Here as elsewhere we find paradox in the United States. Pluralist consensus theorists have long celebrated the low-pressure, non-ideological quality of usual politics in America, holding it up as a major virtue. Yet, as these reports make clear, violence is indeed "as American as apple pie" and has been so throughout much of our history. Moreover, a large part of it has been of the direct-action variety with clear political overtones. Thus turn-of-the-century European socialists who visited the United States were regularly horrified at the extent of violence in—and directed against—the labor movement, a violence of which the activities of the left wing of the I.W.W. and the Ludlow massacre of 1914 in Colorado were good examples. The tradition of political violence in the United States obviously has complex roots, as the specialized monographs reveal. But its survival into our own time is in a sense difficult to square with a simple-minded variant of such conventional arguments as the "frontier thesis"—if for no better reason than that other societies with very recent frontier experiences, notably Australia and Canada, show no real counterpart to the American experiences of the 1960s.

We return to our paradox. The United States stands in the front rank of advanced industrial—indeed post-industrial—societies. It has a political regime whose stability and endurance has been endlessly celebrated. Yet during the 1960s it experienced higher levels of political or politically relevant turmoil than any other advanced Western society. The comparisons—except, happily, in the rate of deaths in civil strife—are more appropriately not with other advanced societies, but with underdeveloped nations, particularly some in Latin America.

Major political violence during the 1960s and early 1970s involved, for the most part, two groups: blacks in urban ghettos, and students and other white radicals who tended to rise in response to specific government policies, particularly those involving the Vietnam war. To some extent ghetto riots seem clearly enough a response to environmental conditions which many in the ghetto regard (with reason!) as intolerable. Williams' analysis of the 1965 census in Cleveland provides a sense of the sociological dynamics at work in the city's "crisis ghetto." The growing gap between middle-class and poor which he describes also shows up in preliminary 1970 census findings for New Jersey, particularly for blacks in the city of Newark. But environmental conditions are wholes; they don't come in bits and pieces. One interesting finding about the Detroit riots which Parmenter discusses is that a remarkable number of rioters and sympathizers were in no sense "the poorest of the poor," either in income, job classification or education. This finding tends to support the point which is discussed in some detail by Boesel et al. here: that a state approaching "cold civil war" exists between the ghetto community as a whole and the power instruments of

whites, police, employers, ghetto merchants, public school teachers, and social workers—especially between the community and the police. In short, something involving a sense of separate national identity has been growing in black ghettos, where social compaction is not cross-cut by close relationships with the white community outside.

In more than one sense, ghetto riots can be seen as both manifestations of this separate identity and as transition points through which it passes during its formation. Boesel et al. point out something which the commission reports have stressed again and again: whites tend to regard the issues of the ghetto largely if not exclusively in terms of weaknesses in the black culture (family structure, community norms, etc.) which disqualify American blacks from effective participation in white society and which move them toward criminal, deviant, and socially ineffective behavior. The commission reports—and most social scientists as well—stress the extraordinary extent to which ghetto-ization has been a vicious cycle of impoverishment, discrimination, and hopelessness. If the black community has major problems of what whites, from a technetronic, rationalist point of view, call social pathology, it is also profoundly true that the black community remains very largely what white America and its institutions have made it. Such a view corresponds to the old European joke that every country gets the Jews it deserves. There is much sociological wisdom in this jest; but it is, after all, no joking matter.

The other groups which have been particularly involved in political or politically-relevant violence have been, very broadly, students and para-student groups in and around major university centers. Here also one finds several contributing factors. First, as with ghetto blacks, there have been immense and historically recent and rapid transformations in social conditions. As blacks made the staggering transition, mostly after 1945, from Southern agriculture to central city, so the postwar period has seen a tremendous increase in the size of the "education industry" and its student consumers. More than 40 percent of the college-age group now attends at least a year of college, up from about one-eighth before World War II. The growth of the higher education industry has compacted together critical masses of university students and others who choose to live in the penumbra of the university community: in the Boston area alone, there are no fewer than a quarter million such people. As their life situation promotes intense interaction, so does their increasing cultural difference in life-styles and values vis-a-vis the outside "adult" community. As the higher education industry has grown—particularly since 1960—it has also become bureaucratized and impersonal. One of the most persistent and telling criticisms which students and educational reformers have been making is that prestige professors at prestige institutions have run away from the classroom to government-funded research and other outside projects, leaving the students to be taught by graduate assistants. The latter, in turn, are for similar reasons as likely to be alienated from the "knowledge factory," Clark Kerr's "multiversity," as the undergraduates they teach.

But there is more to it than that. Universities are, to a unique degree, emporia of ideas. At least as often outside the classroom as in it, students learn to think in abstract terms. They are exposed to intellectual currents which, interacting with their life situation and the policies of "big organizations" all the way up to the White House, are profoundly subversive of traditional American political formulas and constraints. Of course, students are in no sense monolithic as a group. Yet there is enough of a combination of a specific economic and social life situation, separate subculture, and physical density in student communities to provide the preconditions for what Marx called a *Klasse für sich,* a class which has become self-conscious of its own identity. Such a class becomes an autonomous political force in its own right. For this class, as for black Americans, the riot and turmoil of the late 1960s were a stage of development in the building of "class" consciousness.

Official institutions of the established order have contributed massively to the shaping of this consciousness. Parmenter's discussion here—amplified elsewhere in John Hersey's account of the Algiers Motel massacre in Detroit—suggests the causal importance of police behavior in helping to ignite ghetto rioting. The Chicago Democratic convention riots in 1968, discussed by the Walker Commission, are a similar classic case of a "police riot" in modern times. In the former case, one need not condone the police harassment and casual brutality directed against the black community to realize that the police are placed in a most difficult psychological condition: they feel hostility everywhere, they feel that it is possible for anything to happen to them at any moment, they are in a state of permanent if usually suppressed warfare with the residents. Yet the kinds of social class backgrounds from which policemen come, no less than the training which they receive, provide them with no clues to the causes of this hostility. There is a parallel with the British troops in Londonderry who, pushed to the

limits of their psychological endurance in a deadly hostile community, perpetrated the massacre of January 1972. The consequence of such bloody encounters between "legitimate" authority and a community which views the authority as an alien force of military occupation is the radical politicization of the affected community. It can be supposed that the Kent State slayings of 1970 would have the same long-term effects on the nationwide student community and, through the media, on many others as well.

The case of the Chicago police riot in 1968 is somewhat different, however. Again there seems to have been the same pattern of loss of control in official use of force, arising from a state of acute psychological anxiety among the police—and this in a police force supposed to have exceptionally "professional" standards and whose recruiters have made serious efforts to exclude sadistic men from its ranks. But the context must also include another form of repression by constituted authority: the rigid control of the Democratic convention by "old politics" forces committed to Lyndon Johnson's Vietnam policy and to securing the nomination for Hubert Humphrey at all costs. There is no greater study in contrast than that of the atmosphere and events outside *and inside* the convention halls of 1968 and 1972; and the contrast is by no means accidentally related to the differences in processes and outcomes within the Democratic party of 1968 and 1972.

One significant thing occurred in the area of riots and disorders since the Kent State shootout of 1970: as of this writing, they have largely ceased. There is remarkably little *detailed, precise* social science theory which can explain why waves of disorders occur at one point in time rather than earlier or later, or why they stop happening, or when (if ever) they are likely to resume again. Off-the-cuff explanations for the sudden decline in mass protest and rioting abound: students are "tired of radical protest," blacks and others have seen that ghetto riots hurt only themselves, or they fear that the Nixon administration would respond with much more indiscriminate official violence than did the Johnson administration. At Kent State and Jackson State the police and/or national guard gave the students a "whiff of grape," and they have grown apathetic as a result. There may well be much to support these views. Certainly a President who responds to pictures of Kent State by asking why it is that the young have no respect for authority cannot be said to have come to terms with the larger problem.

But if one regards such disorders as part of a sea-change in political and social consciousness, as a transition stage in the development of the class-for-itself, then their perhaps temporary cessation may lend itself to a broad explanation, even though we may be unable to predict subsequent events with any precision. What appears as "anarchism" in life style and behavior then turns out to look very much like the first stage in a longer process. In this process members of the affected group tend to slough off formerly accepted social norms and behavior which inhibit the development of their consciousness of a discrete social identity, and they eventually acquire values and commitments which are relevant to their perception of their real position in the social and political structure. What appears to be—and actually is—violent mass protest and civil disorder on one level can be an integral part of the solidification of social identity on another. But, as the studies in this Part make clear, it also closely reflects the inability of the established political regime to accommodate demand from emerging groups, classes, or even, to use Michael Harrington's term, "substitute proletariats."

When one turns to a special form of political violence, the political assassination, one finds W. J. Crotty's analysis useful, revealing as it does that random factors appear to play a much larger role than appears true in civil disorders. This should not occasion surprise. In many assassinations, the deed was done or attempted by individual psychopaths, from Guiteau, the assassin of President Garfield in 1881, through Bremer, the would-be assassin of George Wallace in 1972. Such individualized acts of violence clearly fall into the larger problem of American criminal violence as a whole rather than into a problem of politics. But Crotty also suggests that some assassinations, at least, tend to be concentrated in periods of major social upheaval: that is, while many *individual acts* may be regarded as random, they are not *bunched chronologically* in a completely random way. Such a finding, limited as it must be, conforms with the view that an increase in politically related violence and deadly encounters is associated with disorganizations of the cultural-norm pattern which occur in periods of critical socio-economic transition. Still, in view of the extreme visibility of the American President in the political system and the very high levels of criminal violence which appear endemic in the United States, it is rather surprising that assassinations have not been far more common in our political life.

As we have attempted to point out, contemporary civil disorders owe their causes in large degree to protest against large-scale institutions which are perceived by the protestors as repressive and hostile to their vital interests. It may well be that, viewed historically, such upheavals have more often than not been concentrated in special periods of American political development—that they are often precursors of critical realignment in parties, policy agendas, and institutions. It would be risky to argue that the protestors in Grant Park in 1968 were McGovern delegates, or even McGovern workers in 1972. It does seem evident, however, that the combined effects of events inside and outside the 1968 Democratic convention so discredited the self-closed "old politics" within that party that it made the crucially important response: it reorganized its internal processes, opening them up to its most important growth constituencies. By doing so, it created the conditions in which Senator McGovern's nomination in 1972 became a possibility. McGovern himself became the embodiment of the aspirations of many of these growth constituencies within the party. He was able to construct an organization, relying heavily on the immense vitality and commitment of college youth, which forged his victory in the primaries and in the convention. He was able to do this because, of all contestants for the nomination, only he realized that the shape of American politics and the location of its "center" had shifted radically.

This reading of events suggests that the interface between "usual politics" and mass protest or direct action is subtle and evolving, but nonetheless *there*. The latter tends to arise when the former provides, through its own rigidity, no legitimate channel for the political mobilization of new social groups or classes. It is by no means true that all direct action produces "results" from the political system which encounters the demands of those doing the protesting. There can be little doubt, however, that it has often enough contributed significantly to volatilizing the public at large, and that by doing so it has made its own contributions to critical realignment in American politics. It may turn out in retrospect that the phasing out of civil disorder after 1970 was not a manifestation of apathy but of a regrouping of forces among the groups involved. Certainly the upheavals of power within the Democratic party from 1972 onward suggest precisely that.

Cleveland's Crisis Ghetto

Walter Williams

The riot in the Hough section of Cleveland, Ohio, occurred in July 1966. Not much more than a year earlier, in April 1965, the Bureau of the Census had conducted a special census for Cleveland that showed unexpected social and economic changes in the five years since 1960. What was most significant was a sharp economic polarization among the city's Negroes. A substantial number had moved up to a more affluent life; but the group in the worst part of the ghetto was at a level of poverty that was actually *below* the one recorded in 1960. Who rose and who stayed behind, and why?

What is most startling about the changes revealed by Cleveland's special census is their magnitude. These five years saw rapidly rising real income and falling unemployment for the city as a whole—but not for the very poor. The gap between haves and have-nots widened strikingly; and the most rapid widening was among Negroes—between those outside the slums who were rising, beginning finally to cash in on the American dream, and those still in the hard-core ghetto, on limited rations of income and hope.

In the special census nine neighborhoods at the bottom economically were grouped together and called the "Neighborhood." (See map.) The rest of the city, in which the prospering middle and upper classes are concentrated, was called the "Remainder of Cleveland." In Cleveland, however—as in the Inferno—there are different levels on the path downward, and one area of the Neighborhood is especially bad. This is the "Crisis Ghetto." It is predominantly Negro. Hough is part of it—on the edge.

The group that rose most swiftly in the period 1960-1965 were the Negroes who did not live in the Neighborhood. In 1960 they numbered 22,000. By 1965 their number had almost doubled. In all Cleveland they had achieved the greatest economic gains, showing that the door of opportunity, for some at least, was opening wider. (And also providing a convenient, but unwarranted, rationalization against help for the less fortunate—for if some Negroes could rise so quickly through their own efforts, why not all?)

At the opposite end of Cleveland's economic spectrum we find a grim picture. The number of Negro children in poor female-headed households increased sharply. By 1965 nearly two-thirds of these poor Negro youths in female families were in the Crisis Ghetto. Further, the Crisis Ghetto's average resident was in worse economic straits than in 1960. Unemployment was higher, income lower, and a larger percentage of the population was poor.

In relative terms the Crisis Ghetto was further away from the rest of the city than in 1960 in terms of major economic indices. For instance, the income gap between the Crisis Ghetto and the next economic stratum (the other five sections of the Neighborhood) had spread visibly. The range of median real incomes for the four sections of the Crisis Ghetto and the five sections in the rest of the neighborhood was as follows:

Range of Median Incomes	1960	1965
Crisis Ghetto	$3,170-4,900	$3,000-4,160
Rest of Neighborhood	$5,450-6,230	$5,460-6,500

Hence the top of the Crisis Ghetto income range is now $1,300 short of the next economic tier, in contrast to $550 in 1960. And that next tier itself had suffered in income terms over the five-year period relative to the Remainder of Cleveland.

Thus, at least in Cleveland, the census validated our fears of the emerging "two Americas." If this portrays what is happening in other cities, it is most disturbing.

The Crisis Ghetto's potential for generating earned income has declined a great deal since 1960. Those economic units with lowest earning potential—female-headed families

and aged people—have increased in absolute numbers, while those with the greatest earning potential (younger male-headed families) have diminished sharply. The Crisis Ghetto has become a concentration point not merely for the poor, but for the hard-core poor—those with least hope or opportunity of being anything else.

The Widening Gap

The increasing distance between Cleveland's majority and its disadvantaged segment is frequently hidden in the overall economic indices of the city. Averaging the increasingly prosperous and the stable poor seems to give a "rise" to everybody. But the almost unchanged poverty rate between 1960 and 1965 masks within different groups large movements that have further split the population. Between 1960 and 1965, the poverty rate:

—declined markedly among male-headed families while it increased among female-headed families;

—fell for white people, but remained almost unchanged for Negroes;

—yet showed a much greater decline (almost 40 percent below the 1960 level) for non-Neighborhood Negroes than for any other group (the whites outside the Neighborhood experienced a 12 percent decrease);

—and rose sharply in the Crisis Ghetto while it fell in the Remainder of Cleveland.

Another important change was in the *kinds* of poor families and poor people in the Crisis Ghetto. Between 1960 and 1965, the number of poor people fell by roughly 14,000. But members of Negro female-headed families increased by almost 12,000 persons (all but the merest handful of whom were found in the Neighborhood) while persons in families headed by Negro males and white males and females decreased by 26,000. As a consequence of these population changes in the five-year period, members of Negro female-headed families increased from one-fifth to one-third of Cleveland's poor. And in 1965, 60 percent of these poor, Negro, female-headed family members lived in the Crisis Ghetto.

Changes in the structure of industry have hurt the Crisis Ghetto. As Louis Buckley notes in discussing the plight of the low-skilled city laborer:

The changes in the demand for labor in our central cities have been in the direction of expansions of industries requiring well educated white collar workers and a relative decline in the industries employing blue collar unskilled and semi-skilled workers.

Many of these modern industries have fled to the suburbs.

Unfortunately, public transportation has not followed, so ghetto residents have difficulty getting out to suburban jobs.

Further, an increasing percentage of the Crisis Ghetto's residents are in families whose heads have the least likelihood of increasing materially their earned income. In general, the two groups with the most limited economic potential are family units (our definition of unit includes single persons living alone) headed by women and by the aged. These groups rose significantly over the five-year period as a percentage of the Crisis Ghetto population. (See the tables.) Not only do these two groups seem *least* likely to earn much more than at present—but they seem the *most* likely group to suffer an actual as well as a relative decline in earned income. In short, they have the lowest chance to improve their financial position, and the highest probability of declining. Once a unit in this limited potential group becomes poor, by definition, it is likely to remain so. This persistent poverty is the eroding evil. Real income in the Crisis Ghetto declined by 2 percent for male-headed families and 15 percent for female-headed

---

A NOTE ON THE STUDY

The special census of Cleveland of April 1965 described in this article is the *only* detailed census of a major city available at mid-decade. Further, comparable information from other cities will not be forthcoming in the near future. We do have a study of the same period for certain low-income areas in Los Angeles, including Watts, but not for the rest of the city. Thus, the Cleveland census is the only available study showing in detail the dynamics of change in a major American city since 1960—in this case, a city which had riots not much more than a year after the census was taken.

---

families between 1960 and 1965. At the end of the five-year period unemployment rates for both men (14.6 percent) and women (17.2 percent—up over one-third since 1960) were higher, standing at nearly three times the city's average; and the poverty level had risen from 36 to 40 percent. In 1965 the average Crisis Ghetto inhabitant was worse off than he had been in 1960, both absolutely and relative to others in the city.

These facts have major implications. On the one hand, those with economic strength or potential *can* flee the Crisis Ghetto. (True, if Negro, they may only be allowed to escape to a better Negro area.) But is is also clear that entrapment in the Crisis Ghetto springs directly from poverty. The price over the wall is primarily money, not skin color. However, once poverty has locked one into the Crisis Ghetto, the chances of being forced to remain—

and the bad consequences of remaining—are greater than if one lived in any other area of the city.

Population Decline

The Crisis Ghetto population declined by about 20 percent during the five years (from 170,000 to 134,000 persons), and this exodus might seem to imply an explanation for the decline and the change. After all, if the more able, above-average people leave, averages should move down.

But exodus, by itself, cannot explain enough. Certainly the population decrease cannot be used to explain the absolute *increases* since 1960 of a few hundreds in the number of female-headed families, and of some 3,000 poor persons in such families. Yet that is what happened; and we have no pat explanation for it.

Nor does the population decrease necessarily counterbalance the possible adverse effects coming from the declining economic situation, particularly the rise in weak economic units as a part of the total population. These people seem likely to face the Crisis Ghetto over an extended period of time. What are the consequences?

The deleterious effects of a hard-core ghetto spread beyond the economy to the total environment—to schools, to street associations, to the preservation of life itself. This last point was driven home when three Washington medical schools threatened to pull out of the D.C. General Hospital because the meager budget provided almost medieval services. Even to be sick in the Crisis Ghetto is far more dangerous than in the suburbs. So, from birth to death the ghetto marks each person, and cuts his chances either to escape or survive. The Crisis Ghetto lacks the precise boundaries and imposed restrictions of the European ghettos of the past; but it is, nevertheless, an existing reality that limits and blights the lives of its inhabitants as effectively as did the old ghettos and pales.

Is this pattern confined to Cleveland? Only in Cleveland was a special census made for the city as a whole. But figures available for 1960-65 for South Los Angeles (which includes Watts and in an economic sense is like the Cleveland Neighborhood) also show a decrease in real income per family, a small increase in the percent of poor people, and a decrease in the male and increase in female unemployment rates (the Crisis Ghetto differs only in that it shows a very small male unemployment increase). Further, Negro female family members became a far more significant proportion of South Los Angeles poor (we do not have city-wide data) increasing from 37 percent to 48 percent. While the number of poor people in Negro female-headed households rose by 9,500 (roughly 25 percent) the number of poor among white male, white female, and Negro male-headed families all decreased.

At the national level poor Negro female-headed family members have increased both absolutely and as a proportion of the total poor population. For 1960 and 1966, the number of poor persons (in millions) for these categories was as follows: (Data furnished by Mollie Orshansky.)

| | 1960 | | 1966 | |
	Number in millions	% of total poor	Number in millions	% of total poor
Negro female-headed family members	3.2	8%	3.8	12%
All other poor persons	35.7	92	28.9	88
Total poor persons	38.9	100	32.7	100

The non-Neighborhood Negro has advanced greatly in the five years between the two censuses—more, as noted, than any other Cleveland group. Of course, this great improvement can be partly explained by residential segregation. The white on the rise goes to the suburbs—and out of the Cleveland census area—while his Negro counterpart must stay in the city. Still, there is no doubt that the Negroes escaping the Neighborhood are advancing as a group more rapidly than any within the city limits, and closing in on the Remainder of Cleveland whites. Even more striking than their increasing prosperity were their increasing numbers—from 22,000 to 41,000. They now account for 15 percent of the Negro population.

The Cleveland data indicate that economic discrimination has declined in Cleveland since 1960. Is this only in the upper and middle level jobs or has discrimination lessened across the board? I believe it may have lessened somewhat across the board; but this may not help the Crisis Ghetto Negroes unless direct action is taken to overcome their difficulties. Any decrease in overt economic discrimination, of course, is encouraging. However, it is absurd to think that this change *alone*—even if the reduction in discrimination had been far greater than I expect it was in Cleveland—will set right all the damage of the past. The liabilities of the Crisis Ghetto Negroes caused by past discrimination —poor education, lack of skills, poor health, police records—would still hold them back in the job market. In fact, the reduction in discrimination *alone* may exacerbate the split between the various strata of Cleveland Negroes.

Earlier discrimination possibly served as a lid for the advancement of *all* Negroes, squeezing them closer together in income and opportunity despite differences in skills and potentials. But once the lid was lifted, especially during boom years, the more skilled, educated, and able rose much more rapidly than the others. So the gap widened. Unless something is done the more able Negroes should continue

Real Income per Family

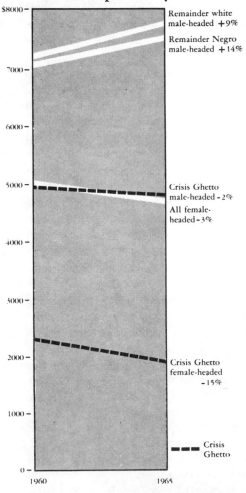

Unemployment Rates

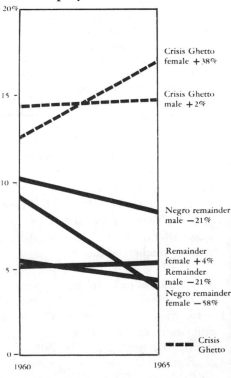

to widen their lead until they too become part of the symbols of success that have so far evaded the Crisis Ghetto Negroes and make failure ever more visible and disturbing.

At the opposite pole, though population in the Crisis Ghetto declined by one-fifth, Negro female-headed families increased by 8 percent, children in these families by 25 percent (16,900 to 21,000), and children in *poor* Negro female-headed families by 30 percent (13,100 to 17,000). Of the 21,000 children of female-headed families in the Crisis Ghetto, 17,000 are living below the poverty level. And it is this increasing group of female-headed families that suffered the largest real income decline of the five-year period, falling from $2,300 to $1,950 per family per year. That is, at the later survey date (1965), the average Crisis Ghetto female-headed family had an income *per week* of just over $37.50.

The implications of these statistics are appalling. There were 3,900 *more* poverty-stricken children in the ghetto in 1965 than 1960—in a population 36,000 less—and there is no reason to believe that this trend is not continuing or accelerating. These children can do least to improve their condition—yet they must have a tremendous influence on the future of the Neighborhood, and of all Cleveland.

Poor Negro children in female-headed families are the great tragedy of the Crisis Ghetto. They constitute 13 percent of all persons there, 30 percent of all the children. They make up over half of the members of the poor limited-potential families.

There has been tremendous movement in and out of the Crisis Ghetto—at least four out of every ten departed or died in the five years. But the option of movement is not a random phenomenon affecting all equally. It seems available at will to some and almost completely closed to others—and most tightly closed to adults with limited economic potential, and their children.

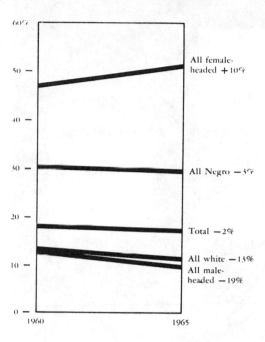

Percent of Cleveland Families in Poverty

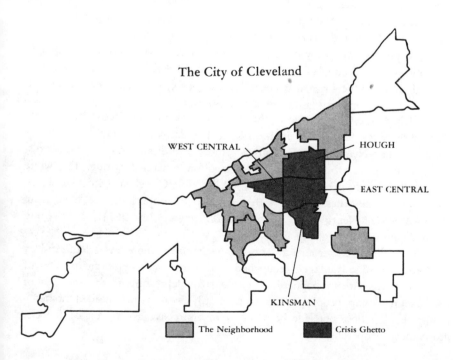

The City of Cleveland

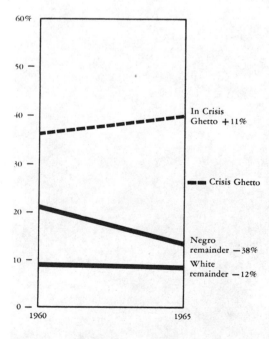

403

the haves and the have-nots

"The years between 1960 and 1965 saw rapidly rising real income and falling unemployment for the city of Cleveland as a whole—but not for the very poor. The gap between the haves and the have-nots widened strikingly."

Although the percentage of people with limited economic potential in the Crisis Ghetto is about twice as large as the population in the Remainder of Cleveland, the percentage of poor among them—standing at nearly 25 percent—is about *five* times as large.

Recent prosperity has removed many from the rolls of the needy, but those remaining may be far more discontented than when most of their neighbors were also poor. "Relative deprivation" is a very real force. For example, the classic study of this phenomenon made during World War II showed that there was more jealousy and dissatisfaction in an Air Force fighter squadron noted for rapid promotions ("boy colonels") than in a military police unit with few promotions. This feeling of being ignored, discriminated against, and isolated, while all around others rise, may create a far more explosive situation than when many are in the same boat, as during the Depression.

The Cleveland Census reveals the city's contrasting prosperity and decay. Sharp differences emerge within the Negro population. The rapid income increase for non-Neighborhood Negroes probably indicates less economic discrimination. Also, while residential segregation remained strong, the white flight to the suburbs opened up some of the desirable Cleveland residential areas. For example, Lee Miles, an area with many expensive dwellings, changed from 28 to 72 percent Negro in five years (21,000 Negroes by 1965). Many strong economic units fled the ghetto.

As many fled to better circumstances, others became more ensnarled. And by 1965 the most disadvantaged group had grown to a very significant portion of the total Crisis Ghetto population. Particularly depressing is the increase of poor Negro young people in the economically weak female-headed homes—young people whose bondage becomes more oppressive as the rest of the city grows more prosperous.

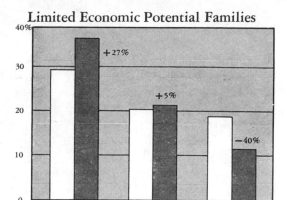

Limited Economic Potential Families

1960
1965

Crisis Ghetto +27%
Remainder +5%
Negro remainder −40%

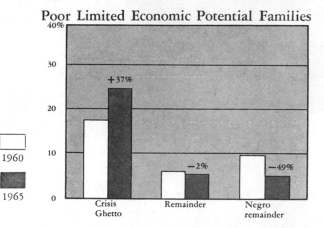

Poor Limited Economic Potential Families

Crisis Ghetto +37%
Remainder −2%
Negro remainder −49%

Income and Incentive

What can be done? What can be our long term goals?

The ghetto male, frequently with limited skills, enters the job market with grave liabilities. Often the job does not pay him enough to support his family and has little prospect of leading to a living wage. The longer the man works, the longer he fails as a provider. His marriage will frequently deteriorate. As Elliot Liebow has suggested in *Tally's Corner,* the unprovided-for family becomes a continuous symbol of a man's inability to fulfill the demands of his society—to be a man. So he opts out, and the sparse existence of the female-headed family has begun.

Job and training programs for men in the Crisis Ghetto are thus a first order need. Employment that yields a living wage over time seems to be the best bet for *preventing* family break-up, and *re-establishing* stable families.

Many broken homes, however, are not going to be re-established. Consequently, the female-headed family, as the Cleveland data show so starkly, will face a particularly exposed financial position. The mother may well seek a relationship with a man that has some prospect of offering family stability and also additional income. Unfortunately, the "eligible" males are often the failures from prior marriages. The woman enters a tenuous relationship with the very unrealistic hope that it will work into a real family situation. The result is often another child.

Programs thus must be aimed at providing greater economic stability to the female-headed family. Job programs should be readily accessible for women as well as men. This means that major efforts for establishing day care centers are needed. Yet, work is not the answer for all these women. Also needed are better programs of income maintenance which will provide the family a reasonable income.

It is clear that our long run goals should be to prevent the breakup of families. But, many families are beyond the prevention of this sort. Further, the Negro mother has shown remarkable strength as a family head. Her great weakness has been in producing sufficient income, and the resultant poverty has had an adverse effect on the family. If these deficiencies can be overcome by work or transfer income, many of these mothers may be able to properly motivate their children. If freed from poverty, the inner strength of the matriarchal Negro family may begin to assert a positive effect upon the Crisis Ghetto.

Income increases from work and transfer payments are vital, but I believe that we must go beyond income programs to effect basic institutional changes in both the larger community that includes the Crisis Ghetto and the ghetto itself. A city must provide adequate education, health, and other services for all its residents. Further, direct community action must help Crisis Ghetto residents end the growing social decay in that area. As Richard A. Cloward and Lloyd E. Ohlin observed in *Delinquency and Opportunity,* the hard-core ghetto community must be structured to provide both social control and legitimate avenues of social ascent. That is, the neighborhood community—the Crisis Ghetto—must be a sound base of opportunity. The resident of the Crisis Ghetto must be able to form a realistic belief in a decent life.

We see the alternative in current trends. The poor in the Crisis Ghetto are falling further behind. Not only distance is building up between the two poles, but tension as well—as with electrodes approaching a sparking point.

If what is happening in Cleveland is also happening in other cities, we must multiply this tension, and the danger signals, by a large factor. If by inaction we consign the misery of the parents in the Crisis Ghettos to their children, the sickness of the central cities must fester and grow worse. Hough may be a pale prelude to other, greater Houghs—a short dramatic prologue, announcing that the tragedy has begun.

White Institutions and Black Rage

David Boesel, Richard Berk, W. Eugene Groves, Bettye Eidson and Peter H. Rossi

Five summers of black rebellion have made it clear that the United States is facing a crisis of proportions not seen since the Great Depression. And one of the root causes of this crisis, it has also become clear, is the performance of white institutions, especially those institutions in the ghetto. Some of these institutions—police and retail stores, for example —have done much to antagonize Negroes; others, such as welfare departments and black political organizations, have tried to help and have failed.

Why have these white institutions helped engender black rage? One way to find out might be to study the attitudes of the men working for them—to discover what their personnel think about the racial crisis itself, about their own responsibilities, about the work they are doing. Therefore,

at the request of the National Advisory Commission on Civil Disorders (the riot commission), we at Johns Hopkins University visited 15 Northern cities and questioned men and women working for six different institutional groups: major employers, retail merchants, teachers, welfare workers, political workers (all Negro), and policemen. All of the people we questioned, except the employers, work right in the ghetto, and are rank-and-file employees—the cop on the beat, the social caseworker, and so on.

Employers' Social Responsibility

The "employers" we questioned were the managers or personnel officers of the ten institutions in each city that

406

employed the most people, as well as an additional 20 managers or personnel officers of the next 100 institutions. As such, they represented the most economically progressive institutions in America. And in their employment policies we could see how some of America's dominant corporate institutions impinge on the everyday lives of urban Negroes.

Businessmen are in business to make a profit. Seldom do they run their enterprises for social objectives. But since it is fashionable these days, most of the managers and personnel officers we interviewed (86 percent, in fact) accepted the proposition that they "have a social responsibility to make strong efforts to provide employment for Negroes and other minority groups." This assertion, however, is contradicted by unemployment in the Negro community today, as well as by the hiring policies of the firms themselves.

Businessmen, as a whole, do not exhibit openly racist attitudes. Their position might best be described as one of "optimistic denial"—the gentlemanly white racism evident in a tacit, but often unwitting, acceptance of institutional practices that subordinate or exclude Negroes. One aspect of this optimistic denial is a nonrecognition of the seriousness of the problems that face black people. Only 21 percent of our sample thought that unemployment was a very serious problem in the nations' cities, yet 26 percent considered air pollution very serious and 31 percent considered traffic very serious. The employers' perspective is based upon their limited experience with blacks, and that experience does not give them a realistic picture of the plight of Negroes in this country. Employers don't even think that racial discrimination has much to do with the Negroes' plight; a majority (57 percent) felt that Negroes are treated at least as well as other people of the same income, and an additional 6 percent felt that Negroes are treated *better* than any other part of the population.

This optimistic denial on the part of employers ("things really aren't that bad for Negroes") is often combined with a negative image of Negroes as employees. Half of those employers interviewed (51 percent) said that Negroes are likely to have higher rates of absenteeism than whites, so that hiring many of them would probably upset production schedules. Almost a third thought that, because Negro crime rates are generally higher than white crime rates, hiring many Negroes could lead to increased theft and vandalism in their companies. About a fifth (22 percent) thought that hiring Negroes might bring "agitators and troublemakers" into their companies, and another one-fifth feared that production costs might rise because Negroes supposedly do not take orders well.

The employer's views may reflect not only traditional white prejudices, but also some occasional experience he himself has had with Negroes. Such experiences, however, may stem as much from the employer's own practices and misconceptions as from imputed cultural habits of Negroes. As Elliott Liebow observed in his study of Negro street-corner men *(Talley's Corner),* blacks have learned to cope with life by treating menial, low-status, degrading jobs in the same way that the jobs treat them—with benign nonconcern.

Most of the employers believe that Negroes lack the preparation for anything but menial jobs. A full 83 percent said that few Negroes are qualified for professional jobs, and 69 percent thought that few are qualified for skilled positions. When it comes to unskilled jobs, of course, only 23 percent of the employers held this view. The employers seem to share a widespread assumption— one frequently used as a cover for racism—that for historical and environmental reasons Negroes have been disabled to such an extent as to make them uncompetitive in a highly competitive society. And while it is certainly true that black people have suffered from a lack of educational and other opportunities, this line of thinking—especially among whites—has a tendency to blame the past and the ghetto environment for what is perceived as Negro incompetence, thus diverting attention from *present* institutional practices. So, many employers have developed a rhetoric of concern about upgrading the so-called "hard-core unemployed" in lieu of changing their employment policies.

To a considerable extent our respondents' assessment of

Negro job qualifications reflects company policy, for the criteria used in hiring skilled and professional workers tend to exclude Negroes. The criteria are (1) previous experience and (2) recommendations. It is evident that because Negroes are unlikely to have *had* previous experience in positions from which they have long been excluded, and because they are unlikely to have had much contact with people in the best position to recommend them, the criteria for "qualification" make it probable that employers will consider most Negroes unqualified.

Negroes Get the Worst Jobs

In short, the employers' aversion to taking risks (at least with people), reinforced by the pressure of labor unions and more general discriminatory patterns in society, means that Negroes usually get the worst jobs.

Thus, although Negroes make up 20 percent of the unskilled workers in these large corporations, they fill only a median of one percent of the professional positions and only 2 percent of the skilled positions. Moreover, the few Negroes in the higher positions are unevenly distributed among the corporations. Thirty-two percent of the companies don't report Negroes in professional positions, and 24 percent do not report any in skilled positions. If these companies are set aside, in the remaining companies the median percentage of Negroes in the two positions rises to 3 percent and 6 percent respectively. Further, in these remaining companies an even larger percentage (8 percent in both cases) of *current* positions are being filled by Negroes—which indicates, among other things, that a breakthrough has been accomplished in some companies, while in others Negro employment in the upper levels remains minimal or nonexistent.

Even among those companies that hire blacks for skilled jobs, a Negro applicant's chances of getting the job are only one-fourth as good as those of his white counterpart. For professional positions, the chances are more nearly equal: Negro applicants are about three-fourths as likely to get these jobs as are white applicants. It seems that Negroes have come closest to breaking in at the top (though across all firms only about 4 percent of the applicants for professional positions are Negro). The real stumbling-block to equal employment opportunities seems to be at the skilled level, and here it may be that union policies—and especially those of the craft unions—augment the employers' resistance to hiring Negroes for and promoting Negroes to skilled positions.

What do urban Negroes themselves think of employers' hiring practices? A survey of the same 15 cities by Angus Campbell and Howard Schuman, for the riot commission, indicates that one-third (34 percent) of the Negro men interviewed reported having been refused jobs because of racial discrimination, and 72 percent believed that some or many other black applicants are turned down for the same reason. Almost as many (68 percent) think that some or many black people miss out on promotions because of prejudice. And even when companies do hire Negroes (presumably in professional positions), this is interpreted as tokenism: 77 percent of the black respondents thought that Negroes are hired by big companies for show purposes.

The companies we studied, which have little contact with the ghetto, are very different from the other institutions in our survey, whose contact with the ghetto is direct and immediate. The corporations are also up-to-date, well-financed, and innovative, while the white institutions inside the ghetto are outdated, underfinanced, and overloaded. In historical terms, the institutions in the ghetto represent another era of thought and organization.

Ghetto Merchants

The slum merchants illustrate the tendency of ghetto institutions to hark back to earlier forms. While large corporations cooperate with one another and with the government to exert substantial control over their market, the ghetto merchant still functions in the realm of traditional laissez-faire. He is likely to be a small operator, economically marginal and with almost no ability to control his market. His main advantage over the more efficient, modern retailer is his restricted competition, for the ghetto provides a captive market. The difficulty that many blacks have in getting transportation out of the ghetto, combined with a lack of experience in comparative shopping, seems to give the local merchant a competitive aid he sorely needs to survive against the lower prices and better goods sold in other areas of the city.

The merchants in our study also illustrate the free-enterprise character of ghetto merchandising. They run very small operations—grocery stores, restaurants, clothing and liquor stores, and so on, averaging a little over three employees per business. Almost half of them (45 percent) find it difficult to "keep up with their competition" (competition mainly *within* the ghetto). Since there are almost no requirements for becoming a merchant, this group is the most heterogeneous of all those studied. They have the widest age range (from 17 through 80), the highest percentage of immigrants (15 percent), and the lowest educational levels (only 16 percent finished college).

Again in contrast to the large corporations, the ghetto merchant must live with the harsh day-to-day realities of violence and poverty. His attitudes toward Negroes, different in degree from those of the employers, are at least partly a function of his objective evaluations of his customers.

Running a business in a ghetto means facing special kinds of "overhead." Theft is an especially worrisome problem for the merchants; respondents mentioned it more frequently than any other problem. There is, of course, some basis in fact for their concern. According to the riot commission, inventory losses—ordinarily under 2 percent of sales—may be twice as great in high-crime areas (most of which are in ghettos). And for these small businesses such losses may cut substantially into a slender margin of profit.

Thus it is not surprising that, of all the occupational groups interviewed in this study, the retail merchants were among the most likely to consider Negroes violent and criminal. For example, 61 percent said that Negroes are more likely to steal than whites, and 50 percent believed that Negroes are more likely to pass bad checks. No wonder, then, that black customers may encounter unusual surveillance and suspicion when they shop.

Less understandable is the ghetto merchant's apparent ignorance of the plight of ghetto blacks. Thus, 75 percent believe that blacks get medical treatment that is equal to or better than what whites get. A majority think that Negroes are not discriminated against with regard to treatment by the police, recreation facilities and so forth. Logically enough, 51 percent of the merchants feel that Negroes are making too many demands. This percentage is the second-highest measured (the police were the least sympathetic). So the merchants (like all other groups in the survey except the black politicians) are inclined to emphasize perceived defects in the black community as a major problem in their dealings with Negroes.

The shaky economic position of the merchants, their suspicion of their Negro customers, and the high "overhead" of doing business in the ghetto (because of theft, vandalism, bad credit risks) lead many merchants to sell inferior merchandise at higher prices—and to resort to other stratagems for getting money out of their customers. To elicit responses from the merchants on such delicate matters, we drew up a series of very indirect questions. The responses we obtained, though they no doubt understate the extent to which ghetto merchants provide a poor dollar value per unit of goods, are nevertheless revealing. For example, we asked the merchants to recommend various ways of "keeping up with business competition." Some 44 percent said that you should offer extra services; over a third (36 percent) said you should raise prices to cover unusually high overhead; and the same number (36 percent) said that you should buy "bargain" goods at lower prices, then sell them at regular prices. (To a small merchant, "bargain goods" ordinarily means "seconds," or slightly spoiled merchandise, because he doesn't do enough volume to gain real discounts from a wholesaler.) A smaller but still significant segment (12 percent) said that one should "bargain the selling price with each customer and take whatever breaks you can get."

The Campbell-Schuman study indicates that 56 percent of the Negroes interviewed felt that they had been overcharged in neighborhood stores (24 percent said often); 42 percent felt that they had been sold spoiled or inferior goods (13 percent said often). Given the number of ghetto stores a customer may visit every week, these data are entirely compatible with ours. Since one-third of the merchants indicated that they were not averse to buying "bargain" goods for sale in their stores, it is understandable that 42 percent of the Negroes in these areas should say that at one time or another they have been sold inferior merchandise.

It is also understandable that during the recent civil disorders many Negroes, unable to affect merchants by routine methods, struck directly at the stores, looting and burning them.

Teachers in the Ghetto

Just as ghetto merchants are in a backwater of the economy, ghetto schools are in a backwater of the educational system, experimental efforts in some cities notwithstanding.

Negroes, of course, are most likely to be served by outmoded and inadequate schools, a fact that the Coleman Report has documented in considerable detail. In metropolitan regions of the Northeast, for example, 40 percent of the Negro pupils at the secondary level attended schools in buildings over 40 years old, but only 15 percent of the whites did; the average number of pupils per room was 35 for Negroes but 28 for whites.

The teachers covered in our survey (half of whom were Negro) taught in ghetto schools at all levels. Surprisingly, 88 percent said that they were satisfied with their jobs. Their rate of leaving, however, was not consistent with this. Half of the teachers had been in their present schools for no more than four years. Breaking the figures down year by year, we find that the largest percentage (17 percent) had been there only one year. In addition, the teachers' rate of leaving increased dramatically after they had taught for five years.

While the teachers thought that education was a major problem for the cities and especially for the ghettos, they did not think that ghetto schools were a source of the difficulty. A solid majority, comparing their own schools with others in the city, thought that theirs were average, above average, or superior in seven out of eight categories. The high quality of the teaching staff, so rated by 84 percent of the respondents, was rivaled only by the high quality of the textbooks (again 84 percent). The one doubtful area, according to the teachers, was the physical plant, which seemed to them to be just barely competitive; in this respect, 44 percent considered their own schools below average or inferior.

The teachers have less confidence in their students than in themselves or their schools. On the one hand, they strongly reject the view that in ghetto schools education is sacrificed to the sheer need for order: 85 percent said it was not true that pupils in their schools were uneducable, and that teachers could do little more than maintain discipline. On the other hand, the teachers as a group could not agree that their students were as educable as they might be. There was little consensus on whether their pupils were "about average" in interest and ability: 28 percent thought that their pupils were; 41 percent thought it was partially true that they were; and 31 percent thought it was not true. But the teachers had less difficulty agreeing that their students were *not* "above average in ability and . . . generally co-operative with teachers." Agreeing on this were 59 percent of the teachers, with another 33 percent in the middle.

The real problem with education in the ghetto, as the teachers see it, is the ghetto itself. The teachers have their own version of the "Negro disability" thesis: the "cultural deprivation" theory holds that the reason for bad education in the ghetto is the student's environment rather than the schools. (See "How Teachers Learn to Help Children Fail," by Estelle Fuchs, September, 1968.) Asked to name the major problems facing their schools, the teachers most frequently mentioned community apathy; the second most-mentioned problem, a derivation of the first, was an alleged lack of preparation and motivation in the students. Fifty-nine percent of the teachers agreed to some extent that "many communities provide such a terrible environment for the pupils that education doesn't do much good in the end."

Such views are no doubt detrimental to education in the ghetto, for they imply a decided fatalism as far as teaching is concerned. If the students are deficient—improperly motivated, distracted, and so on—and if the cause of this deficiency lies in the ghetto rather than in the schools themselves, then there is little reason for a teacher to exert herself to set high standards for her students.

There is considerable question, however, whether the students in ghetto schools are as distracted as the teachers think. Events in the last few years indicate that the schools, especially the high schools and the junior high schools, are one of the strongest focuses of the current black rebellion. The student strike at Detroit's Northern High School in 1966, for example, was cohesive and well-organized. A boycott by some 2,300 students, directed against a repressive school administration, lasted over two weeks and resulted in the dismissal of the principal and the formation of a committee, including students, to investigate school conditions. The ferment in the ghetto schools across the country is also leading to the formation of permanent and independent black students' groups, such as the Modern Strivers in Washington, D.C.'s Eastern High, intent on promoting black solidarity and bringing about changes in the educational system. In light of such developments, there is reason to think that the teachers in the survey have overestimated the corrosive effects of the ghetto environment on students—and underestimated the schools' responsibility for the state of education in the ghetto.

Social Workers and the Welfare Establishment

Public welfare is another area in which old ideas have been perpetuated beyond their time. The roots of the present welfare-department structure lie in the New Deal legislation of the 1930s. The public assistance provisions of the Social Security Act were designed to give aid to the helpless and the noncompetitive: the aged, the blind, the "permanently and totally" disabled, and dependent children. The assumption was that the recipient, because of personal disabilities or inadequacies, could not make his way in life without outside help.

The New Deal also provided work (e.g., the W.P.A.) for the able-bodied who were assumed to be unemployed only temporarily. But as the Depression gave way to the war years and to the return of prosperity, the massive work programs for the able-bodied poor were discontinued, leaving only those programs that were premised on the notion of personal disability. To a considerable extent today's Negro poor have had to rely on the latter. Chief among these programs, of course, is Aid for Dependent Children, which has become a mainstay of welfare. And because of racial discrimination, especially in education and employment, a large part of the Negro population also experiences poverty as a permanent state.

While most of the social workers in our survey showed considerable sympathy with the Negro cause, they too felt that the root of the problem lay in weaknesses in the Negro community; and they saw their primary task as making up the supposed deficiency. A hefty majority of the respondents (78 percent) thought that a large part of their responsibility was to "teach the poor how to live"—rather than to provide the means for them to live as they like. Assuming disability, welfare has fostered dependency.

The social workers, however, are unique among the groups surveyed in that they are quite critical of their own institution. The average welfare worker is not entirely at one with the establishment for which she works. She is likely to be a college graduate who regards her job as transitional. And her lack of expertise has its advantages as well as its disadvantages, for it means that she can take a more

straightforward view of the situations she is confronted with. She is not committed to bureaucracy as a way of life.

The disparity between the welfare establishment and the average welfare worker is evident in the latter's complaints about her job. The complaints she voices the most deal *not* with her clients, but with the welfare department itself and the problems of working within its present structure—the difficulty of getting things done, the red tape, the lack of adequate funds, and so on. Of the five most-mentioned difficulties of welfare work, three dealt with such intra-agency problems; the other two dealt with the living conditions of the poor.

There is a good deal of evidence to support the social worker's complaints. She complains, for example, that welfare agencies are understaffed. The survey indicates that an average caseload is 177 people, each client being visited about once a month for about 50 minutes. Even the most conscientious of caseworkers must be overwhelmed by such client-to-worker ratios.

As in the case of the schools, welfare has engendered a countervailing force among the very people it is supposed to serve. Welfare clients have become increasingly hostile to the traditional structure and philosophy of welfare departments and have formed themselves into an outspoken movement. The welfare-rights movement at this stage has aims: to obtain a more nearly adequate living base for the clients, and to overload the system with demands, thus either forcing significant changes or clearing the way for new and more appropriate institutions.

Black Political Party Workers

Usually when segments of major social institutions become incapable of functioning adequately, the people whom the institutions are supposed to serve have recourse to politics. In the ghetto, however, the political machinery is no better off than the other institutions. Around the turn of the century Negroes began to carve out small niches for themselves in the politics of such cities as Chicago and New York. Had Negro political organizations developed along the same lines as those of white ethnic groups, they might today provide valuable leverage for the ghetto population. But this has not happened. For one thing, the decline of the big-city machine, and its replacement in many cities by "nonpolitical" reform governments supported by a growing middle class, began to close off a route traditionally open to minority groups. Second, black politicians have never been regarded as fullfledged political brokers by racist whites, and consequently the possibility of a Negro's becoming a powerful politician in a predominantly white city has been foreclosed (the recent election of Carl Stokes as Mayor of Cleveland and Richard D. Hatcher, Mayor of

Gary, Indiana, would be exceptions). Whites have tended to put aside their differences when confronting Negro political efforts; to regard Negro demands, no matter how routine, as racial issues; and hence to severely limit the concessions made to black people.

Today the sphere of Negro politics is cramped and closely circumscribed. As Kenneth B. Clark has observed, most of the Negroes who have reached high public office have done so *not* within the context of Negro politics, but through competition in the larger society. In most cities Negro political organizations are outmoded and inadequate. Even if, as seems probable, more and more Negro mayors are elected, they will have to work within the antiquated structure of urban government, with sharply limited resources. Unless things change, the first Negro mayor of Newark, for example, will preside over a bankrupt city.

Our survey of Negro political workers in the 15 cities documents the inadequacy of Negro politics—and the inadequacy of the larger system of urban politics. The political workers, understandably, strongly sympathize with the aspirations of other black people. As ghetto politicians, they deal with the demands and frustrations of other blacks day after day. Of all the groups surveyed, they were the most closely in touch with life in the ghetto. Most of them work in the middle and lower levels of municipal politics; they talk with about 75 voters each week. These political workers are, of course, acutely aware of the precipitous rise in the demands made by the black community. Most (93 percent) agreed that in the last few years people in their districts have become more determined to get what they want. The stongest impetus of this new determination comes from the younger blacks: 92 percent of the political workers agreed that "young people have become more militant." Only a slight majority, however (56 percent), said the same of middle-aged people.

Against the pressure of rising Negro demands, urban political organizations formed in other times and on other assumptions, attentive to other interests, and constrained by severely limited resources, find themselves unable to respond satisfactorily. A majority of the political workers, in evaluating a variety of services available to people in their districts, thought that all except two—telephone service and the fire department—were either poor or fair. Worst of the lot, according to the political workers, were recreation, police protection, and building inspection.

In view of these respondents, the black community has no illusions about the ability of routine politics to meet its needs. While only 38 percent of the political workers thought that the people in their districts regarded their councilmen as friends fighting for them, 51 percent said that the people considered their councilmen "part of the city government which must be asked continually and re-peatedly in order to get things done." (Since the political workers were probably talking about their fellow party members, their responses may have been more favorable than frank. A relatively high percentage of "don't know" responses supports this point.)

Almost all the Negro politicians said that they received various requests from the voters for help. Asked whether they could respond to these requests "almost always, usually, or just sometimes," the largest percentage (36 percent) chose "sometimes"—which, in context, is a way of saying "seldom." Another 31 percent said they "usually" could respond to such requests, and 19 percent said "almost always." Logically enough, 60 percent of the political workers agreed that in the last few years "people have become more fed up with the system, and are becoming unwilling to work with politicians." In effect, this is an admission that they as political workers, and the system of urban politics to which they devote themselves, are failing.

When economic and social institutions fail to provide the life-chances that a substantial part of a population wants, and when political institutions fail to provide a remedy, the aspirations of the people begin to spill over into forms of activity that the dominant society regards either as unacceptable or illegitimate—crime, vandalism, noncooperation, and various forms of political protest.

Robert M. Fogelson and Robert D. Hill, in the *Supplemental Studies* for the riot commission, have reported that 50 percent to 90 percent of the Negro males in ten cities studied had arrest records. Clearly, when the majority of men in a given population are defined as criminals—at least by the police—something more than "deviant" behaviour is involved. In effect, ghetto residents—and especially the youth—and the police are in a state of subdued warfare. On the one hand, the cities are experiencing a massive and as yet inchoate social rising of the Negro population. On the other hand, the police—devoted to the racial status quo and inclined to overlook the niceties of mere law in their quest for law and order—have found a variety of means, both conventional and otherwise, for countering the aims of Negroes. In doing so, they are not only adhering to the norms of their institution, but also furthering their personal goals as well. The average policeman, recruited from a lower- or middle-class white background, frequently of "ethnic" origins, comes from a group whose social position is marginal and who feel most threatened by Negro advances.

The high arrest rate in the Negro community thus mirrors both the push of Negroes and the determined resistance of the police. As the conflict intensifies, the police are more and more losing authority in the eyes of black people; the young Negroes are especially defiant. Any type of contact between police and black people can quickly lead to a situation in which the policeman gives an order and the Negro either defies it or fails to show sufficient respect in obeying it. This in turn can lead to the Negro's arrest on a disorderly conduct charge or on a variety of other charges. (Disorderly conduct accounted for about 17 percent of the arrests in the Fogelson-Hill study.)

Police Harassment Techniques

The police often resort to harassment as a means of keeping the Negro community off-balance. The riot commission noted that:

Because youths commit a large and increasing proportion of crime, police are under growing pressure from their supervisors—and from the community—to deal with them forcefully. "Harassment of youths" may therefore be viewed by some police departments—and members even of the Negro community—as a proper crime prevention technique.

The Commission added that "many departments have adopted patrol practices which, in the words of one commentator, have 'replaced harassment by individual patrolmen with harassment by entire departments.'"

Among the most common of the cops' harassment techniques are breaking up street-corner groups and stop-and-frisk tactics. Our study found that 63 percent of the ghetto police reported that they "frequently" were called upon to disperse loitering groups. About a third say they "frequently" stop and frisk people. Obviously then, the law enforcer sometimes interferes with individuals and groups who consider their activities quite legitimate and necessary. Black people in the ghetto—in the absence of adequate parks, playgrounds, jobs, and recreation facilities, and unwilling to sit in sweltering and overcrowded houses with rats and bugs—are likely to make the streets their front yards. But this territory is often made uninhabitable by the police.

Nearly a third of the white policemen in our study thought that most of the residents of their precinct (largely Negro) were not industrious. Even more striking about the attitudes of the white police working in these neighborhoods is that many of them deny the fact of Negro inequality: 20 percent say the Negro is treated better than any other part of the population, and 14 percent say he is treated equally. As for their own treatment of Negroes, the Campbell-Schuman survey reported that 43 percent of the black men, who are on the streets more than the women, thought that police use insulting language in their neighborhoods. Only 17 percent of the white males held this belief. Of the Negro men, 20 percent reported that the police insulted them personally and 28 percent said they knew

someone to whom this had happened; only 9 percent and 12 percent, respectively, of the whites reported the same. Similarly, many more blacks than whites thought that the police frisked and searched people without good reason (42 percent compared to 12 percent); and that the police roughed up people unnecessarily (37 percent as compared to 10 percent). Such reports of police misconduct were most frequent among the younger Negroes, who, after all, are on the receiving end most often.

The policeman's isolation in the ghetto is evident in a number of findings. We asked the police how many people —of various types—they knew well enough in the ghetto to greet when they saw them. Eighty-nine percent of the police said they knew six or more shopowners, managers, and clerks well enough to speak with, but only 38 percent said they knew this many teenage or youth leaders. At the same time, 39 percent said that most young adults, and 51 percent said that most adolescents, regard the police as enemies. And only 16 percent of the white policemen (37 percent of the blacks) either "often" or "sometimes" attended meetings in the neighborhood.

The police have wound up face to face with the social consequences of the problems in the ghetto created by the failure of other white institutions—though, as has been observed, they themselves have contributed to those problems in no small degree. The distant and gentlemanly white racism of employers, the discrimination of white parents who object to having their children go to school with Negroes, the disgruntlement of white taxpayers who deride the present welfare system as a sinkhole of public funds but are unwilling to see it replaced by anything more effective—the consequences of these and other forms of white racism have confronted the police with a massive control problem of the kind most evident in the riots.

In our survey, we found that the police were inclined to see the riots as the long range result of faults in the Negro community—disrespect for law, crime, broken families, etc.—rather than as responses to the stance of the white community. Indeed, nearly one-third of the white police saw the riots as the result of what they considered the basic violence and disrespect of Negroes in general, while only one-fourth attributed the riots to the failure of white institutions. More than three-fourths also regarded the riots as the immediate result of agitators and criminals—a suggestion contradicted by all the evidence accumulated by the riot commission. The police, then, share with the other groups—excepting the black politicians—a tendency to emphasize perceived defects in the black community as an explanation for the difficulties that they encounter in the ghetto.

The state of siege evident in many police departments is but an exaggerated version of a trend in the larger white society. It is the understandable, but unfortunate, response of people who are angry and confused about the widespread disruption of traditional racial patterns and who feel threatened by these changes. There is, of course, some basis for this feeling, because the Negro movement poses challenges of power and interest to many groups. To the extent that the movement is successful, the merchants, for example, will either have to reform their practices or go out of business—and for many it may be too late for reform. White suburbanites will have to cough up funds for the city, which provides most of them with employment. Police departments will have to be thoroughly restructured.

The broad social rising of Negroes is beginning to have a substantial effect upon all white institutions in the ghetto, as the situation of the merchants, the schools, and the welfare establishment illustrates. Ten years ago, these institutions (and the police, who have been affected differently) could operate pretty much unchecked by any countervailing power in the ghetto. Today, both their excesses and their inadequacies have run up against an increasingly militant black population, many of whom support violence as a means of redress. The evidence suggests that unless these institutions are transformed, the black community will make it increasingly difficult for them to function at all.

Breakdown of Law and Order

Tom Parmenter

Spokesmen and public men, preachers and newspaper columnists need only open their mouths in the face of a Detroit or a Newark or a Watts and the phrase "breakdown of law and order" comes rolling out. The cliche has much to commend it to such men. Certainly neither "They're breeding like hamsters down there" or "We need to set up a pilot program" quite covers the situation and until the time comes to say "We must appoint a committee" nothing is quite so appropriate as "breakdown."

Cliches are convenient. No one in love or in mourning uses anything else. And as shorthand expressions of public figures they make the work of a reporter lighter. The danger comes when the cliche becomes reality, when it turns into an explanation. In the case of Detroit and the other urban riots, "breakdown of law and order" means looting and snipers, soup lines, broken windows and broken lives, corpses and sirens, and calling out the troops. This is the meaning of the phrase to the public men who use it, but the phrase may have another meaning to the Negroes of Detroit.

I spent several days in Detroit as the riots were running down gathering material on encounters with the police. What appears below is not the truth that may eventually emerge from trials, grand-jury investigations, and committees, but the truth as perceived by those involved in the events.

The Detroit riots started in a police raid on what is known locally with self-conscious quaintness as a blind pig, an after-hours tavern. The police began to move the eighty patrons to the precinct station for booking and downtown to jail. The police guard around the building attracted a crowd even at 5 a.m. Someone smashed the window of a squad car. Within minutes the crowd began to move down 12th Street breaking windows and looting.

A shoe store was torched and the crowd grew. One of the first official acts of the police commissioner was to block off Belle Isle Park, the island which saw the worst of the 1943 riot. Despite the trouble, the night police watch went off duty as usual at 8 a.m. and the day watch came on. At the same time, things began to quiet down a bit. The crowd milled around the streets, good-tempered if sarcastic. The police increased their guard.

"They were intimidating the hell out of the streets, man," said a Negro community organizer who was on 12th Street that Sunday morning. "It was the most insane thing you'd want to see. They just occupied 12th Street. Ninety God-damn degrees, Sunday morning, and they just occupy that street. They thought about pulling off but they waited until too late. The tension was bad, man. And the police recognized it and said, 'Well, maybe we'd better get out of here a little bit,' you know? Between 9 a.m. and the time they pulled some of the police out, that's when it really got going. Cats was walking up and down the streets drinking blood and saying 'We're going to burn it. We're going to smoke it up and we don't want nobody down there talking no shit.'"

"It was just too late. It would have erupted sooner or later. There was nothing to do *then*. I mean it was all over. What they should have done when they busted that blind pig and these cats broke in those three stores, they should have boarded those stores up and got the hell out of there and then sent some detectives in there or something. But these cats boarded the damned things up and blocked off 12th Street and when people came out in the morning here they are with shotguns on the God-damned streets. If that's not the most stupid thing. They just made mistake after mistake. And they miscalculated in so God-damn many areas. I mean it can only go so long. I mean the probability of this kind of thing happening under the *law enforcement* process here in Detroit.

It was time for something to happen. These cats have gotten away with so much shit, man. They ran down Negroes on *horses* in Belle Isle last year, man. There was no riot until these cats started it. They tried to start the riot four days earlier down on Butternut."

The incident referred to took place about three miles from the blind pig. A disturbance had started over a disorderly conduct arrest. "They called in the rest of the dogs down there, man. In four minutes, it was 20 squad cars in that block. Police was all over the place, you know. And there they was with these shotguns, all prepared with riot tactics. It was an integrated crowd standing around watching, you know. It was irresponsibility. Four days later they did the same damned thing on 12th Street but they was in the wrong part of town. It blew up.

"The *whole thing* was showing force. That's all they was doing was showing force, intimidating purposely. The policy of showing force went straight on to the other end, man. Three hours after these cats were showing force with the Detroit police department down here on 12th Street, the law had broke down completely."

The riot started again in full force about noon on Sunday. A young man described for me his usual way of life and his part in the riots. Call him Arthur.

"I'm making more money than the average white man with a white collar job," he said.

"How is that?"

"Well, I make mine."

"Hustling?"

"Well," he smiled and went on, "I do a little bit of everything. I don't steal for it. I don't rob nobody. I mean I can't go to jail unless somebody tell on me, you understand? And I don't think they're going to tell on me because they love me."

"How did you hear about the riot?"

"I heard a friend of mine say, 'Hey! They rioting up on 12th.' I said what are they doing and he said *looting.* That's all it *took* to get me *out* of the house. He said the police was letting them take it; they wasn't stopping it; so I said it was time for me to get some of these diamonds and watches and rings. It wasn't that I was mad at anybody or angry or trying to get back at the white man. If I saw something that I could get without getting hurt, I got it."

Arthur's assertion that he wasn't trying to get back at anyone was not assured. He did agree that he was stealing.

"This is nothing but pure lawlessness. People are trying to get what they can get. They *have* been *denied* these things and when the first brick was thrown, that's all it took. Let's get it while we can get it. They were trying to get all they could get. They got diamonds here, they got money here, they got clothes here and TV's and what not. What could they do with it when they bring it out except sell it to each other? That's all. They're just getting something they haven't got. I mean, I bought me some clothes from somebody. I have exchanged whiskey and different things for different things. You know, something I wanted that I didn't have. This was a good way to get it. *I really enjoyed myself.*

"I didn't get caught until Sunday night. I got caught because I was going into one of them little bitty stores instead of going in one of them big stores. I went to a stocking store because I was going to get my girl friend some stockings. I had three or four hundred pair under my arm when I come out. They told me to put 'em down.

"Before that the police weren't stopping me. What have we got them for? They *could* have stopped it. I'd come up and I'd have an armful of clothes or a bagful of diamonds and he'd say, 'Having fun?' I'd say 'Plenty of it.' I'd take them on and go back and get some more. If he had pulled a gun and said drop it it would have been dropped. I wouldn't have picked up nothing else. But they seemed to be enjoying seeing 12th Street tore down."

"Why?"

"For the prostitutes. That's the *only* reason. It's more prostitutes than it is people living there.

"I thought it was a lot of fun. People see'n what they could get for nothing and they went out and got it. It wasn't no race riot. They was white and Negro both going in stores and helping each other pass things out. Having a good time. Really enjoying themselves until them *fools* [snipers] started shooting. I hope they can get them because they're stopping me from making my money.

"Before that you didn't even have to go in a store to get nothing. All you had to do was tell people you saw with a bunch of stuff, 'Hey buddy, let me get some of that.' They'd give you some. One guy had ten suits and I had two; he gave me three. That's the way it was. It wasn't no organized stuff. Everybody was trying to get in it. I went in one place there was about 10 hands in a safe trying to get the money. Like I said, I really enjoyed myself.

"The only thing was that we had a minority group that was going around burning. I really do believe it was organized. They waited until stuff got going. See? What they tried to do was shoot off a few police officers and see if everybody would get armed. That's ridiculous."

Urban Frontier Justice

The snipers in Detroit 1967—there were snipers there in 1943 as well—attracted a great deal of attention, and not only from adherents of devil theories. It is widely believed by Detroit officials that fewer than a dozen snipers —white and Negro—ever fired a gun in Detroit during the riots. Although police reports make frequent mention of sniper fire in the area of a number of the riot deaths, even the daily tally issued during the riots by police attributed only two deaths to sniper fire. In comparison, 22 deaths were attributed to shootings by police, soldiers, private guards, and store owners. Of these, 14 were killed by the Detroit police. All the deaths occurred after the first day of looting described above.

Three of the deaths for which the police nominated snipers as a probable source may become a greater cause celebre than the riots themselves. Three days after I gathered most of the following material, the deaths hit the front pages of the Detroit papers. The implication was police execution. Since then, several investigations of the incident have been announced.

The first police reports implied that three youths had been killed in an exchange of gunfire between police and snipers in an annex to the Algiers Motel. (The annex is located on a pleasant tree-lined street not at all untypical of Detroit's Negro neighborhoods.) No guns were found in the rooms where the bodies were found, however, and the police were informed of the deaths anonymously—not by an official source.

One witness was Michael Clark, 19. His roommate, Carl Cooper, 17, was killed. "There was no shooting around the motel at all. We was just sitting in the room doing nothing. The first shooting I knew about came from the cops. I looked out and there was a state trooper pointing a rifle up into the window. Carl ran down the hall. I guess they shot him downstairs. That's where the body was. He was dead when we got down. They said they was going to shoot us one at a time. Called us niggers. I heard them shoot Fred Temple after they took him out. They just kept on beating us and beating us all the time. Then they told me to come into a room and they pointed a gun in my face. Told me to lay down and then he shot. He shot above me. I don't know why he didn't shoot me. Then I heard another shot across the hall. I guess that was Aubrey Pollard when they shot him. I don't know why they did it. I got out of there. But I'm going to testify. I've already talked to the detectives."

Cooper's funeral was a Jessica Mitford affair held in a funeral home so "tasteful" that it looked like an architect's drawing rather than a building in use. Clark was one of the pallbearers. "I knew Carl since we was little kids."

Cooper's family and friends seemed the sort known as "the good people of the Negro community." They were decorous people, well-dressed and driving good cars. They were not necessarily middle class, but they were urban people, not poverty-stricken Southern migrants dressed uncomfortably in their mail-order suits and Sunday dresses. The body was lying in an open coffin. The minister offered his comforting best to a background of weeping. After everyone had passed the body, curtains were drawn across the front of the room, hiding the pulpit and the body. Suddenly, the room erupted in a surge of emotion. Women screamed and several charged the curtain only to be led away by attendants. The family seating section lost all semblance of regularity as women began to rock back and forth and soon everyone was moving around the room. The funeral director eyed his watch; another cortege was waiting to move into the chapel. The women who had been led away went back into the room. The minister offered more words and then the curtains were reopened and Clark and the other pallbearers moved the coffin out to the hearse.

The stories about investigations of the death were not yet public, but they were common knowledge among the several hundred gathered for Cooper's funeral. In fact, the stories were being heard all over the West side soon after the deaths early Wednesday. Arthur, the hustler quoted above, hangs around the Algiers and although he was unwilling to admit it to himself, it was only happenstance that he was not killed himself.

Arthur wasn't at Cooper's funeral, although he said he was closer to him than to the other two who were killed. His ambivalence about race is apparent as he talks about politics and grief. "I think Johnson is for the Negroes. He has to be to be President. I would be for anybody in the world if they was going to elect me President. Everybody's talking about Abe Lincoln freeing the slaves but there was only one man who was really for the Negroes and that was Kennedy. You see what they did to him. That's the only man—white man, black man, green man— that I ever cried for when he got killed. That was the man."

"Did you cry over these kids?"

"Naw. I didn't cry over them. I mean, that's life. They wasn't doing anything for me. Kennedy was trying to help me. I felt bad about them, but the first thing that hit my mind was, 'I'm glad it wasn't me.' That's the only thing I thought about."

His first words when asked about the shootings were, "It was murder. They just murdered them boys. They just happened to be with these white girls, all of them sitting up in the room together. That's what it was. We was standing outside and the guard here at the motel said it's curfew time and we had to get in. So they went around with them and we went on in our place. That's the deal.

"There were plenty of cops around. When we opened the door to see—we heard some shooting—just a crack more or less and a shotgun or a rifle came into the door and told us to come on out of there. That's what we did. I didn't know who it was and I didn't care. I was coming out even if it had been a sniper, but I was coming out.

"When the other bunch come downstairs one of them was in the hall already dead. That's Carl. I know for a fact that Carl was not the kind of guy to be raising no whole lot of hell. If a policeman put a drop on him he's going to raise them up like he's supposed to. He was dead. They killed him. Then they shot the other two and then just called downtown and said it's three bodies up in back of the Algiers. They didn't do no reporting other than that, no numbers or saying they was policemen or nothing.

"There wasn't any rioting or anything closer than six blocks away. I did hear about some blank pistol or something being shot but that wasn't close." [Newspaper reports stated that Cooper had a starter's pistol, but none was found.]

Arthur continued: "I think it must be because the white girls was in the room with them. I really do. It was just cold-blooded murder. They asked the girls, 'Which one of you white whores is fucking one of these black niggers?' Before the girl could say something he hit her in the head. He beat her down. They hit her in the head with the rifle."

A second young man—he gave his name as Boston Blackie and said he was a pimp—broke into the conversation. "I'm going to tell you what the whole deal was. They probably didn't know how it happened, seeing these white girls in this room with these Negroes. They didn't give nobody a chance to explain themselves. All cops are probably prejudiced to an extent. This girl that was hit told me the officer was in the late thirties or early forties. She said he seemed like he was nuts. She said he came in talking that shit about a white woman in there. At first I didn't believe it when I heard it. Then I was sick when I came over and found out. They said this one guy who

was giving the orders seemed like he was mentally unbalanced or something. The dude *had* to be crazy. He was talking about who wants to die first the girls or the fellows. She thought he was going to shoot her, too, after he hit her on the head."

Arthur continued: "They had us all out there in the court by the swimming pool. They didn't tell us to lay down or nothing. I asked *them* if there was going to *be* any shooting to let me lay down. I didn't want to be standing up because they had jeeps out here with these 50 calibers pointed this way and I didn't want them to shoot me. I was already scared of being shot at. It was a half hour after they laid us down that we found out that the boys was dead. One of the security guards around the motel walked one of the girls back to her room and when they walked in the hallway the boys was in there dead. The police had gone.

"They left the bodies here. You wouldn't expect them to stay after committing murder. The boys was laying down when they shot them. They looked for bullet holes and couldn't find them till they looked on the floor.

"I really thought Michael was dead. That's what they told me. I really thought he was dead until he showed up today. He came in here and said, 'Well, I'm not dead, y'all.'

"Now why did all this happen? What kind of shit is this? They don't turn in no report on who they are or nothing. That's nothing but murder. That's all it was and all it could be.

"If the boys *was* up there shooting *out* the window, *get on up there* and shoot *in* the window. Don't be just shooting all over the place. They could kill anybody. They had the boys in there and they had them up against the wall. They could have called the paddy wagon or whatever they wanted and took them downtown. They didn't have to kill the boys. They had no business over there. They wasn't doing shit in that room. They wasn't even playing cards like we was. They said they heard some shots and that's all it took. If I had had a cap pistol they'd be liable to come in there shooting instead of saying 'what is it' or 'come on out.' They just went in shooting."

"They just went in shooting." The words were repeated to describe one of the last deaths in the riot. The following material was gathered less than an hour after the death, at the same time that the street was hearing it first. An inquest or trial may turn up a different and perhaps more correct story, but a story that will be heard by dozens as compared to the far greater number who heard the story as it appears here.

Of all those killed in the riots in Detroit, regular army paratroopers killed one, this one. The national guardsmen killed three, according to a police summary. Policemen are accustomed to working alone or with a partner. The closest they get to tactics—and it happens rarely in the normal course of police work—is surrounding a house with a single man holed up inside. Soldiers, on the other hand, rarely work in units smaller than a squad. The paratrooper who killed Ernest Roquemore this night—by accident it would seem—was one of the few army men who had been removed from his unit and assigned to a police car. The policeman he was working with wounded a youth and two girls, 13 and 17, with his personal hunting weapon, a 16-gauge shotgun.

Police said they were looking for loot. One of the injured girls had been visiting the apartment of her brother where the shootings took place. Their father is talking.

"My wife was talking to my daughter on the phone when it happened. My wife just heard a shot on the phone. She said, 'John, please, something done happened already. Please go over to Hal's house (which is my son). Somebody's done shot somebody.' I got here as fast as I could and they wouldn't let me in. They said it was looting. There was some looting around the corner, but my son, he don't believe in looting. Like they said that furniture was looted. But that furniture wasn't looted. I've got to pay. I've got the receipt. My son put $800 down on that furniture and he still owes $592. They wouldn't let him get it because he owes for an automobile. So I had to co-sign for him. I got the book here. We paid regular. They said he had to put that heavy payment down for the furniture.

"They said there was somebody in there with a gun. Maybe there was, but I didn't see him. Then they said they was some marijuana. I don't know."

Roquemore, 19, a resident of the building, was shot accidentally while the paratrooper was firing at an armed youth who was running away. He was not caught, but police said they found a packet of marijuana on the stairs.

The father continued: "They just bust in there without saying nothing to nobody. Now I come over here and they won't tell me anything. They said, 'Well, you can't go in there.' I said, 'Why not? I want to see who's hurt because my son stays here. I want to see what's the matter.' They said, 'Naw, you have to stay on the side.' Then this Negro soldier, he said, 'Look, do like they say. Don't get yourself involved. Take it easy. So many of my people getting killed already.' I stood back there. I obeyed them. Then I waited and they tried to take the furniture out.

I got the book right here. I'm waiting for them now. They can't take that furniture out because it belongs to my son.

"I don't know about that marijuana or that looting or what. I don't see where that give them the right to be shooting when they come in the house. They should find out who's *in there* first.

"There's four people shot. They said somebody had a gun. But didn't nobody up there shoot at nobody. Maybe they thought somebody was breaking in and then if I had a gun I might get it out. But the policemen didn't say nothing. They just came in shooting.

"This is worser than the thing, the raid, that started the riots. Didn't nobody do nothing but they just go in there shooting. Then they want to say, 'How come the colored man get down wrong?' That make any man do something wrong."

The Frontier Organizers

The institution of the booster, the organizer, is a familiar one. One corporation front man I know introduces himself as "the vice president in charge of joining good causes." The adherents of this institution—which include the Babbitt, the PR man, the associate minister, and other assorted icon polishers—have generally been hired for their winning smiles and friction-free personalities.

More recently, the institution has been enlivened by a band of men who neither smile much nor avoid friction. Although Detroit may have been a little behind other cities, it is now home to a number of black community organizers. These men saw the riots as an opportunity to assert leadership in building a community. They were excited by the riots and proud of them in a way, but they were also depressed at the implication that rioting might present more opportunities than community organization.

Frank Ditto came to Detroit from Chicago just a month before the riots to work for a new group called CESSA, Churches on the East Side for Social Action. He was in Newark at the Black Power convention when the riots broke out in Detroit. He had gained fame in Chicago as the leader of 150 consecutive days of miles-long marches through the streets, ending each night at the home of Mayor Richard J. Daley. One of the first friends Ditto made in Detroit was Rennie Freeman, the executive director of the West Community Organization, an older counterpart to CESSA in the area that was most seriously hit by the riots. Whenever Ditto and Freeman meet they give one another the Black-Power secret grip, a variation on Indian wrestling.

Freeman was working on 12th Street when the riot began to emerge. John Conyers, the Negro Democrat who represents the West Side in Congress, asked Freeman to help quiet the crowds shortly before noon on Sunday. Freeman tells the story:

"Conyers and his functionaries came down here talking to me saying, 'Will you help?' I said, 'Man, I'll help you if you do the right thing.' He said, 'Well, I'm going to get a bullhorn down here and get these cats off the streets. We don't want anybody hurt.' So I said no. He said, 'What are you doing down here then? What are you here for? Do you want a riot?' You've got all these brothers down on the street corner and as I told Conyers, 'If you go up and down 12th Street with a bullhorn trying to tell all the colored folks to get off *their* street when these cops are standing out here with shotguns and bayonets, what's going to happen is that the people are going to turn against *you*.' I said I'd help if the police were going to get out, too, but I think even at that point it was too late. The young brothers was out there and they didn't dig it *at all*.

"I started walking down the street with the cat and here I am with John on one side and this functionary on the other. I said to myself, 'Well, hell, I'm not walking down here with these armband Negroes. What do I look like riding up and down 12th Street telling these cats to get off the street with these functionaries? John just can't comprehend that the disorganized brothers have something to say. He thinks that if you aren't organized you have nothing to say. So he made the mistake, but at that he was the only cat down there. None of these other Negro politicians was there. Conyers was the only one."

Regardless of the difficulty of organizing the "disorganized brothers," both Ditto and Freeman place their faith in organization. Said Ditto, "To be honest with myself, having been oppressed and subjected to all the dehumanizing factors of American life as a black man, I very well could have been out there burning, looting, and sniping. I see more point in organizing than I do in looting. It's more constructive. This kind of thing here, the rioting, runs out of gas in four or five days. With an organization when you get weak and tired you know that you have someone beside you who you can lean up against and still keep going on."

Ditto's mood varied widely. In an interview given a television reporter while the riots were still going on, organization, except in a special sense, was not foremost in his mind.

"Is this organized or a spontaneous thing?" the reporter asked.

"It's a combination of both. It was spontaneous in the sense that it was caused by just another incident of police brutality. It was organized in the sense that it has been going on more than four hundred years and the black folks have been organized for four hundred years to fight for survival."

He was even willing during the riots to take a real-politik view of the loss of Negro lives and property in the riot.

"The way that society looks at these things, we would say it's unfortunate, but the United States is dropping napalm bombs on women and children over in Viet Nam and no one has anything to say about it. I mean, this is a state of war. This is the price of war. You might get killed and I might get killed and who gives a damn?"

A few days later, Ditto encountered two young hustlers who had enjoyed the rioting, but who were unwilling to extract any political moral from it.

"If they wanted to do something, really wanted to cut it up, why did they do it down here," one said. "In all these soup lines and burned apartments up and down 12th Street, all I see is colored people in a fix. They should have gone up to Grosse Pointe. Get in their cars and go up there and riot. That'd show somebody something. Not like this; this didn't show the white people nothing."

Organization was not for the hustlers. "The white man's got everything," one said. "I'd like to get in on it but I can't get in on it so I get around it. What's the old saying, 'God bless the child that's got his own'? The Negroes have just got to get out and get theirs like I'm getting mine. Let them go for theirself."

Ditto didn't like it. "Do you realize that just 150 years ago when black babies were born and brought into the earth the slave master would snatch them away from their mother and send them off to some other plantation as soon as they were old enough? They separated brothers and sisters and fathers and sons. Negroes don't stick together because of the psychological brainwashing they've been through for hundreds of years."

"I'll tell you one thing," the hustler replied. "It would have been hard to get me over here at all if my brother in Africa hadn't been selling me for some beads."

Despite this sort of apathy, Ditto and Freeman were planning to try to bring together young Negroes like these—and others even tougher and less articulate—with the hope of formulating a program of police-community relations. Freeman explained, "We've got to strike while the iron is hot. Right now nobody knows what the hell to do. But the brothers can tell them what to do without hesitating. The brothers know what needs to be done.

"They aren't going to hear it from these Uncle Tom preachers. They don't even know what the *gossip* is on 12th Street. This is the time to organize. Everybody's together if you leave out the Toms. The Negroes in the community belong to what's happening, man. Those rioters was running down the streets and I see these middle class people standing out on the porches giving the Black Power sign. You know, women in house dresses giving the fist. And it is clear that this thing about the lower class being disenchanted is bullshit. Negroes are disenchanted. It's not just the cats that have got the guts to throw the bricks that's pissed off. Everybody is pissed off. There these chicks are that sit on the PTA boards giving the Black Power sign when there's smoke all around. Even the Toms break down and cry. They just don't have no goddam guts. That's the only difference."

This was on one of their hopeful days. The next day, after attending the funeral of a Negro youth apparently killed by police during the rioting, Ditto's mood was one of despair. "I've had people treat me like that cigaret butt there just because I'm black. I could very easily be on the other side of the street with a 30-30 rifle. I have this fight with myself every day. I keep having this hope that people will somehow come to their senses. I don't know what I'll be doing a year from now. I might give up on this organizing. I just don't know what I'll do."

Confrontation at the Conrad Hilton

The Walker Commission

A police riot. A reporter coined that phrase in attempting to capsulize the melee involving Chicago police and demonstrators in Chicago's Grant Park last August during the Democratic National Convention. Now the words have been immortalized by *a Chicago study team on assignment from the President's Commission on the Causes and Prevention of Violence. The task of the study team was to find out what happened in Chicago and why. The result of its 53-day investigation was a documented report* released December 1, entitled "Rights in Conflict," and bearing the name of a Chicago corporate attorney, Daniel Walker, who directed the investigation throughout and insisted on its immediate and unexpurgated publication despite pressure from some on the violence commission who wanted obscenity in the report toned down and publication delayed until at least next spring.

The report is based on 3436 statements of eyewitnesses and participants taken by the Walker committee and by the FBI. Those interviewed included police officers, National Guardsmen, United States Army personnel, demonstrators and their leaders, government officials, convention delegates, news media representatives and bystanders. The staff also viewed about 180 hours of motion picture film provided by television networks and local stations, the Chicago police department and others. More than 12,000 photographs were examined and official police and National Guard records were reviewed.

It is important to note that although individual members of Students for a Democratic Society, and other allied organizations linked to the National Mobilization Committee to End the War in Vietnam, were interviewed, the organizations themselves refused to cooperate with the study team. Thus, there is a likelihood in the report of considerable under-reporting of mass spontaneous violence.

Violence marked police-demonstrator relations from beginning to end of the convention, but none was so vicious as the bloody clash Wednesday evening, August 28, in front of the Conrad Hilton Hotel, where many delegates were staying and where the presidential campaign headquarters of Senator Eugene J. McCarthy was located. The following story is taken from the Walker Commission report. It is the step-by-step, indeed—nearly blow-by-blow account of events leading to the clash.—The editors

By about 5 p.m. Wednesday the U.S. Attorney's report says about 2000 persons, "mostly normally dressed," had already assembled at the [Conrad] Hilton [Hotel]. Many of these were demonstrators who had tired of waiting out the negotiations and had broken off from the marchers and made their way to the hotel. It appears that police already were having some difficulty keeping order at that location. Says the U.S. Attorney's report: "A large crowd had assembled behind the police line along the east wall of the Hilton. This crowd was heavily infiltrated with 'Yippie'

THE PARTICIPANTS

"There were of course, the hippies—the long hair and love beads, the calculated unwashedness, the flagrant banners, the open lovemaking and disdain for the constraints of conventional society. In dramatic effect, both visual and vocal, these dominated a crowd whose members actually differed widely in physical appearance, in motivation, in political affiliation, in philosophy. The crowd included Yippies come to 'do their thing,' youngsters working for a political candidate, professional people with dissenting political views, anarchists and determined revolutionaries, motorcycle gangs, black activists, young thugs, police and secret service undercover agents. There were demonstrators waving the Viet Cong flag and the red flag of revolution and there were the simply curious who came to watch and, in many cases, became willing or unwilling participants.

To characterize the crowd, then, as entirely hippie-Yippie, entirely "New Left," entirely anarchist, or entirely youthful political dissenters is both wrong and dangerous. The stereotyping that did occur helps to explain the emotional reaction of both police and public during and after the violence that occurred.

Despite the presence of some revolutionaries, the vast majority of the demonstrators were intent on expressing by peaceful means their dissent either from society generally or from the administration's policies in Vietnam.

Most of those intending to join the major protest demonstrations scheduled during convention week did not plan to enter the Amphitheatre and disrupt the proceedings of the Democratic convention, did not plan aggressive acts of physical provocation against the authorities, and did not plan to use rallies of demonstrators to stage an assault against any person, institution, or place of business. But while it is clear that most of the protesters in Chicago had no intention of initiating violence, this is not to say that they did not expect it to develop." From the summary of the Walker Commission report.

types and was spitting and screaming obscene insults at the police."

A policeman on duty in front of the hotel later said that it seemed to him that the obscene abuses shouted by "women hippies" outnumbered those called out by male demonstrators "four to one." A common epithet shouted by the females, he said, was "Fuck you, pig." Others included references to policemen as "cock suckers" and "mother fuckers."

A short time later a reporter noticed a lot of debris being hurled from one of the upper floors of the Hilton. He climbed into a police squad car parked in the area and with the aid of police binoculars saw that rolls of toilet paper were coming from the 15th floor, a location he pinpointed by counting down from the top of the building. He then went to the 15th floor and found that the section the paper was coming from was rented by Senator McCarthy campaigners. He was not admitted to the suite.

If Dellinger's marchers in Grant Park now moved to the Hilton area, an additional 5000 demonstrators would be added to the number the police there would have to control.

The Crossing

At about 6 or 6:30 p.m., one of the march leaders announced by loudspeaker that the demonstrators would not be allowed to march to the Amphitheatre. He told the crowd to disperse and to re-group in front of the Conrad Hilton Hotel in Grant Park.

Police in the area were in a far from cheerful mood. A neatly dressed sociology student from Minnesota says he stepped off the sidewalk onto the grass and two policemen pulled their billy clubs back as though ready to swing. One of them said, "You'd better get your fucking ass off that grass or I'll put a beautiful goddam crease in your fucking queer head." The student overheard another policeman say to a "hippie-looking girl of 14 or 15, 'You better get your fucking dirty cunt out of here.'" The growing feeling of entrapment was intensified and some witnesses noticed that police were letting people into the park but not out. The marshals referred to the situation as a "trap."

As the crowd moved north, an Assistant U.S. Attorney saw one demonstrator with long sideburns and hippie garb pause to break up a large piece of concrete, wrapping the pieces in a striped T-shirt.

Before the march formally disbanded, an early contingent of demonstrators, numbering about 30 to 50, arrived at the spot where Congress Plaza bridges the Illinois Central tracks at approximately the same time as a squad of 40 National Guardsmen. The Guard hurriedly spread out about three feet apart across Congress with rifles at the ready, gas masks on, bayonets fixed.

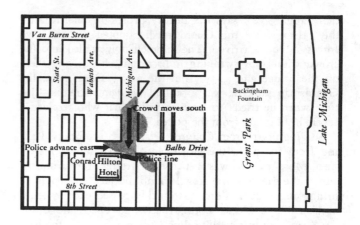

Now as the bulk of the disappointed marchers sought a way out of the park, the crowd began to build up in front of the Guard. "I saw one woman driving a new red late-model car approach the bridge," a news correspondent says: "Two demonstrators, apparently badly gassed, jumped into the back seat and hoped to get through the Guard lines. Guardsmen refused to permit the car through, going so far as to threaten to bayonet her tires and the hood of her car if she did not turn around. One Guardsman fired tear gas point blank beside the car."

The crowd's basic strategy, a medic recalled, was "to mass a sizeable group at one end of the line," as if preparing to charge. Then, when Guardsmen shifted to protect that area, a comparatively small group of demonstrators would push through the weak end of the line. Once the small group had penetrated the line, the medic says, members would "come up behind the Guardsmen and taunt them, as well as push and shove them from the rear." A Guard official said later that his men were attacked with oven cleaner and containers filled with excrement.

As the crowd swelled, it surged periodically towards the Guard line, sometimes yelling, "Freedom, freedom." On one of these surges a Guardsman hurled two tear gas canisters. Some of the tear gas was fired directly into the faces of demonstrators. "We came across a guy really badly gassed," a college coed says. "We were choking, but we could still see. But this guy we saw was standing there helpless with mucous-type stuff on his face, obviously in pain."

An Assistant U.S. Attorney says he saw "hundreds of people running, crying, coughing, vomiting, screaming." Some woman ran blindly to Buckingham Fountain and leaped into the water to bathe their faces. The Guard medic quoted earlier says he was again assaulted by demonstrators when he went into the crowd to treat a man felled by "a particularly heavy dose of tear gas."

"In Grant Park, the gassed crowd was angered . . .

more aggressive," says the history professor. Shortly after the gassing, says the Guard medic quoted earlier, "two forces of police arrived. They immediately waded into the crowd with clubs swinging indiscriminately, driving them off the bridge and away from the area." Once more, the Guardsman said, he was assaulted by demonstrators—this time when he tried "to treat an individual who received a severe head injury from the police."

Surging north from Congress Plaza to a footbridge leading from the park, the crowd encountered more Guardsmen. More tear gas was dispensed. Surging north from the site of the gassings, the crowd found the Jackson Boulevard bridge unguarded. Word was quickly passed back by loudspeaker "Two blocks north, there's an open bridge; no gas." As dusk was settling, hundreds poured from the park into Michigan Avenue.

The Crowd on Michigan Avenue

At 7:14 p.m., as the first groups of demonstrators crossed the bridge toward Michigan Avenue, they noticed that the mule train of the Poor People's Campaign was just entering the intersection of Michigan and Jackson, headed south. The wagons were painted, "Jobs & Food for All."

The train was accompanied by 24 policemen on foot, five on three-wheelers, and four in two squadrols. A police official was in front with the caravan's leaders. The sight of the train seemed to galvanize the disorganized Grant Park crowd and those streaming over the bridge broke into cheers and shouts. "Peace now!" bellowed the demonstrators. "Dump the Hump!" This unexpected enthusiastic horde in turn stimulated the mule train marchers. Drivers of the wagons stood and waved to the crowd, shouting: "Join us! Join us!" To a young man watching from the 23rd floor of the Hilton Hotel, "the caravan seemed like a magnet to demonstrators leaving the park."

The Balbo-Michigan Crowd Builds Up

When the crowd's first rank reached the intersection of Balbo and Michigan, the northeast corner of the Hilton, it was close to approximately 2000 to 3000 demonstrators and spectators. The police were armed with riot helmets, batons, mace, an aerosol tear gas can and their service revolvers (which they always carry). Behind the police lines, parked in front of the Hilton, was a fire department high pressure pumper truck hooked up to a hydrant. Pairs of uniformed firemen were also in the vicinity. The growing crowds, according to the U.S. Attorney's report, were a blend of "young and old, hippies, Yippies, straights, newsmen and cameramen," even two mobile TV units.

From within the crowd were rising the usual shouts from some of the demonstrators: "Hell no, we won't go!" . . . "Fuck these Nazis!" . . . "Fuck you, L.B.J.!" . . . "No more

war!" . . . 'Pigs, pigs, pigs." . . . "The streets belong to the people!" . . . "Let's go to the Amphitheatre!" . . . "Move on, Move on!" . . . "You can't stop us." . . . "From the hotel," recalls a student, "people who sympathized were throwing confetti and pieces of paper out of the windows and they were blinking their room lights."

Isolated Incidents

Occasionally during the early evening, groups of demonstrators would flank the police lines or find a soft spot and punch through, heading off on their own for the Amphitheatre. On the periphery of the Hilton and on thoroughfares and side streets further southwest, a series of brief but sometimes violent encounters occurred.

For example, says the manager of a private club on Michigan Avenue, "a large band of long-haired demonstrators . . . tore down the American flag" overhanging the entrance to the club "and took it into Michigan Avenue attempting to tear it."

At about 7 p.m. from the window of a motel room in the 1100 block of South Michigan, a senator's driver noticed a group of demonstrators walking south, chanting: "Hell no, we won't go!" and "Fuck the draft." They were hurling insults at passing pedestrians and when one answered back, the witness says, "five demonstrators charged out of Michigan Avenue onto the sidewalk, knocked the pedestrian down, formed a circle around his fallen body, locked their arms together and commenced kicking him in a vicious manner. When they had finished kicking their victim, they unlocked their arms and immediately melted back into the crowd. . . ."

Back at the Conrad Hilton

Vice President Humphrey was now inside the Conrad Hilton Hotel and the police commanders were afraid that the crowd might either attempt to storm the hotel or march south on Michigan Avenue, ultimately to the Amphitheatre. The Secret Service had received an anonymous phone call that the Amphitheatre was to be blown up. A line of police was established at 8th and Michigan at the south end of the hotel and the squads of police stationed at the hotel doors began restricting access to those who could display room keys. Some hotel guests, including delegates and Senator McCarthy's wife, were turned away.

By 7:30 p.m. a rumor was passing around that the Blackstone Rangers and the East Side Disciples, two of Chicago's most troublesome street gangs, were on their way to the scene. (This was later proven to be untrue; neither of these South Side gangs was present in any numbers in either Lincoln Park or Grant Park.) At this point, a Negro male was led through the police line by a police officer. He spoke to the police officer, a city official and a deputy superintendent of police. He told them that he was

THE ARRESTS

Chicago police arrested 668 persons in connection with disturbances during the convention week. Fifty-two persons were in possession of weapons when arrested. The weapons consisted primarily of rocks and bricks, but police also arrested nine demonstrators with knives, two with guns, two with machetes and one with a bayonet.

Two-thirds of the Arrests Were Made of Persons From 18 to 25 Years Old, With Men Outnumbering Women 8 to 1.

Age	Arrested	Percentage of Total
17 and Under	64	9.6
18-20	221	33.1
21 25	221	33.1
26 and Over	157	23.5
Not Reported	5	0.8
	668	100.0%

Forty-three Percent of the Arrested Were Employed, Representing a Wide Range of Occupations Including Teachers, Social Workers, Ministers, Factory Laborers and Journalists.

Occupation	Arrested	Percentage of Total
Employed	287	43.0
Student	218	32.6
Unemployed	133	19.9
Not Reported	30	4.5
	668	100.0%

The Majority of Those Arrested Were Male Residents of Metropolitan Chicago, But Police Records Listed Persons From 36 States, Washington, D.C. and Five Foreign Countries.

Residence	Arrested	Percentage of Total
Chicago City	276	41.4
Out of State	291	43.5
Chicago Suburban	74	11.1
Other Illinois	14	2.0
Not Reported	13	1.9
	668	100.0%

Less Than 1/6 of Those Arrested Had Previous Records.

Sex	Age 17 and Under	Age 18-20	Age 21-25	Age 26 and Over	Total
Male	4	26	45	35	110
Female	0	2	4	2	8
	4	28	49	37	118

More Than 4/5 of the Previous Arrests Were For Misdemeanors.

Charge	Arrests	Percentage of Total
Felony	39	11.5
Misdemeanor	277	81.5
Narcotics	24	7.1
	340	100.0%

in charge of the mule train and that his people wanted no part of this mob. He said he had 80 people with him, that they included old people and children, and he wanted to get them out of the mob. The police officer later stated the group wanted to go past the Hilton, circle it, and return to the front of the hotel where Reverend Ralph Abernathy could address the crowd.

In a few minutes, Reverend Ralph Abernathy appeared and, according to the police officer's statement, "said he wanted to be taken out of the area as he feared for the safety of his group." The police officer directed that the train be moved south on Michigan to 11th Street and then, through a series of turns through the Loop, to the West Side.

A policeman on Michigan later said that at about this time a "female hippie" came up to him, pulled up her skirt and said, "You haven't had a piece in a long time." A policeman standing in front of the Hilton remembers seeing a blond female who was dressed in a short red minidress make lewd, sexual motion in front of a police line. Whenever this happened, he says, the policemen moved back to prevent any incident. The crowd, however, egged her on, the patrolman says. He thought that "she and the crowd wanted an arrest to create a riot." Earlier in the same general area a male youth had stripped bare and walked around carrying his clothes on a stick.

The intersection at Balbo and Michigan was in total chaos at this point. The street was filled with people. Darkness had fallen but the scene was lit by both police and television lights. As the mule train left, part of the group tried to follow the wagons through the police line and were stopped. According to the deputy superintendent of police, there was much pushing back and forth between the policemen and the demonstrators.

Continual announcements were made at this time over a police amplifier for the crowd to "clear the street and go up on the sidewalk or into the park area for their demonstrations." The broadcast said "Please gather in the park on the east side of the street. You may have your peaceful demonstration and speechmaking there." The demonstrators were also advised that if they did not heed these orders they would face arrest. The response from many in the crowd, according to a police observer, was to scream and shout obscenities. A Chicago attorney who was watching the scene recalls that when the announcements were broadcast, "No one moved." The deputy superintendent then made another announcement: "Will any non-demonstrators, anyone who is not a part of this group, any newsmen, please leave the group." Despite the crowd noise, the loud-speaker announcements were "loud and plainly heard," according to an officer.

While this was happening on Michigan Avenue, a separate police line had begun to move east toward the the crowd from the block of Balbo that lies between Michigan and Wabash along the north side of the Hilton.

Just as the police in front of the Hilton were confronted with some sit-downs on the south side of the intersection of Balbo and Michigan, the police unit coming into the intersection on Balbo met the sitting demonstrators. What happened then is subject to dispute between the police and some other witnesses.

The Balbo police unit commander asserts that he informed the sit-downs and surrounding demonstrators that if they did not leave, they would be arrested. He repeated the order and was met with a chant of "Hell no, we won't go." Quickly a police van swung into the intersection immediately behind the police line, the officers opened the door at the rear of the wagon. The deputy chief "ordered the arrest process to start."

"Immediately upon giving this order," the deputy chief later informed his superiors, "we were pelted with rocks, bottles, cans filled with unknown liquids and other debris, which forced the officers to defend themselves from injury. . . . My communications officer was slugged from behind by one of these persons, receiving injuries to his right eye and cheekbone."

The many films and video tapes of this time period present a picture which does not correspond completely with the police view. First, the films do not show a mob moving west on Balbo; they show the street as rather clean of the demonstrators and bystanders, although the sidewalks themselves on both sides of the street are crowded. Second, they show the police walking east on Balbo, stopping in formation, awaiting the arrival of the van and starting to make arrests on order. A total of 25 seconds elapses between

their coming to a halt and the first arrests.

Also, a St. Louis reporter who was watching from inside the Haymarket lounge agrees that the police began making arrests "in formation," apparently as "the result of an order to clear the intersection." Then, the reporter adds, "from this apparently controlled beginning the police began beating people indiscriminately. They grabbed and beat anyone they could get hold of."

"The crowd tried to reverse gears," the reporter says. "People began falling over each other. I was in the first rank between police and the crowd and was caught in the first surge. I went down as I tried to retreat. I covered my head, tried to protect my glasses which had fallen partially off, and hoped that I would not be clubbed. I tried to dig into the humanity that had fallen with me. You could hear shouting and screaming. As soon as I could, I scrambled to my feet and tried to move away from the police. I saw a youth running by me also trying to flee. A policeman clubbed him as he passed, but he kept running.

"The cops were saying, 'Move! I said, move, god dammit! Move, you bastards!'" A representative of the ACLU who was positioned among the demonstrators says the police "were cussing a lot" and were shouting, "Kill, kill, kill, kill, kill!" A reporter for the *Chicago Daily News* said after the melee that he, too, heard this cry. A demonstrator remembers the police swinging their clubs and screaming, "Get the hell out of here." . . . "Get the fuck out of here." . . . "Move your fucking ass!"

The crowd frantically eddied in a halfmoon shape in an effort to escape the officers coming in from the west. A UPI reporter who was on the southern edge of the crowd on Michigan Avenue, said that the advancing police "began pushing the crowd south." A cherry bomb burst overhead. The demonstrators strained against the deputy superintendent of police's line south of the Balbo-Michigan intersection. "When I reached that line," says the UPI reporter, "I heard a voice from behind it say, 'Push them back, move them back!' I was then prodded and shoved with nightsticks back in a northerly direction, toward the still advancing line of police."

"Police were marching this way and that," a correspondent from a St. Louis paper says. "They obviously had instructions to clear the street, but apparently contradicting one another in the directions the crowd was supposed to be sent."

The deputy superintendent of police recalls that he ordered his men to "hold your line there" . . . "stand fast" . . . "Lieutenant, hold your men steady there!" These orders, he said, were not obeyed by all. He said that police disregarded his order to return to the police lines—the beginning of what he says was the only instance in which he personally saw police discipline collapse. He estimates that ten to 15 officers moved off on individual forays against demonstrators.

The Clash

Thus, at 7:57 p.m., with two groups of club-wielding police converging simultaneously and independently, the battle was joined. The portions of the throng out of the immediate area of conflict largely stayed put and took up the chant, "The whole world is watching," but the intersection fragmented into a collage of violence.

Re-creating the precise chronology of the next few moments is impossible. But there is no question that a violent street battle ensued.

People ran for cover and were struck by police as they passed. Clubs were swung indiscriminately.

"I saw squadrons of policemen coming from everywhere," a secretary said. "The crowd around me suddenly began to run. Some of us, including myself, were pushed back onto the sidewalk and then all the way up against . . . the Blackstone Hotel along Michigan Avenue. I thought the crowd had panicked."

"Fearing that I would be crushed against the wall of the building . . . I somehow managed to work my way . . . to the edge of the street . . . and saw police everywhere.

"As I looked up I was hit for the first time on the head from behind by what must have been a billy club. I was then knocked down and while on my hands and knees, I was hit around the shoulders. I got up again, stumbling and was hit again. As I was falling, I heard words to the effect of 'move, move' and the horrible sound of cracking billy clubs.

"After my second fall, I remember being kicked in the back, and I looked up and noticed that many policemen around me had no badges on. The police kept hitting me on the head."

Eventually she made her way to an alley behind the Blackstone and finally, "bleeding badly from my head wound," was driven by a friend to a hospital emergency room. Her treatment included the placing of 12 stitches.

A lawyer says that he was in a group of demonstrators in the park just south of Balbo when he heard a police officer shout, "Let's get 'em!" Three policemen ran up, "singled out one girl and as she was running away from them, beat her on the back of the head. As she fell to the ground, she was struck by the nightsticks of these officers." A male friend of hers then came up yelling at the police. The witness said, "He was arrested. The girl was left in the area lying on the ground."

A *Milwaukee Journal* reporter says in his statement, "when the police managed to break up groups of protesters they pursued individuals and beat them with clubs. Some police pursued individual demonstrators as far as a block . . . and beat them. . . . In many cases it appeared to me that when police had finished beating the protesters they were pursuing, they then attacked, indiscriminately, any civilian who happened to be standing nearby. Many of these were not involved in the demonstrations."

In balance, there is no doubt that police discipline broke during the melee. The deputy superintendent of police states that—although this was the only time he saw discipline collapse—when he ordered his men to stand fast, some did not respond and began to sally through the crowd, clubbing people they came upon. An inspector-observer from the Los Angeles Police Department, stated that during this week, "The restraint of the police both as individual members and as an organization, was beyond reason." However, he said that on this occasion:

There is no question but that many officers acted without restraint and exerted force beyond that necessary under the circumstances. The leadership at the point of conflict did little to prevent such conduct and the direct control of officers by first-line supervisors was virtually non-existent.

The deputy superintendent of police has been described by several observers as being very upset by individual policemen who beat demonstrators. He pulled his men off the demonstrators, shouting "Stop, damn it, stop. For Christ's sake, stop it."

"It seemed to me," an observer says, "that only a saint could have swallowed the vile remarks to the officers. However, they went to extremes in clubbing the Yippies. I saw them move into the park, swatting away with clubs at girls and boys lying in the grass. More than once I witnessed two officers pulling at the arms of a Yippie until the arms almost left their sockets, then; as the officers put the Yippie in a police van, a third jabbed a riot stick into the groin of the youth being arrested. It was evident that the Yippie was not resisting arrest."

"In one incident, a young man, who apparently had been maced, staggered across Michigan . . . helped by a companion. The man collapsed. . . . Medical people from the volunteer medical organization rushed out to help him. A police officer (a sergeant, I think) came rushing forward, followed by the two other nightstick-brandishing policemen and yelled, 'Get him out of here; this ain't a hospital.' The medical people fled, half dragging and half carrying the young man with them. . . ."

During the course of arrests, one girl lost her skirt. Although there have been unverified reports of police ripping the clothes from female demonstrators, this is the only incident on news film of any woman being disrobed in the course of arrest.

While violence was exploding in the street, the crowd, wedged behind the police sawhorses along the northeast edge of the Hilton, was experiencing a terror all its own.

Early in the evening, this group had consisted in large part of curious bystanders. But following the police surges into the demonstrators clogging the intersection, protesters had crowded the ranks behind the horses in their flight from the police.

From force of numbers, this sidewalk crowd of 150 to 200 persons was pushing down toward the Hilton's front entrance. Policemen whose orders were to keep the entrance clear were pushing with sawhorses. Other police and fleeing demonstrators were pushed from the north in the effort to clear the intersection. Thus, the crowd was wedged against the hotel, with the hotel itself on the west, sawhorses on the southeast and police on the northeast.

Films show that one policeman elbowed his way to where he could rescue a girl of about ten years of age from the vise-like press of the crowd. He cradled her in his arms and carried her to a point of relative safety 20 feet away. The crowd itself "passed up" an elderly woman to a low ledge.

"I was crowded in with the group of screaming, frightened people," an onlooker states, "We jammed against each other, trying to press into the brick wall of the hotel. As we stood there breathing hard . . . a policeman calmly walked the length of the barricade with a can of chemical spray [evidently mace] in his hand. Unbelievably, he was spraying at us." Photos reveal several policemen using mace against the crowd. "Some of the police then turned and attacked the crowd," a Chicago reporter says. A young cook caught in the crowd relates that:

"The police began picking people off. They would pull individuals to the ground and begin beating them. A medic wearing a white coat and an armband with a red cross was grabbed, beaten and knocked to the ground. His whole face was covered with blood."

As a result, a part of the crowd was trapped in front of the Conrad Hilton and pressed hard against a big plate glass window of the Haymarket Lounge. A reporter who was sitting inside said, "Frightened men and women banged . . . against the window. A captain of the fire department inside told us to get back from the window, that it might get knocked in. As I backed away a few feet I could see a smudge of blood on the glass outside."

With a sickening crack, the window shattered, and screaming men and women tumbled through, some cut badly by jagged glass. The police came after them. "A patrolman ran up to where I was sitting," said a man with a cut leg. "I protested that I was injured and could not walk, attempting to show him my leg. He screamed that he would show me I could walk. He grabbed me by the shoulder and literally hurled me through the door of the bar into the lobby. . . .

"I stumbled out into what seemed to be a main lobby. The young lady I was with and I were both immediately set upon by what I can only presume were plainclothes police. . . . We were cursed by these individuals and thrown through another door into an outer lobby." Eventually a McCarthy aide took him to the 15th floor.

In the heat of all this, probably few were aware of the Haymarket's advertising slogan: "A place where good guys take good girls to dine in the lusty, rollicking atmosphere of fabulous Old Chicago. . . ."

There is little doubt that during this whole period, beginning at 7:57 p.m. and lasting for nearly 20 minutes, the preponderance of violence came from the police. It was not entirely a one-way battle, however.

Firecrackers were thrown at police. Trash baskets were set on fire and rolled and thrown at them. In one case, a gun was taken from a policeman by a demonstrator.

"Some hippies," said a patrolman in his statement, "were hit by other hippies who were throwing rocks at the police." Films reveal that when police were chasing demonstrators into Grant Park, one young man upended a sawhorse and heaved it at advancing officers. At one point the deputy superintendent of police was knocked down by a thrown sawhorse. At least one police three-wheeler was tipped over. One of the demonstrators says that "people in the park were prying up cobblestones and breaking them. One person piled up cobblestones in his arms and headed toward the police." Witnesses reported that people were throwing "anything they could lay their hands on. From the windows of the Hilton and Blackstone hotels, toilet paper, wet towels, even ash trays came raining down." A police lieutenant stated that he saw policemen bombarded with "rocks, cherry bombs, jars of vasoline, jars of mayonnaise and pieces of wood torn from the yellow barricades falling in the street." He, too, noticed debris falling from the hotel windows.

A number of police officers were injured, either by flying missiles or in personal attacks. One, for example, was helping a fellow officer "pick up a hippie when another hippie gave [me] a heavy kick, aiming for my groin." The blow struck the officer partly on the leg and partly in the testicles. He went down, and the "hippie" who kicked him escaped.

In another instance, a Chicago police reporter said in his statement, "a police officer reached down and grabbed a person who dove forward and bit the officer on the leg. . . . Three or four fellow policemen came to his aid. They had to club the demonstrator to make him break his clamp on the officer's leg." In another case, the witness saw a demonstrator "with a big mop of hair hit a police officer with an old British Army type metal helmet." The reporter said he also heard "hissing sounds from the demonstrators as if they were spraying the police." Later he found empty lacquer spray and hair spray cans on the street. Also he heard policemen cry out, "They're kicking us with knives in their shoes." Later, he said, he found that demonstrators "had actually inserted razor blades in their shoes."

By 8:15 p.m., the intersection was in police control. One group of police proceeded east on Balbo, clearing the street and splitting the crowd into two. Because National Guard lines still barred passage over the Balbo Street bridge, most of the demonstrators fled into Grant Park. A Guardsman estimates that 5,000 remained in the park across from the Hilton. Some clubbing by police occurred; a demonstrator says he saw a brick hurled at police; but few arrests were made.

Wild in the Streets

Now, with police lines beginning to re-form, the deputy superintendent directed the police units to advance north on Michigan. He says announcements were again made to clear the area and warnings given that those refusing to do so would be arrested. To this, according to a patrolman who was present, "The hippie group yelled 'fuck you' in unison."

Police units formed up. National Guard intelligence officers on the site called for Guard assistance. At 8:30 the Secret Service reported trucks full of Guard troops from Soldier Field moving north on Michigan Avenue to the Conrad Hilton and additional units arrived about 20 minutes later. The troops included the same units that had seen action earlier in the day after the bandshell rally and had later been moved to 22nd Street.

By 8:55 p.m., the Guard had taken up positions in a U-shaped formation, blocking Balbo at Michigan and paralleling the Hilton and Grant Park—a position that was kept until 4 a.m. Thursday. Although bayonets were affixed when the troops first hit the street, they were quickly removed. Explains a Guardsman who was there: "The bayonets had gotten in our way when we were on the Congress Street bridge." At one point, a demonstrator tried to "take the muzzle off" one of the Guardsmen's rifle. "All the time the demonstrators were trying to talk to us. They said 'join us' or 'fuck the draft.' We were told not to talk to anyone in the crowd." One Guard unit followed behind the police as a backup group.

With the police and Guard at its rear, the crowd fractured in several directions as it moved away from Balbo and Michigan. Near Michigan and Monroe another casualty center had been set up in the headquarters of the Church Federation of Greater Chicago. This, plus the melding of the crowds northbound on Michigan and east-bound on Monroe, brought about 1,000 persons to the west side of Michigan between Adams and Monroe, facing the Art Institute. There were few demonstrators on the east side of Michigan.

At 9:25 p.m., the police commander ordered a sweep of Michigan Avenue south from Monroe. At about this same time the police still had lines on both the west and east sides of Michigan in front of the Hilton and additional National Guard troops had arrived at 8th Street.

At 9:57 p.m., the demonstrators still on Michigan Avenue, prodded along by the southward sweep of the police, began marching back to Grant Park, chanting "Back to the park." By 10:10 p.m., an estimated 800 to 1,000 demonstrators had gathered in front of the Hilton.

By then, two city street sweeping trucks had rumbled up and down the street in front of the hotel, cleaning up the residue of violence—shoes, bottles, rocks, tear gas handkerchiefs. A police captain said the debris included: "Bases and pieces of broken bottles, a piece of board (1″ × 4″ × 14″), an 18-inch length of metal pipe, a 24-inch stick with a protruding sharpened nail, a 12-inch length of ½-inch diameter pipe, pieces of building bricks, an 18-inch stick with a razor blade protruding . . . several plastic balls somewhat smaller than tennis balls containing approximately 15 to 20 sharpened nails driven into the ball from various angles." When the delegates returned to the Hilton, they saw none of the litter of the battle.

As the crowd had dispersed from the Hilton the big war of Michigan and Balbo was, of course, over. But for those in the streets, as the rivulets of the crowd forked through the areas north of the hotel, there were still battles to be fought. Police violence and police baiting were some time in abating. Indeed, some of the most vicious incidents occurred in this "post-war" period.

The U.S. Attorney states that as the crowd moved north on Michigan Avenue, "they pelted the police with missiles of all sorts, rocks, bottles, firecrackers. When a policeman was struck, the crowd would cheer. The policemen in the line were dodging and jumping to avoid being hit." A police sergeant told the FBI that even a telephone was hurled from the crowd at the police.

In the first block north of the Hilton, recalls a man who was standing outside a Michigan Avenue restaurant, demonstrators "menaced limousines, calling the occupants 'scum,' telling them they didn't belong in Chicago and to go home."

As the police skirmish line moved north, and drew nearer to the squad cars, the lieutenant said, he saw several persons shoving paper through the cars' broken windows—in his opinion, a prelude to setting the cars on fire. A theology student who was in the crowd states that "a demonstrator took a fire extinguisher and sprayed inside the car. Then he put paper on the ground under the gas tank. . . . People shouted at him to stop." To break up the crowd, the lieutenant said, he squirted tear gas from an aerosol container and forced the demonstrators back.

"Two or three policemen, one with a white shirt, advanced on the crowd," one witness said, "The white-shirted one squirted mace in arcs back and forth before him."

A cameraman for the *Chicago Daily News* photographed a woman cowering after she had been sprayed with mace. A *News* representative states that the officer administering the mace, whom the photographers identified as a police lieutenant, then turned and directed the spray at the cameraman. The cameraman shot a photograph of this. The police lieutenant states that he does not remember this incident.

A priest who was in the crowd says he saw a "boy, about 14 or 15 white, standing on top of an automobile yelling something which was unidentifiable. Suddenly a policeman forced him down from the car and beat him to the ground by striking him three or four times with a nightstick. Other police joined in . . . and they eventually shoved him to a police van."

A well-dressed woman saw this incident and spoke angrily to a nearby police captain. As she spoke, another policeman came up from behind her and sprayed something in her face with an aerosol can. He then clubbed her to the ground. He and two other policemen then dragged her along the ground to the same paddy wagon and threw her in.

"At the corner of Congress Plaza and Michigan," states a doctor, "was gathered a group of people, number between 30 and 40. They were trapped against a railing by several policemen on motorcycles. The police charged the people on motorcycles and struck about a dozen of them, knocking several of them down. About 20 standing there jumped over the railing. On the other side of the railing was a three-to-four-foot drop. None of the people who were struck by the motorcycles appeared to be seriously injured. However, several of them were limping as if they had been run over on their feet."

Reporter Witnesses Attack

A UPI reporter witnessed these attacks, too. He relates in his statement that one officer, "with a smile on his face and a fanatical look in his eyes, was standing on the three-wheel cycle, shouting, 'Wahoo, wahoo,' and trying to run down people on the sidewalk." The reporter says he was chased 30 feet by the cycle.

A few seconds later he "turned around and saw a policeman with a raised billy stick." As he swung around, the police stick grazed his head and struck his shoulders. As he was on his knees, he says someone stepped on his back.

A Negro policeman helped him to his feet, the reporter says. The policeman told him, "You know, man I didn't do this. One of the white cops did it." Then, the reporter quotes the officer as saying, "You know what? After this

is all over, I'm quitting the force."

An instant later, the shouting officer on the motorcycle swung by again, and the reporter dove into a doorway for safety.

Near this same intersection, a Democratic delegate from Oklahoma was surrounded in front of his hotel by about ten persons, two of them with long hair and beards. He states that they encircled him for several minutes and subjected him to verbal abuse because they felt he "represented the establishment" and was "somewhat responsible for the alleged police brutality." The delegate stood mute and was eventually rescued by a policeman.

At Van Buren, a college girl states, "demonstrators were throwing things at passing police cars, and I saw one policeman hit in the face with a rock. A small paddy wagon drove up with only one policeman in it, and the crowd began rocking the wagon. The cop fell out and was surrounded by the crowd, but no effort was made to hurt him."

At Jackson, says the graduate student quoted earlier, "People got into the street on their knees and prayed, including several ministers who were dressed in clerical garb. These people, eight or ten of them, were arrested. This started a new wave of dissent among the demonstrators, who got angry. Many went forward to be arrested voluntarily; others were taken forcibly and some were beaten. . . . Objects were being thrown directly at police, including cans, bottles and paper."

"I was in the street," a witness who was near the intersection states, "when a fire in a trash basket appeared. . . . In a few minutes, two fire engines passed south through the crowd, turned west on Van Buren and stopped. They were followed by two police wagons which stopped in the middle of the block. As I walked north past the smaller of the two wagons, it began to rock." (The wagon also was being pelted by missiles, the U.S. Attorney states, and "PIGS" was painted on its sides.)

"I retreated onto the east sidewalk," the witness continued. Two policemen jumped out of the smaller wagon and one was knocked down by a few demonstrators, while other demonstrators tried to get these demonstrators away. The two policemen got back to the wagon, the crowd having drawn well back around them." The U.S. Attorney's report states that one of the policemen was "stomped" by a small group of the mob.

A young woman who was there and who had attended the bandshell rally earlier in the afternoon states that the crowd rocked the wagon for some time, while its officers stayed inside. "Then," she says, "the driver came out wildly swinging his club and shouting. About ten people jumped on him. He was kicked pretty severely and was downed. When he got up he was missing his club and his hat."

A police commander says that at about this moment he received "an urgent radio message" from an officer inside the van. He radioed that "demonstrators were standing on the hood of his wagon . . . and were preparing to smash the windshield with a baseball bat," the commander recalled. The officer also told him that the demonstrators were attempting to overturn the squadrol and that the driver "was hanging on the door in a state of shock." The commander told the officer that assistance was on the way.

"I heard a '10-1' call on either my radio or one of the other hand sets being carried by other men with me," the U.S. Attorney states, "and then heard, 'Car 100-sweep!' [Car 100 was assigned to the police commander.] With a roar of motors, squads, vans and three-wheelers came from east, west and north into the block north of Jackson."

"Almost immediately a CTA bus filled with police came over the Jackson Drive bridge and the police formed a line in the middle of the street," says a witness. "I heard shouts that the police had rifles and that they had cocked and pumped them. Demonstrators began to run."

"I ran north of Jackson . . . just as police were clearing the intersection and forming a line across Michigan," says the witness quoted above. "The police who had formed a line facing east in the middle of Michigan charged, yelling and clubbing into the crowd, running at individuals and groups who did not run before them."

"As the fray intensified around the intersection of Michigan and Jackson, a big group ran west on Jackson, with a group of blue-shirted policemen in pursuit, beating at them with clubs," says the U.S. Attorney's report. Some of the crowd ran up the alleys; some north on Wabash; and some west on Jackson to State with the police in pursuit."

An Assistant U.S. Attorney later reported that "the demonstrators were running as fast as they could but were unable to get out of the way because of the crowds in front of them. I observed the police striking numerous individuals, perhaps 20 or 30. I saw three fall down and then be overrun by the police. I observed two demonstrators who had multiple cuts on their heads. We assisted one who was in shock into a passer-by's car.

"A TV mobile truck appeared . . . and the police became noticeably more restrained, holding their clubs at waist level rather than in the air," a witness relates. "As the truck disappeared . . . the head-clubbing tactics were resumed."

One demonstrator states that he ran off Michigan Avenue on to Jackson. He says he and his wife ran down Jackson and were admitted, hesitantly, into a restaurant. They seated themselves at a table by the window facing onto Jackson and, while sitting at the table, observed a group of people running down Jackson with policemen following them and striking generally at the crowd with their batons. At one instance, he saw a policeman strike a priest in the head with a baton.

At the intersection of Jackson and Wabash, said a student whose wife was beaten in the race from Michigan, "the police came from all four directions and attacked the crowd. Demonstrators were beaten and run to the paddy wagons. I saw a black policeman go berserk. He charged blindly at the group of demonstrators and made two circles through the crowd, swinging wildly at anything."

An Assistant U.S. Attorney watching the action on various side streets reported, "I observed police officers clearing people westward . . . using their clubs to strike people on the back of the head and body on several occasions. Once a policeman ran alongside a young girl. He held her by the shoulder of her jacket and struck at her a few times as they were both running down the sidewalk.

A traffic policeman on duty on Michigan Avenue says that the demonstrators who had continued north often surrounded cars and buses attempting to move south along Michigan Avenue. Many males in the crowd, he says, exposed their penises to passers-by and other members of the crowd. They would run up to cars clogged by the crowd and show their private parts to the passengers.

To men, the officer says, they shouted such questions as, "How would you like me to fuck your wife?" and "How would you like to fuck a man?" Many of the demonstrators also rocked the automobiles in an effort to tip them over. A policeman states that bags of feces and urine were dropped on the police from the building.

As the crowd moved south again on Michigan, a traffic policeman, who was in the vicinity of Adams Street, recalls, "They first took control of the lions in front of the Art Institute. They climbed them and shouted things like, "Let's fuck" and "Fuck, fuck, fuck!" At this same intersection, an officer rescued two Loop secretaries from being molested by demonstrators. He asked them, "What are you doing here?" They replied, "We wanted to see what the hippies were like." His response: "How do you like what you saw?"

Old Town: The Mixture as Before

While all that was going on in and around Grant Park, Lincoln Park on Wednesday was quiet and uncrowded: but there was sporadic violence in Old Town again that night. Two University of Minnesota students who wandered through the park in the morning say they heard small groups of demonstrators saying things like "Fuck the pigs," and "Kill them all," but by this time that was not unusual. They also heard a black man addressing a group of demonstrators. He outlined plans for the afternoon, and discussed techniques for forming skirmish lines, disarming police officers, and self defense.

Also during the morning Abbie Hoffman was arrested at the Lincoln Hotel Coffee Shop, 1800 North Clark, and charged with resisting arrest and disorderly conduct. According to Hoffman's wife, Anita, she and her husband and a friend were eating breakfast when three policemen entered the coffee shop and told Hoffman they had received three complaints about an obscene word written on Hoffman's forehead. The word was "Fuck." Hoffman says he printed the word on his forehead to keep cameramen from taking his picture.

Most of the violence against police, from all reports, was the work of gang-type youths called "greasers." They dismantled police barricades to lure squad cars down Stockton Drive, where one observer says "punks engaged in some of the most savage attacks on police that had been seen." Ministers and hippies in the area were directing traffic around the barricades and keeping people from wandering into the danger area. Two ministers in particular were trying to "keep the cool."

Back at The Hilton

By 10:30 p.m., most of the action was centered once more in Grant Park across from the Hilton, where several hundred demonstrators and an estimated 1,500 spectators gathered to listen to what one observer describes as "unexciting speeches." There was the usual singing and shouting. Twice during the evening police and Hilton security officers went into the hotel and went to quarters occupied by McCarthy personnel—once to protest the ripping of sheets to bandage persons who had been injured and a second time to try to locate persons said to be lobbing ashtrays out of the windows. But compared to the earlier hours of the evening, the rest of the night was quiet.

In Grant Park, the sullen crowd sat facing the hotel. Someone with a transistor radio was listening to the roll call vote of states on the nomination and broadcasting the count to the rest of the throng over a bullhorn. There were loud cheers for Ted Kennedy, McCarthy, McGovern and Phillips ("He's a black man," said the youth with the bullhorn.) Boos and cries of "Dump the Hump" arose whenever Humphrey received votes. "When Illinois was called," says the trained observer, "no one could hear totals because of booing and the chant, 'To Hell with Daley.' "

During this time the police line was subject to considerable verbal abuse from within the crowd and a witness says that both black and white agitators at the edge of the crowd tried to kick policemen with razor blades embedded in their shoes. Periodically several policemen would make forays into the crowd, punishing demonstrators they thought were involved.

At about "Louisiana," as the roll call vote moved with quickening pace toward the climax of Humphrey's nomi-

nation, the crowd grew restless, recalls a trained observer. About this same time, according to the Log, the police skirmish line began pushing the demonstrators farther east into the park. A report of an officer being struck by a nail ball was received by police. Film taken at about this time shows an officer being hit by a thrown missile, later identified as a chunk of concrete with a steel reinforcement rod in it. The blow knocked him down and, as he fell, the crowd cheered and yelled, "More!" The chant, "Kill the pigs," filled the air.

"At 'Oklahoma,' " recalls an observer, "the Yippie on the bullhorn said, 'Marshals ready. Don't move. Stay seated.' "

"The front line rose [facing the police] and locked arms, and the others stayed seated. Humphrey was over the top with Pennsylvania, and someone in the Hilton rang a cow bell at the demonstrators. Boos went up, as did tension. A bus load of police arrived. Others standing in front of the Hilton crossed Michigan and lined up behind those in front of the demonstrators.

"The chant of 'Sit down, sit down' went out. An American flag was raised on a pole upside down. Wandering began among demonstrators and the chant continued.

Shortly before midnight, while Benjamin Ortiz was speaking, National Guard troops of the 2/129 Inf. came west on Balbo to Michigan to replace the police in front of the Hilton. "For the first time," says an observer, "machine guns mounted on trucks were pulled up directly in front of the demonstrators, just behind the police lines. The machine guns, and the Guard's mesh-covered jeeps with barbed wire fronts made the demonstrators angry and nervous. Bayonets were readied. In films of this period the word "pig" can be seen written on the street.

"Ortiz continued, 'Dig this man, just 'cause you see some different pigs coming here, don't get excited. We're going to sleep here, sing here, sex here, live here!' "

As the police moved off, one of the first Guard maneuvers was to clear demonstrators from Michigan's east sidewalk. This was done to allow pedestrian traffic. The crowd reacted somewhat hostilely to the maneuver, but by and large, the demonstrators semed to view the Guard as helpless men who had been caught up in the events and did not treat them as badly as they had the police. Having secured the sidewalk, the guards shortly retired to the east curb of Michigan Avenue. A line of "marshals" sat down at the edge of the grass at the feet of the guards. Access to the hotel was restored and people began to move from the hotel to the park and vice versa. By now, there were an estimated 4,000 persons assembled across from the Hilton. Most of the crowd sat down in a mass and became more orderly, singing "America" and "God Bless America." McCarthy supporters joined the crowd and were welcomed.

By 12:20 a.m., Thursday, the crowd had declined to 1,500 and was considered under control. By 12:33 a.m., the police department had retired from the streets and the Guard took over the responsibility of holding Michingan from Balbo to 8th Street. At 12:47 a.m., another conting- ent of Guard troops arrived at the Hilton. Delegates were returning and were being booed unless they could be identified as McCarthy or McGovern supporters. Those delegates were cheered and asked to join the group.

The crowd grew in number. By 1:07 a.m., the Secret Service estimated 2,000 persons in the park across from the hotel. Ten minutes later the crowd had grown by another 500. Those in the park were "listening to speeches— orderly" according to the log.

The Violence Commission: Internal Politics and Public Policy

Jerome H. Skolnick

The 1960s are already infamous for assassinations, crime in the streets, student rebellion, black militancy, wars of liberation, law and order—and national commissions. We had the Warren Commission, the Crime Commission, the Riot Commission and the Violence Commission; and the point about them was that they were among the major responses of government to the social dislocations of the decade. Millions of people followed the work of these commissions with interest and gave at least summary attention to their reports. Social scientists were also interested in commissions, though skeptical about their value. Most would probably agree with Sidney and Beatrice Webb's description of Royal Commissions, "These bodies are seldom designed for scientific research; they are primarily political organs, with political objects."

I share this view, yet I have worked with three commis-

sions, albeit under very special arrangements guaranteeing freedom of publication. The discussion that follows is partly analytical and partly autobiographical, especially where I discuss my work as director of the task force on "Violent Aspects of Protest and Confrontation" for the Violence Commission. If the autobiography stands out, that is because I did not participate in commissions to observe them. I studied the phenomena at issue—crime, police, protest and confrontation—not commissions. Still, my experience may be helpful in understanding commission structures, processes and dilemmas.

Constituencies

Commissions have three functioning groups: commissioners, the executive staff, the research staff, with overlapping but distinctive interests.

Andrew Kopkind has recently written that President Lyndon B. Johnson chose the 11 commissioners for his National Advisory Commission on Civil Disorders because of their remarkable qualities of predictable moderation. The Violence Commission, chaired by Dr. Milton Eisenhower, was perhaps even more predictably "moderate" than the Riot Commission. It included a member of the southern and congressional establishment, Congressman Hale Boggs; Archbishop, now Cardinal, Terence J. Cooke, Francis Cardinal Spellman's successor; Ambassador Patricia Harris, standing for both the political woman and the Negro establishment; Senator Philip A. Hart, Democrat of Michigan, associated with the liberal establishment in the Senate; Judge A. Leon Higginbotham, a Negro and a federal judge from Philadelphia; Eric Hoffer, the president's favorite philosopher, presenting the backlash voice of the American workingman; Senator Roman Hruska, Republican of Nebraska, a leading right-wing Republican; and Albert E. Jenner, Jr., prominent in the American Bar Association and in Chicago legal affairs. In addition, there was Republican Congressman William M. McCulloch of Ohio, who had served on the Kerner Commission and was the only overlapping member of both commissions. In response to criticisms that the Riot Commission contained no social scientists, Dr. W. Walter Menninger was appointed, although he is a practicing psychiatrist and not a social scientist. Finally, there were Judge Ernest W. McFarland, the man whom Lyndon Baines Johnson had replaced in the House of Representatives, and another Texan, Leon Jaworski, a close personal adviser to the president and a prominent and conservative lawyer.

Obviously, the commissioners themselves cannot perform the investigative and analytical work of the commission. Commissioners are chosen because apparently they represent various economic and political interests, not because they have distinguished themselves as scholars or experts. In fact, they do not "represent" anyone. What they best mirror is a chief executive's conception of pluralist America.

Moreover, even if a commissioner should have the ability to do the research, he or she usually has other demands on their time. Inevitably, then, the staff of the commission does the work—all of the leg work and the research and most of the writing of the final report, with, of course, the commission's approval.

The staffs of both the Riot Commission and the Violence Commission were similar. The executive staff, working out of Washington, was charged with getting the research and writing job done and with organizing the time of the commission. In each case, the director of the executive staff was a leading Washington attorney who had ties with the Johnson administration, David Ginsburg for the Riot Commission, Lloyd Cutler for the Violence Commission. Moreover, younger attorneys were named as their closest associates.

There had been considerable friction in the Riot Commission between the research staff and the executive staff, as well as between both and the commissioners. According to Andrew Kopkind, the social scientists under Research Director Robert Shellow drafted a document called "The Harvest of American Racism" which went further than most top staff officials thought prudent in charging that racism permeated American institutions. "Harvest" characterized the riots as the first step in a developing black revolution in which Negroes will feel, as the draft put it, that "it is legitimate and necessary to use violence against the social order. A truly revolutionary spirit has begun to take hold . . . and unwillingness to compromise or wait any longer, to risk death rather than have their people continue in a subordinate status." According to Kopkind, both Ginsburg and Victor Palmieri, his deputy director, admitted that they were appalled when they read "Harvest." Shortly after its submission many of the 120 investigators and social scientists were "released" from the commission staff in December 1967 (on public grounds that money was needed to pursue the war in Vietnam). But Kopkind says that there is every reason to believe that the "releasing" was done by Palmieri (with Ginsburg's concurrence) because of the failure of Shellow's group to produce an "acceptable" analytical section. The commissioners them-selves are reported to have known little of the firing or of the controversy surrounding it but were persuaded by Gins-burg to go along with it.

I tell this story only because it bears on the central ques-tion of what effects, if any, informed researchers and writ-ers can have on the final reports of commissions, the pub-lic face they turn to the world. Kopkind, for example, ar-gues that the "Harvest" incident proves that the *Kerner Re-port* would have been "liberal" regardless of events pre-ceding its final writing. He concludes, "The structure of the Commission and the context in which it operated sug-gest that its tone could have hardly been other than 'liberal.' The finished product almost exactly reproduced the ideo-logical sense given it by President Johnson more than half a year earlier. The choice of Commissioners, staff, consul-tants and contractors led in the same direction." Yet that outcome is not at all evident from the rest of Kopkind's analysis, which argues, for example, that the commissioners were selected for their predictable moderation, that one commissioner, Charles Thornton, attempted to torpedo the report just before its launching and that the findings of the report were patently offensive to President Johnson. It is at least arguable that the "liberalism" of the final report was not inevitable, that it might have been far more on the conservative side of "moderate" and that the "Harvest" document had something to do with moving it to the Left.

The Eisenhower Violence Commission

When Senator Robert F. Kennedy was assassinated and the president appointed yet another commission, many ob-servers were suspicious. Was this the only response that Washington could give to domestic tragedy? Even the press gave the Violence Commission unfavorable publicity. The commissioners seemed even more conservative than the riot commissioners. Some considered the commission a devious plot by President Johnson to reverse or smudge the inter-pretation of civil disorders offered by the Riot Commission.

Furthermore, what could the Violence Commission say that hadn't already been said by the Riot Commission? The distinction between civil disorder and violence was not, and still isn't, self-evident. Moreover, because of the flap over the firing of the social scientists on the Kerner Commission, many of that community were deeply and un-derstandably dubious about the possibility of doing an in-tellectually respectable job under commission auspices.

The executive staff saw this problem and coped with it, first, by establishing the position of research director, so

that social scientists (James F. Short, Jr., jointly with Mar-vin Wolfgang, as it turned out) occupied a place in the hierarchy of the executive staff, a club usually limited to corporation lawyers. Authority still rested with the execu-tive director, but the research directors performed four im-portant functions; they initiated the commission policy of independent task forces with freedom of publication; they helped select the social science staff; they served as liaison between the social scientists, the executive staff and the commissioners; and they served as good critics and col-leagues.

Furthermore, they promoted another departure from Kerner Commission practice, namely that social scientists and lawyers are the co-directors of task forces.

Some additional comments are warranted here because organizational structures and rules may seriously influence intellectual autonomy. University social scientists with little legal or governmental experience may assume that freedom to write and publish follows from well-intentioned assur-ances of future support. Yet as one experienced man with whom I shared a panel recently put it: "He who glitters may one day be hung."

The social scientist must understand the ways he can be hung and protect himself accordingly. First, his materials can be used and distorted. Second, his name can be used, but his material and advice ignored. This is particularly possible when social scientists hold highranking but rela-tively powerless titles on the commission. Ultimately, they are placed in the dilemma of seeming to endorse the final product. (In the Violence Commission, for example, the names of James F. Short, Jr., and Marvin Wolfgang seem-ingly "endorse" the scholarly merit of the final report. In addition, the presence of a recognized social science staff does the same. To this extent, we were all "co-opted," since none of us, including Short and Wolfgang, were responsi-ble for the final report.) Third, he may experience subtle (sometimes not so subtle) pressures to shape or present his findings in favored directions. Finally, his work may be suppressed.

In general, one receives maximum protection with a *writ-ten* contract guaranteeing freedom of publication. Beyond that, however, experienced Washington hands can be quite charming—which holds its own dangers for one's intel-lectual independence.

From the very beginning, the executive staff expressed some doubts about the ultimate impact the commission's own report would have on public policy, or even the shape it would take. Recall that this was the summer of 1968, following the assassination of Senator Kennedy and before the national conventions of both parties. Who could foretell what future event would have what future impact on national politics? Who could, with confidence, predict the nominees for the presidency, the victor and his attitude toward the commission?

Task Force Reports

Like the able corporation lawyers they are, the executive staff came up with a prudent primary goal, a set of books called *Task Force Reports,* which they hoped could be a solid contribution to understanding the causes and prevention of violence in America. I call this goal prudent because it set a standard that was at least possible in theory. From these studies, it was felt, the commission would write its own report; the initial idea was to have each task force report provide the materials for a summary chapter for the commission report.

Modest as this plan was, it soon ran into difficulty. Commissions are usually run at a gallop. With all the best intentions and resources in the world, it is virtually impossible to complete eight books of high quality in five months, particularly when no central vision controls the research and writing. Our own report, *The Politics of Protest,* was completed on time, but we worked under enormous pressure. Still, we had several advantages.

First, a shared perspective among key staff members contributed to a fairly consistent analysis. We shared a deep skepticism about counterinsurgency views of civil disorder as a form of "deviant" pathology that needed to be stamped out as quickly as possible. On the contrary, we assumed that insurgents might conceivably be as rational as public servants. Our approach was influenced, first, by subjectivist and naturalistic perspectives in sociology, which lead one, for instance, to take into account both the point of view of the black rioter and to assume his sanity, and to assume as well the sanity of the policeman and the white militant. Second, we were influenced by revisionist histories of America, which see her as a more tumultuous and violent nation than conventional histories have taught us to believe. Finally, we were influenced by social historical critiques of the theory of collective behavior, which interpret seemingly irrational acts on the part of rioters as forms of primitive political activity, and by an emphasis upon social history in understanding such collective behavior as student protest, rather than upon analysis of "variables."

Another advantage in favor of our task force was that our headquarters was at the Center for the Study of Law and Society at Berkeley. This kept us away from the time-consuming crises of Washington, although the tie-line kept us in daily touch with events there. In addition, the center and the Berkeley campus offered a critical mass of resources that probably could not be duplicated anywhere else. Our location, then, combined with my status as independent contractor with the commission, offered a degree of independence unavailable to the other task force directors. For example, the staff members of our task force were not required to have a White House security clearance.

Finally, the staff was far from unhappy about working for a national commission. Those involved, regardless of expressions of skepticism, were not opposed to making a contribution to a national understanding of the issues involved. My contract with the government, and its contract with me, assured the staff that its best understanding of the issues would be made public.

Given time limitations, it was impossible to undertake the original research one would need for a large-scale social science project. My inclination, shared by the research directors and the executive staff, was to recruit a staff experienced in research on the areas under study. We saw the five-month period as an opportunity to summarize findings rather than to undertake original investigation.

We did, however, conduct original interviews with black militants and with police. As can be imagined, these interviews were not easily obtained. For black militants our interviewer was a man with extensive connections, but who stipulated that he would interview only if we agreed to listen to and not transcribe the tapes and make no notations of who was being interviewed. The interviews substantiated much that we suspected and served to sharpen our analytical outlook. Similarly, the interviews we held with policemen—conducted, incidentally, by a former policeman—served to fill gaps in our thesis that the police were becoming an increasingly politicized force in the United States.

I should also add that our emphasis on social history and political analysis seemed to violate some of the expectations of some portions of our audience.

Audiences and Hearings

The Politics of Protest staff worked with three audiences in mind. First, we were concerned with trying to persuade the commissioners of the validity of our findings and the validity of our analysis. They were our primary audience. Our second was the general public, an audience we had little confidence in being able to influence except,

perhaps, through persuading the commissioners. Most reports have a limited readership—and *The Politics of Protest* isn't exactly *The Love Machine*. So our third audience was the academic community and the media representatives. In the long run, the university had to be our major audience, since the report is scholarly and the media treated with publication as news, quickly displaced by other stories.

The audience for the hearings was both the commissioners and the general public. Several members of the executive staff believed that one reason the Kerner Commission failed to gain public acceptance was its failure to educate the public along the way. The "predictably moderate" commissioners had been emotionally moved in the hearings, especially by representatives of the black communities of America, but the public had never been allowed to hear this testimony. Consequently, the Violence Commission hearings were made public, and each task force was given three days for hearings.

Hearings are a form of theater. Conclusions must be presented to evoke an emotional response in both the commissioners and the wider television audience. In this respect, the planners of the hearings can be likened to the author and director of a play with strategy substituting for plot. Yet strategies can and do go awry, and so the outcome of the play is not determined, nor can one guarantee whether the effect on the audience will be tragedic or comedic.

A staff tries to get across a point of view on the subject matter. At the same time, however, it is also expected to be "objective," that is, lacking a point of view. The

expectation is that staff and commissioners will walk along fresh roads together, reaching similar conclusions. This expectation derives from the image of a trial. Such an adjudicatory model must, however, be largely fictional. The "judges," the commissioners, already have strong views and political interests, though they are supposed to be neutral. The staff, too, is supposed to lack opinions, even though it was selected because of prior knowledge.

Since strategy substitutes for plot, there really are only three possible outcomes. The play may be a flop, that is, the staff perspective is not communicated; or the perspective is communicated, but unemotional so as to merely make a record; or emotional engagement is achieved. Here social science as theater reaches its ultimate art.

Commissioners are used to hearings, are used to testimony and probably cannot be moved in any new direction unless emotionally engaged. Commissioners are culturally deprived by the privatized life of the man of power. Whatever may have been their former backgrounds, commissioners are now the establishment. They may be driven to and from work, belong to private clubs and remain out of touch with the realities of the urban and political worlds they are assumed to understand. They are both protected and deprived by social privilege.

Moreover, their usual mode of analysis is legalistic and rationalistic. Not intellectuals, they are decision makers interested in protecting the record. Furthermore, they are committed to the prevailing social, economic and political structures, although they will consider reforms of these structures and may well be brought to see contradictions within them. In addition, they are affiliated with certain political and social interests. Consequently, there are practical limits to the possibilities of persuading any of them to a novel position.

The public is another audience for the hearings, but there are also constraints on teaching the public. All that "public hearings" means is that the media are present, not the mass of the public, and the media reports only the most dramatic messages. Also, commissioners themselves become part of the cast. The TV will register an exchange between a witness and a commissioner. So a strategist (director) must anticipate what that exchange might be.

Finally, the presence of the press alters the atmosphere of the hearing room. We held mostly public hearings and some hearings in executive session. With the television cameras and the radio people and the newspaper people present, the commissioners were stiff and formal. When the press left, the commissioners visibly relaxed.

Given these conditions, how does one go about casting? First, we tried to present witnesses who represented a variety of points of view. That was elementary. But within that framework we had to decide: what kinds of witnesses representing what kinds of points of view will bring the most enlightened position with the greatest effect both on the commissioners and on the general public?

There are practical limitations in hearings. Obviously, it may not be possible to get the witness you want, or to get him for a particular day. Ira Heyman, general counsel, and I were given three days for hearings to discuss the antiwar and student movements, black militancy and the responses of the social order. This was not enough time for any of these topics to be adequately discussed. The one day of hearings on black militancy was especially inadequate, although undoubtedly the most exciting. It was also the most difficult to arrange, the most trying and the most rewarding.

Hoffer vs. the Black

First, there was some question as to whether any well-known black militant would have anything to do with the Violence Commission. Even if he should want to, anybody who stepped forward to represent the militant black community could be charged with playing a "personality" game and disavowed as representing even a segment of the black community. After much thought, we decided on Huey P. Newton, minister of defense of the Black Panther party as a widely acceptable representative of black militancy. He was willing to cooperate, politically minded and seeking opportunity to present his point of view.

Herman Blake, an assistant professor of sociology at the University of California at Santa Cruz, joined me in interviewing Newton and was to present the interview to the commissioners. Although Blake would not officially be representing the Panthers, Newton knew him, knew of his work and trusted him to make an accurate analysis of the tape of the interview that was to be played to the commission.

As it turned out, there was no problem at all. Both Blake and I, in Charles Garry's presence, interviewed Newton in the Alameda County Courthouse Jail where he was being held while standing trial for the alleged murder of an Oakland policeman.

The Newton tape, and Blake's testimony, produced an emotionally charged confrontation between Blake and Eric Hoffer and a dignified censure of Hoffer by Judge Higgin-

botham, vice-chairman of the commission.

Mr. Hoffer: I tell you there is rage among the Negroes on the waterfront. It is at the meetings when they get together. Suddenly they are repeating a ritual. A text. You are repeating it. Now I have . . . I don't know of these people, where they were brought up. All my life I was poor and I didn't live better than any Negro ever lived, I can tell you. When I was out picking cotton in the valley the Negroes were eating better than I did, lived in better houses, they had more schooling than I did . . .

Mr. Blake: Have you ever been called a nigger?

Mr. Hoffer: Let me finish it. By the way, the first man in the U.S. I think who wrote about the need to create a Negro community was in 1964 when I . . .

Mr. Blake: Why do you stop calling it a community then?

Mr. Hoffer: I say that you have to build a community. You have to build a community and you are not . . .

Mr. Blake: We can't build a community with white people like you around telling us we can't be what we are.

Mr. Hoffer: You are not going to build it by rage. You are going to build it by working together.

Mr. Blake: You are defining it.

Mr. Hoffer: They haven't raised one blade of grass. They haven't raised one brick.

Mr. Blake: We been throwing them, baby, because you been out there stopping them from laying bricks and raising grass.

Judge Higginbotham: Mr. Chairman . . .

Dr. Eisenhower: Mr. Blake . . .

Mr. Jenner: Would you do me a personal favor and stay for a moment, Mr. Blake?

Judge Higginbotham: Mr. Chairman, if I may, I feel compelled because I trust that this Commission will not let statements go in the record which are such blatant demonstrations of factual ignorance that I am obliged to note on the record how totally in error Mr. Hoffer is on the most elementary data.

The McCone Commission, headed by the former director of Central Intelligence, who I assume while he may not be the philosopher which Mr. Hoffer is, that he is at least as perceptive and more factually accurate. The McCone Commission pointed out that in Watts, California, you had unemployment which ran as high as 30 and 40 percent. Sometimes 50 percent among youth. It pointed out in great detail [that] in the Watts area you had the highest percent of substandard housing any place in L.A.

If my colleague, Mr. Hoffer, who I would like to be able to call distinguished, would take time out to read the data of the McCone Report, which is not challenged by anyone, based on government statistics, at least the first portion of his analysis would be demonstrated to be totally inaccurate, and I am willing, as a black man, to state that what I am amazed at is—that with the total bigotry, patent, extensive among men who can reach fame in this country —[not] that there has been as little unity as there has been. It is surprising that there has been as much.

I think that Mr. Hoffer's statements are indicative of the great racist pathology in our country and that his views are those which represent the mass of people in this country. I think that what Toynbee said that civilizations are destroyed from within, that his comments are classic examples of proving that.

Dr. Eisenhower: Mr. Blake, only because we have two other distinguished persons to testify this afternoon, I am going to conclude this part of our testimony. I want you to know that I personally had some questions to ask you but my good friend Judge Higginbotham asked precisely the questions in his part that I had intended to do. So on behalf of the Commission I thank you for your willingness to come, for your candor, for being with us and I accept the sincerity and truth of what you said to us.

Mr. Blake: Thank you.

That day, I think it is fair to say, was the most emotional day of the hearings for the Violence Commission. Eric Hoffer was an exemplary witness for the depth of racism existing in this country. No wealth of statistics could have conveyed as well to the other commissioners and to the public in general what racism meant to the black man.

Yet Hoffer is also a popular public figure. Moreover, only a minute or so of the hearings was shown on national television. There, Hoffer was seen shouting at a bearded black man in a dashiki. It is doubtful that much enlightenment was achieved by the televising of that exchange. I believe that in the long run the reports themselves will have a far greater impact than the TV time allocated to the hearings.

A first draft of *The Politics of Protest* was sent off to the executive staff of the commission on 27 December 1968, approximately five months after the initial phone call from Washington. They received the report with mixed feelings. They were, I know, impressed with the magnitude and quality of the report, but it violated the kinds of expectations they had about commission reports. We were clearly less concerned about "balance" and "tempered" lan-

guage than we were about analytical soundness, consistency and clarity. Some of the commissioners were described to me as "climbing the walls as they read it." And this did not make an easy situation for the executive staff. They suggested in January that it be toned down, and I did *not* tell them to go to hell. I listened carefully to their suggestions and accepted most of them concerning language and tone. But I did not alter the analysis in any of the chapters. I.F. Stone was later to call our analysis "Brilliant and indispensable," and a *Chicago Tribune* editorial ranked it alongside the *Walker Report* as "garbage."

The Impact of Commission Reports

Since the report was published, I have often been asked the question: Of what use is all this? Does it actually contribute to public policy? My answer is, I don't know. *The Politics of Protest* apparently made little impact on the commission itself. It was cited only once in the final report of the commission, and then out of context. But the book has been given considerable publicity, has been widely and favorably reviewed and has been widely adopted for classroom use. The major audience for *The Politics of Protest* will probably be the sociology and political science class, although more than most books on this subject it will find its way into the hands of decision makers.

The Politics of Protest will also provide an alternative analysis to the main report of the Violence Commission. Naturally, we think our analysis is more pointed, more consistent, more scholarly and more directed to the historical causes of American violence than the commission's own report, which adopts a managerial, counterinsurgency perspective that looks to symptoms rather than causes. But history will tell. Reports sponsored by commissions are ultimately intellectual documents subject to the criticism that any book or investigation might receive.

Yet they are something more as well. Despite the increasing tendency among radicals and intellectuals to challenge the usefulness and integrity of commission reports, they do tend to create an interest over and above that of similar work by individual scholars. One can even point to a series of commission reports that have had an enormous impact—those used by Karl Marx in developing his critique of capitalist production. Without the narrative provided by these commissions, Marx's *Capital* would have been a much more abstract and predictably obscure document and simply would not have attracted the readership it did. Marx himself, in his preface to *Capital,* offers an accolade to these investigative commissions.

Commission reports, whatever their analytical strictures, defects or omissions, come to have a special standing within the *political* community. If a social scientist or a journalist gathers "facts" concerning a particular institution, and these facts are presented in such a way as to offer a harshly critical appraisal of that social institution, the gathering and the analysis of such facts may be called "muckraking." But if the same or a similar set of facts is found by a commission, it may be seen as a series of startling and respectable social findings.

And herein lies the essential dilemma posed by the commission form of inquiry. On the one hand, we find a set of high-status commissioners whose name on a document will tend to legitimize the descriptions found therein; and on the other hand, precisely because of the political character of the commissioners, the report will be "balanced" or "inconsistent" depending on who is making the judgment. A commission, upon hearing one expert testify (correctly) that there is darkness outside and another testify (incorrectly) that the sun is shining will typically conclude that it is cloudy.

Nevertheless, whatever facts are gathered and are presented to the public, they are in the public domain. No set of facts is subject only to one interpretation and analysis. Surely it was not in the minds of the commissioners of inquiry in nineteenth-century England to provide the factual underpinning for a Marxist critique of capitalist production. Yet, there was no way to stop it. So my point is simply this: to the extent that a commission of inquiry develops facts, it necessarily has done something of social value. Its interpretations can be challenged. How those facts and how those interpretations will be met and used depends upon the integrity and ability of the intellectual community.

For Further Reading

OVERVIEW

The Constitution and What It Means Today by Edward S. Corwin (Atheneum, 1963).

The End of Liberalism by Theodore Lowi (W. W. Norton, 1969).

The Death of the Past by J. H. Plumb (Houghton Mifflin, 1971).

PART ONE. SOCIAL SCIENCE AND PUBLIC POLICY

The Military Establishment: Its Impacts on American Society by Adam Yarmolinsky (Harper & Row, 1971).

Reporting on the Social State of the Union (Mondale)

Social Indicators edited by Raymond A. Bauer (M.I.T. Press, 1966) attempts to describe a system of social indicators and the uses or drawbacks that might develop if a national social indicator system were set up.

Action under Planning: The Guidance of Economic Development edited by Bertram Gross (McGraw-Hill, 1967) treats economic planning in a context of social planning and social reaction to innovation.

PART TWO. PUBLIC OPINION AND THE CRISIS OF TRADITIONAL PARTY POLITICS

Hopes and Fears of the American People by Albert H. Cantril and Charles W. Roll (Universe, 1971).

Revolutionary Change by Chalmers Johnson (Little, Brown, 1966).

Computers, Polls, and Public Opinion (Abelson)

"Political Behavior" by David O. Sears in Gardner Lindzey and Elliot Aronson's edited volume, *The Handbook of Social Psychology*, Vol. 5 (Addison-Wesley, 1968).

Candidates, Issues, and Strategies: Computer Simulation of the 1960 and 1964 Presidential Elections by Ithiel de Sola Pool and Samuel Popkin (M.I.T. Press, 1965).

"Simulation of Social Behavior" by Robert P. Abelson in Gardner Lindzey and Elliot Aronson's edited volume, *The Handbook of Social Psychology*, Vol. 2 (Addison-Wesley, 1968).

Theories of Cognitive Consistency: A Sourcebook edited by Robert P. Abelson, Elliot Aronson, et al. (Rand McNally, 1968).

The 480 by Eugene Burdick (McGraw-Hill, 1964).

American Voting Behavior edited by Eugene Burdick and Arthur Brodbeck (Free Press, 1959).

Life, Time and the Fortunes of War (Wright)

The Press and the Cold War by James Aronson (Bobbs-Merrill, 1970).

Public Opinion and Foreign Policy by James H. Rosenau (Random House, 1961).

The Political Beliefs of Americans by Lloyd Free and Hadley Cantril (Simon and Schuster, 1968).

The "Liberation" of Gary, Indiana (Greer)

Black Awakening in Capitalist America by Robert L. Allan (Doubleday, 1969) remains the single best work on black political power, with an excellent treatment of the problems of co-optation.

Black Political Power in America by Chuck Stone (Bobbs-Merrill, 1968) is a detailed appriasal of the severely limited role of black Americans in the governmental apparatus.

The State in Capitalist Society by Ralph Miliband (Beacon Press, 1969) contains, in addition to a general analysis of the relation of governments to economic elites, an excellent description of how government bureaucracies resist efforts at change by newly elected radicals.

Los Angeles Liberalism (Maullin)

Television in Politics by Jay G. Blumler and Denis McQuail (Faber and Faber, 1968).

The Los Angeles Riots: A Socio-Psychological Study edited by Nathan Cohen (Praeger, 1970).

The Electoral Process edited by Kent M. Jennings and Harmon L. Ziegler (Prentice-Hall, 1966).

Election 1968—The Abortive Landslide (Burnham)

The Responsible Electorate by V. O. Key, Jr. (Harvard University Press, 1966).

Elections and the Political Order by Angus Campbell et al. (John Wiley & Sons, 1960).

The End of American Party Politics (Burnham)

The American Party Systems edited by William N. Chambers and Walter Dean Burnham (Oxford University Press, 1967).

The End of Liberalism by Theodore Lowi (W. W. Norton, 1969).

Congressmen and the Electorate by Milton R. Cummings (Free Press, 1967).

Critical Elections and the Mainsprings of American Politics by Walter Dean Burnham (W. W. Norton, 1970).

PART THREE. NATIONAL POLICY ELITES AND THEIR POLITICS

The Semisovereign People: A Realist's View of Democracy in America by Elmer E. Schattschneider (Harper & Row, 1961).

The Unheavenly City: The Nature and the Future of Our Urban Crisis by Edward C. Banfield (Little, Brown, 1970).

The President: Office and Powers by Edward S. Corwin (New York University Press, Fourth Edition, 1957).

The Best-Known American (Greenstein)

Children and Politics by Fred I. Greenstein (Yale University Press, 1965).

Children and the Death of a President by Martha Wolfenstein and Gilbert Kliman (Doubleday, 1965).

The Two Presidencies (Wildavsky)

Congress and the Presidency by Nelson W. Polsby (Prentice-Hall, 1965) is a fine short study of executive-legislative relationships.

The Common Defense by Samuel P. Huntington (Columbia University Press, 1963) remains the best study of presidential participation in defense policy-making.

The White House Staff Bureaucracy (Lacy)

Presidential Power by Richard E. Neustadt (John Wiley & Sons, 1962) remains the most useful conceptual treatment of the presidency.

Executive Branch Lobbying in Congress (Murphy)

Legislative Liaison: Executive Leadership in Congress by Abraham Holtzman (Rand McNally, 1970).

"The Congressional Committee System and the Oversight Process" by Thomas P. Jahnige (*Western Political Quarterly*, 1968: 227–39).

"The Political Economy of Geographical Distribution of Federal Funds: The Mid-West Case" by Thomas P. Murphy (*Administrative Science Quarterly*, September 1969: 435–439).

Science, Geopolitics and Federal Spending by Thomas P. Murphy (D. C. Heath, 1971).

An Administrative History of NASA, 1958-1963 by Robert L. Rosholt (National Aeronautics and Space Administration, 1966), pp. 290–298, 346.

Women in Congress (Gehlen)

"Sexism on Capitol Hill" (*Washington Newsletter for Women*, September 1969).

Remarks by Representative Shirley Chisholm (*Congressional Record:* May 21, 1969).

Riot Commission Politics (Lipsky and Olson)

From Race Riot To Sit-In: 1919 and the 1960s by Arthur T. Waskow (Doubleday, 1966) is an historical and comparative study of race riots of the World War I period with emphasis on the Chicago Commission of Race Relations' investigation into the 1919 Chicago race riot.

Race Riot at East St. Louis: July 2, 1917 by Elliott M. Rudwick (Meridan Books, 1966) is a thorough study of a major race riot including analyses of four separate investigations into riot causes and remedies.

PART FOUR. INNOVATION, PRIORITIES, AND PROBLEMS IN NATIONAL PUBLIC POLICIES

Setting National Priorities: The 1973 Budget by Charles L. Schultze et al. (Brookings Institution, 1972).

In Critical Condition by Edward M. Kennedy (Simon and Schuster, 1972).

Toward A National Urban Policy by Daniel Patrick Moynihan (Basic Books, 1970).

Apartheid U.S.A. (Lowi)

The Death and Life of Great American Cities by Jane Jacobs (Random House, 1963) critiques the profession and ideology of planning. Once hotly disputed, her charges against planning as irrational and counterproductive have gained in credibility as urban crises mount.

Building the American City by the National Commission on Urban Problems (Praeger, 1969).

Politics, Planning and the Public Interest by Martin Meyerson and Edward C. Banfield (Free Press, 1955) is the first and best study of the local politics of public housing.

Public Housing—The Politics of Poverty by Leonard Freedman (Holt, Rinehart & Winston, 1969) reviews the politics and policies of housing and evaluates some of the black power and separatism issues that have emerged in the field.

Fair Housing Laws—Unfair Housing Practices (Eley)

Equality and Beyond: Housing Segregation and the Goals of the Great Society by George and Eunice Grier (Quadrangle Books, 1966) is perhaps the best brief discussion of housing segregation in this country and of public and private measures to combat it.

Death of the American Dream House (Sternlieb)

Levittowners by Herbert J. Gans (Pantheon Books, 1967).

Blue Collar World by Arthur B. Shostak and William Gombey (Prentice-Hall, 1965).

Working-Class Suburb by Bennett Berger (University of California Press, 1960).

Day Care Centers (Steiner)

The Employed Mother in America by F. Ivan Nye and Lois W. Hoffman (Rand McNally, 1963).

An Ideal Health Care System for America (Roemer)

In Failing Health: The Medical Crisis and the AMA by Ed Cray (Bobbs-Merrill, 1970).

The Plot Against the Patient by Fred J. Cook (Prentice-Hall, 1967).

Doctors in Hospitals: Medical Staff Organization and Hospital Performance by Milton I. Roemer and Jay W. Friedman (Johns Hopkins Press, 1971).

Professional Dominance: The Social Structure of Medical Care by Eliot Friedson (Aldine-Atherton, 1970).

Health Care in Transition: Directions for the Future by Anne R. Somers (American Hospital Association, 1971).

Cooling Out the Economy (McMahon)

Economic Report of the President (Superintendent of Documents, 1971) analyzes the needs of the economy from the perspective of the President's Council of Economic advisors.

Readings in Money, National Income, and Stabilization Policy by Warren L. Smith and R. L. Teigen (Richard D. Irwin, Revised Edition 1970) contains judiciously selected articles by Samuelson, Harry Johnson, Ackley, Okun, Hymans, Friedman, and others, with excellent introductions concerning fiscal policy.

Tax Cut in Camelot (Stein)

Economic Advice and Presidential Leadership by Edward Flash (Columbia University Press, 1965) treats the role of the Council of Economic Advisors both before and during Camelot.

New Dimensions of Political Economy by Walter W. Heller (W. W. Norton, 1967) views the episode discussed in Stein's article from a viewpoint other than his.

Private Initiative in the Great Society (Long)

A Great Society? by Bertram M. Gross (Basic Books, 1968).

Area and Power: A Theory of Local Government edited by Arthur Maas (Free Press, 1959).

Community Leadership and Decision-Making (University of Iowa Extension Bulletin, 1967) contains the proceedings of the Third Annual Urban Policy Conference of 1968.

PART FIVE. AMERICAN JUSTICE AS VIEWED FROM THE BOTTOM

Justice Stumbles Over Science (Bazelon)

Insanity and the Criminal Law: From M'Naghten to Durham, and Beyond by Simon E. Sobeloff (*American Bar Association Journal*: 41, September 1955).

The Family and the Law by Joseph Goldstein and J. Katz (Free Press, 1965).

Crime and the Criminal Law by Barbara Wooten (Stevens & Sons, 1963).

Psychoanalysis, Psychiatry and Law by J. Katz, J. Goldstein, and A. Dershowitz (Free Press, 1967).

Child Convicts (Lerman)

Delinquency and Social Policy edited by Paul Lerman (Praeger Publishers, 1970) presents further evidence and discussion of injustice, ineffective correction, police discretion, and other topics relating to adult behavior vis-a-vis young people.

Borderland of Criminal Justice: Essays in Law and Criminology by Frances A. Allen (University of Chicago Press, 1964) was frequently cited by the U.S. Supreme Court in the *Gault* decision. This perceptive legal scholar examines legal and social consequences of the American predilection for attempting to criminalize social problems.

Children and Youth in America edited by Robert H. Bremner (Harvard University Press, 1970).

Juvenile Defenders for a Thousand Years: Selected Readings from Anglo-Saxon Times to 1900 edited by Wiley B. Saunders (University of North Carolina Press, 1970).

The Child Savers: The Invention of Delinquency by Anthony M. Platt (University of Chicago Press, 1969).

Children in Urban Society: Juvenile Delinquency in Nineteenth-Century America by Joseph M. Hawes (Oxford University Press, 1971).

Task Force Report: Juvenile Delinquency and Youth Crime and *Task Force Report: Corrections*, both by the President's Commission on Law Enforcement and the Administration of Justice (U.S. Government Printing Office, 1967).

Varieties of Police Behavior by James Q. Wilson (Harvard University Press, 1968).

Crime, Victims, and the Police (Ennis)

The Challenge of Crime in a Free Society (U.S. Government Printing Office, n.d.) is a report by the President's Commission on Law Enforcement and Administration of Justice.

The American Jury by Harry Kalven, Jr., and Hans Zeisel (Little, Brown, 1966).

PART SIX. LOCAL GOVERNMENT AND COMMUNITY CONTROL

The Governmental Process: Political Interests and Public Opinion by David B. Truman (Alfred A. Knopf, 1951).

Beyond the Melting Pot: The Negroes, Puerto Ricans, Jews, Italians, and Irish of New York City by Nathan Glazer and Daniel P. Moynihan (M.I.T. Press, First Edition 1963, Second Edition 1970).

Rent Strikes (Lipsky)

Dark Ghetto by Kenneth B. Clark (Harper & Row, 1965) explores the implications of powerlessness in the ghetto for the psychology of individuals and the viability of political movements.

Neighborhood Groups and Urban Renewal by J. Clarence Davies, III (Columbia University Press, 1966) is one of few systematic studies of the interaction of political organizations and city agencies at the neighborhood level.

The Symbolic Uses of Politics by Murray Edelman (University of Illinois Press, 1964) is a highly suggestive study of the symbolic meaning of government activity and the ways such activity affects political consciousness and activism.

Militant Civil Servants in New York City (Piven)

Confrontation at Ocean Hill-Brownsville: The New York School Strikes of 1968 edited by Maurice R. Berube and Marilyn Gittell (Praeger, 1969).

City Politics by Edward C. Banfield and James Q. Wilson (Harvard University Press and M.I.T. Press, 1963).

Governing New York City by Wallace S. Sayre and Herbert Kaufman (Russell Sage Foundation, 1960).

Negro Neighbors (Ross, Crawford, and Pettigrew)

"Educating the American Negro" by Virgil A. Cliff in John P. Davis' edited volume, The American Negro Reference Book (Prentice-Hall, 1966).

The Negro American edited by Talcott Parsons and Kenneth B. Clark (Houghton Mifflin, 1966) draws together essays by authorities in virtually every realm of race relations.

A Profile of the American Negro by Thomas F. Pettigrew (D. Van Nostrand, 1964) places school desegregation in perspective through analyses on black crime, intelligence, health, personality, protest, and prospects.

Strangers Next Door: Ethnic Relations in American Communities by Robin M. Williams, Jr. (Prentice-Hall, 1964) is an extensive, thoughtful investigation of group relations in four small cities.

PART SEVEN. THE LIMITS OF USUAL POLITICS

To Establish Justice, To Insure Domestic Tranquility: Final Report of the National Commission on the Causes and Prevention of Violence by Milton Eisenhower (Praeger, 1970).

Report of the President's Commission on Campus Unrest (Avon Books, 1970).

History of Violence in America edited by Hugh D. Graham and Ted R. Gurr (Praeger, 1969).

Assassination and Political Violence: A Staff Report to the National Commission on the Causes and Prevention of Violence by James F. Kirkham et al. (Praeger, 1970).

Report of the National Advisory Commission on Civil Disorders (Bantam Books, 1968).

Supplemental Studies for the National Advisory Commission on Civil Disorders by Robert M. Fogelson and Robert D. Hill (U.S. Government Printing Office, 1968) reports on sociological studies of racial attitudes in fifteen large cities, the white institutions located in these cities' ghettos, and the characteristics of arrestees in major riots.

Shoot-Out in Cleveland: Black Militants and the Police by Louis Masotti and Jerome R. Corsi (Praeger, 1969).

Assassination and the Political Order by William J. Crotty (Harper Torchbooks, 1971).

Cleveland's Crisis Ghetto (Williams)

Negroes in the Cities by Karl E. Taeuber and Alma F. Taeuber (Aldine-Atherton, 1965) includes a wealth of statistical data on black migration problems and racial segregation in large urban areas.

The Moynihan Report and the Politics of Controversy by Lee Rainwater and William L. Yancey (M.I.T. Press, 1967) discusses the Moynihan controversy, including the debate over poverty versus cultural inheritance.

Planning for a Nation of Cities edited by Sam Bass Warner, Jr. (M.I.T. Press, 1966) contains useful chapters on the problems of transition from country to city.

Tally's Corner by Elliot Liebow (Little, Brown, 1967) is an anthropological field study of black street-corner men which seems relevant to the study of family formation by females.

Confrontation at the Conrad Hilton (The Walker Commission)

Miami and the Siege of Chicago by Norman Mailer (World Publishing Co, 1968).

Rights in Conflict: Convention Week in Chicago, August 25–29, 1968: A Report by Daniel Walker (E. P. Dutton, 1968).

The Violence Commission (Skolnick)

The Politics of Protest (The Report to the National Commission on the Causes and Prevention of Violence) by Jerome H. Skolnick (Simon and Schuster, Clarion Books, 1969).

The Contributors

ROBERT P. ABELSON ("Computers, Polls, and Public Opinion") is professor of psychology at Yale University and associate director of the Yale Program in Communication and Attitude Change. He is a member of the Research Board of Simulmatics Corporation.

DAVID L. BAZELON ("Justice Stumbles Over Science") is chief judge of the United States Court of Appeals for the District of Columbia. He is also a lecturer in the Department of Psychiatry at the Johns Hopkins School of Medicine and clinical professor of psychology at George Washington University.

RICHARD BERK ("White Institutions and Black Rage"), a lecturer in sociology at Goucher College, is currently studying the relation of black militancy and civil disorders to the actions of city officials and major institutions. He has conducted research on politics and the poor and has done a study of ghetto retail merchants.

DAVID BOESEL ("White Institutions and Black Rage"), a research associate with the Group for Research on Social Policy at Johns Hopkins University and an analyst for the Kerner Commission, has done a study on ghetto riots for the Department of Government at Cornell University.

THOMAS CRAWFORD ("Negro Neighbors") is assistant professor in the Department of Psychology at the University of California at Berkeley.

ALAN J. DAVIS ("Sexual Assaults in the Philadelphia Prison System and Sheriff's Vans") is a partner in the Philadelphia law firm of Wolf, Block, Schorr and Solis-Cohen. A former editor of the *Harvard Law Review*, he specializes in civil and criminal trial law.

Robert P. Abelson

Judge David L. Bazelon

David Boesel

Alan J. Davis

MATTHEW P. DUMONT, JR., ("Down the Bureaucracy") is a psychiatrist serving as director of the Division of Drug Rehabilitation in Massachusetts' Department of Mental Health. He has written numerous articles on community health and social problems and is the author of a book, *The Absurd Healer*.

BETTYE K. EIDSON ("White Institutions and Black Rage") is associate professor of sociology at the University of Michigan. She has conducted research on government programs for the unemployed, as well as studying community structure and conflict in fifteen U.S. cities.

LYNN W. ELEY ("Fair Housing Laws—Unfair Housing Practices") is assistant chancellor of extension at the University of Wisconsin and professor of political science at the University of Wisconsin at Milwaukee. He is co-editor of *The Politics of Fair Housing Legislation: State and Local Case Studies*.

PHILIP H. ENNIS ("Crimes, Victims, and the Police") is professor of sociology at Wesleyan University in Middletown, Connecticut. He was formerly senior study director at the National Opinion Research Center, and he directed a study on criminal victimization for the President's Crime Commission.

WILLIAM GAMSON ("How to Lose a Referendum") is professor in the department of political science at the University of Michigan, Ann Arbor. He is the author of *Power and Discontent* and *SIMSOC: Simulated Society*.

FRIEDA L. GEHLEN ("Women in Congress") is an assistant professor of sociology at Purdue University. Her field of interest is general social organization with emphasis on politi-

Matthew P. Dumont, Jr.

Lynn W. Eley

Frieda L. Gehlen

Philip H. Ennis

Edward Greer

Fred I. Greenstein

Alex B. Lacy, Jr.

Irving Louis Horowitz

cal sociology, the sociology of education, and a general overview of American society.

FRED I. GREENSTEIN ("The Best Known American") is professor and chairman of the government department at Wesleyan University in Middletown, Connecticut. He is the author of *Introduction to Political Analysis* (with R. E. Lane and J. D. Barber), *The American Party System and the American People, Children and Politics, Personality and Politics* (with M. Lerner), and *A Source Book for the Study of Personality and Politics*. In September 1973 he will be Henry Luce Professor of Politics, Law and Society at Princeton University.

EDWARD GREER ("The 'Liberation' of Gary, Indiana") is director of the Urban Affairs Program at Wheaton College in Norton, Massachusetts. He is editor of *Black Liberation Politics*.

W. EUGENE GROVES ("White Institutions and Black Rage"), a member of the Group for Research on Social Policy at Johns Hopkins University, is presently conducting a detailed analysis of policing in the ghetto. With Peter H. Rossi he is planning a survey of social conflict arising from drug use on college campuses.

ANDREW HACKER ("Votes Cast and Seats Won") is professor of political science at Queens College of the City University of New York. He is a consultant to The Brookings Institution and the author of *The Congressional Districting, The Study of Politics, The Corporation Take-Over* and *The End of the American Era*.

JEFFREY HADDEN ("The Making of the Negro Mayors") is professor of sociology and urban studies at Tulane University. He has written extensively in the areas of urban studies, religion, and the family. Among his major books are *A Time To Burn* (with L. H. Masotti, K. F. Siminatore and J. Corsi), *The Gathering Storm in the Churches* and *Religion in Radical Transition* (editor). He is a contributing editor to *The Christian Ministry* and has been a research consultant to the Danforth Foundation, Educational Testing Service, the National Council of Churches, and the National Urban Coalition.

IRVING LOUIS HOROWITZ ("Social Science Yogis and Military Commissars" and "The Life and Death of Project Camelot") is distinguished professor of sociology at Rutgers University. He is editor-in-chief of *Society* magazine and director of *Studies in Comparative International Development*. Among his recent books are *Foundations of Political Sociology, Three Worlds of Development* (2nd edition), and *Cuban Communism* (2nd edition) published by Transaction.

HERBERT JACOB ("Winners and Losers") is professor of political science at Northwestern University. He is the author of *Debtors in Court*.

ALEX B. LACY, JR. ("The White House Staff Bureaucracy") is dean of the School of Urban Studies at Georgia State College. In addition to studying the staff of the White House, he does research on urban policy issues.

PAUL LERMAN ("Delinquents Without Crimes") is associate professor of social work at Rutgers University's Graduate School of Social Work. He teaches courses on delinquency and social policy, social welfare policy, and research. His major interest is in understanding societal responses to youthful deviance.

SEYMOUR MARTIN LIPSET ("The Wallace Whitelash" and "The President, the Polls, and Vietnam") is professor of government and social

Paul Lerman

Michael Lipsky

Norton E. Long

relations at Harvard. Among his many books are *Agrarian Socialism, Union Democracy, Social Mobility in Industrial Society, Political Man, The First New Nation*, and *Revolution and Counter-Revolution*.

MICHAEL LIPSKY ("Riot Commission Politics" and "Rent Strikes") is associate professor of political science at Massachusetts Institute of Technology and a staff associate of the Institute for Research on Poverty. He has written *Protest in City Politics*.

NORTON E. LONG ("Private Initiative in the 'Great Society'") is director of the Center of Community and Metropolitan Studies at the University of Missouri in St. Louis. He is author of *The Polity*.

THEODORE J. LOWI ("Apartheid U.S.A.") is senior professor of American Institutions at Cornell University and author of *The End of Liberalism*.

WALTER W. McMAHON ("Cooling Out the Economy") is associate professor of economics at the University of Illinois at Urbana, where he teaches macroeconomic analysis. He is currently engaged in research on the economics of investment in education and human resources.

THEODORE R. MARMOR ("Why Medicare Helped Raise Doctors' Fees") teaches public policy courses at the University of Minnesota. The author of *The Politics of Medicare* and editor of *Poverty Policy*, he is interested in welfare state politics.

LOUIS H. MASOTTI ("The Making of the Negro Mayors") is professor of political science and urban affairs and director of the Center for Urban Affairs at Northwestern University. In addition to publishing many other books and articles, he has co-edited *Suburbia: Cities of the Seventies* and *The Suburbanization of the City*.

RICHARD L. MAULLIN ("Los Angeles Liberalism") is California's

Theodore J. Lowi

Walter W. McMahon

Theodore R. Marmor

Louis H. Masotti

Seymour Melman

Thomas P. Murphy

Richard L. Maullin

Walter F. Mondale

Stuart S. Nagel

deputy secretary of state. He has studied the significance of revolutionary violence in Colombia and also works on the management of election campaigns on a volunteer basis.

SEYMOUR MELMAN ("Pentagon Bourgeosie") is professor of industrial engineering at Columbia University. Among his many books are *The War Economy of the United States*, *Pentagon Capitalism: The Political Economy of War*, and *Conversion of Industry from a Military to Civilian Economy*.

WALTER F. MONDALE ("Reporting on the Social State of the Nation") has been U.S. senator from Minnesota since 1964. He serves on Senate committees on space, agriculture, banking and currency, and aging. He led the fight for passage of the fair housing bill and fair warning law requiring manufacturers to notify automobile owners of safety defects.

FRANK MUNGER ("Changing Politics of Aid to Education") is professor of political science at the University of North Carolina, Chapel Hill. He is an editor of *Studies in Comparative Politics* and the author of *American State Politics: Readings for Comparative Analysis*.

THOMAS P. MURPHY ("Executive Branch Lobbying in Congress") is professor of government and politics and executive director of the Institute for Urban Studies at the University of Maryland. He has written numerous articles and four books: *Pressures Upon Congress—Legislation by Lobbies; Metropolitics and the Urban County; Emerging Patterns in Urban Administration;* and *Science, Geopolitics and Federal Spending*.

STUART S. NAGEL ("The Tipped Scales of American Justice") is professor of political science at the University of Illinois and a member of the Illinois bar. He is the author of

451

Legal Process From a Behavioral Perspective.

DAVID J. OLSON ("Riot Commission Politics") is assistant professor of political science and director of undergraduate studies at Indiana University. He has conducted a number of studies on the impact of racial violence and has published several articles in social science journals. He is also co-editor of and a contributor to *Black Politics: The Inevitability of Conflict.*

TOM PARMENTER ("Breakdown of Law and Order") is a free-lance writer and editor. He was a Russell Sage fellow at *trans-Action* (now *Society*) magazine and was editor of *Inequality in Education*, the bulletin of the Harvard Center for Law and Education.

THOMAS PETTIGREW ("Negro Neighbors") is professor in the Department of Social Psychology at Harvard University. He is the author of *A Profile of the Negro American* and *Racially Separate or Together.*

FRANCES FOX PIVEN ("Militant Civil Servants in New York City") is professor of political science at Boston University and was associated with the founding of the National Welfare Rights Association. She is co-author of *Regulating the Poor: The Functions of Public Welfare* and is currently working on a book analyzing contemporary movements of the poor in the United States.

EARL RAAB ("The Wallace Whitelash") is director of the Jewish Community Relations Council of San Francisco. He has taught at San Francisco State College and the University of California at Berkeley. With Seymour Martin Lipset he wrote *Prejudice and Society* and *The Politics of Unreason: Right-Wing Extremism in America, 1790–1970.*

David J. Olson

Frances Fox Piven

Albert J. Reiss Jr.

Milton I. Roemer

ALBERT J. REISS, JR. ("Police Brutality") is professor of sociology at the University of Michigan and chairman of the department. He served on the President's Commission on Law Enforcement and the Administration of Justice and the National Advisory Commission on Civil Disorder. He has written extensively on deviant behavior.

MILTON I. ROEMER ("An Ideal Health Care System for America") is professor of public health at the University of California at Los Angeles and professor of preventive and social medicine at the UCLA Medical School. He has written many books and articles on the social aspects of medicine.

PETER H. ROSSI ("White Institutions and Black Rage") is chairman of the Department of Social Relations at Johns Hopkins University and director of the Group for Research on Social Policy. He has recently co-authored *The Education of Catholic Americans* and *The New Media and Education.*

J. MICHAEL ROSS ("Negro Neighbors") is assistant professor of sociology at Boston University. He is especially interested in computer applications for political data.

ROBERTA S. SIGEL ("Citizens Committees") is professor of political science at the State University of New York at Buffalo. She is editor of *Political Socialization: Its Role in the Political Process, the Annals*; and *Political Process*; and *Learning About Politics: Studies in Political Socialization*. In addition, she has written *The Political World of Adolescents.*

ROBERT A. SKEDGELL ("How Computers Pick an Election Winner") has been with CBS radio and television since 1939 as writer, news editor, reporter, producer, and ad-

Peter H. Rossi

Roberta S. Sigel

Jerome H. Skolnick

Herbert Stein

Gilbert Y. Steiner

George Sternlieb

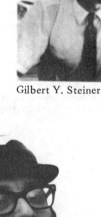

Arthur I. Waskow

Aaron Wildavsky

ministrator. Currently he is director of Broadcast Research at CBS News.

JEROME H. SKOLNICK ("The Violence Commission") is professor at the University of California at Berkeley's School of Criminology and acting chairman of the Center for the Study of Law and Society. He was director of the Task Force on Violent Aspects of Protest and Confrontation of the National Commission on the Causes and Prevention of Violence and has written *The Politics of Protest*.

HERBERT STEIN ("Tax Cut in Camelot") was appointed by President Nixon to the Council of Economic Advisors. He is a senior fellow at The Brookings Institution and is a contributor to its compendium of papers, *Agenda for the Nation*. He has also written *The Fiscal Revolution in America*.

GILBERT Y. STEINER ("Day Care Centers") is senior fellow and director of the Government Studies Program at The Brookings Institution and has long been a consultant to state and local governments. His most recent books are *The Congressional Conference Committee*, *Legislation by Collective Bargaining*, *Social Insecurity: The Politics of Welfare*, and *The State of Welfare*.

GEORGE STERNLIEB ("Death of the American Dream House") is professor of urban and regional planning and director of the Urban Studies Center at Rutgers University. Among his many published works are three Transaction Books: *The Affluent Suburb: Princeton; The Zone of Emergence: A Case Study of Princeton, New Jersey;* and *The Ecology of Welfare*.

VICTOR THIESSEN ("The Making of the Negro Mayors") is assistant professor of sociology at Case Western Reserve University. He is currently conducting research in political sociology and the sociology of religion.

ARTHUR I. WASKOW ("Community Control of the Police") is with the Institute for Policy Studies in Washington, D.C. He is the author of *From Race Riot to Sit-In, Bush Is Burning* and *Freedom Seder: A New Haggadah for Passover*.

AARON WILDAVSKY ("The Two Presidencies") is dean of the Graduate School of Public Policy at the University of California at Berkeley. A prolific author and editor, his most recent books are *Implementation: The Economic Development Administration in Oakland* (with Jeffrey Pressman) and *Buying Outdoor Recreation: Budgeting and Evaluation in Federal Recreation Policy* (with Jeanne Nienaber).

WALTER WILLIAMS ("Cleveland's Crisis Ghetto") is professor of public affairs and director of research at the Institute of Governmental Research, Graduate School of Public Affairs, at the University of Washington in Seattle. His most recently published works are *Social Policy Research and Analysis: The Experience of the Federal Agencies; The Struggle for a Negative Income Tax;* and *Evaluating Social Programs: Theory, Practice and Politics* (co-editor).

Walter Williams

Frederick M. Wirt

James D. Wright

FREDERICK M. WIRT ("The Politics of Hyperpluralism") is a research political scientist at the Institute of Governmental Studies and lecturer at the School of Education of the University of California at Berkeley. He has written *Politics of Southern Equality: Law and Social Change in a Mississippi County*.

JAMES D. WRIGHT ("Life, Time, and the Fortunes of War") is a doctoral candidate in sociology at the University of Wisconsin. His research interests include social mobility and political ideology, the sources of right-wing political support and the extent and causes of popular political cynicism.

WALTER DEAN BURNHAM (editor of this volume and author of "Election 1968—The Abortive Landslide" and "The End of American Party Politics") is professor of political science at Massachusetts Institute of Technology. He has written a number of articles on American electoral politics and voter alignments and is the author of *Presidential Ballots, 1836–1892* and *Critical Elections and the Mainsprings of American Politics*. With William N. Chambers he has co-edited *The American Party Systems*.

Walter Dean Burnham

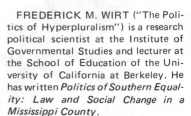